www.wadsworth.com

wadsworth.com is the World Wide Web site for Wadsworth Publishing Company and is your direct source to dozens of online resources.

At *wadsworth.com* you can find out about supplements, demonstration software, and student resources. You can also send e-mail to many of our authors and preview new publications and exciting new technologies.

wadsworth.com
Changing the way the world learns®

FIFTH EDITION

A Practical Study of Argument

Trudy Govier

Wadsworth
Thomson Learning™

Australia • Canada • Mexico • Singapore • Spain • United Kingdom • United States

Philosophy Editor: Peter Adams
Assistant Editor: Kara Kindstrom
Editorial Assistant: Mark Andrews
Marketing Manager: Dave Garrison
Print Buyer: April Reynolds
Permissions Editor: Bob Kauser

Production Service: Hal Lockwood
Copy Editor: Cathy Baehler
Cover Designer: Annabelle Ison
Text and Cover Printer: WebCom, Ltd.
Compositor: Publishers' Design and Production
    Services, Inc.

Printed in the United States of America
1 2 3 4 5 6 7   04 03 02 01 00

Library of Congress Cataloging-in-Publication Data
Govier, Trudy.
    A pratical study of argument / Trudy Govier.—5th ed.
        p.   cm.
    Includes bibliographical references.
    ISBN 0-534-51976-8
    1. Reasoning.   2. Logic.   I. Title.
    BC177.G65 2000
    168—dc21   00-038191

Wadsworth/Thomson Learning
10 Davis Drive
Belmont, CA 94002-3098
USA

For information about our products, contact us:
Thomson Learning Academic Resource Center
1-800-423-0563
http://www.wadsworth.com

International Headquarters
Thomson Learning
International Division
290 Harbor Drive, 2nd Floor
Stamford, CT 06902-7477
USA

UK/Europe/Middle East/South Africa
Thomson Learning
Berkshire House
168-173 High Holborn
London WC1V 7AA
United Kingdom

Asia
Thomson Learning
60 Albert Street, #15-01
Albert Complex
Singapore 189969

Canada
Nelson Thomson Learning
1120 Birchmount Road
Toronto, Ontario M1K 5G4
Canada

Contents

8   Deductively Valid Arguments: Propositional Logic   253

9   An Introduction to Inductive Arguments   298

10   Analogies: Reasoning from Case to Case   350

Preface

This book is intended for all those who are interested in arguments and in arguing, and especially for university and college students taking courses designed to improve their ability to understand, construct, and criticize arguments. My goal has been to present enough theory to explain why certain kinds of argument are good or bad and enough illustrations and examples to show how that theory can be applied in practice. I present an integrated treatment of cogent arguments and fallacies, of formal and informal techniques of analysis, of theory and practice. Many real world illustrations are included, and extensive exercises accompany each chapter. Some exercises are answered within the text, while the remainder are answered in a manual available to instructors.

My interest in the theory and practice of natural argumentation stems from an occasion many years ago when someone asked me to review a proposed text on informal fallacies. At the time, I was teaching an elementary course on formal logic to a large group of students for whom it was compulsory and, it appeared, irrelevant. The greater practicality of the informal logic, and the real-life examples I found in that manuscript, fascinated me. I began to study other texts in the field and developed my own course on practical reasoning. Based on a synthesis of four existing texts, that course was successful. But the awkwardness of the synthesis seemed to call for a new book. As I worked further in the area, my interest developed and extended to exploring some of the many philosophical issues posed by the shift from formal logic to the analysis of arguments expressed in natural language.

The first edition of this text was written between 1982 and 1984, the second in 1986, the third in 1990, and the fourth in 1995. This edition, the fifth, was written in the summer of 1999. The book combines a detailed treatment of good and bad arguments in natural language with a solid treatment of two central areas of formal logic: categorical logic and propositional logic. The first edition was novel in its combination of discussions of cogent and fallacious arguments, its synthesis of topics from formal and informal logic, and its sustained effort to present a coherent general theory of argument, within which the study of various types of argument could be located. This synthesis is common to all editions. Because some other authors in the field subsequently followed a similar route, the combination of topics is less unusual than it was previously. In addition to the interpretation and evaluation of arguments, the book also treats themes pertinent to the construction of cogent arguments.

Three problems commonly experienced by students of argument and critical thinking are taken very seriously in this text:

Finding and Interpreting Arguments   In order to critically evaluate an argument, it is necessary to have a clear sense of what that argument is. In practice, for written arguments, this means finding the conclusion and premises in a spoken or written text. Students often find this matter difficult. I spend considerable time on it in Chapter 2, which teaches a standardizing technique in some detail. Chapter 2 also includes a treatment of indicator words, implicit premises and conclusions, subarguments, argument structure, and other related topics.

Having Confidence in Argumentative Procedures   For many students, if an issue is not one of straightforward fact, it is a matter of "mere" opinion, and in an area of opinion, no distinction can be made between well supported and poorly supported or between correct and incorrect. The topic of opinion is explicitly addressed in the first chapter. Students are advised that opinions and beliefs can be supported by evidence and reasons. They can be supported well or badly, and one can learn to distinguish which is which. This book offers hundreds of examples, most on topics of serious concern, that illustrate this point. This text has been used extensively in the United States and Canada. In addition, it has been used outside North America. For this reason, I have made a special effort to select examples that will be interesting to a wide audience and that presuppose relatively little detailed knowledge of the political and social circumstances of any single country. When appropriate, points of background knowledge have been included with examples or expository text.

In the many exercises, students work to develop disciplined critiques of a variety of arguments. At some stages, they are asked to develop their own arguments or to fill in needed reasons. The sorts of arguments studied in this book are integral to the study of many areas—including law, physical and social science, administration, ethics, and various humanities disciplines such as literature, history, and philosophy. The importance of cogent argumentation is a persistent theme in this book. I hope that study in a critical thinking or practical argument course and work with a book such as this one will give the students a solid and enduring appreciation for the ubiquity and importance of argument and the grounds for drawing the distinction between good arguments and poor ones.

Using Argument Skills after the Course Is Over   Textbooks have to use fairly short examples, and one problem faced by many students and instructors is that of *transfer*. How can concepts and skills developed for short textbook examples be applied in further work, where we are considering not just a paragraph or two, but a whole essay, or even a whole book? New to the third edition was a chapter directly confronting this transfer problem. Preserved in later editions and supplemented by five essays for analysis, the final chapter of this text offers detailed practical advice to help students use the techniques and standards of argument interpretation and analysis as the basis for their own critical analysis of an essay-length work. A sample essay, included in the chapter, is analyzed and evaluated according to the methods suggested.

Features New to the Fifth Edition

- A discussion of evaluating Internet sources of information is included (Chapter 5).
- The role of charity as a principle of interpretation is discussed (Chapter 2).
- Emotion and its possibly distracting role in argument evaluation are explored (Chapter 6).
- The importance of the dialectical context of argument is explained, and an emphasis is placed on the significance of objections and alternative positions (Chapter 3).
- The topic of pseudoprecision is included (Chapter 9).
- The fallacies of composition and division are explained (Chapter 9).
- There is an explanation of the nature and purpose of operational definitions (Chapter 4).
- The problem of jargon and elitist language is treated (Chapter 4).
- The fallacy of appeal to tradition is included (Chapter 6).
- All essays for analysis have been changed.
- Examples have been updated throughout.
- A number of incidental errors have been corrected.
- Chapter 7 has been shortened.

Where relevant, references are made to my recent book of theoretical essays, *The Philosophy of Argument* (Newport News, VA: Vale Press, 1999). Readers interested in further exploring points of theory may wish to consult that work.

The Instructor's Manual for the third edition was prepared by myself and Michael Reed of Eastern Michigan University. I have prepared the two subsequent manuals myself, with the able editing assistance of Risa Kawchuk in the case of the present manual. The Instructor's Manual offers overview summaries of each chapter, along with answers to exercises not answered in the text and suggestions concerning quiz and examination questions.

Acknowledgments

I have benefited from studying other texts in this field, from my participation in conferences on argumentation held at the University of Windsor, Brock University, and the University of Amsterdam, from writing and reading papers in the journal *Informal Logic*, and from discussions with students and colleagues over many years.

The treatment of analogies in this book derives originally from John Wisdom's "Explanation and Proof," (commonly known as the Virginia Lectures). I am grateful to Professor Wisdom for kindly granting me permission to study the manuscript of these lectures at a time when they were not in print. Carl Wellman's *Challenge and Response: Justification in Ethics* (Carbondale, IL: Southern Illinois University Press, 1971) also greatly influenced my ideas. The term *conductive argument* is taken from his work.

Students in Philosophy 105 at Trent University, in a graduate seminar on theory of argument at the University of Amsterdam, and in adult education courses in Calgary and Vancouver have helped me a great deal—both by expressing their enthusiasm for the study of argument and by asking challenging and penetrating questions about my ideas and techniques. Special mention must go to Derek Rasmussen whose enthusiasm for the subject has persisted, through greatly shifting life circumstances, over a period of nearly two decades. I have benefited considerably over the years from being able to discuss theoretical and pedagogical points with J. Anthony Blair, Ralph Johnson, David Hitchcock, David Gallop, Bernard Hodgson, Barrie McCullough, Bela Szabados, Frans van Eemeren, Rob Grootendorst, Jonathan Adler, Alec Fisher, James Freeman, Janet Sisson, and Marius Vermaak. Thanks also to users of this text who have sent queries and comments over the years.

Through their enthusiastic commitment to the development of informal logic and argument studies, J. Anthony Blair and Ralph Johnson of the University of Windsor have contributed greatly to this area of study—not only in their teaching and writing, but through the editorship of the *Informal Logic Newsletter*, later to be the journal *Informal Logic*, and their hard work in organizing international conferences. I owe them a great deal—as do many others who work in this area. I am grateful to Frans van Eemeren and Rob Grootendorst and their colleagues for the enormous energy they put into organizing conferences at the University of Amsterdam in 1986, 1990, 1994, and 1998. Similarly, I wish to acknowledge the hard work of Hans Hansen of Brock University and Chris Tindale of Trent University, in organizing conferences on argument held at Brock University (Ste. Catherine's, Ontario) in 1995, 1997, and 1999.

Wadsworth's philosophy editors, Kenneth King, Tammy Goldfeld, and Peter Adams, have given much helpful assistance over the years. Wadsworth's Mindy Newfarmer was helpful in discussing plans for the fifth edition and providing supportive publisher's materials, and I appreciate Kerri Abdinoor's work in connection with the Instructor's Manual. I would also like to thank the following manuscript reviewers for their helpful comments and suggestions for this new edition: Morton Schagrin of SUNY, Fredonia, Brian Domino of Eastern Michigan University, George Rainbolt of Georgia State University, Frank Fair of Sam Houston State University, and Istvan Berkeley of the University of Southwest Louisiana. Users may wish to seek out Wadsworth's philosophy resource center web site at http://philosophy.wadsworth.com.

I owe much to my "troubleshooters," Cary MacWilliams for the third and fourth editions and Risa Kawchuk for the fifth edition. Their critical questions, creative suggestions, and careful proofreading were enormously helpful.

As before, my greatest debt is to my husband, Anton Colijn, who, in addition to coping with the domestic stress resulting from the burden of writing a large manuscript at home, has been involved in the planning and writing of all five editions. Without his patient listening, discussion of themes and examples, continued enthusiasm for the subject, contribution of examples, and considerable assistance with computer matters, this book could not exist.

chapter one

What Is an Argument? (And What Is Not?)

THIS IS A BOOK ABOUT ARGUMENTS. It is about the nature of arguments—what arguments are and the different structures they have—and about the standards for judging arguments to be good or bad. It is about understanding the arguments other people give, evaluating those arguments, and constructing good arguments of your own. Arguments are found where there is some controversy or disagreement about a subject and people try to resolve that disagreement rationally. When they put forward arguments, they offer reasons and evidence to try to persuade others of their beliefs. Consider the following short argument:

> War is a legitimate instrument of foreign policy whenever the survival of the nation is at stake, because the purpose of foreign policy is to preserve the nation.

In this argument, a claim about the legitimacy of war is made; that is the **conclusion** of the argument. And a reason for that claim is put forward; that is the **premise** of the argument.

Argument and Opinion

A natural question to ask is how argument is related to opinion. Many people think that if an issue is controversial, what somebody thinks about it is just a matter of opinion and that there is no point in trying to give reasons for or against opinions, so argument is pointless whenever we are dealing with opinions. They think of opinions as being purely a matter of individual choice and not subject to any sort of critical evaluation. Such slogans as "Everyone has a right to his opinion" and "Well, that's your opinion," may suggest that, on controversial topics, people think in whatever way they wish, without evidence or reasons having anything to do with the matter. However, these ideas about opinions are oversimplified.

To think about this issue, we must first explore what an opinion is. An **opinion** is a belief, typically not fully supported by evidence, on a matter where we expect several different views to be held. For example, people have different opinions on the legitimacy of war as a tool of foreign policy. Some are of the opinion that war is never legitimate. Others hold the opinion that war is legitimate in certain extreme circumstances, as for example when the survival of one's country is in jeopardy. Still others have the opinion that war is legitimate whenever it is undertaken to protect profound values such as universal human rights. Another opinion is that war is legitimate whenever national interests are at stake. Evidence and reasons based on background theories are relevant to all these opinions and to the feelings and beliefs that surround them. However, evidence and reasons do not fully prove that one or another claim on this topic is right. Yet people do hold different beliefs, or opinions, about the legitimacy of war. Those opinions are discussed, are important in their own right, and make an important difference to policy decisions and to human lives.

Usually when we hold opinions, we are aware that they are our opinions, that we cannot prove or demonstrate them to be true, and that other people hold different opinions. If we are sensitive to the possibility of disagreement and the fact that others have views different from our own, we do not accept our opinions in quite the wholehearted way that we accept less controversial beliefs. Opinions can be formed with or without evidence, for good reasons or poor ones. On issues such as the legitimacy of war, opinions may be linked to theories and beliefs, and other opinions, on related topics. For example, different views on the legitimacy of war may stem from different views about such related matters as the value of human life, the nature of the nation-state, the legal and moral significance of national sovereignty, the existence of human rights, and the right to self-defense. Relevant facts may be cited to back up opinions. On the issue of the legitimacy of war, relevant facts would concern such matters as the effects of modern weaponry on the environment, the past effectiveness of negotiation and conflict resolution techniques when employed as alternatives to the use of violence, and the numbers and proportions of civilians killed in wars.

As human beings living in an uncertain world, we cannot avoid having opinions. Like our beliefs and our claims to knowledge, our opinions affect our actions. Politically and legally, we are free to hold any opinion at all. But from the point of view of logic and evidence, we cannot say that all opinions are equal. Some opinions are mere opinions, reactions based on little more than a gut response. A view that war is legitimate because violence gets people what they want has little credibility if it is based only on viewing adventure movies. This view is, to be sure, an opinion, and a person who holds it has the legal right to think it and to express it to others, claiming it as "my opinion." But that opinion has little credibility as contrasted to an opinion based on systematic theorizing about premises and a careful appraisal of relevant factual evidence.

What we think is important: it can be a matter of life and death. Even if something is "a matter of opinion," that is no reason to think hastily about it. We should seek well-founded and sensible opinions, grounded in factual accuracy and coherent and plausible background theories. We may hold any opinion we wish; we may hold completely arbitrary opinions, which have no good basis in reason and evidence. But there is little point in being careless and freewheeling about our opinions. Even though we are in some sense "entitled to our opinion," even when it is arbitrary or carelessly grounded, such an opinion will be of little interest to others and little service to ourselves. Concerning controversial issues there are pertinent evidence and theories that may be evaluated as reliable or unreliable and these grounds may provide better or worse reasons to back up our opinions. The point of arguing and evaluating arguments is to reach opinions based on reasoned reflection and good judgment.

Although we all hold opinions, this does not mean that all issues are *merely* a matter of opinion. Nor does the fact that we have different ideas on an issue demonstrate that there is no distinction between credible and careless opinions. Sometimes people say, "It's all a matter of opinion," suggesting in a misleading way that there is no reliable relevant information, that no reasons bear on the case, and that one opinion is just as good as another. In practical terms, however, people recognize that there is a distinction between truth and falsity, or between better and worse grounds for decisions and beliefs. For example, when choosing a college or university, or buying a car, people look for information, evidence, reasons, and arguments and try to make the best-informed and most sensible decision possible.

Nothing can assure us that our opinions are true. However, we can use and evaluate arguments to help us gain more credible and useful opinions, and to more fruitfully discuss our opinions with others. In this book, we hope to convince you that having an opinion is an occasion to begin thinking and arguing, not an excuse for not doing so.

Opinions on important controversial matters can and should be defended by rational arguments. Rational arguments can be analyzed and evaluated in a careful, logical way, and then be used to support opinions. You can do better than say, "That's just your opinion" when someone disagrees with you. You can learn to critically assess the reasons for the view and defend your positions with solid arguments. By arguing carefully, and responding carefully to the arguments put forward by others, you can work to discover which opinions are reasonable.

What Is an Argument?

An **argument** is a set of claims a person puts forward in an attempt to show that some further claim is rationally acceptable. Typically, people present arguments to try to persuade others to accept claims. The evidence or reasons put forward in defense of a claim are called the premises of an argument. An argument may have several premises, or it may have only one. The claim being defended in the argument is called its conclusion. An argument, then, is composed of one or more premises and a conclusion.

Let us return to the example about war, cited earlier:

> War is a legitimate instrument of foreign policy whenever the survival of the nation is at stake (conclusion) because the purpose of foreign policy is to preserve the nation (premise).

In this argument, as in others, the arguer does not merely say what he thinks or offer his opinion. He gives you a reason for this opinion or belief.

Sometimes the word *argument* is used to mean dispute or fight as in the sentence "The parents got into so many arguments over the child's problems that finally they stopped living together." In ordinary speech, this use of the word *argument* is quite common. In this book, however, the word *argument* is not used to refer to a fight or dispute. Rather, an argument is a reasoned attempt to justify a conclusion. Both kinds of argument—rational arguments and fights—have a connection with disagreements between people. When they use rational arguments in the sense of offering reasons, people respond to disputes by trying to reasonably justify their opinions or beliefs in an attempt to rationally persuade others that their opinions or beliefs are correct. When they fight, people do not restrict themselves to words and efforts to persuade by reason. Instead, they shift to other tactics—even, sometimes, to the use of force and physical violence.

It's important to keep the two senses of the word *argument* distinguished from each other. This book is not about verbal or physical fights. It is not even primarily about disputes. Here our concern is with the logical structure of arguments, their evaluation as cogent or not cogent, and their prospective usefulness as tools of rational persuasion. In the first few chapters, we concentrate on understanding what arguments are and how they are stated. We then move on to the task of evaluating arguments—offering and explaining standards that you can use to determine how good or bad an argument is.

Here is another example of an argument:

> There are no international police. It takes police to thoroughly enforce the law. Therefore, international law cannot be thoroughly enforced.

This argument has two premises (the first two statements) and a conclusion (the third statement). We can make the structure of premises and conclusions clearer by setting the argument out as follows:

1. There are no international police.
2. It takes police to thoroughly enforce the law.
Therefore,
3. International law cannot be thoroughly enforced.

In this argument, statements (1) and (2) support statement (3), which is the conclusion of the argument. The word *therefore* introduces the conclusion.

Let us look at a somewhat more complex example, taken from a letter to the editor of a newspaper. The letter deals with the issue of deficit reduction as a main goal of government. The author argues that cutting back on government expenditure is by itself not enough to be a worthy national goal.

> I am getting sick and tired of what seems to have become the Miserly Society, in which cutbacks and deficit reduction are present as our most worthwhile national goals. Think of it—the Magna Carta does not include a balanced-budget clause. In the Gettysburg Address there is not one mention of the deficit. The motto of the French Revolution was not "Liberté, egalité, responsabilité financière." If we really want to make Canada a better place for all of us, we will have to realize that there is more to having a country than balancing the books, and being able to make more stuff cheaper than anyone else.[1]

At the end, the author states his conclusion, which is that there should be more to national goals for Canada (and presumably any other country) than balancing the books economically. Before that, he states his premises. He seeks to support his view of deficit reduction by alluding to three famous national accomplishments: the Magna Carta, an English charter establishing protections for individuals under the law; the Gettysburg Address, an inspiring speech by the American president Abraham Lincoln; and the values of the French Revolution, which were liberty, equality, and fraternity, not liberty, equality, and financial responsibility. These landmark historical achievements of nation-states dealt with fundamental human values, and had nothing to do with debt, deficit, or accounting procedures. The author is arguing that because these achievements had everything to do with ideals and nothing to do with deficit reduction, deficit reduction is an inadequate and uninspiring goal for a nation-state. (We will not say at this point whether his argument is good or poor; the point is simply that this passage does contain an argument.)

A person who tries to persuade you by rational argument will claim that because the premises are true or acceptable, the conclusion should be accepted. The argument is put forward as an attempt to rationally persuade, on the basis of premises offered to an audience, that a stated conclusion is one that should reasonably be accepted. The arguer is saying, in effect,

Premise 1
Premise 2
Premise 3 . . .
Premise N
Therefore,
Conclusion

In effect, the arguer is claiming that she has given cogent reasons in her premises to support her conclusion, and that those premises render the conclusion rationally acceptable. Therefore, a person hearing or reading her argument has good reasons to accept the conclusion. In this model, the N and the dots indicate that arguments may have any number of premises—from a single premise to many. The word *therefore* indicates that the conclusion is being inferred from the premises supporting it.

Therefore is one of many words that logicians call **indicator words**. Other words such as *thus, so, consequently,* or *for these reasons* might have been used instead.

Indicator words suggest the presence of an argument. Some indicator words come before the premise or premises of an argument; others come before its conclusion. Indicator words are not part of the content of the premises or the conclusion. Rather, they serve to indicate which statements are premises and which are conclusions. In doing so, they indicate the direction of the reasoning in the argument. In attempting to rationally persuade people of her conclusion, an arguer in effect asks her audience to reason *from* the premises *to* the conclusion.

Here are some of the many indicator words and phrases that come before the premises in arguments:

PREMISE INDICATORS

since	on the grounds that
because	for the reason that
for	as indicated by
follows from	may be inferred from
as shown by	may be derived from
given that	may be deduced from

Consider another short example:

Universities need to have faculty who will do research, *because* there are few other institutions that support research.

In this example, the conclusion is that universities need to have faculty who will do research. The premise is that there are few institutions other than universities that support research. The indicator word is *because*. It comes before the premise, indicating that the premise is intended to provide rational support for the conclusion.

Here is another example:

It is a pity that career counselling and psychotherapy are viewed as separate disciplines, *since* both are often needed to help people realize their vocational ambitions.[2]

In this example, *since* is an indicator word that comes before the premise (both are often needed…) and helps us follow the direction of the argument. The conclusion comes before the indicator word and the premise comes after it.

Here are some of the words and phrases that come before conclusions in arguments:

CONCLUSION INDICATORS
therefore
thus
so
hence
then
it follows that

it can be inferred that
in conclusion
accordingly
for this reason (or for all these reasons) we can see that
on these grounds it is clear that
consequently
proves that
shows that
indicates that
we can conclude that
we can infer that
demonstrates that

Consider the following argument:

Kurt Godel, one of the most famous theoretical logicians of all time, was deeply disturbed by the suspicion that people were trying to poison him. This paranoia *demonstrates that* being theoretically profound does not always give a person the common sense to lead an ordinary life.

In this example, the indicator expression *demonstrates that* precedes the conclusion and shows us the structure of the argument.

Here is another example, in which *for these reasons we can see that* is the indicator expression that introduces the conclusion:

The number of Buddhists in North America is steadily growing, and business with countries such as Japan and India, which have large Buddhist populations, is increasingly significant in North America. *For these reasons we can see that* understanding Buddhism has practical as well as spiritual value.

Sometimes the word *and* may precede these conclusion indicators, as in expressions such as *and therefore* or *and accordingly*. In such cases, *and* itself is not an indicator word: it merely connects clauses or sentences.[3]

Both to understand other people's arguments and to construct and present clear arguments ourselves, it is important to be clear about the distinction between the premises and the conclusion. The conclusion is the claim or statement that is in dispute and that we are trying to support with reasons. The premises are other claims, which offer evidence or reasons intended to support the conclusion. The arguer claims that because the premises hold, the conclusion should be accepted. The argument can be used to justify the conclusion by reasons or in an attempt to persuade others, by reasons, that the conclusion is true or acceptable.

Where and How Do You Find Arguments?

Indicator words can often help you to find arguments, because they show that one claim is being given rational support by others. Consider the following examples:

(a) Human beings are neither naturally good nor naturally evil. *The reason is clear to see:* human beings become either good or evil because of the lives they lead, which in turn are the result of choices they make in this world.

(b) *Since* the meaning of a word must be understood by all the people who use that word, the meaning of a word cannot be a mental image in only one person's head.

(c) There is life somewhere in the universe as well as here on earth, *for* the universe is infinite and it can't be true that in an infinite universe only one place has the special features needed for life.

In example (a) the conclusion is "human beings are neither naturally good nor naturally evil." The indicator words are *the reason is clear to see*, which introduce the premise that human beings become good or evil as a result of choices they make. Whether human beings are naturally good or evil is an example of a matter on which a person might be said to have an opinion. In example (a) that opinion is backed up by reasons relating good and evil to choice and way of life. In example (b) the word *since* introduces the premise that tells you why the conclusion (that is, "the meaning of a word cannot be a mental image") is supposed to hold. In example (c) the conclusion is "there is life somewhere in the universe as well as here on earth," and the word *for* introduces the reasons offered for this claim. In these examples, the indicator words reveal that arguments are being offered and help to show the premises and conclusions.

It is not always as straightforward as this to find the premises and conclusions of arguments. There are several complications. First, not all arguments contain indicator words. It is possible to argue without inserting indicator words between the conclusion and the premises or before the premises. You can see this by changing example (c) only slightly, in such a way that essentially the same argument is presented, but the indicator word is omitted. Consider example (d):

(d) *John:* I think the earth is the only place in the universe where life has developed and can flourish.

Mary: I doubt it. The universe is infinite. It can't be that in an infinite universe, only one place has special features needed for life. There is life somewhere else in the universe as well as on earth.

In example (d) Mary replies to John and asserts all the claims asserted in example (c). We can understand which claim is her conclusion because of the conversational context that is given in the example. John makes a claim; Mary says she doubts it; she then tells John why she doubts it, in effect trying to rationally persuade him that there is a basis for her doubt. That is to say, Mary gives reasons for her view, which is different from John's view. Even though she does not use the word *for*, or any other logical indicator word, she is nevertheless offering an argument, and her conclusion is the conclusion put forward in example (c). This example illustrates the fact that arguments do not necessarily contain indicator words.

Another complicating factor about arguments and indicator words is that many of the indicator words such as *so, since, because, for, thus,* and *therefore* can also occur outside arguments. Their presence in a speech or written passage does not always mean that the speech or passage contains an argument. For example, the words *since* and *for*, which are important and common premise indicators, can also serve other functions.

Consider, for instance, the following examples:

(e) Since last week there have been three substantial dust storms in the Sahara.
(f) Susan did the word processing for Deborah.

In example (e), the word *since* introduces a period of time; it is not a logical indicator for a premise. In example (f), the word *for* is a preposition showing the beneficiary of Susan's work; it is not a premise indicator either. Words listed above as premise indicators and conclusion indicators typically have that function, but they do not always have it.

To be able to spot arguments, you have to develop your sense of context, tone, and natural logical order. Being able to understand the basic structure of an argument in terms of its conclusion and supporting premises is a matter of seeing when people are trying to justify claims rationally and which claims they are trying to justify. In practical situations, there is relatively little difficulty in determining that people are offering arguments because, as part of the situation, you know which claims are in dispute. Suppose you are a union member and you are trying to get a raise. Whether indicator words are used or not, you are likely to know what the conclusion of the union's argument is going to be: the workers should be given a raise. In offering arguments to management, the union tries to persuade them, on the basis of reasons, that the raise is feasible and appropriate. (Attempts at rational persuasion will end, and efforts in the direction of nonrational persuasion begin, if members stop the discussion and go on strike.)

Finding conclusions and premises in written texts may be more difficult than when you are engaged in a situation where oral arguments are being used. One possible source of difficulty lies in the fact that you may know less about the situation or context in which the argument is put forward. To understand whether a written passage contains an argument and what claims in the text are the premises and the conclusion of the argument, we may need background knowledge about the context in which the passage was written. Indicator words can be helpful. When there are no indicator words in a text, it may still contain an argument if some statements in the text are best interpreted as providing reasons, support, or evidence for others. One clue to the presence of argument is an indication that a claim put forward has been disputed and is thus in need of support. If someone says, "Jane has long insisted that such and such is the case, but actually, such and such is false," it will be natural for him to follow his contention that Jane's view is false by giving reasons. If he does this, he offers an argument. Similarly, in the example offered earlier about deficits and government goals, the author was clearly replying to a view he did not hold: the view that getting costs down is the primary and sufficient goal of government.

People may construct arguments when there is little controversy about the conclusion, to see whether a good justification could be given for beliefs that are not, in fact, disputed. For instance, philosophers have constructed complicated arguments for conclusions such as that material objects exist outside human minds, or events have an order in time. Few people have practical doubts about these conclusions. However, these beliefs are so fundamental in our picture of the world that the question as to how they can be supported by reasons and evidence is profound and important. One way of exploring those foundations is to construct and examine arguments that can be put forward to support them. In this context, argument construction and argument evaluation serve as methods of inquiry and investigation.

If you are trying to determine whether a speech or a passage contains an argument and you are having some difficulty interpreting it, you can start by asking yourself what the conclusion would be if it were an argument. Is something in dispute? Or is a possible dispute being considered? Is a claim normally taken for granted explored by someone who is putting forward various reasons for it? Reflecting on what is at issue in the context—what is being disputed or supported— may guide you to the conclusion. If you cannot find a stated conclusion and you do not think a conclusion is suggested by the passage, then there is likely no argument. If you think you have found a conclusion, you then see whether other claims are offered as evidence or reasons to support it. If there is a good reason to regard the writer or speaker as trying to persuade others that a claim is true, then the speech or passage contains an argument. Casual conversations about practical problems or public issues, scientific research papers, meetings, political speeches and lectures, letters to the editor, academic books and articles, and advertisements are all natural homes for arguments.

Why Are Arguments Important?

Since some nonarguments are perfectly acceptable and some arguments are poor, we cannot in general say that one speech or text is more rational than another, merely because it contains more arguments. This leads us to the general questions why, and in what ways, arguments are important. In general, arguments are no better or worse than other forms of communication; they are merely different, serving a different purpose. The lack of an argument is a fault in serious contexts where disputable claims are being put forward as true. For instance, if a political analyst were to claim that the next U.S. president will be African American and offer no evidence, this would be a flaw in her account. The claim might be true, but people would not accept it as true unless they saw considerable support for it. However, many claims don't require argument; they are claims on which people agree anyway or claims for which arguments have been given in other places. It would be perfectly appropriate, for instance, for a political analyst to claim that the United States will have another presidential election in the year 2004 and give no supporting argument, because these elections are regularly held every four years, and elections were held in 1992, 1996, and 2000.

Why all the fuss about arguments? The general answer is that unlike descriptions, jokes, stories, exclamations, questions, and explanations, arguments are attempts to prove or justify a claim. We use arguments when we try to rationally persuade others of our beliefs and opinions. The processes of justification and rational persuasion are important both socially and personally, and for both practical and intellectual reasons. When we give arguments, we try to show reasons for believing what we do, and in doing so, we gain an opportunity to explore the strength of these reasons. When we evaluate other people's arguments, we think critically about what they claim and their reasons for claiming it. Arguing and evaluating arguments are indispensable parts of critical thinking—of carefully examining our beliefs and opinions and the evidence we have for them.

Careful attention to the arguments of people who disagree with us can help us understand why they think as they do. It may give us good reason to rethink our own position; by attending to the arguments of other people, we may find reason to conclude that we are wrong. Finding out that we are wrong may sound unpleasant, but it is of fundamental importance. If we never consider reasons why we might be wrong, we have no possibility of knowing that we are right. To understand what we believe, we have to understand and consider why we believe it. The processes of listening to, evaluating, and constructing arguments provide the best way to do this.

Arguing back and forth is an approach to disagreement. It is nearly always more reasonable and less dangerous than some of the common alternatives such as cutting off all communication, weeping, shouting, making threats, or physically attacking someone. When parties disagree about a claim or theory, when they have different opinions, they can try to persuade each other by reasons. If back-and-forth argument is pursued honestly and sincerely, one or both may change their views so that the disagreement is resolved. Even if agreement is not achieved, the process will help them better understand each other.

Some people say, "He has not given us any argument at all," when they really mean that someone has offered faulty arguments. In effect, they are using the word *argument* to mean *good argument*. We do not follow that usage in this book. In our sense of *argument*, a person has offered an argument if he or she has put forward premises in an attempt to justify a conclusion. In our sense of the word *argument*, arguments may be evaluated as either good (offering cogent reasons) or poor (failing to offer cogent reasons). Given that the premises are put forward by an arguer as backing up a conclusion, it is an open question whether they in fact do so. When you have gained the ability to criticize these arguments step by step, you will have an important strategy for persuading others to come around to your point of view. You will also be far better equipped to understand their point of view and see how they are led from some beliefs to others. Furthermore, you will be better able to reflect on your own beliefs and the reasons for them.

In addition, arguments are significant in contexts in which knowledge is being constructed. We want to know how well justified a theory or claim is, and we can find out by assessing the arguments that are (or can be) offered to support a position. A careful understanding of these arguments is extremely important when we are deciding whether to accept a new position. It also helps us to better understand positions we already accept. Sometimes it can lead us to revise them.

The question whether emotion, faith, authority, or beauty constitutes a viable alternative to reason and rational argument has often been raised. Many people believe that in some contexts, such as religion or love, arguing is beside the point, and the careful use of reason is inappropriate. We have the right feelings or we do not, and that is all there is to it. But even in these profoundly spiritual and emotional areas, where trust and faith are crucial to our experience, it would be going too far to say that reason and argumentation are irrelevant. We need reason to explore the limits of our trust and faith. Many thinkers have, for instance, tried to prove the existence of God by reason and have used reason in the process of interpreting religious texts such as the Bible, the Torah, and the Koran. As for love, where is the lover who did not, at some time, try to weigh evidence to determine how the loved one feels about him or her?

Whether intuition and feeling are viable alternatives to reason or valuable supplements is a profound topic, one about which many books have been written. Our view on this topic—which we cannot explore in any real depth here—is that intuition and feeling are indispensable supplements to reason, but they cannot replace it. Trying to justify human beliefs by reason, arguing for and against claims that are in dispute, is an indispensable intellectual task, central to human existence. Careful reasoning from acceptable premises to further conclusions is the best method of arriving at decisions and beliefs because this method is the most likely to lead to accurate beliefs and sensible decisions. Only the method of reason is based on the need to respect standards of evidence and logical principles. Because this method is more reflective, more careful, and more systematic than the others, it has the greatest chance of getting things right.

The main purpose of this book is to cultivate your ability to construct and evaluate arguments. These are not new things, of course. In all likelihood, you have been doing these things nearly all your life. To improve skills you already have, we will direct your attention explicitly toward things that you normally take for granted. What is likely to be new for readers working through this book are the experiences of thinking reflectively about these natural activities and working to articulate and defend general standards used to judge arguments as good or poor.

What Isn't an Argument?

Even the most rational speakers and writers do not offer arguments all the time. Sometimes they simply make statements, and those statements are neither premises nor conclusions. Sometimes they make exclamations, expressing feelings. Or they raise questions, describe events and problems, explain occurrences, tell jokes, and so on. In none of these cases are they trying to justify conclusions as true on the basis of supporting reasons.

Consider the following:

(a) In 1999, there were between 160,000 and 190,000 Jewish settlers living in the West Bank.
(b) I can't stand broccoli!
(c) What were the causes of World War I?
(d) It was a crisp and frosty September morning, but so many problems occupied their minds that the beauty of the day went unappreciated.

None of these sentences express arguments. Example (a), is simply a statement of fact, put forward in an article "The Irrelevance of a Palestinian State," by Anthony Lewis.[4] Example (b), expresses a feeling of distaste. Example (c), raises a question rather than stating or claiming anything. Example (d), offers no argument; it merely describes a situation, saying how it was on that morning in September. In none of these sentences do we find an attempt to persuade people of a conclusion; therefore, none of them expresses an argument. The sentences serve other purposes: expressing, questioning, and describing.

Let us look at several longer passages that do not contain arguments and see just why they do not. The following excerpt is taken from a newspaper editorial:

> It's not the sort of chatter you hear at cocktail parties, but the muscle fibres of the cockroach are almost human. Really. That's why biologists at Atlanta's Emory University are teaching cockroaches to jog. They attach little weights to the roaches' legs and send them racing along the treadmill.
>
> Frankly, we're leery about doing anything that might give the insects an edge. It's hard enough trying to catch the little sprinters without having to listen to them wheezing behind the walls after a five-meter workout. But we shouldn't carp; there's always a chance the roaches will adopt not only the jogging, but the jogger's healthy lifestyle and scrupulous diet. If they start by keeping decent hours and giving up greasy foods, we'll be satisfied.[5]

This passage does not contain an argument. It first gives a humorous report of some research at Emory University and then expresses, in jocular terms, some possible risks and benefits of the research—to the insects and us. The writer obviously regarded the research as rather silly, and the style and tone of his editorial express that view. But he did not argue for it: no serious reasons are given as to why this kind of research is not worthwhile. (Probably the writer thought the point was too widely agreed-on to bother arguing about.) Because the writer merely expressed his views in a witty and entertaining way and did not try to persuade us by reasons of the truth of any conclusion, the passage does not contain an argument.

Another example of a passage that contains no argument is taken from *Greenlink*, a news magazine circulated by Greenpeace:

> The air reeked of oil. But as far as I could see, there was nothing but seemingly pristine snow stretching to the horizon. As I began walking towards the distant trees, my footprints in the snow turned brown. Suddenly, with a sucking noise, I sank knee deep into the thick black oil. I was on the edge of an oil "lake," only one of dozens of such lakes in the Russian Arctic republic of Komi, and part of one of the largest oil spills in history.[6]

Here the author, Kevin Jardine, tells of his trip to the Russian republic of Komi to check into reports of oil spills. At first he thought he could see only clear snow, but then he saw brown and began to sink into the ground. There was oil under the snow. Because Jardine simply describes his own experiences, the passage does not contain an argument.

Arguments are fascinating, and getting the knack of identifying and criticizing other people's arguments can be entertaining and fun. In fact, it is easy to get so carried away by the feeling of intellectual power gained through this activity that you start to see arguments everywhere—even where there aren't any. Although arguments are important and common in ordinary life, politics, work, and academic studies, we have to remember that much of what is written and said is not argument at all. Rather, it is pure statement, description, explanation, exclamation, questioning, storytelling, gentle ridicule, or any of a number of other things. Passages with these functions can be perfectly respectable, intellectually and rationally, without containing any arguments.

Arguments are needed when views are controversial and persuasion is attempted. If Kevin Jardine were debating the safety of oil and gas development in Russia with representatives of multinational corporations, they might ask him to prove that there had been serious oil spills in Russia. He would then have to document the point, and he might use his own experiences in the republic of Komi as part of a larger argument. The passage in *Greenlink,* however, was not an argument. To say this is not to point out any fault, it is just another kind of passage. Similarly, the passage about cockroaches jogging had no argument, and again, this does not imply any fault. The author of that work presented some amusing facts and entertained us. His readers probably do not need to be persuaded that teaching cockroaches to run a treadmill has little utility. Since neither passage contains an argument, it would not be appropriate to try to find premises and a conclusion in either one. Nor would it make sense to accuse either author of using a poor, or weak, argument.

If a writer or speaker does not put forward an argument, he or she obviously does not put forward a poor argument or a good one. To evaluate arguments critically, we must first be able to identify them. This means that we must distinguish between those speeches or passages that contain arguments and those that do not. For those passages containing an argument, we have to identify the conclusion and the premises. In this book, because our special focus is on argument, we sometimes refer to speeches or texts that do not contain argument as **nonarguments.** There are many types of nonargument, including descriptions, stories, jokes, exclamations, questions, and explanations. Because in some contexts, explanations may be confused with arguments, they are discussed in more detail below.

EXERCISE SET

Exercise 1: Part A

For each of the following passages, determine whether it does or does not contain an argument, and give reasons for your judgment. If the passage does contain an argument, indicate the conclusion. *Answers to exercises marked with an * are provided in the back of the book.*

1. People don't want to hear it or believe it, but the truth is, war doesn't kill mainly soldiers. In twentieth-century wars, more than 90 percent of those killed have been civilians.

*2. The sun was setting on the hillside when he left. The air had a peculiar smoky aroma, the leaves were beginning to fall, and he sensed all around him the faintly melancholy atmosphere that comes when summer and summer romances are about to end.

3. Some people who came to North America from India for economic reasons are now returning to India from North America, again for economic reasons.

*4. Any diet poses some problems. Here's the proof. If the diet does not work, that is a problem. But if the diet does work, there is still a problem. If the diet works, then the dieter's metabolism is altered. An altered metabolism as a result of dieting means a person will need less food. Needing less food, the person will gain weight more easily. Therefore, after successful dieting, a person will gain weight more easily.

5. The system was technologically advanced, and yet it was remarkably easy to use.

*6. "A computer then calculates the patient's bone density. Readings are compared to those of a standard for people of the same age, sex and body type. Using a classification system developed by the World Health Organization, physicians express the risk of osteoporosis as a T-score.

People with a minus one T-score are considered at low risk for fracture, while those with T-scores of minus one to minus 2.5 are considered to have osteopemia, or low bone mass."
(Advertisement "Unraveling the Mystery of Soft Bones," in the *New York Times Magazine*, June 20, 1999)

7. Everybody who dreams is asleep. When a person is asleep, he cannot control his mind so as to plan things. Therefore, dreams cannot be controlled by a person who is dreaming.

8. "The tradition of stand-up comics grew out of the coffeehouses of Greenwich Village in the early fifties. Now there are at least six chains in the United States, bringing laughter, of sorts, to all parts of the country."
(Toronto *Globe and Mail*, May 2, 1990)

9. "Now it is manifest by the natural light that there must be at least as much reality in the efficient and total cause as in the effect of that cause. For where, I ask, could the effect get its reality from, if not from the cause?"
(Rene Descartes, "Third Meditation," as translated by John Cottingham, in *Rene Descartes: Meditations on First Philosophy with Selections from the Objections and Replies* [Cambridge, England: Cambridge University Press, 1986], p. 28)

*10. "If all goes well, the reactor and the steam generators in a nuclear power plant of the pressurized-water variety maintain a stable, businesslike relationship such as might obtain between two complementary monopolies. The reactor can be thought of as selling heat to the steam generators."
(Daniel Ford, *Three Mile Island: Three Minutes to Meltdown* [Middlesex, England: Penguin, 1982])

11. "You not only need to control it (toxic radioactive substances) from the public, you also need to keep it away from the workers. Because

the dose that federal regulations allow workers to get is sufficient to create a genetic hazard to the whole human species. You see, these workers are allowed to procreate, and if you damage their genes by radiation, and they intermarry with the rest of the population, for genetic purposes it's just the same as if you irradiate the population directly."
(Quotation from medical physicist John Gofman, cited in Leslie Freeman, *Nuclear Witnesses* [New York: Norton, 1982])

12.   "If you want to be successful in business on a long-term basis, you must match your operational expertise with an ethical code of conduct practiced in every phase of your business. No exceptions! Why? Because history has proven that ethical businesses succeed in the long run and, to put it bluntly, because business ethics can be measured in dollars. Sooner or later, unethical businesses get caught."
(Jacqueline Dunckel, *Good Ethics, Good Business* [Vancouver: Self-Counsel Press, 1989], p. 2)

*13.   "Like our ancestors of a thousand years ago, we still war and pray and worry about who our children will marry. We still laugh at bad jokes and loud farts and scary noises that turn out to be nothing. We flirt and steal and mourn our dead. Nothing there has changed. But when you look at today's science and technology— how the solar system is put together, the wonders of refrigeration, antibiotics, the theory of evolution, liver transplants, the structure of the atom, nylon, television—we are very different. Our powers are different. Our global consciousness is different. Our wealth, both intellectual and material, is different."
(Editorial in the Toronto *Globe and Mail*, January 6, 1999)

14.   "I shall pass through this world but once. If, therefore, there be any kindness I can show, or any good thing I can do, let me do it now; let me not defer it or neglect it, for I shall not pass this way again."
(Attributed to Stephen Grellet, cited in *The Penguin Dictionary of Quotations* [London: Penguin Books, 1960], p. 179)

*15.   "An ant is crawling on a patch of sand. As it crawls, it traces a line in the sand. By pure chance the line that it traces curves and recrosses itself in such a way that it ends up looking like a recognizable caricature of Winston Churchill. Has the ant traced a picture of Winston Churchill? A picture that depicts Churchill? Most people would say, on a little reflection, that it has not."
(Hilary Putnam, "Brains in a Vat," in *Reason, Truth, and History* [Cambridge, England: Cambridge University Press, 1981])

16.   "Britain is no longer a Christian country and makes no pretence of being one. Churches are being closed throughout the nation. On Sundays in London's West End, the congregations are in the shops, some of which do booming business. There is as little attention paid to God in Britain as in Cuba. We see emerging there the grim paganism of twentieth-century life."
(Patrick O'Flaherty, in "A Growing U.K. Religion: Animal Worship," Toronto *Globe and Mail*, February 10, 1986)

17.   "In what respect are we superior to the brute creation, if intellect is not allowed to be the guide of passion? Brutes hope and fear, love and hate; but without a capacity to improve, a power of turning these passions to good or evil, they neither acquire virtue nor wisdom. Why? Because the Creator has not given them reason."
(Mary Wollstonecraft, "Vindication of the Rights of Men," in *A Wollstonecraft Anthology*, edited by Janet Todd [Bloomington: Indiana University Press, 1977], p. 73)

*18.   "When Lee Bass was just 16, his father sent him from the comfort and security of his family home in Fort Worth, Texas, to take part in a wilderness leadership program in South Africa. One experience in particular etched itself on his mind: being forced to clamber up a tree in fear for his life as a charging rhinoceros chased him. "That sort of thing tends to make an impression on you," he recalls with a smile. Today, at 38, Bass is a rich man, with corporate interests extending from oil and chemicals to investment,

property, and construction. In an earlier time, a man in his position might have become a big-game hunter....[I]t came as something of a surprise to find Bass recently at a meeting in Australia with fellow conservationists committed to saving rhinos from extinction under the banner of the International Rhinoceros Foundation."
(From Bob Beale, "The Rhino Meets Its Matchmaker," as printed in *World Press Review,* July 1994)

19.   *Background:* In the summer of 1978, Andrew Young was the American ambassador to the United Nations. Young, an African American, made the controversial statement that there are large numbers of political prisoners in the United States. In the public uproar that followed, African American activist Jesse Jackson contended that Young's statement was quite correct:

 " 'Some may debate the diplomacy and timing used by Ambassador Young, but the truth and accuracy of his statement is beyond question,' Jackson told the Leavenworth prisoners.

 " 'Thousands are in jail because they are too poor to pay bail bond,' Jackson said. 'Thousands are in jail because of delayed trials. Thousands are in jail because they were not tried by a jury of their peers. That is political.' "
(Calgary *Herald,* July 17, 1978)

 As he is quoted here, did Jackson offer an argument?

20.   *Background:* Here Metta Spencer, editor of *Peace* magazine, is interviewing Richard Falk, professor of Politics and International Affairs at Princeton University.

 Metta Spencer: I think we should give some thought to the lack of democracy in the process of globalization. I know you are doing some writing on this issue. Tell me your suggestions.

 Richard Falk: Basically it's important to allow citizens—voluntarily organized—to participate more directly in the decision-making institutions of the world. This means challenging the influence of global market forces and trying to force states to take account of what their citizens want, as well as what the global market prescribes in terms of efficiency and profit mar-

gins and so on. This is partly an educational matter. People need to learn that the global market is creating a non-sustainable human future by promoting a consumerist ethos that can't be realized without destroying the foundation of life on Earth.
(*Peace* magazine, November/December 1994, p. 11)

Exercise 1: Part B
In each of the minidialogues below, construct an argument for the second character, so that they give reasons for their claim. Then, indicate the conclusion and premises of the arguments you have constructed. *Note:* Of course, it is better to construct good, cogent arguments than poor ones, but we have as yet said nothing about what makes an argument good or poor. Construct an argument that you think is at least superficially reasonable and sensible.

1.   *John:* You should get a small car to save on gas.
 Bill: I disagree. Small cars are just not safe on the highway.

2.   *Sue:* Have you ever read *Gone with the Wind*? It's a very good book for getting a better understanding of American history, because it tells about the Civil War from the point of view of people on the losing side, and that is a perspective that is not so often heard. Also, it is so vivid that it helps you remember war by presenting it in human terms.
 Penny: I didn't think so. I read the book but I thought it was long and boring.

3.   *Chris:* Reconciliation is something that can only happen between individuals, so it makes no sense at all to talk about national reconciliation—say between blacks and whites, or between natives and nonnatives.
 Paul: I can't see why you are saying that, because groups need to get together and cooperate every bit as much as individuals do.

4.   *Rosita:* I am going to enroll in a course in German. I really think that German is going to become much more important as a world lan-

guage, now that East and West Germany have reunited. In a few years, Germany will be the economic powerhouse of Europe.

Don: Well, that's interesting, but I think you are wasting your energy. There's only one international language of business, and it's English.

5. *Fred:* I just read a review of the concert our choir did last weekend. The review was pretty negative. The guy didn't like our soloist, and he said the tenors were off-key. Boy, do those critics make me mad! Probably none of them can sing a note—or do anything else for that matter. But they can sure go all out attacking other people who try to do creative things! I don't know why newspapers hire these guys in the first place. They are completely unnecessary.

Kathy: I disagree. Critics play a valuable role.

6. *Jim:* Genetically altered foods could be really dangerous, because the alterations could have effects far into the future, on things like the human immune system and even human genetic structure. If I can avoid eating genetically altered foods, I sure will.

Jan: I think these foods are safe enough. I'd be willing to eat them.

7. *Melissa:* There is no point in saving for retirement when you are only in your twenties, because it is just too unpredictable what the world will be like in fifty years or so, when you would need the money.

Shadeep: I don't know. Well, actually, I think you're wrong.

Argument and Explanation: What's the Difference?

Some of the indicator words that may appear in arguments may also appear in explanations. Although explanations resemble arguments in several ways, there are important differences between them. As we have seen, in an argument, premises are put forward as grounds to justify a conclusion as true. In an **explanation**, on the other hand, claims are put forward in an attempt to render a further claim understandable—to offer an account as to why it is true. Explanations are offered on the assumption that the fact, situation, or event being explained exists, and the question is why or how it came into existence. Much has been written about the nature of explanations. In this book, we concentrate on the logic of arguments, not on explanations, and look at explanation only in a preliminary way. Our main purpose is to clarify the distinction between explanations and arguments.

We have seen that arguments are formed of premises and conclusions, which may naturally be arranged as:

Premise 1
Premise 2
Premise 3 . . .
Premise N
Therefore,
Conclusion

It can be difficult to distinguish arguments and explanations because they both can be set out in a similar way and they both give reasons. In arguments, the premises are intended to provide *reasons* to justify the conclusion, to show that the conclusion is plausible or true. In explanations, statements having a role parallel to that of the premises usually describe *causes* or factors that show how or why a thing came to exist. Still, many of the same indicator words used in arguments are also used in explanations. Words such as *therefore, so,* and *thus,* which often precede the conclusion of an argument, may also point to a statement of something to be explained. The word *because,* which is often used before the premises of arguments, is also to be found in explanations.

Consider, as an example of an explanation, the following:

> The window had been shut all summer and the weather was hot and damp. So the room smelled awfully musty when he returned.

Here the word *so* introduces a statement describing what is explained: the mustiness of the room. The passage does not contain an argument; there is no attempt to prove or give evidence that the room smelled musty. Rather, the passage contains an explanation of what is assumed to have been a fact: that the room smelled musty. The first sentence offers information that would show how the room came to be musty. The word *so* connects the causes cited for it being musty with the fact that it is musty. The writer is not trying to justify or back up a claim, as he would do in an argument. He is not trying to prove that the room was musty. Rather, he is assuming that it was musty and attempting to explain why it came to be musty.

In an explanation, someone tries to show how something came to be. Typically, explanations are given by citing causes of the event, fact, or thing to be explained. The explanations may naturally be set out as:

> Factor (1)
> Factor (2)
> Factor (3)…
> Factor N
> Therefore,
> Fact or event *x* came to be.

Any number of factors may be cited in an explanation. Often, the factors cited in an explanation are causal factors; the fact or event is explained by citing causes that produce it.

Here is another example of a causal explanation:

> She had difficulty completing the examination because she has an eye problem that affects her reading. In addition, the room was noisy, making it difficult to concentrate.

In this example, the word *because* precedes two phrases that mention causal factors (eye problems and noise affecting concentration) which explain her difficulty in completing the examination.

Sometimes, instead of offering reasons for their beliefs, people explain what caused them to hold these beliefs. In doing so, they explain themselves but make no attempt to justify their beliefs as acceptable. You can see this in the following example, based on a speech given by a political science professor.

> You know, I am one who has a positive sense of the things that government can do. And I'll tell you why I feel this way. I grew up in Britain after World War II and the government was doing a lot. When I was a child, we had a hot lunch program and a milk program in our school. It helped me a lot and it helped many other children too. Later I won a state scholarship. It was only because of that scholarship that I was able to go to university, and that's how I came into my present career. So it was natural for me to believe that the state is a positive force that can play a positive role in people's lives.[7]

In this passage, the word *so*, which may indicate the conclusion of an argument, plays another role. It precedes the description of a belief that is explained, not justified. The speaker is not trying to argue that state intervention in people's lives is generally good. When he made these remarks, he was introducing himself to an audience. As part of his self-introduction, he described his own background and explained, in terms of the circumstances of his own life, why he believes that state intervention in the economy can have good effects. His explanation of his feelings, given his own experience, is not an argument. The fact that there is an explanation for his attitude based on his life experience neither supports his belief nor refutes it. He offered the explanation to introduce a broader and more general analysis of the role of government in society.

Causal explanations offer an account of how and why things came to be as they are. There are at least two additional types of explanation: explanations by purpose and the explanation of meaning. Explanations by purpose offer an account of why something makes sense by fitting a phenomenon into a recognizable pattern or relating it to a human purpose. For example, we might explain why a mother with three sons is having another baby by saying that she would like to have a daughter. This explanation appeals to her *motives* for having the baby. Another type of explanation is involved when we explain the meaning of words. Explanations of meaning are not put forward in causal terms; typically, we explain what a word means by using other words that mean the same thing. We can explain what the word *sibling* means by saying that a sibling is a brother or a sister. A definition like this is an explanation, but it is not a causal explanation. It is an explanation of the meaning of a word, in this case the word *sibling*. It says nothing about the causes or effects of being a sibling.

Because some explanations cite motives or purposes, and others offer an account of the meaning of words, it not entirely accurate to think of explanations simply as being causal. There are various kinds of explanations. But even though thinking of explanations as causal is an over-simplification, it may be helpful to think along these lines for a little while. A great many explanations are causal, and the ones that are hardest to distinguish from arguments tend to be causal. Think initially of explanations as saying what the *causes* of something are and of arguments as offering *reasons* purporting to show that a claim is true or acceptable. That contrast makes it easier to sense the general difference between explanation and argument.

Arguments offer justifications; explanations offer understanding. Even though reasoning is used both in arguments and in explanations, and even though the same indicator words may appear in both, they have different purposes.

Here are three imaginary dialogues that bring out the different purposes of argument, explanation, and description. Suppose that two businessmen, Smith and Wilson, have a business that offers second mortgages. Wilson takes the business into a town called Slumptown, where people have little money to buy homes and as a result, there is a great demand for second mortgages. Wilson and Smith operate profitably in Slumptown for several years, but then the economy of Slumptown worsens, and many people are forced to default on their mortgages. The two men lose heavily. We can imagine the following dialogues between them:

DIALOGUE I

Wilson: Well, it's too bad we lost so much, but you can't win all the time. I just don't understand how it happened.

Smith: Actually, it's perfectly understandable. The causes of our good business in Slumptown were the poverty of the people and the bad job market there. Because people could not quite afford the houses they bought, the market for second mortgages was good. And yet these factors did indicate how vulnerable Slumptown's economy was. When the powerful XYZ company laid off workers, people in Slumptown were worse off than before, and they just couldn't keep up with the payments on their houses. It is easy to see what led to our losses in Slumptown.

Smith offers no argument here; he is explaining why he and Wilson lost their money. Now look at Dialogue II, which contains an argument, but does not contain an explanation.

DIALOGUE II

Wilson: We were unlucky in Slumptown. Perhaps we should transfer the firm to Hightown, down the road. In Hightown, there are plenty of jobs, the real estate market is booming, and people are crying out for second mortgages.

Smith: That would be a mistake, I think. Hightown is different from Slumptown in many ways, but it is similar in having a vulnerable economy. All of the economic activity in Hightown depends on one aircraft parts firm, which is expanding at the moment. If the firm loses a contract with Nigeria, it will have to lay off thousands of workers, and Hightown's economy will be severely affected. In such a situation, Hightown would become another Slumptown, and we would have the same problem with defaults all over again.

This time Smith does offer an argument. He gives reasons against taking the business to Hightown because he and Wilson do not initially agree on what should be done. In Dialogue I, both Smith and Wilson knew they suffered losses—there was no need to justify that proposition—and they were discussing what might have caused their losses. In Dialogue II, they initially disagree. Smith then tries to persuade Wilson that moving to Hightown would be unwise, and he gives premises—reasons to support that conclusion.

Passages that do not contain arguments may contain explanations, or they may contain descriptions, suggestions, jokes, questions, illustrations, and so on. We have emphasized explanations not because all nonarguments are explanations, but rather because explanations most closely resemble arguments and are hardest to distinguish from them.

To see an illustration of a passage that is neither an argument nor an explanation, consider a third dialogue about Slumptown and Hightown.

DIALOGUE III

Wilson: I found the contrast between Slumptown and Hightown quite amazing. In Slumptown, things looked so drab and messy. Windows were boarded over, even on the main street. People looked drab, too. It seemed as though the slowed-down economy even affected their clothing and the expression on their faces. Nothing much seemed to be happening, and people never seemed to have any energy. In Hightown, on the other hand, downtown shops were busy and there were no empty retail spaces on the main street. The people seemed colorful and lively. On weekends, there were lines for movies, active bars, and even lively amateur theater and music groups.
Smith: I know what you mean. I noticed those things, too. The difference was quite striking, wasn't it?

In Dialogue III, Wilson describes his perceptions and ideas of Slumptown and how they contrasted with those of Hightown. He is not trying to explain anything or trying to argue.

We have suggested, in the above discussion of the distinction between argument and explanation, that a set of claims can be either an argument or an explanation and never both at once. Unfortunately, things are not quite this simple. Two qualifications must be made. The first, which you will soon discover for yourself, is that some passages seem to be classified either as arguments or as explanations, depending on what you assume about the situation or context in which they are made.

Here is a simple example:

(a) Carol is the best math student in the class because she is the only student in the class who is going to a special program for gifted students.

Suppose that you read this passage and assume that the person making the statement is trying to persuade others that Carol is the best math student. As an arguer, that person would then be giving as evidence for his conclusion the claim that Carol goes to a special program. If you make this assumption about the context, you will see in it the following argument:

Premise: Carol is the only student in the class who is going to a special program for gifted students.
Therefore,
Conclusion: Carol is the best math student in the class.

On the other hand, you could make some different assumptions about the context in which the statement is made. Suppose you assume that the speaker is talking to a group of people, all of whom already agree that Carol is the best math student in the class. In such a context, there would be no point in arguing for that claim, because there is no need to try to rationally persuade anyone that it is true; the people spoken to already believe it. Those people might be interested in a suggested explanation as to how it came to be that Carol is the best math student in the class. Assuming this context, you would naturally interpret statement (a) as an explanation.

It would go like this:

> Proposed explaining factor: Carol is the only student in the class going to a special program for gifted students.
> This is why (that is, this explains or is the cause why),
> Carol is the best math student in the class.

As this example illustrates, statements and short passages taken out of context can sometimes be interpreted either as explanation or as argument. If someone quotes such a passage and asks you whether it contains an argument, you may not know what to say. You can think about different contexts in which the statements might be made and try to determine the most likely context. You can then make an assumption that this is the context, and base your interpretation on this assumption. (When you do this, it's important to recall that you have made an assumption and what that assumption is.)

Another problem that arises is rather rare but will be mentioned here in the interest of completeness. Occasionally, the very same statement or set of statements can serve both as argument and as explanation. This happens because the same premises that constitute evidence will also, by coincidence, serve to explain why the conclusion is true.[8] Here is an illustration:

1. A policy will be nearly impossible to apply if a key term used to state it is vague and unclear.
2. In the corporation's policy on ethical conformity, *ethical conformity* is a vague and unclear term, not given any precise meaning.
   Therefore,
3. The corporation's policy on ethical conformity is nearly impossible to apply.

Suppose that the context is one in which we do not believe (3), and (3) is in dispute. Then we would naturally read the passage as an argument intended to show that (3) is true. But suppose that we know (3) is true, and we are wondering why it is true. We are asking what causes the policy on ethical conformity to be so hard to apply. We can then read the passage as an explanation; we will understand (1) and (2) as showing the causes why (3) is true. We might even read the passage both ways: first as an argument put forward to rationally persuade someone of (3), then as an explanation of (3), granting that one has accepted (3) as being true. Cases like this are rather unusual and are considered here only in the interest of theoretical accuracy. They point to issues that are rather interesting, but too complex to be explored here.

In subsequent chapters, we try to avoid these cases where explanation and argument are threaded together. In practical life, you know more of the context than you are given in a logic textbook, and it is easier to judge whether an explanation or an argument is being put forward. Here, you have to use your background knowledge and sense of what needs to be rationally justified to try to determine whether an argument is being offered.

EXERCISE SET

Exercise 2: Part A

For each of the following passages, state whether it does or does not contain an argument. If you think that the passage does contain an argument, briefly state why and identify its conclusion. If you think that the passage is a nonargument, state why.

1.   The cause of the traffic jam was an abandoned truck in the center lane of the freeway.

2.   It is not essential to be tall to be good at basketball. This point is quite easy to prove. Just consider that basketball teams often have players of average height who make contributions to the game through fast running and expert passing.

3.   Good health depends on good nutrition. Good nutrition requires a budget adequate to buy some fresh fruits and vegetables. Therefore, good health requires a budget adequate to buy some fresh fruits and vegetables.

*4.   "Einstein's relativity principle states that the laws of physics—that is, the way individual measurements relate to one another—must be the same for everyone, but this does not mean that everyone's measurements of the same event will be the same. Most of my measurements of an event—if I happen to be moving relative to you—will look different from yours, but when I fit all my measurements together into a certain pattern, both our patterns will agree. These invariant patterns are the laws of physics, the same for all observers. Physics consists largely of the search for such patterns—ways of putting together observations that disagree to form structures that are the same for everyone."
(Nick Herbert, *Faster Than Light: Superliminal Loopholes in Physics* [New York: New American Library, 1988], p. 25)

*5.   We know that males and females have different hormones. Now scientists have discovered that these hormones affect verbal and spatial abilities that are connected with different sides of the brain. Given this evidence, it is likely that men's brains are organized differently from women's.

6.   "Don't despair. It doesn't help...and you don't have time."
(E-mail advice to a medical student, cited in the Toronto *Globe and Mail*, May 23, 1995)

7.   Some people find it easier than others to admit that they are wrong, because they are more secure about themselves and can own up to making a mistake without feeling as though they are deeply inadequate.

8.   Human beings are not the only animals that communicate with each other. It is well known that dolphins, whales, and elephants communicate with each other.

9.   Only if they are effective workers on teams can today's young people hope to fit into the modern corporation. These young people from a highly competitive private school are not effective workers on teams, so there is no way they

are going to fit into the modern corporate environment.

*10. Because she was an only child, she did not develop the independence necessary to care for herself. Even at seven, she was unable to put on her own skates, for example.

11. *Background:* The following passage is taken from *Harpur's Heaven and Hell* by Tom Harpur. Harpur describes a speech in which the speaker attributed his surviving a serious air crash to the power of prayer. He disputes the claims made by the speaker.

" 'Prayer is as important as it was centuries ago,' said Norman Williams, a man who survived the 1977 mid-air collision of two jets in the Canary Islands in which 593 people were killed. Williams credits his survival to his widowed mother's prayers with him before he undertook the journey. 'My Bible-believing mama asked me to pray with her for a safe return, and I did,' he said. 'That's what made the difference.' Does he think for one moment that none of the 593 or their families were praying for safety? Does he presume that somehow the others—some of whom, he said, were cursing as their plane burst into flames—were of less concern to God than he? Was Pastor Dietrich Bonhoeffer not praying when his Nazi captors led him out and hanged him in Flossenburg, just two days before the allies liberated the town? Did no one in Auschwitz, or Buchenwald, or Dachau pray before being sent to the crematorium? The plain fact of the matter is that bad things happen just as regularly to 'good' people as to anyone else."
(Tom Harpur, *Harpur's Heaven and Hell* [Toronto: Oxford University Press, 1983], p. 29)

*12. If a person knows in advance that his actions risk death, then if he voluntarily takes those actions, he is accepting a risk of death. These conditions surely apply to mountain climbers, so we can see that mountain climbers accept a risk of death.

13. "The only way you could license nuclear power plants and not have murder is if you could guarantee perfect containment. But they admit they're not going to contain it perfectly. So licensing nuclear power plants is licensing murder."
(John Gofman, in Leslie Freeman, *Nuclear Witnesses* [New York: Norton, 1982])

*14. *Background:* The following passage is taken from Edward C. Banfield, *The Moral Basis of a Backward Society*. Banfield is describing life among peasant people in a small Italian village called Montegrano, as it was in the early 1950s.

"In part the peasant's melancholy is caused by worry. Having no savings, he must always dread what is likely to happen. What for others are misfortunes are for him calamities. When their hog strangled on its tether, a laborer and his wife were desolate. The woman tore her hair and beat her head against a wall while the husband sat mute and stricken in a corner. The loss of the hog meant they would have no meat that winter, no grease to spread on bread, nothing to sell for cash to pay taxes, and no possibility of acquiring a pig the next spring. Such blows may fall at any time. Fields may be washed away in a flood. Hail may beat down the wheat. Illness may strike. To be a peasant is to stand helpless before these possibilities."
(Edward C. Banfield, *The Moral Basis of a Backward Society* [Chicago: Free Press, 1958], p. 64)

*15. *Background:* This passage is taken from the essay "On Liberty," by the nineteenth-century philosopher John Stuart Mill who defends freedom of speech.

"The peculiar evil of silencing the expression of an opinion is that it is robbing the human race; posterity as well as the existing generation; those who dissent from the opinion still more than those who hold it. If the opinion is right, they are deprived of the opportunity of exchanging error for truth. If wrong, they lose, what is almost as great a benefit, the clearer perception and livelier impression of truth, produced by its collision with error."

16. *Background:* This passage is taken from Avishai Margalit, *The Decent Society*. The author

is offering an account of Jean Paul Sartre's theory of human nature.

"Humans have no nature in the sense that they have no set of character traits or tendencies that uniquely determine the course of their lives. Every human being has the radical possibility of starting life anew at any moment irrespective of his life's previous course. This freedom to shape one's life is, in another sense, the only nature humans have, in contrast to other animals and things. Humans have no character, but they do have a nature in this sense."

(Avishai Margalit, *The Decent Society* [Cambridge, MA: Harvard University Press, 1996], p. 117)

17.   *Background:* In the period 1979–1982, Nestlé, a multinational corporation manufacturing chocolate, cocoa, coffee, and infant formula, was accused of overly aggressive advertising of infant formula in developing countries. Critics charged that because mothers in these countries were vulnerable to pressure to copy a Western way of life, they were encouraged to switch unnecessarily to infant formula instead of breast-feeding their babies. Due to unsanitary conditions, use of formula frequently caused illness or even the death of children.

"No one questions that marketing of infant formula in the Third World can pose serious problems. Everyone, including the infant formula industry, agrees that breast-feeding provides the best and cheapest nutrition for babies. Also, mothers who are lactating are less likely to conceive. Breast-feeding also helps to space out births. Therefore, marketing practices should not induce mothers who otherwise would be willing and able to breast-feed to switch to the bottle."

(Herman Nickel, "The Corporation Haters," reprinted in Eleanor MacLean, *Between the Lines* [Montreal: Black Rose Books, 1981], p. 91)

*18.   "His voice seemed suffocated and my first impulses, which had suggested to me the duty of obeying the dying request of my friend in destroying his enemy, were now suspended by a mixture of curiosity and compassion. I approached this tremendous being. I dared not again raise my eyes to his face, there was something so scaring and unearthly in his ugliness. I attempted to speak, but the words died away on my lips. The monster continued to utter wild and incoherent self-reproaches."

(From Mary Wollstonecraft Shelley, *Frankenstein* [New York: Scholastic Books, 1981—first published in 1817], pp. 266–267)

*19.   "The kids are rarely overpowered by life's adversities because they set up safety valves to release the mental anguish caused by their personal hang-ups. Lucy, for example, flaunts her femininity so she can cope with life more easily. Charlie Brown eats peanut butter sandwiches when he gets lonely. And Frieda wheedles compliments to restore her faith in herself and in her curly hair. Snoopy, unashamed, straps himself to his doghouse and mentally shrugs off most anything he can't handle."

(From Jeffrey H. Loria, *What's It All About, Charlie Brown?* [Greenwich, CN: Fawcett Publishers, 1968], p. 12)

Exercise 2: Part B

1.   Think of a particular person, such as a friend, relative, or co-worker whom you know quite well, and list five claims that you might at some time wish to explain to that person. Now list five different claims that you might at some time wish to justify to that person by offering an argument.

2.   Look at the two lists that you have constructed for question 1. What makes it reasonable to put a claim on one of the lists rather than the other? (That is, how do you say whether the claim would be more appropriately explained or justified to your friend?)

CHAPTER SUMMARY

Even though there are various opinions on controversial matters, we can seek to support our own opinions and understand other people's opinions by the process of rational argument. To argue on behalf of an opinion or belief is to put forward evidence or reasons in an attempt to show that it is true or plausible. Arguments have two basic parts: premises and conclusions. In understanding and constructing arguments, it is particularly important to distinguish the conclusion from the premises. Indicator words can help us do this: words like *therefore, thus, so, because,* and *since* tell us which claims are to be justified by evidence and reasons, and which other claims are put forward as premises to support them. Indicator words are not infallible signs of argument because some arguments do not contain indicator words, and some indicator words may appear outside the context of arguments.

Arguing and arguments are important as rational ways of approaching disputes and as careful critical methods of trying to arrive at the truth. Speeches and texts that do not contain arguments can be regarded as nonarguments. There are many different types of nonargument—including description, exclamation, question, joke, and explanation. Explanations are sometimes easily confused with arguments because they have a somewhat similar structure and some of the major indicator words for arguments are also used in explanations. Explanations should be distinguished from arguments, however, because they do not attempt to justify a claim, or prove it to be true.

Review of Terms Introduced

Argument   A set of claims put forward as offering support for a further claim. An argument is composed of the supporting claims and the supported claim. A person offers an argument when he or she tries to justify a claim by offering reasons for it.

Conclusion   In an argument, the claim for which premises are intended as support. It is this claim that the arguer tries to make credible.

Explanation   An account showing, or attempting to show, how it came to be that a fact or an event is the way it is. Frequently, explanations are given by specifying the causes of an event. An explanation is one kind of nonargument.

Indicator words   Words such as *for, since, thus, therefore,* and *because* typically used in arguments to indicate that a person is reasoning from premises to a conclusion. However, these words may also occur in explanations and elsewhere. They do not appear only in arguments.

Nonargument   A passage or speech that does not contain an argument.

Opinion   A belief typically about a matter open to dispute, where there is not full proof and others have different ideas. Often people are aware that their opinions are not fully backed up by evidence and hold less firmly to them than to other beliefs for which there is more conclusive evidence, less disagreement, or both.

Premise   A supporting reason in an argument. It is put forward as being acceptable and providing rational support for a further claim.

Notes

1. Letter to the Toronto *Globe and Mail*, May 26, 1995.
2. Jack Muskat, "Do What You Love—But Plan for It Carefully," Toronto *Globe and Mail*, May 22, 1995.
3. For a discussion of *and* as a logical connective between statements, see Chapter 8.
4. Anthony Lewis, "The Irrelevance of a Palestinian State," *New York Times Magazine*, June 20, 1999.
5. Editorial in the Toronto *Globe and Mail*, October 23, 1980. Reprinted with the permission of the *Globe and Mail*.
6. Kevin Jardine, "Canadian Oil on Russian Soil," *Greenlink*, Vol. 3 (1995) no. 1, p. 1.
7. David Thomas, address on Community; conference sponsored by the Calgary Institute for Local Initiatives, Calgary, Canada, May 13, 1995.
8. *For instructors.* I discuss the distinction between argument and explanation in a theoretical paper entitled "Why Arguments and Explanations Are Different" in Trudy Govier, *Problems in Argument Analysis and Evaluation* (Providence, RI: Foris, 1987). The point that the same statements can, on the same interpretation, serve both as argument and as explanation is made by S. N. Thomas in his teachers' manual for the second edition of *Practical Reasoning in Natural Language* (Englewood Cliffs, NJ: Prentice-Hall, 1983). Thomas contends that we should dispense with the distinction between argument and explanation altogether. In the essay referred to, I offer a number of reasons for not taking this view.

chapter two
Pinning Down
Argument Structure

I N MOST OF THE EXAMPLES in the last chapter, we could readily determine which claims were the conclusions of arguments and which were their premises. Most examples were relatively short and worded in a straightforward way so that the line of reasoning used in the argument was easy to follow. However, things are not always quite so clear. We sometimes have to look closely at passages and listen closely to speeches to see the line of reasoning. In this chapter, we look at the problem of identifying the premises and conclusions of arguments and see how important it is to examine carefully the particular manner in which arguments are stated. We also examine several different ways premises can support conclusions.

To evaluate an argument, we must first understand just what the argument is. That means understanding the premises and the conclusion and how the premises are supposed to support that conclusion. If we rush into the task of evaluating an argument and deciding whether we agree with the conclusion before we take the time to understand what the premises and conclusion of the argument are, we are likely to think too quickly and make mistakes.

Standardizing an Argument

To understand an argument more accurately, it is helpful to set out its premises and conclusion in a simple standard format such as the following:

Premise 1
Premise 2

Premise 3 . . .
Premise N
Therefore,
Conclusion

We'll call this standardizing an argument. To **standardize** an argument is to set out its premises and conclusion in clear, simple statements with the premises preceding the conclusion. By numbering the premises and the conclusion, we can refer to specific statements in an efficient way. We can simply refer to (1) or premise (1) instead of copying out all the words. We can say such things as, "The author uses statements (1), (2), and (3) to defend statement (4)." Standardizing arguments gives us a clear view of where they are going and forces us to look carefully at what the arguer has said. When we come to the more advanced stage of criticizing arguments, we will find standardizing extremely helpful, because it allows us to see which stage of the argument our criticisms affect and which parts of a speech or passage are essential in the attempt to establish the conclusion.

Here is a simple example:

It is a mistake to think that medical problems can be treated solely by medication. Medication does not address psychological and lifestyle issues. Medical problems are not purely biochemical. They involve issues of attitude and way of life.

In this example, the conclusion is stated before the premises. It is the first sentence: "It is a mistake to think that medical problems can be treated solely by medication." Three premises are offered as support for this conclusion: "Medication does not address psychological and lifestyle issues;" "Medical problems are not purely biochemical;" and "They (medical problems) involve issues of attitude and way of life." To write the argument to show the reasoning from the premises to the conclusion, we reorder the sentences: here (1), (2), and (3) are the premises and (4) is the conclusion. Standardized, the argument looks like this:

1. Medication does not address psychological and lifestyle issues.
2. Medical problems are not purely biochemical.
3. Medical problems involve issues of attitude and way of life.
Therefore,
4. Medical problems cannot be treated solely by medication.

The order of the sentences has been changed because it is a convention in logic, when we set out someone's argument, to state the conclusion after the premises. This order represents the fact that the conclusion emerges from the premises as a claim that is supposed to be supported by those premises. Interestingly, though, in speech and in writing, conclusions are often stated first and then followed by supporting reasons. Thus, the reversal that we have used in setting out this standardization is often necessary. Note also that the conclusion is written in a more simplified style, replacing "it is a mistake to think that . . ." with the denial of the claim in question.

So far we have described arguments as though each one were self-contained. Actually, arguments often proceed in stages in such a way that what is a premise in one argument is the conclusion in another. Premises may be defended in subarguments, so that there are really several arguments in one. A **subargument** is a subordinate argument inside a main one, in which a premise in the main argument is defended.

Consider this example:

> A computer cannot cheat in a game, because cheating requires deliberately breaking rules in order to win. A computer cannot deliberately break rules because it has no freedom of action.

As in the previous example, we need reversal of order for the standardization. The argument can be set out as follows:

> 1. A computer has no freedom of action.
> Thus,
> 2. A computer cannot deliberately break rules.
> 3. Cheating requires deliberately breaking rules.
> Therefore,
> 4. A computer cannot cheat.

The premises supporting the claim that a computer cannot cheat are that cheating requires deliberately breaking rules and a computer cannot deliberately break rules. This argument is found in the first sentence and in the first part of the second sentence in the unstandardized example. The direction of this argument is indicated at several points by the word *because*.

There is a subargument structure in this example. The premise that a computer cannot deliberately break rules is itself supported by a reason: a computer has no freedom of action. The argument can be diagrammatically represented as shown in Figure 2.1.

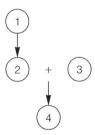

FIGURE 2.1

In this example, premise (1) is offered as support for premise (2), which is the conclusion in the subargument, sometimes called a subconclusion. Then, in the main argument, premises (2) and (3) are offered in support of the conclusion, (4). The same statement "A computer cannot deliberately break rules" serves the roles of both premise and conclusion, since it both supports and is supported.

From a practical point of view, it is easy to see why subarguments are necessary and useful. When you use an argument, you are trying to rationally persuade others of your belief, trying to convince them, on the basis of evidence or reasons, that your claim is correct and should be accepted. You use premises in an attempt to justify your conclusion and persuade your audience that it should be accepted. You are, in effect, asking your audience to accept your premises and to reason from them to the conclusion. If your audience doesn't accept the premises, there is little in the argument to convince them. When you need to use a premise that you anticipate your audience may not readily accept, that is the time for a subargument. You can back up the premise so that it will be more reasonable, and your whole argument will be more convincing. In the previous example, for instance, many people might not find it obvious that computers cannot deliberately break rules. The subargument is an attempt to give a reason for that claim.

To speak of the premise or the conclusion or the argument in the example about whether computers can cheat is somewhat unclear, because there are two different arguments involved. Thus two different sets of conclusions and premises can be identified. The argument from (1) to (2) is one argument, and the argument from (2) and (3) to (4) is another. However, the main point of the passage, or the **main conclusion,** is (4). The entire structure, with subargument and all the statements, we will refer to as the **whole argument**.

There is no theoretical limit on the number of subarguments that can be used as parts of an argument. We might, for example, find an argument like the one shown in Figure 2.2. In this structure, (1) is offered as support for (2), which is offered as support for (3); there is thus a subargument and a subsubargument. (9) is offered as support for (4); (10) is offered as support for (5); (4) and (5) together are supposed to support (6). The main argument is from (3) and (6) to (8). This example is given to illustrate the point that subarguments, subsubarguments, and so on are perfectly possible. There are contexts in which such structures are useful and important. In most practical situations, though, it is not advisable to use too many subarguments, since people may find your arguments hard to follow. In this book, we will not explore such elaborate structures.

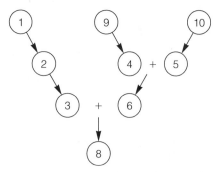

FIGURE 2.2

Here is an example in which there is a simple subargument structure. The author, Stephen Jay Gould, is a Harvard professor and science writer. He is discussing the issue of whether the human species is special, and whether it is a matter of false pride (hubris) to think of it as being unique.

> It is not mere hubris to argue that *Homo sapiens* is special in some sense—for every species is unique in its own way. Shall we judge among the dance of the bees, the song of the humpback whale, and human intelligence?

Although this is a short passage, it contains a main argument with a subargument. As in the previous example, the written order is the reversal of standard logical order. The second sentence in the passage is a rhetorical question. It is written in the form of a question, but it is a question to which the author assumes we know the answer. (Shall we judge . . . we shall not.) Rhetorical questions, which seek to impose a particular answer on the reader or listener, are another way of making statements.

Standardized, the passage looks like this:

1. We should not judge between the dance of the bees, the song of the humpback whale, and human intelligence.
Thus,
2. Every species is unique in its own way.
Therefore,
3. It is not mere hubris to argue that *Homo sapiens* is special in some sense.

Here, the main conclusion is supported by a single premise, which, in turn, is the conclusion of a subargument with a single premise.

Another interesting pattern is one in which the same premise or premises may be used to establish two distinct conclusions, so that one argument may appear to have two conclusions. Here is an example, adapted from the political philosophy of John Locke.

> Labor is the basis of all property. From this it follows that a man owns what he makes by his own hands and the man who does not labor has no rightful property.

This example is a statement of John Locke's theory of the moral basis of a right to private property. Locke believed that the human entitlement to private property was based on human labor. In the previous argument, "from this it follows that" is a phrase indicating inference. There is a single premise: labor is the basis of all property. From this premise, two conclusions are inferred: a man owns what he makes by his own hands and a man who does not labor has no rightful property. There is no subargument here, because Locke's premise is not supported by any other premise, and neither conclusion can be used to support the other. In fact, we cannot even really say that there is a main argument here. Strictly speaking, there are two distinct arguments, each of equal weight. The wording of the two arguments is compressed; they are stated together so that the common premise is stated only once, and then two different conclusions are drawn from it.

The two arguments can be standardized as:

1. Labor is the basis of all property.
Therefore,

2. A man owns what he makes by his own hands.
and
1. Labor is the basis of all property.
Therefore,
3. A man who does not labor has no rightful property.

We can diagram this argument in two different ways (see Figure 2.3).

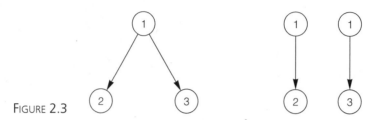

FIGURE 2.3

The diagram on the left of Figure 2.3 shows both conclusions emerging from a single premise, in a divergent way. The diagram on the right shows two arguments, each with the same premise.

From Colloquial Writing to Standardized Form

Standardization is useful because it enables us to identify conclusions, premises, and subargument structures. But these are not the only benefits of standardization. A major benefit is that we isolate the premises and conclusion from parts of the surrounding text that may not contain argument at all. In addition—as we saw in the case of the previous rhetorical question—we put premises and conclusions that may be expressed in indirect or unusual ways into straightforward sentences making claims.

To see the greater clarity that results when we standardize an argument, let us look at a lengthier example. The following passage is from a book about fund-raising for nonprofit groups. The author, Joyce Young, an experienced fund-raiser, wrote the book to offer advice to others.

> It may be that the general manager takes a very dim view of your group and has turned you down before. Should you try to approach the head office directly? In most cases the answer is no because the people at the head office are going to be very, very reluctant to go over the head of the local manager on a local matter. In fact, the head office might well send such a letter back to the general manager to draft a reply! Then the general manager will take an even dimmer view of your group.[1]

The first two sentences set the issue that the argument is about—whether a fund-raiser who has been refused by a local manager should go over the head of a local office to approach the head office directly. The beginning of the third sentence, "the answer is no," expresses the conclusion that fund-raisers should not go over the head of a local manager to the head office in a case where a local office has refused them before. Two reasons are given in support of this conclusion. The first is that the head office does not like to go over the head of a local manager on this sort of issue (this premise is stated after the logical indicator word *because* in the third sentence). The second is that the head office might send your letter back to the local manager, who would then be less impressed by the group.

The argument can be standardized as follows:

1. Head offices do not like to go over the heads of local managers on fund-raising issues.
2. If a head office receives a request over the head of a local manager, it may well send the letter back for that local manager to compose a reply.
3. If a local manager receives a letter back from a group the manager has previously turned down, a letter that the group has sent to the head office by going over the manager's head, the manager's impression of that local group is likely to be worse than it was before.

Therefore,

4. It is not a good idea for fund-raisers to go over the head of a local manager who previously refused them to request money directly from the head office.

We can see from the standardization which statements are used as premises and what the conclusion is. The standardization also helps to indicate how the author reasoned from the premises to the conclusion.

Here is a further example, taken from the Christian writer and religious theorist, C. S. Lewis:

> Creatures are not born with desires unless satisfaction for those desires exists. A baby feels hunger. Well, there is such a thing as food. A duckling wants to swim: well, there is such a thing as water. Men feel sexual desire: well, there is such a thing as sex. If I find in myself a desire which no experience in the world can satisfy, the most probable explanation is that I was made for another world. If none of my earthly pleasures satisfy it, that does not prove that the universe is a fraud.[2]

Here Lewis is offering an argument. What is the point he is trying to establish? He talks about babies and ducklings and sex: this is to indicate that there are creatures on earth who are born with desires that can be satisfied on this earth. The examples seem to be his basis for saying that we do not have desires unless they can be satisfied. Lewis goes on to consider what would be the case if people were to have desires that could not be satisfied in this world. Most likely, he says, those beings would be made for another world. The last sentence in the passage virtually repeats this point in different words. This is the point Lewis is trying to establish: it is his conclusion.

The claims about the desires of babies, ducklings, and humans (sex) are used to back up his general premise about creatures being made with desires that can be satisfied (this is a subargument), and it is from that general premise that he seeks to derive his main conclusion. We should note that the conclusion is not that people are made for another world. (As a Christian, Lewis probably believed that, but he does not assert it in this passage.) Lewis asserts that if people have desires that can't be satisfied in this world, they are probably made for another world. ("If I find in my-self a desire which no experience in the world can satisfy, the most probable expla-nation is that I was made for another world.") It's important to notice that the main conclusion is qualified by the words *if* and *probable*. In standardized form, Lewis's argument looks like this:

1. The desires of babies who are hungry, ducklings who want to swim, and men who desire sex can be satisfied in this world.
So,
2. Creatures are not born with desires unless satisfaction for those desires exists.
Therefore,
3. If people find in themselves desires that no experience in the world can satisfy, then the most probable explanation for this is that they were made for another world.

It is worth noting what we had to do to Lewis's original paragraph to get this clear argument out of it. First, we had to look at the logical flow of the passage and identify the main conclusion. Second, we had to decide which parts of the passage were stated as reasons intended to back up that conclusion and put these into the most natural logical order; we also had to recognize the subargument structure. Third, we had to abbreviate and simplify Lewis's prose, putting it into clear, com-plete statements that could be used as premises. These tasks are not always easy to do. People write and speak in a way that is more disorganized (and more interest-ing) than the "(1) and (2), therefore (3)" format that is best to work with when we are evaluating arguments. They word statements in the form of questions and com-mands, repeat themselves, include background and aside remarks, tell jokes, wander off the topic, and so on. These elements of colloquial writing are eliminated when we put the argument in standardized form.

A passage may contain an argument even though it also contains sentences that are not premises or conclusions in that argument. Strictly speaking, background in-formation and material inserted just for added interest or for humor are not parts of the argument because they are neither premises nor conclusions. For example, a speaker or author may take some time to introduce the topic or to define the terms before offering an argument on an issue. He may explain the views of others, to set a context for his own. He or she may insert personal comments such as "It has al-ways amazed me that . . ." or "My interest is chiefly in . . ." or "I'm sick and tired of . . ." or "I've long been interested in . . ." Such expressions are not parts of an ar-gument in the sense of being its premises or conclusion. Thus they do not belong in the standardization. Often passages require considerable shortening and editing be-fore we can represent them as arguments in standard form. It takes practice to learn to do this. The work may seem picky and annoying, but it is worthwhile because standardizing arguments is an important skill that is helpful in many contexts. Working to acquire this skill, you are forced to read or listen with a view to deter-mining the main point of a passage or speech.

Practice in standardizing trains you to ask why the author or speaker is saying what he or she says. What reasons is this person offering to support his or her claims?

If there is no argument, you will not find a conclusion and premises. That too is a discovery worth making. If the claims made are controversial and require support, the fact that there is no argument given for them constitutes a strong criticism.

The following is a repetitive, disorganized example that illustrates the need to standardize and the simplification you can achieve by setting out the central argument in standardized form:

> In the letter "Any group could abuse children," in response to Professor Edward Shorter's column referring to the "great child abuse scam," Dr. J. Jacobs suggested: "Would it not be better to disturb the feelings of 99 families in the hope of finding one family who needed help in preventing further child abuse?"
>
> In my "unprofessional" opinion as a mere full-time mother of three, I would say that families have been "disturbed" too much for far too long by far too many professionals and that is why incidents of child abuse have increased by 34 percent in the past year.
>
> The professionals may not want to admit the possibility, but I believe that all the anti-parent, anti-family attitudes that gushed from the International Year of the Child campaign last year probably have a lot to do with that 34 percent increase in incidents of child abuse.
>
> The "professional observers of human nature" don't seem to understand just how much stress and pressure you have injected into North American families, bombarding young struggling parents with one shelling of modern philosophy and psychology after another for decades now.
>
> These "professionals" have not only brought stress, but distress into many families. Parents have been told so much that they don't know what to do any more. They have been conned into believing that their parents didn't raise them properly and they can't possibly trust their own instincts or judgments about what is right or wrong for their children.
>
> I say to all the "professionals" who've been minding everybody's business but their own: Let parents return to being intelligent individuals who desire to make their own judgments about what is best for their own children; stop trying to "diagnose and treat" us as though we were one great massive lump; and stop making us feel like criminals for spanking a child—maybe some of them won't feel so frustrated that they end up abusing them.[3]

This is a rather rambling letter. The author does seem to be arguing. As the first paragraph tells us, she has written to oppose a suggestion made by a Dr. Jacobs, and she tries to give some basis for her stance. The conclusion may be found in her opposition to Jacobs's view: she believes that professionals should not risk disturbing ninety-nine families in the hope of finding the one family in one hundred that would need help in preventing child abuse. (Check back to the first two paragraphs.) The author contends that professionals disturb parents and that parental disturbance is probably a major cause of child abuse. These points are made in the second, third, and fourth paragraphs of the letter. The fifth and sixth paragraphs try to provide some justification for the claim that professionals have harmed parents. Parents mistrust their own judgment because of extensive professional literature, and they feel like "criminals" when they spank their children because of the attitudes professionals take.

These are the main points. If you look back at the letter, you will see that it is quite repetitive. You don't need to state the same point more than once in the premises. Nor do you need to insert such expressions as "in my 'unprofessional' opinion as a mere...mother" and "I say to all the 'professionals.'" In these phrases, the author is adding a kind of editorial commentary to her substantive remarks. She is expressing her reaction rather than stating substantive reasons for her view. Obviously, there will be many deletions before we get a clear model with only the premises and the conclusion. The following version is reasonably accurate and tolerably short:

1. Professionals have made parents mistrust themselves and their own judgments about their own children. (fifth paragraph)
2. Professionals have brought stress and distress into many families. (fourth and sixth paragraphs)

Thus,

3. Professionals have probably brought about an increase in the incidence of child abuse. (second and third paragraphs)

Therefore,

4. Professionals should not risk disturbing ninety-nine families hoping to find the one family in one hundred whom they might help.

We now have a simple version of the original. Premises (1) and (2) are offered in support of (3) in a subargument; then (3) is offered in support of (4). This version is much shorter and clearer than the original. Should there be flaws in the argument, they will appear more clearly in the standardized version. But it is wise, in a case such as this one, to look back at the original when you are about to accuse the author of a major mistake in arguing.

We won't make any comment on the merits of this argument yet because in this chapter our job is to concentrate on identifying the premises and conclusions and seeing the basic structure. The evaluation of argument presumes this kind of structural understanding: you cannot accurately determine whether the premises give good reasons to support a conclusion unless you know just what the premises are and what the conclusion is.

General Strategies for Standardizing Arguments

1. Read the passage carefully several times, making sure that you understand it.
2. Confirm that the passage you are dealing with actually contains an argument. It contains an argument if, and only if, the author is trying to support a position with claims offered in its defense.
3. Identify the main conclusion or conclusions and any subargument structures. Indicator words should help. Often the context is helpful, particularly when one person argues against another. Typically in that case, one person's conclusion will be the denial of the other person's position; and the person denying another's position will offer reasons for doing so.

4. Identify those statements in the passage that are put forward as support for the main conclusion and any subconclusions. It is helpful at this stage to look at the statements in the passage and ask yourself which ones could plausibly give support, or be thought of as giving support, to the conclusion you have identified.

5. Omit any material that serves purely as background information—for example, introductory or editorial remarks.

6. Omit material that you have already included. This instruction applies when the same premise or conclusion is stated several times in slightly different words, except in two circumstances. First, if this happens when the different wording indicates first a premise and then a conclusion in the same argument do put the statement twice in your standardized version. (As we will see later, this situation means there is a serious flaw in the argument.) Second, you may wish to do this if a statement is first the conclusion in a subargument, and then serves as a premise in the main argument. In other circumstances, don't repeat the statement.

7. Omit such personal phrases as "I have long thought," "in my humble opinion," and so on. These are not part of the content of the argument but are stylistic indicators of the author's direction.

8. Number each premise and conclusion, and write the argument in the standard form with the premises above the conclusion.

9. Check that each premise and conclusion is a self-contained complete statement. This means that premises and conclusions should not include pronouns such as *he*, *my*, *it*, and *this*. Instead, the appropriate nouns should be used. Also, premises and conclusions should be in the form of statements—not questions, commands, or exclamations.

10. Check that no premise or conclusion itself expresses a whole argument. For instance, if one premise says, "John has lied before so he is unreliable," you need to break down this premise further into (1) John has lied before and (2) John is unreliable. In the structure (1) will be shown as supporting (2) in a subargument. The subargument will not be shown if you write "John has lied before so he is unreliable" as a single premise.

11. Check your standardized version against the original to see whether you have left out anything essential, or included anything that, on reflection, you think should not be included.

EXERCISE SET

Exercise 1: Part A

Examine the following passages to determine whether they contain arguments. For those passages that do, represent the argument in a clear, standard form, numbering premises and conclusion(s).

Remember, if a passage does not contain an argument, it does not contain premises or a conclusion either. Should you find passages that are nonarguments, simply indicate that is the case and briefly state why. For arguments, note any subarguments and indicate which is the main conclusion.

*1.   If a car has reliable brakes, it has brakes that work in wet weather. The brakes on my car don't work very well in wet weather. You can see that my car does not have reliable brakes.

2.   "An impression first strikes upon the senses, and makes us perceive heat or cold, thirst or hunger, pleasure or pain of some kind or other. Of this impression, there is a copy taken by the mind, which remains after the impression; and this we call an idea."
(David Hume, *A Treatise of Human Nature* [edited by L. A. Selby-Bigge; Oxford: Clarendon Press, 1965], p. 8)

*3.   When unemployment among youth goes up, hooliganism and gang violence go up too. So unemployment is probably a major cause of these disruptions. People who say gang violence is caused by drugs have got it all wrong.

4.   Exercise benefits the circulation, and diabetes is a disease which tends to inhibit circulation, giving rise to circulatory problems. Therefore, for diabetics, regular exercise is particularly important.

*5.   Every logic book I have ever read was written by a woman. I conclude that all logicians are women.

6.   "The investigation of the truth is in one way hard, in another easy. An indication of this is found in the fact that no one is able to attain the truth adequately, while, on the other hand, no one fails entirely, but everyone says something true about the nature of things, and while individually they contribute little or nothing to the truth, by the union of all a considerable amount is amassed."
(Aristotle, *Metaphysics*, 993a27–b19)

7.   Either the butler committed the murder or the judge committed the murder. Since the

butler was passionately in love with the victim, it was not he who committed the murder. Therefore, the judge committed the murder.

8.   Why did twentieth-century scientists conclude that the ether posited by nineteenth-century scientists does not exist?

*9.   *Background:* The following passage is taken from an article about the archaeopteryx, a type of dinosaur.
     "Its [that is, the archaeopteryx's] main feathers show the asymmetric, aerodynamic form typical of modern birds. This similarity proves that the feathers of Archaeopteryx must have been used for flying."
(Peter Wellnhofer, "Archaeopteryx," *Scientific American*, May 1990, p. 70)

*10.   "Science, since people must do it, is a socially embedded activity."
(Stephen Jay Gould, *The Mismeasure of Man* [New York: Norton, 1981])

11.   Canada and the United States are vast countries that depend on road and air transport to a far greater extent than smaller countries in western Europe, such as France and the Netherlands. In these European countries, rail service can be more economically run than in Canada or the United States, simply because distances are shorter and populations are more concentrated. In North America, where rail systems do less business, are less modern, and are more expensive, more shipping is done by air and road. Air and road travel require extensive government support, but are necessary when vast distances are involved. Therefore, North Americans are not wasteful of money or energy for transport as compared to western Europeans.

12.   "Since we are not under an obligation to give aid unless aid is likely to be effective in reducing starvation or malnutrition, we are not under an obligation to give aid to countries that make no effort to reduce the rate of population growth that will lead to catastrophe."
(Peter Singer, "Famine, Affluence, and Morality," in *World Hunger and Moral Obligation*, ed. William Aiken

and Hugh LaFollette [Englewood Cliffs, NJ: Prentice-Hall], 1977)

*13.   "The source of much of California's shak-iness is, as any school child knows, the San An-dreas fault. On a geological map, it isn't hard to find, but in ground truth—as geologists call their legwork—the fault can be elusive. Serpen-tine and secretive, it lurks just below the surface along six-sevenths of California's length. A 650-mile crack in the earth, it cuts, largely unnoticed and often intentionally ignored, through almost every other geological feature of the state."

(Shannon Brownlee, "Waiting for the Big One," *Dis-cover*, July 1986, p. 56)

14.   "Of the varied forms of crime, bank rob-bery is the most satisfactory to both the individ-ual and society. The individual of course gets a lot of money, that goes without saying, and he benefits society by putting large amounts of cash back into circulation. The economy is stimulated, small businessmen prosper; people read about the crime with great interest, and the police have a chance to exercise their skills. Good for all."

(From Harry Harrison, *The Stainless Steel Rat Saves the World* [Lindhurst, NJ: Putnam Press], 1972)

*15.   "Apart from a few oddities such as the Venus flytrap and the mimosa, most plants do not visibly react when you touch them. Don't be deceived. If recent experiments at the Stanford University Medical Center are anything to go by, plants may even respond to physical stimuli at a genetic level. Janet Bram and Ronald W. Davis have found several genes in a common labora-tory plant called *arabidopsis*, a member of the mustard family, that are turned on when the plant's leaves are gently touched. The response starts within 10 minutes after stimulation and lasts more than an hour."

(Biological Sciences Reports, *Scientific American*, May 1990, p. 32)

Hint: Assume that the conclusion is ex-pressed in the first two sentences taken together and look closely at the role of "don't be deceived."

16.   "No one has a right to use a relatively unreliable procedure in order to decide whether

to punish another. Using such a system, he is in no position to know that the other deserves punishment: hence he has no right to punish him."

(Robert Nozick, *Anarchy, State, and Utopia* [New York: Basic Books, 1974], p. 106)

17.   *Background:* The following passage is taken from a book about children's allergy problems and how they can cause behavior problems.

   "It is always surprising and most gratifying to observe how the family tensions diminish after the true cause of the child's problems are recog-nized and resolved. Many families can cope satis-factorily once they understand why the child acts the way he does and once they know that help is available. Months to years of unacceptable behav-ior, however, lead to conditioned responses which are no longer acceptable after the child improves. Family counselling is often indicated, and most effective after the cause of a child's previous diffi-culties has been eliminated. There is no way, for example, that a child can be evaluated fairly while he is hostile and hyperactive from eating some problem food, smelling a problem chemical, or inhaling an airborne allergen."

(Doris J. Rapp, *The Impossible Child* [Tacoma, WA: Life Sciences Press, 1986], p. 58)

Exercise 1: Part B

In some of the following dialogues, the main ar-guer could profitably use a subargument to back up a premise used in his or her main argument. Indicate for which dialogues a subargument would be useful and which premise needs to be supported, on the basis of the dialogue given. Then try to construct a suitable subargument that will help make the arguer's case more convincing to the audience. In each case, assume that the main arguer is the first speaker and the audience is the second speaker.

1.   *Mary:* I don't care what they say about free-dom of religion and all that. When that school decided to let a Sikh girl wear a six-inch dagger because the Sikhs said it is part of their religion to wear a ceremonial dagger, they just made the wrong decision and that is all there is to it. There

is no proper place for weapons in our schools. So kids should not be allowed to wear daggers—whether they are supposed to be part of somebody's religion or not.

Joe: I can see your point in a way, Mary, but what about kids who carry knives to protect themselves from other kids? What are you going to say about that? I don't see what basis you have for being so sure that weapons have no place in schools.

*2. *Juan:* Opinion polls have a terrible effect on the electoral process. I think they should simply be forbidden during the two or three weeks prior to an election.

Peter: Why do you think that?

Juan: The problem is, the polls get all the attention, and they take attention away from the main issues. They even take away attention from the competence and integrity of the candidates themselves. All the attention goes to what people say about the candidates, to who's leading and so on.

Peter: Isn't that how democracy is supposed to work?

Juan: I don't think so. Democracy requires that people make an informed decision as to which candidate can best deal with the important issues, and they vote according to that decision. Polls work against that kind of decision. Therefore, polls work against democracy. And for that reason, their publication should be restricted in the few weeks right before an election.

Peter: OK, I can kind of see what you are driving at. But why do you think polls work against people getting information about candidates? Don't they work to give people information?

*3. *Catherine:* Did you hear about the man in California who wants to have his brain cut out and frozen? He has a brain tumor, you see, and he wants to live forever, but he is due to die in

about six months. This guy believes that someday doctors will know how to cure the tumor—they can't do it now—and he wants to have his brain frozen. Then someday, he thinks, when doctors have the cure, the head can be thawed and attached onto another body. He'll come to life again.

Nancy: You're kidding!

Catherine: No, really.

Nancy: That guy really has the courage of his convictions, doesn't he? Imagine asking people to cut your head off and freeze it. Gross!

4. *Susan:* I just don't think you should rely on experts. Lots of so-called experts don't know what they are talking about.

Peter: Why do you say that?

Susan: Well, for one thing they disagree with each other a lot. For another, they change their minds. And to make things even worse, they can be bought.

Peter: They can be bought? Gosh, why would you say that?

*5. *Don:* Allergies are a major health problem today, but my grandmother says people hardly ever heard of them when she was growing up sixty years ago.

Al: Really? I wonder why not.

Don: Maybe doctors just didn't know enough.

Al: You mean people had a lot of allergies, but doctors didn't diagnose them?

Don: Yeah. Or maybe people hadn't even heard of allergies much, so when they had problems such as itchy eyes, stomachaches, and sniffly noses, they just accepted it.

Al: That could be. People today may just expect a higher standard of health than they did back then.

Don: They probably do. We're all just too spoiled.

Important Details about Conclusions

Location of Conclusions

To put an argument in standardized form, you have to know what its conclusion is. Identifying the conclusion is even more basic than identifying the premises, because your sense of the point of the passage will make you decide that certain statements are merely background or asides and that others are intended to support the author's point. It would be nice if we had some definite rules about where conclusions had to be stated—if, for instance, speakers and writers always had to state their conclusions last, or if they always had to state them first. Unfortunately, there are not any rules like this, and as language works, the conclusion in a passage or a speech can come at any point. It may be first, as in the following:

> (a) The film *Patch Adams* was an illuminating portrayal of medical education because it highlighted the importance of treating patients as people and not just as the locations of diseases.

The conclusion of (a) is "The film *Patch Adams* was an illuminating portrayal of medical education."

Or it may be last, as in the following:

> (b) Humans were said to be the only animals that use tools. Now it has been discovered that other animals use tools as well. For instance, chimpanzees use sticks to dig for termites, which they then eat. Thus, we cannot prove that humans are unique on the basis of their use of tools.

The conclusion of (b) is "we cannot prove that humans are unique on the basis of their use of tools."

A conclusion may also be stated in the middle of a passage, with supporting premises on either side of it. Here is a passage exemplifying that arrangement:

> (c) Rats who are only occasionally rewarded for behavior become frantically anxious to repeat the behavior to obtain a reward. We can see that inconsistent behavior toward children is likely to make them frantically anxious, because it is well established that children respond to punishment in much the same way animals do.

The conclusion of (c) is "inconsistent behavior toward children is likely to make them frantically anxious." This structure has the conclusion between two premises. Argument (c) is worth standardizing:

> 1. Rats who are only occasionally rewarded for behavior become frantically anxious to repeat the behavior to obtain a reward.
> 2. Children respond to punishment in much the same way animals do.
> Therefore,
> 3. Inconsistent behavior toward children is likely to make them frantically anxious.

The premises must be linked to offer support for the conclusion. In (c) they are stated on either side of that conclusion. Since this kind of arrangement may be difficult for some readers and listeners to understand, we would not, in general, advise that you use it when constructing your own arguments. Putting the premise either first or last is usually clearer. In fact, when an argument is substantial, conclusions may be stated twice: both at the beginning and at the end of a substantial speech or passage. This style is often suitable when there are subarguments or many premises. The repetition serves to emphasize the fact that the conclusion is the main point, the basic theme that the arguer wishes to communicate and on which he or she wishes to persuade the audience. When a conclusion is stated twice, it is usually worded slightly differently each time, to avoid monotonous repetition.

Varying passage (b) a little to produce (d), we have an illustration of how this technique works:

> (d) Some people have claimed that human beings are different from all other species because they are the only animals that can use tools. But this isn't right. It's easy to see why: other animals use tools too. For instance, chimpanzees use sticks to dig for termites, which they then eat. Humans are not unique in their use of tools.

In (d), the phrase "but this isn't right" alludes to the first statement, because "this" refers to the claim that human beings are the only animals that use tools. Thus, "but this isn't right" says, in effect, that humans are not the only species that use tools, which is the claim made in the conclusion, "humans are not unique in their use of tools." The conclusion, or main point, is stated twice, in different words each time.

There is no simple recipe for picking out the conclusion of an argument when you are studying speeches or writings. You have to read carefully—or listen carefully, if it is an oral argument—and try to determine what the main claim is. It is a matter of getting the primary drift of what is said. When constructing your own arguments, you can help your audience by stating conclusions clearly at either the beginning or the end of the presentation; by using clear indicator words such as *therefore*, *so*, or *thus*; and by repeating your conclusion (stating it both before and after the premises) when your argument is substantial and lengthy.

Scope and Commitment in Conclusions

Conclusions may be more or less sweeping in scope, and it is important to notice this aspect because the kind of evidence that is needed to support the conclusion will vary accordingly. It is easy to understand this phenomenon from a commonsense point of view. Compare the following four statements, which might be conclusions of an argument:

> (a) All dance students have a good sense of rhythm.
> (b) Most dance students have a good sense of rhythm.
> (c) Many dance students have a good sense of rhythm.
> (d) Some dance students have a good sense of rhythm.

Clearly, evidence would have to be much stronger to support (a) than to support (d). When you identify the conclusion in an argument, try to determine its scope.

The conclusion may be about one particular individual or situation, in which case the issue of scope does not apply. But often arguments are about categories or groups of things, in which case it is important to note whether the arguer is making a universal claim about all in the group, a generalization about most or many members, or a claim about some of them.

Another crucial point about conclusions is the **degree of commitment** with which they are put forward. An author or speaker may state her point emphatically, with no qualification whatsoever. On the other hand, she may make the point more tentatively, saying only that it is probably true, or could be true. What is said matters very much for proper understanding; obviously, it will make a difference to our evaluation of the argument. For instance, much better support will be needed for a **categorical conclusion**, such as "Exercising will cause weight loss," than for a more tentatively expressed conclusion, such as "Exercising may be one factor that assists in bringing about weight loss." The former statement firmly and categorically makes the claim that exercising will bring about this result, whereas the latter is so qualified "may be one factor" that it scarcely makes any claim at all. Better evidence would be needed to support the former claim than the latter.

When constructing arguments yourself, it is a good idea to think about how strongly you are committed to your conclusion. Do you wish to maintain that something definitely is the case? That it is very likely the case? Or merely that it might be the case? The strength of evidence you require to put forward a convincing argument will vary depending on the degree of commitment you wish to indicate, as well as on the scope of the conclusion.

Here is an example in which it is especially important to note that the author is putting forward only a tentative, or qualified, conclusion. We will misunderstand him if we fail to see this.

> The malaise within English studies, like the university's other complaints, has been described as a temporary crisis in the evolution of a venerable and necessary institution. Yet it should be remembered that both the university and its departments have not always existed, and that during their tenure they have not always served as indispensable channels for the flow of the cultural stream. Less than a hundred years ago, English studies hardly existed. Moreover, when they replaced classical studies, that discipline passed quietly into desuetude while hardly anyone noticed. *It is not at all inconceivable*, given the history of the humanities, that English studies, though at present the seemingly irreplaceable guardian of the Western cultural tradition, should decline to the current marginal status of the classics.[4]

The author is comparing the role of English studies to that of the classics and suggesting, on the basis of this comparison, that the fate that met the classics might possibly befall English studies also. The conclusion of this passage comes at the end, where it is to be found in the statement: "It is not at all inconceivable…that English studies … should decline to the current marginal status of the classics." It's important to note that this author has not claimed that English studies *will* decline, or that they *ought to* decline. He merely says that "it is not at all inconceivable . . . that

English studies . . . should decline." In other words, their decline is a possibility; they *might* decline. This is a very qualified, or tentatively stated, conclusion.

Some arguments have sweeping claims, categorically stated, as their conclusions. Others have conclusions that are restricted in scope, or are put forward in a tentative, qualified way, as being likely, probable, or possible. One might think that arguing on behalf of claims is something we do only when we have a definite position that we want to support. But this idea is not correct. It is possible, as in the preceding example, to argue for a qualified position. A qualified, or tentative, conclusion is still a conclusion and in some contexts it will be worth arguing for. One might, for instance, argue that it is desirable to reflect on some matter, such as the structure of taxation laws. To claim that it is desirable to reflect on taxation laws is to make a modest claim: it is not to say that taxes should be higher or that they should be lower, or even that they need reform. Still, there are contexts in which such a conclusion could need support and would be worth arguing for—as, for instance, when a possible anomaly or injustice in present laws had been discovered.

It would be useful if people always used words such as *definitely, must be, might be, probably, possibly,* or *perhaps* in front of their conclusions, and if they were also clear as to whether they were talking about all, most, many, or some of the members of a group. If we always had explicit indications of the degree of commitment and scope of the conclusions claimed, we would have a clearer idea of what arguers are asserting and the strength of evidence needed. Unfortunately, many speeches and passages are not explicit in these ways. We often have to infer from the tone of a passage and the context in which it appears just how firmly the arguer is asserting the conclusion. When we are constructing our own arguments, we can try to make our conclusions clear by indicating scope and commitment.

Unstated, or Missing, Conclusions

Another important point about conclusions is that sometimes they are not stated at all. This may strike you as an odd thing for us to say. After all, didn't we define an argument as a set of claims put forward to defend a conclusion? If that's what an argument is, a conclusion is by definition part of every argument. Why, then, are we now telling you that in some arguments the conclusions aren't stated? This happens not because such arguments lack conclusions but because they have **unstated conclusions**. The conclusions are suggested by the stated words as they appear in the context.

Here is an example:

Joe: Did you hear about the frozen embryo case? A couple had some of her eggs fertilized by his sperm in a test tube. Embryos started to develop and they had them frozen. The idea was to implant the embryos in her uterus so they could have a baby. So anyway, these embryos were frozen, and then the couple got divorced. They're involved in a court case trying to determine who owns the embryos.

> *Fred:* Who owns them? That makes me sick! Embryos are developing human beings with all the genetic material necessary for human life. Nothing that has all the genetic material needed for human life is property that can be owned.

In this dialogue, Fred is shocked at the idea of a court case in which a husband and wife would dispute about which one of them owns frozen embryos. The very idea of ownership in this context implies that the embryos, which have all the material needed for human life, are property. Clearly, Fred does not regard embryos as property. In fact, he gives a reason for this view, which he clearly maintains though he does not state it. In the context of the dialogue, Fred has given an argument with an unstated conclusion. The argument is:

> 1. An embryo has all the genetic material necessary for human life.
> 2. Nothing that has all the genetic material necessary for human life is property.
> Therefore,
> <u>3</u>. An embryo is not property.

The stated premises link to support the conclusion, (<u>3</u>), which was unstated. We underline (<u>3</u>) here because it is something we have added to the argument.

We have to be sure that a person intends to argue if we are going to add a conclusion. If we were willing to add conclusions to any statements or passages, we could turn just about anything into an argument. We have to be careful. When the conclusion is not stated, but is strongly suggested by the statements that are made or by the context in which the speech or passage appears, we have a missing conclusion. To standardize the argument in such a case, we have to write in the conclusion.

Another example may be found in a short letter about evolutionary theory written to the popular science magazine *Discover*. The author of this letter refers to Carl Sagan, a well-known scientist and supporter of evolutionary theory. At the time this letter was published, Sagan's television series *Cosmos* had occasioned a number of letters to the magazine.

> Could evolution ever account for the depth of intellect that Carl Sagan possesses? Not in a billion years.[5]

The author strongly suggests here that evolutionary theory is incorrect. But he does not state this specifically. Rather, he states that there is something evolutionary theory could not account for: Carl Sagan's intellect. The tone of the passage is argumentative. (Could it? No.) The issue is one of public controversy, and the writer is suggesting that the failure of the theory to account for Sagan's intellect marks it as an inadequate theory. Given the implication, the context, and the tone, it seems appropriate to regard the letter as an argument with a missing conclusion. To regard it as an argument, we have to supply a conclusion, because there is no argument without a conclusion. The standardized version of the argument looks like this:

> 1. Evolution could never account for the depth of intellect that Carl Sagan possesses.
> Therefore,
> 2. Evolutionary theory is incorrect.

Conclusions may be unstated for various reasons. Sometimes, the point will seem too obvious to bother making after reasons have been stated. Sometimes, the conclusion is indirectly expressed in exclamations and questions. In these cases, even though the conclusion is not explicitly stated in any direct way, it is at least partially expressed. Occasionally, the conclusion is unstated for stylistic reasons: a suggestion or an implication may be more effective than an outright direct statement.

There are contexts, however, where the conclusion is not directly stated because it can be more easily insinuated. That is, the arguer may believe that his or her message is more likely to be accepted if it is suggested or insinuated than if it is stated outright. There can sometimes be something a little sneaky about unstated conclusions, especially in some contexts. Consider, for instance, the advertisement. The conclusion or message of most advertisements is that we who hear or read the ad should buy the product mentioned. (There are, of course, variations: we may be urged to rent or lease something, or to change our lifestyle; or the ad may be an "image" ad, trying to improve the image of a company, person, or institution.) To state, "You should buy product X" or "Company Y is a good company" may be too blatant and obvious. People who hear or read this statement are conscious of it and may reject it; there is nothing subtle in the appeal. A subtle appeal may more easily escape the attention of the reader or listener and creep unevaluated into his or her consciousness. For this reason, advertisements are a natural home for unstated conclusions. Reading ads and trying to supply them with **missing conclusions** can be an entertaining and valuable exercise.

Here is one well-known advertisement with a missing conclusion:

> The bigger the burger the better the burger. The burgers are bigger at Burger King.

The missing conclusion is that the burgers are better at Burger King. Another advertisement with a missing conclusion is the following:

> One good night's sleep every night. Why buy a Dreamworks Mattress? We can customize each side of the mattress meeting individual requirements. We strengthen individual springs where your body needs it to maintain correct spinal alignments so that you wake up refreshed and feeling good. Hypoallergenic covers eliminate dust mites and greatly reduce breathing difficulties. (Dreamworks Mattress Corp.[6])

The advertisement shows a photo of a dog on a mattress. The clear implication of this advertisement is that to get a comfortable night's sleep, you should buy one of these mattresses. In effect, this claim is an unstated conclusion. When we add to the original, as we do by inserting the missing conclusion, we should make sure that we can justify the addition by checking our version against the context and wording of the original.

EXERCISE SET

Exercise 2: Part A

Assume that each following statement is a conclusion in an argument. Comment on the degree of commitment indicated in the statement: very tentative, somewhat tentative, quite definite, very definite. Briefly explain your reasons for your answer by pointing out those words on which it is based and saying what you think they mean in the context of the statement given.

*1. Few teachers are likely to enjoy junior high school teaching, if the stories my daughter has to tell are anything to go by.

2. The woolly mammoth is not the only creature to have become extinct.

3. Earthquakes will do great damage to American and Canadian cities on the West Coast in the next two decades.

*4. Hip replacements are probably beneficial to most patients who receive them.

5. Perhaps theoretical work in physics is handicapped by a shortage of resources to fund expensive experiments.

*6. There's no doubt about it: abortion is murder, pure and simple.

7. I would estimate that there are few blind students who are entirely comfortable in classes designed for the sighted.

8. Accountants prefer clients who submit tax returns promptly.

9. A degree in computer science will get you a better job than a degree in history.

*10. Allergies could be aggravated by general environmental problems, especially that of air pollution.

Exercise 2: Part B

In each of the following passages, state whether an argument is given. If so, identify the conclusion. Do you think any of these passages should be interpreted as expressing an argument with an unstated conclusion? If so, which ones? What is the unstated conclusion, and what are your reasons for reading it into the passage?

1. "In projecting energy consumption, let us first consider just the United States, which consumes much of the world's energy and is to some extent representative of the industrialized regions of the world. Before projecting into the future, let us look back at what has happened in the past."
(John C. Fisher, *Energy Crises in Perspective* [New York: John Wiley, 1974], p. 19)

2. *Background:* The following comments are made on the issue of how we might achieve world peace:
    "Would you feel more secure now if Toronto were armed? Are you less secure now that Toronto doesn't maintain an army in case Hamilton invades? We haven't ended conflict between individuals or cities; we've just found other ways of dealing with it."
(J. S., Toronto, as quoted in James Freeman, *Thinking Logically* [Englewood Cliffs, NJ: Prentice-Hall, 1988], p. 340)

*3. *Background:* The following are comments about what is said by the use of pictures, as contrasted with statements.
    "Logicians tell us . . . that the terms 'true' and 'false' can only be applied to statements, propositions. And whatever may be the usage of critical parlance, a picture is never a statement in that sense of the term. It can no more be true or false than a statement can be blue or green."
(E. H. Gombrich, in *Art and Illusion*, as quoted in Erving Goffman, *Gender Advertisements* [New York: Harper and Row, 1979], p. 14)

*4. *Background:* In this passage, John Hardwig discusses the importance of trust among scientists engaged in cooperative research.
    "Often . . . a scientific community has no alternative to trust, including trust in the

character of its members. The modern pursuit of scientific knowledge is increasingly and unavoidably a very cooperative enterprise. Cooperation, not intellectual self-reliance, is the key virtue in any scientific community. But epistemic cooperation is possible only on the basis of reliance on the testimony of others: scientific propositions often must be accepted on the basis of evidence that only others have."

(John Hardwig, "The Role of Trust in Knowledge," *Journal of Philosophy* 88 [1991], pp. 693–708)

*5. *Background:* The following is excerpted from a short passage on fashion that appeared in *Avenue* magazine for June, 1999:

"Clunky platform sandals. Undoubtedly, we have the Spice Girls to thank for bringing the platform shoe back into our collective fashion consciousness. But just because those girls have perfected the inexplicable ability to walk, dance and perform in ridiculously stacked heels doesn't mean this is something you should try at home, even with parental supervision. Just take one look at the teetering teens trudging around town on their poor blistered feet and you'll see why flat, colorful, comfortable Keds have never gone out of style."

6. *Background:* This passage was printed in the Letters section of *Time*:

"As a German citizen born at the war's end, I agree with essayist Michael Kinsley on what America needs to do to help Eastern Europe consolidate its newborn democracies. But having lived for years in South America, I wonder why his brilliant reasoning that the U.S. is duty-bound to give financial aid has not been applied with more emphasis to neighbors in Latin America. They desperately need money and help, rather than bullets like the ones used in Panama, in order to cement progress."

(Einardo Bingemer, Rio de Janeiro, in *Time*, March 12, 1990)

*7. *Background:* The following passage is taken from an introductory philosophy book written for college and university students:

"Now consider what happens when you repeat the word *chair* silently in your mind. Just say *chair* to yourself over and over. Don't look at anything—close your eyes. . . . Right now, before you go on to the next paragraph, spend a few minutes repeating the word silently to yourself.

"What happens? The longer you listen to yourself repeating the word 'chair,' the more the meaning starts to dissolve. First the one meaning turns ambiguous—you hear the other words that compose the word *chair*, like *hair* and *air*. Next, the unity of that mental sound dissolves as the end of one repetition slurs into the next. Eventually, all meaning dissolves. You hear just uninterpreted mental imagery—sounds without meaning."

(Daniel Kolak and Raymond Martin, *Wisdom Without Answers* [Belmont, CA: Wadsworth, 1989], p. 42)

*8. *Background:* The following passage treats an aspect of the trade-off between quantity and quality in communications industries:

"There is some hope that as the structure of the mass media is altered by video cassette recorders, communication satellites, and cable television, the same media used to produce formula programming will be used to create more meaningful artistic experiences. While a number of companies were optimistic that fine arts programming was feasible, economics still guides and strangles most attempts to escape from the trap of formula. In 1981 William S. Paley, then the chairman of the board at CBS, began CBS Cable with the intention of producing high-quality cultural programming. CBS Cable went out of business in 1982 after losing more than thirty million dollars. The same fate awaited the Entertainment Channel with its BBC and Broadway productions. Tele-France USA gave up in September 1982 in its attempt to present French cultural programs."

(From Gary Gumpert, *Talking Tombstones and Other Tales of the Media Age* [Oxford and New York: Oxford University Press, 1987], p. 35)

Important Details about Premises

Ways Premises Support Conclusions

The subargument structures illustrated above were mostly based on a simple argument structure where a single premise supports each conclusion. Many arguments have more than one premise. Where this is the case, it is important to understand how the premises combine to support the conclusion. They may either link or converge to support it. In either case, it is important to think of premises together when trying to understand and evaluate an argument. When people begin to analyze arguments, a common mistake is to consider premise support for the conclusion by looking at only one premise at a time. This approach is not correct because it ignores the fact that when an argument has several premises, its premises combine, in various ways, in the arguer's attempt to support the conclusion.

This working together is especially easy to see when the premises are linked. Linked premises can support the conclusion in the argument only when they are taken together. In a linked argument, no single premise will give any support to the conclusion without the others. To see how this works, consider the following example:

1. Vulnerability to heart disease is either inherited or environmental.
2. Vulnerability to heart disease is not environmental.
Therefore,
3. Vulnerability to heart disease is inherited.

We can reason from the combination of (1) and (2) to get the conclusion, (3). But if we were to argue either from (1) alone or from (2) alone, the argument would not make much sense. To support (3), (1) and (2) must be linked (see Figure 2.4).

Figure 2.4

It is common for premises to work together by linking. Before leaving the topic, let us look at one further example:

1. A country in troubled times is like a ship in a storm.
2. A ship in a storm needs a strong, capable captain.
Therefore,
3. A country in troubled times needs a strong, capable leader.

Here again, premises must link if they are to support the conclusion. Without (2), (1) would have no chance of supporting the conclusion, and without (1), (2) would have no chance of supporting it. To understand how the argument works, you have to see that both premises are needed. When you evaluate the argument, this will be very important; if you evaluate without appreciating the way the premises are interdependent in their support, you will miss the point.

Linked support contrasts with **convergent support**. Here, too, we have to consider premises together to understand the argument. But with convergent support, the relationship between the premises is less tight. A conclusion is to be supported by several different premises, each of which states a separate reason or separate piece of evidence that the arguer thinks is relevant to his or her case. In a convergent structure, the premises are all put forward to support the conclusion, but they are not so interdependent that one would be unrelated to the conclusion without the others. We could take away a premise or two and still have some argument left, although the resulting argument would be weakened and less rich in detail.

Consider the following example:

1. Setting aside apartments for adults and keeping out children discriminates against people with children.
2. Setting aside apartments for adults and keeping out children encourages single childless people to pursue an overly selfish lifestyle.
Therefore,
3. Apartments should not keep children out.

Here, either (1) or (2) by itself could provide some reason for the conclusion. Having both reasons together does, however, strengthen the argument. This argument would be diagrammed as shown in Figure 2.5.

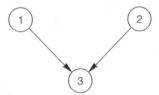

FIGURE 2.5

There are, then, two basic facts to understand about the way in which premises support conclusions. First, premises should be considered together in their support. Second, they may be linked or convergent. In the latter case, it would be possible to see each premise as providing a separate reason or separate bit of evidence in support of the conclusion, but the whole argument requires us to think of these separate strands together, as the weight of support accumulates. Convergent support is discussed further in Chapter 11, and various types of linked support are treated in detail in Chapters 7, 8, 9, and 10.

EXERCISE SET

Exercise 3

Assume that each of the following passages represents an argument. Identify the premises and the conclusion. For all cases where there is more than one premise, indicate whether you think the premises would link or converge to support the conclusion. If there are subarguments, identify them and comment on the pattern of support in the subargument.

1.   There is no point in getting your first elementary education in some other language if your native language is English, because the language of your first elementary education is the one that you will know best. English is the language of world business and world scholarship. For that reason, fluency and skill in English are highly advantageous. They should not be sacrificed in the interests of apparent political or personal advantages one might get from early immersion studies in another language.

*2.   Individuals are not reliable in their judgments, and groups are made of individuals, so groups probably are not reliable in their judgments either.

3.   Virtue is something that is valued because of the kinds of comparisons we make between people. If all people shared all good qualities equally, there would be no such thing as virtue.
(Adapted from philosopher Thomas Hobbes)

*4.   The black hole is a key scientific concept that is virtually impossible for nonexperts to comprehend. The notion of antimatter, required to account for what happens in nuclear explosions, is a real metaphysical paradox. And there is no understanding of what causation means when we come to the context of elementary physical particles. Thus we can see that modern physics is a mysterious subject indeed.

5.   There must be angels because there are so many unexpectedly good turns of events in the world, and the most natural way for many people to explain such events is to say that they have been brought about by angels.

6.   Language is necessary for communication, and communication is necessary for advancement. Therefore, language is necessary for advancement. Any attempt to censor language could restrict advancement. This is why the censorship of books is always wrong.

*7.   "Why can't my right hand give my left hand money?—My right hand can put it into my left hand. My right hand can write a deed of gift and my left hand a receipt.— But the further practical consequences would not be those of a gift. When the left hand has taken the money from the right, etc., we shall ask, "Well, and what of it?"
(Ludwig Wittgenstein, *Philosophical Investigations* [translated by G. E. M. Anscombe, Oxford: Basil Blackwell, 1963], p. 268)

8.   There can be no life without change, for stagnation is death.

9.   "The motions of the stars proceed in a fixed order. The succession of the seasons also proceeds according to fixed laws. The change from day to night takes place without variation. We can see from these facts that nothing is better organized than the universe."
(Adapted from the Roman writer Cicero in *De Inventione*)

*10.   If a word could mean just anything, or could be used in any old way, there would in fact be no meaning at all. So language requires rules. To have a rule, we have to have more than one person following a rule. That's because a single person could make anything he wanted be right, and his so-called rule would not really be a rule at all. Thus private language is impossible.
(Adapted from philosopher Ludwig Wittgenstein)

The Problem of Missing Premises

Sometimes we may have the impression that the author of an argument has left out something important that he must have been implicitly claiming to support his case. It seems as though there is some additional material that should be there to fill the gap—but it is not stated. Arguments can have **missing, or unstated, premises**, just as they can have missing conclusions. However, there are some differences; the matter of missing premises is more complex and controversial than that of missing conclusions.

What makes an argument appear to have a missing premise? It is that, as stated, the argument strikes us as having a hole or gap—a hole that we could fill in quite naturally if we added another premise to those the arguer has already stated. For example, many children argue that dads know more than moms because they are taller than moms. That is, children infer greater knowledge from greater height. This strikes most adults as quite an unreasonable jump in logic. You can fill in the gap if you realize that these children are relying on a premise that they haven't stated: namely, taller people know more than shorter people. When you hear or read an argument and think that it has one or more missing premises, you are perceiving a logical gap that you would like to fill in.

What makes the problem of missing premises tricky is that we can't fill in every gap we perceive in other people's arguments just so that we can build up those arguments into something we find clear. We want to find missing premises when there really are some, but we don't want to rewrite other people's arguments just to suit our own sense of how things should hang together. When we see a gap in an argument, how do we know that the author was omitting exactly the premise that we would want to use to fill in that gap? The difficulty is to balance our own sense of logical direction with due respect for what other arguers actually said and meant. It is hard to strike the right balance here, and this makes the problem of missing premises one of the most difficult in the theory of argument. In fact, even trained philosophers and logicians disagree quite vehemently about it. In this book, we take a cautious approach to the problem, because we think it is too easy for people to read into arguments things that they want to find there and, as a result, to misinterpret what others have to say. We urge that you add missing premises sparingly, paying careful attention to what arguers really said or wrote, and being sure to justify any additions by reference to the material that is present.

The question of whether to add missing premises arises when you see a gap in an argument as stated. You will then see that this gap could be filled in, making the flow of the argument much more natural and clear, if a particular missing premise were written in. When this arises, write down what you think is a missing premise and then look carefully at what the author has actually said. Make sure that you can justify the addition of the premise with reference to the wording and context that are actually there. This will prevent you from wandering too far from the stated text and turning other people's arguments into your own.

You have a different situation if you are listening to someone present an argument and you think that she is relying on unstated premises. This is an easier case because you can simply ask her whether she is using the premises you see as missing as part of her argument. If she is, she can say so; if she is not, you can point out what you think is a logical gap in her argument. In the case of written arguments, even when you think that by adding premises you can improve an argument, you should not do this unless you can justify it with reference to the stated text and any background knowledge you may have about what the author would accept.[7]

Our policy amounts to this: no supplementation without justification. The reason for this restriction is that we appraise other people's arguments to find out how strong their reasons are for their particular conclusions. If we start adding extra premises whenever we don't find the logical flow of an argument natural, we will end up wandering away from the arguments we started with and working on new arguments, which we have invented ourselves. In doing this, we will risk reading our own minds into other people's reasoning and, possibly, failing to understand what those others really have to say. We will look at several examples so that you can get a sense of how this policy is applied.

Here is an argument that can be considerably clarified by the addition of a missing premise. As we shall see, in this case, there is sufficient basis in the stated material for adding that premise.

DON'T TAKE THE ADVICE OF THE NUCLEAR ESTABLISHMENT ON THE ISSUE OF NUCLEAR SAFETY

The people that make and run nuclear power plants have assured us that there will never be a major catastrophe. But manufacturers of nuclear reactors also make toasters, dryers, washers, and television sets, and other household appliances. These simple appliances are not completely reliable and there is much less reason to believe that complex nuclear reactors are completely dependable.

Remember: We're talking about millions of lives and billions of dollars in property damage.[8]

The stated premises and the conclusion are as follows:

1. Manufacturers of nuclear reactors make toasters, dryers, washers, and other simple household appliances.
2. Toasters, dryers, washers, and other simple household appliances made by the manufacturers who also make nuclear reactors are not completely reliable.
So,
3. Complex nuclear reactors are very unlikely to be completely reliable.
4. Unreliable nuclear reactors could cause millions of lives to be lost and billions of dollars to be lost in property damage.
Therefore,
5. We should not take the advice of the nuclear establishment when it assures us that nuclear energy is safe.

You can see that there is a subargument here. Premises (1) and (2) link to support (3); then (3) and (4) link to support (5).

In this case, we'll concentrate only on the subargument, since that is where the issue of a missing premise arises. In (1) the author deals with appliances such as toasters, which he says are "simple." In (2) he states that these simple appliances are unreliable. From these statements, he concludes in (3) that nuclear reactors, which are complex, are less likely to be reliable than the simple appliances made by the same companies. What is missing here is an explicit assertion that complex items are less likely to be reliable than simple items made by the same company. This claim is never overtly made, but it is strongly suggested in the author's wording when he says, "These simple appliances are not completely reliable and there is much less reason to believe that complex nuclear reactors are completely dependable." "Much less reason," in this context, suggests:

> 6. Companies are less likely to make complex items that are reliable than they are to make simple items that are reliable.

The subargument may be regarded as having (6) as a missing premise. It moves from (1), (2), and (6) to (3), instead of from (1) and (2) to (3). By adding (6) as a missing premise, we make the structure of the original argument clearer, for we can see how the fallibility of toasters is supposed to be related to the fallibility of nuclear reactors. The added statement is underlined to indicate that it is something we have placed in the argument in the process of analyzing it.

Another example with a missing premise is the following argument put forward by C. S. Lewis:

> And immortality makes this other difference, which by the bye, has a connection with the difference between totalitarianism and democracy. If individuals live only seventy years, then a state or nation, or a civilization, which may last for a thousand years, is more important than an individual. But if Christianity is true, then the individual is not only more important but incomparably more important, for he is everlasting and the life of the state or a mere civilization, compared with his, is only a moment.[9]

If we used the stated material only, the argument would look like this:

> 1. If Christianity is true, then the individual is everlasting.
> 2. States and civilizations are not everlasting.
> Therefore,
> 3. If Christianity is true, the individual is incomparably more important than the state or the civilization.

Let us check back to the original passage to see whether this standardized version is accurate. The first part of the first sentence of the paragraph introduces the topic; to this introduction Lewis adds an aside (beginning with "which by the bye"), which is not strictly speaking part of the argument. The second sentence states what Lewis regards as a consequence of non-Christian views: what would follow if individuals lived only seventy years. But the author's main concern is with the consequences of the Christian view; the alternative view is included as part of the background and is not really a premise or conclusion. The word *but* indicates a return to his main line of thinking: he spells out the consequence of Christianity for the importance of the individual. This is his main point and his conclusion.

The author's conclusion is qualified in an important way. Lewis does not state here that Christianity is true, but that *if* it is true, the individual is incomparably more important than the state or civilization. The word *for*, an indicator word in that sentence, introduces the reasons for the conclusion: the individual would be everlasting and the state or civilization would not. Our standardization omits the background and the aside and contains only the premises and the conclusion.

In this passage, Lewis reasoned from the everlasting life of an individual, under the Christian hypothesis, to the greater importance of that individual. In reasoning this way, he seems to be committed to the belief that everlasting life makes for greater importance. We can see this commitment because everlasting life is the only feature of the individual referred to, and it is said to make him or her "incomparably more important" than states or civilizations, which are not everlasting. We might consider adding as a missing premise:

4. Everlasting entities are more important than those of merely finite existence.

We have seen that Lewis is committed to (4) by other things he says and by the direction of his argument; adding (4) will make the argument much clearer. It will then look like this:

1. If Christianity is true, then the individual is everlasting.
2. States and civilizations are not everlasting.
4. Everlasting entities are more important than those of merely finite existence.
Therefore,
3. If Christianity is true, the individual is incomparably more important than the state or the civilization.

Statement (4), which has been added, should be underlined. Premises (1), (2), and (4) link to support (3).

This standardization of the argument will be helpful when we come to evaluate Lewis's reasoning, because having that missing premise written out clearly will bring it to our attention. The missing premise, now inserted as (4), seems rather disputable. One reason it is good to have this premise spelled out is that when we come to evaluate the argument, we will wish to reflect carefully on that premise to see whether we regard it as plausible and whether it should be accepted. (Missing premises are often disputable, and important to state for that reason, in addition to reasons of structural clarity.) At this point, however, we'll continue to concentrate our energies on standardizing arguments—on identifying their stated and unstated premises and conclusions, and not on appraisal. In later chapters, when we study the evaluation of arguments, we will see how important unstated premises can be in the evaluation of arguments.

One further example of an argument with a missing premise is the following:

In fact, the ordinary orange is a miniature chemical factory. And the good old potato contains arsenic among its more than 150 ingredients. This doesn't mean natural foods are dangerous. If they were, they wouldn't be on the market.[10]

This argument was part of an advertisement put out by a food-processing company. The overall thrust of the advertisement was that there is no general difference, so far as safety is concerned, between naturally grown and artificially manufactured foods. What we have shown here is a subargument used on the way to establishing that more general conclusion. The advertisement stated (first quoted sentence) that natural foods such as oranges and potatoes contain chemicals; this is said to associate these foods with processed foods. But many of us now think that foods containing chemicals are dangerous, and the ad wishes to assure us that they are not. This is the conclusion: "This doesn't mean natural foods are dangerous." The reason in support of this conclusion is offered in the final sentence. The first two sentences contain the larger argument of the ad; the last two contain the subarguments, which will be the focus of our attention here:

1. If natural foods such as potatoes and oranges were dangerous, they would not be on the market.
So,
2. Natural foods such as potatoes and oranges are not dangerous.

Now if you look at the reasoning from (1) to (2), you will see that the ad depends on an obvious fact: such natural foods as potatoes and oranges are on the market. Consider the following as a missing premise:

<u>3.</u> Natural foods such as potatoes and oranges are on the market.

The addition of this premise makes the structure of the reasoning very clear. Since (<u>3</u>) is a matter of common knowledge, which the advertiser certainly would have accepted, there is no danger of writing in something that he or she didn't believe. This is a case in which the unstated premise is something so well-known both to the arguer and to the intended audience that it does not even seem worth saying. In fact, the obviousness of a given claim is often a reason for not bothering to say it or write it. The argument as stated here has (<u>3</u>) as a missing, or unstated, premise. When that premise is added, the supplemented argument has two premises, (1) and (<u>3</u>), which link to support the conclusion, (2).

In this example about potatoes and oranges, the missing premise was not suggested by the wording used in the original. It was added on the grounds that it is such an obvious matter of fact that the arguer would have been sure to accept it. It is legitimate to add a missing premise if the wording of the text or speech provides good reasons for doing so, or if that premise is required to make the argument fit together and it is something that the arguer would accept. In other examples, we have a choice between seeing a gap in reasoning and adding something that is not specifically suggested by actual wording or a matter of common knowledge. We sense a gap, sense that the arguer's reasoning cannot be followed through as it is stated, and sense that there must be a missing premise, because we assume that the arguer is following through a line of thought that has a logical coherence to it. Here is a simple example:

1. Eileen could not carry a tune at the age of eight.
Therefore,
2. Eileen is probably tone deaf.

When we come to interpret what people say and write, we assume that people are in general capable of reasoning and putting forward connected ideas. We assume that, by and large, people put forward claims on the assumption that these claims are coherent, relevant, and potentially interesting to others—their readers or listeners. If anyone were to argue along the lines above, he would effectively be assuming a general connection between not being able to carry a tune at the age of eight and being tone deaf. Without such a connection, there would be no point in citing this information about Eileen not being able to carry a tune at age eight and following it with the claim that Eileen is probably tone deaf.

We can make the argument logically clearer, and fill in the apparent gap, by spelling out the connection that has been assumed. But this raises the question: What exactly has an arguer committed himself to if he puts forward the above argument? The arguer would not need to assume that *all* such people have this problem, because the conclusion includes the word *probably*. Because of the direction of the reasoning, and because of this qualifying word, we can justifiably add a missing premise to the effect that *most* people who cannot carry a tune at the age of eight are tone deaf. The resulting argument will then be:

1. Eileen could not carry a tune at the age of eight.
<u>3</u>. Most people who cannot carry a tune at the age of eight are tone deaf.
Therefore,
2. Eileen is probably tone deaf.

Criticism of the argument would no doubt be directed to this unstated claim, (<u>3</u>), which is open to question. This added premise is somewhat more plausible than another we could have added, which would also have served to link the stated premise with the stated conclusion. Consider:

<u>4</u>. All people who cannot carry a tune at the age of eight are tone deaf.

This statement is less plausible than (<u>3</u>) because it makes a more sweeping claim, a claim that is more sweeping than the argument demands and that is easily refuted. When adding premises, we have to be careful not to make the original argument worse than it is. (If we do this, interpreting an argument so as to make our standardized version less cogent and credible than the original argument, we offer a faulty interpretation and commit something called the straw man fallacy, which is discussed in Chapter 6.) In the interests of accurate and fair interpretation, when we see a need to add an unstated premise, we should select the most plausible premise to link the stated premises to the stated conclusion. We should select a premise that is a matter of common knowledge and would almost certainly be accepted by the arguer for that reason (for instance, the premise that foods such as potatoes and oranges are on the market), or a premise that the arguer is logically committed to because of the material that he has put forward in just so many words.

In short, missing premises should be added under the following conditions:

1. There is a logical gap in the argument as stated.
2. This logical gap could be filled by inserting an additional premise.
3. This additional premise is either something that the arguer accepts or something to which he or she is committed. Evidence that an arguer accepts a claim can either be found in the wording of the surrounding text or it can be based on the fact that the claim is a matter of common knowledge or belief—something that nearly everybody would accept. Evidence that an arguer is committed to a claim can be based on the direction of the reasoning, which shows that only by such a commitment can the arguer move from the stated premises to the stated conclusion.
4. Statements inserted as missing premises should be as plausible as possible, consistent with the previous conditions.[11]

In general, we urge caution about adding missing, or unstated, premises. If you add more than two or three missing premises to a short passage, you are beginning to construct your own argument rather than standardizing that of the arguer.

The Principle of Charity in Argument Interpretation

In interpreting an argument, we should make every effort to be fair to the arguer by not worsening his argument by adding material that would make it less credible, or deleting material that would make it more credible. We should attempt to keep our standardized version reasonably close to the exact words used. Otherwise we will begin to construct a new argument of our own, as opposed to understanding the argument put to us by another person. Sometimes, it is suggested that we go further in the direction of *charitable* interpretation, interpreting a speech or a written passage so as to render it as plausible and reasonable as possible. Such generous interpretive **charity** has been claimed to be the fairest thing to the speaker or author. However, this very generous charity can lead us away from accuracy if it is taken too far. The danger is that we may seek to improve someone else's speaking or writing, but in doing so, read in too many ideas of our own and move too far away from the original words and thoughts.

In an essay entitled "Logic and Conversation," H. P. Grice set out what he called a Cooperative Principle for conversations and other verbal exchanges. In this essay, Grice pointed out that when people talk to each other, or write for each other, they do not simply make disconnected remarks. People communicate for some purpose—and what they have to say is connected, in virtue of that purpose. For this reason, Grice claimed, people generally try to give what information is needed, avoid falsehoods or claims for which there is no evidence, avoid unclear language, and make claims relevant to the topic at hand. If we did not in general try to do these things, communication—whether in conversation or in writing—would not be possible.[12]

A principle of restrained, or Modest Charity, similar to Grice's Cooperative Principle, can be urged for the special communicative activity of arguing. In general, it may be presumed that people who are stating arguments, and responding to each other's arguments, are trying to give good reasons for claims they genuinely believe, and are open to criticism concerning the merits of their beliefs and their reasoning. Generally, when people offer arguments, they seek to communicate information, acceptable opinions, and reasonable beliefs. Most of the time, people are at least trying to offer good arguments in which the premises lead in some reasonable way to the conclusion. When we come to interpret the arguments of others, we should bear this point in mind, and not represent arguments as flawed or implausible unless we have checked to make sure that there are good reasons for doing so. A principle of Modest Charity can be recommended. If your standardization of an argument is such that the argument seems to make no sense at all, or to contain wild leaps in logic, check the original text again to make sure that you have not been unfair to the arguer.

EXERCISE SET

Exercise 4
Assume that each of the following passages states an argument in which the final sentence is the conclusion. In each case, determine the premises of the argument. Are there any unstated premises? If so, what are they?

1.   If pollution could kill, we'd have been dead long ago. Alarmists are exaggerating the seriousness of pollution.

*2.   Butterflies need warm air and sunlight to breed. So the conservatory at the zoo is a perfect place for them.

3.   Either many species of animals are going to become extinct in the near future or zoos are going to become more active in breeding programs for species preservation. We've got to give up our selfishness and do what's right for nature. Breeding programs are a must for zoos on an endangered planet.

4.   Democracy is the only form of government that provides a mechanism for the accountability of a government. Furthermore, it is the only form of government that offers a good chance of a nonviolent transition between a government and its successor. Thus democracy is the best form of government.

*5.   If God had meant us to fly through the air, we would have been born with wings. People aren't meant to fly.

6.   "I found out she's a librarian. So she's highly intelligent."
(From a cartoon)

7.   Young people are often bored. They do crazy, sometimes criminal, things out of boredom. So the way to cut the crime rate among youth is to give them some meaningful activities to do.

*8.   We speak of the competitiveness of countries, but this way of speaking is based on a mistake. Only businesses compete, in the economic sense, and a country is not a business.

9.   Photographs can be altered and the techniques for doing so are increasingly sophisticated, due to the use of computers. For this reason, photographs are not a reliable guide to what reality was like in the past. You can see a man and his children in a picture, with no wife beside him, and yet in the original picture his wife (whom he has now divorced) was there. He had her eliminated with sophisticated alteration techniques.

*10.   Understanding another person's ideas requires really listening to her and trying to experience the world as she experiences it. If we can't do this, we're never going to resolve conflicts and get rid of social problems. The prospects of working out conflicts, for a full resolution, are quite gloomy.

Exercise 5
(a) For each of the following examples, decide whether the passage contains an argument. If it does, then (b) represent the argument in a standardized form with the premises preceding the conclusion. (c) Check carefully to see whether any passage requires either a missing conclusion or a missing premise. (d) Indicate any subarguments. (e) If you add material that is not explicitly stated by the author, give interpretive reasons for doing so.

*1.   If you've eaten a banana, you've eaten everything in Nutrasweet.

2.   High blood pressure is a real health hazard. Therefore, anyone who is overweight should get to work and reduce.

3.   Anyone who has been drinking heavily should refrain from driving a car. So people should not drive home from New Year's parties.

*4.   The crime rate among teenagers is going up. Can we believe that drug use is declining if teenage theft is on the rise?

5.   If people were truly unselfish, they would give as much to worthy charities as they save for their old age. But do they? You tell me!

6.   Many women who consider themselves to be altos are actually sopranos with a relatively undeveloped upper range.

*7.   Secondhand smoke can cause minor health problems to nonsmokers, because some nonsmokers suffer from headaches, runny noses, and itchy eyes as a result of exposure to smoke. I can tell you, it is downright irritating to suffer a headache for a day just because some inconsiderate person has smoked in an elevator! And secondhand smoke can cause lung cancer even in nonsmokers who are regularly exposed to smoke. We have good reason to ban smoking in public places.

8.   We all hope to grow old someday, and when we grow old, we will need the services of retailers, manufacturers, politicians, dentists, doctors, nurses, and many other personnel. These people will provide us with what we need, and they will help to care for us. Who will they be? Only a few, if any, will be our own children. The rest will be other people's children. Thus, we all have a personal stake in educating other people's children. Anyone who says, "I am willing to pay to educate my own children, but not other people's children" is making a serious mistake.

*9.   "Dr. Joyce Brothers visited Weight Loss Clinic and went home impressed. It's one thing for us to tell you that we offer a superb weight loss program. But it's even more impressive when Dr. Joyce Brothers does the talking:

'One of the problems I'm asked about most often is overweight. If I could put together the best possible weight loss program, I'd make sure it was run by trained professionals…counsellors and nurses, who were not only dedicated…but enthusiastic about helping each individual client achieve success. A program like the one at Weight Loss Clinic.'

"Dr. Joyce Brothers was impressed. There's no reason why you shouldn't be."
(Advertisement, Toronto *Star*, February 25, 1981)

*10.   *Background:* In 1978, Russian dissident novelist Alexander Solzhenitsyn made a widely publicized speech criticizing the materialism of Western societies. He said,

"If humanism were right in declaring that man is born to be happy, he would not be born to die. Since his body is doomed to die, his task on earth evidently must be of a more spiritual nature."

(As quoted in the Calgary *Herald*, July 6, 1978)

11. The *Challenger* shuttle explosion could not have been caused by a leaky valve. If the valve had leaked, the instrument panel would have registered it. Since the only other possibility is an expanded, overheated O-ring, that must have triggered the explosion.

*12. *Background:* The following is taken from Plato's dialogue, *Meno* (80a) (translated by W. C. K. Guthrie, in Edith Hamilton and Huntingdon Cairns, editors, *Plato: Collected Dialogues*)

"Socrates, even before I met you they told me that in plain truth you are a perplexed man yourself and reduce others to perplexity. At this moment I feel you are exercising magic and witchcraft upon me and positively laying me under your spell until I am just a mass of helplessness. If I may be flippant, I think that not only in outward appearance but in other respects as well you are exactly like the flat sting ray that one meets in the sea. Whenever anyone comes into contact with it, it numbs him, and that is the sort of thing that you seem to be doing to me now. My mind and my lips are literally numb and I have nothing to reply to you."

13. "The application of the physical and biological sciences alone will not solve our problems because the solutions lie in another field. Better contraceptives will control population only if people use them. New weapons may offset new defenses and vice versa, but a nuclear holocaust can be prevented only if the conditions under which nations make war can be changed. New methods of agriculture and medicine will not help if they are not practiced, and housing is a matter not only of buildings and cities but of how people live. Overcrowding can

be corrected only by inducing people not to crowd, and the environment will continue to deteriorate until polluting practices are abandoned. In short, we need to make vast changes in human behavior, and we cannot make them with the help of nothing more than physics or biology, no matter how hard we try."

(B. F. Skinner, *Beyond Freedom and Dignity* [New York: Bantam Books, 1971], p. 2)

14. "Everyone who exercises to improve his muscles knows that what is physical can be altered by behavior. The brain is a physical organ; as such, we have every reason to expect that it can be altered by behavior and cultural patterns. Work with retarded infants, in which great strides have been made by the technique of extra stimulation to 'exercise' the brain, is an illustration of the truth of this claim."

(Rose Kemp, "Male and Female Brains," unpublished essay)

*15. "It is important that we understand how profoundly we all feel the needs that religion, down the ages, has satisfied. I would suggest that these needs are of three types: firstly, the need to be given an articulation of our half-glimpsed knowledge of exaltation, of awe, of wonder; life is an awesome experience, and religion helps us understand why life so often makes us feel small, by telling us what we are smaller than. . . . Secondly, we need answers to the unanswerable: how did we get here? How did 'here' get here in the first place? Is this, this brief life, all there is? How can it be? What would be the point of that? And, thirdly, we need codes to live by, 'rules for every damn thing.' The idea of god is at once a repository for our awestruck wonderment at life and answer to the great questions of existence, and a rulebook too. The soul needs all these explanations—not simply rational explanations, but explanations of the heart."

(Salman Rushdie, "Is Nothing Sacred?" in *GRANTA 31* [Spring 1990]: p. 104)

16. *Background:* The Yanomami are Amazonian Indians living in the rain forest. In an article

called "Priests, Levites, Samaritans and the Yanomami," Bob Sharpe discusses conservation and so-called primitive societies, exploring the issue of whether such societies should be preserved, regardless of their moral practices. The essay appeared in *Cogito 1992* (Volume 6, issue 1) pp. 24–28.

"The Yanomami, we are told, murder one another. We are advised not to intervene. But why should we treat the Yanomami differently from other peoples? We do not generally condone the Iraqi's murder of their Shiite compatriots in the South (of Iraq). The Iraqis too are a different culture from ours: is it unwarranted interventionism to insist that our moral values should apply? Yet many of us do feel morally outraged by the behavior of Saddam Hussein's henchmen."

17.   The following dialogue is taken from a cartoon:

"Did you ask Kelsey out for a date?"

"Nope. I found out she's a librarian, which means she's highly intelligent. Therefore, I'm sure she's only interested in highly intelligent guys. That rules me out!"

"No it doesn't!"

"It doesn't? Gee, thanks, Patrick!"

"They say opposites attract! Maybe she goes for simpletons."

(How many main arguments can you find here? Are there any subarguments? Set out all main arguments in standardized form.)

CHAPTER SUMMARY

Understanding the structure of an argument is fundamental if we are to evaluate it correctly. A good awareness of argument structure is also useful when we construct arguments, because knowing what the structures are helps us to make our own arguments clearer. When we consider a speech or a written passage, there are a number of distinct stages in identifying an argument. First, we have to make sure that there is an argument—that is, that the speech or text is one in which the author is trying to support a claim or claims by putting forward other claims as evidence. Then, we have to identify the conclusion and listen or look carefully to determine what scope and degree of certainty are being claimed. Even when a passage is basically argumentative, there may be parts that are not argumentative; examples would be background information, remarks that are asides, explanations, and jokes. In identifying the premises of an argument, we have to omit these nonargumentative aspects, restricting ourselves to those claims that are put forward in an attempt to support the conclusion. Some premises may, in turn, be supported, in which case there is a subargument structure.

When there are several premises in an argument, those premises support the conclusion together and will have to be considered together when we come to appraise the argument. In the linked pattern of support, the premises are interdependent in the way they support the conclusion; if we did not consider them together, they could provide no support at all. In the convergent pattern of support, on the other hand, one premise alone could provide some support to the conclusion, but the various premises, together, are intended to cumulate so as to offer more support. Linked and convergent support can be found in main arguments or in subarguments.

Either conclusions or premises may, on some occasions, be unstated. Sometimes, then, when we write a standardized version of an argument, we will include statements that are not in an original text, at least not in so many words. Whether we add conclusions or premises, we should be careful to find justification for what we are doing in the stated text. We should underline any such added statements to remind ourselves that they were not strictly present in the original. In interpreting arguments, and in particular in adding unstated conclusions or premises, we should apply a principle of reasonable charity. On the presumption that people who offer arguments are seeking to be reasonable and to provide information supported by logically connected ideas, we should not represent their arguments as implausible or unreasonable unless there is compelling evidence, in a speech or text, for doing so.

The standardized argument, with premises, any missing premises, conclusion, and any missing conclusion, should be arranged in logical order. That is, the premises should precede the conclusion. If there are subarguments, the premises of the subargument should precede that conclusion too. Putting it all together, we can see that really grasping the structure of an argument can be a complex process. It may involve deletion (of material that is not argument), addition (of unstated premises and conclusions), rewording (so that premises and conclusions are stated in clear language), rearranging (so that premises are stated leading to the conclusion, with subarguments fitting in appropriately along the way), and interpretive judgments (regarding charity and plausibility).

Review of Terms Introduced

Categorical conclusion   Conclusion stated in such a way that it is reasonable to attribute a high degree of commitment to the arguer.

Charity   Principle of interpretation. On a very generous principle of charity, not supported here, we would make out an argument to be as reasonable and plausible as we could, always giving the arguer the benefit of the doubt. On a more modest principle of charity, recommended in this text, we would avoid attributing to an arguer loose reasoning and implausible claims unless there is good evidence, in his speech or writing, for doing so.

Convergent support   A kind of support where premises work together in a cumulative way to support the conclusion, but are not linked. The bearing of one premise on the conclusion would be unaffected if the other premises were removed; however, the argument is strengthened when the premises are considered together, since more evidence is then offered.

Degree of commitment (to conclusion)   Level of commitment, on the part of the arguer, to the conclusion that he or she is putting forward. The arguer may claim that something is definitely the case, that it is probably the case, that it is perhaps the case, or that it might be the case.

Intermediate conclusion   A premise in an argument, used to defend a main claim, but one that is itself defended in a subargument. The intermediate conclusion can be thought of as a conclusion that is reached along the way to the main conclusion.

Linked support   A kind of support where premises are interdependent in their support for a conclusion; when premises are linked, the removal of one would affect the bearing of the others upon the conclusion.

Main conclusion   The main claim defended in an argument.

Missing, or unstated, premise   A premise not stated in just so many words but suggested by the context, wording, and natural logical order of a passage and needed to fill a gap in the reasoning. *Note:* Missing premises should be supplied only when there is a clear interpretive justification for doing so.

Qualified conclusion   Conclusion stated in such a way that it is reasonable to attribute less than a high degree of commitment to the arguer.

Scope (of conclusion)   Quantity of members of a group or category the conclusion is about. Scope is indicated by such words as all, most, many, and some.

Standardizing (an argument)   Picking the conclusion and premises of an argument from a passage and setting them up in a standard simple format with the conclusion at the end.

Subargument   A smaller argument within a larger one, in which a premise of a main argument is itself defended.

Unstated, or missing, conclusion   A conclusion not put into words but suggested by the context, wording, and natural logical order of a passage. *Note:* Unstated conclusions should be added only when there is a clear interpretive justification for doing so.

Whole argument   Argument for a main conclusion, including all subarguments used to support any premises.

Notes

1. Joyce Young, *Fundraising for Non-Profit Groups* (North Vancouver, BC: Self-Counsel Press, 1978), p. 112.
2. C. S. Lewis, *Mere Christianity* (New York: Macmillan, 1953), p. 106.
3. Letter to the Toronto *Star*, October 25, 1980.
4. Peter Shaw, "Degenerate Criticism," *Harper's,* October 1979, pp. 93–99.
5. Letter to *Discover*, November, 1980.
6. Advertisement in *Avenue* magazine (Calgary, Alberta), June, 1999.
7. Cited in the *Informal Logic Newsletter,* Examples Supplement for 1980.
8. Cited in the *Informal Logic Newsletter,* Examples Supplement for 1980.
9. C. S. Lewis, *Mere Christianity,* p. 80.
10. Advertisement by the Monsanto Chemical Company, in *Harper's,* October 1980. This argument can be regarded, in addition, as implying the further conclusion that having chemicals in it does not make a food dangerous. In order not to unduly complicate the discussion here, I have deliberately omitted discussing this further implication in the text.
11. I am grateful to Allan Spangler for suggestions at this point. The problem of missing premises

is so difficult and yet so basic that it poses real problems for textbooks. It is a challenge to say something that is complex enough to be accurate and yet simple enough to be comprehensible at an early stage in the course. I discuss the problem of missing premises at length in my *Problems of Argument Analysis and Evaluation*

(Dordrecht, NL and Berlin: Foris/de Gruyter 1987). See especially Chapters 5–7 of that work.

12. P. F. Grice, "Logic and Conversation," in P. Cole and J. L. Morgan, editors, *Syntax and Semantics 3: Speech Acts* (New York: Academic Press, 1975).

chapter three

When Is an Argument a Good One?

W<small>E ARE NOW READY TO PROCEED</small> to the stage of evaluating arguments, which means reasoning toward informed judgments about their quality. Many different issues bear on the evaluation of arguments. We cannot study them all simultaneously. The approach we have chosen in this book is to introduce the basic conditions of good argument first in a fairly general way, and then more fully explain related details later. In this chapter, we work at a general and fairly simple level. As you use the conditions developed here, you will come to appreciate the need for the more detailed and more complete explanations that are given in subsequent chapters.

The ARG Conditions

There are basically two aspects of argument evaluation: the evaluation of the premises and the evaluation of the reasoning from premises to the conclusion. Arguments that are deemed to be satisfactory in both regards may be called good, strong, compelling, convincing, sound, or cogent. Here we use the term *cogent* as our basic term of argument evaluation. If the premises of an argument are rationally acceptable and if, in addition, they provide rational support for the conclusion, the argument is **cogent**.

The basic elements of a cogent argument, referred to here as the **ARG conditions,** are as follows:

1. Its premises are all acceptable. That is, it is reasonable for those to whom the argument is addressed to believe these premises. There is good reason to accept the premises—even if they are not known for certain to be true. And there is no good evidence known to those to whom the argument is addressed that would indicate either that the premises are false or that they are doubtful. (General points about the **acceptability of premises** and some common pitfalls in this area are treated in Chapter 5.)

2. Its premises are properly connected to its conclusion. Traditional logicians have spent most of their time and energy on this condition. The condition may be usefully subdivided into two parts:

   a.   The premises are genuinely relevant to the conclusion; that is, they give at least some evidence in favor of the conclusion's being true. They specify factors, evidence, or reasons that count toward establishing the conclusion. They do not merely describe distracting aspects that lead you away from the real topic. (The concept of relevance, and some common fallacies of relevance, are explored in greater depth in Chapter 6.)

   b.   The premises provide sufficient or good grounds for the conclusion. In other words, considered together, the premises give sufficient reason to make it rational to accept the conclusion. This statement means more than that the premises are relevant. Not only do they count as evidence for the conclusion, they provide enough evidence, or enough reasons, taken together, to make it reasonable to accept the conclusion. (We delve further into various sorts of good grounds in Chapters 7–11.)

The subdivision occurs in condition (2) because the distinction between relevancy and sufficiency is a basic and useful tool in understanding and criticizing arguments. It can happen that a premise is relevant to the truth of a conclusion but not sufficient to provide good grounds for it. For example, suppose that a person cites her own recovery from cancer after a treatment program as a premise to support a conclusion that the treatment program would be generally effective for cancer patients. She has given in that premise evidence that is relevant to her conclusion and does count in a small way toward showing that the conclusion is true or acceptable. After all, she was a cancer patient, she recovered after the treatment, and she may have recovered because of the treatment. But her evidence is not sufficient: this premise alone cannot provide good grounds for her general conclusion. She is only one among many millions of cancer patients, and furthermore, the fact that her recovery *followed* the treatment does not show that her recovery was *the result of* the treatment. We distinguish the **relevance of premises** from the sufficiency of grounds because it is quite possible for a premise to be relevant to the conclusion without providing good grounds, as this example illustrates.

On the other hand, if the premises provide good grounds, or sufficient evidence or reasons to make it rational to believe the conclusion, they will be relevant as well. If they give enough evidence (sufficient grounds) to make the conclusion rationally acceptable, they will at least give some evidence (be relevant) in support of that conclusion.

If its premises are relevant to its conclusion but are not sufficient to render it acceptable, an argument could be strengthened by adding more information similar in type to that offered in the premises. For instance, if the cancer patient had access to studies about the general effectiveness of the treatment, and were able to offer evidence that a number of people had recovered following this treatment, her argument would be strengthened. If the premise stated evidence that was not relevant to the conclusion at all, adding more evidence of a similar type would not improve the argument.

Argument cogency requires:

A. acceptability-(1)
R. relevance-(2a)
G. adequacy of grounds-(2b)

You can keep these basic conditions of argument cogency firmly fixed in your mind by noting that the first letters, when combined, are ARG—the first three letters of the word *argument*.

Among formal logicians, who symbolize arguments in a rather mathematical way before attempting to evaluate them, the term *cogent* as defined here is not commonly used. Instead, the term *sound* is used. While the term *cogent*, as defined in this book, is quite common in texts on practical argumentation, our usage differs from that of formal logicians. Since some readers may later pursue courses in formal logic, we will briefly explore the nature of this difference and explain the reasons for it. In formal logic, a **sound argument** is one in which all the premises are true and they provide logically conclusive support for the conclusion. Logically conclusive support, or deductive entailment, will be explained in more detail, in Chapters 7 and 8. For now, let's just say that if the premises of an argument deductively entail its conclusion, then it is logically impossible for the premises to be true and the conclusion false. Such an argument is known as deductively valid, or sometimes simply as valid, which is one of the two conditions for argument soundness.

Here is a simple example of a deductively valid argument:

1. Either interest rates will go down or inflation will go up.
2. Interest rates will not go down.
Therefore,
3. Inflation will go up.

In this argument, it is logically impossible for the conclusion to be false if the premises are true. Thus, if true, the premises provide complete support for the conclusion. In a situation where the premises were true, the argument would be sound in the traditional sense of the term. Any sound argument is a good argument.

There are several basic reasons why we do not use *sound* in this book as the most general term for evaluating arguments. One reason is that there are a number of ways premises can support a conclusion: deductive entailment is not the only one. The second reason is that the concept of truth in the traditional account of soundness poses problems. In arguments, what is really important is not so much that the premises be true but that we know them to be true or—if knowledge is not obtainable—that we have good reasons to believe them. As we will see in more detail in Chapter 5, many important arguments have premises that are plausible and accepted by the arguer and the audience but that we would hesitate to say are true in an absolute sense.

It would be confusing to define *sound* in a new sense, because we would then be giving a definition that was at odds with common practice. Such a departure would make this book hard to study in conjunction with some other texts and major works. Thus we use *cogent* as the most general term for argument evaluation. In this book, good arguments are called cogent arguments; poor arguments are not cogent. Nearly all arguments that are sound in the traditional sense are cogent in the sense to be defined here.[1] However, there are many arguments that pass our standards for cogency that are not sound in the sense of having true premises and being deductively valid. These include arguments in which the reasoning from the premises to the conclusion is legitimate and sensible, but not deductively valid, and arguments in which the premises are acceptable claims for which we have reasonable evidence, but which we do not know to be true.

More on the (R) and (G) Conditions: Reasoning from Premises to Conclusions

Deductive Entailment

Deductive entailment is a relationship between statements. If statement A deductively entails statement B, then it is logically impossible for A to be true and for B to be false. If several statements conjoined together—for example, A, C, and D—deductively entail B, then it is logically impossible for all of A, C, and D to be true and for B to be false. In virtue of this relationship of entailment, you can reason from the entailing statement or statements to the entailed statement. If the entailing statements are the premises of an argument and the entailed statement is its conclusion, the R and G conditions are satisfied.

To illustrate the relationship of deductive entailment, consider only two statements, one of which entails the other. If statement (1) is true and entails statement (2), then this relationship logically guarantees the truth of statement (2).

In each of the following pairs, statement (1) entails statement (2):

(a) 1. Advertising does not always contain statements.
2. Advertising does not always contain false statements.

(b) 1. All prolonged conflicts involve emotions.
2. The prolonged conflict between Catholics and Protestants in Northern Ireland involves emotions.

(c) 1. People do not understand that police personnel are often afraid when
       approaching scenes of crime.
    2. People misinterpret what makes police personnel act as they do when
       there is a crime.

In each case, (1) entails (2) because it would be impossible for (1) to be true and
(2) false. This is not to say that (1) is true in any given case. We are saying only that
if (1) is true and (1) deductively entails (2), then (2) is also true, as a matter of logical necessity.

Any argument in which the premises, taken together, entail the conclusion is a
deductively valid argument and satisfies conditions (2a) and (2b). That is, if the conjunction of the premises deductively entails the conclusion, the argument satisfies (R)
and (G) because it is valid. Valid reasoning is correct reasoning, so the premises of
such an argument do support the conclusion. They support it in the sense that if
they are true, the conclusion must be true as well. And if they are reasonable to accept, they will render the conclusion reasonable to accept. Thus, provided that an
argument is valid, to determine whether it is cogent, you only have to determine
whether its premises are acceptable.

A **conjunction** is one statement connected to another using *and*—or another
word implying *and*, such as *but* or *yet* or *also*. Suppose that an argument has two
premises, as in the following case:

1. A mathematical proof is an intellectual exercise.
2. Some computers can do mathematical proofs.
Therefore,
3. Some computers can do an intellectual exercise.

The conjunction of these two premises is as follows: a mathematical proof is an intellectual exercise and some computers can do mathematical proofs.

The argument uses these two premises to reach the conclusion:

3. Some computers can do an intellectual exercise.

This argument is deductively valid because the conjunction of its premises deductively entails its conclusion. It is impossible for the premises to be true and the conclusion false. Thus, granting the premises, the conclusion must be true. More
generally, if the premises are acceptable, then, since they provide logically conclusive
grounds for the conclusion, the conclusion is acceptable as well.

In any argument in which the premises deductively entail the conclusion, the
(R) and (G) conditions are satisfied. The only condition left to assess is the (A) condition. If it is also satisfied, the argument is cogent.

Deductive entailment is so complete and elegant a connection that when we
have it there is no need to consider separately the relevance of premises and the issue
of whether they provide good grounds for the conclusion. Deductive entailment is
an all-or-nothing thing; the premises either entail the conclusion or they do not. If
they entail it, the argument is deductively valid. In cases where premises deductively
entail the conclusion, they provide relevant grounds that are also sufficient or good

grounds, so that the (R) and (G) conditions are satisfied simultaneously. If the premises do not deductively entail the conclusion, the argument is not deductively valid. Its premises are irrelevant from the point of view of **validity**, so any support they give would have to be of some other type. (Deductive entailment is discussed again, in considerably more detail, in Chapters 7 and 8.)

Appraising arguments, and theorizing about that task, would be considerably simpler if deductive entailment were the only way of satisfying the (R) and (G) conditions. But it is not: claims can be supported in argument by means other than logical entailment. We could not give an accurate or plausible general theory about arguments if we limited ourselves to those involving deductive entailment as the relationship between premises and conclusion.

There are at least three other ways in which premises may be properly connected to a conclusion: inductive support through **empirical generalization**, analogy, and conductive support.

Inductive Support through Empirical Generalization

Suppose that you have met eighty students who have graduated from a particular high school with about 1,500 students and every single one of them has received good grades in mathematics. You infer that the next student you meet from that school will also have received good grades in mathematics. When you make this inference, you use premises about your past experience of members of a group (in this case, graduates of school X whom you have already met) to reach a conclusion about your future experience of members of that group (in this case, all graduates of school X—including any whom you may meet in the future). When you reason in this way, you are in effect constructing for yourself a simple inductive argument.

1. All the students I have met who have graduated from school X got good grades in mathematics.
So, probably,
2. All students who have graduated from school X got good grades in mathematics.

Inductive reasoning is based on the presumption that unobserved cases are likely to resemble observed cases—or, in other words, that our experience is likely to be fairly uniform, that things and events in the world have a regularity, intelligibility, and connection.

Another type of inductive argument may be stated. Consider:

1. The eighty students I have met, who graduated from school X, all have good marks in mathematics.
2. The best and most natural explanation for the fact that all eighty students I have met from school X got good marks in mathematics is that mathematics is well taught at school X.
So probably,
3. Mathematics is well taught at school X.

Life depends on such inductive reasoning. The connection between what we have experienced and what we expect to experience is not that of deductive entailment. There would be no logical impossibility in the next student from school X being weak in mathematics, despite all your past experience with its mathematically capable graduates. As we shall see in more detail when we explore inductive reasoning further in Chapter 9, no inductive argument can show beyond a shadow of doubt that its conclusion is true. Obviously, your expectations could be wrong; your experience might change. If it changed significantly, that is, if you met a number of graduates who were weak in mathematics and had not received good grades in the subject, then you would re-think your conclusion and would look for another explanation for the fact that the first eighty students you met were so adept in the subject.

Analogy

Suppose you want to know whether a once-a-month birth control shot is safe (you have just invented it), but for legal and moral reasons you cannot test it on people. You get some rats and do an experiment. As things turn out, fifty of your two hundred rats develop breast cancers. You reach two conclusions: (1) the birth control shot caused breast cancer in rats, and (2) the birth control shot might cause cancer in humans. Your argument for conclusion (1), based on your experiment, will be an inductive argument for a causal conclusion. (This sort of argument will be discussed further in Chapter 9.) Your argument for conclusion (2) is also inductive, but it is an inductive argument of a special type. It is based on **analogy,** in this case the analogy between the rat's physical system and the human being's physical system. You are reasoning from one species to another that is compared with it. This is reasoning by analogy. As this example suggests, reasoning by analogy occurs rather frequently in science. It also occurs in law, ethics, and administration. If a verdict has been pronounced on one case (for example, it has been decided that case (a) counts as negligence), we may reason that because case (b) is relevantly similar to case (a), it should count as negligence as well. Provided that the cases you compare are relevantly similar, the link between premises and conclusion is a proper one. Relevance is explained in Chapter 6, and analogy is examined in more detail in Chapter 10.

Conductive Support

Suppose you are considering a decision about suitable office space for an activist group. You want to decide what the ideal space would be. You think about the group's needs, which are many and varied, and start listing desirable features: centrality, low cost, acceptable decor, comfort, adequacy of heating and cooling, proximity to related groups, and so on. Then you find a space. To argue that it is suitable, you point out which of the relevant features it has. If it has several, you may wish to conclude that it is a suitable place. In these arguments, we often have to deal with pros and cons. A crucial aspect of evaluating conductive arguments is thinking of counterarguments—factors or reasons that would count against the conclusion. In **conductive arguments**, the premises are put forward as supporting the conclusion convergently, not in a linked way. Conductive arguments are treated in more detail in Chapter 11.

As this discussion shows, the (R) and (G) conditions, which have to do with the reasoning from the premises to the conclusion, may be satisfied in a variety of ways. The traditional account of argument soundness required that an argument have true premises and a deductively valid inference from its premises to its conclusion. This traditional account, although valuable for arguments in mathematics and logic, is too narrow to apply plausibly to a wide variety of arguments used in science, the humanities, law, administration, and everyday life. In these areas, there are many important and rationally persuasive arguments in which premises are not known for certain to be true and in which the connection between premises and conclusions is something other than deductive entailment.

Using the ARG Conditions to Evaluate Arguments

By using the ARG conditions, you can assess the cogency of an argument. That is, you can determine, on the basis of a reasonable, stage-by-stage evaluation, how good the argument is—how strong the support is that it gives to its conclusion. You first put the argument into a standard form so that you can see exactly what its premises and conclusion are. Then you determine whether the premises are acceptable.

Suppose that the audience to whom the argument is addressed is you. You should ask yourself whether you have good reason to accept the premises on which the argument is based. If you are inclined to accept the premises, ask yourself why you do. If you do not accept them, the argument cannot possibly provide you with a good basis for accepting its conclusion. An argument moves from its premises to its conclusion, and you will not get anywhere without a starting point.

If the premises are passable on the (A) condition, you move on to (R). Ask yourself whether the premises are relevant to the conclusion. How, if at all, do they bear on it? If the premises have nothing to do with the conclusion, they can't be properly connected to it, and (even if acceptable) they can't give you any reason to think that the conclusion is true. An argument with irrelevant premises is a poor argument; it fails on (R) and cannot be cogent.

If (A) and (R) are satisfied, you move on to (G). Ask yourself whether the premises, taken together, provide adequate grounds for the conclusion. Premises that are acceptable and relevant may fail to provide sufficient grounds for the conclusion; they may offer an appropriate sort of evidence but fail to give enough of it. If this is a problem, then (G) is not satisfied and the argument is not cogent.

A cogent argument passes all three conditions of ARG. All its premises must be acceptable. They must be relevant to its conclusion. And taken together they must provide adequate grounds for that conclusion. If any one of these conditions is not satisfied, the argument is not cogent. It does not offer strong support to the conclusion.

We shall now look at some examples and see how the ARG conditions can be used to evaluate them. We will look at examples of arguments that fail each of the ARG conditions, one at a time, and see how this failure makes the argument unsuccessful in giving rational support to its conclusion. This procedure is used for the sake of simplicity. In fact, arguments do not have to fail on just one of the ARG conditions. They may fail with respect to more than one condition at once. For example, the premises of an argument might be both unacceptable in their own right and logically irrelevant to the conclusion, in which case the argument would have failed on conditions (A) and (R) at once—and it would have failed on (G), since any argument that fails on (R) will fail on (G). On the other hand, an argument may meet all the conditions and be cogent.

Failing on the (A) Condition

Consider this argument, based on a letter that appeared in *Time* magazine:

> There can be no meaningful reconciliation of science and religion. I'll tell you why. For one thing, their methods are diametrically opposed. Science admits it has no final answers, while religion claims to have them. And furthermore science, despite its excesses, has gone far to liberate the human spirit; religion would stifle it.[2]

Before evaluating this argument, we have to identify its conclusion and premises. The conclusion is the rather controversial claim announced in the first sentence: There can be no meaningful reconciliation of science and religion. The second sentence serves as a logical indicator that the following sentences are going to offer reasons for that conclusion. The third and fourth sentences form a small subargument: the fourth sentence gives a reason for the third sentence—that their methods are opposed. There is, then, a subargument in these two sentences, both of which deal with the methods of science and religion. The final sentence specifies a quite different contrast between science and religion with regard to their effects (liberation) and intentions (to stifle the human spirit). The premises are put forward so as to convergently support the conclusion. The writer argued for the conclusion that science and religion are not reconcilable by contrasting them in two ways—with regard to their methods and to their actual or intended effects. His point about methods is defended in a subargument.

The argument would look like this in standardized form:

1. Science admits to having no final answers, while religion claims to have final answers.

So,

2. The methods of science and religion are diametrically opposed.
3. Science has helped to liberate the human spirit, whereas religion would stifle the human spirit.

Therefore,

4. There can be no meaningful reconciliation of religion and science.

Given this argument, should we be convinced of the author's conclusion? Has he shown that there can be no meaningful reconciliation between science and religion? Note that the conclusion is stated in strong terms, with no qualifications. To evaluate, or appraise, the argument, we seek to determine whether it is cogent. We do this by working through the ARG conditions stage by stage.

First, consider the acceptability of the premises. Premises (1) and (3) are undefended premises, and they must be acceptable as stated if the argument is to work. There is a problem with (1), which seems to be false as stated. Premise (1) is categorical in its tone and sweeping in scope. It draws a very sharp contrast between science and religion. When we think about it, we can see that this contrast is exaggerated and is not borne out by a careful consideration of various religions and scientific theories. Some scientific theorists (for example, Isaac Newton, author of gravitational theory) have claimed to have the final answers to the questions they asked. On the other hand, some religious thinkers have made no such claim. Buddhist thinkers, for instance, characteristically see religion as the cultivation of individual peace of mind and harmony with the natural universe. They do not regard religion as a body of doctrines giving definitive answers to a set of specific questions. Thus (1) is not acceptable. For this reason, (2) is not adequately defended, since it is supposed to get its support from (1)—so (2) here would also appear to be unacceptable. Now look at (3). Here the author used more qualified terms. He says science has gone far to liberate the human spirit and that religion would stifle it. But even when these qualifications are considered, the author is overstating the contrast between science and religion. Like (1), (3) is untrue to the facts. There are scientists who seek to use scientific knowledge to control human beings, and there are religious leaders who seek to encourage the spiritual development of religious adherents. Thus premise (3) is also unacceptable.

We can conclude that this argument fails miserably on the (A) condition. All of its premises are disputable in the light of common knowledge about the roles that science and religion have played in human history. The author has overdrawn his contrasts and has been insensitive to the concrete detail that, if recalled, would force dramatic qualification of his claims. The argument is not a cogent argument because it fails on the (A) condition, and all three conditions must be met if the argument is to be cogent.

Failing on the (R) Condition

We shall now move on to consider an argument that fails on the (R) condition. The following passage was printed as a letter to the editor of *World Press Review*. The author discusses articles the magazine had previously printed, from publications outside the United States, which had criticized the witholding by the United States of its United Nations dues. (These were withheld because the United States did not approve of some policies of the United Nations and its agencies.) The author is arguing that the United States was justified in what it did and that the foreign publications were too critical of U.S. policy.

> Some foreign publications are unduly critical of my country. I believe the U.S. was justified in withholding its U.N. dues. At least twice, the Soviets have withheld theirs when they did not approve of U.N. policies (peace actions in Korea and what is now called Zaire). The foreign press did not get very worked up about it. U.N. members have constantly found fault with the U.S. They abuse us on the one hand and expect handouts on the other. Parents of adolescents face similar problems.
>
> I personally never insist on respect from anybody, but those who do not give it to me need not bother asking me for any financial help.[3]

The argument in this passage can be standardized as follows:

1. The Soviets have twice withheld U.N. dues when they did not approve of U.N. policies.
2. U.N. members have constantly found fault with the United States.
3. U.N. members who abuse the United States and then expect handouts are like adolescents.

Thus,

4. The United States was justified in withholding its U.N. dues.
5. When the Soviet Union withheld U.N. dues, the foreign press did not get very worked up about it.

Therefore,

6. Foreign publications criticizing the United States for withholding U.N. dues are being overly critical.

There are two arguments for the two conclusions: first the subargument from (1), (2), and (3) to (4) and then the main argument from (4) and (5) to (6) (see Figure 3.1).

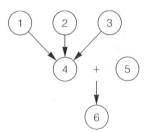

FIGURE 3.1

We shall discuss only the subargument here.

If we try to evaluate the premises for acceptability, problems arise because we would need to do historical research to determine whether they are true, or probably true. Without checking, we may not know whether, as the author claims, the Soviet Union (now Russia) did in fact withhold U.N. dues. This claim would be relatively easy to check. But in fact, the argument has such serious problems of relevance that it is not necessary to do this checking.

To see the problems of relevance in this example, we need to look at some of the language used. Let us consider the meaning of the conclusion the arguer is trying to defend. He is trying to show that the United States was justified in withholding its U.N. dues. Dues are not charity; they are costs of membership, imposed according to an agreed-on formula. Premise (1), about the Soviets, is irrelevant to the conclusion because it contains no information about the United States that could bear on the conclusion. If we knew that the Soviets had been in similar circumstances to the United States and that they had been right to withhold their dues, this premise would be relevant—but we know no such thing, and it is unlikely that the author believes this. His tone, as well as the way Soviet behavior was usually referred to in Cold War discussions, makes it more likely he thought the Soviets were quite wrong. And if premise (1) says that the Soviets were wrong in withholding dues, this point cannot show, or give any evidence at all, that the Americans were right to withhold them. Nor is premise (2) strictly relevant to the conclusion. Dues have been agreed on and are owed; the fact that others criticize a country is not relevant to the existence of this obligation.

In the third premise, the first thing to look at is the word *handout*. This word is emotionally quite negative. A handout is something the recipient does not deserve and, by implication, should not receive. No evidence has been given that the money the United States was to have given the United Nations was charity in any sense, much less a negative sense. There is an important and crucial distinction between a handout and dues owed, and when we appreciate this distinction, we can see that the third premise too is irrelevant to the argument.

In this argument, the premises are not relevant to the conclusion. Thus the argument is not cogent, whether its premises are acceptable or not. Similarly, we need not consider the (G) condition. If premises are not even relevant to the conclusion, they cannot possibly provide good grounds for it.

Failing on the (G) Condition

We now move to another example—this time one that satisfies (A) and (R) but fails on (G). It goes as follows:

> We arrived at the park gate at 7:25 P.M. at which time the cashier gleefully took money for admission. Upon entering the zoo and walking across the bridge, the loudspeaker was stating that the zoo buildings were closing at 8:00 P.M. We asked if we would not get a pass for the following day. The answer was no. In summary, it is easy to see that Calgary is anything but a friendly city, but rather out to rake off the tourist for all they can.[4]

The writer of this letter received shabby treatment at the Calgary zoo and is inferring, or drawing the conclusion, from this fact that Calgary is an unfriendly city that is out to exploit tourists. His argument is simple:

1. Some tourists were given unfriendly treatment at the Calgary zoo.
Therefore,
2. Calgary is an unfriendly city, out to exploit tourists.

Whether the premise is true we cannot know for sure; the writer is describing his personal experiences. He is likely to have had these experiences: let us grant the (A) condition. The premise is clearly relevant to the conclusion; if one person (a cashier) in one Calgary institution (the zoo) is unfriendly to tourists, this is some minimal evidence for the general conclusion that the whole city is unfriendly. It does count toward establishing that conclusion. Hence the (R) condition is also satisfied. But when we come to the (G) condition and ask how good the grounds are for the conclusion, the argument obviously breaks down. The unfriendliness of a single individual in a single institution is not adequate evidence to establish the unfriendliness of a city as a whole. The argument passes on (A) and (R) but fails on (G). It is not a cogent argument.

Satisfying All Three Conditions

We now move on to look at an argument that is cogent and that passes all three conditions. This example comes from an essay on education written by the British philosopher Bertrand Russell.

> Freedom, in education as in other things, must be a matter of degree. Some freedoms cannot be tolerated. I met a lady once who maintained that no child should ever be forbidden to do anything, because a child ought to develop its nature from within. "How about if its nature leads it to swallow pins?" I asked; but I regret to say the answer was mere vituperation. And yet every child, left to itself, will sooner or later swallow pins, or drink poison out of medicine bottles, or fall out of an upper window, or otherwise bring itself to a bad end. At a slightly later age, boys, when they have the opportunity, will go unwashed, overeat, smoke till they are sick, catch chills from sitting in wet feet, and so on— let alone the fact that they will amuse themselves by plaguing elderly gentlemen, who may not all have Elisha's powers of repartee. Therefore, one who advocates freedom in education cannot mean the children should do exactly as they please all day long. An element of discipline and authority must exist.[5]

Russell is arguing that some element of discipline and authority must exist in education. (Another way of stating this point is that freedom must be a matter of degree, rather than being absolute.) He states this point several times in the first two sentences and in the final two sentences. The incident about the woman Russell met is not really a premise; it is a story about someone who held a view with which Russell himself disagreed. He describes the episode as a way of explaining the view he doesn't hold and (by contrast) his own view. The vivid and various ways boys can come to harm need not all be mentioned in the standardization of Russell's argument, for his point is simply that they can easily come to harm—whether this is by overeating, or catching chills, or whatever won't really matter so far as the fundamental point of the argument is concerned.

The argument can be standardized as follows:

1. Both younger and older children, left to themselves, can easily come to physical harm.
2. Older children, left to themselves, often are very annoying to adults.

So,

3. Children simply cannot be left to do as they please all day long.

Therefore,

4. There must be some element of discipline and authority in education.

There is a subargument structure here: the first two premises are intended to support the third one, and that is intended to support the conclusion of the main argument. The undefended premises, then, are (1) and (2). Both are clearly acceptable; these are matters of common knowledge; hence the (A) condition is satisfied. And they are clearly relevant to (3): that unsupervised children will naturally harm themselves and others are two good reasons for not just leaving them to do as they please all day. The (R) condition is satisfied.

Furthermore, the (G) condition is also satisfied in this subargument. These are compelling reasons. The subargument passes all of the ARG conditions and is cogent; thus (3) is acceptable, since it is defended by a cogent argument. The final assessment will depend on whether (3) is properly connected to (4). Does it provide relevant and adequate grounds for (4)? To fully explain the relevance of (3) to (4), it helps to recall that children in western European societies (about whom we can presume Russell would have been writing) spend a substantial portion of their time in the educational system. To have no discipline and authority in education would in effect leave these children to their own devices for a considerable portion of their time—contrary to what we accepted in (3). Thus (3) not only is acceptable but is properly connected to (4), because it is relevant to it and provides adequate grounds for it. Since the subargument is cogent and the main argument is cogent, the entire argument is cogent.

The Significance of Argument Evaluation

It is important to note what you have shown when you show that an argument is not a cogent one. You have shown that the author of the argument failed to support his or her conclusion with adequate reasons. The conclusion is not justified by the reasoning the author put forward. If you have evaluated an argument of your own and found it not to be cogent, you may have discovered that you do not have good reasons for one of your opinions or beliefs.

To evaluate an argument as not cogent is to object to the argument as a whole, not just to the conclusion. If you show that an argument is not cogent, you show that its premises do not provide rationally adequate grounds for its conclusion. However, this process of evaluation does not show that the conclusion itself is false or unacceptable. The conclusion might be true. There might be other evidence showing it to be true, even though the argument you considered did not.

Suppose a person were to argue this way:

1. Jones offered a poor argument for the conclusion that old growth forests in Oregon, northern California, and British Columbia are in danger.
Therefore,
2. Old growth forests in Oregon, northern California, and British Columbia are not in danger.

Such an argument would be faulty. It would fail on the (G) condition; the grounds offered are not adequate. If a person were to argue in such a way, he would have only the flimsiest of evidence for his conclusion. After all, Jones is only one person among many. The fact that he happened to come up with a poor argument on a topic does not show that there are no good arguments for the conclusion he sought to reach on that topic.

To show that someone's argument is faulty is to show that the conclusion put forward is not well supported by the evidence. It is to show that one particular argument has failed to be cogent, and that is all. It is important to remember that you have not refuted a claim or a theory simply because you have shown that one or more of the supporting arguments for it are faulty. To refute a conclusion, you would have to come up with an independent argument supporting the denial of that claim. Often this task of refutation is harder than simply finding faults in the argument for the original conclusion. To go back to the example about the old growth forests in the North American northwest, you would have to show logging practices and human settlements and so on in this area are not threatening the survival of these forests. That is more of a task than finding fault with some particular argument for the conclusion that they are endangered. Finding a flaw in an argument for some claim, X, does not show that not-X is true or acceptable.

EXERCISE SET

Exercise 1

Assess the following arguments using the ARG conditions as you are able to understand them at this point. There may be several arguments in combination; if so, specify your comments accordingly, noting each subargument and then pulling together your remarks to appraise the combined structure. The first arguments are pre-standardized to make your work easier. In the case of arguments that are not standardized, carefully standardize them before applying ARG. For the purposes of this exercise, do not add missing premises or conclusions. If you think that you do not have enough background knowledge to determine whether premises are acceptable, omit the (A) condition and concentrate on (R) and (G).

1. *The Sibling Rivalry Case*
    (1) People who have a brother or sister are in a different family situation from those who do not have a brother or sister.

(2) People who have a brother or sister have to compete with their sibling for the parents' attention, whereas those who are only children do not have to compete with a sibling for this attention.

(3) Competing for a parent's attention is a phenomenon that can bring out emotions of jealousy, anger, and inadequacy.

Therefore,

(4) Jealousy, anger, and inadequacy can arise in people with brothers and sisters more readily than in people who are only children.

2. *The Animal Rights Case*

(1) Animals are not human beings.

(2) Animals do not speak language as human beings do.

(3) Animals do not have the same advanced cultures and technologies as human beings.

Therefore,

(4) Animals do not have any moral rights.

3. *The Aggression Case*

(1) People have given their children war-related toys for many centuries.

(2) Children have often enjoyed playing cowboys and Indians and using toy soldiers and related playthings.

(3) Not every child who plays with war toys becomes a soldier.

Therefore,

(4) War toys have no tendency whatsoever to make children less sensitive to violence.

*4. *The Philosophy Instructor Case*

(1) The textbooks selected for the philosophy course were difficult to read.

(2) The assignments for the philosophy course were difficult to complete.

(3) Many students do not enjoy studying philosophy.

Therefore,

(4) The instructor in the philosophy course was not competent in his knowledge of philosophy.

5. *The Case of Fashion and Formality*

(1) The wearing of formal, as opposed to informal, clothes does not alter who a person is or what that person can do.

(2) The wearing of formal clothes means that clothes cost more money than they would if informal clothes were worn.

(3) The wearing of formal clothes means that the upkeep of clothes takes more time than it would if informal clothes were worn.

Therefore,

(4) The custom of wearing formal clothes every day in work environments is not desirable.

*6. *The Success of Technology Case*

(1) People thought an atomic bomb was impossible, and we made atomic bombs.

(2) People thought flying machines were impossible, and we made airplanes.

(3) People thought that landing a man on the moon was impossible, and we landed a man on the moon.

(4) People think getting an adequate vaccine against AIDS is impossible.

Therefore,

(5) We will discover an adequate vaccine against AIDS.

7. *The Case of Evolutionary Selfishness*

(1) Any action can be interpreted as being something the agent wants to do.

So,

(2) Any action can be interpreted as selfish.

And,

(3) Any action that can be interpreted as selfish is selfish.

(4) Any action is, ultimately, the effect of the genetic structure of the agent who performs it.

Therefore,

(5) Our genes make us do selfish things.

8. *A Professor Generalizes about Psychology Students*

(1) Students in my present psychology class do not work as hard as students in my psychology class last year.

Therefore,

(2) Students at the university in general are not working as hard this year as they did last year. And,

(3) Affluence and low standards in the high schools produce poor work habits in students.

*9. *Polls on a Doctors' Strike*

(1) In a poll, 75 percent of the people questioned said that they think people who perform essential services do not have a right to strike.

(2) Doctors perform essential services.

So,

(3) Polls indicate that 75 percent of people think doctors do not have a right to strike.

*10. There are only two kinds of thinkers. There are those who analyze, who like to pull problems apart and reduce them to basic simple units. Then there are those who synthesize, pulling together all sorts of different materials to bring about novel results. Therefore, all thinking is about how wholes result from parts.

*11. In schools in Cuba, girls far outdo boys in their achievements. Cuba is a socialist state in which equality of the sexes is a matter of law. In Cuba it is even a legal requirement for men to do their share of the housework! Therefore, we can see that under socialism and true equal opportunity, women show up as superior to men.

12. Marijuana should not be illegal, because it is less harmful than alcohol, and alcohol is legal.

13. Geese and ducks should not be fed in the winter, because feeding them encourages them to remain in northern climates from which they would normally migrate at that time.

14. *Background:* The following comments are taken from "Madison Avenue Medicine," an ethics column by Randy Cohen that appeared in the *New York Times Magazine* for June 27, 1999. Cohen is discussing the question of whether doctors should advertise. He says,

"Advertising is always a dubious means of education, since it involves the testimony of interested parties. And while patients need information, that need will not be met by transform-

ing the doctor/patient relationship into the McDonald's/burger-eater relationship."

*15. Competition results in the best system for all. We can easily see why this is the case if we consider how small businesses operate. If a town has only one bakery, the baker can make buns, pies, and muffins just as he wishes and charge the highest prices customers will tolerate. But if there are two or three bakeries, customers can select the best products at the lowest prices. With competition, there is pressure to bring quality up and prices down, which benefits consumers. Therefore, competitiveness is a force for good and should not be eliminated.

16. *Background:* The following statements were made from Russian cosmonaut-engineer A. Feoktisov, who is quoted in "Eclipsed," an article about the American and Russian space programs, by Bill Keller. (*New York Times Magazine*, June 27, 1999)

"We had a lunar program because the Americans had a lunar program. When I speak of the stupidity of the Soviet program, the same applies to the American program. These decisions were not made by scientists. They were made by politicians. And for what? . . . From an engineering standpoint, the Apollo program was quite an accomplishment. But what was the result? They brought back a few hundred kilograms of rocks. We got absolutely no information about the origin of the moon, for example. The Americans wasted $25 billion for prestige. For $25 billion, they might have done something more interesting."

17. *Background:* The following excerpt is from Brian Skyrms, *Choice and Chance: An Introduction to Inductive Logic*, 3rd ed. (Belmont, CA: Wadsworth 1986), p. 123.

"Science is concerned with patterns which recur throughout the universe, rather than with gossip about a particular spatio-temporal region. This concern flows from the essential pursuits of science: explanation and prediction. Science always explains an event by showing it, in some way, to be an instance of a general pattern, rather than just a freak occurrence."

The Challenge of Argument

Someone arguing for a conclusion on the basis of premises is trying to make a reasonable case for something she believes. She thinks there are good reasons for the claim she is defending in her conclusion, and she is trying to rationally persuade others of this claim by giving evidence and reasons for it in her premises. She tries to use premises the audience will believe and reasoning that will lead the audience from those premises to the conclusion. When things work ideally, she offers a cogent argument to an audience that can understand it, accepts it, and as a result is rationally persuaded of her conclusion. Thus, argument can serve as a fundamental tool of rational persuasion.

In effect, an arguer putting forward an argument does these three things:

1. Asserts the premises
2. Asserts that *if* the premises are true (or acceptable) the conclusion is true (or acceptable)
3. Asserts the conclusion

In the ideal case, the argument is a cogent one; the audience accepts the premises, understands and accepts the accuracy of the reasoning from the premises to the conclusion, and, being rationally persuaded, is led to accept the conclusion. If the audience does not accept the conclusion, it finds some error either in the premises or in the reasoning.

What we call the challenge of argument is to construct and respond to arguments in ways that are appropriate to this basic structure. When we offer arguments, we should make every attempt to put forward true or reasonable premises that offer solid grounds for our conclusion. When we consider other people's arguments, we should think through the premises and reasoning given and base our acceptance or rejection of the conclusion on this reflection. It is especially important to respond to the argument offered when we disagree with the conclusion. Arguing on the basis of premises to a conclusion is a natural and common human activity. Nevertheless, there are some responses to it that fail to take the basic nature of argument into account. A temptation is to ignore arguments to conclusions with which we disagree.

A surprisingly common mistake when offering arguments is to put forward premises that state or presuppose the conclusion. In such a case, the premises are too logically close to the conclusion to be able to support it. This mistake is often called begging the question and will be explained in more detail in Chapter 5. Following a recent study of argument skills, based on substantial interviews with 160 subjects ranging in age from 14 to 69, researcher Deanna Kuhn found that only half of these subjects were able to offer genuine evidence for their beliefs about the causes of school failure, unemployment, or recidivism. (Recidivism is the repeated commission of crimes by those who have been released from prison.) The other subjects offered only pseudoevidence that in effect presupposed that the conclusion was true. Pseudoevidence is what appears to be evidence, but could not be genuine evidence, because it is too closely related to the conclusion claim to provide any support for it. If you are trying to show that people should not smoke in public places (your intended conclusion) and you use as a premise the claim that people have no right to smoke in public places, you have offered no real evidence for your conclusion. You have offered only pseudoevidence.

The following excerpts from one of the interviews cited in Deanna Kuhn's book illustrate the problem of pseudoevidence. In this interview, the subject has stated that the cause of recidivism is that crime has been rewarding for the ex-prisoner. His conclusion is that ex-prisoners go on to commit more crimes because this is what they want to do.

> *Interviewer:* How do you know that this is the cause?
>
> *Subject:* Because (1) I think if they want to become good citizens, they would . . .
>
> *Interviewer:* If you were trying to convince someone else that your view that wanting to stay in crime is the cause, what evidence would you give to try to show this?
>
> *Subject:* Well, I would get some evidence of people that did commit crimes and went to jail and now are good honest citizens . . . There are many . . . Some should still be in jail. They shouldn't let them out at all. (2) The crimes they commit . . . there is no excuse for them.
>
> *Interviewer:* Just to be sure I understand, can you explain exactly how this shows that wanting to stay in crime is the cause?
>
> *Subject:* Well, they always blame it on environment and how they are brought up, and I can remember, I can state that crime and the burning of buildings that you have throughout the United States today . . . (years ago this did not happen; now things are different . . .) It's the element, the people that come in. (3) They don't want to better themselves . . . (3a) People don't want to change . . .
>
> *Interviewer:* Is there anything someone could say or do to prove that what you've said is what causes prisoners to return to crime?
>
> *Subject:* Anybody that's been in jail and have repeated convictions . . . they've always been in jail, so what did he get out of it? (4) They get room and board and they really don't make an honest living. And you and I, the taxpayer, maintain these people. It comes out of our taxes.

The numbered statements all *presuppose* that people who commit crimes and go to prison want to do this—and this is a problem, because that is the conclusion that the subject is trying to support. Despite considerable persistence, the interviewer is unable to lead the subject to put forward premises that could genuinely support the conclusion. The problem is that all the claims put forward as evidence assume what he is supposed to be arguing for: which is that recidivism is caused by prisoners' not wanting to change, wanting to remain in jail, or wanting to continue committing crimes.[6]

According to Kuhn, more than half of the subjects interviewed indicated some version of this problem of pseudoevidence. They were unable to offer cogent arguments to support their claims, because when they attempted to justify their beliefs, they were unable to state any reasons for them that did not, in effect, presuppose the very conclusions they were attempting to support. Kuhn suggests that the subjects were so committed to their beliefs that they could not formulate any evidence that did not already presuppose those beliefs. They were unable to meet the challenge of argument. The frequency of the problem of pseudoevidence in this research indicates the importance, both in constructing arguments and in evaluating them, of keeping the fundamental distinction between the premises and the conclusion firmly in our minds.

Another common mistake occurs when people attempt to respond to the arguments offered by others. This is the mistake of ignoring the premises and the reasoning—in effect, just ignoring the argument—and evaluating the conclusion directly. People often listen or read only partially. When they come to a claim they disagree with, they simply reject it without checking to see whether the speaker or arguer has given reasons for it—reasons that should be taken into account before the claim is just rejected. Or, alternately, they hastily judge that an entire speech or passage is sensible and well-reasoned, merely because they agree with the conclusion. They fail to check whether the premises used are plausible and whether the reasoning is good or poor. It is extremely important to separate your evaluation of the argument from your prior belief about its conclusion. Someone who offers you an argument is giving you reasons or evidence to accept a claim. If you look directly at the conclusion and accept or reject it wholly on its own, you are, in effect, ignoring the argument. You are failing to respect the other person by leaving out his or her reasons for thinking as he or she does, and you are depriving yourself of an opportunity to think, reflect, and possibly change your mind.

Consider the following dialogue as an example:

DIALOGUE I

Peter: Mountain climbing is a terrific sport. It gives people a chance to get out in beautiful country, it gives them good exercise, it builds really strong arm and leg muscles, and it requires great teamwork.

Susan: A great sport? Isn't it kind of dangerous?

Peter: More than any other sport I know it builds both health and teamwork.

Susan: I don't know. I've heard about a lot of climbing accidents.

Peter: Furthermore, you aren't going to find a better sport for aerobic strength and arm and leg muscle development.

Susan: Mountain climbing is really risky. I just can't see the point. And besides, why should the public have to pay when these mountain climbers get into trouble? The forest rangers are in there with helicopters and heaven knows what else, and it all costs taxpayers' money.

Peter: Come on, don't be such a nervous Nellie. We're going out next weekend, and I was going to ask you to come. But I guess I won't. Obviously, you're not the type.

Here Peter and Susan ignore each other's arguments to the point where they seem about to lapse into a quarrel. Peter puts forward four reasons why he thinks mountain climbing is a terrific sport: it gets people out in beautiful country, it provides good exercise, it builds strong arm and leg muscles, and it requires great teamwork. Susan obviously doesn't agree with Peter's claim. She states another view, also based on an argument: mountain climbing isn't a good sport because it is too unsafe.

But read the dialogue again. Note that Susan does not respond at all to Peter's argument. It is as though he did not use premises at all; she disagrees with his claim about mountain climbing, and she reacts to his argument by disagreeing with the conclusion instead of considering his reasons and how they might support what he has to say. Peter responds in kind and ignores Susan's argument. The dialogue thus shows the two characters talking at cross-purposes. Each is trying to defend a point of view with reasons but ignoring the reasons put forward by the other. It does not seem likely that either will convince the other or that they will resolve the dispute by coming to a third view. These people fail to connect in that they do not address each other's reasons and evidence. Each goes on thinking what he or she did before, making no effort to reflect on whether the other person's statements might provide reason to change his or her point of view. This sort of reaction is a common way of avoiding the challenge of argument.

What could Susan and Peter have done to better meet the challenge of argument? Compare Dialogue II with Dialogue I to get some idea.

DIALOGUE II

Peter: Mountain climbing is a terrific sport because it's so good for muscle development and teamwork. Also, you see wonderful scenery when you're mountain climbing.

Susan: I doubt that mountain climbing is better for developing muscles than some other sports like soccer and tennis. Is it better for developing teamwork than football, baseball, or basketball? I can see why mountain climbing attracts people, in a way, but I think it's too risky to be a good sport to take up.

Peter: I'm not saying it's the only way to develop muscles and good teamwork. You could do this through other sports, of course. But mountain climbing is a challenge, and it's so much fun and gives you such a sense of achievement. When you put these together with the good exercise and teamwork, you've really got something. As for risk, why do you think mountain climbing is so risky?

Susan: It's those stories you see in the paper every summer about how the forest rangers have to go out and use helicopters to rescue mountain climbers who go out on ledges and so on.

This time, Susan considers Peter's argument and asks him how several of his premises are supposed to support his conclusion. She mentions her own view that mountain climbing isn't such a great sport because it is too risky. And Peter responds to her argument by asking her why she thinks it is risky. He is, in effect, questioning her premise (politely) and asking for a subargument. Whether or not Peter convinces Susan in the end, we can see that much more information is being exchanged. The situation seems less likely to degenerate into a quarrel.

We are sometimes tempted to react to argument as though all we had to do was evaluate the conclusion. We are unwilling to allow ourselves to be rationally persuaded; we are, in effect, presuming that what we believe before we heard the argument is correct and that we can use our beliefs to directly evaluate the conclusion without thinking through any premises put forward to support that conclusion. Our temptation is to respond positively to an argument whenever we agree with its conclusion and respond negatively to an argument whenever we disagree with its conclusion. When we do this, we behave like Susan and Peter in Dialogue I: we just don't want to follow the thinking through. We are tempted by the shortcuts of dogmatic rejection or hasty agreement, and shut our minds to the possibility of **rational persuasion.** The temptation to evaluate arguments by focusing solely on their conclusions should be resisted, because it deprives us of any opportunity to change our mind on the basis of an argument. This opportunity is a valuable one. It can genuinely open our minds and give us new information.

How can another person's argument lead you to change your mind? Suppose you are inclined to disagree with, or feel some doubt about the conclusion, but you identify premises put forward to support it and you find that you do accept those premises. You then think the argument through, from premises to conclusion, and try to see how the arguer has reasoned from the premises to the conclusion. If the premises logically support the conclusion, and they seem to be true or acceptable, then you are, in effect, judging that the argument is cogent and provides you with rational support for a conclusion with which you did not previously agree. You have good reason to change your mind. If you do not change your mind, you should, at least, begin to think further about the issue and examine the argument to see whether you can identify the point where it has gone wrong.

Given the pressures of time that often face us, there are some arguments that we are unable to respond to. If an issue is relatively insignificant, it may be all right to ignore an argument; we cannot argue over everything. In this book, since our goal is to practice constructing, understanding, and evaluating arguments, we try to meet the challenge of argument whenever it arises.

It is probably more common to reject or ignore arguments when we disagree with the conclusion than when we agree with it. We tend to focus on things we agree with and ignore what we disagree with. Psychologists have studied and documented this human tendency, which they refer to as the "confirmation bias." But having a true or acceptable conclusion is not enough to make an argument a good one; to say that the conclusion is true or acceptable is not to say that any ARG condition is satisfied—much less that all of them are! A good argument must have true or acceptable premises (A) and correct reasoning from those premises to the conclusion (RG). The challenge of argument is to reason through, to appraise the premises and the legitimacy of the reasoning from those premises as a basis for forming our judgment about the conclusion. A convincing argument may give us good reason to change our mind. To think clearly and accurately and to approach issues with an open mind, we should be alert to this possibility.

Suppose that you are absolutely convinced by common experience that the conclusion of someone's argument should not be accepted. In such a case, you will be inclined to say that there must be something wrong with the argument. But then your task is to find out what that is. It is not enough to reject the argument merely on the grounds that you do not like its conclusion. You should find something wrong either with its premises or with its reasoning—or both. If you cannot do this, you should reconsider your views. To truly meet the challenge of argument, you should respond to arguments as attempts to give reasoned support for conclusions. This means doing your own reasoning to determine whether you dissent from the premises, or the reasoning, or both—that is, to determine why you disagree. If you are unwilling to accept someone's conclusion on the basis of his or her argument, you should have reason to reject the premises, or the reasoning from the premises to the conclusion, or both. To criticize an argument merely on the grounds that you do not agree with its conclusion is not an adequate response.

EXERCISE SET

Exercise 2: Part A

Read the following dialogues. In each one, the first character gives an argument and the second character responds to it. Find those cases in which the second character's response meets the challenge of argument and indicate that it does. Find those cases in which the second character's response does not meet this challenge and indicate that it does not. In each case, explain the basis for your answer.

*1. *Caroline:* Mathematics is the most important subject you can study at a university. First, it is completely precise. There is always just one right answer to every question, and you can prove beyond any doubt that that answer is the right one. Second, by doing proofs in mathematics, you learn standards of rigor and exactness. Third, mathematics is the basis of all the sciences—physics, geology, chemistry, engineering, even biology. You can't do these if you don't understand mathematics. It is surely unfortunate that mathematics is so badly taught and that many people don't like it.

Bob: I hate math and I always will. My math teacher in elementary school was the crabbiest teacher I ever had. She could never explain anything, and the whole class was lost. I never caught up. If math becomes a requirement, colleges and universities will soon be empty of students.

2. *Alan:* Animals think and feel. Why should anybody doubt this? After all, when I know that other humans think and feel, I know this only because I make inferences from human behavior, from the things that human beings do. Well, animals exhibit intelligent and sensitive behavior just as humans do. So animals think and feel too.

David: I disagree. The premise you use ignores the very important role language plays in our understanding of other people. Dogs and lions can't talk, so any basis we would have for attributing thoughts to them is shaky. It's far less adequate than our evidence for the existence of thoughts in other people.

3. *Jim:* A mediator should be completely neutral between the two parties in a dispute. If he is

on the side of either party, the process will be unfair to the other party. In addition, the disadvantaged party will probably detect the lack of neutrality and then the mediation won't work. Neutrality is probably the most essential of all qualities for a mediator to have.

Roger: You're wrong. Sympathy is much more important—and concern that the conflict be resolved.

4. Prahdeep: I get so frustrated with these modern novels in which there are shifts of time frame and shifts of narrator all over the place. I think a good novel should be enjoyable to read, and these kinds of novels just aren't enjoyable, because it is too hard to follow them. So they aren't any good. Old-fashioned novels, which were more logical and organized, and easier to follow, were much better.

Juan: I don't agree. First of all, I don't think the standard for what makes a novel good is that it should be easy to read and readers should enjoy it. There are other standards, in terms of style, what aspects of reality are captured in the novel, and what its message is. Secondly, you may be unusual in your inability to follow modern novels. These books do sell, which suggests that lots of other people are able to read them and follow them. Maybe you should try to develop your tolerance for a little chaos. After all, the world itself is pretty chaotic, isn't it?

5. *Steve:* I would never let myself be hypnotized by anyone, for any reason.

Peter: Why not?

Steve: Too much is at stake. I just don't trust anyone that much. When you let somebody hypnotize you, they are getting right inside your mind, and they have a lot of potential to control you. Hypnosis is dangerous because it opens your mind to too much outside influence.

Peter: I can see what you mean but I don't know; hypnosis helped me a lot when I was quitting smoking. I used it once for dental work too, and it was great.

6. Alex: Michel and Marie-Jeanne are really having marriage problems. I think they should get counselling. It really worked well for some other friends of mine, and since Michel and Marie-Jeanne have several children, it would be really unfortunate if they split up.

Sheila: I don't know, Alex, I wouldn't suggest it if I were you. Just because counselling worked for some people you know, that doesn't mean it would work for everybody. Michel and Marie-Jeanne have no doubt thought about, and worked on, their own problems, and an inept counsellor could do more harm than good. There are lots of bad counsellors out there. As for the kids, you know people say children are better off with divorced parents than with quarrelling unhappy parents.

7. *James:* The earth is very much affected by all the creatures that live on it—the human race is only one. Animals and plants affect the earth's atmosphere. Water, too, is affected by what all the creatures do, and the earth adapts. The earth can adapt to changes all these creatures make in it. It is as though the earth and all the living creatures on it constitute a single vast organism.

Richard: I disagree. In an organism, the parts more or less adapt to the needs of the whole. But plants and animals do not adapt to the needs of the earth. Quite the contrary, in fact. They can reproduce until their numbers are disproportionate and harmful.

(Adapted from "Gaia: The Smile Remains, but the Lady Vanishes," *Scientific American*, December 1989, p. 34)

8. *Susan:* I don't think that man should have been sentenced to death for committing the murder—even if he does seem like a really awful character. Actually, I am against capital punishment in general, for three reasons. First of all, the state expresses disrespect for human life when it is involved in executions. Secondly, it does happen that innocent people are convicted of crimes and die for crimes they never even committed, which is morally intolerable. And thirdly, people who commit crimes do so because they have disturbed backgrounds and they often are not fully responsible for what they do.

Bruce: Gosh, I didn't know you were such a knee-jerk liberal and so soft on crime. People who have committed murders deserve to die. Capital punishment is not only justified, it is absolutely required for justice.

Exercise 2: Part B

For those examples in which the second character did not respond to argument in Part A, attempt to construct a response that would properly recognize the challenge of argument and would satisfy the ARG conditions.

Evaluating Arguments and Constructing Your Own Arguments

The tasks of evaluating arguments, responding to arguments, and constructing your own arguments are closely connected. When you decide that someone else has offered a poor argument and you give an appraisal of the argument to show which of the ARG conditions are not satisfied, you are actually offering an argument yourself. If you are really meeting the challenge of argument, there are three possible responses to an argument put to you by another person.

1. *Reasoned Acceptance.* You may agree with the argument and accept the conclusion. You are then deeming it to be a cogent argument, and allowing yourself, on the basis of the cogent argument, to be rationally persuaded of the truth of the conclusion.
2. *Reasoned Rejection.* You may find some problem with the argument because it does not satisfy the ARG conditions. In this case, you contend that the first argument is not cogent because there is some flaw in it. You should have an argument of your own showing that it is wrong, and why.[7]

Ultimately it is impossible to respond to the challenge of argument without constructing arguments yourself. Even if you do agree, it is worth thinking the argument through to understand why you agree.

In our explanation of what makes for a good argument, we have tended to emphasize critically responding to other people's arguments. But it is worth noting that when you use the ARG conditions to evaluate arguments, you will end up constructing your own arguments, because you will be giving reasons for your conclusion that the argument is or is not cogent. When you determine that another's argument is not cogent, you are using the ARG conditions as tools of criticism. The critique that you work out can itself be put forward as an argument.

Consider the following general example:

1. The arguer used an unacceptable premise.
2. The arguer's second premise is irrelevant to the conclusion.

So,

3. The argument given fails on the (A) condition and on the (R) condition.

Therefore,

4. The argument offered is not a cogent argument.

In this case, you yourself need to defend premises (1) and (2) in subarguments, because it is up to you to show why a premise put forward is unacceptable, or irrelevant. Saying, "It's false," or "It's unacceptable," or "It's irrelevant" does not do the whole job. You have to have reasons for thinking so. (In most cases, the person who offered the argument would have thought that its premises were acceptable and relevant; otherwise, it is unlikely that he or she would have used them.)

When you offer your own argument, you are moving beyond applying critical labels to someone else's argument. You have to explore and state your own reasons for your critical judgments. At this point, you are constructing your own arguments. Your arguments, to be good ones, will themselves have to satisfy the ARG conditions. Avoid the problem of pseudoevidence. Make sure that what you say about the original argument is acceptable and relevant and that it provides adequate grounds for your judgment that the original argument is not cogent.

Textbooks on argument, such as this one, include many examples of short arguments written by a wide variety of people. Students working through the textbook are asked to analyze these examples. This process of analysis and criticism is highly practical for academic studies and in everyday life. However, the practice can lead us to forget that there are two sides to the practice of argument. There is the matter of evaluating other people's arguments, and there is the matter of becoming good at constructing arguments yourself. The most natural way to construct cogent arguments is to concentrate on the ARG conditions and check your arguments accordingly. The ARG conditions are tools for argument construction as well as for argument criticism. Try to use premises that are acceptable—both to you and to those who will be hearing or reading your argument. Be careful to observe the distinction between the premises and the conclusion and make sure that your premises do not restate, or presuppose, your conclusion. Have a keen sense of which conclusions you are trying to defend, and make sure that what you have to say is either relevant to those conclusions or clearly stands out as a background, or an aside. Make sure there are enough relevant premises to provide adequate grounds for your conclusions.

You may have noticed that many of the arguments invented here to illustrate various themes in this book are much easier to follow than the real arguments quoted from letters to the editor and from nonfiction works. With the real arguments, sometimes it seems as though most of your work comes in standardizing, rather than in appraisal. You cannot apply the ARG conditions until you have a clear argument to apply them to. If you find this matter difficult, spend some time reviewing Chapter 2. The difficulties we may experience in standardizing can teach us something when we come to construct our own arguments, and that is the importance of making ourselves clear. Obviously, when we compose a public speech or an essay, we will not number our premises and conclusions. But we can introduce important conclusions with useful phrases such as "I wish to argue that" or "What I am trying to show is," and we can state conclusions clearly either at the beginning or end of what we have to say. We also can clarify terms that could be misinterpreted by the audience whom we are addressing. The various things that cause problems of interpretation or weak arguments when they appear in other people's writing also can appear in our own work, and we should strive to eliminate them. Becoming a competent critic of other people's arguments and gaining the ability to argue clearly oneself are opposite sides of the same coin.

The Dialectical Context

Usually when you put forward arguments to try to rationally persuade other people of your views, you will do so in a context where there is a controversy of some kind. The **dialectical context** is the context of discussion and deliberation about an issue.[8] In this dialectical context, there will be different positions, positions which are alternative to your own and which are held by other people. There will also be objections to your own position and the argument you have put forward to defend it.

When you offer an argument that you believe to be cogent, you are putting forward premises in an attempt to defend a conclusion—a conclusion that other people dispute. That is to say, your position is one position among a number of possible ones; it is a position to which there are alternatives. You may be inclined to think of alternatives in a yes/no or agree/disagree way. You might think to yourself, "well, there are two sides to every question." To think this way gives some understanding of alternatives, but in fact it is an over-simplification. For many issues there are far more than two sides. As an example, consider a controversy that has been an intense one in North America for more than three decades: abortion. There are many different positions taken by people on this matter. Some believe (1) that abortion amounts to murder and is always wrong; others (2) that abortion is morally permissible early in pregnancy, say up to four months; others (3) that abortion is morally wrong but should be legally permissible in early months whenever the expectant woman feels that she needs it and some number of doctors will support her in that decision; and still others (4) that abortion is both morally and legally permissible and should at any time be a matter of choice for the expectant woman. We have already located four different positions in the abortion debate: there are more.

This case illustrates the point that claims about disputed issues are made in a dialectical context where they have competitors—alternative positions. If you have a position on the abortion issue, yours will be one of a number of alternative possibilities. If you construct and put forward an argument to support your position, you imply in doing so that your position is preferable to these alternatives, that it is rationally defensible in the public debate in which various other positions are also contenders. When you are constructing and reflecting on your own argument, it is often helpful to be aware of the fact that there are alternatives and that other people think about the issue in different ways. Being sensitive to these alternatives and reflecting carefully on them, to the extent that you can, are likely to improve your argument. We suggest that when you are constructing an argument, you reflect in a general way on the alternatives to your own position. Try to think about how you would argue against at least one of those alternatives.

There are bound to be objections to your argument, and it is useful when constructing the argument to consider what some of those objections might be, and how you would handle them. What should be of greatest concern is objections against the argument itself (not against the conclusion detached from the premise, or you as an arguer, or your circumstances). Such objections are those that would cast doubt on the cogency of your argument. You should ask yourself: Could someone plausibly object to your premises, claiming that they are false or problematic? In effect, could someone plausibly contend that your argument does not satisfy the (A) condition? Could someone plausibly object that your premises are actually irrelevant to the conclusion, implying that the (R) condition is not satisfied? Or that, while relevant, your premises do not provide good and sufficient grounds for the conclusion, so that (G) is not satisfied? If you think through possible objections, in this framework, before formulating your argument, you have a good chance of improving it. How objections may be understood and how we may deal with them is discussed further in Chapter 11.

EXERCISE SET

Exercise 3: Part A
Construct your own arguments in response to two of the following questions after critical examination and reflection. (*Note:* Read the example before doing the exercise.)

(a)   Should English literature and composition be compulsory subjects in the first year of college and university programs?

(b)   Should people feel free to cheat on their income tax because the government is so big that the amount involved won't make any difference?

(c)   Should North America (Canada, the United States, and Mexico) have one common currency, which would be the United States dollar?

(d)   Should people enroll in courses that they want very much to take, in circumstances where studying these things is unlikely to get them a job?

(e)   Should women keep their maiden names after marriage if they wish to do so?

Strategy for doing this exercise: First, think about the question you have selected to discuss, and think about your tentative response to it. Next, think about your reasons for wanting to answer in this way. Write them down. Now, look at what you have written and organize it into a clear argument. Then proceed to the dialectical stage, and consider one objection to your own position and one alternative position. State the objection and state how you would answer it. State an alternative position, state what reasons could be given for that alternative position, and state how you would respond to an argument in favor of that position. Now re-evaluate your original argument to see whether thinking through the objection and the alternative position have led you to see any need to revise it. Revise it if you deem this to be appropriate.

Example: Question: Is nuclear energy necessary?

First response: Nuclear energy is necessary.

Reasons: Nuclear energy would not have been developed unless experts thought it was necessary and, by and large, energy experts know what is likely to be needed; oil, gas, and coal are alternative sources of energy, and they are not going to last forever; growth in manufacturing, which is important to give people jobs, will require more energy; we can get virtually unlimited amounts of energy from small amounts of uranium, so nuclear energy has virtually unlimited potential and can meet these needs.

Possible objection: What experts think is not always right.

Alternative position: Nuclear energy may not be necessary under some conditions.

Reasons for alternative position: We could change our habits so that we do not consume so much energy (much is wasted); solar and wind energy may be viable alternatives to oil, gas, coal, and nuclear energy; perhaps if we put massive resources into researching solar and wind energy, we would find vast potential there too; solar and wind energy do not pose the safety hazards nuclear energy does.

Resulting argument: (*Note:* This argument is an amended version of the first argument; amendments are based on considerations as to how premises and conclusion should be clarified and qualified because of the considered objection and alternative.)

1. Energy experts used to think nuclear energy

was needed, and they were probably right in the judgments they made, considering the time at which these were made.

2. Coal, oil, and gas are the major alternatives to nuclear energy, and they will not last forever.

3. Solar and wind energy probably will not have the same potential for expansion as nuclear energy.

4. We need vast amounts of energy to keep economies going and give people jobs.

So, probably,

5. Nuclear energy is necessary unless there is successful research on how to develop solar and wind energy.

Note any subarguments, and clearly mark the premises and conclusions in your final argument. Then rewrite your argument in more natural language as though it were an essay, a report for a work environment, or a letter to the editor of your local newspaper.

Exercise 3: Part B

Show that the arguments you constructed in response to Part A satisfy the ARG conditions of argument cogency.

Exercise 3: Part C

Ask a friend in the course to evaluate your argument. Note disputed points, if any, and either revise your position to accommodate these or defend your position with subarguments.

CHAPTER SUMMARY

Our general term for argument evaluation is *cogent*. A cogent argument is one in which the premises are acceptable (A), are relevant to the conclusion (R), and, considered together, provide good grounds for the conclusion (G). These three conditions of cogency are called the ARG conditions. They are readily remembered, since A, R, and G are the first three letters of the word *argument*. According to the theory of argument adopted in this book, a cogent argument, one in which all three of the ARG conditions are satisfied, is a good argument. An argument that fails to be cogent is poor, or weak.

The (R) and (G) conditions can be satisfied in various ways that are discussed in more detail in later chapters of this book. These are deductive entailment, inductive support, analogy, and conductive support.

If an argument fails to satisfy the ARG conditions, then it is not cogent and it fails to rationally support its conclusion. It is important to note that this is not to say that its conclusion is unacceptable, just that this particular argument does not support it. The conclusion might be shown to be acceptable by some different argument. If you evaluate an argument using ARG and find that it is not cogent, then you know only that this one argument has failed to support the conclusion; you don't know whether the conclusion is false or unacceptable.

Traditionally, logicians have tended to define good arguments as sound, where *sound* means having true premises that deductively entail the conclusion. We do not use the term *sound* in this sense to explain what a good argument is, because we think the traditional account is too narrow. It does not apply plausibly to many arguments in which the premises appear to support the conclusion by some logical relationship other than deductive entailment. In addition, requiring premises to be true is probably too strict. What is more reasonable in a practical sense is to require that they be rationally acceptable, that is, that we have a good basis for believing them.

The challenge of argument is to meet an argument on its own terms, that is, to meet it as an argument. What this means is avoiding the temptation to judge arguments only in terms of whether we previously agreed or disagreed with their conclusions. Someone who offers an argument is offering reasons to support a case, and we should respond on that basis. If we do not wish to accept the conclusion, we should work through the argument to find out where and why we disagree with it. Are the premises wrong? Is the reasoning unacceptable? Either we accept the conclusion on the basis of the argument, we give reasons for finding that the argument is not cogent, or we admit that we have a problem and a subject for inquiry; there is a cogent argument for a conclusion we do not accept.

Using the ARG conditions gives you a basis for your own critical arguments. In fact, to evaluate an argument using ARG is implicitly to argue yourself: you are finding reasons to support an evaluation of the argument you are considering. The ARG conditions are, in addition, valuable tools to use when you are constructing your own arguments. You can use them to check up on yourself. Try to make sure that your premises are rationally acceptable, are relevant to the conclusions you are trying to support, and combine to give good grounds for those conclusions.

An argument is put forward in a context in which an issue is being explored or discussed. This context may be referred to as its dialectical context. When constructing arguments, you may improve their quality by considering at least one alternative position to the position you defend, and at least one objection to your argument.

Review of Terms Introduced

Acceptability of premises   Premises of an argument are acceptable provided there is appropriate evidence, or reasons, to believe them.

Analogy   Comparison based on resemblances. When the premises are connected to the conclusion on the basis of an analogy, the premises describe similarities between two things and state or assume that those two things will be similar in further ways not described. The claim is made that one of the things has a further property, and the inference is drawn that the other thing will have the same further property.

ARG conditions   The conditions of a cogent argument. The premises must be: (1) acceptable, (2a) relevant to the conclusion, and (2b) when considered together, provide sufficient grounds for the conclusion. For an argument to be cogent, all ARG conditions must be satisfied.

Cogent argument   An argument in which the premises are rationally acceptable and also properly connected to the conclusion. This means they are relevant to the conclusion and, considered together, provide good grounds for it.

Conductive argument   An argument in which premises (nearly always several in number) describe factors that are supposed to count separately in favor of a conclusion because each is relevant to it. Typically, in conductive arguments we deal with matters on which there are pros and cons.

Conjunction   Connection of two or more statements using the word *and* or another word or symbol equivalent in meaning.

Deductive entailment   Most complete relationship of logical support. If, and only if, one statement entails another, then, given the truth of the first statement, it is impossible that the other should be false. In an argument, the premises deductively entail the conclusion if, and only if, given the truth of the conjunction of the premises, it would be logically impossible for the conclusion to be false.

Dialectical context   The context of controversy and discussion in which an argument for a conclusion about a disputed issue is formulated and put forward.

Empirical generalization   When premises are connected to a conclusion on the basis of an empirical generalization, the premises describe observations about some cases, and the conclusion, which is more general, attributes the same features reported in the premises to a broader range of cases.

Goodness of grounds   Sufficiency of premises to provide good reasons or full evidence for the conclusion. Premises offer sufficient grounds if, assuming that they are accepted, and are relevant to the conclusion, they are sufficient to make it reasonable to accept the conclusion.

Rational persuasion   Causing someone to come to believe a claim by putting forward good reasons, or a cogent argument, on its behalf.

Relevance of premises   Premises of an argument are relevant to its conclusion provided they give at least some evidence, or reasons, in favor of that conclusion.

Sound argument   An argument in which the premises are true and deductively entail the conclusion.

Validity   Connection between premises of an argument and its conclusion in the case where the premises deductively entail the conclusion. Any argument in which the premises deductively entail the conclusion is deductively valid. The terms *deductively valid* and *valid* are used as equivalent in meaning within logic, although outside logic valid is sometimes used with other meanings.

Notes

1. *For instructors.* An exception would be an argument of the form '*p*; therefore '*p*, where *p* stands for a true statement. Such an *argument* is sound in the sense that it has a true premise that deductively entails its conclusion. But it is not cogent as defined here, because *p*, though true, would not be acceptable in any argumentative context in which it was being offered as a reason for itself. Why not? Because if *p* is the conclusion, *p* is in question, or needs to be justified. Given this questionability, *p* is for that very reason not acceptable as a premise. This consequence of the present account of cogency is an attractive one.

2. Based on a letter that appeared in *Time* magazine on February 26, 1979. Several indicator words have been added to make the structure of this argument more clear.

3. Letter to the *World Press Review*, December, 1988. Because of its dissolution in 1991, the Soviet Union is no longer a member of the United Nations. Its successor state is Russia.

4. Letter to the Calgary *Herald*, July 5, 1978.

5. Bertrand Russell, "Freedom Versus Authority in Education," in *Sceptical Essays* (London: George Allen and Unwin, 1953), p. 184.

6. Deanna Kuhn, *The Skills of Argument* (New York: Cambridge University Press, 1991), pp. 71–72. Inserted numbers have been added to Kuhn's text. What Kuhn refers to as pseudo-evidence is more commonly called "begging the question." (See Chapter 5.)

7. Because a cogent argument may not provide an absolute proof for a claim, one might urge addition of a third possibility here such as having reasons to suspend one's judgment. One might admit that there are good reasons to support the conclusion and yet not be rationally persuaded. Thus one might at this point suspend judgment on the acceptability of the conclusion. At this point, the conclusion and the argument offered for it have become subjects for future inquiry. Because contexts in which we need absolute proof are comparatively rare, and to avoid encouraging people to ignore arguments, I have not included this third possibility in the main body of the text.

8. I owe my interest in the dialectical context of an argument to Ralph Johnson who explores the 'dialectical tier' in his book *The Rise of Informal Logic* (Newport News, VA: Vale Press, 1996.) I have discussed Johnson's ideas about dialectical obligations to address alternative positions and objections to them in *The Philosophy of Argument* (Newport News, VA: Vale Press, 1999). See especially "Progress and Regress on the Dialectical Tier" and "Becoming Dialectical: Two Tiers of Argument Appraisal?"

chapter four
Looking at Language

LANGUAGE IS AN ESSENTIAL TOOL of thought, one whose effects go very deep. In constructing, understanding, and evaluating arguments, language is important at every stage. Words can be used so as to assist in our understanding, or they may obscure issues and contribute to careless thinking. A good sense of the meanings of words used and their role in persuasion is extremely valuable.

Generally it is far easier to use language than to think about it. Language is so much a part of us that we are accustomed to using it unreflectively. Yet it is important to reflect on language and gain some basic tools to analyze its use, because language plays an absolutely central role in shaping our thought. Our choice of terms affects which aspects of reality we attend to and which we ignore. It shapes our attention and helps us construct our picture of the world. Language does not merely enable us to refer to things and facts. It allows us to label or describe reality; it shapes and expresses our interpretations and attitudes and affects our responses to reality.

One preliminary way of thinking about language is to relate words to things in the world, and to think of the meaning of a word as the thing that it points to. We may wish to think of words as names of things. If you have a dog called "Fido," well, his name is Fido. It might seem that you can easily explain his name and thus explain what you mean by "Fido," just by pointing to your dog. In this simple case, there would seem to be a one-to-one relationship between a *word* and a *fact* in the world. In his early work, the philosopher Ludwig Wittgenstein held a theory of meaning that was rather like this. He thought of a sentence as having a kind of pictorial form, enabling a sentence to depict objects and facts in the world. Wittgenstein had been influenced by an account of a court case in Paris where motor vehicle accidents were reconstructed using dolls and toys to make models of the events. Dolls and toys represented people and vehicles. Analogously, Wittgenstein thought of words as representing facts in the world. A sentence such as "The blue truck hit the brown car" would be considered to have words pointing directly to aspects of the world. For instance, the word *blue* would point to the color of the truck, the word *truck* to the truck, *brown* to the color of the car, *car* to the car, and so on.

Note here that when we are speaking about a word, or **mentioning** that word, we put it in quotation marks, italics, or a distinct typeface. By doing so, we indicate that the word is being mentioned, not used. Consider the following example:

(a) The word *truck* refers to a kind of vehicle.

In (a) the word *truck* is mentioned. All the other words are used.

Wittgenstein later came to believe that his early theory was incorrect. You can begin to see one fundamental problem with this theory if you ask yourself what the words *the* and *hit* would point to in the example "The blue truck hit the brown car." There is just no obvious answer. Wittgenstein's later view was that words are used for many different purposes, not just to refer to things. He came to believe that we can best understand what words mean by closely studying the various ways in which they are used.[1] To think of the meaning of words as things or as facts in the world is not correct. This kind of theory may seem natural when we first begin to think about language. It is helpful in reminding us that a word is not a thing (there is a difference between "Fido" and Fido). Nevertheless it is too simplistic to be correct. Some words refer to things, but others have different functions—referring to actions, serving to classify, directing attention, expressing emotions, connecting, facilitating abstraction, and so on.

We can begin to appreciate the effect language has on our thinking if we consider some of the language of politics. To call a change of government a *coup*, for instance, is quite different from saying it is due to an *intervention*. The first term implies that an internal group took over the government in a sudden bid for power; the second implies that outside forces had a role. An argument about a *coup* in Nigeria would set the stage for one sort of political discussion, one about an *intervention* for quite another.

One might argue about whether certain events constitute an intervention or a coup—and people do. Responding to such disputes, we may feel impatient and wish to say, "Get on with it. What's in a word?" The answer to this last question is "more than you would think"— in fact, sometimes almost everything.

Often language plays so many roles at once that a whole political theory or ideology seems to be captured in a single term. Here is an important illustration. The official Chinese press termed the massive student demonstrations it violently suppressed in Tiananmen Square in June 1989 the work of rebels and counter-revolutionaries. The term *counter-revolutionary* in this context refers back to Marxist-Leninist theory. The original Communist revolution (victorious in mainland China in 1949) is seen as an uprising by working and peasant classes that was in the true interests of the people; it was in 1989, and is still, understood as being for the good of the people. Given this idea of what revolution is, counter-revolutionaries are seen as wicked reactionaries working against progress for the people. Argument will hardly be necessary to prove that counter-revolutionaries are wrong. The very term *counter-revolutionary* will carry that message to those trained in Marxist-Leninist theory. In fact, the evolution of the government's reaction to the student movement can be traced in shifts in the words used to describe it. First it was a *movement*, then a *disturbance*, then a *turmoil*, and finally, a *counter-revolution*.[2] The term *movement* is neutral; the others express growing degrees of disapproval culminating, just before the violent government reaction, in *counter-revolution*.

Even terms that might seem at first glance to be devoid of such profound political implications can shape and express deep attitudes on matters of considerable social importance. An example is *he* used as an indefinite pronoun; another is *man* used to represent human beings in general. According to older works on grammar, *he*, *man*, and *mankind* can properly be used to represent human beings of either sex. However, since these words are also used to represent male human beings specifically, there is a permanent possibility of confusing the inclusive meaning (man as male or female) and the more specific meaning (man as male).

An illustration of the **ambiguity** between gender-specific and gender-neutral senses of the word *man* is provided by the comments of Richard Holloway, an Anglican archbishop. Holloway, of Edinburgh, Scotland, urged his church not to condemn people for having adulterous affairs. His reason was that, as he put it, "Man was born to have many lovers."[3] Because of the possibility of interpreting *man* here either in the gender-inclusive way or in the male-specific way, this comment is quite ambiguous. Did Archbishop Holloway mean to say that men (males) were born to have many lovers? Or did he, rather, mean to say that human beings, both men and women, were born to have many lovers? Either way, the comment probably provoked considerable comment in the church. But its meaning is quite unclear because of the ambiguity created by his use of the word *man*.

Another illustration of confusion between inclusive and non-inclusive uses of the masculine is provided by the following passage, taken from a 1980 book offering advice on writing style. The author is advising writers to keep their style simple because a cluttered style will mean that readers will easily be distracted from the work. He says:

> Who is this elusive creature the reader? He is a person with an attention span of about twenty seconds. He is assailed on every side by forces competing for his time: by newspapers and magazines, by television and radio and stereo, by his wife and children and pets, by his home and his yard and all the gadgets that he has bought to keep them spruce, and by that most potent of competitors, sleep. The man snoozing in his chair with an unfinished magazine open on his lap is a man who was being given too much unnecessary trouble by the writer.[4]

In the sentence beginning "He is a person" we might suppose—and the author himself might claim—that the word *he* is being used inclusively, to refer to readers both male and female. But as the paragraph goes on, it is clear that the male-specific meaning of *he* has taken over. This reader can only be male, because he has a wife! The passage illustrates how words may guide our thinking. It is most unlikely that William Zinsser, who wrote this passage, actually assumed that all readers are men, or that he intended to communicate such an assumption to his readers. Nevertheless, in using *he* to refer to the general reader and then lapsing into a set of assumptions about *him* extending to a domestic scene where the reader has a wife and clearly has to be a man, Zinsser did communicate that assumption.

These examples are two of many that illustrate how specifically male meanings of such words as *he*, *man*, and *mankind* easily intrude into contexts where people seek to use those terms in gender-neutral and more inclusive ways. The idea that *man* and related words can be used in a way that is truly inclusive is not plausible. Several decades of discussion on the matter have led most publishers and stylists to recommend clearer language. For instance, in contexts where we wish to refer to men and women, *he or she* can be used instead of *he*, and *humanity* or *human beings* should be used instead of *mankind*.

These problems with *man* and *he* illustrate the powerful role language plays in directing our attention and in framing issues. The power of language in these respects is a large and fascinating topic. We cannot treat it fully here, but we do explain some basic points about language with a special emphasis on those most pertinent to argument.

Definitions

When we think of clarifying the meaning of terms, what first comes to mind, probably, is the matter of definitions. The demand "define your terms" is often heard. Some disputes seem impossible to resolve because people mean different things by words or cannot agree on meaning. Words such as *democracy, justice, freedom, imperial,* and *colonial* have powerful emotional associations and are defined in different ways by people of differing beliefs.

Many people find it annoying and picky to have to discuss and argue about definitions, but in fact, they can be quite important. In recent decades, advances in medical technology have made it necessary to redefine *death* as the absence of brain activity rather than the cessation of heartbeat or respiration, as was used in an older definition. The new definition is important. Without it, doctors who remove a heart from a traffic victim could be charged with murder. If the heart is still beating, the person from whom the heart is removed would still be alive in the old sense. Provided that the brain is no longer functioning, the person would be dead in the new sense, though his or her heart was still beating and still suitable for use in a transplant.

The modern definition of *death* is the result of more than a mere decision that the word will begin to mean something different from what it meant before. It is not just a matter of people standing up and saying, "Well, *death* used to be defined as the stopping of the heartbeat; now we are going to define it as cessation or drastic slowing of brain activity." The new definition of *death* is not purely arbitrary: it has important practical and theoretical consequences. It was made necessary by the technology of life-support systems that can keep some human bodies breathing and operating for a long time when there is too little brain activity for consciousness. The new definition is based on the belief that consciousness is more essential and definitive of human life than are breath and pulse—as well as an interest in legally and morally obtaining viable organs for transplants.

It is not necessary to define every term, of course. Many words are easy enough to understand. We live in a culture where people use words in regular, predictable ways, and the context in which words are used often helps to identify the meaning. If, for instance, you tell someone to shut the door, you do not normally need to define the words *door* and *shut*. In most situations when such simple words are used, we readily understand each other.

Even when words have several different meanings, the context of a conversation will often make it clear which meaning is the right one. The word *strike*, for instance, can have various meanings, as you can see by looking at the following four sentences:

(a) The nurses went on *strike* in June and did not go back to work until late July.
(b) According to the rules of baseball, if a batter fails to hit the ball, after three *strikes*, he is out.
(c) If someone *strikes* her on the face, she is going to *strike* back.
(d) When he is hurt, he is likely to *strike* back in anger and say something cruel, in an attempt to hurt someone else.

In (a) a *strike* is a refusal to work, a tactic employed in a labor dispute; in (b) it is a failed attempt to hit the ball, in baseball. In (c) it is the physical movement of the arm, to hit another person; in (d) it is an aggressive, but not physically aggressive, gesture against another person. The meaning in (d) is related to that in (c). In (d) the reference is to someone striking back in anger by making a hurtful remark, as distinct from using his arm in a physical move to hurt the other. That strike is a metaphorical one. In (c) the word *strike* is used literally, whereas in (d) it is used metaphorically, or figuratively.

We are all capable of using and understanding words that have multiple meanings. We can use and understand words without defining them, without even thinking about them, because we learned to do so as children and because we use words in the context of a life and culture that is familiar to us. Language is part of our social life; we often know what to expect in particular situations, and we can sense what is meant without searching for definitions. Trying to define all our terms would be a hopeless task because we need some words to define others. We look for a definition when we see a claim or argument that is hard to understand or seems strange and implausible, or when there is a practical problem whose solution depends on our having an explicit definition. We begin then to wonder what certain important words mean.

As an example of a case where a definition would help to clarify a statement, consider the following. Suppose a person from England tells you that in England only the children of the upper classes go to public schools. This is an amazing statement from the point of view of North Americans. In North America, public school means school supported by taxpayers and open to all children. In some areas, parents are dissatisfied with public schools and select private schools for which they must pay tuition fees (usually at least several thousand dollars annually). Such parents are usually comparatively wealthy. The statement about England is surprising against this background. It would surely be odd if only well-off people sent their children to public schools. The oddity of this consequence should lead us to suspect that there is some confusion in language. Is the expression "public school" used differently in England? In fact, it is. In England, public schools are "endowed grammar schools—usually boarding schools—preparing students for university" (*Abridged Oxford English Dictionary*, 4th ed., [1951]). Public schools in England are roughly equivalent to private schools in North America. Given this different definition, the claim that seemed so peculiar makes perfect sense.

When evaluating claims and arguments, we may seek definitions for terms in which an issue is presented. We will seek definitions if we find those terms unclear or if we suspect that, in the context in which they are used, there is some confusion about their meaning. Various kinds of definitions can be given, and it is useful to distinguish the different types. Different kinds serve different purposes and should be evaluated by different standards, deriving from those purposes.

Ostensive Definitions

It can, in some cases, be difficult to describe accurately the use of words. Sometimes it is hard to "catch" the sense of a word by using other words. We would like, if we could, to get outside language and explain a word by pointing to the world itself. Ostensive definition is one way in which we try to do this. In an ostensive definition of X, we explain what X is by pointing to an example of X. We point to something that is X—either a real thing, or a representation of X. For instance, instead of using words to say what *pineapple* means, we might just point to a pineapple and say, "That's a pineapple." The fact that some words can be defined in this way is one of the things that makes the "Fido"/Fido theory of meaning superficially plausible.

As children we learn language by participating in social life and by copying things others say and do. Children are taught many words by having objects pointed out to them. The procedure of **ostensive definition** appears to tie language to the world in a natural and obvious way, letting us escape from what we may feel are "words, words, and more words." Ostension may seem to be the core of language learning because of the way it connects words to the world.

Ostensive definitions are especially useful for sensory qualities that are impossible to capture, or even suggest, in words. To tell someone in words what pineapple tastes like, how a trumpet sounds, or what periwinkle blue is, is virtually impossible. It is so much easier and simpler if you can provide the appropriate example and say, "This is it." The best way to give someone an understanding of what pineapple tastes like is to put a piece of pineapple in his mouth and let him taste it. This procedure would also provide another ostensive definition of what *pineapple* means; the word refers to the kind of fruit that tastes . . . like this.

However, ostensive definition is not as simple as it might first seem to be. It does not avoid all possibilities of misunderstanding. Significantly, when one person defines a term ostensively to another, the person to whom the definition is given will come to a proper understanding only if he knows which features he is supposed to attend to. Suppose that Mary tries to teach Bill what a window is by pointing to a window and saying, "That's a window." Bill may spot something outside the window, such as a dog or a car, and think that Mary is pointing to that instead. If he misunderstands in this way, he will not use the word correctly on the basis of the definition. Another limitation of ostensive definition is that we cannot use the technique to define complex or abstract conceptions. For instance, we might cite a case of justice, but that would not give us a definition of justice.

Reportive, or Lexical, Definition

A **reportive definition** is one that has the goal of accurately describing how a word is used. Its purpose is to state in a clear way the meaning of the word as people use it and to do this by referring to nontrivial, important properties. Reportive definitions are also called lexical definitions. These definitions are intended to capture the **literal meaning** or **denotation** of a word. They do not capture original or new figurative (metaphorical) meanings, although they may note some particularly common **figurative meanings.** Nor are lexical definitions intended to capture the many **connotations**, or associations, that may accompany a word. If you look up *chair* in a dictionary, you will find an account of the various meanings of that word as it is commonly used by speakers of English. This is an account of the various ways in which *chair* can be used. These are the denotations of the word. You will not find an account of the connotations, those associated feelings and ideas that may accompany the word *chair* and that are likely to vary from person to person. To some people, the word *chair* may connote coziness and a fire at home, to others, a rocking chair in which a grandmother sits knitting, to others the slightly grubby reclining chair used by Martin in the television series, *Frasier*. Lexical, or reportive definitions, address denotation (the standard meaning or meanings of a word, as it is actually used), not connotation (the variable associations or thoughts and emotions that are suggested by a word).

A reportive definition of the word *chair* as used to refer to furniture is "a piece of furniture that is to seat one person; it typically has a straight back and is raised from the floor by legs." Such a definition is supposed to describe how people use the word *chair* to refer to pieces of furniture. The definition makes being a piece of furniture and being used to seat one person essential features of chairs, and suggests that having a straight back and being raised by legs are not strictly speaking essential, though they are typical. We don't call stools chairs because stools don't have backs. We don't call sofas chairs because sofas seat more than one person. We do call large bags filled with small pellets "bean bag chairs," because they shape into a kind of back and seat and hold one person, even though they are not raised from the floor by legs. As used for a piece of furniture, the word *chair* poses few problems. It seems relatively easy to give a reportive or lexical definition.

However, even a simple word like *chair* has other meanings, as we can see from the following examples:

(a) The chair called the meeting to order.
(b) The college established a chair in Roman history.

In (a) a chair is a person in charge of a meeting. In (b) it is an endowed professorial position. As we noted with the word *strike* earlier, the context makes clear which meaning is intended. It would not make sense for an item of furniture to call a meeting to order; hence we assume that some other meaning of *chair* is intended in (a). The meaning that would make sense for (a) is that in which the chair is a chairperson, the person in charge of a meeting or group. Similarly, in (b) it would hardly make sense to think of a college as establishing, for a specific scholarly pursuit, either an item of furniture or a presiding person. The meaning that would make sense, and the one that we read into the context here, is that of a chair as an endowed professorial position.[5]

For reportive or lexical definitions, a dictionary is a good place to start. A dictionary seeks to describe how a word is actually used and uses other words to briefly sum up that pattern of usage. If you look up the word *chafe* in the *World Book Dictionary*, you will find that it is a verb. Four meanings are listed: three are literal and one is figurative. The literal meanings are (1) to make sore by rubbing or scraping, as when a stiff collar chafes a man's neck; (2) to rub to make warm, as when a mother chafes her child's hands; (3) to wear away by rubbing or scraping (no example given). The figurative meaning, (4), referring to a common use of *chafe* in a slightly metaphorical way, is to make angry or annoyed, to irritate, as when a brother's teasing chafes a person.

We must remember, however, that even dictionaries sometimes offer imperfect definitions. Because they have to be brief, they may omit features that are important to understanding normal usage. Also, dictionaries may not reflect variation in use in different places and times. For words such as *equality, freedom, democracy, right,* and *justice*—words that represent abstract and profound ideas about which there are different philosophical and political theories—dictionaries are rarely sufficient. In the short space that they are able to allot to a single word, they cannot say enough about the issues and principles involved in these ideas to give a reliable account. For example, the *World Book Dictionary*'s definition of *just* provides relatively little guidance if you are trying to determine what it would mean, from a moral point of view, to claim that a particular law is just. It lists some seven different meanings of *just* as an adjective, with sparse explanation in each case. Summarizing, the meanings are: (1) right, fair; (2) deserved; (3) having good grounds; (4) true, exact, and or correct; (5) in accordance with standards or requirements; (6) righteous; and (7) lawful. These seven possibilities might provide a good beginning, but they do not offer deep understanding of what the justice of a law would be. As this case suggests, it is rarely advisable to cite dictionary definitions as the final word in any serious exploration of philosophical, political, administrative, or legal issues.

Some reportive definitions are open to correction against facts of usage. A reportive definition may be too broad (incorrectly implying that the word can apply to more things than it really does) or too narrow (implying that it applies to fewer things than it really does). For instance, the *Abridged Oxford English Dictionary*, 4th ed., (1951), defines *chair* (in the context of furniture) as "separate seat for one, of various forms." This definition may be criticized as too broad, because it allows a stool to count as a chair. The case of a stool provides a counterexample to the definition; according to the definition, a stool would be a chair, but in ordinary usage, we do not call a stool a chair. A reference to a back is needed to make the definition describe common usage more closely. On the other hand, we have too narrow a definition if we define *chair* as "separate seat for one having a back and four legs" because some chairs have only three legs, and bean bag chairs have none.

In addition to being too broad or too narrow, reportive definitions may be flawed for other reasons, four of which we will mention here. First, they may use terms that are too obscure and, therefore, are not helpful in explaining the meaning of a word. For instance, a definition of eating as "successive performance of masticating, humectating, and deglutinating" would be open to this objection. Anyone who needed a definition of a simple English term such as *eating* would not understand such uncommon words.

Second, reportive definitions may be inadequate if a word that is not essentially negative is defined negatively. It will not be helpful to define a church as a nonschool, because this does not tell us positively what a church is. Generally, it is more useful to be told what a thing is than what it is not. Third, reportive definitions should define by citing features that are significant rather than trivial. To define *human being* as a featherless biped is not a good definition, even though it is true both that human beings are featherless and that most have two feet. The problem with the definition is that these are trivial, not significant attributes of human beings. A definition of *human being* in terms of rationality or essential biological characteristics would be more adequate.

Fourth, reportive definitions may also be inadequate because the word to be defined is repeated in the definition. For instance, if we define *drug* as a "substance commonly used to drug someone" we have a circular definition. The word *drug* is used again in the definition, so no progress in explanation can be made. Circularity is found in such proposed definitions as "Scientists are those who undertake scientific research" or "Philosophers are those intellectuals who study problems that are peculiarly philosophical." Circularity in definitions makes them useless. When the definition uses the term being defined, or one so closely related to it in meaning that it could not be explanatory. When you try to understand a circular definition you are led right back to where you started, to the term you did not originally understand.

Ultimately, obscurity and circularity in definitions depend on the audience for whom those definitions are intended.[6] The examples of obscurity and circularity just mentioned here are so extreme that virtually anybody who needed the definition would find that it did not help to explain the meaning of the term. Other examples might be obscure to some audiences but all right for others, or they might be circular in some contexts but legitimate in others. For instance, one dictionary defines *hocus pocus* as "jugglery, deception, or a typical conjuring formula." Though the words used in the definition are quite advanced, to many people they would be better known than the expression *hocus pocus* itself. This definition could probably be helpful for many people, so it is not hopelessly obscure.

Although there is some context-relativity involved when we appraise reportive definitions, it is nevertheless possible to specify conditions for a good reportive definition in general terms. Using X to represent any word that is being defined, we can define a good reportive, or lexical, definition of X as having the following features:

1. It defines the word X in terms of the essential features that a thing must have to be X, and not in terms of trivial features.[7]
2. It is not couched in negative terms, unless X itself is negative.
3. It is not too broad, or overinclusive. That is, all things that the definition would have us call X are called X in ordinary usage.
4. It is not too narrow, or underinclusive. That is, all things that are called X in ordinary usage are called X according to the definition.
5. It is not too obscure. That is, for the audience to whom the definition is directed, the terms used to define the word X are not more difficult to understand than is the word X itself.
6. It is not circular. That is, for the audience to whom the definition is directed, the terms used to define the word X are not so closely related to that word that the definition fails to explain anything.

When you understand a language and can speak it competently, you have the resources to check reportive definitions of basic terms in that language for yourself. You can use the above points to do so.

When assessing definitions, it is important to note that a definition can fail in several different ways at once. You may be surprised to learn that a proposed reportive definition can be both too broad and too narrow. Suppose we were given, as a reportive definition of the term *swimming pool*, the following: "A swimming pool is an enclosed, artificially constructed area of water intended for public use." This definition would be too broad because it allows wading pools with only six inches of water to count as swimming pools. (We do not ordinarily call such shallow pools swimming pools.) It would be too narrow because it requires that swimming pools be intended for public use. (Some businesses and families have swimming pools that are not open to the public; we still call them swimming pools.)

Stipulative Definitions

A **stipulative definition** is one in which someone specifies what the usage of a word is to be. In stipulating a definition, the person who puts forward the definition creates, broadens, or narrows the bounds of usage. He or she does not seek to describe ordinary usage, as in a reportive or lexical definition. Rather, the person stipulates, or lays down, a meaning for a term. This may be done when the meaning of a word that is in common use is restricted for a special purpose, such as in the context of a technical development of a subject. Also, stipulative definitions are used by those who are inventing new words and giving them meanings.

An example of a stipulative definition is "For the purposes of this scholarship award, *full-time student* shall mean any student enrolled in eight or more semester-length courses in a given calendar year." Such a definition might be stated in the context of a description of a scholarship to explain eligibility conditions. It stipulates, or sets out, how the expression *full-time student* is to be used in the competition for the scholarship. Its purpose is practical—to make applicants and administrators understand who is and who is not eligible for the award. A stipulative definition like this applies only in a limited context. Legal contracts and specific legislation may include stipulative definitions of similar kinds.

Definitions constructed in technical areas may become standard in those fields and may eventually extend to common usage. The American mathematician Edward Kasner defined an expression for the number "10 raised to the 100th power." He called it a *googol*. The word is now found in some contemporary dictionaries. The distinction between blue-collar (factory) and white-collar (office or professional) workers is often supplemented by *pink-collar workers,* a term already in popular use to refer to women workers who occupy secretarial positions with relatively little independent decision-making power. Robert E. Kelley of Carnegie-Mellon University coined the term *gold-collar worker*, defined as "an employee in a brain-intensive business who regards his or her intellect, experience, and inventiveness as monetary assets to be leveraged with respect to relationships with current or potential employers."[8] Presumably, Kelley coined this term because he thinks the creative intellectual worker in a certain business has a distinct economic and social role that makes him or her different from other white-collar workers. Perhaps the term will come into common usage.

We might think that stipulative definitions cannot be criticized. This is an area in which the "Humpty Dumpty" theory of meaning might seem to apply. In Lewis Carroll's work *Alice in Wonderland*, the Humpty Dumpty character insists that he can use words to mean whatever he wants them to mean.[9] The general problem with Humpty Dumpty's theory of meaning is that if a person defines words arbitrarily and uses them all just according to his or her own definitions, nobody else will understand those words. Thus there will be little point to using them at all. We might at first think that if someone created a meaning for a term, that person could do just what Humpty Dumpty wanted to do—make the word mean whatever he or she wanted it to mean. Could something similar to Humpty-Dumptyism apply when one stipulates a definition? Surprisingly, even here the answer is "no." The stipulation succeeds in establishing a meaning only if it sets standards of consistent use. Meaning will depend on general use and on public expectations.

Stipulative definitions are put forward for some particular purpose, and can be assessed on the basis of how well they serve that purpose. A scholarship eligibility condition requiring an eligible person to be a full-time student and defining a full-time student as a "student who is enrolled in at least fifteen semester courses in a calendar year and does no nonacademic work for pay" can be criticized as too demanding and narrow to be fair.

If a stipulated definition becomes popular, the word defined in its new sense then becomes part of public language, and it is open to changes and variations in use just as other words are. The word will appear in dictionaries and can be given reportive definitions, which can be checked for their reliability. Its original author loses his authority as the only person who can say for certain what the word means. For example, if Kelley's term *gold-collar worker* becomes part of our language, it will not be up to him to say, for instance, whether computer programmers are gold-collar workers. This decision will depend both on facts about the creativity and ambitions of computer programmers and on how the expression *gold-collar worker* comes to be used by the general public.

People sometimes seek to win arguments merely by stipulating definitions—a kind of Humpty Dumptyism in the context of an argument. However, this strategy is not a good one. This strategy of argument seeks to substitute a new definition for evidence and reasons. Suppose someone stipulates that resource means "any valuable substance in the earth owned jointly by all the world's people." This arguer can use the word *resources* in this way if he or she wants to do so. But this proposed usage, or personally stipulated definition, does not provide any reason to believe that all the world's people own all the world's resources. The game "Propaganda," which gives examples of various faulty forms of argument, calls such a move "victory by definition" because the person is using a new definition in an attempt to win his case. If he does win, the so-called victory will not be a real one.

Persuasive Definitions

A fourth type of definition is similar in some ways to a stipulative definition, but it is disguised. The fact that a meaning is being stipulated is not obvious, because claims are worded as though they described matters of fact or as though the definition was reportive. We often do not notice that a stipulation is being made, and we all too willingly transfer emotions and attitudes on the basis of the stipulation alone. In a **persuasive definition,** there is an attempt to alter beliefs and attitudes by redefining a term.

Terms such as *real, true, authentic,* and *genuine* are often elements in stating persuasive definitions. If someone tells you that modern abstract art is not real art because real art must depict objects realistically, he is relying on a persuasive definition of *art.* In a persuasive definition there is an attempt to transfer favorable or unfavorable connotations to an activity by shifting the denotation of a word in what is, in effect, a disguised stipulative definition. Implicitly, someone who tells you that modern abstract art is not real art because it is not realistic is defining *art* in a special restricted way to arrive at the conclusion he is seeking. If something is not realistic, this person will not give it the name or status "art." The term *art* tends to be one of praise and implies a certain status. To deny that modern abstract art should not count as art is to imply, among other things, that it has no proper place in museums, art history courses, or expensive art auctions. Someone who has this attitude can express it by denying that abstract art is real art, but such a statement is only a disguised stipulative definition. No reasons are given for refusing to count abstract art as art.

The concept of persuasive definition was first put forward by philosopher Charles L. Stevenson more than sixty years ago. Stevenson was interested in ethics and, in particular, in the way attitudes and beliefs about facts are involved in moral judgments. In his theory of moral language, Stevenson emphasized that some words have a strong emotional component that expresses and also helps to evoke attitudes and emotions. Their connotations are highly positive. People may wish to preserve those connotations while changing the denotation of the word. Terms such as *democracy*, *art*, *justice*, *freedom*, *socialism*, and *security* are particularly common objects of this technique. Stevenson cited an example from a novel by Aldous Huxley, in which a character has seen through an attempt to make prison acceptable by transferring to it the favorable connotations of the word *freedom*.

> But if you want to be free, you've got to be a prisoner. It's the condition of freedom—true freedom.
> "True freedom!" Anthony repeated in the parody of a clerical voice. "I always love that kind of argument. The contrary of a thing isn't the contrary; oh, dear me, no! It's the thing itself, but as it truly is. Ask any die-hard what conservatism is; he'll tell you it's true socialism. And the brewer's trade papers: they're full of articles about the beauty of true temperance. Ordinary temperance is just gross refusal to drink; but true temperance, true temperance is something much more refined. True temperance is a bottle of claret with each meal and three double whiskies after dinner. . . ."
> "What's in a name?" Anthony went on. "The answer is, practically everything, if the name's a good one. Freedom's a marvelous name. That's why you're so anxious to make use of it. You think that, if you call imprisonment true freedom, people will be attracted to the prison. And the worst of it is, you're quite right."[10]

Persuasive definitions can also be used in a negative sense. If we redefine teachers as "nothing but babysitters," or insist that computer programmers are "only hacks," we are implicitly stipulating a negative name, hoping thereby to transfer negative emotions to these roles. In negative persuasive definitions such words as *nothing but*, *mere*, *just*, and *only* are common. The important thing about persuasive definitions is to notice them and not be tricked into transferring favorable or unfavorable attitudes on the basis of someone else's idea of the real, true meaning of a word. Like stipulative definitions, persuasive definitions can have their point. But they should never be a substitute for substantive argument.

Operational Definitions

Operational definitions are a type of stipulative definition. They are most commonly used in the process of scientific study, when it is necessary to define an abstract word in terms of concrete experience. The purpose of an operational definition is to specify a set of operations, or procedures which will be used to determine whether the word applies. An operational definition of *soluble* is: A substance is soluble if, and only if, it dissolves when placed in water. The procedure to test for solubility is to place a substance in water and observe to determine whether the substance dissolves. If it does, it is soluble; if it does not, it is not soluble. Consider another example, this time from the social sciences. A possible operational definition of *rational* would be: "A human being will be defined as rational provided that he or she can achieve a score of 50 or more on a standard IQ test."[11] This definition specifies a procedure that will give measurable results and can be used in a reliable and predictable way. In the operational definition, a key word such as *soluble* or *rational* is defined in terms of the measurable results of a procedure usable by various different observers. An operational definition eliminates the need to rely on subjective impressions, which are likely to vary from one observer to another and be impossible to measure with any precision.

To consider another example, a war is a violent conflict between two parties, usually struggling over resources or political power. But that lexical definition does not tell us how many people have to be killed for a conflict to count as violent and as a war: many conflicts over resources and political power are pursued at length through largely non-violent means, although they are quite intense and may be characterized by sporadic violence. A common operational definition of *war*, intended to address this problem, counts a violent conflict as a war if one thousand or more persons are killed in the conflict in a year's time. By this standard, the conflict between Catholics and Protestants in Northern Ireland, since the late sixties, would not count as a war. The conflict in Bosnia in the mid-nineties would count as a war. Clearly, anyone who is going to generalize about wars needs an operational definition making clear what he or she is going to count as a war and what not.

In virtually any systematic study, it will be necessary to stipulate meanings for central terms in such a way as to provide for reliable criteria of application.

Proposed operational definitions can be criticized on the grounds that the procedures set forward do not adequately reflect important aspects of the meaning of the term they purport to define, so that interpretive problems will arise regarding the results of the study in question. A much-discussed example in this context is the attempt by some researchers to operationally define *intelligence* in terms of IQ tests. This sort of operational definition is a questionable reduction of a complex and evaluative concept to a short-answer style of test. The pre-operationalized, intuitive, concept of intelligence is a difficult one to pin down. It implies value judgments about activities and skills, and it allows for people to be quite intelligent in some respects (conducting their personal relationships, for instance) while they are quite unintelligent in others (doing higher mathematics, for instance). As used in colloquial English, the term *intelligent* allows for flexibility and uncertainty and does not permit precise numerical measurement. This fluidity of the term is quite inconvenient for purposes of scientific research. We can understand the need for some operationalization of a difficult concept such as intelligence. Operationalizing *intelligence* by appealing to measurement on the basis of an IQ test will be a tempting and plausible move for researchers because it allows them to replace a qualitative, rather subjective term with a quantitative one, apparently quite precise. However, issues of qualitative judgment will arise when they and others come to interpret the results of their research.

To see these problems of interpretation and application, suppose that a study based on such an operational definition issues in the conclusion that people who are more intelligent make better use of health care professionals and have a greater life expectancy than those who are less intelligent. To take this result seriously, we will want to ask whether those deemed to be more intelligent by the criteria used in the study really were more intelligent or whether they simply did better on IQ tests. In effect, we are asking whether intelligence can be reduced to results on IQ tests; the question cannot be avoided at this point. Anyone unwilling to accept the operational definition used in the study will for that very reason be unwilling to accept the main conclusion of the study, which is that *more intelligent people* have a longer life expectancy.

This example points to the central issue about operational definitions in the course of scientific research. When the research is in progress, the evaluative, indeterminate, and disputable aspects of the abstract term may not be apparent because they have been temporarily eliminated by the operational definition replacing qualitative considerations by quantitative ones and allowing for measurement. However, those aspects will emerge again when it comes time to interpret and apply the research results. At that point people who are not scientific researchers will be seeking to understand and use the results. Even fairly good operational definitions capture only some aspects of the ordinary meaning of a term. The significance and applicability of a study can be undermined by those aspects that are not captured.[12]

EXERCISE SET

Exercise 1

1. Consult a recent dictionary for reportive definitions of the following words. Are the dictionary definitions open to any criticisms such as being too broad, too narrow, circular, or obscure? If so, explain the problem and fix the definition so that it is more accurate.

    a. geology
    b. wrist
    c. illuminated (adjective)

    d. meander (verb)
    e. generous (adjective; as in "generous person")

2. Construct your own reportive definitions for the following terms and, if possible, have a friend discuss with you their accuracy and usefulness.

    a. pyramid
    b. judge (noun, as court official)
    c. poised

d. efficient
e. creative

3.   Assume that you have a visitor about your own age, from Poland, and you are trying to teach English to this person, who knows only a few words. Of the following words, which do you think you could define by ostensive definition? Which do you think would not be possible to define in this way? Give reasons for your answers.

   a. bed
   b. jam (the food)
   c. jump (verb)
   *d. wisdom
   e. cell phone
   f. chartreuse

4.   Assume that the following statements are put forward as reportive, or lexical, definitions. Test their adequacy according to the criteria previously discussed.

   *a. "Money is a medium of exchange."
   b. "Health is the absence of disease."
   c. "A hawk is a bird of prey used in falconry, with rounded wings shorter than a falcon's."
   *d. "To study is to concentrate very hard with the goal of remembering what you are concentrating on."
   e. "Peace is the absence of war."

5.   Specify appropriate stipulative definitions for the following situations:

   a. You are making a legal agreement to rent a small building. After discussion, you and the landlord have agreed that you will, on the terms of the lease, be able to use the building as a private residence and as the site of a small family business. You want to live there with three friends, not related to you, and he agrees to this. Also, you want to conduct either a modest secretarial business, taking in papers to type, or a small daycare center, admitting five to ten children. He agrees to this, but he does not want you to have a business that will bring a lot of traffic or noisy machinery to the neighborhood. Construct suitable stipulative definitions for

private residence and *small family business* that will serve your purposes and those of the landlord.

   b. Your English teacher has asked you to write an essay comparing the novels of three great twentieth-century English novelists. You wish to write an introduction to your essay, explaining why you have chosen Theodore Dreiser (American), Margaret Atwood (Canadian), and E. M. Forster (British). Give a stipulative definition of great twentieth-century English novelists that will serve your purposes without deviating too far from standard usage.

   Hint: Concentrate on the terms *great* and *English*.

   *c. You own a small orchard and have been experimenting with cross-pollination. By clever experimentation, you have produced a fruit that is a cross between an apple and a pear. Coin a word for your new fruit, and stipulate a definition for it.

6.   Which of the following are persuasive definitions? How can you tell that the definition is persuasive, and what attitudes is the speaker trying to change?

   a. "Reform means having me as your new leader."
(Comment by a candidate for the leadership of the Social Credit party in British Columbia, quoted on CBC television, July 7, 1986)

   b. "With our earth shoes and the lowered heel, you can do pure walking."
(Adapted from an ad popular in the 1970s)

   *c. Coffee is a beverage consumed widely in Europe and North America, and consumed with particular enthusiasm by writers and intellectuals.

   d. "A real woman is one who knows how to please and keep a man."
(Adapted from the politics of Real Women, an antifeminist group)

   *e. A policeman is nothing but a man with a special license from the government to assault or even kill people whose activities he disapproves of.

   f. Mathematics is the most obscure and dismal of the sciences.

   g. The only true national security is one that enables us to respond to any threat at all—physical, cultural or economic, real or perceived. Anything less is pure illusion.

*h. Photography is not art. Authentic art requires artificial reproduction of reality, and photography is a natural reproduction that does not select among those aspects of reality to be presented.

i. I shall mean by *total institution* an institution such as an asylum or prison in which there are physical barriers preventing the free departure of inmates and free entry of visitors.
(Adapted from sociologist Erving Goffman)

j. A radical is nothing but a person with an extreme, implausible, and ruthless plan for reforming society.

*k. A person of integrity is one who will honor his or her commitments.

l. "Men who have fathered children during brief sexual encounters do not have a right to be consulted if the mothers of those children decide to give them up for adoption. For the purpose of adoption law, these men are not parents. They are nothing but casual fornicators."
(Judges in an Ontario Supreme Court case, reported in the Toronto *Globe and Mail*, March 11, 1990)

Further Features of Language

When we come to evaluate arguments and construct our own arguments, clarity is important. Language, which does so much to direct our attention and express and shape our attitudes, can sometimes be unclear in ways that affect the precision and accuracy of statements or arguments. Two important types of lack of clarity are ambiguity and vagueness. Another is the use of obscure jargon that is ponderous and condescending, but conveys no clear meaning at all.

Ambiguity: Syntactic and Semantic

Sometimes we take for granted that we have understood a passage when we have read in only one of several meanings, without clear reason for doing so. In other cases, arguments and claims often gain a spurious plausibility because of hidden ambiguities.

A word or phrase may have several meanings, any of which could fit naturally in the context it is used. It is important to watch for this; if you miss it, you may not understand what is said. A simple example of ambiguity can be seen in the newspaper headline "Home Delivery Sought." As it stands, this headline might refer either to a desire for babies to be born at home rather than in hospitals or a desire for mail to be delivered to private homes rather than to group mailboxes. In such a case, the ambiguity is easily resolved when we read the accompanying story. If the story turns out to be about the postal service, we know which sort of delivery is meant.

A small booklet was published some years ago, with many examples of headlines containing amusing ambiguities and other flaws. Here are several of the many entertaining examples given: "Time for Football and Meatball Stew," "Crisis Held Over at Nuclear Plant," "Aging Expert Joins University Faculty," and "Woman Better After Being Thrown from High-Rise."[13]

There are two basic types of ambiguity: semantic and syntactic.

1.   *Semantic Ambiguity.* In the example "Home Delivery Sought" the ambiguity comes from the fact that the expression "home delivery" could refer to having one's baby born at home or it could refer to having one's mail delivered at home. When we only read the headline, we do not have enough information to guide us to which meaning is intended, so the headline is ambiguous in a misleading way. This is an example of **semantic ambiguity.**

As an example of semantic ambiguity in a profoundly important intellectual debate, consider the oft-heard claim "Evolution is only a theory." In such comments, the word *theory* has at least two different meanings:

Meaning (1): Theory: A theory is a mere speculation that is not fully supported by any firm facts.
Meaning (2): Theory: A theory is a body of scientific principles that are intended to explain observed phenomena.

When people insist that evolutionary theory is "only" a theory and go on to criticize the educational system for teaching evolutionary theory in high school biology, they are appealing to meaning (1) (theory as speculation). The problem is, though, in this sense of *theory*, it is by no means obviously true that evolutionary theory is a theory. In the second sense of theory (theory as a body of scientific principles), it is uncontroversial that evolutionary theory is a theory; indeed, all science is theory in this sense. But in this sense of *theory*, it is completely appropriate to teach theory in science classes.

The comment that evolution is only a theory may sound as though it is plausible and has the implication that evolution should not be the only view taught in biology classes. But the plausibility of the comment arises because we tend to blur together meaning (1) and meaning (2) of the word *theory*. The first meaning would allow the inference that the evolutionary view is not the only one that should be taught; the second makes it obviously true that evolutionary doctrine is theory.

2.   *Syntactic, or Structural, Ambiguity.* Other ambiguities are due to the structure of phrases or sentences—to the way words are put together. These ambiguities arise because a phrase or sentence can quite naturally be interpreted as standing for two or more distinct grammatical structures. A common cause of **syntactic ambiguity** is careless writing.

As a simple example of syntactic ambiguity, consider the following statement:

(a) As Susan was watching her two friends, she saw Mary give Doreen her book.

The syntactic ambiguity becomes apparent if we ask, "Whose book?" The pronoun *her* could refer either to Susan, or to Doreen, or to Mary, and this makes (a) unclear because it is syntactically ambiguous. Sentence (a) could mean that Mary gave Doreen Susan's book, that Mary gave Doreen Mary's book, or that Mary gave Doreen Doreen's book. Strictly, the grammatical rule is that a pronoun refers to the nearest noun; that would mean that the book is Doreen's. But people do not always write and speak according to the strict rules of grammar, so several interpretations are possible. When you are writing, it is important to avoid syntactic ambiguity.

Another example of syntactic ambiguity is found in the previously mentioned headline "Time for Football and Meatball Stew." Here, word order, meaning and reasonable charity in interpretation all indicate that the word *meatball* serves to describe the stew. The headline is amusing because the word *football*, linked to *meatball* by *and*, might be taken also to describe the stew. A football and meatball stew would be highly unusual and quite inedible! A more plausible reading of this title is that the article is going to be about having time for two things. One is football; the other is meatball stew. The ambiguity is structural, or syntactic, because the function of *and* is not clear.

3.   *Ambiguity and Argument: The Fallacy of Equivocation.* Clarification of meanings is crucial in the evaluation of arguments. In arguments, words may be used in such a way that several different meanings are involved. Sometimes the ARG conditions seem to be satisfied only because the ambiguity is not detected. In fact, there is a special fallacy, or mistake of argument, based on problems of ambiguity. This is the fallacy of equivocation. A **fallacy** is an argument that is based on a common mistake in reasoning, a mistake that people tend not to notice. Fallacies tend to be deceptive. That is, although they are not cogent arguments, they often strike people as being cogent, or good. People may be persuaded by fallacious arguments if they do not notice the mistakes. There are many kinds of fallacies, as we will see in later chapters of this book.

The **fallacy of equivocation** is committed when a key word in an argument is used in two or more senses and the premises of the argument appear to support its conclusion only because these senses are not distinguished from each other.[14] Here is an example:

> Any subject taught in the Faculty of Science must be a science. Any science involves the experimental method. Mathematics is taught in the Faculty of Science, so mathematics must involve the experimental method.

Here, the premises seem to entail the conclusion, so the RG conditions seem to be met. Yet the conclusion is false and not acceptable. Mathematics is done by reasoning and definition, without appeal to experience. Is something wrong with the premises of the argument? The premises do seem acceptable. But the word *science* must have a different meaning in the first premise and in the second premise. In the first premise, *science* is used in a purely classificatory way, referring to institutional groupings. In the second, it is used to mean "systematic study dependent on observation and experiment." The premises must link to support the conclusion, and the argument goes through only if *science* has a constant meaning. Since it does not, the argument is an instance of the fallacy of equivocation.

Another example of the fallacy of equivocation is found in the following brief argument, taken from a letter to the *New York Times*. The author is writing in response to an article that had described the activities of Micah White, a high school student who is an atheist and sought to lessen the influence of Christian groups in his high school. The writer, Michael Scheer, is arguing that White could not have been persecuted for his beliefs. He says:

> Micah White says he has "endured persecution" for his beliefs, but an atheist is, by definition, one who lacks beliefs.[15]

In effect, Scheer is arguing:

1. Micah White is an atheist.
2. All atheists lack beliefs.
So,
3. Micah White lacks beliefs.
4. Anyone who lacks beliefs cannot be persecuted for his beliefs.
Therefore,
5. Micah White cannot be persecuted for his beliefs.

The conclusions are not explicitly stated, but they are clearly implicit.

The fallacy of equivocation occurs in the move from (3) and (4) to (5). In the subargument, *beliefs* must in effect mean "religious beliefs expressing commitment to the existence of some kind of divine being." In this sense of *beliefs* it is indeed true by definition that atheists have no beliefs. So in this sense of *beliefs*, White, being an atheist, lacks beliefs. But this sense of *beliefs* is not the one required to make (4) true. The only way it can be impossible to persecute a person for his or her beliefs is for that person to have *no beliefs at all*. A person who does not have religious beliefs may nevertheless have beliefs on many subjects other than religion. Statement (4) trades on two different meanings of *beliefs*. The only way to make this argument work is to understand *beliefs* first in the narrow sense and then in a broader sense. Micah White apparently had beliefs about the separation between church and state, and those were beliefs for which he might have been persecuted. Thus the argument commits the fallacy of equivocation.

An illustration of the broader sense of *beliefs* may be found in the following letter to the Calgary *Herald*, again on the topic of atheism and belief:

> I am an atheist. I do not belong to any group or organization, but I have my beliefs just as any Christian, Jew, Muslim, Taoist, etc., does. These beliefs are mine ... when I read comments claiming that a life without faith is surely an empty and self-serving one, I become a little angry. . . . Please do not assume that atheists are selfish, Christian-hating nihilists whose sole purpose is to destroy the great society that we live in. We—or at least I—simply have a different world view. . . . As you tolerate those beliefs and as I tolerate yours, please allow me mine.[16]

In a case involving the fallacy of equivocation, we may at first think the argument is cogent because we fail to notice that a key term is used ambiguously. Presumably, the person who invented the argument did not notice the different meanings of this key term. However, the person hearing or reading the argument can avoid being taken in by the fallacy by noticing the different meanings and by understanding that the apparent cogency of the argument depends on not distinguishing these meanings. When the premises and conclusion are clearly understood, the ambiguity is apparent and the argument no longer seems cogent. We can see that the ARG conditions are not satisfied.

Seeing how important clarity is in other people's arguments allows you to understand that it will be important in your own arguments too. When constructing your own arguments, you should write carefully and make your statements as unambiguous as possible, avoiding syntactic and semantic ambiguity. If you use a term that has several distinct meanings, you should get clear in your own mind which sense of the term you intend, and do your best to make your meaning clear to your audience.

Vagueness

Vagueness is another example of lack of clarity in meaning. To say that words or statements are **vague** is to say that their meaning is unclear in the sense that it is too imprecise to give information needed in the context where the words are used. With ambiguous words or phrases, the problem is that there are several distinct meanings. With vagueness, the problem is that the word as used fails to convey any distinct meaning. Vagueness is an indeterminacy or lack of distinctness of meaning. Problems of vagueness arise when language is used so imprecisely that we cannot tell what is being asserted and we therefore cannot judge whether it is rationally acceptable.

The problem of vagueness arises when a word, as used, has a meaning that is indeterminate, or fuzzy, and as such is not sufficiently clear to convey the necessary information in that context of use. To contrast vagueness and ambiguity, you might think of words as being used to mark out boundaries. When a word or phrase is used ambiguously, there are several different bounded areas, and we won't know to which of these the word is pointing. When a word or phrase is used vaguely, the boundaries are fuzzy so that we cannot see which area is marked out.

Sometimes vagueness is used as a kind of evasive technique to avoid saying anything definite. Imagine that a factory manager is asked what he is going to do to improve productivity, which has been decreasing, and he replies by saying, "Things are being worked out so that something can be brought into effect at the appropriate moment." He has spoken but has managed to avoid the issue by not really saying anything! Words are strung together, but nothing of substance is communicated. Identifying this kind of vagueness is important because it can help you understand that you have not really been given any information and can press for more genuine information if you need it. Vagueness of this sort is a technique for avoiding issues.[17]

We speak sometimes of words being vague, but this way of speaking is slightly misleading, because vagueness arises from the way a word or phrase is used in a particular context. If the context is one requiring that we be able to determine when the word applies to a thing, and we cannot determine that, the word is used vaguely in that context. Such vagueness will pose a practical problem. However, the very same word might be used in another context in such a way that there is no problem of vagueness.

For example, if a buyer tells a real estate agent that she needs a big house for her family and fails to specify how many bedrooms, bathrooms, and so on she needs, or what kind of square footage she has in mind, she has used the word *big* vaguely. The agent needs guidance as to how many bedrooms, bathrooms, and so on she has in mind. What one means by "a big house" can vary a great deal. If the agent is going to search for houses, he needs more precise guidance than he will get from the unclarified expression "We need a big house." On the other hand, if someone comments that size 18 is big for a man's collar, it is probably not necessary to have further clarification of what is meant by big in this comment. Her point is that the size is larger than average. It is rarely of practical importance to attach a precise meaning to *big* in this context.

Sometimes we don't know whether statements are acceptable because we don't know the relevant facts. For instance, we might not know how many people in New York City are malnourished because we lack factual information about the availability and distribution of food in New York. On the other hand, even if we know many statistics about food distribution and availability, we might still be unable to determine how many people are malnourished because we don't know how severe the deprivation has to be before we should call them malnourished. In this case, our lack of knowledge would be due to unclear language-indecision as to our criteria for using the term *malnourished*, with resulting vagueness.

In arguments, it is essential for the premises and conclusions to have meanings that are sufficiently precise that we can decide whether they are acceptable. If vagueness is so serious that we cannot give a reasonably distinct meaning to a premise or conclusion, this is an important criticism of an argument. Vagueness can be dangerous in legal or administrative contexts because it permits authorities to apply rules selectively. Suppose, for example, that it is illegal to loiter and yet there is no clear specification as to what counts as loitering. In that circumstance, police can—for no substantial reason—charge teenagers or members of racial minorities who are standing to chat or simply walking along with loitering while at the same time they choose to ignore white middle-aged citizens doing similar things.

Just as arguments can get their persuasiveness from ambiguity, some can trade on vagueness. An arguer may begin with a vague term and proceed through his argument applying the term to anything and everything, getting away with it because the term is so vague that it is not easy to say he is wrong. Here is an example:

> There are two types of abuse of children. The first is described as extreme and includes such elements as murder, rape and incest, multiple bruises, broken bones, gross neglect, and starvation. In many instances such abuse is fatal. The second form of abuse is more general and more moderate in that while it neither kills nor fatally wounds, it may do considerable psychological harm. Included in this abuse are parental and professional neglect through ignoring parents, inattentive teachers, and incompetent professionals. In addition, hundreds of children are abused because they are unwanted, poor, or are victims of the

undue expectations of adults, or are subjected to authoritarianism in the name of religion, tradition and discipline, to physical punishment at home and at school, to name calling, to judgmental comparison, to the achievement syndrome, to pornography and violence, and to unnecessary labeling that proves to be detrimental.

Children suffer abuse as well, I think, when budgetary restraints limit daycare or render it of poor quality, deny needed services for the handicapped, close school libraries, and force children to be bussed hundreds of miles a week in unsafe vehicles.[18]

At the beginning of this passage, the author seems to be using *abuse* as it is normally used in *child abuse*: child abuse is deliberate assault against children, or gross neglect of them, resulting in physical harm. But eventually he speaks of moderate abuse, which sounds like a contradiction in terms. It turns out that inattentive teachers and insufficiently funded daycare systems also abuse children, according to this author. By *abuse* now, he must simply mean harm. Note that this is a much less precise meaning than he started out with and that it gives a much broader meaning to *abuse* than the word usually has in contexts where people speak of child abuse. The stretching of language is virtually absurd when the author comes to the point of calling the unnecessary labeling of children abuse. Labeling may not be a good thing, but to use the same term for it and for gross physical beating is to stretch language too much. The differences between gross physical brutality and inappropriate funding for schools are more significant than the similarity the author wants us to attend to.

This author uses the word *abuse* so vaguely that it virtually loses all meaning. He is trying to show that children should be properly cared for, schools and daycare centers should be properly funded, and so on. By saying that children are *abused* when we do not do this, he tries, in effect, to carry over the negative feelings we hold toward abuse in the narrower sense to all these activities.

Emotionally Charged Language

As has already been illustrated, language can become a substitute for rational argument and work to disguise the fact that important and contested claims have not been supported by reason or evidence. Think back to the example about child abuse in the previous section. Whatever child abuse is, we are bound to be opposed to it, because *abuse* has powerful negative associations. You can see the negative emotional charge in the word *abuse* if you imagine that a friend tells you that his dentist abuses him. Most people's dentists hurt them to a degree, at least when the needle goes in to freeze an area before drilling. We do not normally call such hurting *abuse* however. The hurting is done for a beneficial purpose, and not with the intention of bringing harm to the patient. In saying his dentist abuses him, your friend would be making a highly critical remark.

Some weak arguments trade on **emotionally charged language**, which may also be called loaded language. The substitution of emotionally charged language for argument is also quite common. If situations are described in emotionally negative language, the message is implied that something is wrong, whereas if they are described in emotionally positive language, the implication is that everything is fine. Through the use of emotionally charged language, a mood and attitude can be set without any evidence or consideration of alternate possibilities.

Consider the difference between calling a change a "diversion of funds" and calling it a "reform." The introduction of Arabic or Spanish language classes might be regarded as a diversion of funds from the mainstream curriculum by some and as a reform by others. Statements about school policy referring to "this diversion of funds" or "this recent reform" would describe the same facts with a different emotional flavor. The negative term *diversion* would suggest opposing the changes, whereas the positive term *reform* would suggest favoring them. When closings of hospitals are called *reform* of the health care system, those opposed to cuts in health services should stand up and object. To simply label such closings *reforms* is to assume and imply, without any evidence or argument, that they are beneficial to a health care system. That position is a controversial one that requires support by argument. To work out a considered position on issues such as this, we need to describe the issue in relatively neutral terms and objectively consider factors for and against the proposed changes.

It would be unrealistic to insist on universally and completely **neutral language**. Pervasive neutrality may not be possible. Even if it were possible, it would make writing and speaking dreadfully boring. What we should be on the watch for is emotionally charged language that conveys a view on a controversial point where the point is in question and no supporting evidence is put forward. The presence of loaded language in an argument does not always mean that the argument is not cogent.[19] An argument that is basically cogent may be expressed in a strong way that involves the use of some emotionally charged language. Often, however, emotionally charged language replaces argument. No support at all is given for a controversial view, and the emotionally charged language distracts us so that we do not notice that fact.

To see how this works, take a look at the following letter to the Toronto *Globe and Mail* on the topic of corporate advertising in school classrooms in Ontario:

> I read with dismay the column describing another *corporate invasion* into our children's classrooms. Their *insidious battle plan* is working flawlessly. First, we are told repeatedly by *pundits* of all persuasions that schools need more computers or there will not be enough MBAs to *march forth* and compete on the global economy's *battlefield*. Then we are *beaten* into "ad complacency" by ubiquitous media bombardment.
>
> Little wonder, then, that instead of expressing outrage at the recent tactics of YNN and other corporate attempts at *hitting them* while they're young, many parents and school officials welcome this *gross intrusion* into our children's education. When are we going to wake up and *throw the scoundrels out* and reevaluate our *slavish devotion* to technology-based education?[20]

Emotionally negative language is extremely prominent in this letter, as is indicated by all the italicized terms. It appears in the terms *corporate invasion, insidious battle plan, pundits, march forth* (there seems here to be an added element of sarcasm), *battlefield, beaten, hitting them, gross intrusion, throw the scoundrels out,* and *slavish devotion.* Clearly the writer is strongly opposed to advertising in classrooms. Clearly he regards such advertising as an improper involvement of corporations in education. Clearly he is also opposed to the extensive use of computers in contemporary education. Because it is so strongly worded, this letter may attract attention. It is rather entertaining to read, it is certainly not boring, and you might sympathize with the author's views. Note, however, that this letter does not contain evidence or reasons to support the author's views. There is no argument at all: the author provides no reasons to support his strong opinions. The highly emotional language works to convey those opinions, but we should not let this language distract us from the fact that no argument is given.[21]

Euphemism

There is a sense in which **euphemism** is the opposite of emotionally charged language. With emotionally charged language, terms are more emotional than appropriate. Euphemism, on the other hand, involves a kind of whitewashing effect in which descriptions are less emotional than would be appropriate. When a second-hand item is referred to as "pre-enjoyed," we have a euphemism.[22] Bland, abstract, polite language is used to refer to things that would be found embarrassing, demeaning, appalling, or horrible. Euphemistic language functions to desensitize us, to dull our awareness of such things.

In 1946, George Orwell wrote an essay in which he attacked the use of euphemism in political speech.[23] In that essay, "Politics and the English Language," Orwell pointed out the importance of language in framing political issues and helping to determine political attitudes. He argued that people are led to condone political horror partly because of the use of euphemism. If thousands of peasants are evicted from their villages and have to flee on foot, there will be great suffering, but if the whole horrible procedure is called "the rectifying of the frontier," we are encouraged to overlook these painful human consequences. Similarly, when the suffering and death of hundreds of civilians is referred to as "collateral damage" (as was common during the Gulf War of 1991), we will tend not even to realize that it is going on.

Many appalling examples of the sort of thing Orwell was talking about can be found in officially authorized materials in Communist countries. When the Soviet Union (now Russia) invaded Czechoslovakia in 1968, to put an end to a period of open expression, freedom, and change, people were not allowed to refer to the intervention as an invasion. The official way of describing it was as "fraternal assistance." In 1974, a writer for the prominent Soviet literary magazine *Literaturnaya Gazeta* used euphemistic language to refer to the millions of people killed by Stalin in the 1920s and 1930s. Discussing the book *Gulag Archipelago*, in which dissident author Solzhenitsyn had detailed thousands of stories of suffering and murders in

Stalinist prison camps, the commentator branded the author a traitor, acknowledging only that there had been some "violations of Soviet legality" during the period.[24] Millions of false arrests, false trials, interrogations, tortures, and years of desperate suffering were blurred over in an abstract and euphemistic phrase.

When the nuclear reactor at Three Mile Island was close to a dangerous meltdown in 1979, many commentators were still following the nuclear industry in calling the crisis an "incident." This expression is euphemistic in functioning to minimize the seriousness of the situation. In the face of criticism of American nuclear policy from the nuclear freeze movement in 1982, President Reagan called the controversial MX missile system the "Peacekeeper." This name was criticized by opponents of the system, who argued that it was euphemistic and misleading. To think of a missile as a peacekeeper is to direct our attention away from the fact that if it were ever used, millions of deaths would result. The term also encouraged people to assume uncritically that the missile could serve to prevent a nuclear attack. The label encourages us to ignore important questions such as whether such an attack is likely in the first place and whether, if it were likely, the deployment of missiles would be the best way, or even a way, to prevent it.

In the following letter, the writer accuses a newspaper of using whitewashing, or euphemistic language. The issue in question was the shooting and killing of a teenage girl on the communal farm of Wiebo Ludwig in northern Alberta. Ludwig was an outspoken and controversial critic of the oil industry who had been legally charged with acts of violent sabotage. The girl, who was with a group of young people riding through his property at 4 A.M., was shot and killed by someone on his farm. The writer says:

> I cannot believe that the media, after two trucks full of teenagers drove their vehicles and trespassed on a property at 4am after partying all night, still call it a *joy ride. This was no joy ride.* If these teenagers are so bright and scholastic, why did they choose, of all places, the Wiebo Ludwig compound to disturb the night where four girls were asleep in a tent? I cannot believe that these teenagers were entirely ignorant of the publicity and fervor the Ludwig compound has generated over the years. The unwise location choice for teenage partying was fraught with danger and potential for tragedy.[25]

This writer gives reasons for objecting to the term *joy ride*, which she finds euphemistic because it encourages us to ignore the lack of wisdom and riskiness of the choice of the Ludwig property as a place on which to trespass.

Like ambiguity, vagueness, and emotionally charged language, euphemisms sometimes pose no problem. They are harmless and not misleading when the aspects of reality blurred over are things that are not important for us to think about. For instance, if garbage men are called "sanitary engineers," or housewives referred to as "household managers," "homemakers," or "domestic managers" the euphemisms may be pretentious, but are probably harmless. The usage may slightly increase the self-respect of garbage men or housewives and they probably do not adversely affect our understanding of what these people do. Sometimes we realize that expressions are euphemistic and find the fact rather amusing. People joke, for instance, about short people being "vertically challenged" or plump people being "gravitationally challenged."

Sometimes we use euphemisms because we are slightly uncomfortable using more straightforward language. Often the usage is polite and almost certainly harmless. For example, the custom of saying "I need to use the bathroom" instead of "I need to go to the toilet" or (still more frankly) "I need to urinate" or "I need to pee" likely does no harm and is considered to be good manners. How far we want to go in the direction of frank expression and what we regard as euphemistic is a matter of taste and etiquette. It could be argued that even "I need to pee" is somewhat euphemistic, and that a more frank admission would be "I need to piss."[26]

Euphemistic language becomes a block in the way of understanding when the aspects of reality blurred over are aspects that we need to think about. Imprisonment, torture, false arrests, war, foreign policy, nuclear reactor accidents, nuclear weapons policy, property intrusions, and shootings are aspects of life that can bring great suffering. These matters are profoundly important. If euphemistic phrases such as *violations of Soviet legality, Peacekeeper missile,* and *joy ride* gloss over serious harms and risks and discourage us from thinking about them, they are dangerous—just as Orwell warned many years ago.

Clarity and Audience: The Problem of Jargon

When speaking or writing, we should consider whom we are addressing and do our best to ensure that our audience can understand the language we use. That language should be selected so as to be attractive, inoffensive, and clear. It would make little sense to put forward an elegant argument in Portuguese to an audience that did not understand Portuguese. Analogously, it makes little sense to use technical or specialized language when addressing an audience that cannot understand it. In many contexts, such considerations indicate that it is best to use ordinary, everyday language.

Of course, many disciplines—including, as you will have noticed, logic and critical thinking—incorporate specialized terminology. It may be appropriate and necessary to use that specialized terminology in some contexts. For example, in completing exercises in this textbook you may need to use such terms as *cogent argument, non-argument, ostensive definition, missing conclusion, convergent support, lexical definition,* and many others. Friends or colleagues who have not used this textbook to study argument may not understand these terms at all, or may understand them as having slightly different meanings from those explained here. If you are discussing examples or points of theory with your instructor or fellow students, it is entirely appropriate for you to use these technical terms. However, should you wish to explore such issues with others who do not share this background and these definitions, you will do best if you can avoid using such technical terms as these. If you do need to use them, you may wish to employ definitions to make yourself understood.

Most areas of study or activity are characterized by the use of some specialized language. In the lumbering industry, for instance, a *schoolmarm* is a tree split halfway up and for this reason deemed to be unsuitable for cutting. (The term originated in the nineteenth century when it was assumed that all women should get married and those who did not had only one possible occupation: that of schoolteacher or schoolmarm. The tree not cut would stand in a clearing, by itself, and was in this way deemed to be like the lonely schoolmarm.) A *snag* is a dead tree posing a threat to loggers because it might fall down. A tree called a *pole* is one suitable for use as a telephone pole. Such a tree could be worth many thousands of dollars, provided it was cut properly. These terms are easily understood by workers in the lumbering industry and they have a precise, clear meaning. Using such terms, loggers can communicate specific pragmatic messages in a clear and efficient way. In lumbering, shorthand could be particularly important because messages may have to be yelled across distances in the forest, in a noisy environment. People working under pressure in these circumstances need to communicate precisely and effectively.[27]

Such specialized language may be called a *lingo*. It developed to serve specific purposes and is useful—though potentially confusing to outsiders. Someone who did not know the lingo and was told that three schoolmarms were standing in a clearing might be quite confused. Stock trading is another area with a lingo. *Pinwheels*, *gaps*, *black candles*, and *hammers* are terms used to refer to physical characteristics of charts that depict patterns in prices. Some analysis is done by examining charts only, and these terms refer to aspects of the physical structure of charts. Without looking at a chart, traders can communicate aspects of the market by using these terms.

In some areas, technical language gives rise to acronyms. Acronyms are abbreviations, like IMF for the International Monetary Fund, or WHO for the World Health Organization. There are many acronyms in the area of computer science. FTP refers to file transfer protocol, a way of sending files. RAM designates random access memory; ASCII is shorthand for American standard character, a form of transferring text. PPP is point-to-point protocol; www is the world wide web, and html is hyper text mark-up language, used in the construction of web pages. Like other lingo, such acronyms have a precise meaning and serve for convenient shorthand communication between people who know what they mean. To others, however, they are likely to be baffling and to convey little or nothing. When writing or speaking for a particular audience, you should ask yourself how likely that audience is to understand any acronyms, technical terms, or lingo you are using. If the audience is unlikely to understand acronyms or specialized terminology, you should either avoid them or define them, to ensure that you can be understood.

The use of specialized language is often convenient or even necessary. However, it may serve to exclude, and even sometimes to intimidate, those who are unfamiliar with it. Those not knowledgeable about a special area—whether it be lumbering, stock trading, or computer hardware and software—will be unable to understand talk about it until specialized terms and oft-used acronyms have been explained. Without explanation and a kind of initiation into the lingo, communication will not be possible. When you are an insider, it is important to be sensitive to the effect your language and knowledge may have on outsiders and to avoid excluding them by using terms they do not understand.

Jargon is distinguished from technical terminology and from lingo. The word *jargon* is used to convey a negative meaning. Jargon is "confused meaningless talk or writing, gibberish" according to the first meaning cited in the *World Book Dictionary* and "language that is not understood, used in an unfriendly way" according to the second meaning cited. The dictionary advises that the term *jargon* is used to refer to language that is confused and unintelligible. Whereas the *schoolmarm*, the *pole*, and the *IMF* are quite specific entities that can be delineated, described, and even pointed to, what is referred to by terms such as *homology* or *absolute self-identity* is nothing specific or designable. When a sentence or paragraph uses such terms repeatedly, the result is likely to be intimidating, confusing, patronizing, and unclear.

It was such considerations that motivated Denis Dutton, of the University of Canterbury, New Zealand, to sponsor a Worst Writing Contest. Winners and runners-up provide spectacular illustrations of jargon at its worst. The Worst Writing Contest received considerable attention in 1999, being covered in the *Chicago Tribune*, *Lingua Franca*, the *Chronicle of Higher Education*, the Toronto *Globe and Mail*, *The Wall Street Journal*, the *Irish Times*, and a number of other news outlets. The 1998 winner was the following sentence:

> The move from a structuralist account in which capital is understood to structure social relations in relatively homologous ways to a view of hegemony in which power relations are subject to repetition, convergence, and rearticulation brought the question of temporality into the thinking of structure, and marked a shift from a form of Althusserian theory that takes structural totalities as theoretical objects to one in which the insights into the contingent possibility of structure inaugurate a renewed conception of hegemony as bound up with the contingent sites and strategies of the rearticulations of power.[28]

The contest provided other examples of utter obscurity, including references to the "ruse of desire" being "calculable for the uses of discipline" and "the disturbance of a discourse of splitting that violates the rational, enlightened claims of its enunciatory modality." Abstract and ponderous terms were strung together in sentences of intolerable length and complexity. Such prose is obscure, ill-defined, vague, and peculiarly threatening to anyone who thinks he or she might have to try to understand it. A close analysis suggests that nothing at all is expressed. Although no clear meaning can be attached to such passages, language or jargon of this kind can nevertheless be used to patronize and intellectually intimidate people. We may employ too much interpretive charity and assume that writers and speakers who use such language are using difficult and large words to express important thoughts. We may think that such authors and speakers are wise beyond our capacities; we may attribute our failure to understand to our own ignorance. To do so would be a mistake.

In fact, there is reason to suspect that intellectual intimidation through obscurity is one of the major functions of such language. In all likelihood, many who use it are arrogantly trying to show off what they take to be intellectual accomplishments. In such extreme cases of jargon, failure to understand is due not to ignorance on the part of the audience but to the fact that there is no meaning to be understood. Quite simply, nothing is said. Our message is twofold. First, never be impressed by this kind of jargon. Second, never write it yourself.

EXERCISE SET

Exercise 2: Part A

Check the following phrases, statements, and arguments to see (a) whether they contain examples of ambiguity, vagueness, or emotionally charged language. (b) If you find an example of ambiguity, explain which words give rise to this ambiguity and state the possible different meanings. (c) In the case of vagueness, explain where vagueness arises and see whether there is a more precise expression that you can substitute to make the meaning more clear. (d) If you find emotionally charged language, note which terms are emotionally charged. (e) Some passages contain no flaws in language; if this is the case, say so.

1. There are no diseases of the body, only problems of balance. If you think you have something wrong, look for an imbalance and fix it.

2. *Background:* The following is excerpted from an ad that appeared in *Harper's* magazine for October 1989.

"The wailing of quawwali, roller skaters, meta-decibel machine music. Live chickens . . . and let us not forget the goat. THIS IS ART? You betcha! This is the Next Wave Festival. The next frontier of the visual and performing arts. This is a window to Tomorrow. Dazzling. Exhilarating. Controversial. Perhaps even incendiary. (Has there ever been a significant new movement in the arts that hasn't driven traditionalists stark, staring mad?) It happens at the Brooklyn Academy of Music from October 3 through December 3."

*3. *Background:* The following is taken from an ad placed by Amoco Chemical Company in *Harper's* magazine for October 1989. The ad defends plastic products against the charge that they are a major contributor to waste and pollution.

"In addition to environmentally secure landfills and more state of the art waste to energy incinerators, we believe that a significant answer to America's waste problem lies in recycling. Everything recyclable should be recycled. Yard waste. Paper. Metal cans. Glass bottles. And plastics. Although plastics recycling is in its infancy, plastics are potentially more recyclable than alternative packaging materials."

*4. *Background:* Carl Sagan produced a popular science presentation for television, called *Cosmos. Time* magazine printed an extensive article covering the series. The following letter appeared in the wake of *Time*'s story:

"Sagan promotes Sagan and 'Cosmos' promotes Sagan. As he postures before lingering cameras and delivers overdramatic monologues from Star Wars, he skillfully blends fact with fiction, leaving viewers perplexed. By adding gimmicks and schmaltz to fascinating scientific subjects, Sagan cheapens them. This type of presentation imbues science with the razzle-dazzle of show biz and reduces it to bubble gum mentality. Fortunately a flick of the TV dial can leave Sagan out in space."
(Letter to the editor, *Time,* November 24, 1980)

*5.   Nationalism has worked to excuse discrimination, intolerance, and hostility toward others. It is sheer prejudice and nothing more. So nationalism has no proper place in the contemporary world of international politics.

*6.   Homosexual acts must be natural because they are found in the animal kingdom in a variety of species and under a variety of circumstances. People have said that because homosexual acts are unnatural, they are morally wrong. But this view is just mistaken. Homosexual acts are perfectly natural and, therefore, they are good.

*7.   *Background:* The following comments on the high debt situation of some developing countries and the suggestion that some debts should be forgiven (cancelled) is taken from a letter to the *New York Times* that appeared on June 13, 1999.

"Your June 9 editorial "Half-Measures for Poor Nations" was welcome in its call for more generous debt relief for developing countries but did not go far enough. The governments of many of these countries find their progress impeded by the weight of the debt amassed by their predecessors. Too often, those regimes never had any intention of using the loans for the benefit of their people. The money was thrown away in a pursuit of luxury by one thieving despot or another. Worse, it allowed many tyrants to buy themselves more years in power. Despite knowing that this was the case, Western lending institutions made these loans. So to argue that the West should "forgive" some of this debt misses the point. Perhaps it is we in the West who should ask the people who suffered under these despots to forgive us."

8.   *Background:* The following comments are taken from a letter to a magazine, referring to an article it had published about alternate headache and pain pills.

"Using the term 'creative advertising' in the subhead of that article implies that some talent is involved in selling a dubious remedy to an uninformed public. No talent is involved here, just greed."

9.   *Background:* We have seen part of this advertisement already. In this case, concentrate on the use of language, and see whether you think the ad is exploiting ambiguity, vagueness, or loaded language to get a point across. The ad appeared in *Harper's* magazine in October 1978:

"Mother Nature is lucky her products don't need labels. All foods, even natural ones, are made up of chemicals. But natural foods don't have to list their ingredients. So it's often assumed they're chemical-free. In fact, the ordinary orange is a miniature chemical factory. And the good old potato contains arsenic among its more than 150 ingredients. This doesn't mean natural foods are dangerous. If they were, they wouldn't be on the market. All man-made foods are tested for safety. And they often provide more nutrition, at a lower cost, than natural foods. They even use many of the same chemical ingredients. So you see, there really isn't much difference between foods made by Mother Nature and those made by man. What's artificial is the line drawn between them."

10.   "Art is energy. It is a privileged communication that passes between something and the spirit of a human."
(R. Pannell, "Arts Criticism: How Valid Is It?" Toronto *Globe and Mail,* March 3, 1979)

11.   "Physicians in general do not seem to commit suicide at a rate significantly different from that of their nonmedical peers, although, perhaps because of their knowledge of drugs and access to them, their methods of choice are characteristically nonviolent: doctors poison themselves more than twice as often as the lay public, and shoot themselves less often. Psychiatrists, however, show a markedly greater tendency to commit suicide than the population at large or their medical peers."
(Thomas Maeder, "Wounded Healers," *Atlantic,* January 1989, p. 38)

*12.   *Background:* The following appeared in a classified advertisement:

"Have several very old dresses from grandmother in beautiful condition."

13. *Peter:* (before the intermission, when attending a concert) How much longer is it?

Susan: I don't really know. Let's see, there are about three pieces left on the program. Maybe another hour.

Peter: No, Mom, you don't understand. How much longer is it to the intermission?

*14. There's no reason for professors and teachers to try to cultivate independent thinking in their students. Independent thinkers would have to start human knowledge again from scratch, and what would be the point of doing that? There's no point. Students should forget about independence and learn from their masters.

15. *Background:* The following argument was stated in a letter to the Toronto *Globe and Mail*, which appeared on May 27, 1999. At this time, NATO countries, under U.S. leadership, were bombing Serbia because of its policies toward Kosovo Albanians living in the area of Kosovo, a part of Serbia.

"The Oxford dictionary defines "war" as a quarrel between nations conducted by force. Media reports of the NATO campaign against Serbia consistently refer to the conflict as the "Balkan War," the war against ethnic cleansing, etc. This reference has bothered me since the bombing began. How can a one-sided conflict in which NATO shoots at its opponents from afar while the opponent seldom shoots back at NATO be called a "war"? Real wars usually have casualties on both sides, shots fired by both sides, etc. Certainly there have been military and civilian casualties in and around Serbia, but there have been very few NATO casualties. If we are ever to understand why we are in this mess, we need more help from the media."

16. *Background:* The following appeared in a classified advertisement: "For sale: a quilted high chair that can be made into a table, potty chair, rocking horse, refrigerator, spring coat, size 8 and fur collar."

17. "Mauling by Bear Leaves Woman Grateful for Life" (cited in *Squad Helps Dog Bite Victim, The Herald-Dispatch,* September 8, 1977).

18. "Scientists Are at a Loss Due to Brain-Eating Amoeba" (cited in *Squad Helps Dog Bite Victim, The Arizona Republic,* October 5, 1978).

Exercise 2: Part B

Of the following descriptions, which would you say contain euphemisms? Emotionally charged language? Give reasons for your answers. *Note:* Not all examples contain euphemisms or emotionally charged language.

1. There is one sense in which swimming is more vigorous exercise than cycling: when you swim you don't go downhill, and even if you coast, you don't coast for long.

2. The new tax is a device for poverty amelioration.

*3. These illiterate peewee critics have no right to pick away at the trimmings; let's get on to the meat of the matter.

4. The probation officer told her client that if he was not able to keep appointments it would be necessary to consider a reinstatement of his previous situation with reference to penal institutions. The client asked whether he would have to go back to jail. The answer was yes.

5. *Background:* The following is taken from an article "Be more careful with the Balkans," written by Yevgeny Yevtushenko and reprinted from the *New York Times* in the Toronto *Globe and Mail* for May 3, 1999. Yevgeny Yevtushenko is a poet and former member of the Russian parliament. He is criticizing a common Russian attitude to the Serbia-NATO conflict over Kosovo. (Russians tended to side with the Serbs.)

"I can hardly believe my eyes when I see some of Russia's most demagogic politicians express their knee-jerk one-sided solidarity. How can one trust their sincerity when they pound their fists on behalf of Serbia, yet show no solidarity whatsoever with Albanian refugees, nor even their own people—war veterans with their hands out huddled in underground passageways, teachers and doctors who haven't been paid for half a year, miners crashing their helmets on the pavement without a response."

*6.   "A great deal of the universe does not need any explanation. Elephants, for instance. Once molecules have learnt to compete and to create other molecules in their own image, elephants and things resembling elephants, will in due course be found roaming through the countryside."

(Peter Atkins, as quoted by Richard Dawkins, in *The Blind Watchmaker* [London: Penguin, 1988], p. 14)

*7.   The executive was let go from his position. In cutting staff in this way, the company freed his future.

8.   *Background:* In the wake of the shootings that left 15 dead in Littleton, Colorado, many writers to the Calgary *Herald* expressed opinions and offered arguments about the cultural context of the killings, raising questions as to whether similar events could occur in Canada. The following is an excerpt from a letter that appeared on April 26, 1999. .

"Is there any doubt that we must build bulwarks against the rising tide of this numbing junk culture before we are swept away by the rapacious materialism, jingoism and win-at-all-costs idolatry that has gored the hearts of our southern neighbours?"

9.   "Children who are unable to move on to the next grade do not fail. They are retained."
(Teacher)

10.   "If you ask why individuals commit crimes and other acts of dishonesty in the workplace, you will probably get different answers, depending on whom you ask. If you ask a criminologist, you will probably get an answer that concentrates on the characteristics of the individual, which are in turn thought to be shaped by a variety of societal and demographic forces. If you ask a security consultant, you will probably get an answer that concentrates on the characteristics of the immediate situation, particularly

factors that led to the perception that the risk was either high or minimal. If you ask a social psychologist, you will probably get an answer that concentrates on the broader situation, particularly on the attitudes and norms of the individual and the work group."

(Kevin Murphy, *Honesty in the Workplace* [Pacific Grove, CA: Brooks/Cole Publishing Company, 1993], p. 43)

Exercise 2: Part C

Consider the following situation: a school has 500 children enrolled in six grades. The working language of the school is English. However, 100 of the students do not have English as their first language and many of them do not know it when they first enter the school at the age of five or six years. Their native languages are mainly Chinese, Spanish, and Polish. Teachers complain that it is hard to teach reading and writing under these circumstances. Also, they experience problems when they try to communicate with the parents of these English-as-a-second-language students, because the parents speak broken English or none at all. After several years of teacher complaints, the school board decides to hire three extra teachers to teach English as a second language for students in early grades and, in special night classes, for their parents. To pay for the extra language classes, programs in art, music, and physical education are cut back, and school field trips are eliminated.

a. Write a paragraph in which you describe this situation from the point of view of someone favoring the change, using emotionally charged language and (if appropriate), euphemism to do so. Circle each emotionally charged word in your account.

b. Write a paragraph as in (a), but now describe the situation from the point of view of someone opposed to the change.

▬▬▬▬▬▬ CHAPTER SUMMARY

Language helps to direct attention and interpret reality, as well as to describe how things are. Attention to language is important in many areas, including that of argument.

Definitions are not necessary for all terms, but they are useful when there is disagreement centering on words or when the meaning of a claim is unclear. Five types of definition may be distinguished: ostensive, reportive (also called lexical), stipulative, persuasive, and operational.

Ostensive definitions seek to connect language directly to the world by pointing to examples of things. For instance, one might seek to ostensively define the word *lemon* by pointing to a lemon and saying "There, that's a lemon." Ostensive definitions can fail in their purpose if those to whom they are addressed attend to inessential or irrelevant features of the things being defined. They are most appropriate for terms whose meaning is difficult to convey in other words, where pointing to appropriate situations or pictures is possible. Reportive or lexical definitions seek to describe accurately how a word is used. They can be evaluated for its adequacy by general criteria. A good reportive definition must mention features essential to whatever is being defined. In addition, it must be neither too broad nor too narrow, must cite nontrivial features and avoid exclusively negative terms, and must avoid obscurity and circularity.

Stipulative definitions are different in function from reportive ones because they say how a person or group is proposing to use a word. Stipulative definitions are often useful and practically important. They must be appraised according to how well they serve the practical task for which they are designed. Generally, stipulative definitions of words that have ordinary uses are misleading and can cause confusion when they give the words defined meanings that are radically different from those they ordinarily have. Stipulative definitions should not provide the major basis for an argument; issues are never solved merely by proposals to use words in new ways. Persuasive definitions are stipulative definitions masquerading as either reportive definitions or factual statements. They are often characterized by the presence of such words as *true, real, authentic,* and *genuine*—or, when negative, by such terms as *merely, just, only,* or *nothing but.* Persuasive definitions can be deceptive in encouraging us to understand words in new ways, implicitly accepting controversial messages without support from any argument and, often, without our even being aware that we are doing so. Operational definitions define words in terms of procedures that may be applied to give observations and measurements permitting the reliable and objective application of the words defined. They are useful and necessary for scientific research but may be objectionable if they disguise issues of value and interpretation that will be important for the public understanding and application of that research.

Ambiguity may be semantic or syntactic. Semantic ambiguity occurs where words as used have more than one distinct, plausible interpretation and the plurality of possible interpretations is due to these words having various possible meanings.

Syntactic ambiguity occurs where the plurality of possible interpretations is due to the way in which words might be connected. Vagueness occurs when words or phrases are so imprecise as to convey practically nothing at all. In understanding, evaluating, and constructing arguments, it is important to check for ambiguity and vagueness and to assign a clear, consistent meaning to the terms used. The fallacy of equivocation is a mistake in argument that is committed when a key term, or phrase, is used in several incompatible ways and both are required to make its premises or conclusion seem plausible.

Emotionally charged language shapes and expresses positive or negative feelings toward what is being described. Such language is by no means always objectionable; without it, speech and writing would be boring and dull. It is, however, important to note the emotional "charge" in words used, especially when controversial issues are being discussed. It is all too easy to substitute emotionally charged language for evidence and reason and to prejudge issues simply on the basis of terms used. Euphemistic language can be seen as the opposite of emotionally charged language; euphemisms seek to whitewash or cover up aspects of situations and events that are regarded as demeaning, embarrassing, or unpleasant. Sometimes it is important for us to consider these aspects, and in such cases euphemisms present an obstacle to careful thought and understanding.

Review of Terms Introduced

Ambiguity   Language is used ambiguously if, in the context in which a word or phrase appears, it could have any one of several distinct meanings.

Connotation   Associations which accompany a word. Strictly speaking these associations are not part of the meaning of the word. For example, the word *fire* may suggest, or connote, the warmth of a living room fireplace.

Denotation   What a word denotes is what it means, not what it suggests or connotes. For example, the word *chair* in one of its meanings denotes articles of furniture.

Emotionally charged language   Language with strong emotional tone, whether negative or positive.

Euphemism   Bland, polite, usually abstract language used to refer to things that are embarrassing, uncomfortable, terrible, or in some way appalling. Euphemisms disguise these undesirable features.

Fallacy   Argument based on a common mistake in reasoning, a sort of mistake that people tend not to notice. Fallacies are poor arguments but often strike people as being cogent.

Fallacy of equivocation   Fallacy committed when a key word in an argument is used in two or more senses and the premises appear to support the conclusion only because the senses are not distinguished. The argument is likely to seem cogent if the ambiguity is unnoticed.

Figurative meaning   Non-literal, or metaphorical meaning. For example, if we say "she was crushed by his remarks," the word *crushed* is used in a figurative meaning.

Humpty-Dumpty theory of language   View that a speaker can make a word mean anything he or she wants it to mean.

Lexical definition   See reportive definition.

Literal meaning   Meaning that does not involve interpreting any words used in a metaphorical or figurative way; words are used straightforwardly according to lexical meanings. For example, if we say, "she bought a tin of crushed pineapple," the word *crushed* is used in its literal sense, not metaphorically. If we say, "his unkind remarks crushed her spirit," the word *crushed* is used nonliterally—that is to say, metaphorically or figuratively.

Loaded language   See emotionally charged language.

Mention (of a word)   Appearance of word surrounded by quotation marks or in special typeface or script to indicate that the word itself is the subject of the discourse. When a word is mentioned it is not used in the normal way. If we say, "the word *fire* has four letters," the word *fire* is mentioned and not used. The sentence is not about a fire. It is about the word *fire*.

Neutral language   Language with little or no emotional tone.

Operational definition   Definition by means of specification of a procedure that will permit observations and measurement to determine whether the word applies. An example is the definition of *intelligence* in terms of results on IQ tests.

Ostensive definition   A kind of definition in which the meaning of a word is indicated by pointing at a thing to which the word applies.

Persuasive definition   A definition, usually implicit, in which there is an attempt to give a new factual content to a word while preserving its previous emotional associations.

Reportive definition   A definition seeking to describe how a word is actually used. It is tested by reference to the facts of usage. A reportive definition is too broad if it would allow the word to be applied in cases where we would not apply it in ordinary usage. It is too narrow if it would not allow the word to be applied in cases where we would apply it in ordinary usage.

Semantic ambiguity   Ambiguity due to the fact that a word or expression may naturally be interpreted as having more than one distinct meaning. If the ambiguity is found in an expression, it is not due to the structure of the expression but due to the meanings of the words used in it.

Stipulative definition   A definition specifying a new or special use for a word.

Syntactic ambiguity Ambiguity due to the grammar or syntax of a phrase, which can naturally be interpreted as expressing more than one distinct meaning.

Use (of a word)   A word is used, in a phrase or sentence, when it appears without quotation marks or special typeface or script. For example, in the sentence, "The forest fires caused a lot of smoke" all words are used. No word is mentioned.

Vagueness   A word is used vaguely if, in the context in which it appears, we cannot determine what things the word would apply to.

Notes

1. Wittgenstein's early ideas are stated in his *Tractatus Logico-Philosophicus* and his later ideas in his *Blue and Brown Books* and *Philosophical Investigations*. There are many descriptions of these theories and of the shift between them. I offer one in Chapter 10 of *Socrates' Children: Thinking and Knowing in the Western Tradition* (Peterborough and Calgary: Broadview Press, 1997).

2. R. W., Chinese journalist studying in Calgary in the early nineties. R. W. is not named for political reasons. Obviously, he translated the Chinese terms into English equivalents.

3. Reported in the *Daily Telegraph* and then again in the Toronto *Globe and Mail,* May 18, 1995.

4. William Zinsser, *On Writing Well: An Informal Guide to Writing Nonfiction,* 2nd ed. (New York: Harper and Row, 1980), p. 9.

5. Both Grice's principles of cooperation in conversation and the principle of charity are relevant here. Compare the discussion of charity at the end of Chapter 2.

6. This suggests the issue of suitability of language to one's audience, which is discussed below under "Jargon and Lingo."

7. To avoid complications intolerable in a short introductory discussion, I have not discussed Wittgenstein's family resemblance theory here. This omission is not due to my lack of interest in that theory.

8. Quoted in the *Atlantic,* July 1986.

9. Lewis Carroll was also a logician.

10. Aldous Huxley, *Eyeless in Gaza,* as quoted by C. L. Stevenson in "Persuasive Definitions" in *Mind,* 1938.

11. This case is given only as an illustration and is not meant to imply approval either of defining human beings as rational animals or of the use of IQ tests to determine rationality—or even, for that matter, intelligence.

12. This topic is discussed further in Chapter 9.

13. *Squad Helps Dog Bite Victim and Other Flubs from the Nation's Press.* Edited by the *Columbia Journalism Review* (New York: Dolphin Books, 1980.)

14. I have benefited from discussing this topic with Cary MacWilliams, several of whose suggestions have been incorporated here.

15. *New York Times,* June 27, 1999.

16. Stephen Gardner, Calgary *Herald,* July 1, 1999.

17. The technique is especially tempting to politicians and administrators confronted by probing questions.

18. Laurier LaPierre, *To Herald a Child* (Toronto: Ontario Public School Men Teachers Association, 1981), p. 47.

19. This section may be usefully compared with the discussion of emotion as possibly distracting in arguments in Chapter 6.

20. George Hathaway, letter to the Toronto *Globe and Mail,* June 30, 1999. My emphasis.

21. What appears in print as a strong claim made without argument may be the result of editing by newspapers or magazines, shortening material submitted to them. When this happens, the absence of argument or presence of weak argument may be the fault of editors rather than the author. As readers, we can only speculate about such matters. But whoever is responsible— whether it be the original writer or the editor— the effect in such a case is that there are strong opinions, strongly expressed, with no supporting argument. From the reader's point of view, the crucial point is to avoid being won over to the strongly expressed conviction for no good reason—that is, to avoid being led along by the strongly emotional language when there are no arguments given.

22. Sign advertising CDs, displayed in Calgary in August, 1999.

23. Orwell is well known for his discussion of political language in the book *1984*. That book envisages a totalitarian order in which a language called Newspeak has been especially designed in order to make unorthodox thoughts impossible to express.

24. *Literaturnaya Gazeta,* February 8, 1974, as translated and reproduced in the *Current Digest of the Soviet Press* for February 1974. Translation and publication by the American Association of Slavic Studies.

25. Zoe C. T. Preston, letter to the Calgary *Herald,* June 30, 1999. My emphasis.

26. Urged by one of the publisher's reviewers for the fourth edition of this text.

27. I owe these examples, and those from stock trading, to Rob Newman. I have benefitted from discussing this topic with him and with Caroline Colijn and Anton Colijn.

28. Judith Butler, "Further Reflections on the Conversations of Our Time," *Diacritics 27* (1997), pp. 13–15; quoted in Denis Dutton, "Bookmarks," in *Philosophy and Literature,* April 1999, p. 252. Thanks to David Gallop for referring me to this volume.

chapter five

Premises: What to Accept and Why

AN ARGUMENT STARTS FROM PREMISES and uses them to support one or more conclusions. If these premises are not rationally acceptable, then even the most elegant reasoning will not render the conclusion acceptable. When appraising an argument, we have to ask ourselves whether there is a reasonable basis for accepting the premises on which the argument is based.

The Dilemma of Premises

When we say that the premises of an argument are rationally acceptable, we mean that it would be reasonable for the person to whom the argument is addressed to accept them. If you are appraising the argument, then, for the moment at least, that person is you. Of course, the argument might have been intended originally for an audience that was quite different from you in various ways, and premises that would have been acceptable for that audience may not be acceptable to you, since that audience might have had different background knowledge and a different perspective. For our present purposes, however, we will ignore this complication and attend to the acceptability of premises from the perspective of you, the reader, as the audience for the argument. This is the most practical point of view in any case.

If you can accept, that is, believe the premises of an argument without violating any standard of evidence or plausibility, then you find its premises rationally acceptable. But what are reasonable guidelines for evidence and acceptability? And how can you use them to evaluate premises of arguments that might be about any topics at all?

Arriving at general standards that will give complete and detailed guidelines for determining the rational acceptability of premises is not possible because premises, like the arguments they are parts of, can be about anything at all from deserts in Africa to higher mathematics to the warming of the planet—or any topic you can think of. In fact, you may have already noticed this feature when considering the many illustrations and exercises used so far in this book.

It is not possible to say in an absolutely general way and in complete detail what makes premises on all these topics rationally acceptable. Some of the knowledge we need to appraise them will be highly specific. For these reasons, it has until recently been traditional for textbooks on logic and argument to omit the topic of rational appraisal of premises, advising readers that this task falls outside the area of logic. Appraising premises seems to be a topic that could lead the author and readers into digressions on every subject from mountains to mermaids. Let us think for a moment about premises. Premises are statements claimed to be true or rationally acceptable. Premises are like other statements; the only difference is that they are used to support a conclusion. Basically, assessing premises is no different from assessing statements that appear in descriptions, reports, or explanations.[1] We have to think about the sort of evidence that we have in favor of them and, in the light of this evidence, how likely they are to be true. But how do we do this in general? It is a tall order to state and explain standards that will apply to premises on a wide variety of topics.

Despite the challenge of this task, we discuss premise acceptability in this book because we believe that the matter is too fundamental to ignore. As we shall see, a number of general points can be made about what makes premises acceptable and unacceptable. Pulling these points together, we can arrive at a useful approach to determining whether the (A) condition of argument cogency is met. If we neglected to consider premise acceptability and unacceptability, we would have to ignore the (A) condition entirely, leaving us with only (R) and (G), and an incomplete study of argument.

Any argument has to start somewhere. In the context of a given argument, the premises may need defending. When this is the case, a subargument can be constructed. The subargument also will have premises. If its premises need defending, they too can be defended, in a subsubargument. We could ask for a defense of the premises of the subsubargument too, and so on. The situation has the potential for what philosophers call an infinite regress. If we question every claim, and demand an argument for everything we question, justification by argument will be impossible. At some point the process has to stop: not every statement can be defended by appealing to further statements. Some statements must be acceptable without further support.

Claims about an enormous variety of topics are put before most of us every day. We read various books, papers, and magazines; we converse with other people who tell us about all kinds of situations and problems and give us their interpretations and opinions about what is going on. Some of these claims just have to be accepted. We learn language and basic facts from parents and teachers, and we build up a picture of parts of the world beyond our own experience from conversation, books, the press, television, and radio. Without relying on these other people and sources of information, we could have no intellectual competence at all. Yet obviously we cannot simply accept everything we hear and read from every source. Some of the claims we encounter are false, implausible, or inconsistent; some sources are notoriously unreliable. Wholesale acceptance of claims is no closer to being a viable intellectual strategy than wholesale rejection of them.

The problem of when and why we should accept what other people tell us is a general one that arises not only in the context of argument but in all of practical and scholarly life and thought. Since this is a book about argument, we address the problem in one special context: that of the acceptability and unacceptability of premises in arguments.

When Premises Are Acceptable

Our first approach will be to discuss some general conditions in virtue of which claims are acceptable as premises. All comments here apply to stated premises and to missing premises that have been added to an argument for the sorts of reasons discussed in Chapter 2.

Premises Supported by a Cogent Subargument

Clearly, a premise in an argument is acceptable if the arguer has already shown it to be acceptable by a cogent subargument. That means the arguer has supplied evidence or reasons that make it rational to accept that conclusion. Although, as we have seen, we cannot always demand that this condition be met, when it is met, the premise is acceptable. In fact, the argument from Russell, quoted at the end of Chapter 3, illustrates this point. Russell used two premises: that children left alone can easily come to physical harm, and that children left to themselves can be annoying to adults, to support the intermediate conclusion that children simply cannot be left to do as they please all day long.

Premises Supported Elsewhere

An arguer may indicate that a premise is supported in a cogent argument elsewhere, even though he or she does not supply a subargument for it in the argument being discussed. Perhaps the arguer has given good evidence for the claim on another occasion and indicates that. Alternately, the arguer may refer to someone else who has shown the premise to be reasonable.

A common way of doing this, in academic writing, is by footnotes. Claims about specific details such as statistics or particular historical or technical points are often backed up with a reference to a source in which these claims are spelled out and defended. The arguer is, in effect, relying on the authoritativeness of his or her source to back up such claims. If the authority is a proper one, the claim is acceptable. (Conditions of proper authority are described below.)

Premises Known *a Priori* to Be True

So far we have considered claims for which evidence is given, either in a subargument or in an independent argument. But as we have already seen, it is not possible for every claim to be supported by argument. Some claims must simply be acceptable in their own right if arguments are to get off the ground. Among these are claims that can be known *a priori* to be true.

The term *a priori* is a technical one. The words are Latin and mean "from the first." Claims that are **a priori** are knowable "from the first" in the sense that they are knowable before experience, or independent of experience. (The contrasting term **a posteriori** means "from something that is posterior, or afterward" and refers to claims that are knowable only after, or on the basis of, experience.) Claims that are *a priori* are knowable to be true or false on the basis of reasoning and the analysis of the meaning of the words used to make the claim. If we can know *a priori* that a claim is true, then that claim is rationally acceptable. For instance, we can know *a priori* that a person cannot steal his or her own property. We do not need experience to prove this claim: in fact, there is no experience we could have of a person stealing his or her own property. It can be proven by logic that it is impossible for anyone to steal his or her own property just because of what stealing is. To steal is to take something that does not belong to you; a person's own property does belong to him or her; hence that person, the owner, cannot steal it.

To see the contrast between *a priori* and *a posteriori* claims more clearly, consider the contrast between these two statements:

(a) No one can steal his or her own property.
(b) No one can steal Nelson Mandela's property.

As we have seen, claim (a) can be proven true by logic alone. It is *a priori*. We can know, on the basis of reasoning from the concepts of stealing and property, that (a) is true and is acceptable. The case of (b), however, is quite different. To know whether (b) is acceptable, we would have to know what sort of property Nelson Mandela (President of South Africa between 1994 and 1999) has and what safeguards are in place to prevent its theft. Statement (b) is *a posteriori*; it requires evidence from experience—our own or somebody else's. If statement (b) is true, it would be because Mandela's property is especially safe or well-guarded.

If a premise in an argument seems to be a matter of definition or of the relations of concepts, or if it deals with a general issue of mathematics or logic, we can determine whether it is true by reasoning, *a priori*. If it is true *a priori*, then it is acceptable. The following claims, for instance, are *a priori* and would, as such, be immediately acceptable as premises in any argument in which they were to occur:

(a) Technology and art have different purposes.
(b) Contraception is undertaken with the intent of preventing pregnancy.
(c) Thirteen is a prime number.

On the other hand, consider the following statement:

(d) Playing the music of Bach and Beethoven in a park will drive out drug dealers.

Unlike claims (a), (b), and (c), claim (d) is not *a priori*. This claim, taken from a news story about efforts to discourage drug dealers from centering their activities in an Edmonton park, is *a posteriori*, or **empirical.** Whether it is acceptable would have to be determined on the basis of evidence from experience.

Common Knowledge

A premise in an argument is acceptable if it is a matter of **common knowledge.** That is, if the premise states something that is known by virtually everyone, it should be allowed as an acceptable premise. Or, if a premise is widely believed, and there is no widely known evidence against it, it is often appropriate to allow it as acceptable. Society operates on the basis of many statements that people know or believe as a common ground for communication and cooperation. From *a priori* claims and claims provable elsewhere, we would have only a slender basis for communicating and justifying our beliefs. Clearly, the basis of argumentation has to be extended. One main way to do that is to rely on common knowledge.

A simple example of a statement that is common knowledge is:

(a) Human beings have hearts.

Claim (a) is well known and obvious, but it is not *a priori*. It is not from logic and concepts alone that we know human beings have hearts. Experience is required. We can feel our own pulse and, in a sense, know from personal experience that we ourselves have a heart. However, most of us learn from other sources—from parents and teachers, from books on health and biology, and from the mass media, which is full of advice about means to improve the health of our hearts—that human beings in general have hearts. This is an elementary fact about the human physical structure, one known by virtually all adults in our culture.

Here are some other examples of claims that would count as common knowledge:

(b) Stress and fatigue make a person more susceptible to illness.
(c) A car with unreliable brakes is unsafe to drive.
(d) Travel by airplane is faster than travel by train.
(e) Racial discrimination has adversely affected people of color more than it has adversely affected white people.

(f) Argentina is a South American country.

(g) Mountain climbing is a sport requiring good health and strong muscles.

Such claims can be deemed rationally acceptable because they constitute common knowledge. They are not *a priori*, but they are sufficiently and widely known that they have become common knowledge and, as such, are rationally acceptable as starting points in an argument.

What counts as common knowledge is to some extent dependent on audience and context. What is true does not vary depending on what time people live in and what they believe, but what is *known* does. In fact, this point may occur to the critical reader, even with respect to the preceding examples. In certain isolated non-scientific cultures, even the claim that human beings have hearts might not be common knowledge and might need considerable support by argument.

For those who follow international politics, it is common knowledge that the country of Yugoslavia split into several distinct countries during the decade of the nineties and that there was considerable violence involved in this process, as Slovenia, Croatia, and Bosnia separated from Serbia and Montenegro. Clearly, what is common knowledge at one time and place may not be common knowledge at another time and place. Thirty years from now it will still be true that Slovenia, Croatia, and Bosnia separated from the rest of Yugoslavia during this decade, but those matters may have ceased to be common knowledge. At that time, many people may not know in which decade those events occurred. People with little interest in history or European politics may not know that these events occurred at all.

A claim that amounts to common knowledge may come to be disputed, and if it is, it may be appropriate to defend that claim with an argument. Realistically, we have to allow that common knowledge varies with time, place, interests, educational level, and culture. This means that the (A) condition, and argument cogency generally, are considered with some reference to the context in which arguments appear.

Nevertheless we cannot realistically dispense with common knowledge as a condition of premise acceptability. Typically, people who argue back and forth share a culture and a broad background of beliefs and commitments. Arguments go on within this shared context and cannot proceed without it. As we have seen, arguments have to start from premises, and not every premise can be defended in a further argument. Reflecting on the *a priori* true statements illustrated above, you may gain some appreciation of the fact that *a priori* statements alone could not provide an adequate argument in the sciences and in everyday life. *A priori* statements only relate concepts to each other; they do not state facts about the world. Many arguments proceed from premises taken as common knowledge and move on to new conclusions. Even though the common knowledge premises are not as obvious and certain as the *a priori* truths, they should be accepted in virtue of the required social context for arguments.

Here is an example that starts from points of common knowledge and reaches a rather surprising conclusion:

1. There are vast numbers of trees in Brazil.
2. If anyone tried to count all the trees in Brazil, it would be a very long time after he started until he reached the last tree.
3. Before a tree counter finished his counting task, some trees already counted would have died because of fire or human destruction and new trees would be sprouting.
4. Having a number of people count these trees would not avoid these problems of destruction and growth.

So,

5. It is practically impossible to determine, by counting, exactly how many trees there are in Brazil.

Therefore,

6. The question "How many trees are there in Brazil?" is a question that has no practically determinable answer. (See Figure 5.1)

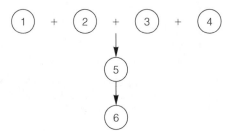

FIGURE 5.1

In this argument, premises (1), (2), and (3) are matters of common knowledge. To deem the argument inadequate by questioning one of these premises would be quite unreasonable. The fourth premise, however, is a different matter. It is not, as such, a matter of common knowledge and does need further defense. But to insist on proof or further evidence for the statement "There are vast numbers of trees in Brazil" is going too far. Someone who takes this kind of stance on the acceptability of premises will soon find that he has no one to argue with and nothing to say.

Testimony

Under some conditions, a claim is acceptable on the basis of a person's **testimony.** That is, a person testifies or tells about something he or she has experienced. Under certain conditions, we accept the claim about that experience as described. From the time we learn language from our parents, accepting what other people tell us is a basic aspect of human life. Our personal experience is limited with respect to both place and time. Other people, in conversation, in writing, and through media such as television, film, and video, communicate a broader experience to us. They tell us of sights, sounds, places, and personal encounters to which we have no independent access. Life would be short and knowledge limited if human beings could not extend their knowledge by relying on the experiences of others.

In many circumstances, if other people tell us they have experienced something, we take their word for it. We trust their word unless we have some specific reason not to do so. We rely on the experience and testimony of other people to broaden our picture of the world. Given the extent of this reliance, it makes sense to begin by assuming that in normal circumstances the word of others is reliable.

Three main factors undermine our sense that a person's testimony is reliable. These are (1) the implausibility of the claim asserted; (2) the poor reputation of the person making the claim or source in which the claim appears; and (3) the claim's having content that goes beyond the personal experience of the person who tells us it is true.

1. *Implausibility of Claims.* If a person claims, as a matter of personal experience, to have witnessed something that is, according to common knowledge or to our own personal related beliefs, extremely implausible, we should doubt his or her testimony merely because of the implausibility of the claim. Even if we know the person asserting the claim and that person is usually honest, accurate, and reliable, if the claim is bizarre or crazy enough, the nature of the claim will make us question the testimony.

For example, if someone tells you that a brand new four-door Chevrolet, in tip-top shape, with no legal holds, is on sale for a thousand dollars, you are not likely to accept this claim. The claim is too implausible, given other things you know about the price of cars. It is too unlikely that anyone would sell such a car for such a low price. You will assume that the person who tells you such a thing is joking, or is mistaken, or is trying to deceive you. If there is a new Chevrolet for sale for a thousand dollars, there is no doubt something wrong with it; either it is a stolen car, or it is in bad repair. What happens in a case like this is that the claim asserted is too implausible to be taken at face value. You have too much independent evidence against it for a single person's testimony to make it believable.

A story involving the rejection of claims because of their implausibility involves a street on which there were three tailor shops, each bearing advertising signs. The sign on the first shop said, "Best tailor shop in the world;" the sign on the second said, "Best tailor shop in the country;" and on the third, the sign said, "Best tailor shop on the street." What was claimed on the first two signs was so utterly implausible that it was not taken seriously by anyone. These claims were too bold, and the two shops that made them were not credible in their advertising. What the third shop claimed, however, was not so implausible—especially given the fact that the other two shops were discredited by their overly bold claims. This claim seemed reasonable: the third shop could well be the best tailor shop on the street.[2]

2. *Unreliability of Person or Source.* People can be unreliable in various ways. The most blatant is lying or deliberate deception. If a person has been known to lie or deliberately deceive others, then it is imprudent to take his or her word for something. Lying and deception, especially about matters of importance, undermine a person's credibility. When people lack credibility, their testimony cannot, in general, be taken to make claims rationally acceptable. Their word has lost its force.

Another possibility is that people may be flawed observers of certain sorts of phenomena; we may know that they are handicapped or biased in relevant ways that make their observations nonstandard and their testimony questionable. For instance, if a person who has poor hearing attends a concert and later argues that the choir was not good because its enunciation of words was unclear, we should not accept his testimony on the point. With poor hearing, he is not a reliable listener at a concert.

Similar points can be made about a person who has such a vested interest in establishing one particular point of view that we lose confidence in the accuracy of his observations. When this happens, we will not wish to accept claims merely on his testimony, even when those claims concern only his experience. We will suspect that he is selecting and interpreting evidence in a one-sided way. An example might be that of an NFL sports fan observing his home team, the Miami Dolphins, play against a rival. He could be so attached to the Dolphins that his observations about the competence and skill of the players on that team, as compared to the other, would not be reliable. Consciously or unconsciously, he selects the better performances of those on the home team and compares them with the more flawed performances of players on the rival team. This kind of bias has been called My Side Bias, and it is very common.

As the name suggests, we should be alert for My Side Bias in ourselves, our own group, as well as in other people. My Side Bias is common in the construction of nationalist histories, which emphasize the occasions on which a group has been heroic or has been victimized by others while downplaying or ignoring those occasions on which it has been less admirable, including those when it has perpetrated crimes against others. This sort of selective attention can lead to biased observations that cannot be the basis for reliable testimony. Our own side is always seen as better than the other, but its merit emerges unreliably because of our selective attention and biased interpretation of what we observe.

Such is our dependence on other people as sources of knowledge and belief that most of us tend, in general, to give a fair amount of credence to the printed word and to media. However, the same qualifications applied to individuals should be applied here too. If a source has printed falsehoods repeatedly in the past, or is strongly biased, these features make it unreliable and inadequate as a source of testimony about other people's experience. A reputable newspaper account of an event such as a traffic accident, change of government, or earthquake is typically accepted as true. Consider, for instance, the following claims, taken from a story in the Calgary *Herald:*

> Negotiations will begin this week to find a way to soften the impact on the Canadian fur industry of a European ban on products obtained through the use of leg-hold traps. The powerful European animal rights lobby says the traps—allowed in Canada—inflict cruel suffering on their victims. Canada argues the ban will "devastate" the livelihood of 100,000 people—nearly half of them natives—whose incomes depend on the fur trade. In meetings at the G-7 summit here, Prime Minister Jean Chretien told leaders of Britain, France and the

European Union that Canada wants the issue settled before the ban takes effect in 15 European countries this fall.[3]

The authors work for *Southam News,* a reputable and fairly reliable news collection agency, and the Calgary *Herald* is a family daily paper, not a tabloid. The story is from Halifax, where the G-7 economic summit had been meeting and where Southam had reporters. There is no particular reason to suspect or disbelieve this story. We might question the Canadian argument, or the European argument (these are not made in the story, only reported). But based on the story, we can simply grant that this dispute is going on, that people are stating these arguments, and that negotiations are going to occur.

We are dependent on the media for knowledge of the occurrence of such events as this one, and other things being equal, we tend to believe what we read in such reports.

In contrast, accounts from notoriously unreliable sources are not accepted in this way, especially when the claims made are themselves extremely implausible. Consider, for instance, the following claims:

> Donald Zenert was viciously gored by a 300-pound buck deer but he survived with only his wits and a penknife by grabbing the animal's antlers and holding on for a wild 90-minute ride. The 33-year-old construction worker was attacked this past February 4 while videotaping deer in Alberta, Canada.[4]

These claims introduced a story in the *National Enquirer,* a tabloid-style paper full of exotic and bizarre stories and widely regarded as unreliable. Though the story was written in the first person and purported to describe Zenert's personal experiences, such testimony, reprinted in such a source, does not render these implausible claims acceptable.

3. *Failure to Restrict Content of Claim to Personal Experience.* A person can testify about what he or she experienced. However, claims that go beyond personal experience to interpretation and judgment cannot be rendered acceptable purely on the basis of testimony. Broadly speaking, a person's experience includes observations, feelings, and memories. It does not include judgments of the value of policies or the causes or meanings of events. If a friend tells you that she often felt angry while attending a particular class, that is a matter of her reaction, something she knows better than anyone else, and something you should generally believe. If she is a reliable, honest person, this claim, which is about her personal experience and based on her personal experience is acceptable simply because she sincerely asserts it. Similarly, if she tells you that a particular professor has a soft voice, that he is strict on deadlines, that he was late on Tuesday, or that he has been discussing classical economic theory for three weeks, you would, and quite reasonably should, accept such statements on the basis of testimony from a reliable person. Such statements describe things that she would be in a position to experience for herself if she has been attending the class.

However, things are different if your friend tells you that this professor is the most dynamic lecturer on campus, or that his analysis of Japanese business practice is extremely sophisticated. At this point, her comments go beyond the nature of her own experience. Whether this professor is the most dynamic obviously involves matters of comparative judgment—furthermore, it is most unlikely that she listened to every professor on the campus. Whether his analysis of Japanese business practice is highly sophisticated will involve knowledge of Japanese business and of other accounts of it, and standards of what it is to have a sophisticated account. These interpretive and evaluative claims cannot be rendered acceptable merely by testimony, because they depend on a broader basis of evidence and the discretion, common sense, and background knowledge of the person making the judgment.

Several examples from a recent book on Africa serve to illustrate this contrast between experiential claims and broader commentary. The author, David Lamb, is an American journalist who spent four years in Africa as bureau chief for the *Los Angeles Times*, traveled widely, and did some independent research. In the following passage, he restricts himself to reporting what was told to him. Lamb describes an interview with Daniel Mwangi, a blind man whom he met in Kenya. He says:

> His problem started when he was six or seven years old—itchy eyelids, blurred vision, headaches. His father thought the boy had been cursed and took him to his friend, a witch doctor. But the practitioner's herbs and chants did not help, and by the time Daniel was thirteen he was totally blind.[5]

In this passage, readers of Lamb's book are offered Lamb's testimony about an interview with Mwangi. Testimony is involved twice: Lamb is telling his readers what Mwangi told him, and Mwangi is telling Lamb how he became blind. In the absence of any special reason to regard either Lamb or Mwangi as unreliable, we would simply accept the story as told. The principles of testimony we have discussed here would recommend accepting the story on the double testimony of the author and the man interviewed.

This passage can be contrasted with others that go beyond testimony to offer commentary and predictions with regard to social and political problems in Africa. Consider, for instance, the following passage from the same book:

> However valuable the church has been in assisting Africa's five million refugees, in helping during times of drought, famine and sickness, it traditionally has acted as a tool of the white establishment. The church did not play an active role in supporting the African's struggle for independence, largely because white clergy in Africa were racist in attitude and approach.[6]

These statements may be correct, and it is absolutely appropriate for Lamb, as a journalist and author, to offer an analysis of these matters. But at this point, the claims made go beyond what we should accept purely on the basis of his testimony. This is because their content goes beyond what the author could experience himself. They state a generalization about the connection between the church and the white establishment and posit an explanation (racism in the church) to explain that connection.

To sum up, claims are acceptable on the word, or testimony, of the person asserting them, unless one or more of the following conditions obtains:

(1) The claims made are implausible.
(2) The person making the claim or the source in which the claim is cited is unreliable.
(3) The claim goes beyond what a single person could know from his or her own experience.

Proper Authority

Sometimes arguments are put forward by people who possess specialized knowledge about a subject. For instance, an African historian might have made the claim about the white church and racism in Africa on the basis of a specialized study of this aspect of African history. Such a person would be an expert, or **authority,** in this area. If he made the claim as an authority, we might, under specific conditions, accept it on his authority.

When people are experts in some area of knowledge, they are said to "speak with authority." An expert has a special role in the construction and communication of knowledge because he or she has more evidence, a more sophisticated understanding of related concepts and theories, greater relevant background knowledge, and—as a result—more reliable judgment in the particular area of expertise than a nonexpert. Under certain conditions, statements or claims are acceptable because reliable authorities or experts assert them.

Accepting a premise on authority is similar to accepting a premise on testimony in one respect: it involves accepting claims because other people have sincerely asserted them. There is, however, an important difference between authority and testimony. Authority requires specialized knowledge in a field where there are recognized standards of expertise. Recognized standards include degrees or professional certificates authorized by licensed and qualified institutions.[7] To be an authority or expert, however, it is not enough just to have one of these degrees, such as a Ph.D. or an M.D. One must also have accomplishments in the area of study— published research or other professional attainment—and one's accomplishments must be recognized as such by other qualified people in that field of study or work. Testimony does not require specialized knowledge: we can all testify about our own experience. Whatever undermines the credibility of testimony (dishonesty, incapacity to make accurate observations, bias, vested interest, and so on) would also undermine authority, because in both cases we are relying on a person to be honest and competent. But because authority, unlike testimony, requires expert knowledge, there are further conditions for the proper use of authority to justify claims.

If we are to accept a claim just because an expert asserts it, that claim must lie within a specific field of knowledge. The person who asserts the claim must be recognized as an expert within that field of knowledge. African history, microphysics, race relations, plant genetics, and child development are specific areas of knowledge. So too are biology, mathematics, theoretical physics, organic chemistry, and engineering—and many other such disciplines. In each of these areas, knowledge has been built up by various researchers and has withstood tests to prove its accuracy. There are established methods to find solutions to problems, and a fair amount of consensus exists among scholars and researchers as to what is correct and incorrect, and what the standards are. Experts have read widely about a phenomenon, made many observations over a period of time, and analyzed an issue closely. For these reasons, they are more likely to have knowledge than the average person.

Some endeavors, although worthwhile and fascinating, cannot be termed areas of knowledge, because there are no methods and principles from which to establish accurate beliefs. There is no agreed-on starting point and no common methods that different people can use to come to the same conclusions. Consider, for instance, such questions as the nature of life on other planets, or the meaning of life, or the existence of free will. These are fascinating topics, and it is worthwhile to think about them. Although there are cogent and noncogent arguments on such matters, there are no established routes to an answer and no systematic body of authoritative beliefs about such subjects. This does not mean that there are no standards of evidence in these areas; there are certainly better and worse arguments. But it does mean you cannot appeal to authority on such matters, for the pure and simple reason that there are no authorities here. You have to think for yourself and work out the answers and responses that seem best to you.

Another important point is that even when there is a systematic body of knowledge, and qualified experts are studying an area using common methods and having some consensus, experts in the area may have different beliefs about particular issues. Consider, for instance, the area of child development. Some experts believe that children do not acquire abstract logical concepts until their early teens, whereas others think that they acquire them as early as six or eight years of age. In the face of such disagreement, you could not hope to show that one of these views is acceptable simply by citing an expert. The experts disagree, so anyone who disputed your claim could just find another expert and argue against you by citing that other expert. Defending a claim on the basis of authority is appropriate only if experts in the area agree.

In addition, the expert cited must be reliable and credible. The expert or authority must not have had his or her credibility undermined by having made dishonest or unreliable claims in the past or by vested interests, such as would result from being paid for favorable testimony by one party to a dispute, by having lied in the past about related matters, and so on.

An especially careful appeal to authority can render a claim acceptable. Such an appeal may be set out as follows:

1. Expert X has asserted claim P.
2. P falls within area of specialization K.
3. K is a genuine area of knowledge.
4. The experts in K agree about P.
5. X is an expert, or authority, in K.
6. X is a reliable and credible person in this context.
Therefore,
7. P is acceptable.

Note here that X is a specific person. A legitimate appeal to authority cannot be an appeal to an anonymous authority.

If we reason to ourselves as in the preceding argument, we have, in effect, constructed our own subargument on behalf of a claim asserted by an expert. If that claim is a premise in an argument, a cogent subargument of the type above will render it acceptable. We have reasoned that we should accept the premise because an expert, or authority, has endorsed it.

Condition (6) concerns the expert's credibility, or worthiness to be believed, and the issues involved are the same as those previously discussed under the topic of testimony.

It used to be thought that people were too ready to trust authorities. Recently, another trend has set in: people are all too ready to distrust authorities. We are not suggesting here that every self-proclaimed expert or professional should be believed. The conditions for proper reliance on authority are, after all, quite strict. Appeals to authority should be evaluated carefully to see that these conditions are met. But people should also be careful not to reject authority in a careless or cavalier manner. The recent populist trend of generalized suspicion toward experts borders on anti-intellectualism and can be hazardous. We can lapse into this way of thinking far too easily, sometimes at great risk to ourselves.

Many people contend, for instance, that the mere fact that some experts are paid and make money from their work gives them a vested interest and makes them lack credibility. Or they argue that because experts are specialized (for example, a specialist in foot disorders cannot tell you whether you have a gum disease) and cannot give all the answers, they do not deserve any respect. Or they think that because experts have made some mistakes, their views are never reliable. None of these common arguments for generalized distrust in experts is cogent—as you will see if you think them over carefully. Accepting such arguments and rejecting established expertise might put us at real risk. For example, as a result of rather widespread distrust in doctors, many people have come to reject Western medicine and seek so-called alternative therapies. But many such therapies are untested and hazardous and supported only by anecdotal evidence—some people believe themselves to have been cured by employing them.[8] There is no good reason in general to think that alternative therapies are likely to be better than established medicine. Even if you believe that traditional medicine has many weaknesses that would not show that alternatives to it have strengths.

Established expertise is based on sustained and careful study and an intellectual tradition. All this is worth something, which we should remember in contexts when we wish to criticize established knowledge and expertise. If we fail to check the credentials of those cited as authorities, we can go too far in accepting authority. But if we hastily infer from the failings of established authorities that untested alternatives will be better, we also can go too far in rejecting authority.

We now consider the matter of **faulty appeals to authority.** To be cogent, an appeal to authority must meet all the conditions listed here: recognized expertise in an area with proper credentials and consensus, agreement of experts on the topic at issue, and the credibility and reliability of the expert cited. If any of these conditions are not met, an appeal to authority does not provide relevant and sufficient grounds to support a claim.

Often people who are authorities in one area make pronouncements in another area in which they are not authorities, in the hope that their expertise will transfer from one area to another. Or others seek to use their expertise in that way, thinking that their name and reputation will carry a claim in an area other than the one where their reputation was established. When this happens, the people cited have as much claim to be taken seriously as anyone else, but no more. An authoritative scientist is not, by virtue of his or her position in the scientific establishment, an authority on the future of humankind or the question of when human life begins. Such issues are broadly philosophical as opposed to scientific, and although philosophers are well qualified to consider these questions, they do not agree among themselves about them. Thus such questions cannot be resolved by appeals to authority.

The dilemma of different parties to a dispute citing their own experts is often seen in the courts. Each side in a dispute engages an expert, who testifies in a way that will suit the case of the side that is paying him or her.[9] In this event, the lawyers for each side will cross-examine each expert witness, and the judge and jury have to try to determine which aspects of the contending expert accounts are correct. They cannot accept all that is said on the basis of authority because to do this would lead to contradictions. Judges have to do their best to really sift through the evidence and expert testimony. In a case in which several experts brought to the court disagree, the judge and jury cannot resolve the issue merely by appealing to the authority of any one of them.

A Note on Internet Sources

For reasons of convenience and efficiency, it has become increasingly common for people to use web sites as a source of information. Caution has to be exercised here, as with any other information source.

It is first of all necessary to determine how reliable the site is. Whose site is it? What sort of information, analysis, value judgement or opinion, are you extracting from the site? If it is the web site of a university or research institute, it is in general a credible information source. The same may be said of sites provided by major and reputable newspapers and magazines. These sites are as reliable as the newspaper or magazine itself. Sites provided by nongovernmental groups may be good for specialized material tied to their interests, and they can provide a valuable corrective to mainstream sources in the case of aspects of issues not thoroughly treated in the mainstream press. However, you have to be careful about selectivity in the case of groups that exist to pursue a specific goal. For example, an environmental group is unlikely to provide information about the jobs that could be lost due to a conservation effort, and an antiwar group is unlikely to provide information about why people who favor a particular war support it. Sites run by such groups gain credibility if they supply information about their own sources of material, or if they provide links to views differing in significant respects from their own.

In the case of organizational web pages, you can probably get reliable information about the organization's activities and basic facts (personnel, mission statement, address and telephone number, expenditures, and so on). But you have to be aware that the web site will be intended to portray that organization in a favorable light. Material from NATO, for instance, will not emphasize accidental civilian deaths in bombing campaigns, or arguments that NATO, as a military alliance, is not a suitable vehicle for peacekeeping efforts.

A major difference between individual web sites and print sources of information lies in the absence of gatekeepers. In the case of a newspaper or magazine, the gatekeepers are editors at various levels, who check material for plausibility, accuracy, writing style, fairness, and tone. Gatekeepers provide some check on material, and knowing they will have to submit to gatekeepers provides some check on the people who write it. The reliability of gatekeepers and the established print or broadcast media for which they work is far from perfect. Nevertheless, writers and editors have accepted a responsibility to make their material as fair and accurate as they can. In addition, newspapers and magazines—and those who write for them—are open to criticism from a wide public. In some areas, they are open to lawsuits if they disseminate incorrect information. In contrast, people can easily arrange to be free of gatekeepers when putting material on the Internet on a private web page or unedited list service. In fact, this is one of the great attractions of the Internet for many people: any person can freely, without hindrance and delay, put material on the net. This aspect of the Internet is positive in providing freedom of expression for many aspiring writers and commentators who could not find space in newspapers and magazines. The "instant publish" feature of the Internet helps to avoid publication costs and delays, which for some journal publications can be several years or more, rendering some material dated even when it is first printed—and inhibiting creative discussion. However, the absence of gatekeepers is negative in several other respects. It has led to a chaotic abundance of material on many topics and—most relevant here—*lack of quality control* in some areas.

Individual or unidentifiable web sites should be approached with great caution. Someone is telling you something. In this respect, a claim made on a web site is like the case of testimony. But you know nothing about the person behind this claim, and you have no cues from interaction, such as you would have if you were conversing with someone. When you are talking with someone—even if it is a stranger just met in a train or other public place—you have some evidence from the encounter that is relevant to that person's honesty and qualifications. And you can ask questions and judge the reply. Obviously, no cues or personal interaction are possible in the case of the Internet, so if a site is not rendered credible in some other way, you should scrutinize any material with care. Claims presented as information should never be deemed credible simply on the grounds that it appears on someone's web site, or can be reached by a link from someone's web site.

Accepting Premises Provisionally

The conditions given so far do not cover all the premises people use in their arguments. As we shall soon see, premises can have features that make them definitely unacceptable, and we will list these. But suppose the following situation occurs. You study an argument, and you cannot judge the premises acceptable on any grounds mentioned here; on the other hand, neither do you have a definite basis for deeming the premises unacceptable, according to conditions about to be explained in the next section of this book. What do you say, then, about the (A) condition of argument cogency?

We recommend deeming the premises provisionally acceptable and then evaluating the argument on (R) and (G). If the argument passes on (R) and (G), then on the basis of a **provisional acceptance of the premises,** you can also **provisionally accept the conclusion.**

Sometimes premises are explicitly provisional. We may want to consider particular theories or hypotheses as a basis for reasoning, just to develop some ideas as to what consequences would follow from them. In such cases, we may speak of granting claims for the sake of argument. For instance, someone might argue as follows:

> Suppose that the number of students entering doctoral programs in electrical engineering in the United States is 2,000 per year, while the anticipated demand for qualified Ph.D.'s in this field, over the next 10 years, is 3,000 per year. If this is the case and continues to be the case, there will be a shortage of 1,000 qualified persons per year. Either that shortage will be met by immigration, or industries will have to train some of their own people.

Here the initial premise about Ph.D. registration is not accepted outright by the writer; it is put forward as a supposition and basis for further reasoning. We can, in this way, grant such a supposition for the sake of argument, reasoning forward on this basis to see what conclusions might emerge.

When we reason on a provisional basis, as in this example, it is important to recognize that the conclusion we reach is entirely conditional on our provisional acceptance of the premises. The previous argument would show that *if* the enrollment in these doctoral programs is as stated and continues at this level, there will be a shortage. In contexts such as these, the word *if* should not be forgotten. The conclusion is acceptable *if* the premises are. We have only provisionally accepted the premises.

Summary of Acceptability Conditions

A premise in an argument is acceptable if any one of the following conditions is satisfied:

1. It is supported by a cogent subargument.
2. It is supported elsewhere by the arguer or another person, and this fact is noted.

3. It is known *a priori* to be true.
4. It is a matter of common knowledge.
5. It is supported by appropriate testimony. (That is, the claim is not implausible, the sources are reliable, and the claim is restricted in content to experience.)
6. It is supported by an appropriate appeal to authority.
7. *It is not known to be unacceptable, as such, and can serve provisionally as the basis for argument.*

Point (7) is italicized to remind us that a conclusion supported by provisionally accepted premises is rendered provisionally acceptable—acceptable if those premises are acceptable.

EXERCISE SET

Exercise 1: Part A

For each of the following statements, (a) determine whether it can be known *a priori* to be true, and (b) explain the basis for your answer.

1. Every triangle has three straight sides.

2. Every grandparent is a parent.

3. Some people predict earthquakes on a grand scale for the west coast of North America during the years 2000–2010.

*4. Everyone who is a biological parent is legally responsible for the well-being of at least one child.

5. "I know of no studies that adequately describe what long-range effects slavery had on Africa, a continent where up to 50 million people, mostly males between the ages of fifteen and thirty-five, were forced to migrate to other worlds."
(David Lamb, *The Africans* [New York: Random House, 1987], p. 149)

6. A number is an expression of quantity.

*7. Either a person is grateful for a favor done him or he is not.

8. "A quarter-million Iraqi children have died under sanctions who would otherwise be alive and healthy."

(Joy Gordon, "Reply to George A. Lopez's 'More Ethical than Not'" in *Ethics and International Affairs 1999*, p. 150)

9. There is a distinction to be made between fraternal twins and identical twins.

*10. No man is an island.

*11. Any action that is caused must result from something that has preceded it.

12. Spending more than two hours a day looking at a computer screen may damage young children's eyes.

13. If a tribe has members who fight with each other over titles and lands to the point of causing each other severe physical injury, then that tribe is not one where expressions of jealousy and aggression are absent.

*14. We need a space station because it is clear we are at a dead end in our ability to understand big questions about life and the universe.

*15. May the Force be with you.

16. Everything that happens has exactly five effects.

17. What goes up must come down.

Exercise 1: Part B

For each of the following claims, (a) try to reach a decision about whether it is acceptable, and (b) state why you think it is acceptable, referring to the conditions of acceptability explained in this chapter.

*1.   Every living animal has some kind of reproductive system.

*2.   Having a previous life would require surviving as a soul during the time interval between several different bodily existences.

3.   Human nature is a mysterious thing, unknowable by social science and a wonder even to human beings themselves.

*4.   Everyone alive today has experienced innumerable past lives.

5.   If exercise leads to a feeling of well-being and a greater zest for life, then exercise is good for you.

*6.   Siamese twins have difficulty leading a normal human life if they are not separated.

7.   Football is an important sport in many North American colleges and universities.

8.   *Background:* The following is taken from a letter to the *New York Times* (June 27, 1999) by Michael Melcher, on the issue of whether it could be appropriate to pay tutors to help children perform better at sports. Melcher is writing in favor of this idea.

   "When I was a child, there were no tutors to help unathletic children like me learn sports. I wish there had been. In 10 years of mandatory physical education, I never played a meaningful part in any team sport. Coaches and team captains sought to minimize possible damage by putting me in nonpositions like roving center-right fielder. I acceded without complaint, wishing to avoid the embarrassment of any contact with a moving ball. Recently, at age 35, I finally learned how to throw a football. It felt as good as if I were 10 years old."

9.   *Background:* The following appeared in an editorial in the Calgary *Herald* for June 16, 1999 on the issue of whether taxi drivers should be tested to make sure they can speak and understand English.

   "Nobody expects cabbies to discourse at great length about current events, but it's only reasonable to assume that, at the very least, the cabbie should be able to understand the address of the passenger's destination and respond to questions about the fare."

10.   *Background:* The following is taken from a short essay, "A Gift to My Father," by Patti Davis, daughter of former U.S. President Ronald Reagan. The essay first appeared in the *New York Times Magazine,* and was reprinted in the Toronto *Globe and Mail* for December 31, 1998.

   "Christmas is supposed to be about giving—not so much the material kind, but giving of the self, the soul, the heart."

When Premises Are Unacceptable

Now that we have described some general conditions that make premises acceptable, we will go on to deal with some things that make them unacceptable.

Easy Refutability

Some premises can easily be refuted. To **refute** a statement is to show that it is false. We can sometimes refute premises by pointing out other knowledge that contradicts the claim made. If, for instance, someone were to say, "No blind student has ever graduated from a university," you could refute him or her by citing just one example of a blind student who has graduated from a university. In this case, you offer a **counterexample.** Any claim that is couched in universal terms and is about all things of a certain type (all men, all women, all problems, all theories, all mammals, . . .) can be refuted by a counterexample. Since the claim is universal, even one counterexample or counterinstance is enough to show that it is false. Claims can be refuted when they are contradicted by experience, testimony, authority, or common knowledge. The technique of counterexample is appropriate when claims are universal in scope—when they say, in effect, that all . . . are . . . or that no . . . are . . . (Such claims are discussed further in Chapter 7.)

Consider some examples of sweeping statements:

(a) The wealthy have no concern for the poor.
(b) Child labor in developing countries is necessary for the survival of families that would otherwise be at the brink of starvation.
(c) If women were political leaders, a nonaggressive style of conducting political business would automatically result.

These statements, all worded in universal terms, are easily refuted. Consider (a), which is couched in unqualified general terms as a statement about "the wealthy." To refute this statement, one has only to find an example of one wealthy person who is concerned about the poor. Since many wealthy persons have left fortunes to foundations devoted to charitable pursuits, statement (a) is easy to refute and is, for that reason, unacceptable. Statement (b) is similarly couched in universal terms. There are no qualifiers restricting the scope of the statement, which appears to be about all forms of child labor in all developing countries. If the statement is interpreted in that way, it is refuted by examples of countries such as Taiwan and Malaysia that made elementary education compulsory, thereby ending the most abusive and debilitating forms of child labor, and were able to do it without worsening the lot of poor families. As for (c), there have been women leaders, such as Britain's Margaret Thatcher and Israel's Golda Meir, who have been hard-line and aggressive in their approach to politics. This statement, too, would have to be qualified to be acceptable. As it stands, it is easily refuted.

At this point it is worth commenting on the common saying "the exception proves the rule." Several centuries ago, the word *proves* meant *test.* If we were to say, "the exception tests the rule" that would be a valid statement: to examine a case that appears to be an exception is a good way of testing a proposed rule. If the apparent exception really is an exception, then the rule is not universally valid; this test has shown that it does not hold up in general. Thus the rule should not be stated in universal terms. If it is stated in this way, the statement of it is refutable, refuted by the exception, and thus shown to be incorrect. If we use the word *prove* in the common modern sense in which *prove* means "show to be true," it is NOT TRUE that the exception proves the rule. A counterexample to a universal claim refutes that claim.

Here is an example of an argument with an easily refutable premise. The example is taken from a discussion of the acceptance of refugees by the United States:

> A century ago an open-ended invitation may have been safe enough. America was a new country then, unfilled. The supply of possible immigrants wasn't so great. Now the huddled masses of the wretchedly poor amount to 800 million. More than three times the U.S. population. It would be insane to invite them all in. Even one percent would be too many.
>
> Variety in a nation is good. So also is unity. But when variety (of which we've always had plenty) overwhelms unity, how are we to keep a complex society like ours running?
>
> When newcomers arrive too fast, they gather into enclaves and resist learning the national language. Immigrants then become the new isolationists. Tribalism becomes a reality: Goodbye, unity![10]

One premise in this argument against admitting refugees to the United States is the following:

> When newcomers arrive too fast, they gather into enclaves, resist learning the national language, and become isolationists.

This premise is rather vague, since it is not clear how fast "too fast" is. But when refugees have come in large numbers to the United States in the past, they have not, in fact, refused to learn the language and adapt to a new life. A great many Hungarians came to the United States in the 1950s and learned English, assimilating into the mainstream of life. Many Italians and Germans did the same thing after World War II. Unless he has a very strict meaning for "arriving too fast," the author has asserted a premise that is not acceptable. We can refute this premise on the basis of common knowledge.

Claim Known *a Priori* to Be False

We saw that some claims can be known *a priori* to be true. In an analogous way, some claims can be known *a priori* to be false. Any such claim is unacceptable and cannot serve as a premise in a cogent argument. Here is an example:

> (a) The man's headache did not hurt him at all.

Claim (a) must be false, and we can see this by reasoning alone. A headache is something that aches, something that hurts a person. It is impossible, by definition, to have a headache that does not hurt at all. A person might have something wrong with his brain, something that did not hurt even though it was an injury or disease, but if it did not hurt, it could not be a headache. There is an inconsistency within (a) between being a headache and not hurting, and because of this **inconsistency,** we can know *a priori* that (a) is false.

Another example of a claim known *a priori* to be false is:

> (b) There are things outside the universe.

The term *universe* refers to everything that exists, so it is impossible for things to be outside the universe. If (b) were a premise in an argument, it would be unacceptable because we can determine *a priori* that it is false.

Inconsistency between Premises

Sometimes an argument will contain a number of premises, and several of these premises will explicitly or implicitly contradict each other. For example, if one premise asserts, "All men are emotionally tough," and another asserts, "Some men are emotionally vulnerable," the argument in which both premises occur has premises that openly, blatantly, and explicitly contradict each other.

As you can imagine, this sort of mistake is too obvious to occur frequently. It is more common for premises to contradict each other implicitly. This means that when we think about what the premises say and make some simple deductive inferences from them, we can derive an explicit contradiction from the premises. If there is either an explicit or an implicit contradiction in the premises of an argument, they are inconsistent and we know they cannot all be true. Hence, as a set, they are unacceptable.

Here is an example of an implicit contradiction:

1. Most mainstream religions began as small sects, which we would today call cults.
2. Sects, cults, and mainstream religions all have beliefs that are not provable by reason and need to be based on faith.
3. Cults are superior to mainstream religions in providing a sense of meaning in life by demanding of their adherents' total devotion and commitment of their life and lifestyle to the movement.
4. Cults, like mainstream religions, respect the freedom of individual men and women to make their own decisions about practical aspects of life, whatever these may be.

Therefore,

5. Cults should not be treated differently in law from mainstream religions (see Figure 5.2).

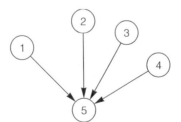

FIGURE 5.2

The implicit contradiction in this argument is between (3) and (4). According to (3), cults differ from mainstream religions because they demand total devotion by the adherent, in his or her way of life. But according to (4), cultures are similar to mainstream religions in permitting adherents to make their own decisions about how to conduct their lives. Total devotion will mean behaving as the cult says; freedom will mean making one's own decisions, which might or might not be in accord with what the cult prescribes. These premises are implicitly inconsistent; thus they are not jointly acceptable. We should not accept both (3) and (4). The argument has unacceptable premises, fails on the (A) condition, and is therefore not cogent.

Vagueness or Ambiguity

To accept premises rationally, we must know what they mean and what sort of evidence would establish them as true. This means that premises must be stated in reasonably clear language. Thus, problems of vagueness or ambiguity can sometimes render premises unacceptable. If a premise is stated in language that is vague or ambiguous to the point where we cannot determine what sort of evidence would establish it, then it is unacceptable as stated. For example, "Dysfunctionality in families is widespread" would be too vague to serve as the premise of an argument without further clarification. Both *dysfunctionality* and *widespread* are extremely vague, as they are used here. Either its meaning will have to be clarified or the argument in which it appears will have to be rejected as not cogent.

Dependence on Faulty Assumptions

Sometimes problems with unacceptable premises are more obvious when we see the **assumptions** underlying those premises. We may suspect that there is something wrong with the premises of an argument but understand what it is when we stop to reflect on why these premises are stated as they are. When we do this, we can see that what the arguer says makes sense only if we grant her a particular assumption or set of assumptions.

Assumptions are not stated premises. Nor are they missing premises. They are presupposed by the argument, and we can see that this is the case by studying the premises.[11] The language of the premises is particularly helpful in this regard. As we saw in Chapter 4, language articulates a framework for classifying and evaluating events. An argument will appear in some such framework, and the wording of its premises will indicate the framework. A word such as *resource*, for instance, indicates that material is to be used and exploited. To call employees "human resources" is to assume that they are there to be used and developed by managers in ways that will suit the purposes of managers. Such an assumption would be most objectionable in the context of a labor negotiation in which managers and employees were participating as equal parties. If the assumption were to be made, premises on which it was based would be unacceptable.

An illustration is found in the following advertisement:

> If you think advertising is a bunch of baloney, why are you reading this ad? You read to learn. Reading brings new ideas and thoughts into your life. It opens up a whole new world. That's what advertising does. It communicates information from one source to another. Advertising gives you the opportunity to make up your own mind by familiarizing you with a product. That's why advertising is a freedom. The freedom to know quality and what is available. You read and listen to advertising to obtain information. Information on just about anything. Including the price of baloney.[12]

This passage is rather repetitive. Its basic point seems to be that advertising is good and useful because it gives us knowledge and information. You can see this in the expressions "It communicates information," "familiarizing you with a product," and "You read . . . advertising to obtain information." The premises, then, are based on the assumption that advertisements consist largely of accurate statements. This assumption is clearly necessary because both information and knowledge can be obtained only if the statements made in advertisements are accurate. The premises assume that advertisements are composed primarily of accurate statements.

Let us spell out that assumption and take a close look at it:

(a) Advertisements are composed primarily of true statements.

There is much evidence against statement (a). In fact, it is easily refuted. Common knowledge is enough to indicate this. Many advertisements contain no statements at all but consist merely of questions, suggestions, pictures, jokes, and so on. Others contain exaggerated or misleading statements, and some even contain statements that are downright false. If the author had tried to prove, or justify, his underlying assumption, he would have faced an impossible task. Instead, the assumption is unstated, or implicit—probably in the hope that readers will not notice it. It is smuggled in through words such as *knowledge*, *learn*, and *information*. You have only to spot this assumption to see that the argument has unacceptable premises and cannot be cogent.

If you can see that the premises of an argument depend on an assumption that is readily refutable or highly controversial, then you know that the argument has unacceptable premises. Looking for background assumptions, which you can then criticize, is a powerful technique for finding flaws in premises. But it should, however, be used with some care. It is all too easy to think you have found assumptions that are not really there. If you think you have spotted a faulty assumption, you should stop to make sure that the premises really do depend on it. If they do, then they are unacceptable.

Premises Not More Acceptable Than Conclusion

The purpose of an argument is to lead an audience from the premises to a rational acceptance of a conclusion. For this purpose to be achieved, the premises of an argument should be more acceptable to the audience than the conclusion.[13] In the context of a particular argument, premises may be unacceptable because they fail in this respect.

Suppose that someone were to argue as follows:

1. The pyramids of ancient Egypt were built with the assistance of creatures from outer space.
Therefore,
2. There has been at least one extraterrestrial civilization that was advanced enough to send some of its members to visit earth.

Such an argument would be extremely unpersuasive because the premise is so improbable. It states a bold claim about a very specific question of history (How were the Egyptian pyramids built?), one that goes against common knowledge and established authority. This premise is most implausible. In fact, it is even less plausible than the controversial conclusion it is used to support.

G. E. Moore, an influential philosopher who taught at Cambridge University during the early 1900s, was famous for attacking the arguments of philosophers on grounds similar to these. Moore noted that some philosophers had invented special theories about how the mind acquires knowledge, or what objects are made of, and other topics. They sometimes used those theories to argue against the beliefs of common sense. Moore maintained that the philosophical theories did not have enough strength to serve as a basis for undercutting common sense. He argued that commonsense claims attacked by such theorists were always more acceptable than the philosophical theories that were used to argue against those claims. Hence, the argument could be reversed. Instead of arguing from the acceptability of the premises to the acceptability of the conclusion, one could argue from the unacceptability of the conclusion to the unacceptability of the premises.[14] Moore considered the views of another philosopher, J. E. M. McTaggart, who had argued that time is unreal. Against McTaggart, Moore argued as follows:

1. If time is unreal, I could not know I had my breakfast before my lunch.
2. I do know I had my breakfast before my lunch.
Therefore,
3. Time is not unreal.

In premise (2) Moore is citing common knowledge, which he uses in his argument to reverse McTaggart's argument. If McTaggart meant to claim that time is unreal and because time is unreal, a person such as Moore cannot know common claims such as that he had his breakfast before his lunch, McTaggart can be refuted. His argument can be reversed. Instead of the "unreality" of time showing that common knowledge is not possible, the fact that common knowledge exists shows that there is something wrong with the theory that time is unreal. In an argument, the audience is supposed to be able to move from the premises to the conclusion. For this to work properly, the premises must be more acceptable to the audience than the conclusion. They cannot be less so.

Sometimes arguments are flawed because a controversial premise is used to support a conclusion that is, in fact, less controversial than the premise. In such a case, the premise is too controversial to be of any use in the context of the argument. This problem arises in the following argument, which was used in a report on education. The author is considering the issue of whether languages other than French and English should be taught in public schools in Canada. (Both French and English are official languages in Canada; in addition to English-speaking and French-speaking people, there are natives and immigrants whose mother tongues include Cree, Ojibway, Greek, Italian, Japanese, Chinese, and many others.) When you read this argument, keep in mind that the author is trying to answer an objection to having other languages taught in public schools.

> It will not surprise anyone that I reject these arguments. A child has the inalien-
> able right to his mother tongue and to his cultural heritage, which not only
> determine who he is, but also who he will be. No school system, therefore, must
> be allowed to interfere with that right. The opposite is also true; everything must
> be done to encourage the child's awareness of his heritage and to develop the
> language skills of his mother tongue. Without these provisions we will merely be
> paying lip service to the multicultural reality of Canada.[15]

The author's whole case here rests on the following premise:

> A child has the inalienable right to his mother tongue and to his cultural
> heritage, which not only determine who he is, but also who he will be.[16]

If we had granted the claim that every child had an inalienable right to his mother
tongue and cultural heritage, we could begin from that claim to argue that schools
should teach all the maternal languages of all the students. But the problem is, this
starting premise is too controversial to serve as the basis for a cogent argument. Obviously, if all children had an inalienable right to their mother tongue, a right that
society had to support at all costs, then schools would have the obligation to teach
many languages. But the author did not give an independent argument for this
sweeping premise, and there are obvious objections to it in costs and the need to
maintain a society with a common culture and efficient communication. As the
premise stands, it is unacceptable. Even though the conclusion can be derived from
it, that does not give the conclusion any real support. To show that a conclusion
follows from a sweeping and unsubstantiated supposition is not to prove that conclusion acceptable.

The Fallacy of Begging the Question

A more specific sort of case in which an argument can go wrong because the premise
is not more acceptable than the conclusion is the fallacy of **begging the question.** An
argument begs the question if one or more of its premises assert the conclusion
(usually in slightly different words) or presupposes that the conclusion is true. This
fallacy was mentioned in Chapter 3, in the discussion of pseudoevidence. Sometimes when the fallacy of begging the question is committed, a person is trying to
prove a conclusion, *C*, and chooses premises that are so logically close to *C* that they
make the same claim in other words. For instance, he might use a premise stating
that no one can appropriately be blamed for a mechanical failure in an attempt to
prove that no one is responsible for the failure. Since the premise just asserts the
conclusion in slightly different words ("cannot appropriately be blamed" and "is not
responsible"), the argument is faulty. It begs, or avoids, the question because it does
not address the issue of whether and why no one can appropriately be blamed. Anyone who disputed the conclusion in this case would also dispute the premise.

It may seem amazing that anyone would ever use or be fooled by a question-
begging argument. And yet this often happens. It happens sometimes because

people are not looking closely, do not have the concept of argument with its premises and conclusion clearly in their minds, or are misled by complicated, ponderous language. In fact, it is quite easy to use a question-begging argument yourself without intending to, especially if you are trying to set out reasons for one of your fundamental and most cherished beliefs. Trying to find premises that will support that belief, you may easily, and quite unwittingly, come up with claims that would be acceptable only to people who already agree with the conclusion you are trying to prove. If this happens, you will have begged the question.

Here is another example. Let us suppose that you use a skateboard and believe that you should be able to do stunts on your skateboard in a prominent square beside a public market. You try to argue this to a friend of yours who has claimed that the municipal prohibition against skateboarding in this place is reasonable since parents often go there with small children, who might suddenly run out and be hurt by a fast-moving person on a skateboard. In discussing the point with your friend, you come up with the following argument:

1. I have a right to use my skateboard in any outdoor public place.
2. The market square is an outdoor public place.
Therefore,
3. I am perfectly entitled to use my skateboard in the market square.

The trouble with this argument is that you assume in premise (1) everything you are trying to prove in your conclusion. This problem can be seen when we think about the expressions "have a right to" and "am perfectly entitled to." These expressions mean exactly the same thing in this context. You have stated as your premise that you have a right to use your skateboard, in an attempt to justify your conclusion that you are entitled to use it. This argument would work if your friend and others who object to people skateboarding had already conceded in advance that you do indeed have this right. But they do not: in fact, this is what they are denying. They think you (and presumably others) do not have any such right because skateboarding can be hazardous to passersby under some conditions. You have, in this context, given an argument that begs the question. Another name for this fallacy is circular reasoning.

An argument in which a premise assumes or presupposes the truth of the conclusion also begs the question. You can see why this would be a problem. In an argument, the writer or speaker is trying to justify the conclusion, trying to give it support, to render it acceptable to someone who does not already accept the conclusion. To the audience, the conclusion is not acceptable at the outset, which is precisely why an argument is needed. If, in offering an argument, the arguer uses premises that assume or presuppose that conclusion, then those premises will not be acceptable either.

A classic example of this type involves an appeal to the authority of the Bible to defend belief in God. (The argument, remember, would be addressed to someone who doubted whether God exists.)

1. The Bible is the word of God.
2. God speaks the truth.
3. According to the Bible, God created human beings and the earth itself, and is a major agent in world history.
Therefore,
4. God exists.

This argument begs the question (or is circular) because all three premises assume or presuppose that God exists, which is just what the argument is trying to prove.

Such cases of begging the question are usually more difficult to spot than instances in which one premise by itself claims the conclusion. The circularity is more subtle and more disguised. But the problem is in essence the same: the premises are not acceptable unless we already accept the conclusion. The argument thus avoids, or begs, the question it should address.[17]

Sometimes, when we are trying to construct arguments for our most basic beliefs, we cannot find premises that do not already require acceptance of the conclusion. When this happens, it is better to admit that we have no argument to prove our fundamental principles than to use arguments that are superficially rational, but beg the question. We can simply admit that we are operating under an assumption that seems reasonable and effective but cannot be fully supported by arguments.

A number of different conditions, then, will show that the premises of an argument are unacceptable.

Summary of Unacceptability Conditions

1. One or more premises are refutable on the basis of common knowledge, *a priori* knowledge, or reliable knowledge from testimony or authority.
2. One or more premises are *a priori* false.
3. Several premises, taken together, produce a contradiction, so that the premises are explicitly or implicitly inconsistent.
4. One or more premises are vague or ambiguous to such an extent that it is not possible to determine what sort of evidence would establish them as acceptable or unacceptable.
5. One or more premises depend on an assumption that is either refutable or highly controversial.
6. For the audience to whom the argument is addressed, the premises are less acceptable than the conclusion.
7. One or more premises would not be rationally acceptable to any person who did not already accept the conclusion. In this case, the argument begs the question.

EXERCISE SET

Exercise 2: Part A

Inconsistencies. Can you detect an inconsistency in any of the following sets of statements? If so, which ones? Explain your judgment.

*1.   Extremely bright students who are good at mathematics often enroll in college majors in mathematics and physics because they can attain high marks in those subjects. However, in most college and university programs, these subjects are unusually difficult and demanding, and that, together with their highly specialized nature, eventually causes some of these students to change their majors.

2.   Squares are rectangles, but not all rectangles are squares.

3.   Most boys have a tendency to shove at age two. Few girls have a tendency to shove at age two unless they are the regular playmates of pushy little boys. A degree of aggression is probably innate in the human species, particularly in the male.

*4.   The economic situation of African Americans in the United States has not improved as much as we might think since the bad old days before the civil rights movement. Even though some African Americans are in successful and conspicuous positions in politics, law, and medicine, it is still true that unemployment affects blacks far more than whites.

5.   The house was built during a period of heavy rains and as a result, untreated wood received considerable moisture. Given this, there is a significant danger that the wood will rot. Since the climate is dry, wood has been the traditional material for home construction. There is no risk of damage from exposure to moisture.

6.   If a woman gives birth to a child, she is responsible for taking care of it. Responsibilities are something we acquire voluntarily. Of course, some children are born as a result of accidents with birth control or even as a result of rape or incest, sexual attacks to which women are involuntarily subjected.

*7.   All goodness derives from God and would not exist without Him. God is good. God created all the goodness in the world. No act can create value. Of many values, goodness is the primary one.

8.   All human beings are omnivorous. Omnivorous beings eat meat and vegetable products. Some human beings are vegetarians. Vegetarians do not eat meat.

*9.   All knowledge depends on proof by argument. Proof by argument requires premises. Those premises must be known to provide the basis for that proof.

*10.   An extraterrestrial civilization that was both technically and morally more advanced than we are would have some reasons to come to earth and other reasons not to come. Presumably, such a civilization would wish to exhibit its technological innovations to others, and it might wish to communicate its advanced moral standards to others. On the other hand, earth is a repellent place from a moral point of view—full of war, torture, murder, greed, robbery, and hypocrisy. A morally advanced civilization might be too disgusted to wish to visit.

11.   Most babies who are chubby as infants lose the extra weight when they begin to crawl around.

*12.   The civil war in Sierra Leone in the late 1990s was especially brutal. Atrocities were committed by both sides, and mutual forgiveness will be necessary if the country is ever to recover. But the activities of rebel troops, who amputated the arms and hands of many village peoples, leave a legacy of misery, horror, and handicap from which the country will not soon recover. If anything ever is, these deeds may be unforgivable.

*13. The value of every human life is absolute. Life has a sanctity that people are not entitled to violate. We can never justify deliberately taking a life. However, capital punishment is morally permissible, and wars in self-defense are sometimes necessary.

14. An activity need not be financially rewarding to be worthwhile and valuable. There are no salaries for choral singing, playing tennis, or riding on horseback, and yet these activities are enjoyable and worth doing. On the other hand, housework is not valuable, because it is not paid work.

Exercise 2: Part B
Can you refute any of the following statements by counterexample? If so, say which ones, and state the counterexample.

*1. People who have health problems are people who do not take proper care of themselves.

*2. Logic is a masculine pursuit.

3. Class smallness is the ultimate measure of how good a college is.

4. Harm will come to anyone who trusts a stranger.

*5. Watching television is always a waste of time.

6. Increases in immigration typically do not lead to higher unemployment, because the needs of immigrants contribute to greater spending, which strengthens the consumer economy, and because many immigrants start small businesses, they create work for themselves and for others too.

7. Any activity that is undertaken by a committee could be performed equally well by an individual.

8. Computer games are violent and will desensitize those who use them to violence.

*9. Women in Islamic countries never achieve positions of political power.

10. If there are no guns and no high-tech weaponry, there can be no war.

Exercise 2: Part C
Evaluate the premises of the following arguments for acceptability using the criteria explained in this chapter, and explain your answers with reference to these criteria. Also say whether you think any assumptions are faulty. If there is any passage that does not express an argument and therefore contains no premises, say so.

1. Anyone who has the capacity to kill should avoid keeping guns around the house. Actually, when you think about it, we all have the capacity to kill. So no one should keep a gun around the house.

2. Nobody should undertake college education without at least some idea of what he or she wants to do and where he or she wants to go in life. But our world is so full of change that we cannot predict which fields will provide job openings in the future. Given this, we can't form any reasonable life plans. So nobody should go to college.

*3. Withholding information is just the same as lying and lying is wrong, so withholding information is wrong.

4. Nuclear energy has a potential to cause environmental damage that will last for many thousands of years. It is unique in this regard; damage from coal, water, and other electric sources can be serious but are likely to be shorter in duration. Therefore, nuclear energy should be approached with extreme caution.

5. If a law is so vague that it is difficult to know what counts as a violation of it, and if there is really no distinct and clear harm that this law could prevent, then the law should be abolished. Laws that prohibit loitering have both of these defects. The conclusion to which we are driven is obvious: laws against loitering should be abolished.

6.   Every employee should have the right to bargain effectively for his or her salary, and this means that every employee should have the right to strike. Nurses are essential employees. Obviously, this means that nurses are employees. So it is quite wrong for nurses' strikes to be illegal. Nurses should have the right to strike.

7.   A great leader is infallible and can never be wrong. Hitler was clearly a great leader because he could really inspire people to follow him. Yet anyone advocating genocide was clearly wrong, and Hitler did advocate genocide. Therefore, Hitler was not infallible.

*8.   Sex is private and intimate. AIDS has to do with sex. Nothing that is private and intimate should be discussed publicly. So AIDS should not be discussed publicly.

9.   Tennis is a much more demanding game than basketball because it is played either singly or in pairs, which means that a person is moving nearly all the time. Basketball is a team sport, and you can sometimes relax and leave things up to the other members. Also, tennis calls for much more arm strength than basketball.

10.   Either the earth is heating up, or it is cooling down. If the earth is heating up, we can expect more and more forest fires. If it is cooling down, we can expect greater use of electricity and fossil fuels for heating, with resultant demands on the environment. Either way, the environment is going to suffer.

*11.   *Background:* The following letter was written in response to a newspaper article dealing with problems of addiction among doctors:

"When doctors become addicts it is because of "pressures" of their job and the "lack of family life." Yet when illiterate employables become addicts, it is because society has failed to train them for a job. If the housewife becomes addicted, it is because she is not appreciated by her family. Or if it is addicted youth, their problem is lack of parental understanding. That is, no matter what segment of society is addicted, another segment can be blamed, with rational-

ized plausibility. This circular slipping away from personal responsibility is clever, but it is fundamentally unjust. Obviously no one knows why some persons of all strata of society, including the clergy, become addicts. Why cannot the experts admit their problem—the problem of not knowing final causes—instead of producing plausible but innocent scapegoats?"
(Letter to the editor, Toronto *Globe and Mail,* October 8, 1980)

*12.   *Background:* The following is taken from a column by Peter Stockland called "Thanksgiving Not the Time to Turf the Turkeys." The column appeared in the Calgary *Herald* for October 12, 1998. Stockland is arguing that there is no need for moral concern about the killing of turkeys. He says,

"A turkey is a nerve impulse on legs. A turkey minus its head is marginally more brain-dead than one in full possession of its noggin. . . . I remember once coming home to find some of my turkeys standing outside in a deluge of rainwater, too stupid to go back through the open door of a coop that was warm and dry. Another time, I tried a small experiment by using feed to lead some turkeys a short distance from their coop just to see if they could find they way back alone. They couldn't. Flowers know how to open and close. But turkeys can't figure out where they live and eat."

13.   According to D. G., who is a well-regarded scholar on ancient Greek philosophy, Socrates never wrote down his philosophy. Thus, what we know about Socrates comes from those who did write. That means mostly Plato and Xenophon.

*14.   Swimming is the safest form of exercise for the many people who have problems with their joints, such as arthritis, because the water supports the swimmer, and there is no stress on such problem joints as the knee and the ankle.

15.   "Cruelty has a human heart, And Jealousy a human face; Terror the human form divine, And Secrecy the human dress."
(William Blake, "A Divine Image")

16.   "Today your kids can watch Drug Deals, Shootouts, and Sex on TV, or they can learn Spanish, French, German, or Italian. Your choice. They're going to watch TV anyway— four, maybe five hours a day—so why not put some of that time to good constructive use? Order MUZZY today for a risk-free 30-day home trial. MUZZY, the BBC's world-renowned audio-video language course, has already given thousands of 2 to 12 year-olds a huge head start over kids who waste their time watching mindless sitcoms, and worse."
(Advertisement that appeared in *World Press Review*, March 1994)

Exercise 2: Part D

For any two of the following claims, imagine that you have to construct an argument in defense. Specify for each case one or more premises that would be acceptable and one or more that would not be acceptable for this purpose, according to the conditions developed in this chapter. Say which conditions make your premises acceptable or unacceptable in each case.

1.   The United Nations is a necessary world body.

2.   Wars within countries are now a more serious problem for the world than wars between states.

3.   Change is not always the same thing as progress.

4.   A holy book such as the Bible, the Talmud, or the Koran provides a reliable guide to moral behavior and the foundations for law and politics in the modern world.

5.   A good solution to the problem of unemployment is to reduce standard working hours for those who have full-time jobs, so that the extra work can go to those who are unemployed.

6.   A major cause of violent crime among youth is their sense that life has no meaning and there is no future for them.

7.   The ability to evaluate arguments is an important practical skill.

▬▬▬ CHAPTER SUMMARY

Because no account of argument cogency is complete without saying something about which premises to accept and why, we set out some general principles about this matter. These principles apply as well to the acceptability of claims outside argument, with the sole exception of those that relate premises explicitly to the argument's conclusion. Using the principles, we chart a cautious path between wholesale acceptance of claims and wholesale rejection: neither policy is realistic.

There are conditions under which the premises of arguments are acceptable, and there are conditions under which they are unacceptable. These have been stated above, but are repeated here for ease of reference.

Acceptability of Premises

A premise in an argument is acceptable if any one or more of the following conditions are met:

1. It is supported by a subargument that is cogent.
2. It is cogently supported elsewhere by the arguer or another person, and this fact is noted.
3. It is known *a priori* to be true.
4. It is a matter of common knowledge.
5. It is supported by appropriate testimony. (That is, the claim is not implausible, the sources are not unreliable, and the claim is restricted in content to experience.)
6. It is supported by an appropriate appeal to authority.
*7. *It is not known to be unacceptable, as such, and can serve provisionally as the basis for argument.*

Unacceptability of Premises

Premises in an argument are unacceptable if one or more of the following conditions are met:

1. One or more premises are refutable on the basis of common knowledge, *a priori* knowledge, or reliable knowledge from testimony or authority.
2. One or more premises are known, *a priori*, to be false.
3. Several premises, taken together, can be shown to produce a contradiction, so that the premises are inconsistent.
4. One or more premises are vague or ambiguous to such an extent that it is not possible to determine what sort of evidence would establish them as acceptable or unacceptable.
5. One or more premises depend on an assumption that is either refutable or highly controversial.
6. For the audience to whom the argument is addressed, the premises are not more certain than the conclusion.
7. One or more premises could not be rationally accepted by someone who does not already accept the conclusion, so the argument begs the question.

Referring to these conditions you often can decide whether to accept the premises of various arguments. If any one of the conditions of acceptability is met, the premise in question is acceptable. If any one of the conditions of unacceptability is met, it is unacceptable. It is important to recall that provisional premises give you a provisional conclusion, one that is shown acceptable if the premises are accepted.

Review of Terms Introduced

A priori **statement**   A statement that can be known to be true or false on the basis of logic and reasoning alone, prior to experience. If a claim is known *a priori* to be true, it is acceptable as a premise in an argument. If it is known *a priori* to be false, it is unacceptable.

A posteriori **statement**   A statement that cannot be known to be true or false on the basis of logic and reasoning alone. On the contrary, it requires experience or evidence. *A posteriori* statements are also called empirical.

Assumption   A claim, typically of a fairly general nature, that is taken for granted and is presupposed by the premises of an argument. A premise in an argument depends on an assumption if the denial of that assumption would mean that the premise was pointless or could not possibly be true. The assumption is a background belief, usually more fundamental and general than the premise itself.

Authority   One who has specialized knowledge of a subject and is recognized to be an expert on that subject. Appeals to authority are legitimate provided the claim supported is in an area that is genuinely an area of knowledge; the person cited is recognized as an expert within that field; the experts in the field agree; and the person cited is credible and reliable.

Begging the question   A fallacy that occurs when one or more premises either state the conclusion (usually in slightly different words) or presuppose that the conclusion is true. Arguments that beg the question are also sometimes called circular arguments.

Common knowledge   A statement that is known by most people or is widely believed by most people and against which there is no known evidence. What is a matter of common knowledge will vary with time and place, but if, in a given context, a certain claim is a matter of common knowledge, then it is acceptable in that context as the premise of an argument.

Counterexample   A case that refutes a universal statement. For example, if someone said, "All colleges in the United States teach in English," and we were to know of a college in the United States that taught in Spanish, the Spanish college would be a counterexample that would refute the generalization. Note that contrary to what is implied by the common expression, the exception does NOT prove the rule.

Empirical   See *A posteriori.*

Faulty appeal to authority   Argument based on authority in which one or more of the conditions of proper appeal to authority are not met.

Inconsistency   Two statements are inconsistent with each other if, putting them together, we would arrive at a contradiction that can be known *a priori* to be false. For example, "All redheads are hot-tempered" and "Some redheads are not hot-tempered" are inconsistent. (A single statement is also inconsistent if it entails a contradiction. In such a case it is not acceptable because we know *a priori* that it is false.) Explicit inconsistency occurs when the contradiction is apparent on the surface, in the way the statements are worded. Implicit inconsistency occurs when the meaning of the statements allows us to infer, by valid deduction, a further statement that is a contradiction.

Provisional acceptance of conclusion   Acceptance of conclusion because it is related, by proper reasoning, to premises that have been provisionally accepted. In such a case, the conclusion can be said to be provisionally established: if the premises are acceptable, the conclusion is acceptable too.

Provisional acceptance of premises   Tentative supposition of premises in a context where there is no special basis for regarding them as unacceptable.

Refuted   A statement is refuted if and only if it is shown, on the basis of acceptable evidence, to be false. Statements that are completely universal in nature, that are categorical in tone, or both, can often easily be refuted. If they are refuted they are not acceptable as premises in an argument.

Testimony   Typically, statements based on personal experience or personal knowledge. A statement is accepted on the basis of a person's testimony if his or her telling of the statement and certifying it as acceptable is the basis for us to believe it. We can rationally accept what another person tells us on his or her testimony unless (1) the claim is implausible; or (2) the person or the source in which the claim is quoted is unreliable and lacking in credibility; or (3) the claim goes beyond what the person could know from his or her own experience.

Notes

1. *For instructors.* The points made in this chapter about accepting and not accepting premises can be applied directly to the more general subject of accepting and not accepting claims. The sole exception concerns the discussion of premises that are unacceptable as a basis for argument because they are less acceptable than, or too logically close to, the particular conclusion they are intended to support.

2. A true story often told by my mother-in-law, Helen Colijn.

3. "Leg-Hold Row Traps Canada," Calgary *Herald,* June 18, 1995.

4. *National Enquirer,* July 3, 1990.

5. David Lamb, *The Africans* (New York: Random House, 1987), p. 261.

6. Ibid., p. 145.

7. We sometimes also speak of experts in contexts where there are no formal credentials such as degrees. A world-renowned ballet dancer is an expert dancer; a tennis player who has won the world match at Wimbledon is an expert tennis player; and there is some sense in which a person who has built up a successful and highly profitable business is an expert on how to run a business. However, these kinds of expertise, although highly important in their own right, are not prominent in contexts of argument. In

contexts of argument, what is relevant is the citing of authority to justify claims. Being an expert ballet dancer, tennis player, or businessman means having tremendous skill. But such skill may not be accompanied by an ability to articulate and explain what is done and why it is done.

8. Anecdotal evidence is discussed critically in Chapter 9.

9. There are many complicated problems underlying this dilemma, which tends both to discredit experts in general and to confuse juries and judges. One problem is that science demands a higher level of certainty than law. The relevant issues are by no means addressed by the preliminary remarks made here. This topic is mentioned merely as a specific illustration of the general point that when experts disagree, we cannot prove our point merely by citing an expert who is on our side.

10. Garret Hardin, "A Lamp Not a Breadbasket," *Harper's* magazine, May 1981, p. 85.

11. The topic of assumptions is a difficult and complex one that is handled only in a preliminary way here. A complete treatment would include not only assumptions that pertain to premises but also those underlying the identification of the subject of the argument as an

issue, and those underlying the reasoning used in the argument. Here, since our topic is premises, we discuss only those assumptions that are required for the premises to be acceptable.

12. *The Peterborough Examiner,* April 16, 1981. Reprinted with permission of the *Examiner.*

13. This is the aspect of our discussion of premise acceptability that does not apply to claims in general, because of the specific comparison between the content and acceptability of premises and the content and acceptability of the conclusion that those premises are intended to support.

14. This sort of move works only if the argument in question is deductively valid. If the conclusion is false and the premises deductively entail it, then one or more of the premises is false. If the conclusion is unacceptable and the premises deductively entail it, then one or more of the premises is unacceptable. As was noted by a reviewer of the fourth edition of this text, the kind of reversibility Moore pointed to indicates a need to qualify the discussion of the Challenge of Argument in Chapter 3. When rejection of a conclusion is done in the way Moore did, so that this rejection is used to challenge the whole argument by alleging reversibility, to reject the conclusion is not to avoid the challenge of argument.

15. Laurier LaPierre, *To Herald a Child* (Toronto: Ontario Public School Men Teachers Association, 1981), p. 36. LaPierre is considering the argument that students would not have time, in Canadian schools, to learn languages other than Canada's two official languages, French and English.

16. Even if children did have the inalienable right to learn their mother tongue, it would not follow that it was the duty of the schools (as opposed to their parents) to teach it to them.

17. There is a broader use of "begging the question" in which a person may be said to beg the question against another person, or against a position, when he makes the unwarranted and unsupported claim that that person or position is wrong. For instance, someone who argues that interest rates should be kept low so that business can expand might be said to beg the question as to how much effect interest rates have on business activity. This broader use of "begging the question" is not employed in this book.

chapter six
Working on Relevance

WE NOW PROCEED TO DISCUSS the second condition of an argument's cogency: relevance. The concept of relevance is so basic to thought and the development of knowledge that it is difficult to define and explain. But no matter how adequate the premises of an argument are, they cannot possibly support its conclusion unless they are relevant to it. Thus, we have to try to improve our grasp of this fundamental, but elusive, concept.

Characteristics of Relevance

In this section, there are three basic ideas we wish to explain: positive relevance, negative relevance, and irrelevance. First we will explain these ideas in a general way, and then we will offer more precise definitions.

Positive and negative relevance are relationships between statements that exist when one statement has a bearing on the truth or falsity (and therefore on the acceptability or unacceptability) of the other. To say that a statement is **positively relevant** to another is to say that it counts in favor of it. It constitutes evidence or reason for it, or makes it more acceptable. To say that a statement is **negatively relevant** to another is to say that it counts against it, is reason or evidence that it is false, or makes it less acceptable. If a statement is neither positively relevant nor negatively relevant to another, then it is **irrelevant.** It counts neither for nor against the truth of the other statement; it has no bearing on the matter.

Suppose that *B* is the statement that genetically altered foods are dangerous to human health. Now let *A* be the statement that some genetically altered foods have been shown to cause immune system deficiencies in small children. Here we can see that statement A is positively relevant to statement B; if true, A counts in favor of B's being true. That some genetically altered foods have been shown to cause immune system deficiencies in small children is certainly some reason to think that the genetically altered foods are dangerous to human health. Statement B is relevant to statement A here because it offers evidence for A. In this case, that evidence is relevant without being sufficient to establish A as true.

Contrast this situation with one in which we consider another statement, C, instead of statement A. Let us suppose that C is the statement that genetically altered foods were shown to have no short-term damaging effects on the health of any person in a program of some 100 tests. If C is true, that would be reason to think that B is not true. Again it would not be complete proof. But C is negatively relevant to B; C counts against B being true.

A third considered statement, Z, might have nothing at all to do with B. Let's suppose, for instance, that Z is the statement that the Canadian dollar has a value some 30 percent lower than the American dollar. Z, in this case, makes no difference at all to the truth or falsity of B. As far as B is concerned, Z is irrelevant.

Relevance of a premise to a conclusion is not just a matter of the premise having something to do with the conclusion. That is too vague. The idea of going to Europe has something to do with the idea of going to Africa, because both involve travel and expense. In general, however, whether we should go to Europe is irrelevant to the question of whether we should go to Africa. Our going to Europe generally will be neither a reason for going to Africa nor a reason against going to Africa—even though there may be, in some loose sense, a relationship between these two things.

Relevance is such a basic concept in thinking that it is hard to pin it down with an exact definition.[1] For our purposes, the following definitions are adequate:

POSITIVE RELEVANCE

Statement A is positively relevant to statement B if and only if the truth of A counts in favor of the truth of B.

NEGATIVE RELEVANCE

Statement A is negatively relevant to statement B if and only if the truth of A counts against the truth of B.

IRRELEVANCE

Statement A is irrelevant to statement B if and only if the truth of A counts neither for nor against the truth of B.

When there is positive relevance, one statement supports another; when there is negative relevance, it undermines it. When there is irrelevance, there is no relation of logical support or logical undermining between the two statements.

We have defined relevance and irrelevance as relationships between statements. This is to some degree a simplification, because the relationships between statements have to be understood in context. If we shift the context, or make special assumptions, a statement that was irrelevant to another may become relevant. In fact, we can do this with the example about traveling to Europe and traveling to Africa. Suppose we assume that someone is considering traveling to Tunisia, in northern Africa, and to Italy, in southern Europe. Suppose that we know there are inexpensive boat trips from southern Italy to Tunisia. Given all these circumstances, and assuming that the person wants to save money and is not pressed for time, going to the southern part of Europe might turn out to be a reason for going to the northern part of Africa. One could argue that the statement "We are going to Europe" is in that context positively relevant to the statement "We should go to Africa." The context makes a difference here. In this particular context, we can reasonably connect the idea of going to Europe to the idea of going to Africa. In the absence of some special context such as this one, in which there is additional knowledge about connecting matter, the issue of whether we are going to Europe or not is irrelevant to whether we should go to Africa. When you are evaluating relevance in an argument, you have to consider both the context in which the argument occurs and the background information.

The ARG conditions require positive relevance. If the premises in an argument are to support the conclusion, then they must count in favor of that conclusion—they must give some evidence for it, some reason to think that it is true. If the premises are negatively relevant to the conclusion—that is, actually give reason to suppose the conclusion is incorrect—or if they are irrelevant and have nothing to do with it, there is a fault in the argument. Negatively relevant premises may be called counterconsiderations, because they count against the conclusion. They are in effect objections to the conclusion, and these objections may tell against the argument itself. When assessing claims and arguments, it is necessary to evaluate the evidence against them as well as the evidence supporting them. Counterconsiderations, or objections, are important, as has been mentioned already in the discussion of the dialectical context of an argument in Chapter 3, and are discussed further in Chapter 11.

Let us look at some simple examples of positive relevance. In each of the following cases, the first statement is positively relevant to the second:

(a) 1. Jones has appendicitis, gout, and cancer of the bladder.
    2. Jones is not healthy enough to run the 26-mile Boston Marathon.
(b) 1. Basketball is a game in which height is a great advantage.
    2. Basketball is a game for which physical characteristics of players make a substantial difference in ability.
(c) 1. Corporations are able to increase their profits by decreasing their costs.
    2. Corporations have an incentive to decrease their labor costs.

In each pair, the first statement, if true, would provide some reason to suppose that the second statement is true. In each case, to say that (1) is positively relevant to (2) means that if (1) were true, it would constitute evidence in favor of (2). This claim does not say that (1) is true; nor does it say that (1) is complete proof of (2). It merely says that if true, it is some evidence, at least.

Negative relevance is quite different from positive relevance. Consider the following examples of negative relevance:

(d) 1. Jogging often results in knee injuries.
    2. Jogging improves a person's general health.

(e) 1. Between 10,000 and 100,000 deaths are predicted, by doctors and scientists, to result from the Chernobyl nuclear reactor accident in 1986.
2. Nuclear reactors provide a safe form of energy.

In both these examples, statement (1) is negatively relevant to statement (2). That is, if the first statement is true, there is some reason to think the second one is unacceptable.

Now let's examine some simple examples of irrelevance. A statement is irrelevant to the truth of another statement if it has no bearing on that further statement. That is, whether it is true or false makes no difference at all as far as the second statement is concerned:

(f) 1. Browning has aged terribly during the last ten years.
2. Browning's lecture on the history of Canadian-American relations was seriously flawed.
(g) 1. The Virgin Mary is worshiped especially by those in rural Poland.
2. Worship of the Virgin Mary may be a relic of ancient Goddess religions in Africa.
(h) 1. Natural catastrophes such as earthquakes and tidal waves are beyond human control.
2. Human beings have no freedom of choice concerning their actions.

In all these cases, the first claim provides no evidence either for or against the second one: it is completely irrelevant to it. In the flow of natural arguments, irrelevance can easily escape our attention. In (h), for instance, the fact that we cannot control natural catastrophes has no bearing on the question of whether we have freedom of choice regarding our own actions. But because they both refer to the topic of human control, we may fail to see that (1) is irrelevant to (2).

As we saw in Chapter 3, when we discussed the cogency of arguments, the failure of premises to be positively relevant to the conclusion constitutes a serious flaw in an argument. If the premises of an argument, considered together, are irrelevant to its conclusion, or are negatively relevant, the argument is not cogent. Any case in which the (R) condition of argument adequacy is not satisfied will be a condition in which (G) is not satisfied either. (If premises are not even relevant to the conclusion, they cannot provide good grounds for it.) When (R) is not satisfied, even if (A) is satisfied, the argument is not cogent. No relevant or sufficient reasons have been given to support the conclusion.

Some Ways of Being Relevant

Relevance can take many forms, as should be obvious from the very general way we have had to define it. Premises are positively relevant to the conclusion when, if true, they constitute some reason to believe the conclusion is true. There are many ways the truth of one statement can provide us with reason to believe another.

Relevance and Complete Support:
Deductive Entailment and Validity

Except in anomalous cases of purely technical interest, if the premises of an argument deductively entail its conclusion, they are relevant to that conclusion.[2] In such cases, the premises when taken together give full logical support to the conclusion. Relevance in these cases is, in a way, more than relevance because premises, if relevant, also provide good and sufficient grounds for the conclusion. The (R) condition and the (G) condition are satisfied together, in this sort of case. Deductive entailment, then, is one sure way of getting relevance.

Here is an example in which the premises are relevant to the conclusion because the premises together deductively entail it:

> Unilateral disarmament would not work unless all grievances, or hostile emotions, of the neighbors of the unilateral disarmer were zero. Since this is not the case, unilateral disarmament will not work.[3]

The conclusion here is "unilateral disarmament will not work." The reasons given are that for unilateral disarmament to work, there must be no grievances in neighboring countries, and this just doesn't happen.

The argument is very clear as stated, but it can be clarified further if we set it out in standard form as the following:

1. Unilateral disarmament will not work unless the unilateral disarmer has no neighbors with grievances or hostile emotions.
2. Countries for which unilateral disarmament might be proposed do have neighbors with grievances and hostile emotions.
Therefore,
3. Unilateral disarmament will not work.

Since (1) and (2), taken together, deductively entail (3), they provide conclusive reasons for believing (3). Since that is so, they obviously provide some reason to believe (3). They are relevant—and also provide full grounds—since this is a case of deductive entailment. Conditions (R) and (G) are satisfied together, so the cogency of the argument will depend on the (A) condition.

Relevance and Similarity: Analogy

Deductive entailment is not the only way in which the relevance condition can be met. There are various ways in which statements can support each other, as we saw in Chapter 3. One is by an analogy between things described in the statements. The basis of arguments by analogy is that when two things are known to be similar in a number of respects, we may infer that they are similar in some further respect. For instance, if rats and human beings were shown to have similar enzymes and hormones, this would give some reason to suspect a further similarity as to the way the two species digest sugar. We would be arguing on the basis of an analogy between rats and humans if we experimented with doses of sugar on rats and drew a conclusion about the proportionately similar doses on humans.

No argument by analogy can conclusively prove its conclusion, but when an analogy holds and there are appropriate similarities between cases, information about one case is relevant to another. Analogies may be used for many different reasons; usually a prime reason is that one case is better known and more familiar than another. In the case of rats and people, often experiments done on rats would be illegal and immoral if done on people.

Relevance can be established on the basis of a comparison between one area of experience and another (for example, between living together before and after marriage) or between one political situation and another (conflict in Rwanda and conflict in Burundi; the two African states have a similar ethnic mix of Hutu and Tutsi peoples). When we argue on the basis of analogy, the similarities between the two things compared make points about one relevant to our consideration of the other. These basic similarities establish relevance. Arguments based on analogies are not as logically tight as deductive arguments, but their premises are often genuinely relevant to their conclusions because of the close similarities between the things compared.

Relevance and Experience: Inductive Reasoning

In inductive reasoning, extrapolations are made from the known cases to unknown cases. Events that have been experienced are described, and an inference is drawn that future or yet-to-be experienced events will be similar to those already encountered. (Like analogy, induction is based on considering similar cases together.) In inductive arguments of this type, relevance comes from the basic assumption that regularities that have been encountered already will persist. On this assumption, known cases are relevant to unknown ones. Like most analogies, and unlike deductively valid arguments, inductive arguments cannot absolutely prove their conclusions to be true. But they make them likely or probable—at least in the case of strong inductive arguments. The experienced events are relevant to those not experienced, for the inductive assumption is basically reasonable. (Without it, we could not function in the world at all.)

Here is an example of an inductive argument:

Every medication we have developed so far has turned out to have side effects, that is to adversely affect some aspect of human health that it was not intended to affect. Medication M is a recently developed medication. From past experience, we can expect medication M to have some adverse side effects.

A person who used such an argument would be reasoning as follows:

1. Every previously developed medication has had some adverse side effects.
2. Medication M is a recently developed medication.
Therefore, probably,
3. Medication M will have some adverse side effects.

This argument is inductive, in that it projects a past regularity into the future. Medications are developed to address one sort of problem; when they are ingested, they have effects on the human body. These effects are various and—according to premise (1)—have always included some adverse side effects. That is past human experience with medications. Medication M, being a medication like the others developed for a specific purpose is, on the basis of this past experience, expected to have some adverse effects as well.

We expect many aspects of experience to persist over time. The inductive assumption that is behind such arguments makes the data in the premise relevant to the conclusion, though the premise is about past experience and the conclusion is about the future. Of course, in such a case, relevance will not amount to full proof.

Relevance and Reasons

When premises of an argument support the conclusion convergently, or separately, each premise is put forward as, itself, constituting a reason that the conclusion should be accepted. In such a case, the relevance of each premise has to be assessed separately. Such support is distinct from deductive validity, analogy, and experiential induction.

The following letter to the editor provides an example. The writer is trying to show why a particular concert hall should be preserved.

> As a person who, in the past, enjoyed many concerts in the Eaton Auditorium, I am deeply concerned that this fine concert hall may be destroyed. Apart from (1) the historical significance is (2) a need for a hall of its size and fine acoustical properties. (3) It is also in a central location with public transportation available. This is often forgotten when locating cultural and recreation facilities but will become an increasingly important factor. (4) Toronto has become a city of ever-increasing cultural activity and facilities are needed for these diverse interests. (5) Many of us who are concerned sincerely trust that this much-needed facility will be retained.[4]

The author offers a number of separately relevant premises to support her view: (1) the hall is historically significant; (2) the hall is of a suitable size and has good acoustic properties; (3) the hall has a convenient location; and (4) there is a need for cultural facilities of its type in Toronto, where it is located. (See Figure 6.1.) Each of these factors is put forward as being relevant to the author's conclusion. Each

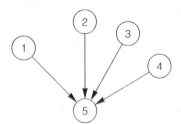

FIGURE 6.1

premise specifies a feature of the hall that would make it serve the purposes a concert hall should serve. The author points to these features to establish the value of the hall as a concert hall and to support her conclusion that the auditorium should be preserved.

In this argument, the premises are relevant to the conclusion because the conclusion is about something that should be done, and the premises each give some reason to do it. Each premise states a reason relevant to establishing that the hall deserves to be preserved. In this example each premise is separately relevant to the conclusion.

We have explained relevance by looking more closely at some of the ways premises can be relevant to a conclusion: by deductive entailment, by analogy (based on similarity of cases), by inductive relationships (based on experience), and as converging reasons. Usually, it is easy to tell in which of these ways relevant premises bear on the conclusion. But even if you cannot tell, the most important thing is to make sure that the premises are relevant somehow. To do this, you have to ask yourself how, and to what extent, the premise would count in favor of the conclusion. What difference would it make to the acceptability of the conclusion if these premises were true? How would they establish the conclusion, or help to establish it? To meet the (R) condition in ARG, the premises must be positively relevant to the conclusion. If they are negatively relevant, or irrelevant, the (R) condition is not satisfied and the (G) condition cannot be satisfied either.

Irrelevance: Some General Comments

If a premise used in an argument is irrelevant to its conclusion, it does not matter one bit whether that premise is true or acceptable; it cannot provide any basis for the conclusion. Obviously, in this case, it cannot possibly provide good grounds for the conclusion. As mentioned previously, an argument that fails on the (R) condition will necessarily fail on (G), and whether it passes on (A) will not matter. From this you can see that irrelevance is a serious flaw in an argument. If you can show that someone else's argument is based on irrelevant premises, you have given a strong objection to it.

An argument in which the premise or premises are irrelevant is sometimes called a **non sequitur.** The Latin words *non sequitur* mean "it does not follow." The premise or premises will not lead you to the conclusion because they are irrelevant to it. The expression *non sequitur* is not used only in connection with arguments. It is often applied to remarks that are surprisingly out of context and seem to have nothing to do with what is going on. Consider:

> *Bill:* The evening air in the mountains had a beautiful cool pine smell. It was wonderful to be there, but unfortunately, we could not spend more time walking around. Perhaps we should drive up again next week, early enough to go for a walk before the lecture.

Shelagh: I wonder whether we'll be home in time to make that long distance phone call before we go to bed.

Bill: Well that's a *non sequitur*! What does a long distance phone call have to do with going for a walk in the mountains?

Another term sometimes used to refer to irrelevance is red herring. A **red herring** is a distracting remark that has no bearing on the topic of discussion and tends to lead people away from the point at issue and distract attention from the fact that the conclusion is not being properly supported. A red herring can be an intentional device to lead people away from an awkward topic, or it can be an unwitting error.

Suppose Mary is discussing her social studies grade with her mother, who is claiming that she does not do enough homework. In responding to her mother, Mary first tries to show that she is doing enough homework by mentioning what she did the day before and how much homework other students do. Then she begins to complain about what was served for supper the night before. In the context, the topic of what has been served for supper, and how good it was or was not, amounts to a red herring. The issue of the quality of yesterday's supper is only a distraction from the real issue. It is irrelevant to the issue of social studies grades and is a red herring as far as that issue is concerned.

It might strike you as amazing that *non sequiturs* and red herrings exist. Don't people know what they are talking about? Can't they stick to the topic? (The answer to this last question is that actually, people are not so very good at sticking to the topic. To explore this matter, try following conversations, panels, and debates with this issue in mind.) Red herrings, *non sequiturs*, and other forms of irrelevance are in fact surprisingly common. In fact, they often deceive unwary audiences. Why? One explanation may be found in the character of the irrelevant material that is introduced. Often the points made are especially interesting, clearly true, or are points of clear agreement between an arguer and the audience. In contexts of controversy, such agreement can seem so important that an audience may forget to ask how the uncontroversial points are related to the topic at hand. Another factor may be that of emotion. As we shall see in more detail later in this chapter, information or ideas that are, in fact, irrelevant may arouse in us such emotions as pity, fear, resentment, anger, envy, or disgust. Sometimes our feelings distract us from the point at issue.

For the present purpose of understanding and evaluating arguments, it does not matter so much what causes people to use or accept arguments containing irrelevance. Our main interest is in understanding what irrelevance is and in learning to recognize some of the common fallacies of relevance.

Logicians have labels for fallacies of relevance that are especially common and interesting. In this chapter, we shall study a number of these fallacies. But we shall not try to learn all of them. This itself can become an irrelevant distraction if the basic goal is to learn to understand and evaluate various types of arguments. You can sometimes sound especially knowledgeable by talking about *non sequiturs* or red herrings, and it is fun to use special fallacy labels, such as *ad hominem*, straw man, guilt by association, and argument from ignorance. Understanding these common types of irrelevance is useful, because studying them makes you better able to spot them. However, our main goal is to recognize irrelevance when we see it. The important thing is to understand that one or more premises are irrelevant, why such premises might be irrelevant, and what difference their irrelevance makes to the cogency of the argument as a whole.

To object to an argument on grounds of relevance is a strong line of criticism. You have to back up the objection by saying why you think the premises used are irrelevant to the conclusion. Presumably, the person who used the argument thought the premises were relevant. If you just say, "What a *non sequitur*!" or "That's irrelevant," it does not put the discussion on a very high level. You have to show how and why such a label applies to the argument you are talking about. All of this serves to emphasize a point we have previously made: criticizing an argument requires that you yourself offer an argument.

EXERCISE SET

Exercise 1: Part A
For each of the following pairs of statements (a) comment as to whether the first statement is relevant to the second, and (b) if you think it is irrelevant, briefly state why.

*1. (a) Elephants have been known to cover the corpses of other dead elephants with leaves and branches, whereas they do not so cover sleeping elephants.

(b) Elephants have a concept of death.

2. (a) In many Third World countries, the governments are run by ill-educated dictators and there is no freedom of the press.

(b) The United States has an admirable and perfectly acceptable system of government.

3. (a) There are tribes in which it is normal and economically useful for two brothers to be married to the same woman.

(b) Marriage as we know it in Western cultures is not a universal human custom.

4. (a) For the conference on conflict resolution, the registration fee will be quite high.

(b) It is unlikely that people with low incomes will attend the conference.

*5. (a) The chemical names of some ingredients of children's snack foods are completely impossible to pronounce.

(b) Some children's snack foods contain dangerous artificial chemicals.

*6. (a) Some French historians dispute whether large numbers of Jews were killed in World War II.

(b) The large number of Jews killed in World War II would have been larger still had it not been for the protective activities of some outstandingly courageous citizens in Holland, France, and Sweden.

7. (a) There are still many social pressures felt by native students in Canadian schools and not felt by white students in Canadian schools.

(b) If there are differences in performance levels between native students and white students in Canadian schools, such differences may not be explained by differences in their capabilities.

8. (a) Swimming places no stress on the knee joints.

(b) Swimming is a safe form of physical exercise for people troubled by problems with their joints.

*9.   (a) Charred rhinoceros bones, thought to be about 300,000 years old, were found in an archaeological site in France.

   (b) Rhinoceri (or rhinoceroses) lived in Europe about 300,000 years ago.

(Based on a report in the Toronto *Globe and Mail*, June 21, 1995)

10.   (a) For many people living in northern Europe, encounters with others whose native language is different from their own are regular and frequent.

   (b) For many people living in northern Europe knowing one or more foreign languages is highly practical.

Exercise 1: Part B

For each of the following passages, (a) determine the conclusion (if any) in each passage, and then (b) indicate any premises that you consider irrelevant to the support of that conclusion. Then (c) state why you think the premise is irrelevant, if you do. *Note:* Not all examples involve irrelevance.

*1.   A number of different religious denominations are represented within the public school system. It is for this reason that the system must be secular, not religious.

2.   Most people take seriously what they have to pay for and take less seriously and are less dedicated to something that other people pay for. Adult students of music pay for their own lessons, whereas children who study music typically have their lessons paid for by their parents. For this reason, in the context of music lessons, we can expect adult students to be more serious and dedicated than children.

3.   *Background:* In 1984, the former prime minister of Jamaica, Michael Manley, published an essay on poverty and underdevelopment in *Harper's* magazine. Manley claimed that poverty in the Third World was a result of imperialism in the colonizing of many countries during the nineteenth century. Thomas Sowell, of the Hoover Institution, wrote objecting to Manley's theory. He said,

"The notion that either the capital or the standard of living in the West depends upon the Third World will not stand the slightest contact with evidence. When the British Empire was at its zenith [peak], around the First World War, more British capital was invested in the United States than in all of Africa or all of Asia outside Australia. The French had more trade with little Belgium than with all its farflung African empire. Germany's trade with its colonies was less than 1 percent of its exports."

(Quoted in "Just What Was Said," Toronto *Globe and Mail*, January 7, 1984)

4.   *Background:* The following report, describing an incident in Falls Church, Virginia, appeared in the Toronto *Globe and Mail*, July 20, 1985.

"A pregnant woman who says she was accused of hiding a basketball under her dress has filed a 600,000 dollar suit against the store that alleged she was shoplifting. A cashier had told her supervisor Ms. Nelson had stolen a basketball and put it under her dress, said Stephen McCarron, Ms. Nelson's lawyer. The lawsuit says Ms. Nelson was given the option of opening her dress or going to the police station. 'I had to disrobe in front of six male security guards and police officers in the store,' said Ms. Nelson. She went into labor shortly after the incident and gave birth to a healthy baby boy, Darius."

   Hint: Does this report contain an argument?

*5.   *Background:* The following is taken from a letter to the editor that appeared in the Toronto *Globe and Mail* for February 9, 1999. The author, Christian Stuhr, is writing to argue that superficial associations between people, sometimes called "degrees of separation" show little about any real connection between them. In interpreting these comments, assume that a missing premise is that there is no significant connection between Stuhr's students and Adolf Hitler.

   "Re: Six Degrees of Separation." So we are all connected more intimately than we think. This is distressing news. While I was at Cornell University, I took a philosophy course from Norman Malcolm. Professor Malcolm was once a student of Ludwig Wittgenstein and remains to this day the philosopher's best-known proponent. A recent study reported that during Wittgenstein's Austrian childhood, he was a school mate of—shudder!—young Adolf Hitler. So I am separated from the fiend of our century by just three steps: Stuhr, to Malcolm; Malcolm to Wittgenstein; Wittgenstein to Hitler. And my students—more than a thousand over the decades—are removed from Hitler by just four degrees. This is most interesting and most disagreeable."

6. Children are unique and sensitive creatures. They are very imaginative, and they are different from adults. Therefore, every child has an absolute right to state-supported education.

7. *Background:* The following passage is taken from a book that describes different sorts of thinkers.

"The most serious Idealist liability derives precisely from the Idealist's greatest strength—reliance on high standards. A typical Idealist blind spot is an inability to recognize just how high those standards are. Sometimes Idealists' standards are set so high that they themselves can't live up to them, not to mention other people."

8. *Background:* The following passage was quoted in the *World Press Review* for July 1994.

"Television in its present form makes it harder, not easier, to understand the world. It's a medium that conveys emotion better than reason, and it has difficulty communicating that which cannot be seen—abstractions as powerful as religious beliefs, ideologies, deficits, foreign languages, and the collective memories, loyalties, and codes of other cultures."

*9. Multicolored fish are more restricted to particular territories than fish of less dramatic coloration. The bright colors serve to warn other fish that they are there. The sense of territory has an important survival function for these fish, and it is indicated by the colors that have

evolved. We can see that a sense of territory is basic in the evolution and nature of higher primates such as humans.

(Adapted from Konrad Lorenz's work on aggression in humans and animals)

*10. *Background:* The following passage is taken from a philosophical book on justifying beliefs in God's existence:

"Suppose religion could be provided with a method of proof. Suppose, for example, that the divine omnipotence was so manifest that whenever anyone denied a Christian doctrine he was at once struck dead by a thunderbolt. No doubt the conversion of England would ensue with a rapidity undreamt of by the Anglican bishops. But since the Christian faith sees true religion only in a free decision made in faith and love, the religion would by this vindication be destroyed. For all the possibility of free choice would have been done away."

(Alastair MacIntyre, *Metaphysical Beliefs* [London: SCM Press, 1957])

11. *Background:* In the late 1970s, university professors in France were accused of incompetence on the basis that students graduating were not well trained. A spokesperson, Francois Chatelet, sought to defend them against this charge. (*Note:* Assume that there is a missing conclusion, which is that professors should not be criticized for giving credits to students who are weak—"idiots.")

"Our degree is not recognized but we have more students than ever. They come because they think they might learn something. Sure there are idiots. And I have given them credits. There are bigger idiots in the Government. Is it up to me to be more rigorous than the electorate?"

(As quoted in the *Canadian Association of University Teachers Bulletin,* September 1978)

12. *Background:* The following was written in response to a proposal to license cats.

"Cats are free spirits, the last really independent creatures around. You can no more license cats than you can license the wind. Dogs may submit to bureaucracy. Cats won't. The same spirit tends to rub off on cat owners. They have enough trouble being pushed around by their cats without being asked to submit to man-made laws. Besides, there's an economic factor. They've never had to buy licenses, so why start? No, it just won't work."

(Quoted by Ralph Johnson in "Charity Begins at Home," *Informal Logic Newsletter,* Vol. iii, No. 3 [June 1981], pp. 4–9)

13.   *Background:* The following letter concerns the issue of what might be the appropriate response by the Catholic church to Catholic public officials in the United States who support abortion rights:

"Both France and Italy, which are overwhelmingly Roman Catholic countries, allow legal abortion. In addition, West Germany and the Netherlands, both roughly half-Catholic, also allow legal abortion. In none of these countries has the national Catholic Church excommunicated or threatened to excommunicate Catholic public officials who are supportive of abortion rights. Charles W. Colson should take note of these facts when he vigorously defends Cardinal John O'Connor's threat to excommunicate American Catholic public officials who support abortion rights. Both he and Cardinal O'Connor must answer the question why Catholic public officials in the United States should be uniquely punished when the Catholic officials of other nations are not similarly threatened. If the Catholic Church is truly universal, shouldn't the hierarchy in the United States practice the tolerance exercised by the Catholic Church in Europe?"

(Letter to the *New York Times,* July 16, 1990)

*14.   *Background:* The following passage is taken from a book review that appeared in the *Atlantic Monthly* in October 1998. The reviewer, David Harvey, is discussing a book about the declining role of the university in contemporary intellectual culture. He is developing an argument for the conclusion that the university has no clear role in contemporary American life. He says,

"What is the point of the University if we realize that we are no longer to strive to realize a national identity, be it an ethnic essence or a republican will? What happens when the culture the university was meant to preserve goes global and transnational along with everything else?"

15.   *Background:* The following excerpt is taken from a letter by Anne Cathrall to *Peace* magazine (March/April 1995) in reply to an article that had appeared in a previous issue.

"In an interview titled "Peace Is the Absence of Fear," Ursula Franklin is quoted as saying, 'Peace is defined not as the absence of war but as the absence of fear.' I assume she means the absence of fear on both sides of a contentious issue. While I agree that this is a necessary condition for peace, I don't think it is sufficient. In the summer of 1990 absence of fear in both Baghdad and Kuwait was a significant factor in Saddam Hussein's decision to invade. Likewise the absence of fear of the collapsing USSR (Soviet Union) emboldened the U.S. to carry out Desert Storm in 1991. Whether considering the continuing Serbian assaults in Bosnia or violence in Canadian schools, it is apparent that people who are truly fearless, because they perceive no-one around who can stop them, and who are in some way aggrieved, can become thugs. Often their victims feel no fear prior to the attack because they didn't see it coming."

16.   *Background:* This is Ursula Franklin's reply to Anna Cathrall's criticism, quoted in Exercise 15.

"I have no argument with the spirit of Anna Cathrall's letter, although I do not think that the bravado of 'to hell with the consequences' that she describes is fearlessness; it is rather recklessness, the absence of accountability, not the absence of fear."

(*Peace* magazine, March/April, 1995)

17.   *Background:* The following passage is taken from Ian Buruma, *The Wages of Guilt: Memories of War in Germany and Japan* (New York: Penguin, 1994), p. 61.

"In 1960, hundreds of thousands demonstrated in Tokyo and other cities against the ratification of a new security pact with the United States. The pact actually reduced American powers in Japan, but it was seen as an example of American intervention nonetheless. People thought, not without reason, that the United States, in collusion with the conservative Japanese elite, was undermining the peace constitution."

Fallacies Involving Irrelevance

A fallacy is a common mistake in arguing, a mistake in the reasoning that underlies an argument. Some fallacious arguments are hard to spot; we may think they are cogent, satisfying the ARG conditions, even though they are not. Fallacies of relevance are mistakes in argument, mistakes that involve irrelevance. There are many different ways of being irrelevant. The specific fallacies of relevance discussed here have been given special names because they are quite common and can be misleading.

Not all fallacies involve irrelevance (R). Begging the question, for instance, involves the acceptability of premises (A). Other fallacies are concerned with the sufficiency of the premises to establish the conclusion (G). In this chapter, however, we are concentrating particularly on relevance and irrelevance, so we shall discuss only fallacies in which the mistake in reasoning is due to mistaking an irrelevant premise for a relevant one.

The Straw Man Fallacy

In Chapter 2, we discussed the interpretation of passages—whether they contain arguments, how to identify the premises and conclusions, and how to decide to add missing premises or conclusions. You were advised not to read in extra premises or conclusions without good evidence that the author of the argument would have accepted them. The policy of interpretive charity was discussed; you should be especially careful if you attribute an implausible or false claim, or a blatantly flawed argument, to a speaker or writer. If you criticize a weak position that an author did not really hold and infer from your criticism that his real position is flawed, you have committed the **straw man fallacy.**

Suppose that someone claims that X is true, and you represent him or her as having claimed Y (a worse or less plausible position or claim than X). You then attack Y and understand or represent yourself as having refuted X, the position that person actually holds. In such a case, you have committed the straw man fallacy. Instead of refuting a real man, you have refuted a "man of straw." A man of straw is easier to knock over than a real man. In believing that your attack is relevant to the real position when it is not, you have committed an error in thinking.

THE STRAW MAN FALLACY

The straw man fallacy is committed when a person misrepresents an argument, theory, or claim, and then, on the basis of that misrepresentation, claims to have refuted the position that he has misrepresented.

To avoid the straw man fallacy, then, you have to interpret other people's claims, arguments, and positions patiently, accurately, and fairly. You have to base your criticisms on the position someone actually holds, not on some other position that (in your mind) is related to it. The best way to avoid the straw man fallacy is to make sure that you direct your comments and criticisms to the actual position held. The actual position held may be quoted, in which case it is put forward in exactly the same words as those used by the person who originally expressed it. Clearly, you cannot misrepresent people by quoting their exact words—though you still need to interpret the quoted material carefully, to avoid error. In addition to being logically committed to exactly what they seriously say or write, people are logically committed to any claim that is deductively entailed by what they seriously say or write. They also have some responsibility for claims that are strongly suggested by what they seriously say or write. It is easiest to go wrong when you are working with what is strongly suggested. You have to make sure that the suggestions are not just in your own mind but are interpretations people would typically make in the context in which the argument or position was stated.

These remarks will be clearer if we see how they apply to a specific example. The Cold War, during which the United States and the Soviet Union (now Russia) regarded each other as intractable enemies, was in a particularly negative phase in the early 1980s. At that time, writer Sidney Lens made the following statement:

> It is mere cliché to say we cannot trust the Russians.[5]

Lens made this comment his theme in a short essay in which he argued that no government should be trusted. He contended that disarmament and foreign policy arrangements had to be made in such a way that international agreements for verification procedures and a strong basis in national interests would supplement trust as the grounds for lasting agreements. His comment is just the sort of thing that could easily be misinterpreted.

Anyone wishing to explore the idea that it is a mere cliché to say that we cannot trust the Russians could quote Lens directly to this effect and by doing so avoid misrepresenting his position. If you wish to reword the comment, you must ensure that what you attribute to Lens is deductively entailed by what he actually said.

Suppose, for instance, you attributed view (i) to Lens:

> (i) It is a mere common saying that the Russians are not trustworthy.

This rephrasing would be quite all right because (i) is merely a verbal variation on the original claim; you get (i) by replacing the word *cliché* with the words *common saying* and replacing the phrase "we cannot trust the Russians" with "the Russians are not trustworthy." The original claim deductively entails (i). In making that claim, Lens was clearly asserting (i). Putting the view as (i) rather than as the original statement would be proper interpretation. You would not commit the straw man fallacy by doing that.

You would venture further in interpretation if you said that Lens had asserted (ii):

(ii) It is false to say that the Russians are not trustworthy.

This remark, (ii), is not deductively entailed by Lens's original comment. It is perhaps suggested by the word *mere* in the expression "mere cliché." A statement that is merely a cliché is one that is only a cliché; perhaps a mere cliché is a statement that is not true. (Being true could be one way of being something more than a cliché.) Whether Lens meant to assert (ii) is debatable.

If we represented Lens as having asserted (iii), we would clearly be misinterpreting his comment:

(iii) The Russians are just as reliable as the British.

No such comparison as this was stated, entailed, or even suggested by the original remark about trusting the Russians, so (iii) would amount to a straw man interpretation. If you interpreted Lens as claiming (iii) and then went on to refute (iii) and claim thereby to have refuted Lens, you would have committed the straw man fallacy.

It is easiest to avoid misrepresenting a theory or position when you have a specific version of it to deal with—as in our example here. You then simply check to see that your interpretation has a firm basis in what was actually said. You do not add premises or conclusions inappropriately, and you proceed with great care in reading into the position anything that is not either explicitly said or deductively entailed by what is said. By taking care in this way, you can avoid committing the straw man fallacy. On those occasions when you are able to compare the author's representation of another position with the original statement of that position, this strategy will help you spot instances of the straw man fallacy.

Let us consider a specific passage and see how easy it can be to commit this fallacy. The following paragraph is taken from a book on building stable, effective relationships:

> But it would be a mistake to define a good relationship as one in which we agree easily, just as it would be a mistake to define a good road as one that is easy to build. While it is easier to build a good road across a prairie than through mountains, a good road through mountains may be more valuable than one across a prairie. Similarly, a good relationship among parties with sharp differences may be more valuable than one among parties who find it easy to agree.[6]

This passage might be misinterpreted in a number of ways. The authors might be represented as arguing from an analogy between roads and relationships. It would then be possible to say that mountain and prairie roads have nothing to do with relationships and that the authors are arguing irrelevantly. However, looking carefully, we can see that the passage does not contain an argument. (The words *while* and *similarly* are not logical indicator words here. *While* has the meaning of *although*, and *similarly* indicates a comparison, but not an argument from analogy.) The example of prairie and mountain roads serves to vividly illustrate the point that the authors are making about relationships; it gives them a way of stating their point, and it is not supposed to support that point.

It is important, too, to understand what the authors are saying about relationships. They are saying that a good relationship between parties with differences may be more valuable than one between parties who easily agree. This is a qualified statement. We would be misinterpreting these authors if we read them as saying that difficult relationships are always more valuable than easier ones. Another misinterpretation would be to read the passage as saying that relationships where agreement comes easily are of no value. The authors do not say this; they say, rather, that such relationships are sometimes of less value than the other sort. If we were to interpret this passage as posing an argument based on an analogy between roads and relationships, or as making a categorical claim about all difficult relationships as compared to all easy ones, or as dismissing the value of relationships where agreement is easy, we could then easily dismiss the authors' ideas as silly. But our criticisms would be misplaced—directed against straw men or women, not real ones.

The straw man fallacy is more difficult to detect when the views being criticized are not quoted explicitly. This happens when the positions discussed are general ones, not identified with the stated ideas of any single specific person. Examples are the environmentalist position on DNA research, feminism, evolutionary theory, the capitalist position on free markets, the belief in free will, and so on. In these contexts, you have to depend on your own background knowledge to determine the real content of the position. In this case the straw man fallacy is less clear-cut than it was in the previous example. But often distortions are quite blatant and detectable even in the absence of explicit quotations.

Consider, for instance, the following example of an advertisement written to criticize the "soft energy" option. Soft energy advocates urge that solar and wind power be developed as environmentally sound alternatives to nuclear power and oil and gas. The advertisement assumes that soft energy advocates want everyone to adopt a rural lifestyle and attacks their view on the basis of this erroneous assumption.

> Wrong for many. That's the reality of 'soft energy'—massive, often unsightly projects. But the dream is appealing partly because it seems small-scale and spread out, like another fantasy of the back-to-nature movement—do-it-yourself farming for everybody. Yet to give every American family of four a 40 acre farm would take more land—including deserts and mountains—than there is in all of the lower 48 mainland states. And such a program would surely mean good-bye wilderness. Besides, what about people who like cities, or suburbs rather than constant ruralism in between? There may be a lot of good in soft energy to supplement conventional power. But we're uneasy with people who insist it will do the whole job and who then insist on foisting their dreams on the rest of us. Especially when their dreams can't stand up to reality.[7]

To detect the straw man fallacy here, you have to ask yourself what the advocates of soft energy are recommending. Their position is that energy sources like the sun and wind are better, environmentally and politically, than nuclear power, oil, or gas. Whether their position is correct is a biological and policy issue about the quantities, costs, and production effects of these various sources of energy.

Soft energy advocates have a position about how energy should be produced. Their position on energy is not a position about farming or lifestyle. The possibility that there is not enough land on the U.S. mainland states for all families of four to have their own farms is completely irrelevant to the merits of the various sources of energy. The advertisement misrepresents the soft energy advocates, changing their position from one about the economics and biology of energy to one about farms and a return to nature. The misrepresented position then becomes vulnerable to attack. As far as the real soft energy position is concerned, the comments in the advertisement are completely irrelevant. No relevant evaluation of the soft energy position is offered in the passage. In contexts where people are arguing against a position, it is wise to be suspicious about how they represent that position. Look carefully to see that the representation is fair.

The *Ad Hominem* Fallacy

Another kind of irrelevance deserving special attention is the *ad hominem* fallacy. The words *ad hominem*, in Latin, mean "against the man." (In the interests of gender inclusivity, it would be more accurate to speak of the fallacy of arguing against the person, but this label is still the standard one.) The **ad hominem fallacy** is one in which a critic attacks a person instead of arguing against the claims, arguments, or theories that the person has put forward. In *ad hominem* reasoning, people try to prove a point by attacking a person who holds the opposite view. Or they criticize a person's personality, background, actions, or situation, and from that they conclude that his or her position is faulty. These debating tactics are almost always mistaken as far as logic is concerned. Yet they are often practically and rhetorically very effective.

Many a proposal has been defeated because the person putting it forward was not the "right" age, sex, race, nationality, ethnicity, or social class, or had some personality trait such as a bent posture, high voice, or unattractive appearance, that was taken to be undesirable. Any argument that begins with a premise to the effect that a person is inadequate in some such way as this and moves to the conclusion that his or her position should not be accepted is grounded on irrelevance. Such arguments are called abusive *ad hominems*. The premises abuse a person by attacking him or her on the basis of some characteristic, and the conclusion states that the person's claims or arguments are not acceptable on the basis of the personal attack.

Implicitly, we are relying on *ad hominem* arguments when we reject a presentation because the person making it does not look presentable and middle class, or when we are skeptical of a view simply because all those who support it are young and have not held responsible jobs. Far too often we connect the merits of theories with the personal qualities of the people who support those theories. These are abusive *ad hominems*.

In other arguments, people are attacked not so much because of their personal traits but because of their actions or circumstances. These arguments are called circumstantial *ad hominems*. An example would be rejecting a doctor's argument against smoking because the doctor herself was a smoker, or rejecting the idea that wages should be kept low because the politician who is supporting this idea himself has a high income.

The following is an example of a circumstantial *ad hominem* argument. The author, Gordon Lowe, reviews a book by Thomas Szasz. Thomas Szasz is an outspoken critic of psychiatry who has for several decades argued in the most categorical terms that mental illness does not exist. Szasz uses the phrase "the myth of mental illness" and argues that no one is really mentally ill. Lowe picks up on this by titling his review "The Myth of Szasz." He makes a number of points against Szasz, the last of which is that Szasz does not live up to his own principles.

> He launches his attack of psychiatry from a unique and special position. He is an M.D., Professor of Psychiatry. . . . He is on the editorial board of at least four medical and psychiatric journals and on the board of consultants of a psychoanalytic journal. That is, he is not only a practising psychiatrist and a teacher of psychiatry, but a veritable pillar of the psychiatric community. What on earth can he tell his students? . . . How can Szasz reconcile what he professes with a professorship? He sees the whole psychiatric subculture as a "medical tragedy" and a "moral challenge," insists that it must be improved, then adds "but we cannot do this so long as we remain psychiatrists." Why then is Szasz still a psychiatrist? . . . His logic is relentless only when he applies it to his colleagues. He appears to regard himself as exempt from his own criticism merely because he is critical.[8]

If Lowe were to go on to conclude that Szasz's theory about psychiatry is incorrect, on the grounds that Szasz himself is personally inconsistent in his support for this theory, he would have committed a circumstantial *ad hominem*: inferring the incorrectness of a claim or position from the personal inconsistency in the person putting forward that claim or position.

Some other *ad hominem* arguments are less obvious and direct. Consider the following excerpt from a column entitled "Emotion Drowns Masculine Logic." The author assumes that logic is something men are good at and women cannot do, and he thinks there is a considerable decline in the quality of public discourse due to the influence of feminism and feminists. He says:

> Syllogistic reasoning (all birds have wings; all crows are birds; therefore all crows have wings) has been the hallmark of vibrant, masculine societies from time immemorial. It has, in particular, been the primary force behind the extraordinary theological, political, social and scientific achievements of Western man. This force is nearly spent, and blame attaches almost entirely to the carping, whining, and *kvetching* of North American feminists who've long complained syllogistic logic offends their social levelling egalitarian ideals and is just an evil imposition by the white, male patriarchy anyway. It's more likely *most feminists are too mentally lazy for such intellectual rigor, but seek to hide this sloth behind a veil of sham do-gooder-ism.*[9]

There are many problems with this passage. Several premises are clearly unacceptable, and there is abundant use of emotionally negative language *carping, whining, sloth*, and *sham*, among others. (In fact the language is offensive and abusive.) There is good reason to accuse the author of committing the straw man (or woman) fallacy if he is accusing feminists as a group of subscribing to the assertion that syllogistic logic is some kind of patriarchal imposition. This passage illustrates the fact that it is entirely possible to commit several different errors in logic at the same time. But our interest at the moment is in the *ad hominem*. If we were to spell out an argument on how the alleged sloth of feminists fits into the picture, and attribute it to the author, it would look something like this:

1. Feminists are too mentally lazy to do logic.
2. Feminists seek to hide their mental laziness behind a veil of sham do-gooderism.

Therefore,

(3) Feminist criticisms of syllogistic reasoning are wrong (see Figure 6.2).

FIGURE 6.2

In this interpretation (3) is inserted as a missing conclusion. We might worry that the argument is so weak that to attribute it to the author would be to commit the straw man fallacy. In this respect, the passage is typical of many that contain *ad hominem* remarks. We may sometimes not know whether to interpret the *ad hominem* material as premises and understand that there is an implicit, or missing, conclusion. If there are no premises and conclusion, there is no argument. On that interpretation, the *ad hominem* content gives no support to the arguer's overall position. If there are premises, and a missing conclusion is assumed, those premises are irrelevant to that conclusion, and there is still no support. In either case, the same fundamental point about relevance can be made: the *ad hominem* comments are not relevant to the substantive issue under discussion.

Discussions of personalities and personal failings only rarely are relevant to discussions of substance. The comments about feminists being mentally lazy are unsubstantiated, would be easily refutable by counterexamples, and are irrelevant to the issue of whether feminists are responsible for lowering the quality of public discourse. They show us nothing about public discourse, logic, emotion, or the syllogism.

We have said that typically premises about personalities do not lend support to conclusions about matters of substance. Now it is time to explain why we have used the word *typically*. By this usage, we suggest that there are some cases in which personality and character considerations are relevant to the logical assessment of theories, positions, and arguments—and indeed there are such cases.

First, sometimes an argument or stance is actually about a person. For instance, a man may contend that he is a suitable candidate to be police chief. Here this person's character is the issue. Thus someone who brings aspects of the candidate's character into the debate is not committing any fallacy of relevance. Suppose someone were to argue the following:

1. McTaggart has repeatedly been accused of assault and of drunk driving.
So,
2. McTaggart does not have a good reputation for compliance with the law.
Therefore,
3. McTaggart is a poor candidate for police chief.

Such an argument would employ relevant premises and would not be *ad hominem*. *Ad hominem* is a fallacy occurring when premises about personal characteristics are used in an attempt to refute claims and positions to which they are not relevant. Here the conclusion is also about McTaggart himself, and premise (2), defended in a subargument, is relevant to it.

The second category of exception is more complicated and takes us back to the discussions of authority and testimony in Chapter 5. *Ad hominem*, authority, and testimony have a certain inverse logical relationship. *Ad hominem* involves the improper use of personal traits to criticize claims, whereas authority and testimony concern the proper use of a person's credible expertise and experience to support views. If you are deciding whether to accept a claim on someone's authority, then aspects of that person's background (his or her other qualifications and experience as a scientist, for instance) and character (his or her honesty, accuracy of observations, and independence) are relevant to this decision. Some aspects are relevant to the question of whether this person does qualify as an authority or is in a position to offer reliable testimony. Others are relevant to the issue of whether the question at hand is one we should be willing to accept on authority.

Consider the following example. Rosalie Berthell is a biologist and statistician who has emphasized that damage to sperm and other human tissue can occur due to radiation, even when radiation is at extremely low levels.[10] Now there is considerable disagreement among biostatisticians and biophysicists as to how the data on low-level radiation effects should be interpreted. Suppose we were to argue as follows:

1. Berthell is a figure whose findings have been disputed by other people in her field.
So,
2. We cannot accept Berthell's claims solely on the basis of her authority as an expert.

Here, the premise is about Berthell as a person, but the argument from (1) to (2) is not an *ad hominem*. Why not? Partly it is because the information in (1) is relevant to (2), as is obvious when we recall our discussion in Chapter 5 about proper appeals to authority. The information that Berthell is someone whose claims have been disputed does not constitute a personal attack on her, and it bears directly on the issue of whether appeal to her authority can be appropriate in this case. We should note that the conclusion in the previous argument is not about low-level radiation as such. It is about whether Berthell's claims about low-level radiation can be accepted solely on her authority.

Reasoning from character and background never establishes points of substance about other topics, but it is relevant to the credibility of a person and thus may be relevant to our decision about how seriously a person's testimony or authority should be taken. It would be *ad hominem* if anyone were to argue as follows:

1. Berthell has no children.
Therefore,
2. Berthell is an unfulfilled woman.
Therefore,
3. Berthell is not an authority on low-level radiation effects.

As a matter of fact, claim (1) is true. But it does not substantiate (2) and in any event (2) would not substantiate (3). Whether Berthell ever had children and whether she might or might not be fulfilled as a woman are claims entirely irrelevant to the issue of whether she is an expert as to the harmfulness of low-level radiation.

Similar points can be made in the context of evaluating testimony. Suppose you must depend on personal testimony to accept a claim. In such a case, you will not be committing a fallacy if you reason that because the person testifying is unreliable as to honesty, accuracy of observation, or independence, the claim cannot be accepted solely on the basis of his or her testimony. Here information about character (past dishonesty, for instance) is relevant to your decision to accept testimony or suspend judgment. Such reasoning is used frequently in courts of law. If a person known to have lied about important matters were to testify in a criminal trial, the defense lawyer would try to bring out his past dishonesty, and it would be sufficient reason not to accept key statements solely on the basis of his testimony.

We can sum up these exceptions and our account of the *ad hominem* fallacy as follows:

THE *AD HOMINEM* FALLACY
A premise about the background, personality, character, or circumstances of a person is irrelevant to the merits of his or her theories and arguments, except in the very special case in which those theories and arguments happen to be about the person.

Specific points about a person's background may bear on the reliability of testimony or the legitimacy of authority. That means that they are relevant to our decision whether to accept his or her claims on testimony or authority even though they are not directly relevant to the question of whether these claims are true or false.

To reason from premises about the backgrounds, personalities, characters, or circumstances of people to substantive conclusions about their arguments or theories is to commit the *ad hominem* fallacy unless the premises are relevant to the conclusion in one of the ways described earlier.

Generally, points about personality and character are irrelevant to the substance of a case. Only in quite special circumstances are they more than rhetorical distractions from the main point.

The Guilt-by-Association Fallacy

We have seen that in the *ad hominem* fallacy, an argument or theory is criticized by means of attacks on the person who holds it. The **guilt-by-association fallacy** is similar, except that in this case the attack on the person is indirect. In this fallacy, comments are made linking a person with a group or movement that is commonly believed to be bad. The implication is that the person himself is also in some sense bad and, usually, that his opinions are incorrect.

Frequently, references to Hitler and the Nazis are used in fallacies of guilt by association—probably because the Nazi movement is one that nearly everyone agrees was terrible. For instance, many who argue against legalizing voluntary euthanasia contend that it is morally evil because it was practiced in Hitler's Germany. This is a guilt-by-association criticism. The fact that something once happened in a terrible context does not show that the thing itself is bad or that it would be bad in all other contexts. To associate advocates of voluntary euthanasia with the Nazis is slander pure and simple. At this point, guilt by association has become vicious.

In the example of defenders of voluntary euthanasia and Hitler's Germany, the connection alleged is wholly fictitious. People who advocate voluntary euthanasia in contemporary North America are not fascists and never supported Hitler. But sometimes, even when a connection is a real one, it does not give a basis for any criticism. When discussing the *ad hominem* fallacy, we saw that only in rare cases are personal characteristics relevant to the substantive issues under discussion. In guilt-by-association fallacies there is a charge against the person on the basis of an association, real or imagined, with a group or movement thought to be disreputable. Such associations are irrelevant to the merits of people's arguments or opinions. Even if someone really is a member of a group that really is disreputable, it is still likely that he has some beliefs not held by the group as a whole, and that the group as a whole has some correct beliefs. Given these possibilities, you obviously cannot get very far by arguing from his "guilt" in being associated with others who hold incorrect beliefs to the conclusion that his beliefs or arguments are wrong.

Here is a case of guilt by association, found in a report describing the responses of Canadian doctors to a study of medical insurance. The study was done by Emmett Hall. Canada has state-supported universal medical insurance, but at the time this argument was written, many doctors had been expressing dissatisfaction with the level of payment they receive from the scheme. They had begun to practice "extra-billing," charging patients more than the state-supported scheme would pay and having patients make up the difference between the two amounts. Hall's report on medical insurance recommended that extra-billing be disallowed for doctors receiving payment from the scheme: doctors would have to bill entirely within the state-supported scheme or opt out of it altogether. To this suggestion, the following response was made:

> Of Mr. Hall's fear that extra-billing will destroy the health care systems and discriminate between rich and poor, Dr. Mandeville said that this is a socialist concept that comes through in a socialist report. Hospitals treat people equally more than any other segment of society. Just look at the hospital.[11]

If Dr. Mandeville is correctly quoted here, then he certainly seems to have committed the fallacy of guilt by association. It comes when he terms the resistance to extra-billing "a socialist concept" and says it is part of "a socialist report."

For free-enterprise doctors, socialism may appear to be a terrible thing, and many of the public in North America have been encouraged to link socialism with communism—and communism with prison camps and secret police. (This link is also guilt by association.) Since it is believed in many circles in North America that socialism is awful, Mandeville tries to dispute Hall's view by linking it with socialism. Linking a person's argument or claim to something undesirable is the classic device of guilt by association. The connection with socialism—real or imagined—does not show that Hall's view was incorrect. It is irrelevant to that issue. Socialism concerns the ownership and control of resources and the distribution of income, whereas Hall was concerned about equality of access to health care. There is no real connection between Hall's proposal and socialism. Even if there were a real connection, it would not show that there is anything wrong with Hall's proposal.

To sum up, we can define the fallacy of guilt by association as follows:

THE GUILT-BY-ASSOCIATION FALLACY

The fallacy of guilt by association is committed when a person or his or her views are criticized on the basis of a supposed link between that person and a group or movement believed to be disreputable. The poor reputation of any group is irrelevant to the substantive correctness of its own views, or of the views of any member of the group, or of the views held by people or groups that may be loosely connected with it.

Guilt by association is often not real guilt or real association. Even when the association is real and the guilt of the associated group is real, it does not transfer logically to every opinion held by the associated person.

It is possible to define a fallacy of virtue by association analogous to that of guilt by association. Just as it is irrelevant to criticize a claim or theory on the basis of an alleged link with a negatively regarded group, it would be irrelevant to try to buttress a claim or theory on the basis of its link with some positively regarded group. Even if the very "best" people believe something or do something, that something may be incorrect. Trying to infer virtue by association would be a fallacy, just as guilt by association is. But virtue by association is not usually mentioned as a distinctive argumentative type.

Fallacious Appeals to Ignorance

There are many things people do not know or have not been able to prove. Sometimes fallacious arguments are based on this ignorance, in which case the **fallacy of appeals to ignorance** occurs. If we do not know something, then that point is often an important one to observe. The problem comes with attempts to infer from the fact that we do not know the claims, the conclusion that they are either true or false. An argument of the type

1. We do not know that statement *S* is true.
Therefore,
2. Statement *S* is false.

is a fallacious argument. The premise is irrelevant to the conclusion because the premise is about what we do not presently know regarding *S* and the conclusion is about *S* itself. Similarly, to argue

1. We do not know that statement *S* is false.
Therefore,
2. Statement *S* is true.

would also be a fallacy. If there are discoveries we have not been able to make, this fact shows only the limits of our knowledge. It does not show how things are in the world, distinct from our beliefs or knowledge about them. It would also be fallacious to argue that since we have no grounds to accept not-*S*, we should accept *S*, or that since we have no grounds to accept *S*, we should accept not-*S*. For instance, from the fact that we do not know that genetically altered foods cause cancer, it does not follow that those foods do not cause cancer. From the fact that scientists have not yet proven beyond all doubt that so-called greenhouse gases are causing climate change on the earth, it does not follow that these gases are not causing such climate change. What follows from ignorance or lack of proof is simply that we do not know.

Slightly more subtle forms of the argument from ignorance occur when people argue from our failure to know the truth or falsity of some claim, *S*, to the conclusion that some further claim, *R*, should be accepted. This sort of error would be committed in the following cases:

(a) (1) We do not know the natural cause of phenomenon X.
Therefore,
    (2) X must have a supernatural cause.
(b) (1) No genetic basis for disease D has been discovered by research scientists.
Therefore,
    (2) Disease D is caused by poor habits and an unhealthy lifestyle.

In both (a) and (b), the premise is irrelevant to the conclusion. The fact that we do not know one thing is not a relevant reason for believing another.

Many issues are such that it is hard to get compelling evidence either way. Think, for instance, of questions about the existence of ghosts, life on other planets, and UFOs, or of the reality of telepathic communication. Because of the nature of these things, it is hard to prove either that they exist or that they do not exist. With ghosts, for instance, people seem to see and hear them, and some events that people want to explain by hypothesizing ghosts as the cause have occurred. However, we cannot get conclusive evidence that ghosts are present on any given occasion, no matter how fervent people may be in their testimony. A ghost is supposed to be an immaterial spirit, representing the soul of someone who has died. Representations such as voices and apparitions that have no known natural cause are often thought to be ghosts. But the problem is that you cannot be sure they are. (To think so would be to make the same mistake as in (a) above—to conclude that something that happens must have a supernatural cause because there is no known natural cause for it.)

In some New Age religions, it is fashionable to believe in reincarnation. People practice something they call "channeling," and think that they are connected with spirits informing them of lives of past selves. To critics they may reply, "You can't show I'm wrong. You can't prove that I didn't have these past lives in which I was a Mongol warrior and a Greek slave maiden." But the fact—if, indeed, it is a fact—that a conclusive *disproof* of a claim about past lives cannot be stated is no reason to believe that the claim a person lived those lives is true. To think that it offered such a reason would be to reason irrelevantly. Ignorance as to disproof cannot be proof or cogent argument. Ignorance is just that: lack of knowledge.

If arguing from ignorance were a sound way to argue, we could both prove and disprove the existence of ghosts! First, we could argue that since we have not been able to prove that ghosts do exist, ghosts do not exist. Then, we could turn around and argue that since we have not been able to prove that ghosts do not exist, they do exist. That is, we could argue from ignorance in two directions and thus arrive at inconsistent conclusions. Obviously, something has gone wrong. The mistake is in thinking that from our inability to definitely confirm or definitely disconfirm the existence of ghosts, we can reach a conclusion about their existence or nonexistence.

To argue that a new product is safe because it has not been proven to be dangerous is to appeal fallaciously to ignorance. This fallacious line of argument has been of great public importance in some policy issues. An important concept in these disputes is that of the burden of proof. **Burden of proof** is not a fallacy; it is a concept related to fallacious appeals to ignorance. The notion of the burden of proof is that there exists an obligation, or duty, to support one's claims.

Where does the burden of proof lie—with those who seek to restrict a product, or with those who seek to market it? Until recently, it has generally been thought that those who would restrict or ban a new product have the burden of proof: it is they who must provide studies to indicate that the product they seek to restrict is harmful.[12] Behind this particular allocation of the burden of proof is probably the assumption that, other things being equal, markets should be free. In the past few years, public thinking on this matter has shifted to some extent, partly due, no doubt, to well-publicized cases of drugs and other products with unforeseen harmful effects. We may see a shift to the idea that those who wish to market new products should first prove, to a rigorous degree, that these products are safe. Issues in this area are fascinating, and rather complex, both from the point of view of logic and from the point of view of public policy. But however the burden of proof is allocated, it is clear that a mere appeal to the failure to demonstrate either harmfulness or safety will not prove the opposite.

Because of the way they are worded and the context in which they appear, appeals to ignorance may be subtle enough to easily escape our attention. Consider, for instance, the following example, taken from a book about bringing up children. The author, A. S. Neill, is trying to show that punishment should never be used:

To say that punishment does not always cause psychic damage is to evade the issue, for we do not know what reaction the punishment will cause in the individual in later years.[13]

Neill suggests that punishment may cause psychic damage in children. His reason seems to be that we do not know what their reaction to punishment received now will be in later years. If this is what Neill is saying, the appeal is to ignorance and it is fallacious. Neill does at least qualify his conclusion, admitting that he knows that our ignorance does not prove that there may be damage. His argument is of the type:

1. We do not know that not-S.
Therefore,
2. S may be true.

If we interpret the conclusion, (2), as claiming only that for all we know, S may be true, then (2) does follow from (1). But if we interpret (2) as claiming that there is some kind of significant likelihood of S being true, that conclusion does not follow. Since Neill is giving a practical argument about how children should be treated, he clearly needs a likelihood that has some practical significance. Thus, in the context of his argument, we should interpret (2) as asserting more than a purely abstract possibility. On this interpretation, (2) is not supported by (1) and (1) is in fact not even relevant to (2). Neill has committed the fallacy of appealing to ignorance.

To spot fallacious appeals to ignorance, use the following procedure:

1. Look for premises with phrases such as "we do not know," "no one has been able to prove," "is not yet confirmed," "has never been discovered," and "has not been shown."
2. Check whether the conclusion asserts that the statement not known is false, or that it is true, or that it is probable or improbable.
3. Check to see whether a further, logically distinct statement is inferred from ignorance of the initial statement.

If (1) is true and either of (2) or (3) is true, the argument amounts to a fallacious appeal to ignorance.

To sum up, the fallacy of appealing to ignorance may be described as follows:

FALLACIOUS APPEALS TO IGNORANCE

An argument exemplifies a fallacious appeal to ignorance if and only if the premises describe ignorance, lack of confirmation, lack of proof, or uncertainty regarding a statement S; and a conclusion about the truth or falsity or probability or improbability of S, or a further statement, is inferred simply on the basis of this ignorance. From ignorance we can infer only lack of knowledge. We cannot infer truth or falsity or objective probability or improbability.

Fallacious Appeals to Popularity

Many arguments are based on popularity. Someone tries to show that a product is good because many people select it or that a belief is correct because many people hold it. Such arguments are flawed because the merits of something are one matter and its popularity another. The problem is that things can be popular for many reasons, and only one of these is their good quality.[14] It would be different if people selected products for only one reason—quality—and if they held their beliefs as a result of only one kind of cause—careful, deliberate evaluation of pertinent evidence. Since this is not the case, popularity is not good evidence either for quality or for truth.

People may choose products because those products are cheap, because they have been well advertised, because they are for sale at a convenient store, because their friends have bought them (another appeal to popularity), or for many other reasons having little to do with the quality of the product. Similarly, they may believe things because they have heard them somewhere, read them in the paper, or picked them up during childhood. A claim may be widely believed only because it is a common prejudice. Thus, the fact that it is widely believed is irrelevant to its rational acceptability.[15]

Arguments in which there is a **fallacious appeal to popularity** are based on premises that describe the popularity of a belief, action, or thing ("Everybody's doing it," "Everybody's buying it," "Everybody believes it," "Well, isn't that what most people think?"), and the conclusion asserts that the belief is true, the action is right, or the thing is good. These arguments are fallacious because the popularity of a belief, action, or product is in itself irrelevant to the question of its merits. The fallacy of appealing to popularity is also sometimes called the bandwagon fallacy, or the fallacy of jumping on a bandwagon.

Here is an example of a fallacious appeal to popularity:

> The perfume of the new millenium. Women of our century choose a subtle feminine fragrance. Carfoor is the most popular choice of the millenial woman. Career women say, "It's feminine, but discrete." Delightful, subtly feminine— and yet you can wear it to work. Work, succeed, and play: you are still feminine and a real woman. Successful women choose Carfoor.

An advertisement of this type contains a number of appeals in emotionally charged language (subtle, feminine, discreet) and a persuasive definition (real women are feminine and, by implication, the sort who wear perfume). It also gives some relevant reasons for Carfoor's attractiveness to career women: it will do for business purposes but is subtly feminine. A major aspect of such an ad, however, is an appeal to popularity. Potential consumers are urged to jump on the bandwagon, do what other real women are doing, and buy the product.

It is equally fallacious to infer that a product or proposal is flawed just because it is unpopular. One nine-year-old boy, told by his mother that he would have to make his bed every day, took a survey of his classmates and discovered that out of the ten he surveyed, nine did not make their own beds. He told his mother that for this reason he should not have to make his own bed. The boy's initiative has to be admired here, but his mother was too smart to be convinced.[16] Similarly, an argument that disco music isn't any good because nobody listens to it anymore would be a fallacious appeal to unpopularity.

FALLACIOUS APPEALS TO POPULARITY

The appeal to popularity is a fallacy that occurs when people seek to infer merit or truth from popularity. It is also known as the fallacy of jumping on a bandwagon or, in Latin, the *ad populam*.

The premise or premises of such an argument indicate that a product or belief is popular. It is endorsed by most people or by almost everybody. The conclusion of the argument is that you should get the product or that you should accept the belief because it is popular. Appeals to popularity (or unpopularity) are fallacious because the popularity of a thing is irrelevant to its real merits. Too many other reasons for selecting products or beliefs exist for the fact of their selection to count as good evidence of quality, truth, or rational acceptability.

Similar to fallacious appeals to popularity are **fallacious appeals to tradition.** In these arguments, the premises claim that some action or practice is traditional or that things have always been done in a certain way. The conclusion claims that an action or policy now is justified because of its conformity to this tradition. To say that something is traditional is to claim that it was common or popular in the past. The fallacy lies in the fact that popularity in the past does not indicate suitability for the present—times and standards may change. This is not to deny that traditions can be worth preserving. Many traditions are valuable, and deserve to be maintained. But when this is the case, there are reasons for preserving the tradition. Perhaps the tradition is beautiful, or articulates emotions treasured by a group, or serves to maintain important memories, for instance. The simple fact that an action or belief has been common in the past and is in that sense traditional is not a relevant reason for endorsing it in the present. Needs and circumstances change. In response, actions and policies may appropriately change as well and we cannot automatically assume that what was good, or deemed good, in the past will be good in the present.

Other Fallacies Involving Relevance

Sometimes an argument of a type that is basically legitimate can be grossly flawed, to such an extent that its premises have no bearing on its conclusion. They are then irrelevant to the conclusion. Thus, examples of what are generally correct types of argument can contain irrelevant premises. Since this is the case, some examples of irrelevance will be discussed in later chapters of this book. For instance, flawed analogies will be discussed in Chapter 10. There are many other fallacies of irrelevance that have been discussed by logicians and philosophers. These include attempts to derive matters of value from matters of fact (termed the naturalistic fallacy); and fallacious attempts to infer quality from origin (termed the genetic fallacy.) To try to describe every kind of irrelevance would be unrealistic and not, in this context, useful. The important thing is to ask yourself how and why premises are relevant to the conclusion they are intended to support, and to note that they are irrelevant, if they are.

Irrelevance, Missing Premises, and Argument Criticism

Criticizing an argument on grounds of relevance is a strong line of criticism, as we have seen. But you have to back up your criticism by saying why you think the premises are irrelevant to the conclusion. If you just say, "That's irrelevant," it does not put debate on a very high level. You should explain why you believe that premises are irrelevant.

Logicians themselves disagree about relevance, but along somewhat different lines. Some claim that when arguments appear to have irrelevant premises, the problem is really that those arguments have missing premises. When these missing premises are added, they will link with the stated premises, and the stated premises will then become relevant to the conclusion. This approach to irrelevance can make even the most blatant cases of irrelevance turn into something else.

For instance, consider the following example of irrelevance:

1. Newman believes that global capitalism is a system unfair to vulnerable people.
2. Newman is an old man.
So,
3. Newman is not worth listening to.
And,
4. Global capitalism is not unfair to the vulnerable.

In this argument, which is an example of the *ad hominem* fallacy, premise (2) is completely irrelevant to conclusions (3) and (4). But some interpreters of argument would claim that we can make such a premise relevant by adding other statements that may be regarded as missing premises. In a move of strongly charitable interpretation, the gap between a premise such as (2) and the conclusions drawn from it can be filled.[17]

Here is one possible reconstruction:

1. Newman believes that global capitalism is a system unfair to vulnerable people.
2. Newman is an old man.
Possible added premise: Old people are not reliable.
So,
3. Newman is not worth listening to.
Further possible added premise: Anything asserted by somebody not worth listening to is false.
Therefore,
4. Global capitalism is not unfair to the vulnerable.

Logicians who use the missing premises approach to relevance and irrelevance would claim that this **reconstructed argument** is better than the original, for it contains no flaw of relevance. The device of adding sweeping statements as missing premises has eliminated the irrelevance. One objection to this interpretive strategy is that the proposed added premises go beyond what was explicitly asserted by the arguer. Another is that the changes do not in the end make a cogent argument out of one that was not cogent. The problem is that the premises added (perhaps out of a sense of interpretive charity) to avoid irrelevance are not acceptable. Whereas the argument we started out with fails on (R), the reconstruction fails on (A). What we have done is move the flaw in the original argument from one place to another.

A major difficulty for the strategy of eliminated irrelevance by ambitious reconstruction is that there are usually a number of different, equally plausible reconstructions. In the previous case, we might have added "Old people make false statements" or "Old people make false statements about economic matters," for instance. Another objection is that if such controversial and sweeping premises were really missing from an argument, that gap would be the mistake of the person who put the argument forward. It is not the responsibility of the audience, or critic, to rectify such errors, and ambitious reconstruction can shift us too far from the original argument in such cases.

If an argument has a flaw of relevance, the extra premises that you would add to reconstruct it without irrelevance will be unacceptable in any case. For practical purposes, our approach and the reconstructing approach do not give very different results. They are, however, quite different from a theoretical perspective.

EXERCISE SET

Exercise 2

For the following examples, (a) determine whether the passage contains an argument. If it does, (b) assess whether the premises are relevant to the conclusion. Then (c) for any premises deemed to be irrelevant, say why you think they are irrelevant and, if appropriate, label the argument as containing straw man, *ad hominem*, guilt by association, appeal to ignorance, appeal to popularity, or appeal to tradition. *Note*: Not all passages contain arguments, and not all the arguments contain mistakes.

*1. *Background:* The following excerpt is taken from Avishai Margalit, *The Decent Society*:

"Among the historical sources of the welfare idea is the notion of the necessity for eradicating degrading treatment of the poor, of the type embodied in England's Poor Laws. The English Poor Laws, in all their transformations

from the time of Elizabeth I, played a part in the use of humiliation as a deterrent against the exploitation of welfare by people looking for a free meal. The idea was that providing people with the bread of charity would encourage laziness and undesired dependence on society. The way to deter lazy people from asking for support was by offering such support under particularly humiliating conditions. Anyone who could accept these debasing conditions would thus be someone without any choice. The phrase 'rogue poor' was an expression of deep suspicion toward the penniless."

(Avishai Margalit, *The Decent Society*, translated from the Hebrew by Naomi Goldblum [Harvard, MA: Cambridge University Press, 1996], p. 223)

2. *Background:* After several years during which the government has cut spending on health care, a provincial union of nurses in the Canadian

province of Quebec has gone on an illegal strike. Jean defends the strike, while Michel opposes it.

Jean: Nurses do important work and the nurses in this province are not paid well. You can see this if you study statistics comparing the provinces. Nurses in Quebec are, on average, the lowest paid in Canada. Our nurses deserve better. They have tried to bargain with the government and failed. It is unfair for them to be denied the legal right to strike and it is perfectly appropriate for them to go out illegally, since the negotiation alternative has pretty well been exhausted.

Michel: I can't believe you're saying this. It's so simple-minded! You're just giving anybody the right to break the law when things don't go their way, and denying that there's any point at all in having laws and the rule of law. What a bleeding heart liberal! You'll be sorry when law and order break down entirely and you can't even safely walk out of your own house. Much less go to a hospital!

*3.   *Background:* Smith and Jones are discussing moral vegetarianism. Moral vegetarianism is the theory and practice of not eating meat for the moral reason that the killing of animals is considered wrong, much in the way we consider the killing of people wrong. Jones defends the idea; Smith attacks it.

Jones: People should not kill animals for food. Animals can feel and be harmed just as humans can. Those being raised for food are often raised in inhumane conditions before they are killed. And, more often than not, they are killed in brutal ways and feel a lot of pain. Besides, people do not need meat to maintain their health. Vegetable proteins, such as the ones in peas, beans, and lentils, will do just as well.

Smith: This idea is ridiculous. Carnivorous animals kill other animals for food. Humans are more than carnivorous; they are omnivorous. Most human beings eat meat. Most human beings always have eaten meat. We do not know what animal consciousness is like, so we must assume that they do not feel pain. Anyway, since animals kill each other, there is nothing wrong with us killing them.

4.   *Background:* The following letter by Erich Toll was printed in the *World Press Review* for July 1994. Toll criticized an article that had appeared in the May issue.

"Pollution: The Price of Progress (May) states that since Europe and the United States polluted heavily during the Industrial Revolution, Asia and the developing world have a right to do the same. Developing nations will serve themselves—and the world—best by learning from the mistakes of the industrial world. He who does not learn from the past is condemned to repeat it, and it is damnation indeed to repeat the ecological devastations of the past."

Hint: Assume that the conclusion is that developing nations should learn from the mistakes of the industrial world.

5.   Nature looks fantastic without clothes. Nobody thinks that seals, penguins, elephants, and birds should be covered in the latest fashion. So why should people wear clothing? Nudity is great!

*6.   *Background:* The following appeared on December 30, 1999 in a letter to the editor of the Toronto *Globe and Mail,* on the issue of whether space is the final frontier of exploration for human beings.

"I count myself among the supporters of research into the unknown, including sorties into the mysteries of biology and the universe beyond us. Space, however, is not our final frontier. I find it unfathomable that more scientific efforts and expenditures have not been devoted to exploring that vast frontier that exists on Earth—that is, our oceans. For example, recent discoveries have suggested that the diversity of life in our oceans may hold the promise of new pharmaceutical interventions in disease treatment. I believe it is as instinctive for humans both to migrate and to seek to view 'up close' that which we can see at a distance as it is for other animals to migrate and to sniff the flora and fauna around them. Regardless of the rationale we invent for doing so, it is a basic force within us, so proven by the myriad armies of explorers and migrants who preceded us."

7. "A major cross-cultural difference in the way people approach problems is the speed at which they act and expect others to act. Americans, particularly in an East Coast business environment, often move at a hectic pace; appointments and travel plans are tightly scheduled. Among other peoples and in other parts of the world, life proceeds more leisurely."

(Roger Fisher and Scott Brown, *Getting Together: Building a Relationship That Gets to Yes* [Boston: Houghton Mifflin, 1988], p. 176)

*8. *Background:* In her book *The Beauty Myth,* author Naomi Wolf argued that women harm themselves when they try to live up to the high standards of beauty implied in most commercial advertising. The following is taken from an interview of Wolf.

". . . something that bothered many readers, including me, was that while Wolf was exhorting her readers not to worry about living up to the heavily marketed ideals of beauty and slenderness, her own heavily marketed book featured a photograph of the author looking, well, beautiful and slender. Can't she see a problem in an attractive woman telling other women not to worry about attractiveness?"

(The *World Press Review,* February 1994)

9. "More than 250,000 hairdressers the world over believe in what L'Oreal Hair Colouring can do for you. What more can we say?"

(Ad cited by R. H. Johnson and J. A. Blair in *Logical Self-Defense,* 2nd ed. [Toronto: McGraw-Hill-Ryerson, 1983], p. 160)

10. *Background:* In this passage, editorialist William Thorsell is arguing that the waging of war is a necessary means of opposing tyrants such as Saddam Hussein. His piece, "The Decisive Exercise of Power," appeared in the Toronto *Globe and Mail* for December 19, 1999.

"In the 1930's the aversion to war in France and the United Kingdom was so pervasive that some pacifists preferred their own subjugation to resistance in the face of violence. Dandies in the best schools developed . . . . eloquent rationales for inaction and appeasement, even treason, to avoid the contest for power that was so obviously rising in Europe. They rejected the wisdom that good and evil are perpetually in conflict, and that it is only for good men to do nothing for evil men to triumph. . . . Remarkably, some of the leading nations in the world still don't appear to 'get it' when Saddam Hussein reappears. At root, it seems to be a matter of non-recognition: They just can't see the man for who he is, just as many people just couldn't see 'Mr Hitler' for who he was (the limits of the parallel noted). If you cannot recognize your enemy, you will not defeat him, except by luck of circumstance, and that will rarely do."

11. *Background:* The following appeared in an article called "Hidden in the Web," by Max Frankel, in the *New York Times Magazine* for July 11, 1999.

"The Times spend several hundred million dollars a year to gather, digest and deliver its unique package of daily news, creating quite a bargain for readers who pay $6 to $10 a week to receive it. Yet the *Times* tells you on its front page that you could also get it all for nothing on the Web. Just punch in www.nytimes.com, read as much as you like, and print out whatever you need to keep. In fact, you get much more on the Web than on paper—including life stock-market and business reports, news updates, school tutorials and an exhaustive calendar of events, tailored, if you wish, to your personal interests. And if the *Times* doesn't satisfy, the Web offers free copies of almost every other American newspaper, down to country and college weeklies, plus the world's main wire services, television newscasts and maybe half the content of half the country's magazines."

12.   *Background:* The following appeared in a letter to the Toronto *Globe and Mail* on December 23, 1998. The issue is comments by a previous writer (Mr. White-Harvey), who had protested the government's handling of crowds of students demonstrating against the visit to Canada of the then repressive leader of Indonesia.

"Mr. White-Harvey taps into a particular vein of mean-spiritedness that seem popular among a certain Canadian demographic today, i.e., that only the opinion of the employed and the tax-paying really counts, and everybody else should just shut up. Or perhaps he is disappointed that those university students at APEC, being not yet enslaved to the rat race which alone, he implies, can bestow full citizenship, may have made a small contribution to the popular removal of an abusive dictatorship the Canadian establishment had seemed only too comfortable with. Since we must indulge in cheap stereotypes, Mr. White-Harvey, let me contribute my own: Lawyer jokes are funny; lawyers, it would seem, are not."

*13.   An art college should be administered by a professor or instructor of art, for only someone who knows art can understand art students, art standards, and the special problems an art college has.

14.   *Background:* The following appeared as an advertisement in the magazine *Miss Chatelaine* in February 1976. A large photograph of Wolfman Jack, a popular rock disc jockey at the time, accompanied the advertisement:

"When those pimples pop up, you should break out the Clearasil Ointment. Listen—if you use a cleanser, that's fine. But I know how you feel when those pimples pop up. So lay out some acne medication on those pimples. Break out the Clearasil Ointment. Clearasil goes right after those acne pimples. Dries 'em up, helps heal 'em up, and that's just for starters. Clearasil hangs right in there—for hours—just soppin' up that extra oil you usually get with pimples. It's

Canada's number-one selling acne medication. Take it from the Wolfman. Pimples . . . I've been there. I know."

*15.   *Background:* The following appeared in the *New York Times* for July 11, 1998, in response to an article about whether Hillary Clinton was sufficiently "a real New Yorker" to stand for election for a Senate position in that state.

"M.L. doesn't fully explain what constitutes a 'real New Yorker.' Is it birth, property ownership, voter registration or mere residency that makes one obtain this coveted mantle? Regardless of one's politics, no one can say that Hillary Rodham Clinton isn't a strong effective advocate for what she believes in. I'd much rather have someone of her stature and position represent me than allow a lesser individual to make it to the Senate based solely on the accident of birth or a current address."

16.   *Background:* The following question and proposed answer are taken from a book on dream interpretation. Assume that the question posed in the first sentence is one that the authors are trying to answer in the rest of the passage, and determine whether what they say is positively relevant, negatively relevant, or irrelevant as an answer to the question.

" 'Can we use dreams to enhance our creativity and inventiveness?' I generally respond to this question by pointing out what a remarkably creative and inventive occurrence the dream itself is. Every dream is unique. The dreamer is expressing what has never been expressed before. He is effortlessly, but nevertheless creatively, transforming something vaguely felt into a visual display, which both captures and radiates the feelings involved. Everyone has a touch of the poet in him, even if it only comes out in a dream."

(Montague Ullman and Nan Zimmerman, *Working with Dreams* [Boston: Houghton Mifflin, 1979], p. 23)

17.   *Background:* The following paragraphs are excerpted from a letter to *Peace* magazine (January/February 1995) by Alan Weatherley. Weath-

erley is criticizing a previous article that had advocated replacing armed troops with civilians.

"The statement that 'where (warring) parties have agreed to suspend hostilities, they can be kept from combat by a corps of civilians' raises important ethical questions.

In fact, what basis is there for this statement? Why should anyone suppose given the recent experiences of U.N.-brokered exercises in peace-keeping that violent, mutually hostile forces, often including ill-led rabbles of uncertain political or ideological persuasion, would display the slightest respect for, or restraint towards, a corps of civilian peacekeepers? Imagine the arrival of such a corps, replete with food, medicines (including drugs), bed, tents, drinking water. Who could doubt that the more undisciplined fringe members of opposing armies would simply loot the corps' supplies for whatever they desired? Hostage taking, murder, and rape could be assumed. Why should anyone think otherwise?"

18.   *Background:* The following is taken from an article entitled "Brazen Lies about Islam," by Mustapha Mahmoud. The article appeared in the *World Press Review* for July 1994. Mahmoud argues that true Muslims are no threat to anyone and lays out an interpretation of the Western cultures.

"In contrast (to Muslim societies) secular civilization is based on the principle that you are free to do whatever you wish as long as you do not hurt others. You have only this life to live, so make the best of it: indulge your body and satisfy your desires without any guilt. In that culture, perverts enjoy the same rights as the righteous. They have their own clubs and are free to promote their abominations. They have also closed the doors of churches and mosques so they will not be bothered by religion."

19.   *Background:* The following appeared in a letter to the *New York Times,* July 11, 1999. The writer is commenting on a statement by Mark McGwire, who opposed having the New York Mets open the year 2000 baseball season in Tokyo on the grounds that the World Series was supposed to be American.

"Has McGwire forgotten baseball's history? When I was growing up, major league baseball was played by white players on 16 teams in 10 American cities, all but one in the North and east of the Mississippi. And the leagues had the nerve to play a championship series they called the World Series. Things improved, beginning with the acceptance of the first black American as a major league baseball player. Later, the leagues added Toronto and Montreal—not yet the 'world,' but at least international. Today, the major leagues have players from other countries, including Japan and Korea. Some of these players are teammates of McGwire."

Emotional Appeals, Irrelevance, and Distraction

Some texts on argument include in their discussion of fallacies appeals to pity and appeals to fear. (In Latin the appeal to pity is called the *ad misericordiam* and the appeal to fear, or force, is called the *ad baculum*.) Recent discussions of arguments appealing to pity, or to fear raise some interesting questions.

So far as pity is concerned, consider the following arguments:

(a) You should give me an A on my paper, because if I don't get an A, I won't be admitted to law school and all the hard work I have done for this degree will be wasted.

The instructor is urged to give the student an A on the grounds that without the A, the student will be in a pitiable condition. However, this condition of the student is irrelevant to the merits of the paper and the issue of which mark it deserves. Similar comments can be made about the following argument:

> (b) You should give me a strong recommendation for tenure and a promotion, because if I don't get these, I won't be able to pay my mortgage and I and my family will be out on the streets without a roof over our heads.

Whether a lecturer deserves a strong recommendation for tenure and promotion depends on his qualifications and skills at teaching and research. The attempt to evoke pity or sympathy here is irrelevant to the issue of his merits.

The question may be posed whether a charitable appeal showing a picture of a destitute child and asking for funds constitutes a fallacious appeal to pity. One problem that arises in many such cases is that there is no explicit argument. Often the picture is doing most or all of the work, somehow expressing a strong, but wordless appeal. Where there is no argument, there can be no fallacy—but somehow we may feel that we are being won over to this appeal by emotions. A second issue about appeals to pity is whether pity always should be irrelevant to what we say and do. In many respects, pity and related emotions such as sympathy and compassion seem to be highly desirable emotions. They draw our attention to the suffering of others, and encourage us to be sensitive to each other, responding to the needs of vulnerable people. Is it plausible to think that appeals to pity are always irrelevant to our attitudes, beliefs, and actions?

Analogous issues arise with regard to fallacious appeals to force or fear.[18] Force may be alluded to, in an explicit or implicit threat. The idea is to intimidate the listener or reader and through this intimidation win him or her over to some belief. In some cases, an appeal to fearsome consequences clearly takes the place of any relevant reasons for a claim. Consider, for instance:

> (c) You had better believe in God, because if you do not, when you die you will go straight to Hell and suffer eternal damnation.

In (c) there is an appeal to force and an attempt to inspire belief by fear instead of offering evidence. No reason is given in (c) to support the claim that God exists. Instead, there is only the idea that fearsome consequences will ensue if you do not accept this belief. The attempt to inspire fear takes the place of relevant premises.

In other cases, the matter is more subtle and ambiguous. The argument may be quite implicit. Furthermore, it may be difficult to detect the difference between logically irrelevant attempts to persuade by intimidating (manipulation) and logically relevant warnings that an action may have negative consequences. There may be a fine line between a relevant warning and a threat. Consider, in contrast to (c), another case, (d). In (d) a woman writes to her colleague about his taking on extra obligations apart from his regular job. She expresses concern that he may be overburdening himself and may be unable to fulfill regular teaching duties and prior commitments, including some that he has made to her. She says:

> (d) If you don't understand how much time and energy these things are going to take, your other work will suffer, including possibly the work we are doing together.

Statement (d) may be interpreted as her warning to him: these negative consequences are likely; you should take them into account. On the other hand, it might
be interpreted as a threat and appeal to her power, an attempt to intimidate him:
I will not work further with you if you take on too many outside obligations. (If
he wants and needs her cooperation on projects, she may be in a position to make
such a threat.) On the latter interpretation, (d) is an irrelevant appeal to power,
and amounts to an attempt by her to intimidate him into accepting her view of his
obligations.

A further point about argument and appeals to emotion is that pity and fear are
by no means the only emotions to which we appeal in our attempts to persuade each
other. Instead of appealing to pity, one might appeal to envy—"these people are better off than you; shouldn't something be done about it?" Instead of appealing to fear
one might appeal to hope, as in:

   (e) You had better believe in God, because if you do so, when you die you will
        go to Heaven and experience eternal bliss.

Like (a), (e) offers no evidence or reasons for believing in God's existence. The expectation is that one will hope and want to go to Heaven and will be led, through
this hope and desire, to believe in God. There is a wide range of emotions that can
be appealed to in attempts to persuade. The list of emotions that may be appealed
to in attempts to persuade includes at least the following: pity, sympathy, compassion, empathy, envy, fear, hope, guilt, unhappiness, grief, rage, resentment, revenge,
hatred, pride, shame, joy, excitement, anxiety, and insecurity. No doubt there are
many more. These emotions may be exploited. Many advertisements cultivate, and
then prey on, our sense of insecurity, on our fear that we are not as beautiful or successful as we should be. Such ads state or suggest that we can improve our inadequate selves if we buy the product in question.

How emotions are to be understood and how they may be related to our beliefs
and actions is an important and complex issue. We cannot explore this issue in
depth here. It would not be correct to say that emotions are always irrelevant to our
thinking and our actions. Language and images that evoke emotions may provide a
useful role in bringing our attention to an issue, providing one motive for actions,
or stimulating thought. But even when emotions are legitimate and not manipulated, they are not in and by themselves good reasons for belief or action. In any case
where language or images evoke in us emotions—whether of pity, fear, guilt, insecurity, resentment, excitement, hope, or whatever—we should pause to ask what
our feelings are, why we have those feelings, and what we are implicitly or explicitly
being urged to do in virtue of those feelings. What claim or claims are explicit or
implicit? What claims are we accepting? And why? Are any reasons given in support
of those claims?

Even in those contexts in which emotions are relevant to our beliefs, actions,
and lives, they cannot by themselves take the place of relevant reasons. What is wor-
risome about strong appeals to emotion—inside or outside arguments—is that such

appeals can so easily be distracting. They tend to distract us from relevant reasons, or—worse yet—from the fact that no relevant reasons are given. In this way, appeals to pity, fear, and other emotions may serve the interests of irrelevance.

CHAPTER SUMMARY

We began to explain relevance by distinguishing between positive relevance, negative relevance, and irrelevance. For the ARG conditions, positive relevance is required: in a cogent argument, the premises must be positively relevant to the conclusion. That means they must count in favor of the conclusion; if true or acceptable, they must provide evidence or reason that the conclusion is true or acceptable. If the premises are negatively relevant to the conclusion, that is, if they count against it, they obviously cannot support it in a cogent argument. In addition, premises must not be irrelevant to the conclusion; if they do not support its truth or acceptability at all, the argument is seriously flawed. For argument cogency, the premises must be positively relevant to the conclusion.

Ways in which the premises of an argument can be positively relevant to its conclusion include deductive entailment, analogy (similarity of cases), inductive support (presumption that examined cases provide a basis for expectations about unexamined ones), and providing reasons (factors that are reasons to think a claim true).

The irrelevance of premises to the conclusion constitutes a serious flaw in argument. Allegations of irrelevance should be supported and explained. It is not a good criticism of an argument simply to say that the premises are irrelevant and leave it at that.

There are a number of important and interesting fallacies involving irrelevance. These include straw man, *ad hominem*, guilt by association, fallacious appeal to ignorance, and fallacious appeal to popularity, tradition, pity, or force. When irrelevance occurs, it can be mended or remedied by a reconstruction of the argument using one or more additional premises that link the premise with the conclusion. However, such a procedure is of little real use, because the added premises are virtually always unacceptable.

Emotion can be a distracting factor in argument, or a factor that leads us to accept claims for which no evidence or reasons are presented. When this happens, an emotional appeal is taking the place of rational persuasion.

Review of Terms Introduced

Ad hominem **fallacy**   A fallacy committed when an irrelevant premise about the background, personality, or character of a person is given in an attempt to show that the person's theories or arguments are false or unacceptable. Such premises about personality and background are relevant only if the person himself or herself is the issue in question (as in an election) or if the reliability of his or her testimony or authority is at stake.

Burden of proof   Obligation, or duty, to support one's claims by argument and evidence. The burden of proof is usually said to rest on the party introducing a claim that needs proof. Various principles can be proposed as to which sorts of claims need proof, and these will give different ideas of where the "burden of proof lies," as we put it colloquially.

Emotional appeal   Use of emotion in language or imagery in such a way as to stimulate feelings and avoid the need to give reasons and evidence to support a belief or a conclusion to the effect that some action should be undertaken.

Fallacious appeals to ignorance   Arguments in which there is either an appeal to our ignorance about S in an attempt to show that not-S is true or probable, or an appeal to our ignorance about not-S in an attempt to show that S is true or probable.

Fallacious appeals to popularity   A fallacy in which one reasons from the popularity of a product or belief to a conclusion about its actual merits. Also called the popularity fallacy, the bandwagon fallacy, or *ad populam*.

Fallacious appeal to tradition   A fallacy in which one reasons from the fact that a practice, action, or belief has been common in the past to a conclusion about its merit in the present.

Guilt-by-association fallacy   A fallacy committed when a person or a person's views are criticized on the basis of a supposed link between them and a person or movement believed to be disreputable.

Irrelevance   A statement is irrelevant to the truth of another statement if and only if its truth or falsity neither counts in favor of the truth of that other statement nor counts toward that other statement's being false. If the truth of one statement is irrelevant to the truth of another, it is neither positively relevant to it nor negatively relevant to it.

Negative relevance   A statement is negatively relevant to the truth of another statement if and only if its truth would give some reason or evidence for the falsity of that other statement. That is, if the first statement were true, that would count in favor of the second one being false.

Non sequitur   An argument in which the premise has no bearing on the conclusion. '*Non sequitur*' is a Latin phrase used to refer to irrelevance; it means "it does not follow."

Positive relevance   A statement is positively relevant to the truth of another statement if and only if its truth would give some evidence or reason to support the truth of that other statement. That is, if the first statement were true, that would count in favor of the second one being true.

Reconstructed argument   An argument in which the inferences (or steps) have been made more orderly, logical, and sensible by the addition of extra premises. Where the unreconstructed, or original, argument had a fallacy of relevance, the reconstructed argument will not. Typically, however, premises added to produce such a reconstruction are unacceptable.

Red herring   A premise or remark that is irrelevant to the conclusion or issue being discussed, so that it tends to distract people and lead them away from the topic at issue.

Straw man fallacy   A fallacy committed when a person misrepresents an argument, theory, or claim, and then, on the basis of that misrepresentation, claims to have refuted the position the person has misrepresented.

Notes

1. *For instructors.* Relevance here is defined using the notion of truth. There is no contradiction between this definition and the replacement of truth by acceptability in the ARG conditions. To say that acceptability is to replace truth in the conditions of an argument's cogency is not to say that truth is to be eliminated as a central epistemic and logical concept. I have benefited from the discussion of relevance in James Freeman's textbook *Thinking Logically: Basic Concepts for Reasoning* (Englewood Cliffs, NJ: Prentice-Hall, 1988) and from discussions with J. Anthony Blair and David Hitchcock. There are complex technical problems about defining relevance that cannot be dealt with here. I owe my understanding of some of these problems to John Woods. Some improvement on the definition offered in the chapter can be made by the following amendments:

   (a) S is positively relevant to X if and only if either the truth of S counts in favor of the truth of X, or the falsity of S counts in favor of the falsity of X, or both.

   (b) S is negatively relevant to X if and only if either the truth of S counts in favor of the falsity of X, or the falsity of S counts in favor of the truth of X, or both.

   (c) S is irrelevant to X if and only if S is neither positively relevant to X nor negatively relevant to X.

   In this account, "counts in favor of" is taken as an undefined term and is understood as a connection logically weaker than that of material implication. For the purposes of argument analysis, the simpler definition offered in the chapter is adequate, since premises are put forward as true or acceptable, not as false.

2. *For instructors.* The qualification is intended to cover cases of formal implication such as '$P \cdot -P$' therefore Q' and 'P; therefore $P \lor R$'. In such cases, it is arguable that there is entailment without relevance. However, instances of such relationships are not likely to be found in naturally occurring arguments in ordinary language, and the complications arising from them are in any event beyond the scope of this book.

3. Adapted from a letter to the Toronto *Globe and Mail,* February 8, 1982.

4. Letter to the Toronto *Star,* April 8, 1981.

5. Sidney Lens, "The Most Dangerous Cliché," *The Nation,* September 11, 1982, p. 210.

6. Roger Fisher and Scott Brown, *Getting Together* (Boston: Houghton Mifflin, 1988), p. 5.

7. Advertisement cited by Harrowsmith, September 1980.

8. I owe this example to Douglas Walton, who cited it in his *The Arguer's Position: A Pragmatic Study of* Ad Hominen *Attack, Criticism, Refutation, and Fallacy* (Westport, CN: Greenwood Press, 1985), p. 284.

9. Peter Stockland, "Emotion Drowns Masculine Logic," Calgary *Sun,* January 17, 1995. Thanks to Janet Sisson for this example. (My emphasis in quotation.)

10. Leslie Freeman, *Nuclear Witnesses* (New York: Norton, 1981) contains fascinating background information on this case.

11. Toronto *Globe and Mail,* September 4, 1980, p. 1.

12. It would be an exaggeration to say that the burden of proof has rested entirely on those who would object to a product as harmful. There are legal requirements for potential products, especially those involving chemicals and pharmaceuticals, to undergo rather stringent tests. However, such tests do not include long-term effects and have been criticized on various grounds.

13. A. S. Neill, cited by Richard Robinson in "Arguing from Ignorance," *Philosophical Quarterly 21,* (1971), pp. 97–107. Note that to criticize Neill's argument is NOT to say that punishment of children is desirable or good, much less that corporal punishment of children is legitimate.

14. It can happen that things become popular because they are, in some respect, good. But this is not always the case. In any event, the point at issue here is whether things can be shown to be good because they are popular.

15. Appeals to the popularity of beliefs should not be confused with the notion of common knowledge developed in Chapter 5. The difference is that the belief whose popularity is appealed to is not universal in a culture, nor is it basic and elementary. Typically, its content is somewhat controversial, speculative, or normative. But it is claimed to be popular.

16. Thanks to Michael and Doreen Barrie for this example and to Cary MacWilliams for calling my attention to the fallacy of appealing to unpopularity.

17. I argued against strong charity, and in favor of moderate charity, when discussing interpretation in Chapter 2.

18. My interest in this topic and some of my ideas about pity and force arose from reading Douglas Walton's *The Place of Emotion in Argument* (University Park, PA: Pennsylvania State University Press, 1992). I also benefited from hearing John Woods lecture on the *ad baculum* fallacy at a conference at M.I.T. in July, 1994.

chapter seven
Deductions: Categorical Logic

W E HAVE DISCUSSED two of the three conditions of an argument's adequacy: acceptability and relevance. We now move on to the (G) condition to see various ways in which premises may work together to provide good and sufficient grounds for the conclusion. In this chapter and the next, our goal is to become clearer about deductively valid arguments by learning about some simple forms of arguments in which the premises deductively entail the conclusion.

Deductive Relations

One statement deductively entails another if and only if it is impossible for the second one to be false, given that the first one is true. That is, the state of affairs in which statement (1) is true and statement (2) is false is logically impossible. That a person is a sister deductively entails that she is female, because it is a logical impossibility for a person to be a sister and not be female. A logical impossibility is a state of affairs that could not exist.

When an argument is deductively valid, it is impossible for all the premises to be true and the conclusion false. An argument such as this is entirely adequate as far as the (R) and (G) conditions are concerned, so any question about its cogency must involve the acceptability of its premises. Many arguments that are deductively valid owe their validity to their logical form. In formal logic, various forms of argument are tested for their logical validity. The logically relevant features of the structure of an argument represented by formalizing it in a particular way then, appealing to rules of formal validity, the formal version of the argument is evaluated. If it passes the tests, then, assuming that the formal version has represented its logically significant features, the argument is valid.[1]

Here is a simple example of a formally valid argument:

1. All consistent opponents of killing are opponents of capital punishment.
2. No opponents of capital punishment are orthodox traditional Catholics.
So,
3. No consistent opponents of killing are orthodox traditional Catholics.

This argument is deductively valid by virtue of its *categorical* form. That is, the deductive connection between the premises and the conclusion depends on the way in which the categories of things are related to each other in the premises and in the conclusion.

The connection here depends on the relationships between *all* and *none*—inclusion in, and exclusion from, groups. Leaving out some words, we can rewrite this argument as:

All . . . are . . .
No . . . are . . .
Therefore,
No . . . are . . .

Now we will replace the omitted words with letters. Let C equal consistent opponents of killing; let O equal opponents of capital punishment; let T equal orthodox traditional Catholics. These letters represent categories of things. It is a good idea to keep a record or dictionary as a reminder of which letter represents which category. The argument can be written as follows:

All C are O.
No O are T.
Therefore,
No C are T.

In this argument, the connection between the premises and the conclusion depends on the way *all* and *no* and the categories are related. Any argument that was accurately formalized as having the same logical form would be deductively valid as well. Consider the following:

1. All mammals are creatures that bear their young alive.
2. No creatures that bear their young alive are creatures that lay eggs.
Therefore,
3. No mammals are creatures that lay eggs.

This second argument has the same logical form as the original example and is deductively valid in virtue of its form.

The formal validity of an argument is quite distinct from the truth, or acceptability of its premises. A good argument must satisfy all three ARG conditions. Deductively valid arguments satisfy (R) and (G) but may fail to satisfy (A).

One further thing to note is that it is not always by virtue of logical form that deductive relations hold. Sometimes one statement deductively entails another by virtue of its meaning. For instance, the statement "Roberta is a sister" entails "Roberta is female" because of what it means to be a sister.[2] It is logically impossible for anyone to be a sister and not be female. The meanings of the terms *sister* and *female* are what make the inference from the first statement to the second a deductively valid inference.

Simple deductive relationships based on form and meaning are essential in our understanding of written and spoken language. Indeed, we have been presupposing these relationships all along in this text—just as we presuppose them in all understanding of language. Whenever we scrutinize a passage to see whether it contains an argument, or ask how to best represent its premises and conclusions in clear simple language, we are, in effect, asking what is and what is not deductively entailed by what was said.

You can intuitively grasp the fact that:

(a) 1. All *S* are *M*.
    2. No *M* are *P*.
    Therefore,
    3. No *S* are *P*.

is a form representing a deductively valid argument. Similarly, you can intuitively grasp the fact that,

(b) 1. Either *A* or *B*.
    2. Not *B*.
    Therefore,
    3. *A*.

is a deductively valid argument. Example (a) is deductively valid because of relations of category inclusion and exclusion, which are the topic of this chapter. Example (b) is deductively valid because of relations between propositions, which are the topic of Chapter 8. If most people could not intuitively appreciate and respond to such facts, formal systems would not have developed at all.

Our logical intuitions can be usefully systematized, explained, and developed through the articulation of formal systems in logic, which develops and systematizes our intuitive understanding. When arguments depend on their form for deductive validity, we can represent them in a symbolic way that will reveal that form without representing the specific content of the argument. Then, using rules dealing only with formal relationships, we can determine the deductive validity of the symbolized arguments. Often this technique is helpful and enlightening because the content of an argument may distract us from formal relationships.

Formal logic is a highly developed and intricate subject, and there are many excellent texts in the field. This book does not treat formal logic in great detail. In our treatment, we concentrate on aspects of the subject most pertinent to ordinary speech and writing, and we emphasize the application of formal techniques to arguments you may find in ordinary speech, in everyday life, and in the study of a variety of subjects.

Four Categorical Forms

Categorical logic uses *all, some, are,* and *not* as its basic logical terms. These terms are used to tell, in a general way, how many members of one category are included in, or excluded from, another category. In our simple example, we considered the following argument:

1. All consistent opponents of killing are opponents of capital punishment.
2. No opponents of capital punishment are orthodox traditional Catholics.
So,
3. No consistent opponents of killing are orthodox traditional Catholics.

In this argument, both premises and conclusion are in categorical form. That is, they are statements in which a subject category is connected to a predicate category. The first statement makes a universal affirmation, whereas the second two state universal negations.

UNIVERSAL AFFIRMATION

All *S* are *P*. (All the members of the *S* category are included within the *P* category. Example: All sisters are female persons.)

UNIVERSAL NEGATION

No *S* are *P*. (All members of the *S* category are excluded from the *P* category. Example: No sisters are male persons.)

For convenient reference, logicians call the universal affirmation an *A* statement and the universal negation an *E* statement. Not all statements in categorical form are universal. There are two further categorical forms:

PARTICULAR AFFIRMATION

Some *S* are *P*. (Some members of the *S* category are included in the *P* category. Example: Some sisters are pianists.)

PARTICULAR NEGATION

Some *S* are not *P*. (Some members of the *S* category are excluded from the *P* category. Example: Some sisters are not pianists.)

The **particular affirmative** is referred to as the *I* statement and the **particular negation** as the *O* statement. These shorthand ways of referring to the categorical forms come from two Latin words: *affirmo* and *nego*. *Affirmo* means "I affirm" and is the source of *A* and *I*, which are positive. *Nego* means "I deny" and is the source of *E* and *O*, which are negative.

The four categorical forms are arranged in a square called the **Square of Opposition** (see Figure 7.1).

The opposition is apparent when we look at the diagonals on the square. Each proposition is the **contradictory** of the one diagonally opposed to it: if all *S* are *P*, then it must be false that some *S* are not *P*; and if no *S* are *P*, then it must be false that

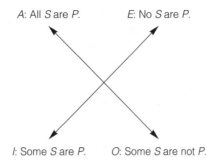

FIGURE 7.1

A: All S are P.   E: No S are P.

I: Some S are P.   O: Some S are not P.

some S are P. When one statement is the contradictory of another, the two always have opposite truth values; if one is true the other is false, and vice versa.

The A and E statements are contraries; that is, they cannot both be true. They can, however, both be false. (For example, "All roses are yellow" and "No roses are yellow" are contraries. They cannot both be true but they can both be false. In fact, both are false.) The I and O statements are **subcontrary statements.** They cannot both be false, but can both be true. (For example, "Some roses are yellow" and "Some roses are not yellow" cannot both be false. They can both be true—and in fact both are true.)

The A and E statements are fully universal. They are true only under the condition that every single member of the subject class is included in the predicate class (A) or excluded from the predicate class (E). That is, an A statement states that every member of the subject category is included in the predicate category, and an E statement states that everything in the subject category is excluded from the predicate category. A technical way of putting this is to say that in both A and E, the subject term is distributed. A term is **distributed,** in a categorical statement, if the statement says something about every item falling under that term. In an A statement, the predicate term is not distributed, although in an E statement, it is. Compare, for instance, the A statement "All sisters are female persons" with the E statement "No sisters are male persons." In the A statement, "female persons" is not distributed, because the statement is not about all female persons. It does not say that all female persons are sisters. However, in the E statement, "No sisters are male persons," the predicate term *male persons* is distributed. All the sisters are excluded from the entire male category; if no sisters are male persons, then no male persons are sisters.

The I and O statements do not include or exclude the whole subject category, only part of it. But the word *part* needs further explanation here, because it has a specific technical meaning at this point. Part or some of a category is interpreted as meaning "at least one" for the purposes of categorical logic. The I statement "Some men are fathers" does not make an assertion about all men. It says that at least one man is a father. Similarly, the statement that some men are not fathers (an O statement) does not make an assertion about all men. In the I and O statements, the subject term (S) is not distributed because these statements are not about all the items within the subject category. In the I statement, the predicate term is not distributed either. For instance, "Some men are fathers" says that the classes of men and fathers overlap. There are some men in the father category. This tells us something about part of the father category but not about all of it. However, in the *O* statement, the predicate term is distributed, because the subject items are, in effect, excluded from the entire predicate category. If we say, "some men are not fathers," those men are outside the entire father category.

Natural Language and Categorical Form

A number of useful formal rules of inference can be applied to statements in categorical form. These rules can be extremely helpful in getting deductive relationships straight. But to use them, we have to be working with statements that are in categorical form. The rules do not necessarily apply to other statements. Few statements in English or other natural languages are spoken or written in perfect categorical form. Many statements in natural languages are basically of the subject/predicate type, and these statements can be put into categorical form. Because our purpose in this text is practical, we shall emphasize the relation between natural wording and categorical form.

The Universal Affirmative: *A*

The *A* statement (**universal affirmative**) in categorical form begins with the word *all*. The word *all* is followed by a noun or noun phrase specifying a category of things; the category is followed by the word *are* or another form of the verb *to be*, which in turn is followed by another noun or noun phrase specifying a category of things. Strictly speaking, the sentence "All dogs have tongues" is not in categorical form, because the predicate is not a category of things. To put that sentence in categorical form, we would have to rewrite it so that the predicate term specifies a category, as for instance in "All dogs are creatures that have tongues." In a somewhat similar way, many sentences in English can be put into the form of *A* statements with slight linguistic alterations. (You must be careful, however, that the statement as reworded captures the meaning of the original one.)

Consider, for instance, these statements, which are all variations of the form "All *S* are *P*."

> Any *S* is *P*.
> Every single *S* is *P*.
> The *S*s are all *P*s.
> Whatever *S* you look at, it is bound to be a *P*.
> Each *S* is a *P*.
> *S*s are *P*s.
> An *S* is a P.
> If it's an *S*, it's a *P*.
> Only a *P* can be an *S*.

All can be translated into A statements as "All *S* are *P*."

Often statements are made in such a way that it is not explicitly said whether the statement is universal or particular. Look at these statements, for instance:

A monkey has a tail.
Zebras have stripes.
A bachelor is an unmarried man.
A lender is in an advantageous position when interest rates are high.
Wars lead to civilian deaths.
Nurses are overworked.
Men feel uncomfortable talking about emotions in close relationships.

All these sentences are of the subject/predicate type. But as they stand, none are in categorical form. To put them in categorical form, we would have to determine whether the intent is to make a universal or particular statement. We would have to make sure we have two categories of things and not just an adjective or adjectival phrase in the predicate and we have to render them so that the connecting verb is a form of the verb *to be*. The results for these statements would look like this:

All monkeys are creatures with tails.
All zebras are creatures with stripes.
All bachelors are unmarried men.
All lenders are persons or institutions that are in an advantageous position when interest rates are high.
All (?) wars are events that lead to civilian deaths.
All (?) persons who are nurses are persons who are overworked.
All (?) men are persons who feel uncomfortable discussing emotions in close relationships.

Sometimes, as in the last three cases here, merely asking whether the statement is universal or particular can be an important critical step. Often people make unqualified statements without making it clear whether they wish to make an assertion about all of the category or part of it. We often hastily make statements about all wars, all members of some occupational group, all men, or whatever without pausing to think about what we really mean to say. It is important to recall at this point that fully universal statements are of a logical type that makes them open to refutation by a single counterexample. Often, they should be qualified. It is false that all men feel uncomfortable discussing emotions in close relationships, although it may be true that most, or many, or some men feel uncomfortable in that situation.

We can be led into accepting stereotypes by an uncritical response to unqualified statements. For instance, if we hear that homeless people are alcoholics, we may naturally accept the statement as a universal generalization. We may do so because the statement seems to be borne out by some encounters we have had with homeless people. Strictly speaking, our cases show that an *I* statement (*Some* homeless people are alcoholics) is true. But the *A* statement (All homeless people are alcoholics), which is now "Homeless people are alcoholics" may easily and carelesssly be interpreted, is false. People may come to be homeless for many different reasons. *Most, many,* or *some* are quite different from *all*. **Stereotyping** people—putting them into categories and making universal judgments about all members of the category—is generally to be avoided. It is intellectually careless and, all too often, ethically and politically dangerous as well.

Statements in which the word *only* is used are implicitly universal. Consider this example:

Only students fluent in French are permitted to enroll in Laval University.

Let us allow *F* to represent "students fluent in French" and *U* to represent "people allowed to enroll in Laval University." The statement may be written in simpler form as:

Only *F* are *U*.

We have to rewrite this as an *A* statement to represent it in the terms of categorical logic, because the four categorical forms do not let us use the word *only*. The right way to do it is as follows:

Only *F* are *U* = All *U* are *F*.

You will understand why this representation makes sense if you reflect that if only students fluent in French are allowed to enroll, then we know that all students allowed to enroll will be fluent in French. Think about this example carefully. Statements like this can easily confuse people. They may want to interpret them as saying:

Only *F* are *U* = (?) All *F* are *U* (*Wrong!*)

Reflecting on this erroneous representation, you are likely to detect the error. It says that everyone fluent in French can enroll at Laval, but that is not what the original statement asserted. (It would imply that fluency in French is all that is needed, that no knowledge of other subjects such as history, science, or mathematics at the high school level is required.) The original statement, saying that admission requires French, leaves open the possibility of other requirements, but asserts that all admitted will have fluency in French, because without it, they would not have been accepted by the university.

The Universal Negative: *E*

There are also many different ways of expressing *E* statements (**universal negative**) in English. Consider the following:

Not a single whale can fly.
Whales can't fly.
None of the beings who are whales can fly.
There never was a whale that could fly.
No whale can fly.
Whales are not able to fly.

All of these sentences are variations of the following:

No whales are creatures that can fly. (No *W* are *F*.)

This last statement is in proper categorical form; it has two categories of things plus *no* and *are*.

There are some other cases that people occasionally find tricky. For instance:

Not all lawyers are rich. (not an E statement)

Here, it is crucial to note that *not all* does not mean *none*. The statement that not all lawyers are rich is the denial of an *A* statement (All lawyers are rich). As such it is the assertion of the *O* statement, not *E*. The words *not all* before the subject should *not* be translated as *none*.

One type of statement that is easy to confuse with the "not all" statement is "All . . . are not . . ." Statements of this type are ambiguous and can be very confusing in some contexts. Consider the following:

All athletes are not tall.

This statement could be read as the *A* type and would then appear in categorical form with the *not* taken as part of the predicate: "All athletes are nontall." On this interpretation, it attributes a property (that of being nontall, that is, being other than tall) to all athletes. However, "All athletes are not tall" may also be interpreted as expressing an *O* statement. On this interpretation, *not* applies to the whole sentence, which is equivalent to "Not all athletes are tall." On this interpretation the statement asserts that some athletes are not tall. On the first interpretation "All athletes are not tall" is false, and on the second interpretation it is true. Thus you can see that the ambiguity is an important one. Clearly it makes all the difference to the acceptability of the statement. If you come across statements of the type "All *A* are not *B*" you have to estimate whether an *A* statement or an *O* statement is being asserted.

Consider the proverb "All that glitters is not gold." If we take it to mean "All that glitters is nongold," (an *A* statement) it says something false. After all, some gold things glitter. Suppose we take it to mean that "Not everything that glitters is gold." "Some things that glitter are things that are not gold" is an *O* statement and it is true.

The Particular Affirmative: *I*

The I statement (particular affirmative) asserts that some things in the subject category are also in the predicate category. In categorical logic, *some* means at least one, or more; no distinction is made between many, most, several, or just one. The word *some* is used to mean any number of members of the category that is greater than none and less than all.

One trick about *I* statements is to be aware of what they are not saying. Typically, when we use them, we suggest more than we actually assert. For instance, imagine a professor who remarks that some of her former students graduated from university. People who hear the comment are likely to think, "Well, if she is saying that some graduated, she must mean that some did not graduate. Otherwise why would she tell us some did?" Strictly speaking, however, she has not said this. She has said only that some did graduate, and according to the interpretation given in categorical logic, that statement will be true if she has at least one former student who did graduate. The *I* statement is asserted; the *O* statement is not asserted. Whether any of her ex-students failed to graduate cannot strictly be inferred, on this interpretation.

When an indefinite article such as *a* or *an* precedes the subject, the statement made can be either universal or particular. We already saw some examples in which there is a universal intent, as in "A monkey has a tail." In contexts in which the statement clearly refers to an indefinitely specified individual, as in:

> A pianist gave a concert.

the sentence should be put into categorical form as *I*:

> Some pianists are persons who gave a concert.

Categorical logic allows us to speak of all, some, or none of the items in a category. It does not allow us to speak of individuals as such. Note how verb tense is handled in this example. The categorical forms are indifferent to verb tense and must express it by specifications within the predicate category: here it appears in the framing of the predicate category as "persons who gave a concert."

The Particular Negative: *O*

We have seen that *not all* before the subject is a way of denying the universal affirmation, and thus is a way of asserting the particular negation: *O*. Thus:

> Not all mammals live on land.

goes into categorical form as:

> Some mammals are not creatures that live on land.

Just as *I* often suggests *O,* but does not assert it, *O* often suggests, but does not assert *I*. A person who says, for instance, that some readers of science fiction are not computer hackers is likely to be interpreted as saying, in addition, that some readers of science fiction are computer hackers. But strictly speaking, he is not saying this. This claim is only suggested by his comment: it is not said and not deductively entailed. (In deductive logic, we do not take what is merely suggested to be part of the content of people's remarks.)

In *O* statements, the word *not* must perform the function of excluding some items in the subject category from the predicate category. The word *not* should not be replaced by a negative particle within the predicate category. The statement:

> Some teachers are persons who are not happy with their work.

is not a statement of the *O* form. It is an *I* statement that happens to have a predicate category (persons who are not happy with their work) with a negative particle inside it.

EXERCISE SET

Exercise 1

(a) Translate the following sentences into categorical form and state which of the four forms—*A, E, I, O*—you have used. Be prepared to defend your answer. (b) If you think that any sentence is ambiguous as to which of the categorical forms it exemplifies, say so and explain why. *Note:* You are not required to discuss whether the statements are true or false, acceptable or unacceptable, but merely to write them in categorical form as *A, E, I,* or *O.*

1.   Every grand piano is expensive.

*2.   A student came to the office asking to be excused from the final examination.

3.   No research scientists have time for lengthy summer vacations.

4.   The early bird gets the worm.

*5.   Only the rich can afford to stay at London's prestigious hotels.

*6.   Some evangelists are not poets.

7.   A rolling stone gathers no moss.

8.   At least one winning athlete was from the state of Maine.

9.   No lakes near Miami are seriously polluted.

*10.   Not all textbooks are boring.

11.   Some books of literary criticism are not best-sellers.

*12.   Mathematicians love abstraction.

13.   Some real estate agents do not get rich.

14.   A place for everything, and everything in its place.
    Hint: Use two statements.

*15.   A woman with a job outside the home and no assistance with household work is burdened with at least two jobs.

*16.   Any friend of yours is a friend of mine.

17.   "Life is just one damned thing after another."
(Elbert Hubbard)

18.   "Reading is sometimes an ingenious device for avoiding thought."
(Sir Arthur Helps)

*19.   A rose by any other name would be as sweet.
    Hint: Complete the predicate term.

*20.   "Ours not to wonder why, ours but to do or die."
(Shakespeare)
    Hint: Use two statements.

Venn Diagrams

The meanings of the *A, E, I,* and *O* statements can be shown on diagrams in which circles represent the categories of things. These diagrams are called **Venn diagrams,** after the nineteenth-century English philosopher and logician John Venn. Venn diagrams are helpful because they enable us to visually show the meanings of the *A, E, I,* and *O* statements and to understand the logical relationships using simple pictures.

Venn diagrams offer a system for representing whether there is something or nothing in an area of logical space. Logical space is represented in circles and parts of circles. To indicate that there is nothing in an area of logical space, we shade in the area. To indicate that there is something, we put an x in the space.

Look at the following two overlapping circles. We call the circle on the left the S circle, because it represents the subject category, and that on the right the P circle, because it represents the predicate category. When we make the circles overlap, we have three areas for the categories S and P. There is area (1) for those things that are S and are not P, area (2) for those things that are both S and P, and area (3) for those things that are P and are not S. Things that are not P and not S would be outside the circles entirely (see Figure 7.2).

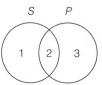

FIGURE 7.2

To show an A statement, we have to indicate its meaning by marking the relevant areas of logical space. The A statement says, "All S are P." If all S are P, then there are no S outside the P category. To indicate this relationship on a Venn diagram, we shade in area (1), as follows (see Figure 7.3):

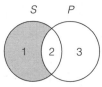

FIGURE 7.3

For instance, if S were the category of sisters and P were the category of female persons, the (true) claim that all sisters are female persons would be represented on this diagram of the A statement. The area of sisters who are not female is shaded in to represent the fact that nothing is in it.

For the E statement, we need to indicate that no S are P. That is, there is no overlap between the categories. On the Venn diagram, area (2) represents the overlap; the space in area (2) is part of both the S circle and the P circle. The E statement says that there is nothing in it; to represent this, we shade in area (2). For example, suppose that S were the category of women and P were the category of men. Then consider the E statement "No women are men." Area (2) represents those women that are men; there are none. Area (2) is shaded in to indicate that this logical space is empty (see Figure 7.4).

The I statement, "Some S are P," says that there is at least one thing that is both S and P. That is, the overlap area, area (2), does have something in it. We represent this by putting an x in area (2). If S is the category of men and P is the category of

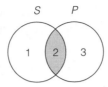

FIGURE 7.4

fathers, then the *I* statement says, "Some men are fathers." There is something in area (2); the *x* placed there indicates the fact that there are men who are fathers (see Figure 7.5).

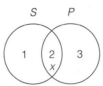

FIGURE 7.5

The *O* statement, "Some *S* are not *P*," says that there is at least one thing in the *S* category that is not in the *P* category. To indicate this, we put an *x* in area (1), which is the space for things that are *S* but are not *P*. If *S* is the category of men and *P* is the category of athletes, then the *O* statement relating these categories is "Some men are not athletes." That is, there are men outside the athlete category, as is indicated by the *x* in area (3) of the diagram (see Figure 7.6).

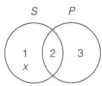

FIGURE 7.6

As we shall see, Venn diagrams are useful in showing logical relationships between categorical statements and in determining the validity of some arguments that can be expressed in categorical form.

Rules of Immediate Inference

We are now in a position to see some of the formal rules of categorical logic. First we will look at rules for **immediate inference**. If you have two statements, and the first deductively entails the second, then you can immediately (that is, without intermediate steps) infer the second from the first. There are a number of operations involving the *A, E, I,* and *O* statements. These are common and important, and some will give us valid immediate inferences.

Conversion

The **converse** of a statement in categorical form is constructed by transposing (changing the positions of) its subject and predicate. Thus:

STATEMENT	CONVERSE OF STATEMENT
A: All *S* are *P.*	All *P* are *S.*
E: No *S* are *P.*	No *P* are *S.*
I: Some *S* are *P.*	Some *P* are *S.*
O: Some *S* are not *P.*	Some *P* are not *S.*

For the *E* and *I* statements, the original statement and its converse are logically equivalent. For instance, if no men are women, then no women are men; this illustrates the relationship of **logical equivalence** between an *E* statement and its converse. If some sisters are women, that is to say that some women are sisters; this illustrates the relationship of logical equivalence between an *I* statement and its converse. Logically equivalent statements deductively entail each other. When two statements are logically equivalent, either they are both true or they are both false. It is impossible for one to be false given that the other is true. You can see that the converse is logically equivalent here, in all likelihood, but in any case the logical facts can be represented neatly on Venn diagrams. The *E* statement and its converse look like Figure 7.7:

   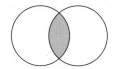

FIGURE 7.7   *E:* No *S* are *P.*   *Converse of E:* No *P* are *S.*

The *I* statement and its converse look like Figure 7.8:

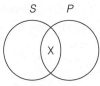   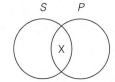

FIGURE 7.8   *I:* Some *S* are *P.*   *Converse of I:* Some *P* are *S.*

The conversion of *A* and *O* statements does not result in statements logically equivalent to the originals. By looking at these figures and Figure 7.9, you will be able to see why.

Many people mistakenly believe that there is a logical equivalence between an *A* statement and its converse. This is a common source of errors in reasoning. Consider the claim "All professional tennis players are professional athletes." This statement is true. But its converse, "All professional athletes are professional tennis

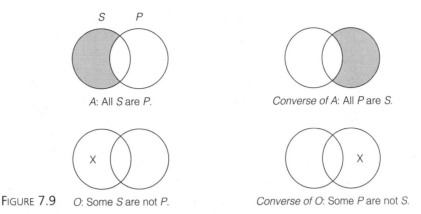

FIGURE 7.9   O: Some S are not P.   Converse of O: Some P are not S.

players" is false. To consider another example, we may reflect that it is true that all Christians are religious believers, but false that all religious believers are Christians.

Contraposition

To **contrapose** a statement in categorical form, you first convert it and then attach a *non* to each category. It works like this:

STATEMENT	CONTRAPOSITIVE OF STATEMENT
A: All *S* are *P.*	All non-*P* are non-*S.*
E: No *S* are *P.*	No non-*P* are non-*S.*
I: Some *S* are *P.*	Some non-*P* are non-*S.*
O: Some *S* are not *P.*	Some non-*P* are not non-*S.*

An *A* statement says that all *S* are *P.* Its contrapositive says that all non-*P* are non-*S.* Given the *A* statement, the contrapositive must be true because if it were not true, there would be a non-*P* that was an *S,* which would be **contrary** to what the *A* statement asserts. Consider the *A* statement "All doctors are educated persons." Its contrapositive "All noneducated persons are nondoctors" is logically equivalent to it.

As for *O* statements, consider, for instance, "Some musicians are not teachers." Its contrapositive is "Some nonteachers are not nonmusicians." To say that some nonteachers are not nonmusicians is to say that some nonteachers are musicians. This is the equivalent of the original statement. Both *A* statements and *O* statements are logically equivalent to their contrapositives.

The contrapositives of *E* and *I* statements are not logically equivalent to these statements. The *E* statement, no *S* are *P,* has as its contrapositive, no non-*P* are non-*S.* These statements say quite different things. The first says that the two categories *S* and *P* do not intersect at all; there are no items in both at once. The second says that what is outside the *S* category does not intersect at all with what is outside the *P* category—a quite different thing. (Compare "No cats are dogs" with "No nondogs are noncats." The first is obviously true: nothing that is both a cat and a dog exists in this world. The second is obviously false: a piece of chocolate cake, for instance, is both a nondog and a noncat.) If one statement is true and the other is false, they cannot possibly be logically equivalent to each other.

The *I* statement, some *S* are *P,* has as its contrapositive the statement that some non-*P* are non-*S*. These statements are not logically equivalent. The *I* statement asserts that there is at least one thing that is in both the *S* and *P* categories. Its contrapositive, on the other hand, asserts that there is at least one thing that is outside both categories. Compare the *I* statement "Some cats are fluffy creatures" with its contrapositive "Some nonfluffy creatures are noncats." In this instance, both statements happen to be true. You can no doubt think of at least one fluffy cat, so you can see that the *I* statement is true. As for a nonfluffy noncat, many things fit this rather strange description—from swimming pools to loaves of bread! Even though in this case the *I* statement and its contrapositive are both true, they are not logically equivalent. They do not entail each other and there are other examples in which an *I* statement is true and its contrapositive is false.

Obversion

Obversion is an operation that can be performed on all four kinds of categorical statements to produce a logically equivalent statement. To obvert a statement in categorical form, you do two things. First you add a *non* to the predicate category to form the complement of that category. (For example, the complement of the category musicians is nonmusicians.) Then you change the statement from negative to affirmative, or vice versa. This means you change the quality of the statement (whether it is negative or affirmative).

The obverse of "All choir directors are musicians" is "No choir directors are nonmusicians."

STATEMENT	OBVERSE OF STATEMENT
A: All *S* are *P*.	No *S* are non-*P*.
E: No *S* are *P*.	All *S* are non-*P*.
I: Some *S* are *P*.	Some *S* are not non-*P*.
O: Some *S* are not *P*.	Some *S* are non-*P*.

Contradictories

You will have noticed, perhaps, that *A* and *O* work in the same way: for *A* and *O* statements, conversion does not produce a logically equivalent statement, whereas contraposition does. Also, *E* and *I* work in the same way: for *E* and *I* statements, conversion does produce a logically equivalent statement, whereas contraposition does not. These relations exist because the *O* statement is the denial of the *A* statement, and the *I* statement is the denial of the *E* statement. *A* and *O* are contradictory to each other; so are *E* and *I*. The truth of one statement entails the falsehood of the other. If it is true that all swans are white, it must be false that some swans are not white. And if it is true that no tennis players are pianists, it must be false that some tennis players are pianists.

These relationships of contradiction are extremely important and useful. The *A* and *E* statements, being universal, are open to refutation by counterexample. We have already discussed this kind of refutation in Chapter 5. Often you find people making unguarded and cavalier generalizations, such as "No people with Ph.D. degrees are unemployed." To refute such a statement, you have only to find one person—just one—who has a Ph.D. and is unemployed. If you do, the *I* statement, "Some people who have Ph.D.'s are unemployed," is true, and the *E* statement, "No people who have Ph.D.'s are unemployed"—which is its contradictory—is false. People who categorically assert *A* and *E* statements make themselves vulnerable to such refutation. More qualified statements, such as "Few people who have Ph.D.'s are unemployed," are not so vulnerable to refutation.

Summary of Rules of Immediate Inference

1. *Conversion.* (To create the converse of a statement, transpose its subject and predicate.) All *E* and *I* statements are logically equivalent to their converse. No *A* or *O* statements are logically equivalent to their converse.
2. *Contraposition.* (To create the contrapositive of a statement, transpose its subject and predicate and negate both.) All *A* and *O* statements are logically equivalent to their contrapositive. No *E* or *I* statements are logically equivalent to their contrapositive.
3. *Obversion.* (To create the obverse of a statement, change its quality from positive to negative or from negative to positive and form the complement of its predicate.) All statements in categorical form are logically equivalent to their obverse.
4. *Contradiction.* If *A* is true, then *O* is false, and vice versa. If *E* is true, then *I* is false, and vice versa (see Table 7.1).

TABLE 7.1

Statement Form	Operation			
	Conversion	Contraposition	Obversion	Contradiction
A	NLE	LE	LE	NLE
E	LE	NLE	LE	NLE
I	LE	NLE	LE	NLE
O	NLE	LE	LE	NLE

Note: LE indicates that the statement formed by the operation is logically equivalent to the original statement. NLE indicates that the statement formed by the operation is not logically equivalent to the original statement.

EXERCISE SET

Exercise 2: Part A

For each of the following statements, put it into proper categorical form and say whether it is *A, E, I,* or *O*.

*1. The pilgrims who came to Massachusetts left England of their own free will.

2. "A robot would behave like a robot."
(Paul Ziff, "The Feelings of Robots," in *Minds and Machines,* ed. Alan R. Anderson [Englewood Cliffs, NJ: Prentice-Hall, 1964], p. 1)

*3. Some technological innovations are not needed.

4. Well, at least some committees are not efficient.

*5. Not all professors are impractical.

6. Any musician needs an accurate sense of rhythm.

*7. Art is the pursuit of beauty and truth.

*8. "Nationalism is an extreme example of fervent belief concerning doubtful matters."
(Bertrand Russell, *Sceptical Essays* [London: Unwin Books, 1935], p. 12)
   Hint: You need not try to represent "is an extreme example of" in categorical form.

9. "A radical is a man with both feet firmly planted in the air."
(Franklin Delano Roosevelt)

*10. "The proles are not human beings."
(Character in George Orwell novel, *1984*)
(*Note:* By *proles* Orwell means proletarians or members of the lowest working class in society.)

11. "All is in flux; nothing stays still."
(Heraclitus, a pre-Socratic philosopher)
   Hint: Use two statements.

12. A republic has to be small.

13. No laundromat can face onto the main street.

14. "If it doesn't say Kellogg's on the box, it isn't Kellogg's in the box."
(Advertising slogan.)

Exercise 2: Part B

For each of the following statements (a) put into categorical form, then (b) form the converse and the contrapositive. (c) State whether the converse and the contrapositive are logically equivalent to the original in each case. (Use the *A, E, I, O* labels, and use letters for the formal representation of categories. For instance, "All humans have backbones" would be "All *H* are *B*," where *H* represents the category of humans and *B* represents the category of creatures with backbones. The converse would be "All creatures with backbones are humans"—a statement of the *A* form. The contrapositive would be "All noncreatures with backbones are nonhumans"—also a statement of the *A* form. The converse is not logically equivalent to the original statement, but the contrapositive is logically equivalent to it.)

*1. Only experts understand the new technology.

2. All milk needs to be pasteurized.

3. Some conflict resolution systems are not adversarial in character.

*4. Whales are in danger of extinction.

5. In countries of the Southern hemisphere, winter comes in July and August.

*6. Some court procedures are so complicated as to be very inefficient.

*7. Some students are not competitive.

*8. No Russian authors are insensitive to nature.

9. Every dog has its day.

10. Some armies have been involved in undercover operations.

Exercise 2: Part C

For each of the following statements, put the statement into categorical form and then form the contradictory.

*1. The advice given to young parents by so-called experts is unreliable.

2. No expert knows everything.

*3. Some crops are best grown on land that has been left fallow for one season.

4. Some conflicts are not resolvable by negotiation.

*5. The only productive and innovative scientist is the one who enjoys freedom of thought and is not afraid to risk pursuing a new idea.

6. The British and Irish governments continued to debate.

7. All statements in categorical form are logically equivalent to their obverse.

Contrary and Contradictory Predicates and False Dichotomies

The results of obversion often sound very unnatural to the sensitive English ear because the *non* attached to the predicate category to form its complement results in a term that is not common in natural English. No doubt you noticed this when working through Part A of the preceding exercise. Because *non* so often has an unnatural ring, people are often inclined to alter it and substitute ordinary words that seem to be equivalent to it in meaning.

For instance, given:

(1) All bankrupt persons are nonhappy persons.

many people would be inclined to substitute:

(2) All bankrupt persons are unhappy persons.

However, statements (1) and (2) here are not logically equivalent. The reason for this lack of equivalence is that the category of unhappy things is a narrower one than the category of nonhappy things. The nonhappy include all who just fail to be happy—whether they are in a neutral (neither happy nor unhappy) state, or whether they are the kinds of things that just could not be either happy or unhappy because the very idea would not make sense. (A carrot or a cloud could not be unhappy, though such things are nonhappy.) We can see that *nonhappy* and *unhappy* do not mean the same thing.

For any predicate, *P*, we can construct a **complementary predicate**, non-*P*, such that these two predicates are the basis of contradictory statements. Two statements are *contradictory* if and only if the truth of one entails the falsity of the other and one of them must be true. For example, let the predicate in question be *beautiful*. We can construct the complementary predicate *nonbeautiful*. Any item in the universe must necessarily be either beautiful or nonbeautiful. For every entity it will be true that it is either beautiful or nonbeautiful. But it is crucially important to note here that *nonbeautiful* does not mean the same as *ugly*. It is not true that every item in the universe is either beautiful or ugly. The terms *beautiful* and *ugly* are opposites, but they are not complementary predicates in the logical sense that anything that fails to be one is the other. The predicates *beautiful* and *nonbeautiful* are complementary predicates. We will call the predicates *beautiful* and *ugly* contrary predicates.

Using **contrary predicates**, we can construct contrary statements, such as "Joan is beautiful" and "Joan is ugly." As is the case with all contrary statements, these two statements cannot both be true. But they can both be false. Supposing that Joan is moderately attractive, then it is false that she is beautiful and it is false that she is ugly.

The reason that obversion will always give you a logically equivalent statement is that you are always forming a complementary predicate by using *non*. You will rarely get a contradictory predicate if you substitute more colloquial terms for the complementary predicate—if you substitute *unhappy* for *nonhappy*, or *ugly* for *nonbeautiful*. Mistaking contraries for logical complementaries is the source of many mistakes. Compare the following lists to see how such mistakes can arise:

COMPLEMENTARY PREDICATES	CONTRARY PREDICATES
happy, nonhappy	happy, unhappy
beautiful, nonbeautiful	beautiful, ugly
intelligent, nonintelligent	intelligent, stupid
prudent, nonprudent	prudent, imprudent
pleasant, nonpleasant	pleasant, unpleasant
healthy, nonhealthy	healthy, unhealthy
friend, nonfriend	friend, enemy
fat, nonfat	fat, thin
good, nongood	good, evil
white, nonwhite	white, black
divine, nondivine	divine, satanic
strong, nonstrong	strong, weak
capitalist, noncapitalist	capitalist, communist

One common result of not being clear about contraries and contradictories is the belief in false dichotomies. We tend very much to classify ideas and situations in terms of an either/or. What makes such thinking tempting is its simplicity. Underlying it, too, however, is a tendency not to distinguish contraries from logical complementaries. It is true, *a priori*, that everything in the universe is either good or nongood and that everyone in the universe is either our friend or our nonfriend. But it is not true *a priori* (or for that matter *a posteriori*) that everything in the universe is either good or evil, that everyone who is not strong is weak, or that everyone is either our friend or our enemy. If we confuse nongood (the logical complementary) with evil (the contrary), the result will be **false dichotomy** or **polarized thinking** in which we will think that everything and everyone is either good or evil. It is not true that everyone who criticizes capitalism is a communist, because accepting communism is certainly not the only alternative to wholeheartedly accepting capitalism. It is quite possible to identify aspects of the capitalist system that merit criticism without thereby accepting communism as an alternative system of social organism. False dichotomies such as "good or evil" or "capitalist or communist" may easily lead us to think in misleading and simplistic division about a highly complex world.

Using or accepting false dichotomies is known as *black-and-white thinking* and is a well-known mistake in thought. Thinking in dichotomies is sometimes also called **binary thinking**. There was a charming joke about it on the Internet in 1995. The joke read: "There are two kinds of people in the world: those who think in binary terms, and those who do not." This remark, which expresses a satire of binary thinking, says that people either do or do not engage in binary thinking. The truth is more complex: people think in binary (and falsely dichotomous) ways sometimes, but in more complex and qualified terms at other times.

Categorical Logic: Some Philosophical Background

Categorical logic was first discovered by Aristotle more than three centuries before the birth of Christ. Seeing the formal relationships between the Greek equivalents of *all are, none are, some are,* and *some are not,* Aristotle formulated rules of inference for simple arguments in which the premises and conclusions were all in categorical form. So impressive was his achievement that for nearly two thousand years most logicians believed that categorical logic was the whole of logic. An important aspect of Aristotelian theory was the belief that all statements—whatever their surface grammatical features—were of the subject/predicate form and that all deductively valid relationships depended on the aspects of logical form that the *A, E, I,* and *O* statements express.

At the end of the eighteenth century, the eminent German philosopher Immanuel Kant still believed that Aristotelian logic was the whole of formal logic. In fact, this belief persisted in many circles until nearly the end of the nineteenth century. However, most modern logicians do not subscribe to this theory: they see categorical relations as some of the important logical relations, not all of them.

Such statements as, "If inflation continues, strikes will increase" and "Either it will be cloudy or it will rain" are not basically subject/predicate statements. They cannot naturally be expressed in categorical form. (Try it for yourself and see. You have to do a lot of fiddling, and the results are not very close to the original in meaning.) There are more useful logical symbolisms to represent these statements. These form part of modern systems of propositional logic, which are introduced in Chapter 8.

In our discussion of categorical form, we did not consider any statements about particular individuals. These statements can be put in categorical form, but only in a rather unnatural way.

Consider the following:

(1) Socrates had three sons.

Using the apparatus of categorical logic, we are unable to talk about Socrates as an individual. We solve the problem of referring to individuals as individuals by inventing a class that only contains one individual. For (1), this would be the class of things identical with Socrates. (There is only one thing in this class. Only Socrates is identical with Socrates.) Thus we represent (1) as (1'):

(1') All persons identical with Socrates are persons that had three sons.

In modern systems of logic, statements about individuals can be symbolized using letters that represent one individual—not a group. Modern logicians do not regard categorical form as the last word insofar as formally representing statements is concerned. Categorical form is a useful representation for some statements in English and other languages, but not for all.

Another interesting difference between ancient and modern theorists of logic concerns the matter of making statements about things that do not exist. Like other Greek philosophers of his time, Aristotle regarded the notion of speaking and reasoning about nonexistent things as irrational and paradoxical. He developed categorical logic on the assumption that its subjects are always things that exist. Aristotle believed that we make assertions only about those things that are real. This view of categorical logic is called the *existential* view.

Most modern logicians do not share this existential view. They point out that we often make statements about things that might or might not exist, and we want our rules of logic to apply to these statements, just as they apply to others. Scientists reasoned about genes and electrons before they knew that such things exist. A scientist who says, "Black holes are invisible," before he or she knows that there is such a thing as a black hole, is saying in effect "If anything is a black hole, then that thing is invisible." The word *if* makes the statement *hypothetical;* the scientist did not commit himself or herself to the claim that there are black holes.

Whereas ancient logicians always interpreted *A* and *E* statements as entailing the existence of things in the subject and predicate categories, modern logicians prefer a hypothetical interpretation in which the nonexistence of things in those categories is left open as a possibility. For the ancient logicians, "All human beings are mortal" carried with it a firm commitment to the claim that human beings exist. This is the existential interpretation.[3] According to the interpretation of modern logicians, "All human beings are mortal" should be interpreted in a hypothetical way. It says only that if anyone is a human, that person is mortal.

In modern logic, *A* and *E* statements can be true, even when there are no members of the subject category. A statement such as, "All students who cheat are liable to penalties imposed by the dean" can be true even if there are no students who cheat. We can make statements about electrons, black holes, mermaids, or unicorns without committing ourselves to the assumption that these things exist. That is, we can do this provided the statements are universal. Modern and ancient logic share the view that the particular statements assert existence. To say that some students cheat is to say that there is at least one student who cheats. This statement commits you to the existence of at least one student.

Who is right in this dispute between ancient and modern logicians? Can we speak and reason about what does not exist? Do we need to? These are large metaphysical questions that we cannot try to answer here. By and large, this book follows the modern view, since this is one you are likely to encounter if you pursue further courses on mathematics and formal logic. In some practical contexts, however, the modern view yields strange results. For example, it prevents us from deductively inferring that some (that is, at least one) lawyers are rich (I) from the claim that all lawyers are rich (A). Surely, you would think, if all lawyers are rich, then some are. But on the hypothetical interpretation of the A statement, we cannot validly infer the I statement from it because the A statement is interpreted as hypothetical and the I statement says *there is* at least one lawyer. We cannot validly deduce the actual from the hypothetical, so in the modern view there will be no valid immediate inference of I from A. The same point holds with E and O. But in the case of rich lawyers, the results may seem strange. You may want to ask, "Aren't some lawyers rich if all are?" The reason the results seem strange is that most of the time, we restrict ourselves in just the way Aristotle did. We talk about things that exist.

We can represent the difference between the ancient view and the modern view with regard to lawyers being rich on a Venn diagram. Diagram A represents the ancient interpretation (existential) of "All lawyers are rich" and diagram B represents its modern interpretation (hypothetical). (See Figure 7.10.)

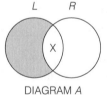 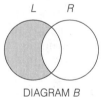

FIGURE 7.10   DIAGRAM *A*   DIAGRAM *B*

In diagram *A,* there is an *x* in the part of the *L* circle (for lawyers) that is not shaded out; the *x* indicates that there are lawyers, which the ancients presumed to be part of the meaning of "All lawyers are rich." In diagram *B,* there is no such *x* because, on the modern interpretation, the existence of lawyers is not presumed by "All lawyers are rich."

The solution to this problem is to step back and ask yourself whether the existence of the subject class should be assumed in the context you are dealing with. If it should, you write that assumption into the universal statement. In the case of the lawyers, you would then understand "All lawyers are rich" as presuming that there are lawyers and saying that all those lawyers are rich. On this understanding of the A statement, you can validly infer the I statement from it. In contexts like these, where it is a matter of common knowledge that the subject category is a category of existing things, we recommend *reading in* an existence assumption and reverting, in a sense, to the ancient view of things. But on the whole, we will work with the hypothetical interpretation, since it is standard in modern logic.

The Categorical Syllogism

A **categorical syllogism** is an argument with two premises and a conclusion, in which the premises and the conclusion are statements in categorical form, and there are three different categories of things involved in the argument. Each of the categories is mentioned in two different statements. The example used early in this chapter to exemplify categorical form is a valid syllogism. Here it is again:

1. All consistent opponents of killing are opponents of capital punishment.
2. No opponents of capital punishment are orthodox traditional Catholics. Therefore,
3. No consistent opponents of killing are orthodox traditional Catholics.

If C represents the category of consistent opponents of killing, and T represents the category of orthodox traditional Catholics, and O represents the category of opponents of capital punishment, then the argument may be formally represented as:

1. All C are O.
2. No O are T.
Therefore,
3. No C are T.

Here T, the predicate in the conclusion, is the **major term.** C, the subject in the conclusion, is the **minor term.** And O, which appears in both premises but not in the conclusion, is the **middle term.** In a syllogism, each term occurs twice. This example is a valid syllogism because the premises, taken together, deductively entail the conclusion.

In fact, Venn diagrams can be used to represent syllogisms, and by this method of representation we can even check the validity of the syllogism. To represent a syllogism in a Venn diagram, you need three circles, one for the major term (P, the predicate in the conclusion), one for the minor term (S, the subject in the conclusion), and one for the middle term (M, which occurs in both premises). You draw the circles as shown in Figure 7.11.

It is customary for S to be drawn on the top toward the left, P on the top toward the right, and M below, between S and P. (This makes sense, since M is the middle term.) A Venn diagram with three circles is more complex than one with only two. There are eight distinct areas, as numbered in Figure 7.11. The reason area (8) is enclosed is to define the complement area, for those things that are neither S, nor P, nor M.

area (1): S, not-P, not-M
area (2): S, not-P, M
area (3): S, P, not-M
area (4): S, P, M
area (5): not-S, P, not-M
area (6): not-S, P, M
area (7): not-S, not-P, M
area (8): not-S, not-P, not-M

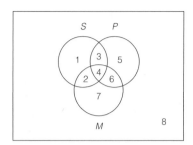

FIGURE 7.11

The Venn diagram has been enclosed in a box to make area (8) a definite space. Strictly, Venn diagrams should always be enclosed in this way, although as a matter of practice, the boxes are often omitted for convenience.

To represent a syllogism on a Venn diagram, we first draw three circles so that the subject term in the conclusion is on the left, the predicate term in the conclusion is on the right, and the middle term is below. We mark each circle with a letter representing the category. (For example, we might mark it *L* for lawyers, *R* for rich people, and so on; try to designate circles in such a way that it is easy to remember what they stand for.)

We represent the information stated in the premises of the argument on the diagram. Premises that are universal in quantity (*A* and *E* statements) should be represented first because, as we shall soon see, their representation sometimes affects how we represent particular premises. Note that we have to shade in several areas to do this. For instance, to represent "All *S* are *P*," we have to shade in area (1) and area (2); these both contain *S*s that are not *P*. To represent "All *S* are *M*," we would have to shade in areas (1) and (3), which contain *P*s that are not *M*. To represent "No *S* are *P*," we have to shade in both area (3) and area (4), which both contain things that are *S* and *P*. If no *S* are *P*, there is nothing in either of these areas. To represent "No *M* are *P*," we have to shade in both area (4) and area (6).

After universal premises have been represented, particular premises (*I* and *O*) should be represented. This is sometimes more tricky. To see why, consider the statement "Some *P* are not *M*." This statement tells you that there are *P*s outside the *M* circle, but it does not indicate whether they should be in area (3) or in area (5). Either one would be all right; it would represent the information that there is at least one *P* that is not an *M*. If one of the areas has been shaded out in the process of representing a universal premise, then the answer is clear: put the *x* in the other. If this is not the case, the *x* should be placed on the line between the two areas, to indicate that you do not have enough information to know if it belongs in area, (3) or (5).

Once you have represented the information from the premises of a syllogism in a Venn diagram, you can use the diagram to tell whether the syllogism is a valid argument. You look at your diagram to see whether the conclusion statement is represented. (In a valid syllogism, the combined information from both premises includes everything that is stated in the conclusion.) You have to look only at the

upper circles on your diagram because the middle term (by definition) does not
occur in the conclusion.

Here is a Venn diagram representation of the argument about Catholics, killing,
and capital punishment, which was cited earlier. As you recall, we had put the argument into categorical form as:

1. All C are O.
2. No O are T.
Therefore,
3. No C are T.

On a Venn diagram, the premises would be represented as shown in Figure 7.12:

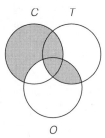

FIGURE 7.12

If we were to represent it separately, the conclusion would look like Figure 7.13:

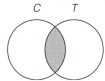

FIGURE 7.13

In the above diagram, all the C that are not O are shaded out because of the information in the first premise, and all the O that are T are shaded out because of the
information in the second premise. To determine whether the syllogism is valid, we
represent the premises on a Venn diagram and then look to see whether the information we have pictured includes what is expressed in the conclusion. Here the conclusion states that there should be nothing in the area that is both C and T. If the
premises entailed the conclusion, then the diagram would show the entire C–T
overlap as shaded out. It does. Thus, the Venn diagram reveals that the argument is
a deductively valid syllogism.

Venn diagrams vividly illustrate something that philosophers and logicians love
to say about deductively valid arguments. In a deductively valid argument, the conclusion is "already contained in the premises." An argument is deductively valid
whenever the premises assert everything needed for the conclusion to be true. In this
way, the truth of the premises makes it impossible for the conclusion to be false. The
Venn diagram for a valid syllogism shows just how this happens. For a valid syllogism, once you have drawn the premises, you need no more drawing to represent

the conclusion: it will already be pictured on your circles. It is irrelevant that areas (1) and (6) are shaded out; these shadings provide information we do not need to check whether the conclusion is true.

Let's look at another syllogism:

1. Some socialists are communists.
2. Some communists are docile puppets of totalitarian regimes.
Therefore,
3. Some socialists are docile puppets of totalitarian regimes.

Here the major term, *D*, represents the category of docile puppets of totalitarian regimes; the minor term, *R*, represents the category of socialists; and the middle term, *C*, represents the category of communists. Formalized, the argument is:

1. Some *R* are *C*.
2. Some *C* are *D*.
Therefore,
3. Some *R* are *D*.

To test the validity of this syllogism using Venn diagrams, we first diagram the premises. Both premises here are of the I form, and this makes our diagram more complicated than before (see Figure 7.14).

Some *R* are *C* and some *C* are *D*.

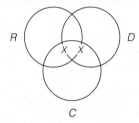

Some *C* are *D*. (The area that is the overlap between *C* and *D* is subdivided into those *CD*s that are also *R* and those that are not *R*.)

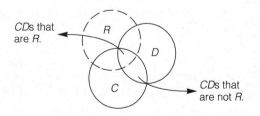

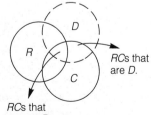

*CD*s that are *R*.

*CD*s that are not *R*.

*RC*s that are *D*.

*RC*s that are not *D*.

FIGURE 7.14   Some *R* are *C*. (The area that is the overlap between *R* and *C* is subdivided into those *RC*s that are also inside *D* and those *RC*s that are outside *D*.)

To use Venn diagrams effectively, you have to be careful not to represent on your diagram more information than the premises state. In this example, the premises do not indicate whether those *R*s that are *C* are also *D;* thus the *x* appears on the line. A similar technique must be used for the second premise. The diagram of these two *I* statements taken together reflects ambiguities that the information in the two premises does not resolve. The premises do not say whether those socialists who are communists are, or are not, among those of the communists who are docile puppets of totalitarian regimes. They assert that some communists are docile puppets, but they make no commitment as to whether these are the same communists who are also socialists. By placing the *x* on the line in these cases, we indicate that there is something in either area that the line separates, but we do not know which.

To see whether this syllogism about the communists and socialists is valid, we look at our diagram to see whether the premises provide the information in the conclusion. The conclusion was "Some *R* are *D*." We look, then, at the *R–D* intersection in the diagram representing both premises. We check whether the diagram guarantees that there will be something in this area. It does not. There is no guarantee that an *x* will be in this area, because the *x*s are on lines, and might both end up in the adjoining areas. Thus the argument is not valid.

To check an argument for validity using these Venn diagrams, you first make sure that it is a syllogism. Then you draw three overlapping circles to represent the three categories on which the argument depends. You represent the two premises on the diagram. Then you check to see whether that diagram expresses the information stated in the conclusion. If it does, the argument is deductively valid. The premises contain enough information to guarantee the conclusion logically. If it does not, the argument is not deductively valid. The conclusion has information that goes beyond what is stated in the premises.

EXERCISE SET

Exercise 3

For each of the following arguments, (a) put the premises and the conclusion into categorical form. Check to see whether the argument is a syllogism. (Remember, in a syllogism, there are two premises and one conclusion. All are in categorical form, and there are exactly three categories in the statements; each category term appears twice.) (b) Test all syllogisms for validity using Venn diagrams. Adopt the hypothetical interpretation.

1. Herpes is a viral infection. Antibiotics are an effective drug only against nonviral infections. Therefore, antibiotics are not effective against herpes.

*2. I don't know why, but some mothers find small children extremely irritating. And some people who find small children extremely irritating just cannot control themselves and suppress their rage. For these reasons, some mothers cannot control themselves and suppress their rage.

3.   Some businesses are harmful to the environment. Anything that is harmful to the environment is ultimately harmful to people. Therefore, some businesses are ultimately harmful to people.

4.   All foods that can be kept on the shelf for several weeks without rotting are foods containing additives. But all foods that contain additives are hazardous to health. Thus, foods with a shelf life of several weeks are hazardous to health.

5.   No one who has poor interpersonal skills will make a good business manager, and many students who are completing their MBA degrees have poor interpersonal skills. So some of these people will not make good business managers.

6.   Some lions are mammals because only mammals give birth to their young alive, and all lions give birth to their young alive.

*7.   Because all well-educated persons can read and all persons who can read have heard of Hitler, there are some well-educated persons who have heard of Hitler.

8.   All zoos are places in which animals may be bred, and no places in which animals may be bred should keep animals in cramped conditions. Thus, no zoo should keep animals in cramped conditions.

*9.   All sunbathing carries with it some risk of skin cancer. Anything that carries with it a risk of skin cancer is dangerous. Therefore, all sunbathing is dangerous.

10.   No test of honesty that can be affected by subjects' control of responses is reliable. Some lie detector tests are tests of honesty that can be affected by subjects' control of responses. Therefore, some lie detector tests are not reliable.

11.   Only those who are fast cyclists can manage the trip from Calgary to Banff. Pedro is a fast cyclist. Therefore, Pedro can manage the trip from Calgary to Banff.

*12.   Some doctors are unhappy. No unhappy people find it easy to express sympathy for others. Therefore, some doctors do not find it easy to express sympathy for others.

13.   Only students who have successfully completed at least one mathematics course can enroll in a physics course. Jim has not completed at least one mathematics course. Therefore Jim cannot enroll in the physics course.

14.   The skeptic is not ashamed to admit his own ignorance. He knows that full knowledge is impossible, and all of us who know that complete knowledge is impossible can certainly admit to our own ignorance without shame.

15.   A tall glass of cold lemonade is better than a Coke.

*16.   Any position in local government that involves power and influence should be allotted on the basis of a municipal election. The position of spouse of the mayor involves power and influence, so it should be allotted on the basis of municipal election.

   Question: Presuming that the mayor sought to avoid this conclusion, which premise of the syllogism should he seek to dispute if he wishes to remain consistent? Or is he compelled by categorical logic to admit that the voters should select his spouse for him?

*17.   Some religious people believe that morality depends on religion. No people who believe that morality depends on religion have a correct understanding of morality. Therefore, some religious people do not have a correct understanding of morality.

The Rules of the Categorical Syllogism

Modeling categorical syllogisms on Venn diagrams gives us a system for checking their deductive validity. Another way of checking the validity of syllogisms involves the use of rules. There are five rules, and if none are broken, the syllogism is a valid deductive argument. To use the rules for the syllogism, you need a good understanding of two technical terms: *distribution* and *middle term*. Whether a term in a categorical statement is distributed depends on whether that statement makes a comment about every item in the category specified by that term.

Distribution of Terms

A: All *S* are *P.* The subject term, *S,* is distributed, and the predicate term, *P,* is not.
E: No *S* are *P.* Both the subject term, *S,* and the predicate term, *P,* are distributed.
I: Some *S* are *P.* Neither the subject term, *S,* nor the predicate term, *P,* is distributed.
O: Some *S* are not *P.* The subject term, *S,* is not distributed. However, the predicate term, *P,* is distributed.

As was explained earlier, the reason that the predicate term is distributed in *O* statements is that the subject category is excluded from the whole predicate category, so that in an indirect way the *O* statement does say something about everything in the predicate category. To say that some men are not fathers, for example, is to say of the whole category of fathers that some men are not in it. The middle term occurs in both premises of a syllogism and does not occur in its conclusion. The middle term enables us to link the premises to logically deduce the conclusion.

The Fallacy of the Undistributed Middle

The middle term is crucial in any syllogism. It must be distributed in at least one premise for the syllogism to be valid. If the middle term is not distributed in either premise, then both premises give information about only some of this category. This means that the predicate term and the subject term cannot be securely related to each other. Consider the following example:

1. All barbers are businessmen.
2. Some businessmen are people in debt.
So,
3. Some barbers are people in debt.

This syllogism is not valid. We cannot validly connect being a barber with being in debt because *businessmen*, which is the middle term, is not distributed in this argument. In the first premise it is the predicate of an *A* statement and is not distributed. In the second premise, it is the subject of an *I* statement and is not distributed. The first premise only alludes to some businessmen, and so does the second premise.

There is no guarantee that the businessmen referred to are the same ones in each case.

The preceding argument illustrates the **fallacy of the undistributed middle,** which is committed whenever a syllogistic argument is used and the middle term is not distributed in at least one premise.

Rules of the Categorical Syllogism

Given an understanding of what distribution is, and what the middle term is, it is easy to understand the rules of the categorical syllogism. These are:

1. For a syllogism to be valid, the middle term must be distributed in at least one premise.
2. For a syllogism to be valid, no term can be distributed in the conclusion unless it is also distributed in at least one premise.
3. For a syllogism to be valid, at least one premise is affirmative; that is, a valid syllogism cannot have two negative premises.
4. For a syllogism to be valid, if it has a negative conclusion, it must also have a negative premise. And if it has one negative premise, it must also have a negative conclusion.
*5. If a syllogism has two universal premises, it cannot have a particular conclusion and be valid.

In the light of our discussion of the ancient (existential) and the modern (hypothetical) interpretations of A and E statements, it should be obvious why the fifth rule is marked with an asterisk. This rule makes explicit the hypothetical interpretation of universal statements. If you are going to use the existential interpretation, then you should drop the fifth rule. Apart from this qualification, to be deductively valid arguments, syllogisms must satisfy the conditions of *all* the rules. If even one is broken, then granting that the argument has been correctly formalized as a syllogism, it is not valid. It is a worthwhile exercise to do several examples from the preceding exercise using these rules instead of Venn diagrams. Your answer should be the same as it was when you used Venn diagrams.

Consider the following syllogism about syllogisms, which we will call Syllogism X.

(1) All invalid syllogisms contain an error. (All I are C.)
(2) This syllogism contains an error. (All T are C.)
Therefore,
(3) This syllogism is invalid. (All T are I.)

Without constructing a Venn diagram, we can easily see that Syllogism X is invalid because the middle term, C, is not distributed in either premise. Syllogism X, then, commits the fallacy of the undistributed middle. Once we have found this out, we need not check any other rules, because the violation of even one rule for the syllogism makes an argument invalid.

Syllogism *X* is a syllogism about syllogisms. In fact, it is a syllogism about itself. It is self-referential, and the property of self-reference is the source of various interesting paradoxes in logic. But Syllogism *X*, though strange, is not a real paradox. If Syllogism *X* strikes you as puzzling that is probably because of its peculiar combination of truth and invalidity. The argument may seem somehow "right," and yet it is invalid. Premise (1) is clearly true. Syllogism *X* (which is this syllogism) does contain an error, so premise (2) is also true. And the conclusion (3) is true, because Syllogism *X* is invalid. So the premises are true and the conclusion is true. The (A) condition for argument cogency is satisfied, due to the truth of the premises. But the (R) and (G) conditions are not satisfied. The example, which is rather amusing in its own right, serves to illustrate again the important point that the truth or acceptability of premises is one thing and the deductive validity of an argument is quite another.

Applying Categorical Logic

If an argument is deductively valid, then the (R) and (G) conditions of argument cogency are perfectly and entirely satisfied; no doubt can be raised on these. If anything is wrong with a deductively valid argument, then it must lie in the premises themselves.

When you read newspapers, magazines, and scholarly articles it is not likely that you will be struck by a conspicuous number of categorical syllogisms. Syllogisms worded as straightforwardly as those we have studied so far in this chapter are comparatively rare in natural discourse. Nevertheless, some clear syllogisms are to be found in contemporary discourse. There are also some arguments that are implicitly syllogistic, though their syllogistic form does not stand out as clearly as you might wish. The rules in this chapter apply only to those statements that are in proper categorical form. A syllogism must have two premises and a conclusion, all in categorical form, and it must involve three distinct categories of things.

To see what may be involved in the application of syllogistic rules, we shall work through an example. This is an argument that the philosopher John Locke used in his defense of religious toleration:

> Speculative opinions and articles of faith which are required only to be believed cannot be imposed on any church by the law of the land. For it is absurd that things should be enjoined by laws which are not in men's power to perform. And to believe this or that to be true does not depend upon our will.[4]

This argument is a valid syllogism, but we have to do some recasting before we can demonstrate this fact.

Locke's conclusion is in the first sentence: "<u>Speculative opinions and articles of faith</u> are <u>things that should not be imposed by law.</u>" The premises are in the next two sentences: "<u>things enjoined by law</u> are <u>things that it is in men's power to per-</u>

form," and "beliefs are not things that depend on our will." Here, as indicated by underlining, we have six categories. Unless we can regard some of these categories as reducible to others, we cannot regard Locke's argument as a syllogism. A syllogism, by definition, is based on three distinct categories of things. We have to look at the differences in wording to see whether we really have the same category described in different words. This does happen in the argument. In this context, *speculative opinions* and *articles of faith* and *beliefs* mean the same thing. Also, "things that it is in men's power to perform" and "things that depend on our will" are the same. Now the only remaining problem concerns the *should* in the first premise. Statements in categorical form must use *are*; therefore, *should* will have to be moved from the linking position to the internal specification of a category.

Once we grasp the necessary variations in wording, the argument may be represented as follows:

1. All things that should be imposed by law are things that depend on our will.
2. No beliefs are things that depend on our will.
So,
3. No beliefs are things that should be imposed by law.

Allowing *B* to stand for beliefs, *I* to stand for things that should be imposed by law, and *W* to stand for things that depend on our will, the argument becomes:

1. All *I* are *W*.
2. No *B* are *W*.
So,
3. No *B* are *I*.

As you can see (check it using Venn diagrams or the rules for categorical syllogisms), this argument is valid. But it takes some reflection and some work to get Locke's original passage into this form. Our reworded argument is less eloquent than Locke's original, but it is much easier to understand. We can show that the argument is deductively valid, and we therefore know that any doubt about its cogency must concern the acceptability of the premises.

Another matter that often arises when we try to spot syllogistic reasoning in ordinary speech and writing is the problem of elliptical syllogisms. Elliptical syllogisms are implicitly syllogistic arguments in which either one premise or the conclusion is not explicitly stated by the arguer. Here is an example:

The bigger the burger, the better the burger.
The burgers are bigger at Burger King.

The point of this advertisement is obviously to convince you that the burgers are better at Burger King. This claim is entailed by the two stated claims. The ad is really a syllogism with a missing conclusion:

1. All bigger burgers are better burgers.
2. All burgers at Burger King are bigger burgers.
So,
3. All burgers at Burger King are better burgers.

This is a valid syllogism.

The question of when you should supply a missing conclusion is not different for syllogisms than it is for other arguments. You have to have reason to believe that the author meant to assert the claim you add. If that claim is, in fact, deductively entailed by what is stated, the author of the argument was clearly logically committed to it, and you are not misinterpreting him or her by adding the conclusion.

Even more common than the missing conclusion in a syllogism is the missing premise. Principles for adding premises and conclusions are the same for elliptical syllogisms as they are elsewhere. (See the section on missing premises in Chapter 2.) It is not appropriate to regard an argument as an elliptical syllogism unless the premise you are going to add is one that will make the argument valid. The very things that make you justified in reading it will relate it to stated material in a valid pattern.

EXERCISE SET

Exercise 4

For the following arguments, (a) identify the premises and conclusions and (if necessary) put them into proper categorical form. If necessary, supply a missing premise or missing conclusion. Then (b) test the arguments for validity using either Venn diagrams or the rules of the syllogism.

*1.   Some problems experienced by human beings in developing countries are the result of climate. No problem that is the result of climate is the result of abuses of human rights. Therefore, some problems experienced by humans in developing countries are not the result of abuses of human rights.

*2.   "Other men die. I am not another. Therefore I shall not die."

(Vladimir Nabokov, *Pale Fire* [New York: Putnam, 1962])

3.   A completely unprejudiced observation is an observation that is made with no goal in mind. But no observation is made with no goal in mind. Therefore, no observation is completely unprejudiced.

4.   Some hockey is highly violent and no activity that is highly violent provides good training for young boys. Therefore, no hockey provides good training for young boys.

5.   Nothing that contains all the genetic information necessary to form a complete human being is mere property. A fertilized egg growing into an embryo contains all the genetic information necessary to form a complete human being. Therefore, a fertilized egg growing into an embryo is not mere property.

*6.   "Among the vowels there are no double letters; but one of the double letters (w) is compounded of two vowels. Hence a letter compounded of two vowels is not necessarily itself a vowel."

(C. S. Peirce, "Some Consequences of Four Incapacities," in *Philosophical Writings of C. S. Peirce*, ed. Justus Buchler [New York: Dover, 1955])

*7.   "The leaders of our country have not told us, the citizens, where they want to lead us. This must mean that they are totally confused themselves."

(Duff Cornbush in the *Canadian*, quoted by Douglas Roche in *Justice Not Charity* [Toronto: McLelland and Stewart, 1970])

8.   "If a much praised government dam was worth the trouble of building, someone would

have been able to build it for a profit. Since it is unprofitable, it must be financed at least in part by taxes."

(From Doug Casey, *Crisis Investing* [New York: Stratford Press, 1980])

9.   A job in an isolated place poses special difficulties, and no job that puts special burdens on the employee should be poorly paid. Therefore, no job that is in an isolated place should be poorly paid.

10.   "Every well-founded inference to an infinite cause is based upon the observation of an infinite effect. But no inference to God's existence from the design in nature is based upon the observation of an infinite effect. Thus, no inference to God's existence from the design in nature is a well-founded inference."

(Adapted from David Hume, "Dialogues Concerning Natural Religion," in *The Empiricists* [New York: Anchor Press, 1974])

11.   Any store that is seeking to sell goods cheaply is going to cut down on staff salaries, and Joe's Department Store is trying to sell goods cheaply, so you can be sure that they are cutting down on staff.

*12.   No one who is lazy will pass the degree in physics, and some students currently enrolled in the physics program are lazy. Therefore some students in the program won't get their degree.

*13.   *Background:* This passage is part of a letter written to oppose the censorship of pornography in Canada:

"A nation that permits, night after night, year in and year out, the showing on TV and in cinemas of murders by the hundreds and thousands, and yet can't show one love-making scene without having it labelled obscenity—that nation is guilty of practicing gross obscenity and hypocrisy, and is consequently without redeeming social value."

(Toronto *Globe and Mail,* April 21, 1984)

Hint: You can find two syllogisms here if you add two extra premises—one for each.

14.   "Our ideas reach no farther than our experience. We have no experience of divine attributes and operations. I need not conclude my syllogism: you can draw the inference yourself."

(David Hume, "Dialogues Concerning Natural Religion," in *The Essential David Hume,* ed. Robert Paul Wolff [Toronto: New American Library, 1969], p. 297)

15.   A person who is truly a good person cannot be a liar. Why not? Because no one who is a liar is worthy to be believed, whereas anyone who is truly a good person must be credible and believable.

(Adapted from Ralph M. Eaton, *General Logic* [New York: Scribner's, 1959], p. 106)

16.   What has been taught to us may feel natural. But what has been taught to us is not natural. So some things that feel natural just aren't.

CHAPTER SUMMARY

Some valid deductive arguments owe their validity to the way in which the key logical terms *all, none, some,* and *not* are used. The relations between these terms are studied in the branch of formal logic known as categorical logic. Relations in categorical logic can be represented on Venn diagrams in which overlapping circles represent various relations between classes of things.

Syllogisms are arguments with two premises and a conclusion, based on three distinct categories, where premises and conclusion are all in categorical form. Syllogisms can be tested for their validity by using Venn diagrams and by applying the rules of the syllogism. To apply categorical logic to the sorts of statements and arguments you would find in magazines, newspapers, and books other than logic text-books, you often have to look closely to see that statements, though not obviously categorical in form, can be rewritten in categorical form. If you can recast statements in this form, categorical logic can be helpful in enabling you to understand logical relationships and to evaluate syllogistic arguments. Like other arguments, syllogisms may have missing conclusions or missing premises.

Review of Terms Introduced

Binary thinking   Thinking in either/or terms; assuming that the things one is thinking about must fall into one of only two classifications. See also false dichotomy, polarized thinking.

Categorical logic   A branch of formal logic in which the basic logical terms are *all*, *some*, *no*, *are*, and *not*.

Categorical syllogism   Argument with two premises and a conclusion, in which the premises and the conclusion are statements in categorical form and there are three different categories of things involved in the argument.

Complementary predicate   Predicate formed by placing *non* in front of an existing predicate. Example: the complementary predicate of *musician* is *nonmusician*.

Contradictory (of a given statement)   That statement that must always be opposite to the original statement in truth value. If the statement is *X,* its contradictory statement is not-*X*. When *X* is true, not-*X* is false, and vice versa. For example, the contradictory statement of "All *S* are *P*" is "Some *S* are not *P*."

Contraposition   A logical operation on a statement in categorical form, in which the statement is converted, and then *non* is attached to each category. For example, the contrapositive of "No *S* are *P*" is "No non-*P* are non-*S*." For *A* and *O* statements, contraposition produces a logically equivalent statement. For *E* and *I* statements, it does not.

Contrary (of a given statement)   A logically related statement that can never be true when the given statement is true, although it can be false when the statement is false. For example, "All *S* are *P*" and "No *S* are *P*" are contraries. They cannot both be true, but they can both be false.

Contrary predicates   Predicates logically related so that nothing can possess both, though things may possess neither. For example, *happy* and *unhappy* are contrary predicates. It is not possible for a thing to be both happy and unhappy, but it is possible for it to be neither happy nor unhappy.

Conversion   A logical operation on a statement in categorical form, in which the order of the terms is reversed. For example, the converse of "All *S* are *P*" is "all *P* are *S*." For *E* and *I* statements, conversion produces logically equivalent statements. For *A* and *O* statements, it does not.

Distribution   When the categorical statement in which the term appears is about all the things within the category that term designates. The subject (S) term is distributed in A and E statements. The predicate (P) term is distributed in E and O statements.

Fallacy of the undistributed middle   Fallacy committed when a syllogism is put forward and it is invalid because the middle term is not distributed in either one of the premises.

False dichotomy   An either/or split that omits alternatives. (For example, to think that everything is either black or white would be to believe in a false dichotomy.) False dichotomies often seem plausible because contrary predicates are mistaken for contradictory ones.

Immediate inference   Inference of one statement directly from another, with no intermediate logical steps.

Logical equivalence   Logical relation between two statements that must necessarily have the same truth value. For instance, "Not all S are P" and "Some S are not P" are logically equivalent.

Major term   Term that appears in the predicate position in the conclusion of a syllogism.

Middle term   Term that occurs in both premises of a syllogism but not in the conclusion.

Minor term   Term that appears in the subject position in the conclusion of a syllogism.

Obversion   A logical operation on a statement in categorical form, in which the prefix *non* is added to the predicate. Then, if the original statement was affirmative, it is made negative. If the original statement was negative, it is made affirmative. Obversion always produces a statement that is logically equivalent to the original one.

Particular affirmative   (I) statement of the form "Some S are P."

Particular negative   (O) statement of the form "Some S are not P."

Polarized thinking   Thinking of the world as divided, along some dimension, into two and only two incompatible and irreconcilable divisions. Examples: good/evil; divine/satanic; strong/weak; masculine/feminine.

Square of Opposition   An arrangement of the four categorical forms. The opposition is apparent from the diagonals on the square.

Stereotyping   Thinking, in an unduly simplistic way, of all members of a class or group as being the same in some fundamental characteristics other than those that define the group. Examples: All Americans resist learning foreign languages; All Canadians love to ski; All Italians eat garlic; All Germans are orderly. Confuses *some* or *most* with *all*.

Subcontrary statements   An *I* statement and an *O* statement with the same subject and predicate. Subcontraries can both be true, but they cannot both be false. Example: Some books are interesting; some books are not interesting.

Universal affirmative   (*A*) statement of the form "All *S* are *P*."

Universal negative   (*E*) statement of the form "No *S* are *P*."

Venn diagram   Diagram in which overlapping circles are used to represent categorical relationships.

Notes

1. *For instructors.* For any evaluation of the formal representation of an argument to tell us whether an argument is formally valid or formally invalid, we must assume that the formal representation of it captures its logically salient structural details. For this reason, formal appraisal presupposes that the task of rendering the argument into formal terms has been carried out accurately. I believe that this presupposition shows that formal logic, in any application to arguments expressed in natural language, presupposes nonformal techniques. An argument may be deemed valid if any formally apt representation of it can be shown valid. But one cannot say it is invalid if any formally apt representation of it can be shown invalid—for invalidity on this interpretation cannot be known to preclude validity on some other interpretation. See T. J. McKay, "On Showing Invalidity," *Canadian Journal of Philosophy 14* (1984), pp. 97–101; and Maurice A. Finocchiaro, "The Positive Versus the Negative Evaluation of Arguments," in *New Essays in Informal Logic,* edited by Ralph H. Johnson and J. Anthony Blair (Windsor: Informal Logic, 1994). Arguments to the effect that argument invalidity in particular cannot be formally demonstrated can be found in J. W. Oliver, "Formal Fallacies and Other Invalid Arguments," *Mind 76,* pp. 463–478; G. J. Massey, "Are There Good Arguments that Bad Arguments are Bad?" *Philosophy in Context 4,* pp. 61–77; and G. J. Massey, "In Defense of the Asymmetry," *Philosophy in Context 4* (Suppl.),

pp. 44–66. My awareness of this issue was heightened by a critical paper presented by Andrew Irvine at the Third International Conference on Argumentation at the University of Amsterdam in June 1994.

2. *For instructors.* One may, of course, insist that such inferences presume universal statements about meaning (in this case, that all sisters are female) and that such presumptions should be regarded as missing premises. This approach is not taken here.

3. The term *existential* as used here should not be confused with *existentialism* or *existentialist.* Existentialism is a school of philosophy, associated largely with movements in France in the 1940s and 1950s, which is based on the idea that human beings have no fixed human nature and define what they are by the ways in which they choose to exist. Jean Paul Sartre and Simone de Beauvoir were leading existentialist thinkers. Sartre was famous for his statement that existence precedes essence, by which he meant that human beings create or define their own essential nature. According to Sartre, our nature comes after our existence and results from choices we make. In contrast to Sartre, Aristotle believed that human beings and other creatures have fixed essences. Aristotle was definitely not an existentialist in the sense in which Sartre was an existentialist.

4. John Locke, "A Letter Concerning Toleration," cited in S. F. Barker, *The Elements of Logic,* 3rd ed. (New York: McGraw-Hill, 1980).

chapter eight

Deductively Valid Arguments: Propositional Logic

ALTHOUGH CATEGORICAL LOGIC is the oldest developed logic in the Western philosophical tradition, it is not now believed to be the most basic part of logic. That role is reserved for **propositional logic,** which deals with the relationships holding between simple propositions or statements and their compounds. In propositional logic, the basic logical terms are *not, or, and,* and *if then.* These terms are used to relate statements and their compounds. The following is a simple example of an argument that is easily formalized in propositional logic:

1. If global warming continues, parts of the polar icecap will melt.
2. Global warming will continue.
Therefore,
3. Parts of the polar icecap will melt.

This argument is deductively valid, but not by virtue of any relations between subjects and predicates. Rather, the conditional relationship between statements makes it valid. In propositional logic, we use letters to represent simple statements. Symbols represent the basic logical connecting words: *not, and, or,* and *if then.* Allowing G to represent "Global warming will continue" and M to represent "Parts of the polar icecap will melt," the preceding argument can be represented in propositional logic as:

1. $G \supset M$
2. G

Therefore,
3. *M*

The symbol ⊃ is used to represent *if then.* Provided that an argument can be accurately formalized in the symbols of propositional logic, we can test its deductive validity by a device called a **truth table.**

Definition of the Basic Symbols
Used in Propositional Logic

In Chapter 7, we noted that in a system of formal logic, we have to define terms more precisely than we would in ordinary natural language. This factor must be remembered when we are working with propositional logic. The symbols –, ·, ∨, and ⊃ stand for *not, and, or,* and *if then,* respectively. But they do not coincide perfectly with all the shades of meaning that these English words have. Rather, they represent a kind of logical core.

Consider the word *not.* Suppose that the letter *W* is used to represent a simple statement, such as "A war was fought in Serbia in 1999." **Denying the statement** that a war was fought in Serbia in 1999 amounts to asserting its contradictory—namely, "A war was not fought in Serbia in 1999." When a single letter represents a statement (in this case, *W*), its contradictory is symbolized by a minus sign preceding that letter, as in –*W*. When *W* is true, –*W* is false; when –*W* is true, *W* is false. (You read –*W* as "not *W*.")

We can represent the simple relationship between any statement and its denial on a truth table, in Figure 8.1:

P	–*P*
T	F
F	T

FIGURE 8.1

This is a simple truth table that defines "–", which is the operator for *not. P* represents any statement that has only two possible truth values. *P* can be either true or false, as is shown in the column on the left. Its denial, –*P*, also has two possible truth values. The truth of *P* and that of –*P* are related, as we can see by reading across the rows. When *P* is true, –*P* is false, and vice versa. If we deny the denial of *P*, we get – –*P*, which is logically equivalent to *P*. The contradictory of "there was a war" is "there was not a war." The contradictory of "there was not a war" is "it is not the case that there was not a war," which is just to say that there was a war.

Now we move on to *and.* Frequently, the word *and* is used to join two statements, as in the sentence:

(a) A war was being fought in Serbia in 1999, and the NATO alliance was one party in that war.

As we saw in Chapter 2, logicians call a combination of statements based on *and* a conjunction. A **conjunction** of two statements is true if and only if both these statements (called conjuncts) are true. That is, statement (a) will be true if and only if it is true that a war was being fought in Serbia in 1999 and it is true that the NATO alliance was one party in that war. If either one of these conjuncts is false, statement (a) will be false, because statement (a) is a conjunction that asserts both conjuncts. Conjunction is represented in propositional logic by "·". This symbol is defined by the truth table in Figure 8.2.

P	Q	$P \cdot Q$
T	T	T
T	F	F
F	T	F
F	F	F

FIGURE 8.2

The truth table for "·" (*and*) is larger than the truth table for "−" (*not*) because we are now working with two different statements, P and Q. Each may have two truth values, so there are four possible combinations of truth values (2 times 2). The truth table must represent all the possible combinations: P and Q both true; P and Q both false; P true and Q false; Q true and P false. That is why it has four rows.

We now move on to *or*. With *and* we conjoin statements. With *or* we disjoin them. That is, we relate them as alternatives: one or the other is true. In a statement such as "Either the husband is the murderer or the lover is the murderer," two simpler statements are disjoined, and the resulting compound statement is called a **disjunction.** The symbol used in propositional logic for the *or* of disjunction is "∨". The symbol "∨" is defined by the truth table in Figure 8.3:

P	Q	$P \vee Q$
T	T	T
T	F	T
F	T	T
F	F	F

FIGURE 8.3

The disjunction "$P \vee Q$" is true when either one of the disjuncts (P, Q) is true. It is also true when both are true. The only case in which the disjunction is false is when both disjuncts are false. You can see this by looking at the bottom row. P is false, Q is false, and $P \vee Q$ is false. (For example, the disjunction "Bosnia is in Northern Europe or Bosnia is in Central America" is false. Bosnia is, in fact, in Southern Europe. Thus it is false that Bosnia is in Northern Europe, and it is false that Bosnia is in Central America.) In any disjunctive statement in which both disjuncts are false, the statement as a whole is false. If one or both disjuncts are true, the statement as a whole is true. These relationships are represented on the truth table, where you will see that the disjunction is true in the first three rows, and false in the last row.

Now for the conditional. A **conditional statement** is one whose form is basically "If such-and-such, then so-and-so." For example, the statement "If it rains, we will not ride on the ferris wheel" is a conditional. The part of the statement that is hypothesized (that is, which immediately follows *if*) is the **antecedent** of the conditional; in the preceding example the antecedent is "it rains." The clause that follows *then* is the **consequent;** in the preceding example the consequent is "we will not ride on the ferris wheel." *A conditional statement asserts neither its antecedent nor its consequent.* Rather, it expresses a link between the two, claiming that if the antecedent is true, then so is the consequent.

For instance, consider the conditional statement "If Joe runs every day, he will become fit." In this conditional statement, the antecedent is "Joe runs every day" and the consequent is "Joe will become fit." The conditional says that *if* the antecedent is true, the consequent will be true also. It says neither that Joe runs every day nor that he will become fit, but rather that these two things are connected. An understanding of conditionals is very important in logic.

In propositional logic, a symbol called the **horseshoe** ($\supset$) is used to express a minimal, but basic, meaning common to all conditionals. There are various sorts of conditionals. Consider:

(a) If a person has a mortgage on his house, he has borrowed money to buy the house. (Conditional based on definition of what a mortgage on a house is.)

(b) If a person has trouble paying a heavy mortgage, he is likely to be under stress. (Conditional based on a causal relationship between a personal circumstance and a state of mind.)

(c) If a person cannot pay his mortgage, he is open to having his house taken over by the bank or person to whom the mortgage is owed. (Conditional based on a legal situation of liability when one fails to repay debts.)

(d) If a person has incurred a debt by taking out a mortgage, he should make every reasonable effort to repay that debt. (Conditional based on the moral principle that one ought to pay one's debts.)

(e) Finally, his banker made a threat, saying "If you don't get that next payment in, we're going to have the locks changed." (The banker's statement is a threat, warning of negative consequences if the payment is not made.)

(f) If you can manage to pay a thousand a month on that mortgage, I'll eat my hat! (Conditional used to assert disbelief in the antecedent, which is indicated by promising, in the consequent, bizarre behavior if the disbelieved claim should turn out to be true.)

All these statements are conditionals, but they differ in significant respects. What they have in common is the relationship between the antecedent and the consequent. Every conditional asserts that given the antecedent, the consequent will hold as well. This connection of truth values between the antecedent and the consequent is the logical core of the conditional relationship. It is this logical core that the horseshoe is intended to capture. Because it is supposed to represent the truth functional antecedent/consequent connection in all the different conditional, the horseshoe may fail to capture certain other aspects of some particular conditionals.

It is probably easiest, for the moment at least, to regard the horseshoe as a technical symbol invented by logicians and learn it in terms of its truth table. When we come to discuss the relation between English meanings and the propositional symbols in more detail, we'll explain why the horseshoe, which is different in important ways from *if then* and related terms, can nevertheless be successfully used to symbolize many arguments.

The horseshoe is technically defined as shown here in Figure 8.4.

P	Q	P⊃Q
T	T	T
T	F	F
F	T	T
F	F	T

FIGURE 8.4

Be sure to learn this truth table. Since the horseshoe does not in all cases correspond to most people's intuitive sense of what is logically correct, you may not understand this connective as easily as the others. It is quite important to remember what "If *P* then *Q*" does not assert. It does not assert that *P*; nor does it assert that *Q*. It does not assert the conjunction *P* · *Q*. It does not assert that *Q* is the only thing that follows from *P*, or that *P* is the only thing that leads to *Q*. As a conditional, "If *P* then *Q*" asserts that if *P* is true, *Q* will be true. That is to say, it will not be the case that *P* is true and *Q* is false.

Using the logical symbols just defined and using capital letters to represent simple statements, we can represent many arguments in an elegant and compact way. Here is an example:

ARGUMENT IN ENGLISH

Either international law will further develop or it will undergo a decline. If international law develops further, the World Court in The Hague will hear more cases regarding disputes between countries. If international law undergoes a decline, then aggravated conflicts between countries will increasingly fall outside the jurisdiction of the law. Therefore, either the World Court will hear more cases regarding disputes between countries, or aggravated conflicts between countries will increasingly fall outside the jurisdiction of the law.

FORMALIZATION OF ARGUMENT

Let *I* represent "International law will further develop" and *U* represent "International law will undergo a decline." Let *W* represent "The World Court in The Hague will hear more cases regarding disputes between countries" and *G* represent "Aggravated conflicts between countries will increasingly fall outside the jurisdiction of the law."

The statements in the English argument can now be represented using these letters and the symbols of propositional logic. The symbolized argument will be:

I ∨ *U*
I ⊃ *W*
U ⊃ *G*
Therefore,
W ∨ *G*

This symbolization is a compact version of the original argument. Once the argument is formalized in this way, we can use a technique involving truth tables to test its deductive validity.

An important matter pertaining to formalization is the matter of brackets. You are familiar with brackets, no doubt, from algebra and arithmetic. There is a great difference between the quantity $(30 + 21)/3$ and the quantity $(30) + (21/3)$. The first quantity is 17; the second is 37. Brackets make an important difference in symbolic logic too. They function much the way punctuation marks do in English—serving to indicate how things are grouped together.

Suppose we wish to express in propositional logic the idea that a person may have either jello or ice cream, but not both, for dessert. We need to use the symbol for *not* so that it applies to the conjunction. We can do this as follows: "You may have jello or ice cream, and not both" is rewritten as "You may have jello or you may have ice cream, and it is not the case both that you may have jello and that you may have ice cream," and that is symbolized as:

$(J \lor I) \cdot -(J \cdot I)$

Look at the second set of brackets in this example. The symbol for *not* is placed outside the bracket because this symbol has the scope of applying to the entire expression within the brackets; it denies the entire conjunction. Suppose that we had simply written:

Wrong: $(J \lor I) \cdot -J \cdot I$

In that case, the symbol "$-$" would deny only that we can have jello. What we wish to deny is that we can have both jello and ice cream. We need the brackets to indicate the scope (extent) of the negation. Similarly, we need brackets around the disjunction to indicate that the disjunction is simply between J and I.

Here are some further examples where bracketing is necessary:

(a) If she is either too busy or not busy enough, she will be unsatisfying as a friend.
$(B \lor -E) \supset U$

In (a), the antecedent of the conditional is the entire disjunction.

(b) If he continues to talk and refuses to listen, he will be a poor conversation partner.
$(T \cdot R) \supset C$

In (b), the antecedent of the conditional is the entire conjunction.

Bracketing serves to group things just the way punctuation marks, especially commas, do in English. It is very important to get brackets right. Look at the English sentence to see the scope of negations and other relationships. An obvious but handy rule about brackets is that if you have an odd number of them, something has definitely gone wrong.

Testing for Validity by the Truth Table Technique

Let's begin by looking at a logically dubious argument. It goes like this:

> If Don is in love with Sue, then Sue is loved by someone. Don is not in love with Sue. Therefore, it is not the case that Sue is loved by someone.

This argument is formally represented as:

$D \supset S$
$-D$
Therefore,
$-S$

In the symbolized version, D represents "Don is in love with Sue" and S represents "Sue is loved by someone." The argument does seem to be a little strange, because it seems to be telling us that if Don does not love Sue then nobody does—which does not seem plausible. (Is there something about Sue that means she couldn't be loved by anyone else? That does not seem to make sense.) We can ask of this argument: Is it deductively valid or not? Our logical intuition does not always tell us these things as clearly as we might like. Assuming that an argument has been correctly formalized using the symbols of propositional logic, we can represent it on a truth table and use a truth table technique to show conclusively whether it is a valid argument in propositional logic.

The argument contains two distinct statement letters, so our truth table will have to have four rows. How many columns it has will depend on the number of distinct statements, and component statements, in the premises and the conclusion. We represent the premises and the conclusion on our table. We calculate truth values for these for all the possible combinations of truth values in the component statements, D and S. Then we check the argument for deductive validity. We have to make sure that in every row of the truth table in which all the premises come out as true, the conclusion also comes out as true. If there is any case where the premises are all true and the conclusion is false, the argument is not deductively valid in propositional logic. If we find even one case where the conclusion comes out false and the premises are all true, the argument is invalid in propositional logic.

Figure 8.5 shows the truth table:

D	S	$-D$	$-S$	$D \supset S$
T	T	F	F	T
T	F	F	T	F
F	T	(T)	(F)	(T)
F	F	T	T	T

FIGURE 8.5

The premises are represented in the rightmost column and in the third column from the left.[1] The conclusion is represented in the fourth column from the left. We check to see where the conclusion turns out to be false. This happens in the first row and in the third row. In the first row one of the premises is false, so the fact that the conclusion is false does not show that the argument is invalid. But in the third row, the conclusion is false and both premises (circled) are true. Thus, there is a case in which the premises are true and the conclusion is false. The argument is not deductively valid.

The truth table test for deductive validity works for any argument that can correctly be expressed in the symbols of simple propositional logic. If you can do this, you can construct a truth table showing all the premises and the conclusion. You then check to see whether there is any row in the truth table where all the premises are true and the conclusion is false. If there is, the argument is not valid. If there is not, the argument is valid.

There are rules for constructing these truth tables. First, you need to know how many rows to have. If n represents the number of distinct statement letters in the argument, then you need 2 to the nth power rows. For two distinct statements, you need 2 times 2 rows; for three distinct statements you need 2 times 2 times 2 rows; for four distinct statements you need 2 times 2 times 2 times 2 rows; and so on. You do not consider a statement and its denial to be distinct statements for the purposes of this calculation because the denial is, technically speaking, a compound statement formed from the original statement. What matters is the number of distinct statement letters.

Second, for the truth table technique to work properly, you must represent on it all the possible combinations of truth values for the statements you are working with. The Ts and Fs in your columns have to be systematically set out in such a way that this requirement is met. Start in the leftmost column and fill half the rows with Ts. (That is, if the truth table has eight rows, fill the first four with Ts.) Then fill the other half with Fs. In the next column, fill one-quarter of the rows with Ts, followed by one-quarter Fs, and repeat. In the third column (if there is one) it will be one-eighth Ts, then Fs, then Ts, and so on. This procedure is a standard one, which ensures that the truth table will represent all the possibilities of truth and falsity combinations for the statements you are working with.

To illustrate the construction of truth tables, suppose that you are setting up a truth table to represent an argument in which the premises and the conclusion require four distinct statement letters: S, C, H, and G. The first four columns of your truth table would be as shown in Figure 8.6.

The next matter is how many columns your truth table needs. It needs at least one for each distinct statement letter, one for each premise, and one for the conclusion. In many cases, inserting additional columns is helpful for clarity and to avoid mistakes. For instance, if you have a premise of the form "$(P \cdot Q) \supset R$," you should have a separate column for "$P \cdot Q$" even if it is neither a premise nor a conclusion in the argument. The reason is that it is a significant component (antecedent of a conditional), and if you enter it separately in its own column, you are less likely to go wrong calculating the truth value of that conditional.

S	C	H	G
T	T	T	T
T	T	T	F
T	T	F	T
T	T	F	F
T	F	T	T
T	F	T	F
T	F	F	T
T	F	F	F
F	T	T	T
F	T	T	F
F	T	F	T
F	T	F	F
F	F	T	T
F	F	T	F
F	F	F	T
F	F	F	F

FIGURE 8.6

Here is another example so that we can study the truth table technique further:

ARGUMENT IN ENGLISH

If John does not practice his singing, he will hinder the work of the choir director. If John hinders the work of the choir director, he should not be allowed to
continue as a member of the choir. As a matter of fact, John does not practice
his singing. So John should not be allowed to continue as a member of the choir.

FORMALIZATION OF ARGUMENT

Let P represent "John practices his singing"; let H represent "John will hinder the
work of the choir director" and let B represent "John should be allowed to
continue as a member of the choir." The argument can be formally represented
as:

Premise 1: $-P \supset H$
Premise 2: $H \supset -B$
Premise 3: $-P$
Therefore,
Conclusion: $-B$

The number of distinct statement letters here is three (P, H, B). Thus we will need 2
to the third, or 8, rows in the truth table in Figure 8.7. We have to represent each
premise and the conclusion.

The columns for the premises and the conclusion are marked with arrows. We
need to check every row in which the conclusion is false, to find out whether all the
premises are true in that row. If this happens, the argument is invalid, because there
is a case in which all the premises are true and the conclusion is false. If it does not
happen, the argument is valid, because there is no case in which all the premises are
true and the conclusion is false.

P	H	B	–P	–B	H⊃–B	–P⊃H
T	T	T	F	(F)	F	T
T	T	F	F	T	T	T
T	F	T	F	(F)	T	T
T	F	F	F	T	T	T
F	T	T	T	(F)	F	T
F	T	F	T	T	T	T
F	F	T	T	(F)	T	F
F	F	F	T	T	T	F

↓ Premise 3   ↓ Conclusion   ↓ Premise 2   ↓ Premise 1

FIGURE 8.7

Using this technique, we can see that the above argument is valid. The conclusion, which is –B, is false in rows 1, 3, 5, and 7, so we have to check the premises for those rows to make sure that at least one of them is false when the conclusion is false. In row 1, premise 2 is false and premise 3 is false. In row 3, premise 3 is false. In row 5, premise 2 is false; and in row 7, premise 1 is false. Thus there is no case in which the conclusion is false and all the premises are true. The argument is valid because all possible cases have been represented on the truth table.

The truth table technique can be quite cumbersome for arguments with more than three distinct statement letters. But it is completely effective: it shows you reliably which arguments are deductively valid in simple propositional logic and which are not.

The Shorter Truth Table Technique

Because the truth table technique is sometimes lengthy and cumbersome, it is convenient to have a shorthand version. The shorter truth table technique is based on the fact that when an argument is invalid then, providing we have formalized it correctly and constructed our truth table correctly, there is at least one row displaying its conclusion as false while all its premises are true. If there is no such row, the argument is valid, because it is impossible for the conclusion to be false when all the premises are true.

To use the shorter technique, we set values of the component statements in such a way as to guarantee that the conclusion will be false. We then see whether we can consistently set values of the premise statements so that the premises turn out to be true. If we can do this, the argument is invalid. If we cannot do it, the argument is valid.

Suppose, for example, that we have the following representation of an argument:

$A \vee B$
$B \supset C$
C
Therefore,
$-A$

The conclusion is $-A$. For this conclusion to be false, A will have to be true. If A is true, the first premise, $A \vee B$, is true regardless of the truth value of B. Making C true makes the third premise true. Given that C is true, the second premise is true whether B is true or false. All these stipulations are consistent with each other. If A is true and C is true, and B is either true or false, the premises turn out to be true and the conclusion is false. Hence the argument is invalid.

Here is another example:

$B \supset D$
$D \supset E$
$B \cdot A$
Therefore,
$D \cdot E$

For the conclusion to be false, at least one of D and E will have to be false. Let us suppose that D is false and E is true. Then, for the first premise to be true, B has to be false. The second premise will be true given that E is true and D is false. The third premise, however, cannot be true, because we have already stipulated that B is false. So this possibility is ruled out. Another way of making the conclusion false is to make D true and E false, but to do so will immediately make the second premise false, so it does not give us a way of finding the conclusion false while all the premises are true.

Alternately, we might stipulate both D and E to be false. But if we do so, we again find that B has to be false for the first premise to be true, and then B cannot be true for the third premise to be true. There is no possible way of making the conclusion false and the premises true. Hence, this argument is valid.

As you can see here, the shorter truth table technique can be very useful. The technique is based on the fact that when an argument is valid, there is no possible way that its conclusion can be false when its premises are true. In using this technique you try to stipulate truth values that will make the conclusion false when the premises are true. If you succeed in doing this, you have shown that the argument is invalid. You have to make sure that you check all the ways in which the conclusion can be false, as we did in the last example. Also, it is necessary to assign truth values accurately and consistently to all the component statements for the technique to work as it should.

EXERCISE SET

Exercise 1: Part A

Symbolize each of the following passages, using statement letters and the symbols –, ∨, ·, and ⊃. Be sure to state which letters represent which English sentences. Example: "Joe skates and Susan swims" is symbolized as "*J* · *S*," where *J* represents "Joe skates" and *S* represents "Susan swims."

1.   Either Fred will be appointed manager or Susan will be appointed manager. If Fred is not appointed manager, he will leave the firm for another company. If Susan is not appointed manager, she will appeal the decision before an arbitration board.

2.   Interest rates are low, properties are for sale at relatively good rates, and it is a good time to get a mortgage.

3.   If it is sunny tomorrow, the mountain hiking will be pleasant. If the hiking is pleasant, it will be a good time to take some souvenir photos. If we do not take souvenir photos tomorrow, we are not going to get any. So if it is not sunny tomorrow, we will have no photos.

   Hint: Use the same statement letter to represent "We are not going to get any photos" and "We will have no photos."

*4.   Either Joshua will organize the demonstration or Noleen will take a petition to all the members of the group. If Joshua organizes a demonstration, media will probably attend, and if Noleen takes a petition to all the members of the group, she is likely to get many signatures.

5.   If Margaret takes out large student loans to go through law school, she will be unable to pay her debts by working as a lawyer when she has finished her studies. If she does not work as a lawyer to pay her debts when she has finished her studies, she will have to work outside law. So if Margaret takes out large student loans to go through law school, she may need to work outside law to pay them back.

6.   If the chairperson does not stand for another term and there is no one else to take over her job, the group will cease to exist.

7.   If the use of refrigerators increases in the Third World and there is no global ban on CFCs in standard refrigerators, then damage to the ozone layer will be extreme. If damage to the ozone layer is extreme, all people with outdoor occupations will succumb to skin cancer. So either people in the Third World will go on doing without refrigerators or we will get a global ban on CFCs or we will have a lot of skin cancer in outdoor workers.

*8.   Both these things are true: extensive public relations efforts are being made on behalf of the nuclear industry, and these efforts are not convincing the public. And if either one of them is true, it is an indication the nuclear industry is in trouble. So the nuclear industry is in trouble.

9.   If the presidency is discredited and the rate of voter participation is low, there is evidence of apathy toward national politics. It's true both that the presidency is discredited and that the rate of voter participation is low. So clearly there is evidence of apathy in national politics. If this evidence exists, we are in big trouble. So we're in big trouble.

10.   If wages go up, corporations have an incentive to leave the jurisdiction. If costs for social benefits go up, they also have an incentive to leave the jurisdiction, and the same is true if environmental standards are raised. If wages go up, or costs for social benefits go up, or environmental standards are raised, there is a chance of strengthening the society. So strengthening the society gives corporations an incentive to leave it.

Exercise 1: Part B

Symbolize each of the following simple arguments and test them for deductive validity using the longer truth table technique. Be sure to stipulate what your statement letters represent.

1. Either the behaviorists are right or the liberal humanists are right. It's been conclusively demonstrated that the liberal humanists are right. So the behaviorists must be wrong.

*2. Provided that you master calculus, you will have no difficulty with the mathematical aspects of first-year university physics. But really, you know, you have mastered calculus successfully. Thus, the mathematical part of the physics course should go smoothly for you.

3. If historical processes lead inevitably to their ends, then human agents make no decisions that affect the course of human history. Yet clearly, human agents do make decisions that affect the course of human history. Thus it is false that historical processes lead inevitably to their ends.

4. Religious believers are inspired by faith or religious believers are inspired by reason. Religious believers are inspired by faith; therefore, they are not inspired by reason.

5. The Weaselhead wildlife area was named, by whites, after a Sarcee Indian called Weaselhead. If whites named an area after Weaselhead, they must have respected him. Therefore, Weaselhead was respected by the whites.

6. Either the murder was voluntarily committed or it was a compulsive action. If the murder was voluntarily committed, the murderer should be sent to jail. If the murder was a compulsive action, the murderer should be sent to a psychiatric institution. So if the murderer is sent to jail, he should not be sent to a psychiatric institution.

7. Either the Russians will develop a respect for the rule of law or Russia will lose what civil order it has. If the Russian government is unable to pay the military and the police, then the military and the police will have no motivation to do a good job, and the Russians will not develop a respect for the rule of law. The Russian government can't pay the police and the military, so Russia is going to lose what civil order it has.

*8. If you are a suitable student of philosophy of science, you know either philosophy or science. You do not know philosophy, and you do not know science. Therefore, you are not a suitable student of philosophy of science.

*9. If medical authorities change their minds too often, people will not be willing to follow their advice about a healthy diet and lifestyle. In fact, people are unwilling to do what doctors say about diet and lifestyle. They have lost their respect for doctors. Therefore, medical authorities have changed their minds too often.

*10. Either the negotiations will be successful, the problem will continue to be unresolved with the situation at a standoff, or the situation will escalate into violence. The negotiations will be successful, so the problem will be resolved.

Exercise 1: Part C
Represent the following arguments in letters and propositional symbols; indicate which symbol represents which statement; and test the arguments for validity using the shorter truth table technique.

*1. If the United States subsidizes grain sales to Russia, then Canadian farmers will receive less than what they presently receive for the grain they sell to Russia. If Canadian farmers receive less than they presently receive for their grain, then some Canadian farmers will go bankrupt. If this happens, Canadian taxpayers will be called on to help support farmers. The United States is going to subsidize grain sales to Russia, so Canadian taxpayers will be called on to help support Canadian farmers.

Hint: Symbolize "this happens" with the same statement letter you use for "Some Canadian farmers will go bankrupt."

2. Jack will take school seriously or he will quit and get a job. Since he will not get a job, he will take school seriously.

*3. Either science teaching will improve, or we are going to have a society that is, effectively, scientifically illiterate. If teachers' salaries are not increased, there will be no chance of attracting good science students into teaching, and if we do not attract good science students into teaching, science teaching will not improve. Governments are cutting funds for education, and if they are doing this, there is no chance of increasing teachers' salaries. I'm afraid, then, that we are going to have a society that is, effectively, scientifically illiterate.

4.   If the prison is well administered, then guards will behave properly, the incidence of rape and drug use will be low, and at least some prisoners will reform as a result of their stay in prison. At least some prisoners have reformed as a result of their stay in prison.

Therefore, it must be true that the prison is well administered.

*5.   Either the murderer used a kitchen knife or the murderer carried an unusually large pocket-knife. If he carried an unusually large pocket-knife, then either he was wearing loose clothing or he would have been noticed by the neighboring observers. The murderer was not noticed by the neighboring observers. If he was wearing loose clothing, either he was very thin or he was not wearing the clothing that was found at the scene of the crime. We know that the murderer was not wearing loose clothing and that he did not use a kitchen knife. Therefore, he was not wearing the clothing that was found at the scene of the crime.

Translating from English into Propositional Logic

So far we have used examples that are relatively easy to put into the symbols of propositional logic. But there are sometimes difficulties in expressing English statements in the symbols of propositional logic. We will work through some of the common problems that arise in connection with the basic connecting symbols.

To illustrate some of the nuances in ordinary language that are not represented in propositional logic, consider the story of two drug stores that were located side by side on a Winnipeg street some years ago.[2] Each had a sign advertising its services to customers. One sign said, "If you need it, we have it," suggesting that the store could meet all the needs of prospective customers. The other said, "If we don't have it, you don't need it," suggesting that the store had selected its goods knowing what people really needed and customers should adjust their needs to what the store supplied. The stores apparently had quite different attitudes to the needs of their customers.

Something interesting is revealed when we represent both slogans in the symbols of propositional logic. Let N represent "You (the customer) need it" and H represent "We (the store) have it." The first sign is represented as "$N \supset H$" and the second as "$-H \supset -N$." In propositional logic, these two statements are logically equivalent. You can check this yourself by making truth tables; truth tables show them to be true and false in the same circumstances. But in terms of public relations and suggestions as to the store's willingness to serve customers, there is a big difference between the signs.

How important are suggested meanings and associations that elude the representations possible in formal logic? The answer is, "It depends." If you are writing poetry or literary essays, giving political speeches, or working for an advertising agency, they are very important. If you are doing proofs in propositional logic or (for most purposes) programming a computer, they are largely irrelevant. Generally, though, to understand what is said, it is important both to grasp the truth functional relations dealt with in propositional logic and to appreciate these additional nuances and connotations that cannot be formalized.

Not

Let us suppose that you have decided to represent a particular English statement in an argument with the letter P. If you represent another English statement in that same argument as $-P$, the second statement must be the contradictory of the first. That is, it must always have the opposite truth value. It cannot merely be the contrary of the first statement. If a statement is true, its contrary must be false. However, it is possible for both a statement and its contrary to be false. Thus a contrary is quite different from a contradictory, which must have the opposite value. For instance, if P represents "Copenhagen is beautiful," then $-P$ cannot be used to represent "Copenhagen is ugly." "Copenhagen is beautiful" and "Copenhagen is ugly" are not contradictory statements. They are contraries. They need not have opposite truth values; they can both be false, as they are if Copenhagen is a city of moderate attractiveness.

A statement and its contradictory must have opposite truth values, and one or the other must be true. If you wish to symbolize one statement as $-P$, when another has been symbolized as P, you must make sure that the two are genuine contradictories and not just contraries. It is important to make sure that the negation applies to the whole statement, P, and not just to some component of it. Consider, for instance, the statement "Zuleikha is friendly to all people" (Z). The denial of this statement ($-Z$) is "It is not the case that Zuleikha is friendly to all people." The negation comes in front of the whole statement. The statement "Zuleikha is friendly but not to all people" is not the denial of Z because in this case, the negation operator has been moved and does not apply to the whole statement.

And

As it is represented and defined on the truth table, the symbol "·" carries no implication that the two statements that it conjoins have any real relationship to each other. That is, if C is "Christine is a mezzo soprano" and R is "The Redskins won the tournament" there is nothing wrong with "$C \cdot R$" from a formal point of view. It says, "Christine is a mezzo soprano and the Redskins won the tournament." The conjunction just asserts both the separate statements and is not intended to suggest that there is any kind of connection between them. But in natural speech and writing, we do not usually conjoin entirely unrelated statements. Usually, we assert two statements together when we believe that they are related in some way. It is important to understand that this aspect of ordinary language is not reflected in propositional logic. Relatively few arguments turn on this particular feature of *and* in English.

Another interesting point about *and* is that in English and other natural languages, the order of the components in a conjunction may be significant. In some contexts, one conjunct may be stated first to imply a sequence in time. In such contexts, the word *and* is used in English to suggest *and then*. The sentence, "The doctor operated and she recovered" suggests that the operation came before the recovery and led to it, whereas, if a similar sentence is worded "She recovered and the doctor operated" the implication is different, and suggests grounds for a malpractice suit! But these differences would not show up on a truth table. In both cases, the statements would be represented as the same conjunction, and they would come out as true or false regardless of the order of the events.

We have to recognize, then, that the formal logic symbol "·" and the English *and* differ. The former never states a temporal relationship, and the latter sometimes strongly suggests one. In any argument or context where the suggested time sequence is important, the symbol "·" would not fully represent the sense of *and*. Another point to be noted is that "·" must be used to conjoin two or more statements. In English, the word *and* is often used this way. But it may also appear between two subjects or between two predicates, as in these examples:

1. Joe and Eugene passed the final examination in university algebra.
2. Jaya mowed the lawn and weeded the garden.

To symbolize these statements, you have to move *and* out of the subject or predicate and construct two simple statements, which you can then link with "·". Thus:

1. Joe passed the final examination in university algebra, and Eugene passed the final examination in university algebra. $(J \cdot E)$
2. Jaya mowed the lawn, and Jaya weeded the garden. $(M \cdot W)$

Sometimes this simple strategy is not appropriate because it may be an important part of the meaning of the statement, in its context, that the subjects performed the activity together. For instance, when we assert that Susan and John got married, we are not simply asserting that Susan got married and John got married; we are asserting that they married each other. This fact will not be represented if we let S represent "Susan got married" and J represent "John got married." (We have to use a single letter to represent the fact that John and Sue married each other, unless we are working in a more complex system of relational logic.) There are other contexts, too, where the togetherness implied by *and* in English will be important to the force of an argument and cannot properly be omitted in the symbolization.

Suppose you try to translate a statement into the symbols of propositional logic that uses *but* or *although* or *yet*, in a conjunctive role. Consider these examples:

3. The summer was delightful, although the mosquitoes were unpleasant at times.
4. Mitesh was a mathematician, but he was sensitive to poetry and all the arts.
5. Evelyn was beautiful and charming, yet she had no real friends.

Each statement is a conjunction of two others and would be symbolized in propositional logic as such, using the symbol for *and*. However, there is something left out in such symbolizations. What is omitted is the contrast suggested by the words *although* in (3), *but* in (4), and *yet* in (5). These words are contrastive in suggesting that what is in the second conjunct is, in view of the first conjunct, not quite what we would expect. That element of contrast cannot be represented in the symbols of propositional logic. The truth table and the conjunction symbol in propositional logic represent only conjunction, pure and simple. Any element of contrast is omitted. Other words that are conjunctive but have contrastive implications of this type are *even though, however, in spite of the fact that, despite,* and *notwithstanding the fact that.*

Or

The notable thing about "∨" as defined in the truth table is that it specifies what logicians call inclusive disjunction. An **inclusive disjunction** is one that is true when both disjuncts are true, as well as when only one of them is true. If you look at the truth table for "∨" you will notice that on the first row, where *P* and *Q* are both true, the compound statement "*P* ∨ *Q*" is also true. In this inclusive sense of *or*, a statement such as:

6. Either the negotiations will be successful or the situation will escalate to the point of violence.

is true when either disjunct is true and when both disjuncts are true. Suppose that the negotiations are successful, but that later the situation escalates to violence for other reasons. Statement (6) would be regarded as true in such a case, given the way "∨" is defined in the truth table. This consequence may seem surprising, and does not always fit well with ordinary usage. In English and in other natural languages, it is common to use and understand *or* and related words in an exclusive sense. We would in all likelihood take statement (6) to mean:

Either the negotiations will be successful or the situation will escalate to the point of violence, and not both.

The exclusive use of *or* implies that one, and only one, of the alternatives will hold. In the case of (6), our background knowledge about negotiations and violence would lead us to assume an exclusive meaning rather than an inclusive one. The inclusive *or* implies that at least one disjunct will be true, and allows that both might be true.

A restaurant menu telling you that:

7. Jello or ice cream may be taken as a free dessert with your meal.

is not usually telling you that you are allowed to have both jello and ice cream. (You doubtless know this, partly from custom and partly from your belief that restaurant owners are in business to make a profit and cannot afford to offer everybody two desserts.) In (7), *or* is used exclusively. If you went to a restaurant and decided to exploit your knowledge of logic, you would almost certainly be unsuccessful if you drew a truth table for the restaurant manager and insisted on having both items for dessert! The same may be said of:

8. Tea, coffee, or milk will be served with the meal.

This statement, similarly, is most plausibly interpreted as exclusive, saying that one or the other or the third will be served—not two and not all three.

We can express **exclusive disjunction** perfectly well using the symbols of propositional logic. Let's see how this works for the example about jello and ice cream.

Let J represent "Jello will be provided as a free dessert with your meal."
Let I represent "Ice cream will be provided as a free dessert with your meal."
The menu is stating:
$(J \lor I) \cdot -(J \cdot I)$

That is, it allows one or the other, not both. *Or* is exclusive: you may have jello or ice cream, but not both.

The inclusive disjunction defined on the truth table for "$\lor$" is standard in propositional logic. When you are symbolizing sentences in which *or* is the connective, use this symbol, representing inclusive disjunction, unless you are sure that an exclusive disjunction is implied. In that case, you have to add *and not both*—indicated by appropriate symbols—to capture the meaning. The other point about "$\lor$" is rather like our point about subjects and predicates linked by *and*. In ordinary speech and writing, you often find *or* between subjects or predicates, as in the following:

9. Taheera or Rachel will help with the gardening.

and

10. Sue will either work in the garden or swim.

But just as "$\cdot$" must link statements in propositional logic, so must "$\lor$". Thus, we have to rearrange the preceding examples as:

9. Taheera will help with the gardening or Rachel will help with the gardening.
    $T \lor R$
10. Sue will work in the garden or Sue will swim.
    $W \lor S$

If Then

With regard to the relation between English and symbols, the horseshoe symbol used to represent *if then* raises fascinating and controversial issues. Let us look again at the truth table in Figure 8.8 that defines the horseshoe connective.

We said that "$\subset$" as defined on this truth table, was a minimal conditional. To see what this means, the first step is to recall that the P and Q on the truth table can represent any two statements at all. Let us stipulate that A represents "Jean Chretien was Prime Minister of Canada in 1998" and B represents "Charles Dickens wrote the

P	Q	$P \supset Q$
T	T	T
T	F	F
F	T	T
F	F	T

FIGURE 8.8

novel *David Copperfield*." As a matter of fact, these two statements are both true. Obviously, they are unconnected with each other. There is no relation by definition, causation, law, morality, threat, or custom between Jean Chretien's political role and Charles Dickens' authorship.

Nevertheless, using the horseshoe to connect A and B, we get the surprising result that the compound statement "$A \supset B$" is true. If Jean Chretien was Prime Minister of Canada in 1998, then Charles Dickens wrote the novel *David Copperfield*. But that statement does not seem to make sense! And yet, look back at the truth table. On the row where A is true and B is also true, $A \supset B$ is true, whatever statements A and B might be. That is just how the horseshoe connective, "$A \supset B$," is defined. And yet it would surely be eccentric—in fact almost a sign of madness—to assert:

11. If Jean Chretien was the Prime Minister of Canada in 1998, then Charles Dickens wrote the novel *David Copperfield*.

Statement (11) here is not the sort of thing anyone would assert because none of the normal connections (definition, causation, law, and so forth) hold between the antecedent and the consequent. Yet if we represent the statement in symbolic logic as "$A \supset B$," statement (11) will turn out to be true, according to the truth table for the horseshoe. How can this be?

The answer is that the horseshoe represents a minimum truth value connection between an antecedent and a consequent. This minimum is as follows: provided the antecedent is true, the consequent must be true. The only case when the minimum conditional is false is the case when the antecedent is true and the consequent is false. For this minimum conditional, there is no requirement that the antecedent and the consequent have any other relationship to each other.

In ordinary life, we are usually concerned with conditionals where there are further relationships between the statements. Because the horseshoe abstracts from these features, it can mislead us. We have to remember that the horseshoe represents the basic conditionality—nothing more. The horseshoe is important in propositional reasoning because it mirrors a core of conditionality that can be precisely defined on a truth table and conveniently related to the other propositional connectives.

To further appreciate puzzling aspects of the horseshoe, look at the two rows of the truth table where P is false. Remember again that P and Q can represent any two statements. This time let's allow P to represent the statement that Argentina invaded the United States in 1999 and Q to represent the statement that salaries for public school teachers in the United States doubled in 1999. Since both statements are in fact false, the combination "$P \supset Q$" turns out to be true. (Check the last row of the truth table to see that this occurs.) But we would never assert—much less believe—that:

12. If Argentina invaded the United States in 1999, then salaries for public school teachers in the United States doubled in 1999.

is true. Statement (12) is entirely contrary to common sense. There is no practical connection, or any other kind of connection, between this invasion, which did not happen, and the salaries of public school teachers.

If you look at your truth table, you will see that because of the way the horseshoe is defined, a statement of the form "$P \supset Q$" will be true whenever its antecedent is false. Since the antecedent of (12) is false, statement (12) as a whole will be true, if we interpret *if then* using the horseshoe. When the antecedent is false, a conditional of the form "$P \supset Q$" will be true, regardless of the content of P and of Q. In some ways this situation is paradoxical. It seems bizarre and unacceptable if we think of the horseshoe as expressing *if then* in English, and it serves as a warning that we should not think of the horseshoe in this way.

Conditional statements like (12), in which the antecedent is known to be false are called **counterfactuals.** The antecedent, being false, is contrary to fact. Note, however, that this is not to say that the whole statement is false or contrary to fact. As we shall see, many counterfactuals are plausibly regarded as being true. In fact, counterfactuals are extremely important both in science and in ordinary life. It is often important to make claims about what would have happened or what would happen if conditions were different from what they are. For example, suppose that gasoline was spilled in the garage, and there was no fire. If a match had been lit in the garage, there would have been a fire. This counterfactual, which is probably true, could be of real importance. (For instance, in a lawsuit it might help to establish negligence on the part of someone who had spilled the gasoline and neglected to clean it up.)

The problem, when we consider representing counterfactuals using the horseshoe, is that in science and in ordinary life we usually distinguish between counterfactuals, thinking that some are true or plausible and others are false or implausible. We do not regard all counterfactuals as equally true, as we would if we understood the conditional relationship in them to be accurately represented by the horseshoe symbol.

Consider:

13. If Hitler had died in childhood, the Jewish population of Poland would be larger today than it is.
14. If Hitler had died in childhood, there would be no threat to the ozone layer today.

We know that Hitler did not die in childhood. Thus both (13) and (14) are conditionals with an antecedent known to be false. Both are counterfactuals. Most of us would find (13) to be plausible, given Hitler's vitriolic hatred of Jewish people and his central role in the anti-Semitic campaigns of the 1930s and in the mass killings of Jews. On the other hand, we would find (14) to be entirely implausible. But if we represent (13) and (14) in propositional logic, using the horseshoe symbol for the *if then* connection, both statements turn out to be true. What has gone wrong? This is an unacceptable consequence. The problem is that counterfactuals cannot properly be represented in propositional logic using the horseshoe.

How counterfactual statements should be understood and what logical apparatus should be used to represent them formally are complex and controversial issues in logic. We cannot explore these issues further here. We mention them to indicate one area where there are recognized limitations to the horseshoe as the symbol for *"if then."*

The core of conditionality represented by the horseshoe can best be understood by looking back at the truth table for "⊃" and focusing your attention on the second line. This line says that for any two propositions *P* and *Q*, when *P* is true and *Q* is false, the horseshoe conditional "⊃" is false. This relationship always holds for conditionals in natural language. To have an illustration of why this makes sense, consider an example. Suppose someone tells you, "If you go to Russia you will see dancing bears in the streets of Moscow." Suppose that you do go to Russia and you do not see any dancing bears in the streets of Moscow. That will show that his conditional assertion was false. This would be indicated if you represented it on the truth table. If the antecedent is true and the consequent is false, the conditional statement is false.

This minimal element of conditionals is most basic for arguments because if we put the horseshoe between the premises and the conclusion of an argument—as in "premise and premise ⊃ conclusion"—we will not be able to move from true premises to a false conclusion. This is what we are trying to avoid when we argue and infer: we do not want to proceed from truth to falsehood.

EXERCISE SET

Exercise 2: Part A
Using ·, ∨, −, and ⊃ and using capital letters to represent component statements, represent the following arguments in the terms of propositional logic.

1. If elephants are domesticated animals and domesticated animals tend to be inbred, then elephants will tend to be inbred if there is not something exceptional about the way they are raised. There is nothing exceptional about the way elephants are raised. We can conclude that elephants tend to be inbred.

2. Only if richer nations come to understand the world food problem can we hope to eliminate famine. If there is no improvement in university education about development issues, the richer nations will not come to understand the world food problem. Thus, if there is not an improvement in university education about world food problems, there is no hope of eliminating famine.

3.   Kimberley is either spying for another company or using this job to move on to a better one. If she is spying for another company, our operations are in jeopardy. If she is using this job to move on to a better one, she is placing our operations in jeopardy and exploiting our company. In either case, she should be fired. You can see, there are good reasons for firing Kimberley.

   Hint: Use the same statement letter, in this context, to symbolize "our operations are in jeopardy" and "she is placing our operations in jeopardy." Do not try to symbolize, "you can see, there are good reasons for."

4.   If there is a global warming effect, and if the burning of fossil fuels contributes to this effect, there is an excellent reason to cut down on the use of cars that use fossil fuels. If global temperatures have risen over the past five years, there must be a global warming effect. And global temperatures have risen over the past five years. We know that the burning of fossil fuels contributes to global warming. Therefore, there is an excellent reason to cut down on the use of cars that use fossil fuels.

*5.   It is not possible to take both French and German in the last year of high school if you take both physics and chemistry, or both chemistry and biology, or both biology and physics. If you take any two of chemistry, physics, and biology, you must take either French or German and not both.

6.   If French is easier than Russian, then if John can learn Russian, John can learn French. John can learn Russian only if he has an aptitude for grammar. John has no aptitude for grammar. Therefore, John cannot learn French.

7.   Choral singing works well only when singers all cooperate and no one tries to be a star and steal the show. If there is a star, that person's voice stands out and spoils the united effect sought by a choir.

*8.   If the land claims disputes are not resolved and the native leaders continue to distrust the government, then either there will be continued nonviolent blockades or there will be an escalation of the problem into terrorist action. If there are continued nonviolent blockades, antagonism between whites and natives will increase, and if there is an escalation of the problem into terrorist action, the whole country will be seriously affected in a most adverse way. Unless the government can inspire more confidence from native leaders, there will be either increased antagonism between natives and whites or adverse effects on the whole country. Somehow, even if land claims disputes are not resolved, native leaders must come to trust the government.

   Hint: Assume that the same statement letter can be used to represent "It is not the case that native leaders continue to distrust the government" and "Native leaders must come to trust the government."

Exercise 2: Part B
Symbolize the following passages, as in Part A, and test arguments for validity using the truth table technique or the shorter truth table technique, as you prefer.

1.   If French philosophy continues to flourish in universities, there will be a pull away from formal logic and philosophy of science among graduate students in philosophy. If there is such a pull, traditional teaching patterns will be upset. And yet, you know, it is quite likely that the attraction of French philosophy will persist. I conclude that we have got to expect some disturbance in traditional teaching patterns.

2.   My husband is not a handsome man, so my husband is an ugly man.

*3.   The book was not a success. So it must have been a failure.

4.   If the four involved parties can agree on a peace accord providing for the disarmament of paramilitary groups, the new political arrangements will be a success. But the four involved

parties cannot agree on a peace accord providing for the disarmament of paramilitary groups. Therefore, the new political arrangements will not be a success.

5. If science is entirely objective, then the emotions and ambitions of scientists have nothing to do with their pursuit of research. But the emotions and ambitions of scientists do have something to do with their pursuit of research. Therefore, science is not entirely objective.

6. If Smith agrees to conduct the choir, the choir will have an excellent director. And if the choir has an excellent director, it may be able to tour Europe next year. Smith has agreed to conduct the choir. So the choir may be able to tour Europe next year.

7. Either the company will move to selling public shares, or it will remain as a limited private company. If the company moves to selling public shares, it will have money for expansion, and if it has money for expansion, it will expand. But the company will remain as a limited private company. Therefore, it will not expand.

*8. International politics is either a difficult academic subject or it is such a mishmash that nobody can understand it at all. If respected academics study international politics, then it is not just a mishmash no one understands. Respected academics do study international politics. So it is not a mishmash. It is a difficult academic subject.

9. The textbook is either accurate and boring or inaccurate and interesting. If the textbook is accurate, it will be widely used. And if it is interesting, it will be widely used. Thus, however things turn out, the textbook is bound to be widely used.

10. If women are drafted, wars will have to provide maternity leaves. If wars have to provide for maternity leaves, war will become impossible. Therefore, if women are drafted, war will become impossible.

11. Either you will not be famous, or you will be famous for doing profoundly lasting things, or you will be famous as a popular star for doing superficial things. If you are an intellectual, you will not be famous as a popular star for doing superficial things. So, if you are an intellectual, you will not be famous at all.

Hint: In the first statement, use the comma as a guide when bracketing.

12. If sex education is successful, children learn a lot about sex, and if they learn a lot about sex, they will know enough to protect themselves from abuse. So either sex education will be successful or children will not know enough to protect themselves from abuse.

13. If morality is entirely relative, torture is as virtuous as charity. But torture is not as virtuous as charity. Therefore, morality is not entirely relative.

14. If learning languages is recognized as important, students will work hard to learn French, Spanish, and Chinese. Students are working hard to learn French, Spanish, and Chinese. Thus, learning languages is of recognized importance.

*15. If Socrates influenced Plato, and Plato influenced Aristotle, then Socrates influenced Aristotle. Socrates did influence Plato, and Plato obviously influenced Aristotle as well, so we can see that Socrates influenced Aristotle.

16. If women are equal to men, then women are as strong as men. But women are not as strong as men. Therefore, women are not equal to men. If women are not equal to men, they have no proper claim to receive salaries as high as men's. But women should receive salaries as high as men's. So women must be equal to men. I conclude that women are both equal and not equal to men.

*17. If Saudi Arabia loses power in the Gulf, the balance of power in that area will be upset. If the balance of power in the Persian Gulf area is upset, then there will be increasing political ambition on the part of fundamentalist Islamic groups. But if Saudi Arabia loses power in the Gulf and is unable to fund fundamentalist Islamic groups, these groups will lose their ability to carry out their ambitions. Saudi Arabia is losing power in the Gulf and will be unable to fund fundamentalist Islamic groups. So fundamentalist Islamic groups are experiencing increasing political ambition while at the same time losing their ability to realize these ambitions.

18.   If Sue and Joel collaborate equitably on the project, both will do a fair share. Both will do a fair share only if their abilities and available time are approximately equal. But if Sue's available time is less than Joel's, they will not both do a fair share. Sue's available time is less than Joel's. Thus, Sue and Joel cannot collaborate equitably on the project.

*19.   If Fred goes on a diet for more than two months, his metabolism will slow down. If Fred's metabolism slows down, he will need less food than he does now. If he needs less food than he does now, he will gain weight on what he eats now. Therefore, if Fred goes on a diet for more than two months, he will gain weight on what he eats now. If the consequence of his dieting is that he gains weight, his dieting is futile. Fred is going to go on a diet for more than two months. So this will be futile.

20.   Either the economy will improve or there will be millions of unemployed young people. The economy will not improve, so there will be millions of unemployed young people. If there are millions of unemployed young people, there is bound to be social unrest. So if the economy does not improve, we can expect social unrest.

Further Points about Translation

Consider the following:

If French philosophy continues to flourish in universities, there will be a pull away from formal logic and philosophy of science among graduate students in philosophy. If there is such a pull, traditional teaching patterns will be upset. And yet, you know, it is quite likely that the attraction of French philosophy will persist. I conclude that we've got to expect some disturbance in traditional teaching patterns.

This argument is a simple deductively valid one, and it can be shown to be valid on a truth table. But to represent the argument in the symbols of propositional logic in such a way that its deductive validity is apparent, we need to gloss over certain verbal and stylistic aspects. The correct representation of this argument in the symbols of propositional logic is:

$$C \supset A$$
$$A \supset D$$
$$C$$
Therefore,
$$D$$

Here C represents "French philosophy will continue to flourish in universities," A represents "There will be a pull away from logic and philosophy of science among graduate students in philosophy," and D represents "There will be some disturbance in traditional teaching patterns." Notice that *C* is expressed in slightly differ-ent ways in the consequent of the first sentence and the antecedent of the second sentence. Also, *D* is expressed in slightly different ways in the conclusion and in the consequent of the conditional in the second sentence. In formalizing this argument, we have made decisions that slightly different English words are equivalent in mean-ing in this context.

This example illustrates the fact that when you are formalizing, you make deci-sions about what you think English sentences mean. You use the same letter to rep-resent two verbally different expressions only when you think that these expressions are functioning to say the same thing. Determining whether these expressions are equivalent can be difficult. But even learning to raise the question is an important step in clarifying meanings. You have to develop your sense for the nuances of lan-guage. Also, if your formalization results in some slurring over of slight differences in meaning, you should check back to see that the omitted aspects do not affect the merits of the argument you are dealing with.

Both . . . And . . .

A statement of the type "Both *P* and *Q*" is easily represented in propositional logic as a conjunction. Here is an example:

(i) Both France and Britain are concerned about the growth of German power in central Europe.

Statement (i) is a conjunction of "France is concerned about the growth of German power in central Europe" (*R*) and "Britain is concerned about the growth of Ger-man power in central Europe" (*B*). To represent (i) in the apparatus of proposi-tional logic, we write:

$R \cdot B$

The same schema for representation can be used for more complex variations of *both . . . and . . . .* Consider:

(ii) Both of these things are true: a high degree of scientific education is needed for a nation to be competitive on the international scene and scientific education in North America is relatively weak.

If we allow *D* to represent "A high degree of scientific education is needed for a nation to be competitive on the international scene" and *W* to represent "Scientific education in North America is relatively weak," then (ii) is formally represented as:

$D \cdot W$

Neither . . . Nor . . .

Consider the following statement:

(i) Neither John nor Susan is able to attend the lecture.

Statement (i) is a compound statement in which the linking words are *neither . . . nor. . . .* In effect, *nor* means "not either . . . or. . . ." If we represent "John is able to attend" by *J* and "Susan is able to attend" by *S,* we can represent (i) as:

$-(J \lor S)$

The same method of representation can also be used when the English does not include *neither* and uses *nor* at the beginning of the second statement, as in (ii):

(ii) The president of the company did not accept responsibility for the problem. Nor did he issue any official statement on the matter.

In (ii) we have two negations. Two possibilities are described, and it is said that neither of them happened—not this, not that. Let *R* represent "The president of the company accepted responsibility for the problem" and *I* represent "The president of the company issued an official statement on the matter." Then, to represent (ii), we write:

$-(R \lor I)$

The formalization here is the same, structurally. It would be too easy to express statement (ii) in English using *neither/nor.* We would say "The president of the company neither accepted responsibility for the problem nor issued any official statement on the matter."

Implies That . . .

Often we speak of statements implying each other. In propositional logic, the implication of one statement by another is represented using the horseshoe. The statement that implies is the antecedent, and the one that is implied is the consequent. Here is an example:

(i) That the United States is the dominant country in NATO implies that NATO policy will always be consistent with United States policy.

To represent this implication statement in terms of propositional logic, let *U* represent "The United States is the dominant country in NATO." Let *C* represent "NATO policy will always be consistent with United States policy." Statement (i) can then be written as a conditional with *U* as its antecedent and *C* as its consequent.

$U \supset C$

Sometimes *implies* is used with grammatical constructions that are not in the form of complete statements, as in the following example:

(ii) Human free will implies the ability to choose what we do.

Here "human free will" and "the ability to choose what we do" are not complete statements. Only complete statements can be represented by statement letters in propositional logic. We can, however, see (ii) as expressing an implication relation between statements. In effect, (ii) is saying:

(ii') That human beings have free will implies that human beings have the ability to choose what they do.

Now (ii'), which has statement components, can be represented in the apparatus of propositional logic. Let H represent "human beings have free will" and let C represent "human beings have the ability to choose what they do." Statement (ii'), and, accordingly, (ii), which is equivalent to it, can be formally represented as:

$H \supset C$

Sometimes we negate statements of implication. When formally representing such negations, you have to be careful to put the negation outside the brackets that surround the conditional. The whole conditional must be denied, not one or more components of it. Consider the following example:

(iii) The fact that he is thin does not imply that he is fit.

Statement (iii) is denying that there is a relationship of implication between being thin and being fit. Let I represent "He is thin" and let S represent "He is fit." Then statement (iii) can be formally represented as:

$-(I \supset S)$

Provided That . . .

We often speak of certain things being the case provided that something else is the case. These kinds of statements are conditionals and can be represented as such in propositional logic. Consider the following:

(i) Freedom of religion is conducive to political harmony, provided that religious groups pay due consideration to those dissenting from their beliefs.

Statement (i) is asserting that freedom of religion makes for political harmony, given a certain condition or, as it is sometimes called, a *proviso*. To represent such a statement using the horseshoe, we make the *proviso* the consequent of the conditional. In the previous example, the idea is that freedom of religion is conducive to political harmony, but only under the condition that religious groups pay due consideration to those dissenting from their beliefs. If we allow C to represent "freedom of religion is conducive to political harmony" and D to represent "religious groups pay due consideration to those dissenting from their beliefs," then statement (i) is represented as:

$C \supset D$

Here is another example:

(ii) Sari can sing soprano parts provided that they do not go higher than A.

The *proviso* here is negative. Let H represent "Soprano parts go higher than A" and S represent "Sari can sing soprano parts." Statement (ii) then becomes:

$$S \supset -H$$

Only If

Consider the following sentence:

(i) Peter is eligible for medical school only if he has studied biology.

Let us allow S to represent "Peter is eligible for medical school" and B to represent "Peter has studied biology." Then the sentence as a whole can be represented, using the horseshoe, as follows:

$$S \supset B$$

Many people want to turn examples like this around:

$B \supset S$ (Wrong!)

This turnaround is wrong because the original sentence states that studying biology is necessary for Peter to be eligible. This sentence means that given that he is eligible, it will be true that he has studied biology; otherwise, he would not be eligible. The turnaround representation, which is wrong, makes a necessary condition of eligibility into a sufficient one. It says that given that he has studied biology, he will be eligible, which is not right. (If you think about how hard it is to get into medical school, this point probably will be obvious. Studying biology is certainly not enough to get a person admitted!)

People are good at understanding the *only if* relationship in practical contexts. Consider the following familiar instruction:

(ii) Pass only from the center lane.

Such an instruction, on a busy highway, is routinely understood and obeyed by drivers.[3] It is an *"only if"* instruction; it is legally permissible to pass (S) only if your car is in the center lane (C). That is, if you are not in the center lane, but in some other lane, you should not pass. The formal representation would be:

$$S \supset C$$

Necessary Condition

A **necessary condition** is one that is needed or required. A sufficient condition is one that is enough to ensure a result. For instance, having oxygen is a necessary condition for human life, but it is not sufficient. On the other hand, having 3,000 calories per day in a balanced diet is a sufficient condition for adequate human nutrition, but it is not a necessary condition. (Less will suffice.) We often find claims about conditions that are necessary for various states of affairs. Consider, for instance:

(i) For human beings, having oxygen is a necessary condition of being alive.

This claim can be symbolized using the horseshoe. Let *H* represent "Human beings are alive" and *O* represent "Human beings have oxygen." Then the relationship of necessary condition can be represented as:

$H \supset O$

To say that having oxygen is a necessary condition of being alive is to say that human beings are alive only if they have oxygen. Life requires oxygen. Thus, from the fact that humans are alive, we can infer they have oxygen. (*H* and $H \supset O$. Therefore, *O*.)

Sufficient Condition

Sufficient conditions are not the same as necessary conditions. Sufficient conditions for a state of affairs will guarantee that a state of affairs exists. For example:

> (i) Striking a match in a well-ventilated room full of gasoline is a sufficient condition for igniting a fire.

Let *S* represent "Someone strikes a match in a well-ventilated room full of gasoline," and let *L* represent "A fire is ignited in a well-ventilated room full of gasoline." To say that *S* is a sufficient condition for *L* is to say that if *S* then *L* which, of course, is represented as:

$S \supset L$

in propositional logic. Given that the match is lit, conditions are sufficient for a fire, so there will be a fire. We should note that sufficient conditions may not be necessary conditions. Lighting a match in a well-ventilated room full of gasoline is not a necessary condition for having a fire in that room because we could get a fire in other ways—by leaving a lighted candle near a newspaper, for instance.

Necessary and Sufficient Conditions

Some conditions are both necessary and sufficient for a given result. For instance, being a female parent is a necessary condition for being a mother, and it is a sufficient condition for being a mother. Consider:

> (i) Tamara's being a female parent is both necessary and sufficient for her being a mother.

If we let *A* represent "Tamara is a female parent" and *B* represent "Tamara is a mother," then we can represent this relationship as:

$(B \supset A) \cdot (A \supset B)$

A conjunction of two conditionals, such as this one, is called a **biconditional.** Necessary and sufficient conditions are represented in a biconditional, as this example illustrates.

Unless

Consider the statement "We will go to the concert unless we run out of time." Clearly, this is a compound statement in which two simpler statements are connected. There is no symbol for *unless* in propositional logic. However, *unless* can be represented by combining symbols for *if then* and *not*. The simplest way to do this is to begin by rewriting the sentence in English, substituting the words *if not* for *unless*. Thus for:

(i) We will go to the concert unless we run out of time.

we write:

(i') We will go to the concert if we do not run out of time.

We can rewrite this statement to put the antecedent first:

(i") If we do not run out of time, we will go to the concert.

Now this statement is easy to render in the formal terms of propositional logic. Let *C* represent "we will go to the concert" and *R* represent "we run out of time." The statement "We will go to the concert unless we run out of time" has been restated as "If we do not run out of time, we will go to the concert," which is formally stated as:

$-R \supset C$

This system for understanding *unless* in the symbols of propositional logic can be mastered quite easily. Usually this method is adequate. A statement of the type "*P* unless *Q*" always asserts at least that "*P* if not *Q*," which is reordered as "If not *Q, P*" and can readily be symbolized.

Sometimes, however, the word *unless* would seem to express a connection stronger than *if not*. Here is an example.

(ii) Don will work this summer unless he wins a scholarship to Oxford.

According to the standard scheme explained above, we would understand (ii) as follows:

(ii') If he does not win a scholarship to Oxford, Don will work this summer.

Let *D* represent "Don will work this summer" and *S* represent "Don wins a scholarship to Oxford." Then (ii') is formally represented as follows:

$-S \supset D$

But this formalization might strike you as not expressing quite enough. Indeed it has struck some critics this way. They think that (ii) also asserts that if he does win the scholarship, Don will not work this summer. (A two-way connection is involved; on this interpretation, there should be a biconditional.) To say that he will work unless he wins the scholarship seems to be saying that winning the scholarship is what would result in his not working. That is, (ii") $S \supset -D$

Statement (ii) seems to express (ii") as well as (ii'), yet only (ii') is represented when we translate *unless* as *if not*.

This possibility poses a question. Do some uses of *unless* express a biconditional? It seems to many native speakers of English that such a statement as "Don will work this summer unless he wins a scholarship to Oxford" says *both* that without the scholarship he will work, and with it, he will not work. Is such a biconditional commonly expressed when *unless* is used? Or is *if not* all that is expressed? This is a tricky question and the answer to it seems to vary depending on the context in which *unless* is used. *If not* is always implied. But sometimes, more seems to be implied, so that a biconditional relationship is being asserted.

Using *if not* will always give you the core meaning of *unless*. If, in a given context, you are absolutely convinced that the additional meaning is there as well, you can represent *unless* using a biconditional, as in the example about Don and his possible scholarship to Oxford.

EXERCISE SET

Exercise 3

Represent the following passages in the formal apparatus of propositional logic, indicating which letters represent which statements, and test the formalized arguments using the longer or shorter truth table technique. *Note:* if a passage does not contain an argument, it need not be symbolized. Just indicate that it does not contain an argument.

*1.   Elephants have been known to bury their dead. But elephants bury their dead only if they have a concept of their own species and understand what death means. If elephants understand what death means, they have a substantial capacity for abstraction. Therefore, elephants have a substantial capacity for abstraction.

2.   Swimming is an excellent form of exercise provided it neither injures joints nor stresses the heart. These conditions are met: it is both true that swimming does not injure joints and true that it does not stress the heart. If swimming is an excellent form of exercise, then swimming regularly will improve a person's general health.

We can conclude that swimming regularly will improve health.

*3.   If it rains all day, the flowers, trees, and grass will benefit from the moisture. If it does not rain all day and if the sun shines, we will enjoy being out. If either the flowers, trees, and grass benefit from the moisture or we enjoy being out, then something good will have come. So if it rains all day, or if it does not rain and the sun shines, something good will have come.

4.   Peter cannot graduate in psychology unless he takes either developmental psychology or experimental design. If he does not take a course in experimental design, Peter will take developmental psychology. So if he does not graduate, Peter will take neither developmental psychology nor a course in experimental design.

*5.   Unless he exercises regularly, his heart condition will not improve. If his heart condition does not improve, he is likely either to have a heart attack or to be at serious risk of one. If he neither has a heart attack, nor is at any risk of one, we can conclude that he exercises regularly.

6. "I was glad about Setsuko's decision to remain at home, for indeed, we had had little opportunity to talk without interruption; and there are, of course, many things a father wishes to know about a married daughter's life which he cannot ask outright. But what never occurred to me that evening was that Setsuko would have her own reasons for wishing to remain in the house with me."

(Kazuo Ishiguro, *An Artist of the Floating World* [London: Faber & Faber, 1986], p. 40)

*7. Unless workers agree not to strike within the next decade, prospects for the recovery of the plant are dim. But unless management agrees to forgo special parking and washroom privileges, workers will not agree not to strike. So there can be a recovery in the plant only if management does its part.

8. The French Canadian folk dance tradition includes many elements of traditional Irish dancing. If a tradition includes Irish elements, then either it will include a significant role for the jig step or it will include a great deal of solo dancing. French Canadian folk dancing does not have much solo dancing. So it must have considerable use of the jig step.

9. Only if there is a good real estate market can Smith hope to sell his house at a reasonable price. If he gets no suitable deal on the house, Smith will either rent it at some loss or declare personal bankruptcy. Declaring bankruptcy is unacceptable for someone in Smith's position. He won't do it. The real estate market is terrible. Thus, we can infer that Smith will rent his house at some loss.

10. Children will be interested in theatre unless the productions are long or boring. If the productions are brief and lively, and the themes are suitable for children, they will like theatre.

  Hint: Assume that "children will be interested in theatre" and "children will like theatre" can be represented by the same statement letter. Assume that "productions are brief" is the contradictory of "productions are long" and that "productions are lively" is the contradictory of "productions are boring."

11. Unless he is a saint, the preacher cannot spend all his time tending to the affairs of others. Unless he is a hypocrite, he cannot both advise others to devote themselves to the affairs of other people and fail to do this himself. The preacher is not a saint. But he does tell others that they should consume their entire lives in devotion to other people, which implies that he is a hypocrite.

*12. Science can be about the objective world only if an objective world exists, and an objective world exists only if there are objects independent of human perceptions and beliefs. If objects exist outside minds, objects are independent of human perceptions and beliefs. Unless tables are inside minds, objects exist outside minds. Tables are not inside minds, so objects do exist outside minds. Therefore, science can be about the objective world.

*13. Either television programs will improve in quality and appeal or the large networks will lose their markets to videos. Television programs can improve in quality only if program budgeting increases, and program budgeting will not increase unless advertisers are willing to pay more. Advertisers are not willing to pay more, and this implies that budgets will not increase. Nor will television programs improve in quality. Thus we can expect the large networks to experience losses.

14. If Joe and Fred are unable to trust each other, they are unable to cooperate on joint projects. If they are unable to cooperate on joint projects, they will be greatly handicapped in what they can do in their business. If, on the other hand, Joe and Fred are able to trust, and are able to cooperate, then they will not be handicapped in what they can do for their business. Joe and Fred are able to cooperate. So they are able to trust each other, and they will not be handicapped in what they can do for their business.

*15.   If the artist is talented, people are likely to admire her work. If she is not talented, they are not likely to admire her work. But whether she is talented or not, and whether they admire her work or not, we do know at least that she gets paid for this work. Her getting paid for the work implies that someone wants to buy it. And someone's wanting to buy it implies that people admire it. Therefore, the artist is talented.

16.   If the problems in the North American economy are due to the demands of workers, then Japanese firms operating in North America will not be able to run profitably. But Japanese firms operating in North America do run profitably. Therefore, the problems are not due to the demands of workers. Problems of firms must be due either to workers or to management. So it is the fault of management.

17.   David is a Nigerian citizen. If David is a Nigerian citizen, then he can legally enter the Czech Republic if and only if he has both a valid passport and a valid visa. David has a valid passport and a valid visa, so he can legally enter the Czech Republic.

*18.   Having a good technical education is necessary to be a good engineer, but it is by no means sufficient. Unless a person is good at teamwork and communication, he cannot be a good engineer. Provided that a person is technically good, cooperatively disposed, and a good communicator, he will be a good engineer. In fact, these three conditions are both necessary and sufficient for being a good engineer.

Simple Proofs in Propositional Logic

Working out validity in propositional logic does not have to be done by truth tables—long or short. You can learn to recognize some basic simple valid argument forms, and you can then show that the arguments you have formalized are valid or invalid by referring to particular forms.

Valid Argument Forms

Here are some of the simple valid argument forms with their standard names:

P; therefore $-(-P)$. Double negation
Also, $-(-P)$; therefore P.
$P \vee P$; therefore P. Tautology
P; Q; therefore $P \cdot Q$. Conjunction
$P \cdot Q$; therefore P. Simplification
$P \cdot Q$; therefore Q. Simplification. (Either conjoined statement may be validly inferred from the conjunction.)
$P \supset Q$; P; therefore Q. *Modus ponens*
$P \supset Q$; $-Q$; therefore $-P$. *Modus tollens*
$P \supset Q$; therefore $-Q \supset -P$. Transposition. Also, $-Q \supset -P$; therefore $P \supset Q$.
$P \supset Q$; $Q \supset R$; therefore $P \supset R$. Hypothetical syllogism
$P \vee Q$; $-P$; therefore Q. Disjunctive syllogism. Also, $P \vee Q$; $-Q$; therefore P.
P; therefore $P \vee Q$. Addition. Also, P; therefore $Q \vee P$. (To see that this rule makes sense, look back at the truth table for "$\vee$" and note again that only one disjunct has to be true for the disjunction to be true.)
$-(P \vee Q)$; therefore $-P \cdot -Q$. De Morgan's rule (a). Also, $-P \cdot -Q$; therefore

$-(P \lor Q)$.

$-(P \cdot Q)$; therefore $-P \lor -Q$. De Morgan's rule (b). Also, $-P \lor -Q$; therefore $-(P \cdot Q)$.

$P \supset Q$; therefore $-P \lor Q$. Implication. Also, $-P \lor Q$; therefore $P \supset Q$.

$P \supset Q$; $R \supset S$; $P \lor R$; therefore $Q \lor S$. Constructive dilemma

$P \supset Q$; $R \supset S$; $-Q \lor -S$; therefore $-P \lor -R$. Destructive dilemma

$-(P \cdot -P)$. Noncontradiction

It will be well worth your while to learn these simple valid argument forms. An easy way to begin is to test each one for validity by the truth table technique. This way you can prove to yourself that they are valid. In addition, a useful exercise is to invent arguments that exemplify each form. By learning the valid forms, you avoid the need to construct truth tables. You can simply recognize many ordinary arguments as deductively valid because they are instances of **modus ponens, modus tollens,** disjunctive syllogism, constructive dilemma, or whatever the case may be.

Examples of Simple Proofs

Sometimes we find deductively valid arguments that proceed by making several valid moves in sequence. We can see that they are valid by seeing that, for example, if we first do *modus ponens* and then disjunctive syllogism, using the premises, we will arrive at the conclusion. This shows us that the conclusion can be validly derived from the premises by a series of steps, each of which is individually valid. This strategy is the basis of proof techniques in more advanced formal logic.

Here is an example:

If Japan makes its airports more convenient for the Japanese public, Japanese tourism in Europe will increase. If Japanese tourism in Europe increases, then either European facilities in key centers will be enlarged or crowding in key centers will occur. Japan is making its airports more convenient for the Japanese public, but European centers are not expanding their tourist facilities. So we can expect crowding in main European tourist centers.

Let M represent "Japan makes its airports more convenient for the Japanese public," E represent "Japanese tourism in Europe will increase," L represent "European facilities in key centers will be enlarged," and C represent "There will be crowding in key European centers." We can then formally represent the argument as:

$M \supset E$ (premise)
$E \supset (L \lor C)$ (premise)
$M \cdot -L$ (premise)
Therefore,
C

The conclusion follows deductively from the premises, and this can be proven with appeals to some of the valid argument forms:

1. $M \supset E$ (premise)
2. $E \supset (L \lor C)$ (premise)

3. $M \cdot -L$ (premise)
4. M from (3) by simplification
5. E from (1) and (4) by *modus ponens*
6. $L \vee C$ from (2) and (5) by *modus ponens*
7. $-L$ from (3) by simplification
8. C from (6) and (7) by disjunctive syllogism

We have validly derived the conclusion from the premises by using valid forms of argument. Since we have constructed a valid proof for the conclusion, based on the premises and valid forms of inference, the formalized argument is valid according to the rules of propositional logic. Provided we formalized the argument correctly, it is valid. We know that the (R) and (G) conditions of argument cogency are met. If the premises are true (or acceptable), the conclusion will be true (or acceptable) as well.

For another example of how these proofs work, consider the following:

Either he will complete his new play or he will achieve success as a political activist. But there is just no way that he can accomplish both. If he completes his play, it will surely be produced. If he achieves success as a political activist, he will be known across the country. Since the production of the play will also bring fame, he is bound to be known across the country.

C = He completes his new play.
W = He will achieve success as a political activist.
R = His play will be produced.
K = He will be known across the country.

(We assume that "The production of a play also brings fame" may be formally represented as "$R \supset K$" in this context.)

The argument may be formally represented as:

1. $(C \vee W)$
2. $-(C \cdot W)$
3. $C \supset R$
4. $W \supset K$
5. $R \supset K$
Therefore,
K

This argument is deductively valid, and this may be shown without a truth table. We show how we can get to the conclusion from the premises, using deductively valid moves:

6. $C \supset K$ from (3) and (5) by hypothetical syllogism
7. $K \vee K$ from (4) and (1) and (6) by constructive dilemma
8. K from (7), tautology

Thus we see how an argument can be shown to be deductively valid by proving the conclusion from the premises in a series of steps. At each step, we appeal to a deductively valid argument form. This procedure is usually more efficient and more intellectually stimulating than writing truth tables. But there is one question that needs to be raised: what if you cannot construct a proof?

When You Cannot Construct a Proof

Sometimes you will not be able to prove an argument valid by using the valid argument forms. There is no series of valid steps that will take you from the premises to the conclusion. When you try to construct a proof and fail to do so, you may suspect that the argument is invalid, but you do not know this for sure. The argument might be valid and your failure to find a proof might be due merely to the fact that you have not hit on the right proof strategy. Thus, these proof procedures do not enable you to show conclusively that a particular argument is invalid. By contrast, for arguments expressible in basic propositional logic, a truth table test for validity will always show you whether the argument is valid or invalid.

It is very important to note the difference between proving an argument valid and failing to do so. If you succeed in constructing a proof in which the conclusion is derived by a series of individually valid steps, then the argument is deductively valid according to propositional logic. Provided that you have formalized it correctly, you have shown that it is valid. But if you cannot find such a proof, your failure to do so does not necessarily mean the argument is invalid. Either the argument is invalid or you have not found the right proof strategy: you do not know which is the case. Thus, the truth table technique has an important advantage: it will always show you whether the argument is valid or invalid. The only problem is that it can be rather cumbersome and involved.

Conditional Proof

A valid argument form not yet listed and of special importance in logic is a **conditional proof.** In a conditional proof, an additional line is introduced as an assumption. This additional claim is then used in just about the way a premise would be, in working through the proof. Conditional proof is often helpful because it gives extra material to manipulate. Anything derived from the premises and the added line introduced as an assumption follows from the premises provided that we allow, in a proper way, for the fact that we have used the assumption. We do this by making the assumption the antecedent of a conditional statement and making what we derived using that assumption the consequent of that statement. (For example, if from P and Q and the assumption X, we could derive Y, then from P and Q, we could derive "If X then Y.")

Here is an example:

1. $B \lor C$ (premise)
2. $R \supset -C$ (premise) We are trying to prove $R \supset B$
3. R (assumption)
4. $-C$ from (2) and (3) by *modus ponens*
5. B from (4) and (1) by disjunctive syllogism
6. $R \supset B$ from steps (3) to (5) by conditional proof

The added premise, R, is introduced into the proof using an assumption; then we get rid of the assumption by making it the antecedent of a conditional statement in the conclusion. What can be derived from the initial premises, in this event, is *if R then B* which is formally represented as $R \supset B$. Conditional proof is an indispensable strategy in constructing proofs, as you will discover if you go on to do more advanced logic.

We may compare the technique of conditional proof with the discussion of provisional acceptance of premises in Chapter 5. There we indicated that when premises are provisionally accepted and a conclusion is seen to be justified on the basis of those premises, what we have really shown is that *if* those premises are acceptable, then the conclusion is acceptable too. Conditional proof involves this kind of reasoning. If from stated premises and assumption *A* we can derive *X,* then from the stated premises, we can derive the conclusion, if *A* then *X.*

The inference rule for conditional proof should be added to the elementary valid argument forms listed earlier. It is written as follows:

P (assume); . . . ; therefore *P* ⊃ *Q* (conditional proof)

In this representation, the dots indicate the intermediate steps that would, using *P* and any other information provided in the premises or previous proof steps, be used to derive *Q*. *Q* itself cannot be derived. It was only derivable on the assumption that *P.* However, the conditional statement $P \supset Q$ does really follow.

In more advanced formal logic, the technique of conditional proof is indispensable. You can use it to derive conditional statements useful in longer proofs. Or the conditional statement itself may be the conclusion you are seeking.

A logical technique related to that of conditional proof is the *reductio ad absurdum.* The name is taken from the Latin and means "reduction to absurdity." In this kind of argument, the premises are "reduced to absurdity" because it is shown that they lead to a contradiction. They entail some proposition of the form of "$P \cdot -P$." No such proposition of this form can be true. (If you do not believe this, construct a truth table for yourself, and you will see how it works out.) If the conjunction of the premises of an argument entails a contradiction, then those premises contain an inconsistency. One or more of the premises must be false. You can use a *reductio ad absurdum* argument to prove a proposition if you start by denying that proposition and then manage to show that its denial leads to a contradiction. (If its denial leads to a contradiction, the denial of its denial must be true, which is to say that the statement itself must be true.) Such a method of proof is often called **indirect proof.** The following is an example of an indirect proof:

1. $K \vee Z$ (premise)
2. $(K \supset Z) \cdot (Q \supset K)$ (premise)
3. K (premise) to prove: $-Z$
4. Z (assumption)
5. $K \supset -Z$ (2, simplification)
6. $-(-Z)$ (4, double negation)
7. $-K$ (6, 5, *modus tollens*)
8. Z (1, 7, disjunctive syllogism)
9. $-Z$ (5, 3, *modus ponens*)

10. $Z \cdot -Z$ (8, 9, conjunction)
11. $Z \supset (Z \cdot -Z)$ (4–10 conditional proof)
12. $-(Z \cdot -Z)$ (noncontradiction)
13. $-Z$ (11, 12, *modus tollens*)

Introducing the assumption Z has enabled us to derive a contradiction, which is denied on line 12. We are thus able to conclude that $-Z$ is true (line 13). We have introduced Z as an assumption, and using that assumption we have been able to produce a contradiction; hence we conclude that the assumption is false. In this example, Z could have been proven in other ways. However, in many cases, indirect proof is the only way to derive a result. The technique is quite powerful.

We have noted *modus tollens* and *modus ponens* as two valid argument forms in propositional logic. Both are basic in human thinking. There are two invalid kinds of arguments that are relatively common and are deceptive because they are so easily confused with *modus tollens* and *modus ponens*. These are:

(1) Invalid move: **affirming the consequent**
$P \supset Q$
Q
Therefore,
P
(Example: If Susan is in Paris, she is in France. Susan is in France, so she is in Paris. Invalid.)
(2) Invalid move: **denying the antecedent**
$P \supset Q$
$-P$
Therefore,
$-Q$
(Example: If Alan is in Rome, Alan is in Italy. Alan is not in Rome, so he is not in Italy. Invalid.)

Both these formal fallacies are relatively common: it is worth learning the names and checking these out for yourself on a truth table so that you see that they are, indeed, invalid argument forms. Other invalid moves have no special names, probably because they are not quite so common as these two.

EXERCISE SET

Exercise 4: Part A

Prove the conclusion on the basis of the premises, using the valid argument forms. In any case where you are not able to derive the conclusion from the premises, use the shorter or longer truth table technique to determine whether the argument is valid.

Hint: Three of the following sequences do not represent a valid argument.

1. $A \supset (B \lor C)$; $B \supset D$; $D \supset G$; $A \cdot -C$; therefore G.

*2. $-A \cdot -B$; $-B \supset C$; therefore C.

3. $-(C \lor D)$; $-D \supset -(H \cdot G)$; $(Q \supset G) \cdot H$; therefore $-Q$.

4. $(A \lor B) \lor (C \lor D)$; $-B \supset -A$; $C \cdot (C \supset -B)$; therefore $-D$.

*5. $(A \lor B) \supset D$; $-D$; $-B \supset (A \supset X)$; $(A \cdot B) \lor X$; therefore X.

6. $A \lor B$; $-B$; $-C \supset -A$; therefore C.

*7. $(D \cdot E) \supset (F \lor G)$; $-D \supset F$; $-(D \lor E)$; therefore $F \lor G$.

8. $-A \supset (B \lor -C)$; $A \supset (C \lor D)$; $A \lor -A$; therefore B.

*9. $A \supset B$; $C \supset D$; $(B \lor D) \supset E$; $-E$; therefore $-A \lor C$.

10. $S \lor -(R \cdot A)$; $-S$; therefore $-A$.

Exercise 4: Part B

Represent each of the following arguments in the symbols of propositional logic. In any example where you believe that the propositional symbols would not capture aspects of meaning crucial to the way the argument works, say why not, and proceed no further. Test symbolized arguments for deductive validity, using either valid inference patterns and a simple proof procedure or the longer or shorter truth table technique.

1. If lightning sometimes causes fires, then if there is increased lightning, we may expect more fires. There is increased lightning. So if lightning sometimes causes fires, we may expect more fires.

2. We cannot worship a god or gods unless we have a capacity to form a concept of the divine, and we cannot have a capacity to form a concept of the divine unless we have a capacity to form concepts that go beyond sense perception. We do worship a god or gods. Therefore, we do have a capacity to form concepts that go beyond sense perception.

3. Most people tend to overestimate the merits of their own actions and underestimate the merits of other people's actions. If people overestimate the merits of their own actions, they do not have an accurate picture of what they themselves do. And if they underestimate what other

people do, they do not have an accurate picture of what other people do. Thus, most people have neither an accurate picture of what they do themselves nor an accurate picture of what other people do.

*4. Understanding is impossible if words refer only to private sensations in the minds of speakers. Since we clearly do understand each other, words are not just references to private sensations.

5. If the media are genuinely democratic, then all citizens have equal access to the media and the media cover all publicly sensitive issues in a fair way. But the media will cover all publicly sensitive issues in a fair way provided only that reporters represent all races, classes, and sexes. This is manifestly not the case. The media do not fairly represent all races. Nor do they represent all economic classes. Nor do they fairly represent women as well as men. Thus the media are not genuinely democratic.

*6. If the world's weather is increasingly erratic, the global warming effect is real. If the world's weather is not increasingly erratic, the global warming effect is not real. The global warming effect is real only if it is measurable, and it is not measurable unless scientific instrumentation is quite elaborate. Because scientific instrumentation is quite elaborate, the global warming effect is measurable. Therefore, the world's weather is increasingly erratic.

7. If people could reason only after someone taught them the logic of the syllogism, then there would have been nobody reasoning before Aristotle discovered the logic of the syllogism. There were people reasoning before Aristotle discovered syllogistic logic. Therefore, it is not the case that people can reason only after someone has taught them syllogistic logic.

(Adapted from John Locke's *Essay Concerning the Human Understanding* [New York: Meridian, 1964])

*8. "I do know this pencil exists, but I could not know this if Hume's principles were true. Therefore Hume's principles are false."

(G. E. Moore, "Hume's Theory Examined," in *Some Main Problems of Philosophy* [New York: Collier Books, 1953])

9.   We cannot suffer after death unless we are conscious after death. We are not conscious after death. Therefore, we cannot suffer after death.

10.   If inflation is brought under control, interest rates will go down and the rate of new business formations will go up. If the rate of new business formations goes up, employment will go up. If employment goes up, more people will be paying taxes, and if more people are paying taxes, there will be more money to support the unemployment fund. But if employment goes up and there is more money to support the unemployment fund, the unemployment fund will run a surplus. Therefore, if inflation is brought under control, the unemployment fund will run a surplus.

11.   If astral projection is possible, then people can project themselves up to a book on a very high shelf and read the title. If astral projection is reliably verified, then people can project themselves up to read in this way and have the event verified by a friend. But people cannot read titles in this way with friends there to verify the event. Therefore, astral projection is not possible.

*12.   The group decided to undertake the action. The group hired Jones to carry out the action. The group funded and directed Jones in carrying out this action. If the group decided on the action, hired Jones, and funded and directed

him in carrying out the action, the group bears responsibility for the action. Therefore, the group bears responsibility for the action.

13.   If children are well trained before the age of five, they seldom lapse into delinquency after the age of five. If women work outside the home, then children will be well trained before the age of five only if daycare centers and kindergartens are extremely well run. Women do work outside the home. Thus, either we have extremely well-run childcare facilities or we risk delinquency in our children.

*14.   She can become a good mathematician only if she studies hard. But she will study hard only if her family life is happy and her general health is good. Good health requires exercise and decent food, neither of which she has. So she will not become a good mathematician.

15.   *Background:* The following argument occurs in Plato's "Symposium," which is a dialogue about the nature and importance of love. At this point in the dialogue, love is personified and referred to as Love, a kind of being, or god. "Mankind," he said, "judging by their neglect of him, have never, as I think, at all understood the power of Love. For if they had understood him, they would surely have built noble temples and altars, and offered solemn sacrifices in his honor; but this has not been done."

(Cited in James Freeman, *Thinking Logically: Basic Concepts for Reasoning* [Englewood Cliffs, NJ: Prentice-Hall, 1988], p. 31)

Propositional Logic and Cogent Arguments

Formal logic is a highly developed technical discipline that we have introduced only schematically in this book. Because our emphasis is on developing practical skills, we stress issues of translation and application while at the same time developing simple formal techniques.

As we noted a number of times, the deductive validity of an argument says nothing about the truth or acceptability of its premises. If an argument is deductively valid, then the (R) and (G) conditions of argument adequacy are fully met. But the (A) condition may or may not be satisfied. It is useful to remember this simple point, because a clearly worded deductively valid argument has a logical flow that makes it seem cogent and sometimes distracts our attention from the fact that the elegant reasoning used is based on false or dubious premises. For mental exercise and in the course of speculation, it is often interesting to see that from some statements, P and Q, we can deductively derive a further consequence, R. But usually this relationship is of little interest in establishing the conclusion unless P and Q are premises we are willing to accept.

The flaw of a dubious premise serving as the basis for impeccably accurate deductive reasoning seems to be particularly prevalent in **dilemma arguments.** These arguments (which, as you will recall, open with a disjunctive premise) are common in debate and in ordinary life. They often appear irrefutable. But the valid form of a dilemma too often serves only to mask the fact that the disjunctive premise on which it is based is false or unacceptable.

Here is an example of a deductively valid dilemma argument that is nevertheless not cogent because of a flawed premise:

> Either the interest rates will come down or there will be a world disaster. In either case I won't have to worry about selling my house. If there is a world disaster, the social fiber of life will be destroyed and selling the house will be no problem. And if there is a fall in interest rates it will be easier for people to buy houses, and selling my house won't be a problem. So, even though the house isn't selling at the moment, I really have nothing to worry about.

The argument begins with a premise that states a false dichotomy. We commented on false dichotomies before, when examining the distinction between contraries and contradictories. In propositional logic, a false dichotomy is readily defined in terms of disjunction. It is a disjunction between two things that are falsely thought to exhaust the possibilities. For instance, the disjunction "John is intelligent or John is stupid" is a false dichotomy. (*Intelligent* and *stupid* are contrary predicates, since there are other alternatives. If John is of average ability, he is neither intelligent nor stupid.)

For the disjunctive premise of the argument about selling the house to be true, there would have to be only two possible courses for world history: that in which there is a world disaster and that in which interest rates come down. If there is even one other possibility, the premise cannot be rationally accepted. (Check back to the truth table for disjunction if you do not understand why. If one disjunct is false, the other must be true for the disjunction to be true.) If you bear this truth table in mind and look closely at the premise, you will see that it is questionable. No one has good reason to believe that interest rates coming down and there being a world disaster are the only two possible futures for our world.

Criticizing dilemma arguments in this way is such a common move that it has a special name. The critic is said to have **escaped through the horns of a dilemma.** She does this by showing a third alternative—by showing that the opening disjunction was not exhaustive, so that the argument was based on a false dichotomy. This sort of problem, which frequently arises with dilemmas, is a nice illustration of the general point that arguments can be "perfectly logical" in the formal sense, exemplifying valid forms, and yet may nevertheless be flawed because they have unacceptable premises.

A further basic point about propositional logic is that it is not always the appropriate tool to use in appraising an argument. It is the appropriate tool only when the connection between the premises and the conclusion depends on the way statements are combined using the basic propositional terms: *or, and, not,* and *if then.* If the force of an argument depends on deductive relations between other terms, or on an analogy, or on empirical evidence for a broader empirical hypothesis, then the argument cannot be properly evaluated by applying the tools of propositional logic. When you represent these other sorts of arguments in propositional logic, you will no doubt find that they are not valid. However, since your symbolization in such cases will not properly reflect the meaning and direction of the original natural argument, this discovery will be of little importance. Propositional and categorical logic are basic and important parts of deductive logic. But they do not apply to all arguments. Arguments that are valid according to the rules of categorical or propositional logic fully satisfy the (R) and (G) conditions. They are cogent provided that their premises are acceptable. Arguments that are not valid according to categorical or propositional logic may be valid within some further formal logic system, or they may be other types of argument—for instance inductive arguments, the subject of Chapter 9, or analogies, the subject of Chapter 10—to which the standards of deductive validity do not properly apply.

CHAPTER SUMMARY

Propositional logic is a basic branch of formal logic in which symbols are used to represent *and, or, not,* and *if then* and letters are used to represent statements. Many arguments depend for their force on relations and connections between these terms. Arguments that can be formally represented in the terms of propositional logic can be tested in various ways for deductive validity.

Three ways of testing propositional arguments for validity are discussed in this chapter: the full truth table technique, the shorter truth table technique, and proof construction. The truth table techniques can be used to show either validity or invalidity. The technique of proof construction does not show invalidity; it can, however, show validity.

In the full truth table technique, arguments are tested on the basis of a full representation on a truth table that has 2 to the power *n* rows, where *n* represents the number of distinct statement variables. The full truth table shows all of the possible combinations of truth and falsity for every statement in the argument. To say that the argument is valid is to say that there is no way that its conclusion can be false given that all of its premises are true. When an argument is valid, there is no row of the truth table showing true premises and a false conclusion.

The full truth table technique is a completely effective one. Given any argument properly formalized in propositional logic, a correctly constructed full truth table will show that it is formally valid or that it is formally invalid. The only problem with the full truth table technique is that it can become rather cumbersome when there are more than two or three distinct statement letters. For instance, if the argument requires four distinct statement letters for its symbolic representation, its full truth table will have 2 to the fourth, or 16, rows. If it has five distinct letters (which is not, in fact, uncommon) the truth table will require 2 to the fifth, or 32, distinct rows. Setting out such a truth table takes quite a lot of time, and with this much information to represent, it is easy to make a careless technical mistake.

The other techniques described are not completely effective in the sense that full truth tables are. The shorter truth table technique requires some ingenuity. To use this technique, you try to set values of true and false for the premises and conclusion to make the argument invalid. That is, you try to set things up in such a way that all the premises turn out to be true and the conclusion turns out to be false, and to do this consistently—giving each distinct statement the same truth value each time it appears in the argument. If there is an assignment in which the premises are all true and the conclusion is false, the argument is invalid. If not, it is valid.

A more elegant technique is that of constructing a valid proof of the conclusion from the premises, using elementary valid argument forms. When you construct a proof, you use a list of elementary forms that you are entitled to appeal to because they are recognized as valid. You move in steps from the given premises toward the conclusion, justifying each move by an appeal to a valid argument form. If you can reach the conclusion in this way, you know that it follows validly from the premises. Proof construction requires insight and ingenuity and is interesting and challenging. You do have a problem, however, if you set out to construct a proof for an invalid argument. You will never succeed, and you will not know whether you have failed because of lack of ingenuity or because the argument is invalid. To find out, you have to use a truth table or another method of showing invalidity.

Deductive validity according to propositional logic shows that the argument meets the (R) and (G) conditions of argument cogency. It does not guarantee that the argument passes on the (A) condition, which has to be determined in another way.

Review of Terms Introduced

Affirming the consequent   An invalid form of inference of the type "$P \supset Q$; Q; therefore P."

Antecedent (of a conditional)   Statement that follows *if* in a conditional of the form "If P then Q." For example, in "If the population increases, the price of housing will increase," the antecedent is "the population increases."

Biconditional   A conjunction of a conditional and its transposition (the conditional that results from transposing the antecedent and the consequent). Example: $(P \supset Q) \cdot (Q \supset P)$

Conditional proof   Proof incorporating an assumption explicitly introduced into the argument and then, in effect, canceled by being represented as the antecedent of a conditional of which the consequent is the conclusion derived from the given premises and the assumption introduced.

Conditional statement   A statement of the form "If P then Q." As such, it does not assert either P or Q. Rather, it asserts a connection between them in the sense that provided P is the case, Q will be the case also. Example: "If the population of Vancouver increases, the cost of housing in Vancouver will increase" does not say either that the population of Vancouver increases or that the cost of housing in Vancouver will increase. It says that *if* the first happens, the second will happen. In propositional logic, the conditional is symbolized as $P \supset Q$.

Conjunction (of statements)   A compound statement in which all the statements are asserted, linked by *and* or an equivalent term. For the conjunction to be true, each component statement or conjunct must be true. The conjunction of statements P and Q is written as $P \cdot Q$.

Consequent (of a conditional)   Statement that follows *then* in a conditional of the form "If P then Q." For example, in "If the population increases, the price of housing will increase," the consequent is "the price of housing will increase."

Counterfactual   A conditional statement in which the antecedent is known to be false. Example: If Hitler had been murdered when he was twenty, World War II would not have occurred. (*Note:* Do not be misled by the term *counterfactual* into thinking that all counterfactuals are false. All have antecedents that are false; however, many counterfactuals themselves are plausibly regarded as true statements.)

Denial (of a statement)   A statement's contradictory or negation. It must have the opposite truth value to the statement. The denial of a statement S is symbolized as $-S$ (not-S).

Denying the antecedent   An invalid form of inference of the type "$P \supset Q$; $-P$; therefore $-Q$."

Dilemma argument   Both constructive and destructive dilemmas constitute valid forms of argument. A constructive dilemma has the form $P \supset Q$; $R \supset S$; $P \vee R$; therefore $Q \vee S$. A destructive dilemma has the form $P \supset Q$; $R \supset S$; $-Q \vee -S$; therefore, $-P \vee -R$. The disjunctive premises of dilemma arguments should be carefully scrutinized for acceptability to ensure that no false dichotomies are involved.

Disjunction (of statements)   A compound statement in which the statements are asserted as alternatives; the connective is *or*. For the disjunction to be true, at least one of the disjoined statements must be true. The disjunction of statement P and statement Q is written as $P \vee Q$.

Escaping through the horns of a dilemma   Showing that a dilemma argument, though valid, is not cogent because it is based on a false dichotomy. This expression is also used when a person shows a dichotomous statement to be false because there is a third alternative; the person is said to have escaped through the horns of a dilemma.

Exclusive disjunction   A disjunction that is true if and only if one and only one of the disjuncts is true. An exclusive disjunction of statements P and Q is represented as $(P \lor Q) \cdot -(P \cdot Q)$.

Horseshoe   A connective written as "$\supset$", used in propositional logic to represent basic conditional relationships. A statement of the form "$P \supset Q$" is defined as false if P is true and Q false, and true otherwise.

Inclusive disjunction   A disjunction that is true if and only if one or both of the disjoined statements are true. The symbol "$\lor$" in propositional logic is used to represent inclusive disjunction.

Indirect proof   Proof of a conclusion by introducing its denial, on the rule of conditional proof, and then deriving a contradiction. Using *modus tollens*, we infer from the contradiction (which must be false) the negation of the statement introduced. That is the denial of the denial of what we set out to prove. This (by double negation) is what we set out to prove.

Modus ponens   A valid argument form, in which from $P \supset Q$ and P, we may infer Q.

Modus tollens   A valid argument form, in which from $P \supset Q$ and $-Q$, we may infer $-P$.

Necessary condition   A condition that is required for another statement to be true. Using the horseshoe, if Q is a necessary condition of P, we would symbolize this as "$P \supset Q$." To say that Q is a necessary condition of P is to say that P will be true only if Q is true.

Propositional logic   That part of logic that deals with the relationships holding between simple propositions or statements and their compounds. In propositional logic, the basic logical terms are *not, or, and,* and *if then.*

Sufficient condition   A condition that is enough to establish a further statement as true. Using the horseshoe, if Q is a sufficient condition for P, we would symbolize it as "$Q \supset P$." To say that Q is sufficient for P is to say that, given Q, P will be true as well.

Truth Table   Set of rows and columns that systematically display the truth values of basic statements and the compound statements formed from them.

Notes

1. Strictly speaking, letters that represent particular statements should not appear at the top of columns on truth tables because the truth table allows for two different truth values for every statement letter. To avoid two levels of symbolization, this technical matter is ignored here, as it is in many other texts.

2. The story of the drug stores was provided by Dr. W. A. McMullen, who saw the signs when he was teaching a logic course at the University of Winnipeg in the early 1960s.

3. The example of the center lane comes from Robert Martin of the Philosophy Department, Dalhousie University, Halifax, Nova Scotia.

chapter nine
An Introduction to Inductive Arguments

W E HAVE EXAMINED the nature of argument, conditions of acceptability and relevance, and some common forms of formal deductive validity. It is now time to take a look at induction.

Philosophical Background

In **inductive arguments,** both the premises and the conclusion are empirical: they are not *a priori* truths or evaluative propositions or propositions recommending what should be done. They predict the way the world will be or, in some cases, retrodict the way it was. An inductive argument is based on some form of **inductive reasoning.** In the most general sense, inductive reasoning is that in which we extrapolate from experience to further conclusions about what will happen. The assumption behind inductive reasoning is that known cases can provide information about unknown cases.

Even those who have not heard of induction, inductive argument, or inductive reasoning rely on induction constantly in everyday life. They assume that cereal, bread, and milk will be nourishing on Wednesday if they were nourishing on Monday and Tuesday, that beds and tables will continue to be stable middle-sized objects, and that people will speak and behave much as they have in the past. People learn inductively by applying past experience to new cases. Inductive learning is absolutely indispensable in everyday life and specialized study.

To appreciate the fundamental nature of induction, we have only to ask ourselves what the basis is for our commonsense beliefs about the world. Why do we believe that in the northern hemisphere January will be colder than August; that a bridge will remain solid when we drive across it; that milkshakes are sweeter than broccoli; that hurricanes are dangerous; that advertising helps sell products; that a government low in the polls a week before the election is unlikely to win that election? In every case, the answer is past experience. Sometimes the evidence comes from our own past experience, and sometimes it comes from the experience of other people, by testimony. (The reliability of testimony was discussed in Chapter 5.) We have experienced various regularities in the world. Reasoning inductively, we assume that what we will experience in the future will be similar to what we have experienced in the past.

Consider this simple inductive argument from the eighteenth-century philosopher David Hume:

1. Every day I can remember, the sun has risen.
Therefore,
2. Tomorrow the sun will rise.

Like all other inductive arguments, this one is not deductively valid. We cannot prove deductively that unexamined cases will resemble the examined ones, or that future mornings will resemble past ones. Here, as in every other inductive argument, there is always some possibility that the conclusion will turn out to be false even though the premises are true. Emphasizing this possibility, Hume elaborated what has been known as the Problem of Induction. However firm our beliefs about the sun rising and other matters established by experience may be, we cannot prove beyond a shadow of doubt that the sun will rise tomorrow. It is possible that it has risen every day we know—and yet that tomorrow it will not rise. The behavior of the sun cannot be guaranteed by the rules of deductive logic.

Does this lack of deductive proof constitute a practical or philosophical problem? If so, can such problems be solved? It is possible to reconstruct the argument about the sun rising (or any other inductive argument, for that matter) to render it deductively valid. We can do this by supplementing the original argument with an additional premise. Consider, for example:

1. Every day I can remember, the sun has risen.
Added premise: The future will resemble the past.
Therefore,
2. Tomorrow the sun will rise.

The argument is now deductively valid. If the premises are true, the conclusion must also be true. However, although the added premise makes the argument deductively valid, it does not fundamentally amend the situation so far as cogency is concerned. There is no way that we can know, in general, that the future will resemble the past, so the added premise is unacceptable. Doubts about the argument have moved from the (R) and (G) conditions to the (A) condition—a phenomenon that we have already had occasion to observe in Chapters 2 and 6. The sweeping generalization incorporated as a "missing premise" cannot be supported by good evidence, and for this reason it is unacceptable. Hume's problem is not solved by this approach: it is only moved from inference to premise. If we knew that the future would resemble the past, then, given our experience of the sun rising in the past, we could prove that it will rise in the future. Here, Hume's problem of induction is embedded in the word *if*. We do not know, nor could we prove, that the future will resemble the past. In a context in which the justification of inductive arguments is in dispute, the added premise begs the question, as Hume pointed out.

The problem of induction has puzzled logicians and philosophers ever since Hume posed it in the eighteenth century. The innumerable responses to the problem are of three basic types. Some philosophers have argued that Hume's discussion of induction constitutes a powerful argument for a kind of fundamental skepticism. Even such basic beliefs as the sun will rise tomorrow, or the binding of the book you are reading will hold it together for the next hour, are founded on induction. In the strictest sense of *know*, we do not know that such beliefs are true. Other philosophers acknowledge that Hume posed a radical challenge to everyday beliefs and science itself, but are not willing to accept the skeptical consequences of Hume's account. They seek to improve on inductive arguments in various ways—by using different versions of the reconstructive approach described above, or by working to develop formal systems of inductive logic.

A third philosophical reaction is to reject the problem as Hume defined it. In essence, this is the stance adopted in this book. In setting out the problem of induction, Hume relied implicitly on a theory of argument and justification. This theory, which presumed that the only good or cogent argument is a deductively valid one, is an especially narrow theory, and as such it is open to criticism. Although Hume had an acutely critical mind and raised many profound questions, he never seems to have questioned this assumption about justification and argument.

Hume's development of the problem of induction can be represented by the following argument:

1. Only deductively valid arguments can demonstrate their conclusion.
2. Inductive arguments, or arguments from experience, are not deductively valid. Therefore,
3. Inductive arguments, or arguments from experience, cannot demonstrate their conclusion.

This argument is a valid syllogism, as you may wish to confirm for yourself. There is, however, a problem with Hume's premises. Although he did a good job of arguing for premise (2), premise (1) is unacceptable, and Hume offered no support on its behalf. It is assumed throughout his writings and never argued for. We reject Hume's problem by refusing to accept premise (1). Contrary to what is claimed in premise (1), there are cogent nondeductive arguments. In fact, we have seen examples of them in this book. Premise (1), then, is open to refutation by counterexample. Hume's problem of induction cannot be solved but it can be "dissolved." To dissolve a problem means to show that it does not arise in the first place. We can eliminate the Problem of Induction if we reject Hume's overriding assumption that a necessary condition of argument cogency is deductive validity.

Could Hume respond by insisting that premise (1) is acceptable on *a priori* grounds, because it is true by definition? We could interpret the word *demonstrate* to make that premise true *a priori*. Then premise (1) would satisfy one of the conditions of acceptability, so Hume would be entitled to insist that it is true and acceptable. Such a definition, however, would amount merely to an insistence that the only way to demonstrate something is by a deductively valid argument. In effect, it amounts to an implicit stipulation, and the stipulation would beg the question in this context. Any "victory" for Hume at this point would be a victory by definition.

Hume was deeply troubled and perplexed by his own conclusions. He realized that we cannot get through life—not even a single hour of a single day of life—without implicitly or explicitly depending on inductive reasoning. We always rely on the general assumption that there are basic regularities and continuities in the world. By nature we are creatures who reason inductively. We naturally and inevitably classify things and operate in life on the principle that things that resemble each other in some respects are likely to resemble each other in further respects. We approach the world on the assumption that there are intelligible patterns within it and relations between causes and effects. Events have causes; hypotheses can be formulated to explain what does and does not happen, and these can be confirmed or disconfirmed.

As Hume himself acknowledged, in every area of life we operate as though there were a distinction to be made between more cogent (strong) and less cogent (weak) inductive arguments. In rejecting wholesale skepticism about induction, we disagree with Hume's generalized theory of argument. But in other ways we agree with Hume. He recognized that in practice induction is the very basis of life, and he himself distinguished between better and worse inductive arguments.

In this book we describe three types of inductive arguments: inductive generalizations, causal inductive arguments, and inductive analogies. Inductive generalizations and causal arguments are explored in this chapter, and inductive analogies are discussed in Chapter 10.

Inductive Generalizations

In **inductive generalizations,** the premises describe a number of observed objects or events as having some particular feature, and the conclusion asserts, on the basis of these observations, that all or most objects or events of the same type will have that feature. Here is a simple example of an inductive generalization:

1. Twenty percent of the 10,000 students at AB University traveled to campus by bicycle in 2000.
So probably,

2. Twenty percent of the 11,000 students who are expected to enroll in AB University in 2001 will use bicycles to travel to campus.

This argument is based on an *extrapolation* of experience from one year to another. The conclusion is inferred on the assumption that the proportion of cyclists in a large group of students will remain constant or nearly so—that 2001 is likely to be similar to 2000 so far as student transportation at AB University is concerned. (The estimate that enrollment will increase by 1,000 in 2000 may also have been based on an extrapolation.) If there were to be a sudden relevant change in circumstances—if, for instance, there were to be several vicious and widely publicized attacks on student cyclists, or if the cost of operating a car were to drop significantly—the strength of this argument would be undermined. In the absence of such changes, the conclusion is well supported by the premises.

Here is another example of an inductive generalization:

1. All the children I have known over the past three decades have begun to talk before the age of two.
2. The seven childcare books I have consulted all indicate that nearly all normal children begin to talk between the first and the second year.
So probably,
4. Your child will begin to talk before the age of two.

Like all inductive arguments, this one is based on experience. Here, however, there is reference both to direct experience and to indirect experience. Premise (1) describes the personal experience of the arguer who apparently has been observing children for some time. Premise (2) describes established beliefs on the topic of children talking, thus incorporating the experience and observations of the authors of these books and the experts they have cited.

You may have been reasoning inductively as you read the example. Based on your own past experience with the way things are numbered, you would expect the conclusion to be numbered (3). If you were reading carefully, you may have wondered why it has been numbered (4). Your inductively grounded expectation was upset, which might have been puzzling. Be assured that this unusual numbering is not the result of a misprint but rather is deliberate. The stated conclusion of this argument is not a generalization but rather a prediction about one particular child. This argument is regarded here as an inductive generalization because we believe that an implicit conclusion, drawn from premises (1) and (2), is the basis for the stated conclusion, (4). The implicit conclusion is:

3. Nearly all children begin to talk before the age of two.

The premises give evidence for the generalization, (3), which is the implicit conclusion of a subargument. The generalization, (3), then serves as a premise to support (4).

Terms such as *probably, in all likelihood,* and *most likely* are often used in inductive arguments. Careful arguers often put such words between the premises and the conclusion, to indicate that the premises only render the conclusion *probable*.

They provide evidence for it—sometimes very good evidence—but they never warrant complete certainty. Inductive arguments do not *prove* beyond a shadow of doubt that the conclusion is true. To understand induction, we must appreciate that it is possible to offer good, strong evidence in favor of a claim without deductively proving that it is true.

The Sample and the Population

There are many variations in inductive generalizations. We may reason from some cases to many, from some cases to all, or from a certain portion of observed cases to a certain portion of the total cases. An example of the latter type is:

1. Figures for 5,000 American and Canadian women studied in the period 1980–1990 indicate that one out of every nine adult women experienced breast cancer at some point in her life.

So probably,

2. One out of every nine adult women in North America will experience breast cancer sometime in her life in the period 2000–2010.

In this argument, a **sample** of 5,000 North American women studied in the period 1980–1990 serves to represent a larger population, that of all North American women in the period 2000–2010. The inductive inference is that the proportion for the population will be the same as it is in the sample.

Sampling is necessary for various reasons. The sheer size of a population may make sampling necessary. But size is not the only factor. The **target population,** or class of things we wish to generalize about, may include events or situations in the past or future. Obviously, these cannot be observed directly. If we wish to make estimations or predictions about them, we have to rely on a sample of events or situations that can be observed.

Often, as in Hume's example about the sun rising, inductive reasoning is used in contexts of **prediction.** We reason from past cases to future ones. However, induction may also involve reasoning from the recent past and present to the distant past. Such reasoning is absolutely fundamental in archaeology and geology. It is sometimes called **retrodiction.** An example of retrodiction would be to argue that because fossils of seashells can be found on a particular region of prairie, the area was once covered by water. We reason backward from present evidence to claims about the past—as distinct from prediction, where we reason forward from present or past evidence to claims about the future. Both in retrodiction and in prediction, we proceed on the inductive assumption that regularities in the world are likely to persist through time.

In inductive generalizations, features that have been observed for some cases are projected to others. Following established practice in statistics and in science, we call the observed cases the sample and the cases we are trying to generalize about the population.

Consider, for example, the following case describing a study by the University of Calgary Department of Economics:

Most Albertans approve of the Klein government's performance to date. Across the province, 56 percent of the 1,004 people interviewed approved of the government's performance, compared to 40 percent who disapproved.[1]

This passage states an inductive argument. The premise is in the second sentence, and the conclusion is in the first sentence. The premise describes a sample: 1,004 Albertans who were interviewed. The conclusion is about "most Albertans." In a study related to voting behavior, we can presume that this means most adult Albertans. A sample of 1,004 people is being used as the basis for making an inductive generalization about some 4 million people. The article noted lower approval ratings when people were questioned specially about cuts to education and health care. There was a substantial gender difference: 65 percent of men approved of the government's performance, whereas only 50 percent of women did. A note indicated that the people questioned were interviewed by telephone between April 28 and May 13, 1995, and that results could be expected to be accurate within 3 percent (plus or minus) nineteen times out of twenty.[2] In other words, there was, on the basis of this study, a 95 percent likelihood that 53 to 59 percent of adult Albertans approved of the Klein government's performance between the end of April and the middle of May 1995.

Sample Representativeness

The clue to reliable inductive generalizations is finding a sample that is **representative** of the population. Informally, this means that the sample is similar to the population in ways relevant to the issue at hand. In the University of Calgary study, the issue was attitudes toward a government that had made deficit-cutting its goal and, in pursuit of this goal, had made extensive cuts to government support of social welfare, education, and health. If the sample was representative of the population, then the people interviewed by telephone were typical of Alberta adults.

Can you think of any questions you would want to raise, on the basis of the information given? You might have noted that people were interviewed by telephone. This means that a person would not be in the sample unless he or she could be contacted by telephone. Thus, homeless people and others inaccessible by telephone would have been excluded. This exclusion could be significant: homeless people, for instance, might themselves have been victims of government cuts in the area of social welfare. The sample, then, was not entirely representative.

In a technical sense, a sample is defined as **random** if every member of the population has an equal chance of being chosen for it. In most circumstances, a random sample is most likely to be representative of the population. If the economists had placed a ticket for every member of the population in a huge basket, shaken the basket, and then picked 1,004 tickets, they would have randomly selected the sample from the population—assuming, that is, that they knew who was in the population and knew that each person had a ticket. In such an event, every member of the population would have had an equal chance of getting into the sample. To have a chance of being selected, a person would not need to be accessible by telephone; homeless people and others inaccessible by telephone would have had tickets like everyone else. To introduce this fiction of a giant raffle is not to fault the economists because they failed to hold one. The story is intended only to illustrate the fact that achieving a sample that is random in the strict technical sense is impossible for populations in the millions.

Improving the Sample

Suppose that you wanted to explore people's beliefs about life after death and you set out to do "person-on-the-street" interviews to explore the beliefs of the people living in your city or town. Doing this would not give you a randomly selected sample; nor would it give you a perfectly representative sample (people who are ill would not be likely to be out on the streets, so they would be omitted), but it would give you a better sample than merely interviewing your personal acquaintances. On-the-street interviews might be the best you can manage for the purposes of your study. To improve your sample, you could interview every fifth person to come around the corner. This strategy would improve sample representativeness by avoiding the danger of interviewing only the more friendly and approachable people.[3] The example indicates the importance of reflecting on the way your sample is selected and on how information comes to you.

If you are distributing a questionnaire and want the responses to provide a sample with information about a broader population, you have to think about several stages in the process. First, you must consider who is going to get your questionnaire. You should try to ensure that your distribution does not omit any relevant subgroup in the population. Suppose, for instance, that you have prepared a questionnaire examining attitudes toward the disabled. It would be a poor strategy to distribute it only to students, only to white-collar workers, or only to women, for instance. Second, you have to consider who is likely to return the questionnaire. Will those who return it be likely to differ in some significant respect from those who fail to return it? If you think such a difference is likely, you might try to counter it—for instance, by offering a small payment for replying or a chance at a prize.

There is a fundamental paradox about sample representativeness and inductive arguments. The sample is perfectly representative if and only if it resembles the population in all respects relevant to the topic being explored. But whether this is the case is something that in practice we can never know. How could we? It is precisely because we are unable to examine the whole population that we are dealing with a sample in the first place. We need inductive arguments because there are cases we cannot examine directly. This means that there are, in the population, unknown cases—and this in turn means that we do not know in detail what the population is like.

Stratified Sampling

Sometimes the technique of **stratified sampling** is used. Suppose that we have a large population, P, and we want to determine how many of this population are likely to do x. We may be able to divide P into relevant subgroups: A, B, and C, where we know what portion of P is in each subgroup. A, B, and C would be based on traits thought to be connected with x. Suppose that the composition of P is 10 percent As, 30 percent Bs, and 60 percent Cs. We can then construct our sample so that it has the same composition, in these respects, as the population. Such a sample is called a stratified sample. Insofar as it reflects the proportions of these relevant subgroups within the population, the stratified sample has a relatively good chance of representing the population.

Polling centers such as the Gallup organization use stratified samples. Because these organizations have been studying such matters as voting habits for a long time, they can obtain reasonably accurate results for populations of many millions from samples of 1,000 to 2,000 people. The stratification is based on past correlations. In the United States, a higher percentage of African Americans than whites tend to vote Democratic; similarly, more older people than younger ones tend to vote Republican, more women than men tend to oppose militaristic attitudes, and so on. Such regularities have persisted for some years. In other cases, where this sort of reliable background knowledge of regularities may not be available, we cannot use stratified sampling in a similarly rigorous way to ensure sample representativeness.

Sample Size

Many people have the intuitive sense that inductive arguments will become stronger insofar as the sample gets larger. Within limits, this is true—but it is not always true. For populations of hundreds of thousands, or even millions, it can be demonstrated that a sample of about 1,000 is large enough to form the reliable basis for an inductive generalization. What is crucial about a sample is not its size but rather its representativeness and the information it contains. In some contexts, substantial increases in sample size produce only relatively small increases in information. What is needed for sample size depends on another factor—the variability of the population. (You can grasp this point informally by supposing that the population does not vary at all with regard to the trait being studied. If this were the case, a sample of *one* would be entirely adequate to represent the population.) The more uniform the population, the stronger the inductive generalization is. To the extent that we have informal reasons to think that the population is quite variable (as we often do for the human population), we should try for the largest sample we can practically obtain. Any sample of less than fifty is unlikely to be useful.

We are seldom in a position to have a precise measure of the variability in the population itself. (This point refers us back to the paradox of sampling: if we were in a position to have knowledge about the whole population, we would not have to consider the sample in the first place.) The greater the variability in the population, the larger the sample that is needed to represent it. If the population is variable, the sample should be larger than it would need to be for a relatively uniform population, and it should reflect the variety in the population.

Variety in samples and populations can constitute serious political and ethical issues. A case in point is the many medical studies that have been done on male subjects alone. Various reasons are given for this research strategy, an especially common one being that female subjects have more variable physiological systems than males because of the effects of the menstrual cycle on their physiology; thus female subjects are more complex to work with. A problem arises, however, if the medical community takes a result demonstrated only for male subjects and uses it to diagnose conditions and prescribe medications for women—as if the result had been demonstrated for the whole adult human population. This is a mistake that can have, and has had, serious consequences for women's health. If a drug has been shown to work in a certain way for 80 percent of males, that says nothing about how it will work for females. Strictly speaking, drugs that have been tested only for males should be regarded as *untested* for females.

The Biased Sample

Occasionally, sampling problems are so severe that the sample demonstrably misrepresents the population. In such cases we speak of a **biased sample.** The sample is selected in such a way that it is bound either to underemphasize or to overemphasize the characteristic being studied. A simple example would be a sample composed entirely of students of literature, where the purpose was to study reading habits in the broad student population. The sample in such a case would be biased because literature students are a self-selected group with regard to love of reading. The sample would over-represent enthusiastic readers.

A computer-users group conducted a survey of its members to find out whether they would prefer to receive the newsletter by regular mail or by electronic mail. Of the membership, 40 percent replied, and of these, 60 percent indicated that they would prefer electronic mail. There was a problem, however; replies were to be submitted electronically. Those who did not like using electronic mail would have been less likely to prefer an electronic newsletter, and therefore less likely to reply. In this case, the bias was a result of careless procedure.

Sometimes bias in a sample is not so innocent; it is a result of deliberate deception. Advertisers, for example, may test group after group of users of a particular brand of toothpaste until they finally find a group in which ten out of ten people have no cavities and are willing to attribute this fact to their choice of brand. Some biased samples are deliberately rigged. An amusing instance occurred in an advertisement for Merit cigarettes. In its unabashed references to good-tasting cigarettes and its omission of any reference to health hazards, this advertisement may now seem dated. Nevertheless its relevance to the issue of rigged sampling remains unchanged.

> "Best-tasting low tar I've tried," report Merit smokers in latest survey. Taste
> Quest Ends. Latest research provides solid evidence that Merit is a satisfying long-

term taste alternative to high tar cigarettes. Proof: The overwhelming majority of Merit smokers polled feel they didn't sacrifice taste in switching from high tar cigarettes. Proof: 9 out of 10 Merit smokers reported they continue to enjoy smoking, are glad they switched, and report Merit is the best-tasting low tar they've ever tried. Merit is the proven alternative to high tar smoking. And you can taste it.[4]

The intended population here is smokers. The sample is smokers of Merit cigarettes. We are not told how many were surveyed, but we are clearly supposed to make an inference as follows:

1. Merit smokers enjoy Merit cigarettes and find them to be the best low-tar cigarettes.
Therefore,
2. Smokers in general will enjoy Merit cigarettes and find them to be the best low-tar cigarettes.

Here the sample has deliberately been selected to be biased. With respect to their attitudes toward Merit cigarettes, smokers of Merit are a self-selected group. Obviously, they would not smoke these cigarettes if they did not like them. The reference to proofs and surveys is supposed to make you think that the advantages of Merits have been successfully demonstrated. But because the sample was so biased, nothing at all has been demonstrated.

Further Illustrations of Problems with Samples

Bearing these considerations about sampling in mind, take a look at this report from a study on attitudes toward sex and competence:

WHEN A MAN TALKS, YOU LISTEN

When you want people to listen, it's what you say and how you say it that counts, right? Not always, report researchers Kenneth Gruber and Jacquelyn Gaebelein. When men and women give identical speeches, the men seem to have a significant edge in capturing an audience's attention.

These findings come from a study involving undergraduates at the University of North Carolina at Greensboro. Gruber, a graduate student, and Gaebelein, a psychologist, prepared videotaped speeches by two men and two women whom a panel of judges had selected for their speaking ability. Each speaker read from an identical script on chess (a topic that previous studies have shown people think of as masculine), interior decorating (thought of as feminine), and skiing (neutral).

Each of 60 student subjects viewed either a man or a woman speaking on one of the topics. Afterward, students' ratings of how informative the speech they heard had been were nearly identical, regardless of the speaker's sex or topic. But both men and women who had seen male speakers recalled more information than those who had seen female speakers.

The researchers think the equal ratings of informativeness may be a byproduct of the women's movement: students may have felt reluctant, consciously or unconsciously, to admit any bias against women. But previous studies have shown that . . . people still expect men to be more competent, intelligent, and knowledgeable than women. If the subjects expected the male speakers to know more, the researchers say, they may well have paid them more careful attention.[5]

In the opening sentences, this report reads as though the findings were universal—about men and women generally. However, since it is obvious that people's attitudes toward competence and sex are likely to vary from one culture to another, we might more charitably assume that the intended population is that of North American adults. This assumption adds some precision to the original. Obviously, this population is large—more than 100 million people. The sample, on the other hand, is decidedly small; it contained sixty people. If we knew that the population was uniform with respect to attitudes on gender roles and competence, this sample size might be adequate. But we do not know this. There is no reason to think that people of various ages, regions, political views, religions, and sexes are similar in their attitudes to gender roles. In fact, experience suggests quite the opposite.

Nor would the researchers, or anyone else, have the background knowledge needed to construct a stratified sample to address the sampling problem. If the researchers had built up a sample using so many Chinese Americans, so many African Americans, so many Native Americans, so many Canadians, so many older and younger people, and so on, they would have improved their sample. It would not, however, be as firmly based as the polls that the Gallup organization and others use for voting predictions, because we do not know which subgroups within the larger population are significant with regard to attitudes about sex roles.

In fact, the sample is seriously unrepresentative. Undergraduates are typically young, educated, less experienced in life, childless, and of a middle class or upper class family background. These features differentiate them from other adults in North America, and it seems likely that some or all of these features would be relevant to attitudes about sexual roles and male and female competence. The argument from reactions found in the sample to reactions likely in the population is inductively weak because the sample is both small and unlikely to be representative of the population. In fact, such problems are of some general interest: many studies in social science are based on samples of undergraduate students. With respect to social attitudes, undergraduate students constitute a poor sample of the adult population.

An influential study of moral reasoning was based on an unrepresentative sample. This case involved the use of males as representative of the entire population. Educational psychologist Lawrence Kohlberg became famous for his studies of moral reasoning, from which he concluded that there is a natural progression in all human beings from self-centered concerns to appeals to universal principles of justice. Kohlberg identified six stages in the process. His work was the basis for much theorizing in developmental psychology and for many programs of moral education for children.

Carol Gilligan, another psychologist, revealed that the interviews on which Kohlberg's theories were based were of eighty-four boys. Despite this sampling bias, Kohlberg and many other researchers who followed him were willing to say that the theory applied to all human beings. Women and girls being human beings, the theory was supposed to apply to them too, even though they had been excluded from the original research. In fact, Kohlberg and his colleagues were willing to infer that many mature women were inferior or "slow" in their moral development because they did not go through the stages that had been identified for boys. Kohlberg's sample was clearly unrepresentative, because it only included boys. Also—a fact not emphasized by Gilligan in her initial criticisms—it failed to represent different cultural, language, and racial groups.[6]

Guidelines for Evaluating Inductive Generalizations

1.   Try to determine what the sample is and what the population is. If it is not stated what the population is, make an inference as to what population is intended, relying on the context for cues.
2.   Note the size of the sample. If the sample is lower than fifty, then, unless the population is extremely uniform or itself very small, the argument is weak.
3.   Reflect on the variability of the population with regard to the trait or property, x, that the argument is about. If the population is not known to be reasonably uniform, the sample should be large enough to reflect what variety there is likely to be in the population.
4.   Reflect on how the sample has been selected. Is there any likely source of bias in the selection process? If so, the argument is inductively weak.
5.   Taking the previous considerations into account, try to evaluate the representativeness of the sample. If you can give good reasons to believe that it is representative of the population, the argument is inductively strong. Otherwise, it is weak.

EXERCISE SET

Exercise 1: Part A

Comment on sample selection techniques for the following issues. If you think the technique, or the situation, will result in an unrepresentative sample being used as the basis for an inductive generalization, suggest ways in which the sample could be made more representative.

*1.   Joe wants to understand whether and how difficulties in finding employment are affecting recent high school graduates in his home state of Wisconsin. He puts a notice on job search bul-letin boards in two major cities, giving his phone number and asking people who are willing to be interviewed to contact him.

2.   Angela wants to study the effects on families of having a family member who suffers from a chronic illness. She consults the College of Physicians and Surgeons, who give her a list of all physicians in her area. She then employs a randomizing technique to pick ten of them from whom she seeks help in getting telephone numbers of chronic patients whose families are likely

to cooperate with her study. After preliminary telephone interviews with 100 people, Angela finds 50 families who agree to participate in in-depth interviews.

*3.   A naturalist is employed to estimate the population of elk in an area of a national park. He begins by finding reports of sightings on four major hiking trails and at two major campsites. He calculates that the area covered is about one-tenth of the total area of the park; the chance of an elk being seen over a one-year period, given the use rate of the park, he calculates at 10 per-cent. There were 20 sightings of elk; hence he estimates the elk population in the area at 2,000.

4.   A real estate agent wants to estimate the number of homes that will come up for sale in a wealthy suburb over the next year. The popula-tion of the suburb is approximately 10,000, and there are approximately 3,000 homeowners. The real estate agent sends out questionnaires to all owners of houses on the five busiest streets, making for a total of 300 questionnaires. From these, she gets 99 returns; 20 of the 99 indicate that they hope to sell their houses over the next year. She calculates that 20 out of 99 is very close to one-fifth; one-fifth of 3,000 is 600, so there should be 600 homeowners in the suburb want-ing to sell in the next year.

*5.   Professor X teaches a compulsory course in military history for history majors, and he has 100 students. Professor Y teaches an optional course in labor history, and he has 15 students. On student evaluations, 60 percent of Professor X's students complain about his course, saying they find it difficult and do not like the assign-ments and the textbooks. By contrast, only 12 percent of Professor Y's students did not like his course. Fully 80 percent rated him as very good or excellent and found the assignments and texts helpful. The remaining 20 percent rated Profes-sor Y as good.

Exercise 1: Part B

Using your own background knowledge, com-ment on the variability you would expect in the following populations, mentioning some of the main respects in which you would expect the population to vary, relevant to the aspect being studied.

1.   Nurses in the United States. (Focus: job satisfaction)

*2.   Situations of elementary school teachers of foreign languages in North America. (Focus: what they find to be successful strategies for dealing with students who pose serious disci-pline problems)

3.   Crops of oats in southern Manitoba and North and South Dakota. (Focus: growth under natural fertilizers as opposed to growth under chemical fertilizers)

*4.   Sea otters in the waters along the west coast of North America. (Focus: evidence, if any, that pollutants in the water, from the growing human population, are adversely affecting the sea otters' health)

5.   Politicians, in North America and western Europe. (Focus: whether politicians significantly differ from nonpoliticians with respect to ambi-tion)

Exercise 1: Part C

For each of the following passages (a) state whether there is an argument based on inductive generalization. If so, (b) identify the sample and the target population and then (c) assess the in-ductive strength of the argument by commenting on the adequacy of the sample. (d) If several claims are supported by the evidence, distinguish them and, when relevant, comment on whether these claims are supported equally well by the ev-idence offered.

1.   In Ireland, disputes between contending Protestant and Catholic groups led to the parti-tioning of the country into Northern and South-ern Ireland, and there is still fighting in Ireland today. In India, disputes between Muslims and Hindus led to the partitioning of the country into India (primarily Hindu) and Pakistan (pri-marily Muslim), and there is much ill will and

some fighting between India and Pakistan. In Vietnam, an attempt to divide the country between communist and noncommunist forces led to continued fighting until the communist forces won a victory in 1975. In Korea, a similar division has led to much animosity, tremendous militarization on both sides of the divide, and occasional border disputes. On the basis of this evidence, we can see that partitioning countries that are experiencing religious or ideological conflict is generally a poor method of resolving conflicts within them. Far from resolving such conflicts, it seems likely to inspire future ones.
(Based on historical arguments given in detail in Robert Schaeffer, *Warpaths: The Politics of Partition* [New York: Basic Books, 1990])

2.   A survey of science students in south Holland indicated that only 65 percent had done any experimental work in conjunction with their high school courses in science. Of the 10,000 students enrolled in either chemistry, biology, or physics in 1998–99, fully 35 percent said they had no experience working in labs and, even of the 65 percent, only one-half had done laboratory work in more than one course. The survey was based on in-school questionnaires filled out by 300 students, half in cities and half in rural areas.
(Constructed example)

3.   In a patch of rainforest in Brazil, approximately 1 square kilometer in size, it has been calculated for that each tree that is removed by selective logging, 27 other trees that are 10 centimeters more in diameter are severely injured and 40 meters of road need to be created. Experts have estimated on the basis of this sample that it will take 70 years for selectively logged forests to again resemble the state they were in when the selective logging was done. Therefore if 400 square kilometers of rainforest were to be logged in this way, approximately 10,800 trees of more than 10 centimeters in diameter would be severely injured. Furthermore, 16,000 meters of road would need to be created. And the rainforest would not recover for some 28,000 years.

(Adapted from "Sustaining the Amazon" by Marguerite Holloway, *Scientific American,* July 1993)

*4.   In a study, 300 adults were questioned about attitudes toward the safety of the nuclear energy industry. Of these, 110 believed that nuclear energy was a safe form of energy and 190 believed that it was unsafe. Of those opposed, 130 were opposed on the grounds that accidents would raise cancer rates. The other 60 were opposed on the grounds that there is no way, known to be safe, of storing nuclear waste over a long period of time. The adults questioned were interviewed in schools, libraries, and office buildings in the south-central United States. We can see from this poll that Americans are now unwilling to accept nuclear energy as safe.

*5.   Linda was not a reliable employee. She was employed for eight months and was supposed to spend five mornings per week in the office. During this time, I went to the office eight times. On four of those occasions she was not in the office because she was, supposedly, working from home. On three of them she was in the office, but her children, who are quite young, were with her, and she was not getting anything done. I don't think we ever got the twenty hours work per week that we were paying Linda for.

6.   *Background:* In *Time* magazine for March 8, 1982, the following advertisement appeared on behalf of MICOM Word Processors. The advertisement was accompanied by a graph, which referred to a 1981 user survey in which 99 percent of MICOM users said they would recommend the system to others. For users of IBM, the graph stated, the figure was 87 percent; it was 89 percent for users of Wang, Xerox, AES, and NBI standalone word processors. When asked if they would recommend MICOM to someone else, 99 percent said yes.

"For the second consecutive year, MICOM 2000/2001 has received the highest rating awarded for overall satisfaction in the prestigious Datapro Survey. The ratings, by users of word processing equipment, ranked the 2000/2001 ahead of all IBM, Wang, Xerox, AES, and NBI standalone word processors. When asked if they would recommend MICOM to someone else, 99 percent said yes."

7.   In a survey of men published in 1982, 50.5 percent of the men questioned said that their favorite sex life would be a marriage in which their wife was their only sexual partner. The results were based on interviews with 4,000 men who were approached primarily in shopping centers and malls, but also in office building complexes, tennis clubs, college campuses, airports, and bus depots. The communities from which subjects were selected varied in affluence.

(Anthony Pietropinto and Jacqueline Simenauer, *Beyond the Male Myth* [New York: New York Times Books])

8.   Ski instructors have the sort of personality one might expect in ambitious career people. Personality tests were given to 78 male and 40 female ski instructors based at glamorous resort spots such as Aspen, Sun Valley, Steamboat Springs, and Vail, all in the United States. The instructors ranged in age from 16 to 62; the average age was 28. Most had been teaching five years or longer and were officially certified. They scored high on ambition, independence, and a propensity for hard work and diligence.

(Adapted from a report in *Psychology Today*, December 1980)

9.   "About one in three Canadians attended a church service during the first week of May. This is down slightly, but not significantly, from the 37% who reported attendance a year earlier. Results are based on 1042 personal, in-home interviews with adults 18 years and over, conducted during the first week of May. A sample of this size is accurate within a four percentage point margin, 19 times out of 20."

(The poll was taken by the Gallup organization for the Canadian Institute of Public Opinion and cited in the Calgary *Herald* for June 28, 1980)

*10.   *Background:* This item is taken from a newspaper story headlined "Three Out of Ten Operations Not Needed: U.S. Nurses."

"New York: Nearly half the nurses surveyed in a nationwide poll claim 3 out of 10 operations are not needed, and many of them say about half of all hospital stays are unnecessary. Eighty-three percent of the nurses polled by the magazine RN, a journal for registered nurses and students, also favored informing patients of less extreme and sometimes less expensive therapeutic alternatives, even if the doctor won't. Based on a national poll of 12,500 nurses, the report provided evidence of a quiet mutiny—in the name of patients' rights—in the nation's hospitals."

(Toronto *Star*, February 15, 1981)

Causal Inductive Arguments

Causal inductive arguments are considerably more complicated than inductive generalizations. Here we consider primarily arguments purporting to establish a cause—that is, arguments in which the conclusion is that one event, or one sort of event, is the cause of another. Typically, the premises of a **causal inductive argument** describe events that are associated or correlated in the sense that they occur together. Under certain conditions, these associations can provide evidence for a causal conclusion. Here is an example:

Whenever he swims in chlorinated water he gets an unpleasant bumpy rash, and whenever he does not swim, or swims in natural water, he does not get the rash. So probably the chlorine in the water is the cause of his rash.

As we shall see, causal arguments present some challenging features. For the moment, we will keep the story simple and suggest that a causal argument be represented as follows:

1. *C* and *E* are regularly associated events.
2. *C* regularly occurs before *E*.
3. The claim that *C* is a cause of *E* is consistent with background knowledge about *C* and about *E*.
Therefore, probably,
4. *C* is a cause of *E*.
(You will better understand what is meant by background knowledge after reading the discussion that follows.)

The nature of causation and the means of verifying causal claims are complex and controversial topics. One thing that complicates the problem is that different things can be meant by *cause*. By *cause* we sometimes mean a necessary condition; sometimes a sufficient condition; sometimes a condition that is both necessary and sufficient; and sometimes something that is a contributory factor. Compare, for instance, the following claims:

a. *C* is a necessary condition, or necessary cause, for *E*. Without *C*, *E* will not happen; $E \supset C$.
b. *C* is a sufficient condition, or sufficient cause, for *E*. Given *C*, *E* is bound to happen; $C \supset E$.
c. *C* is a necessary and sufficient condition, or cause, for *E*. Without *C*, *E* will not happen and given *C*, *E* is bound to happen. Biconditional: $(E \supset C) \cdot (C \supset E)$.
d. *C* is a contributory cause of *E*. (*C* is one of several factors that, together, produce *E*.)

These claims are different from each other in important ways. Claims (a), (b), and (c) make the clearest assertions from a logical point of view. Often, however, it is causal factors (d) that we are trying to discover. Both in ordinary speech and in scientific research, we often speak of a contributory factor, as in (d) as "the cause." If we were using language strictly, such a claim would be an oversimplification. Consider, for instance, the much-discussed claim that high cholesterol in the blood causes heart disease. High cholesterol may be *one contributory factor* to the development of heart disease but there are many other contributory factors, including genetic inheritance, fitness level, and diet.

When we read reports in the media and elsewhere of the results of scientific studies, it is important to check to see whether a causal claim is made. Causal claims are not always stated using the words *cause* and *effect*. Many other words and expressions are used in stating causal claims. Here are some of them:

A produced *B*.
A was responsible for *B*.
A brought about *B*.
A led to *B*.
A was the factor behind *B*.
A created *B*.

A affected B.
A influenced B.
B was the result of (or resulted from) A.
As a result of A, B occurred.
B was determined by A.
A was a determinant of B.
B was induced by A.
B was the effect of A.
B was an effect of A.

When we evaluate inductive arguments, it is crucially important to see whether a causal claim is made. Causal claims require a different justification from inductive generalizations; in addition they have different implications for action.

Mill's Methods

The nineteenth-century philosopher John Stuart Mill proposed methods for discovering causal relationships. Of Mill's methods, three are briefly described here: the Method of Agreement, the Method of Difference, and the Joint Method of Agreement and Difference. As we shall see, Mill's methods have some limitations. However they are still useful in some circumstances.

The Method of Agreement To see how this works, suppose that a group of ten friends visit a restaurant and have a nice dinner. Afterward five of them develop acute stomach pains. They were all in the restaurant together; investigating to find the cause, they begin by operating from the assumption that the stomach pain resulted from what they ate in the restaurant.[7] They ate in the same restaurant, but they did not all eat the same thing. To use Mill's Method of Agreement to explore this topic, they would list what each person ate and then check to see whether there was one food eaten by all the people who suffered from stomach pains. If there were, they would tentatively infer a causal hypothesis: that item was the cause of the stomach pains. In this case, the cause would be a *sufficient condition* (given the background circumstances) of having the stomach pains.

Suppose that Paul, John, Mary, Sue, and David were the ones who became ill, that they ate different main dishes and different desserts, but they all had Caesar salad with a sharp cheese dressing. Given this evidence, there is reason to suspect that the salad or the sharp cheese dressing caused their illness.[8]

It is worth noting that the exploration need not stop at this point. The Method of Agreement can be used to explore the matter further. For example, did other patrons who consumed this dressing suffer stomach pains? If the group were to discover that thirty-five others ate the sharp cheese dressing, and of these only ten experienced ill effects, that would be evidence against their causal hypothesis that the dressing caused the stomach pains. (Perhaps sharp cheese dressing, in conjunction with some other factor or factors, caused the discomfort. Such hypotheses could also be explored using Mill's methods.) The investigating patrons could use the Method of Agreement again with the broader group of fifteen people to try to discover the cause by finding out what, if anything, all these people had in common relative to their illness.

The Method of Difference   As we might expect from its name, in the Method of Difference we are looking for the factor that makes the difference. Suppose that 100 people are exposed to Disease D and of them, only three catch it. Following the Method of Difference, we would seek what feature differentiates these three people from the others. If we could find a property that they shared, and that none of the other people possessed, we would have grounds for the causal hypothesis that the shared characteristic made the difference in catching Disease D. If, for instance, these three people, and only they, had scarlet fever as children, we would tentatively form the hypothesis that having had scarlet fever made them more vulnerable, and that this was a cause (in the sense of necessary condition) of getting Disease D.

The Joint Method of Agreement and Difference   This method consists of using the Method of Agreement and the Method of Difference together. If an aspect, x, is common in all examined cases in which a phenomenon, y, occurs and is absent in examined cases in which y does not occur, then we have some reason to suspect that x is the cause of y. The application of the Joint Method supports the conclusion that x is a necessary and sufficient condition of y. That is to say, $(y \supset x) \cdot (x \supset y)$.

Mill's methods presuppose that there is a cause to be found, and that we have enough knowledge to know what sorts of factors to look for. Using these methods, we arrive at causal hypotheses. There are some pitfalls in the method. An obvious one is that we may have made a faulty assumption when we identified the factors to examine. (Our list of possible factors may have been too short.) In the case of the sharp cheese dressing, for example, it is not hard to imagine various ways in which the causal inference might have gone wrong. The overall assumption that the cause must have been something in the food might be mistaken. Paul, John, Mary, Sue, and David might have all been exposed on a previous day to a certain flu bug, and the stomach pain might have been part of that flu. By concentrating their attention on what was eaten at the restaurant, the friends would miss this factor and reach a faulty causal conclusion. This is not to say that Mill's methods are useless—only that they have to be applied with care. We must remember first that our results are only as good as the assumptions used in formulating the problem, and second, that the conclusion is a causal *hypothesis*.

EXERCISE SET

Exercise 2
Note: Separate instructions are given for each question.

*1.   Joan has had severe allergic skin reactions five times this summer. On the first occasion, she had multiple mosquito bites, had used a new perfumed soap, and was exposed to severe heat. On the second occasion, she had been bitten by a wasp, had used perfumed bubble bath, had been suffering from a mild flu, and had a number of mosquito bites. On the third occasion, she was again bitten by a wasp, had been wearing a new blouse with specially treated fabric, had many mosquito bites, and had slept at a motel where the sheets were laundered with scented soap. The fourth time, she had been exposed to heat, had attended a theatrical performance where she had to sit next to someone wearing powerfully scented cologne, had mosquito bites, and had eaten sharp cheese. On the fifth occasion, Joan had drunk wine, sat next to someone wearing a strong perfume, had been stung by a wasp, and had a number of mosquito bites.

Question: Applying Mill's Method of Agreement, what would you conclude about the cause of Joan's skin problems this summer?

*2.   Using the information in question 1, suppose that you find out that on ten other occasions during the summer, Joan had many mosquito bites but did not encounter any skin problems. Would this lead you to modify the causal hypothesis you reached in question 1? What would be your alternate hypothesis? Which of Mill's methods would you use to try to arrive at an alternate hypothesis?

3.   In question 1, a number of features of Joan's circumstances when she experienced skin problems were described. Only some features of these situations are mentioned. Comment on other aspects that might have been relevant and on the assumptions on which the selection of features seems to have been based.

*4.   Joe and some of his friends like to drink. Joe often has gin and tonic with ice; it makes him feel relaxed and happy. Fred has rum and coke with ice, and that makes him feel good. Peter enjoys scotch on ice, which always makes him feel great. Alan's favorite drink is vodka and orange with ice, which puts him in a pretty good mood. Using Mill's Method of Agreement, what seems to cause the men's relaxed feeling in these

cases? Comment on this result; has anything gone wrong? Can you make any suggestions as to what has gone wrong? Could you reformulate the example to avoid the problem?

5.   Of 200 children attending an inner-city school, 120 failed state examinations at the age of 14, while 80 passed. Of the 80 who passed, 15 received an average grade of over 80 percent. The other 65 received average grades ranging from 60 percent to 70 percent. The school was in a district where many people lived in poverty and there was a high rate of crime and drug abuse. Teachers studying the children's results discovered that none of those who failed had extra tutoring in examination subjects, whereas of the 15 students who achieved an average over 80 percent, all had extra tutoring. Using Mill's methods, what causal hypothesis would you form about the cause of failure? About the cause of high achievement? Can you think of any way in which Mill's methods would lead you to a faulty conclusion in this case?

6.   In the same case as question 5, teachers went on to explore the differences between those students who passed but did not get over 80 percent (65 people) and those who passed and did get over 80 percent (15 people.) In the first group, all were younger siblings in their families; 40 had always attended inner-city schools; and 19 had part-time jobs. In the second group, all were either the oldest children in their family or only children; 10 had previously been in schools in rural areas of the state; and none had part-time jobs. Using Mill's methods, what causal hypothesis would you reach about the cause of high achievement among those passing the examination? Suppose someone were to generalize this causal hypothesis, wishing to extend it to a broader population? What would you say about the strength of an inductive generalization based on the sample in this case?

7.   One hundred fifty students are enrolled in a university course on algebra. Because the available classrooms can hold only 75 students, the class is split in two on the basis of student

timetable convenience. One section is taught by Dr. Smith in person, whereas in the other section students view Dr. Smith's lectures on television. In both sections, two graduate assistants are present; the same two graduate assistants attend each section, do the marking, and conduct tutorials. The textbook is the same for each class. Dr. Smith composes and marks all examinations for both sections. He is widely regarded as an uninspiring lecturer with a rather arrogant and unattractive personality. The live section is held at 9:00 A.M., whereas the television section is held at 1:00 P.M. At the end of the course, students are asked to evaluate it. In the morning section, the average evaluation is 7.5 out of 10 and there is no evaluation lower than 5. In the afternoon section, the average evaluation is 4.5 out of 10 and there is no evaluation higher than 6.

(a) Based on the information given, state two causal hypotheses, based on Mill's Method of Difference, for this result. (b) Of the two hypotheses, which do you think is the more plausible? State reasons for your view. (c) How could you use Mill's methods to do further testing and find out which hypothesis is more likely to be correct?

8. In 12 elections over a 50-year period, there have been 75 candidates for the presidency of Ruritania. Of these, 12 have been successful in that they were elected to the presidency, whereas the remaining 63 were unsuccessful. A study of the 12 successful candidates revealed the following: all were male, all were white, all were rich, all spoke the language of the country with no accent, 9 had previously held political office, 11 were married, and 1 was a bachelor. Among the 63 unsuccessful candidates, all were white and rich; 50 were male, 13 female; 60 spoke without an accent, whereas 3 had accents; 43 were married, 20 single; and 20 held previous office. Based on this information, and using Mill's methods, can you arrive at a hypothesis about the cause of getting elected to the Ruritanian presidency? Why or why not?

Correlations

Correlational claims are based on observations of two distinct objects or events. Researchers look at two aspects of each subject: they first determine whether it is *A* or non-*A,* and then whether it is *B* or non-*B.* The results of such a study may be of three different types:

(i) Positive correlation: if a higher proportion of *A*s than non-*A*s are *B,* then there is a positive correlation between being *A* and being *B.*
(ii) Negative correlation: if a smaller proportion of *A*s than non-*A*s are *B,* then there is a negative correlation between being *A* and being *B.*
(iii) No correlation: if about the same proportion of *A*s as non-*A*s are *B,* then there is no correlation between being *A* and being *B.*

In a sample, researchers try to estimate whether positive or negative correlations are significant. A *significant* correlation is one that is reliable in the sense that it is not likely to have occurred purely by chance. This being the case, there is a strong likelihood that the correlation will persist in the population itself. That is, it is not merely an accident due to the way in which the sample has been selected. Slight positive or negative correlations could be due to accidental variations within the sample. As well as distinguishing between positive, negative, and no correlation, we have to distinguish between those positive or negative correlations that are significant (that is, reliable) and those that are not.

If we were to study 1,000 women and 1,000 men, and we were to find that 55 percent of the women and 46 percent of the men disapproved of the testing of nuclear weapons, the correlation between this attitude and gender would be interesting. Is it significant in the technical sense? Would it hold for other samples of the same population, or for the population as a whole? With this difference in a sample of 2,000, the answer is probably yes. If, on the other hand, the sample size were far smaller, such a gender difference would not be at all significant in the technical sense. For instance, in a sample of only 30 people, small differences in percentages do not mean anything. Three percent of 30 is, after all, only 1 person, and it could easily be that 1 person out of 30 accidentally had some attitude or characteristic.

Correlation and Cause

In this book, we do not try to offer a complete theory of correlation or a complete theory of causation. These topics are too complex to be thoroughly explored here. We only hope to give you some analytical tools so that you can look at causal arguments with a critical eye. A major point, and one that can be easily understood, is that *correlation* is not the same as *causation*. Just because *A* is positively correlated with *B*, that does not mean that *A* is the cause of *B*. Even if we grant that *A* and *B* are positively correlated and that this correlation is significant, it does not follow that the explanation for the correlation is that *A* is the cause of *B*. This is one possible explanation, but there are others as well.

When a correlation between two things is discovered, it is natural to suspect that there is some sort of causal relationship. Often we have background knowledge suggesting this as well. We may find statements to the effect that certain phenomena are "linked" or "have been linked," or are "associated" or "believed to be associated." Such statements state a correlation but *suggest* as well that there is a causal relationship between the phenomena. This implication is unobjectionable so long as the intent is to indicate a causal *hypothesis*. But such usage can be confusing, especially in media reports. If correlational evidence is presented and a causal claim is made or suggested, it is important to note the gap between the evidence and the claim. The (G) condition will be a problem in such a case. Correlational evidence is never adequate grounds to establish the conclusion.

When *linked* and *associated* are used in such contexts, you should ask whether there is evidence to support a causal relationship. The words subtly, and often misleadingly, suggest that there is a causal relationship when, at best, the evidence supports a correlation.

Here is an example that illustrates the problem:

MIGRAINES LINKED WITH SEXUAL AROUSAL

That worn-out line, "Sorry I've got a headache," has long been an easy excuse for avoiding sex. According to the latest medical evidence, however, a headache can actually create a craving for sex. At the 1980 International Headache Conference in Florence, Italy, Dr. Frederico Sicuteri, migraine specialist, reported on a study of 362 migraine patients. Nine percent of women and 14 percent of men felt sexually aroused during their migraine attacks, he said. He speculated that the percentage was probably much higher, but it was a topic that some patients were unwilling to discuss. Among those patients who reported feeling sexually aroused, the erotic sensation usually came near the end of their headaches. Fifty to 60 percent of their headaches were accompanied by arousal. Evidence suggests that headaches and sexual excitement are both linked to an imbalance of serotonin and dopamine, two important neurotransmitters, chemical substances that transmit nerve impulses.[9]

According to this report, Dr. Sicuteri thought that he had found a correlation, and perhaps even a causal relationship, between having a migraine headache and being sexually aroused. But the data seem to have been far from substantiating either such claim. Sicuteri found at most a correlation in a modest number of migraine patients. If we assume that of the 362 patients, half were men and half were women, then (calculating the percents) 16 women and 25 men would have felt the effect. These are small numbers. And even these people felt sexually aroused during only 50 to 60 percent of their headaches. Furthermore, to show that there is a positive correlation between having a migraine and being sexually aroused, a researcher would have to compare people who have migraines with those who do not and see whether there are significantly more aroused people in the former category. This is a problem because *all the people Sicuteri was working with were migraine patients.* Of people who are not suffering from migraines or other headaches, what percent feel sexually aroused at a given time? (Note that the term *sexually aroused* in this context is rather vague.)

According to the report, the correlation pointed to a causal relationship: "a headache can actually create a craving for sex." But the evidence provided is far from supporting a causal hypothesis. First of all, grounds for a general correlation are very weak. Secondly, even if the correlation were supported, that would not by itself indicate a causal relationship. The passage is rather amusing and provides tremendous scope for the exercise of critical thinking. But when all is said and done there is little to be learned from it about headaches and sexual excitement.

If *A* is positively correlated with *B*, then one of the following will be true:

1. *A* causally contributes to *B*. That is, either *A* is the necessary cause, the sufficient cause, or the necessary and sufficient cause of *B*, or it is one of several contributory factors that combine to produce *B*.

Or

2. *B* causally contributes to *A*. That is, either *B* is the necessary or sufficient cause of *A*, or the necessary and sufficient cause of *A*, or it is one of several contributory factors that combine to produce *A*.

Or

3. Some other factor, *C*, is the underlying cause—in one of the senses defined above—of both *A* and *B*.

Or

4. The correlation between *A* and *B* is coincidental.

Given that there are these four possibilities, we cannot simply argue from a positive correlation between *A* and *B* to the conclusion that *A* is the cause, or a cause, of *B*. To do so would be to infer (1) without giving any reason to exclude the alternatives, (2), (3), and (4). Such an inference would be hasty and mistaken. To legitimately infer (1), we must have good grounds for excluding (2), (3), and (4).

These points about correlation and cause mean that arguments based on premises about correlation, used in an attempt to support conclusions about causal relationships, are difficult to construct with accuracy. So many things might be underlying causes of both *A* and *B*. Sometimes it is easy to exclude the possibility that *B* causes *A*; it may happen that *A* comes before *B* or that we already have background knowledge that would rule out this possibility. But for some correlations, even this is not easy.

An example of a dispute about correlation and cause is the following: there is a positive correlation between being overweight and having high blood pressure. What is usually inferred from this correlation is that being overweight is one cause of having high blood pressure—that is, that it combines with other conditions to produce the high blood pressure. From this inference, medical doctors traditionally have made the further inference that patients with high blood pressure can improve their condition by losing weight. However, some critics have urged that these inferences are too hasty. They have pointed out that many of the overweight people whose blood pressure has been observed have been dieting and therefore have been under stress. Also, they point out, our society strongly condemns extra pounds, and makes life difficult for people who are overweight. Perhaps the causal relationship holds between stress and high blood pressure, or between social attitudes, stress, and high blood pressure. Perhaps this is not simply an issue of higher than normal weight and high blood pressure. And of course further complications are possible. There is evidence that a particular gene causes both overweight and adult-onset diabetes. Adult-onset diabetes, in turn, seems to cause high blood pressure. If these hypotheses are correct, then high blood pressure and overweight would, in some cases, have a common genetic cause. Given these multiple factors, which probably interact, it is almost certainly an over-simplification to conclude from a correlation between overweight and high blood pressure that the former causes the latter.

An additional complication in some contexts such as this one is the possibility that a correlation is simply a coincidence. That is a possibility that science can never absolutely rule out; the best that can be done is to improve the sample. If the correlation persists, then it is a general regularity in the world. According to the principles of the scientific method, there must be some explanation for it. But to say this is not to say what that explanation is. Certainly there is no guarantee at all that causal relationships will be simple and clear.

With these points in mind, consider the following report on teenagers' marijuana smoking habits. The report is taken from a text in psychology, which seems at this point not to be taking the distinction between correlation and cause as seriously as it should:

A FRIEND IN WEED IS A FRIEND IN DEED

Among the factors responsible for adolescent students using drugs, one of the most potent is social conformity pressures. A large-scale 1971 survey of over 8,000 secondary school students in New York State revealed that adolescents are much more likely to use marijuana if their friends do than if their friends do not.

To some extent initiation into the drug scene is a function of modelling parental drug use. . . . But the most striking finding was the role that peers played. Association with other drug-using adolescents was the most important correlate of adolescent marijuana use. "Only 7 percent of adolescents who perceive none of their friends to use marijuana use marijuana themselves, in contrast to 92 percent who perceive all their friends to be users." As can be seen, the influence of best friends overwhelms that of parents.[10]

According to this study, there is a positive correlation between perceiving one's friends to use marijuana and using it oneself: 92 percent of those who perceive all their friends to be users use it, whereas only 7 percent who perceive none of their friends to be users use it. The sample is large and this is a huge difference; obviously, the positive correlation is significant. It is clear from the wording of this report that a causal relationship is claimed. The implication is evident in the phrases "among the *factors responsible* for adolescent students using drugs" and "as can be seen, the *influence* of best friends *overwhelms* that of parents." However, no evidence is given for a causal relationship between friends smoking and a teenager smoking, and indeed the distinction between correlation and causation seems to be entirely ignored. The only data presented concern the perception of one's friends smoking and smoking oneself. As described here, the research clearly involved a hasty inference from correlation to cause. No basis is given for excluding other hypotheses that could explain the correlation. These would include (a) the use of marijuana influences one's selection of friends; (b) the use of marijuana influences one's *perception* of one's friends; (c) some underlying cause produces both the marijuana habit and the selection of a certain type of friend; and various others. The passage is an apt illustration of how not to reason from correlation to cause.

Before leaving the topic of correlation and cause, we should say a few words about negative correlation. From the information that *A* is negatively correlated with *B*, we would not, of course, even be tempted to conclude that *A* is the cause of *B*. We might, however, be tempted to infer that *A* prevents *B*. An example of negative correlation is the relationship between breast-feeding and breast cancer in women. Breast cancer occurs less frequently in women who breast-feed their babies than in women who do not breast-feed. On this basis, it has been speculated that breast-feeding in some way prevents breast cancer, or at least inhibits its development. But this too is a causal claim and, like any other, needs more support than purely correlational data. Just as we need additional reasoning and evidence to argue from a positive correlation to cause, we need additional evidence to argue from negative correlation to prevention.

Let us suppose we study 800 people, of whom 400 are highly skilled at playing the piano and the other 400 are unskilled. Now let us say that we study the handedness of students in each group. We are thereby dividing the group with regard to piano-playing skill (highly skilled or unskilled) and handedness (left-handed or right-handed). Let us suppose that of those unskilled at piano playing, 10 percent are left-handed and 90 percent right-handed, whereas of those highly skilled at piano playing, 25 percent are left-handed and 75 percent right-handed. In this sample of students, there is a strong positive correlation between being highly skilled at piano playing and being left-handed. Suppose that we begin to investigate the relationship. For this case, the possibilities are:

a. Being left-handed causally contributes to developing high skill at playing the piano.
b. Playing the piano (frequently enough to become highly skilled) causally contributes to being left-handed.
c. Some underlying factor causally contributes to both left-handedness and high piano-playing skill, or causally contributes to both.
d. The relationship between handedness and piano-playing skill in this sample of students is purely accidental.

To reach the causal conclusion that being left-handed contributes to the development of high skill at playing the piano, without any leaps in logic, we have to give reasons for excluding (b), (c), and (d). We can eliminate (b), for we know that handedness develops before people are old enough to be either skilled or unskilled at playing the piano. This leaves (c) and (d). As for (d), it is partly a matter of sampling. We have to check to see that the 800 students in our sample are representative with regard to handedness, piano-playing skills, and related matters. But granting that the sample is representative, this is all we can do to rule out (d). It represents a remote possibility, one that is less likely as we find better evidence for (a) or (c). Scientific reasoning addresses such claims as (a), (b), and (c); the prospect of utter coincidence as in (d) is something that the scientific method is not able to rule out.

For such a case, then, the real task in reaching a causal conclusion would be to eliminate (c) as an alternative hypothesis. If we want to conclude, on the basis of our data, that left-handedness contributes to piano-playing skill, we have to give grounds for rejecting the possibility that some other underlying cause is responsible for both left-handedness and piano-playing skill. Background knowledge would play a large role in our reasoning. We would not attempt to refute alternative hypotheses about any and every possible underlying cause. Some possibilities would be taken seriously; others would not.

Consider, for instance, two possible alternative hypotheses, H1 and H2:

H1: Having a mother who has been married twice causes both left-handedness and piano-playing skill.
H2: Having the kind of brain in which hemisphere specialization is comparatively limited causes both left-handedness and piano-playing skill.

H2 is suggested by brain hemisphere research, which is confirmed for some other areas (for example, the treatment of some epilepsy patients and stroke victims).

Our background beliefs regarding the significance of the brain in human abilities and behavior also have a bearing on H2. On the other hand, H1 would not be taken seriously as an alternative hypothesis because it seems frivolous. We have no other knowledge that would make H1 likely as an explanation, and it is not worth investigating.

The point of all this is to illustrate how fundamentally *background knowledge* enters into causal reasoning. Background knowledge yields the working distinction between serious and nonserious alternative hypotheses. Experiments cannot be designed to rule out every imaginable alternative explanation. The best that can be done is to show that those alternatives that merit some consideration are not probable.

Background knowledge tends to be more reliable in physical science than it is in social science and reasoning about social problems, though neither in physical science nor in the social studies can background knowledge be regarded as fixed and final. What we refer to here as background knowledge includes well-confirmed theories and beliefs—but these can change in the light of new evidence. Populations (all rocks of a certain type, all earthquakes, all tides, all robins, and so on) tend to be less variable in the physical sciences than they are in the human sciences. For these reasons, causal claims in such disciplines as physics, chemistry, and biology are typically more reliable than causal claims in history, psychology, or anthropology. In many areas of social science, the background knowledge used to differentiate between significant and insignificant alternative hypotheses is open to serious challenge. Sometimes claims used as background knowledge are no more acceptable than the causal conclusions they are used to support. For these reasons, conclusions about causes—and especially conclusions about the causes of complex social phenomena—should be regarded as tentative and subject to revision.

Problems with Premises

The Possibility of Unreliable Observations

As with any argument, the cogency of an inductive argument will depend on the acceptability of its premises as well as on the merits of the reasoning from its premises to its conclusion. The premises of an inductive argument are based on someone's observations. For the argument to have a solid base, those observations have to be reliable. There are circumstances and features that can make observations unreliable. It is easy to see this in your own case. If you are sleepy or ill or worried, you may easily make mistakes in observation, thinking you have seen or heard something that was not there, or forgetting important details, for instance. The same holds for observations by other people. In fact, we described such problems when we discussed testimony in Chapter 5. If the observations on which an inductive argument is based are unreliable in some way, then its premises are not acceptable, and the argument will lack cogency for that reason.

Issues of Classification

In addition to these features about observation itself, there are other ways premises of inductive arguments may be subject to question. One important aspect is that of classification. The premise of an inductive argument alludes to observations under some description or classification. Sometimes it's clear that we have observed something, but it's not clear how we should classify it. (For instance, we may be quite sure we hear sounds from a nearby building and yet not know whether these sounds are music.) We may not be aware of the classificatory decisions that underlie premises in inductive arguments. However, classificatory assumptions and judgments are always implicit in the premises. The premise that all or most observed *X*s have some characteristic presupposes that what has been observed is correctly and appropriately classified as *X*. If the classification of these items as being *X* is incorrect, the premise is unacceptable and the argument is not cogent.

Here is an example that combines the matter of reliable observation with that of classification. Let us suppose that a young woman is feeling insecure and unhappy and that for this reason she frequently interprets other people's jokes and comments as being criticisms directed against her. She might, when considering whether to go to a party, reason to herself as follows:

1. Many times in the recent past I have observed my fellow students laughing at me and making fun of me.
2. The attitudes and behavior of the people at the party are likely to be similar to those of my fellow students.
Therefore, probably,
3. The people at the party will laugh at me and make fun of me.

On the basis of such an inductive argument, this young woman might decide not to attend the party. As with any inductive generalization, we could ask what sample of her experience the first premise is based on, and how representative that sample is likely to be. But something else is involved in this argument. The first premise would be unacceptable if the young woman were making unreliable observations and interpretations of other people's behavior. Often when we are upset and feel sensitive and vulnerable, we overreact to what others say, and we misinterpret it. Strictly speaking, we do not just observe others making fun of us or laughing at us. The unhappy woman in this example has heard jokes and comments and has classified these as "laughing at me" and "making fun of me." If these observations are unreliable and her interpretations are mistaken, her premise is unacceptable. Although the reasoning from behavior in other contexts to behavior at the party might be based on a correct inductive analogy, the argument will break down because it has an unacceptable premise.

The issue of classification is especially apparent when data are plausibly susceptible to several distinct classifications that have importantly different implications. In her book *The Chalice and the Blade*, Riane Eisler describes ancient figurines of large-breasted and broad-hipped women. These figurines were thought by some archaeologists to represent virgins in a fertility cult. Eisler argues that they represent women who have given birth (she thought they were too plump to represent virgins) and that they depict goddesses in an ancient religion worshiping women as givers of life. From premises about these ancient goddess figurines and related evidence, Eisler reasons that ancient divinities were female and ancient social lives exhibited equality between the sexes. (Note that this reasoning is retrodictive.) Archaeologists agree that the figurines have been observed, but there is still some disagreement as to how they are to be classified. Have archaeologists found ancient tokens of fertility worship? Or have they found figurines of life-giving earth goddesses? The different classifications would give premises as grounds for quite different inductive arguments about life in ancient times. Whether Eisler's claims about ancient social life can be supported by archaeological evidence would depend largely on the correctness of her interpretations and classifications.

Questionable Operational Definitions

As we have seen in Chapter 4, scientific research often requires operational definitions of key terms. When such studies are reported in the media, or when they are to be applied as a basis for policy or in some other context, there is a danger of confusing the more common lexical meaning of such terms with the more specialized meaning that has been stipulated as a basis for the research. The resulting unclarity can seriously undermine our reasoning when we seek to understand and apply the research. Especially in social scientific studies, it is important to reflect on—and if possible to find out—how key terms may have been operationally defined. Often key terms refer to abilities or mental operations that are not easily "cashed out" as observable behavior. Often too, terms carry implicit evaluative connotations. For instance, the word *creative* has positive connotations; whereas the word *impulsive* often has negative connotations. To understand studies of creativity or impulsiveness, we would have to understand how these terms have been operationalized and what values have been tacitly presumed in the stipulations that underlie operational definitions.

These issues are illustrated in the following passage, which deals with a controversy about the effects of fast-paced television shows on preschool age children.

> At the University of Massachusetts, Daniel Anderston, Stephen Leven, and Elizabeth Lorch compared the reactions of 72 four-year-olds to rapidly paced and slowly paced segments of *Sesame Street*. The research team observed the children watching differently paced versions, tested them after viewing to measure their *impulsive behavior* and the *persistence* in completing a puzzle, and then observed them during a 10-minute play period. They concluded that there was no evidence whatever that rapid television packing has a negative impact on pre-school children's behavior and that they could find no reduction in *sustained effort* and no increase in *aggression* or in *unfocused hyperactivity*.[11]

Here the italicized terms are terms that the researchers must have formally or informally operationalized. That is, they must have decided which childish behaviors counted as showing impulsive behavior, persistence, sustained effort, aggression, and unfocused hyperactivity and which did not. Suppose that a child had refused to work on a puzzle because she wanted to play on a swing? Would this count as impulsive behavior or persistence? As sustained effort or aggression? Or both? Would such a child be showing unfocused hyperactivity or not? You can see that the results of the study will depend crucially on how these terms have been operationalized. To the extent that operationalizations are questionable, the conclusions are undermined. A peculiar, and logically objectionable, combination of precision and imprecision results when terms that have been loosely operationalized on the basis of contestable value judgments are incorporated into statistical judgments. Imagine, for instance, that someone said, of the previous study.

Only 32 percent of the children showed any unfocused hyperactivity.

To speak of 32 percent is to suggest that there is precision in the results, but given the difficulty in precisely and satisfactorily operationalizing "unfocused hyperactivity" there can be no real precision. What we have in such a context is pseudoprecision.

Pseudoprecision

There is a tendency in our society to be impressed with scientific results, with measurement, and with numbers. Information presented in numerical terms often has a ring of exactness that suggests it is the product of careful and rigorous study, and makes it particularly credible. It is as though the mere presence of numbers shows that the facts presented are accurate and precise. We should, however, be careful about such impressions. Darrell Huff, author of the oft-reprinted book, *How to Lie with Statistics*, offers many examples of **pseudoprecision**—where numbers suggest an exactness and accuracy that is just not there. Many readers will recall being taught about significant digits in science courses. If we multiply two numbers, each accurate to one decimal place, the product will have two decimal places. Thus, we will arrive at a result implying that there has been a measurement accurate to two decimal places. Such a result is not significant and should be rounded off, since it is the result of other figures accurate only to one decimal place. The rounded off result is as precise as the situation permits; we do not have sufficient information to state a result to two decimal places. Doing so would not be precise, though it might appear precise. It would be pseudoprecision in a scientific context. Scientific texts advise against it and tell students how to avoid this form of pseudoprecision.

Examples of pseudoprecision can be found in daily life. A jar of peanut butter, for instance, is labelled as being safe until 10:23 on February 12, 2002. ("Better eat quickly—it's ten o'clock and we still have half a cup left.") Few would be misled by this example, because it is so implausible to think that the peanut butter would spoil at exactly 10:22. This example is merely humorous. Other examples of pseudoprecision may be taken more seriously. For example, a recipe may be stated in terms of cups of flour, butter and sugar, tablespoons full of honey, pinches of salt, and so on. Then, at the end, one is told that the resulting cake has 432 calories per serving, a piece of advice that could be regarded as quite important by someone on a restricted diet. And yet there are two reasons to brand this kind of information pseudoprecise. First, there is the extremely unlikelihood of the ingredients being measured with enough exactness to allow for such a precise calorie count. Second, there is the vagueness, in this context, of the word *serving*. There are many contexts in which it does not matter how big a serving is, but if one is going to count calories or carbohydrate levels, its size will matter.

In contexts where we are reflecting on claims and evaluating information, we should be especially careful to reflect on numbers and ask ourselves where those numbers come from and how exact they are likely to be. We should never let the mere presence of a number lend credibility to a claim. Consider, for instance, this material from an advertisement:

> Research studies show that on the average we listen at a 25% level of efficiency. This is terribly costly. When executives don't listen effectively, communication breaks down. Ideas and information get distorted as much as 80% as they travel down an organization.[12]

The appeal to "research studies" here makes no specific reference; the studies are unidentified and anonymous. For this reason, the advertisement contains a faulty appeal to authority. The idea that "studies" showed something is intended to make it sound as though scientific work is backing up the claims made. For some consumers, this effect is likely to be enhanced by the use of "25%" and "80%." But both numbers are pseudoprecise, in this context. Ask yourself what a 100 percent level of efficiency in listening would be and how you would test for it. Then, if (as is likely) you do not know the answer, go on to ask yourself what a 25 percent level of efficiency would be. Would it be $1/4$ of the first, as the numbers suggest? In this anonymous study, how might someone have measured that people "on the average" listen at 25 percent efficiency? While "listening" and "efficiency" might have been successfully operationalized, without knowing the operationalization, we can give no meaning to such claims as are used in this advertisement. Furthermore these terms are not, in ordinary usage, exact enough to be meaningfully conjoined with numbers. Similar comments can be made about ideas and information being distorted "as much as 80%." Contrary to some first impressions, numbers in this case are not an indication of precision and exactness. Instead, this is a case of pseudoprecision.

Pseudoregularities

Inductive arguments are based on regularities—patterns that are projected from some observed cases to others and (in causal arguments) patterns that are taken to require explanation. For a cogent inductive argument, we need a genuine regularity, not a pseudoregularity. To see what is meant by a pseudoregularity, consider the following example.

Suppose that suddenly, on a Tuesday morning, you suffer from blistered feet, a headache, a backache, and a runny nose. You can classify all these things together:

all are unpleasant minor health problems and all begin on Tuesday. Is there something special, and awful, about Tuesday? For the purposes of inductive generalization or causal reasoning, this is not a useful question to pose. There is nothing in our background knowledge about human customs, days of the week, or physical symptoms that would indicate that "happening on Tuesday" is a relevant similarity concerning human health. Background knowledge would suggest that your symptoms are distinct and likely to have distinct causes. Perhaps your feet are blistered because you walked too far in the heat; your runny nose is due to an allergy; your backache is due to the gardening you did; your headache is due to stress concerning an upcoming examination. These hypotheses are more promising as a basis for exploration than the superficial resemblance of "happening on Tuesday," which is a pseudoregularity.

A **pseudoregularity** is one that is not a proper basis for inductive argument because it is grounded on a similarity that is not scientifically relevant. Pseudoregularities are too superficial to serve as the basis for cogent inductive arguments. When a number of cases are classified and grouped together for the purposes of induction, the classification not only must be interpretively correct (as indicated in the example just discussed) but also must be scientifically relevant. That is, it must be based on some feature that it is reasonable to extrapolate or (in the case of a causal argument) some feature for which we have reason to expect that a single causal explanation can be found.

Suppose we have five events that have one striking feature in common: they are all impossible to explain given present knowledge. We could group them together on this basis (that is, classify them simply as "unexplained events") and then, on the basis of the classification, look for a single explanation for all of them. There is no good reason to think the same thing has caused all of them.

A striking illustration of the phenomenon of pseudoregularity can be found in Erich von Daniken's book *Chariots of the Gods*.[13] Von Daniken cites a number of different unexplained events, including the building of the pyramids and what he regards as "landing strips" at various points around the earth. He argues that extraterrestrial beings visited the earth from other planets, in ancient times. His argument is based on the grounds that this causal conclusion would explain all of these otherwise unexplained events. A major problem with the argument is that the events he groups together are too disparate—rather like the symptoms you experienced on that single Tuesday. Given that there are "landing strips" around the earth (and this itself is a highly questionable classification), and that there are pyramids that could not have been built by unassisted human beings, there is still no good reason to group these events together and seek one causal explanation for them.

Plausible Scenarios

In Deanna Kuhn's study of causal arguments, the plausible scenario was a popular type of pseudoevidence. (Pseudoevidence, you will recall from Chapter 5, is put forward to support a conclusion but cannot genuinely support it because it begs the question.) Subjects interviewed by psychology researchers were asked to give evidence for their opinions about the cause of a phenomenon. Many stated premises offered no real evidence because they described **plausible scenarios** that, in effect, took the conclusion for granted.

To understand this problem in the abstract, suppose that a person believes that C causes E. Someone asks her for evidence to support the claim that C causes E. She responds by stating premises that describe a particular case in which events of type C result in events of type E. She puts the events together in a narrative that makes sense and seems to fit; she describes a plausible scenario, or sequence of events. But such premises cannot provide real evidence for the causal conclusion because they are constructed on the assumption that the causal conclusion is true. They beg the question.

Here is an example in which the subject believes that the cause of school failure is lack of motivation and the interviewer is trying to get her to give an argument for her opinion. A plausible scenario takes the place of genuine evidence.

> *Interviewer:* How do you know that this is the case?
>
> *Subject:* Well, one of my friends in history, she doesn't do her homework, she dreams in class, and she just has such an attitude toward the teacher. She doesn't like the teacher. . . . (When) the teacher says, "Why don't you study for this?" she just says, "I couldn't" or "I didn't want to." But she could do well in her history if she tried.[14]

The subject believes that lack of motivation causes failure; she understands her friend's situation in the light of this belief and tells the story accordingly. She has selected out certain facts about her friend and linked those selected facts to the friend's failure to do well in school. The problem is that this linking presumes the very causal hypothesis that she is supposed to be supporting—the claim that the friend is failing because she is not motivated. This subject would have done better than a plausible scenario with pseudoevidence if she had considered other possible explanations of her friend's failure in history and given reason to reject them.

Causal beliefs are used when we tell stories and when we construct plausible descriptions of how things happen, or how we think they might have happened. In arguments to support causal beliefs, though, we must preserve a degree of detachment and skepticism about these stories if we are to avoid begging the question. If the causal claim is threaded into premises that describe a plausible scenario, the argument will beg the question.

In general, the premises of inductive arguments can be assessed for acceptability as can premises of other arguments. However, the special features of inductive arguments make it useful to watch in addition for unreliable observations, inappropriate classifications, pseudoregularities, and the use of plausible scenarios instead of evidence to back up causal claims.

EXERCISE SET

Exercise 3: Part A
For each of the following examples (a) say whether it contains an inductive generalization, a correlational claim, a causal claim, or none of these. (b) If you believe that there are claims that are ambiguous, as between several of these types, say so and explain why. (c) If a causal claim is not stated, but is implied, point this out. (d) If an example contains an explicit or implicit generalization from a sample to a target population, comment on the sample and the population and the representativeness of the sample.

*1. "Alcoholism has been linked to poor grammar, in a study by speech pathologist P. J. Collins. Nearly twice as often as a control group of nonalcoholics, a group of 39 alcoholic men and women were found to use illogical words and phrases and to speak in fragments."
(Adapted from *Psychology Today*, April 1982)

2. "If you hear the whistling the next time you are riding in an airplane, it might be cause to worry, according to *Omni* magazine. Robert Rudich, an air transportation consultant for the U.S. Federal Aviation Administration, says that of more than 260 voice-recorder tapes from airplanes involved in accidents, both large and small, more than 80 percent of the tapes recorded the whistling of pilots during the last half hour of flight."
(Toronto *Globe and Mail*, March 27, 1981)

*3. "An analysis of other groups shows church attendance is considerably higher in Eastern than in Western Canada, among women, among those living in smaller communities, and among those with a lower level of education."
(Calgary *Herald*, June 28, 1980)

4. "The key to homicides, child abuse and other kinds of violent behavior may be rooted in the most primal instinct—reproduction," says a McMaster University psychologist. That's the

theory of Martin Daly, whose statistical studies show, among other things, that more males are murdered in their peak breeding years than at any other time of life. "Perpetrators of homicides show the same general age characteristics as their victims," Daly said. "It seems the same bunch who are killing are also being killed." Using data compiled from homicides in the United States and elsewhere, Daly noted that a significant percentage of violent disputes between these men involve squabbles over women."
(Calgary *Herald*, December 5, 1979)

5. In the 1960s, the United Church of Canada commissioned a study of the relationship between urban and rural lifestyles, and conservative and liberal theological views. They sent a mail survey to 1,705 laypeople. Of these, 452 were low in urbanism, 1,010 were medium in urbanism, and 243 were high in urbanism. Of the 452 who were low in urbanism, 38 percent held liberal theological views; of the 1,010 who were medium in urbanism, 45 percent held liberal theological views; and of the 243 who were high in urbanism, 66 percent held liberal theological views. Urbanism, then, seems to be associated with liberal theological beliefs.
(Cited by John Burbidge in *Within Reason: A Guide to Non-Deductive Reasoning* [Peterborough, ON: Broadview Press, 1990], p. 85)

*6. "In the period between 1920 and 1970, the United States was a natural laboratory for studying the deterrent effect of the death penalty. Each of the 48 contiguous states had its own system of criminal law and in each region of the country (New England, the South, etc.) some states had the death penalty for murder and some did not. Since the states in each region were comparable with respect to the factors known to influence crime rates, a special deterrent effect of the death penalty would probably

mean lower annual murder rates in the death-penalty states in each region. In fact, no significant difference in murder rates was found in any region between the states which had the death penalty for murder and those which did not."
(Example taken from David Hitchcock, *Critical Thinking: A Guide to Evaluating Information* [Toronto: Methuen, 1983], p. 124)

7.   *Background:* The following report describes an experiment conducted among University of Colorado undergraduates. Participants received simulated monthly checks and were to declare income and pay tax. On the basis of random audits, it was determined whether they had evaded taxes, and penalties for evasion were imposed.

   "Everyone was told (correctly) that his own tax rate was 70 percent. One third of the group was told (falsely) that others paid less taxes than they did; one-third was told that others paid more taxes than they did; and the last one-third was told the truth, that its own rates were the same as everyone else's. Overall the group evaded about one dollar in four of tax. But those who felt they were paying lower rates than everyone else evaded only 12 percent of their tax, while those who felt they were paying more than everyone else evaded nearly one-third of their tax. In the laboratory, and perhaps in life, compliance walks hand in hand with the perception of fairness and equity. Destroy the latter, and whether there are penalties or not, compliance plunges."
(Shloma Maital, "The Tax Evasion Virus," *Psychology Today,* March 1982)

8.   "The risk of cancer in men with the lowest level of vitamin A was 2.2 times greater than for men with the highest level."
(Toronto *Star,* February 6, 1981)

9.   Welfare payments to single males have been reduced by some 200 dollars a month. Is it any accident that the rate of homelessness has increased in our city?

10.   Of young army personnel who served in the Gulf War, 10 percent have experienced nau-

sea, depression and fatigue. Of a comparable group of young people, only 3 percent suffered nausea, depression and fatigue. What was there about this military service that caused such symptoms?

11.   "The theory of evolution is not just an inert piece of theoretical science. It is, and cannot help being, also a powerful folk-tale about human origins. Any such narrative must have symbolic force. . . . Most stories about human origins must have been devised purely with a view to symbolic and poetic fittingness. Suggestions about how we were made and where we come from are bound to engage our imagination, to shape our views of what we now are, and so to affect our lives. Scientists, when they find themselves caught up in these webs of symbolism, sometimes complain, calling for a sanitary cordon to keep them [the webs of symbolism] away from science. But this seems to be both psychologically and logically impossible."
(Mary Midgley, *Evolution as a Religion: Strange Hopes and Stranger Fears* [London: Methuen, 1985], p. 1)

12.   "While other studies had shown that girls often did poorly in mathematics, those in this study were not just any girls. They were the brightest girl mathematicians in the United States—4300 7th and 8th graders who had scored in the top 2 to 5 percent of standardized mathematical tests. But when compared with boys at the top of their classes, these girls consistently averaged lower on the Scholastic Aptitude Tests. At top levels—scores of about 700 out of a perfect 800—boys outnumbered girls by 10 to one. (The ratio of boys to girls participating in the study was 57 percent to 43.)
(Toronto *Globe and Mail,* September 3, 1981)

*13.   "In some cases, it may be logically impossible to study all members of the population. The population may be infinite, or simply not yet available for study. Thus, the psychologist who is studying learning ability in white mice will hope his results, and therefore his inferences, will have some application to all white mice—not just the millions that exist at this

moment, but also the further millions not yet born. He may even hope his results can be generalized to explain human learning."
(Derek Rowntree, *Statistics without Tears; A Primer for Non-Mathematicians* [London: Penguin, 1985], p. 21)

14.   It was the decline in world gold prices that led to the closing of several large South African gold mines. These closings in turn brought about a higher unemployment rate among South African blacks, many of whom have large families dependent on the income of one or two workers in the mines. Thus trends in the world market affected the level of black poverty in South Africa.

Exercise 3: Part B
In the following arguments, state whether any premises would be unacceptable due to unreliable observations, inappropriate classifications, faulty operational definitions, pseudoprecision, pseudoregularities, or the use of plausible scenarios to back up causal claims.

*1.   In a sample of 400 injured birds examined in the Chicago area, 80 percent were found by the examining veterinarians to have skull injuries—possibly from flying into the windows of suburban homes. (Intended conclusion: Most birds injured in North America are injured by flying into windows.)

2.   Students interviewed fifty homeless people in Milwaukee streets. They found most of them to be unfriendly, secretive, and paranoid. (Intended conclusion: Most homeless people are paranoid.)

*3.   I can testify as the mother of one young participant in a summer hockey program that that program was badly run. My nine-year-old son was really unhappy with it. He had a number of problems and complaints, and the leader was always unhelpful.

4.   My manuscript went out to thirty-five publishers, and so far, I have heard from twenty-three of them, none of whom want to accept it for publication. Out of these rejection letters,

twenty have arrived on a Friday. It takes the mail about four days to reach its destination, in my experience, so if you figure it out, these things must have been mailed on Monday. So there must be something about Mondays that makes people reject my manuscript.

5.   All seventy-five calves that had been born in March and survived through the summer were weighed, using the standard veterinary scale, which has been shown to be accurate within 1 kilogram. The average weight gain over a four-month period for these calves was 21.273 kilos. So if I were to raise calves in this area, I could expect a gain of over 21.27 kilos a month next year.

*6.   *Context:* The issue is the cause of arson, when forests were set on fire during a serious drought in the Los Angeles area.
    "It must be the disparity between rich and poor. The cause of this arson is that poor people resent the rich. They can see economic injustice, and it makes them want to destroy those posh homes. If you were a poor person, or a homeless person, and you felt miserable and could hardly survive from one day to the next, wouldn't you resent these people with their posh ocean-view homes and three-car garages? Then you would do something about it: commit arson. You can see what the cause is: people set the fires from resentment of social injustice—that's obvious."

7.   In nineteenth-century Germany, business leaders were overwhelmingly Protestant, according to the sociologist M. Weber in *The Prostestant Ethic and the Spirit of Capitalism*. Something in the Protestant religions of the time made these men want to work hard and achieve conspicuous worldly success.

8.   Members of the new religious sect report, from their own observations, that its leaders are highly spiritual and conscientious and extremely self-sacrificing. Thirty-five members were interviewed by supporters after a two-day rally featuring fasting and extensive religious chants.

9. "Many times in past years, I have dreamed about doing things; then I have gone out and done them, and things have really worked out for me. These dreams had a message, and the message was the truth. They gave me insight, truth, and good advice. In fact, I have measured it, and my most vivid dreams give me the best and most accurate advice. Out of 300 dreams, there were 113 vivid dreams, and 187 less vivid dreams. What does it mean for a dream to be vivid? The most vivid ones are the ones I remember best, and in the most detail. From the 113 vivid dreams, I got advice which I acted on successfully 82 times. From the 187 less vivid dreams, I got advice which I acted on successfully on 31 times. Thus the vividness of a dream shows that it can give accurate advice. Dreams can be a guide to live and the most vivid dreams are the best guide of all."

*10. *Context:* A debate about the cause of younger people (under age thirty) leaving established churches.

These people leave because they are bound up in a materialistic culture, and they don't want to be reminded that there is more to life than a good job, a nice house, expensive computers, and lots of consumer playthings. I have three friends that are like this, and all three left the church. Why? They didn't want to be reminded of war, poverty, and social injustice; they didn't want to give up their Sunday mornings to listen to sermons; and they were working hard to pay off $200,000 mortgages on extravagant houses they didn't need in the first place. It's easy to see that materialism and consumerism in our culture are what cause people to leave the churches.

11. People who use drugs are ill-adjusted and have dysfunctional relationships. So to understand the cause of drug use, we have to understand the factors that make people ill-adjusted and make their relationships dysfunctional.

12. Studies on 300 rats that were fed the new hormone showed that 95 percent reduced their body fat by 10 percent or more. Thus the hormone enables rats to reduce their body fat.

13. A newspaper reported a speech about the effect of various forms of therapy. According to the report, "delinquents who went to psychotherapists had a much better success, showing a 78% improvement. But the fly in the ointment is that those who didn't see anyone had a 72% improvement rate."
(Toronto *Globe and Mail,* September 13, 1980)

Common Fallacies in Inductive Arguments

Hasty Inductive Generalization

A **hasty inductive generalization** is an argument in which the sample is hopelessly inadequate, so that the inference from the sample to the population is not reliable. Often the generalization is based on an exceedingly small sample of cases—sometimes only one or two. A person rather carelessly assumes that the case or cases that have come to her attention are more than just episodes or isolated events. She assumes, without sufficient warrant, that they indicate a general tendency or trend. Hasty generalization is an easy fallacy to lapse into because we are all interested in general knowledge, and yet our own experience is limited and particular. What could be more natural than inferring a general trend from something we witnessed or experienced ourselves?

Consider, for instance, the following short argument:

> In 1974 I visited both Sweden and Denmark and found the Swedes to be gloomy and inhospitable, while the Danes were cheerful and friendly. So Danes are a lot more agreeable than Swedes.

Unless we have some particular reason for regarding the arguer as unreliable, we can accept the premise as testimony; if someone says she had these experiences, we can believe her. Yet the limited sample of Swedes and Danes she would have encountered makes any inductive argument from her experience to a generalization about the attitudes of Danes and Swedes unreliable. As a tourist, one does not meet a representative sample of the population; the sample one encounters is selective (people in service occupations being overly represented) and usually quite small. If one could know that the people one met were representative of the population as a whole, one could generalize from a very small sample. But the problem is, one cannot know this. In this, as in other hasty generalizations, the evidence may be acceptable, and it is relevant to the conclusion but does not provide adequate grounds for the conclusion. The (A) condition for argument cogency may be met; (R) is met; but (G) is not.

In arguments such as this one, the evidence is sometimes said to be purely **anecdotal**, meaning that it is based on anecdotes, or stories of what has happened to a person, as opposed to any systematic effort to obtain a representative sample from the population that the generalization is about. When such arguments are our own, they strike us as extremely plausible, because we have a close sense of our own experience and like to base our beliefs on it. We may be so wedded to our own experience, find it so much a part of ourselves, that we lose our critical perspective and forget that our experience may not be representative. The issue is whether our own personal experience gives a reliable basis for a more general inductive conclusion. It rarely does: our experience gives us only a limited sample of what the world has to offer, and a reliable generalization requires wider evidence.

The *Post Hoc* Fallacy

Perhaps you have heard of this one. The name of this fallacy comes from the Latin expression *post hoc ergo propter hoc*, which means "after this, therefore because of this." Superstitions may have had their beginnings with *post hoc* inferences: a man sees a black cat and then injures his knee, so he infers that it is because he saw a black cat that he injures his knee. With all that we have said about the difficulties that arise when you try to prove a causal relationship, you can no doubt see that any inference of the following type is inadequate:

1. *A* came before *B*.
Therefore,
2. *A* caused *B*.

This is the basic form of the ***post hoc* fallacy**. It is even shakier than an incorrect inference from correlation to cause, for in *post hoc* there is typically only one anecdote or event.

Here is another example of a *post hoc* argument:

1. He talked on the telephone with his father and then did poorly at the job interview.
So probably,
2. He did poorly at the job interview because he talked on the telephone with his father.

The fact that the telephone conversation *came before* the failed interview does not give sufficient evidence for the conclusion that it was this conversation that *caused* him to do poorly. The evidence in a *post hoc* argument is relevant to the conclusion. Suppose the arguer could cite more cases of *A*-events being followed by *B*-events, to claim a general correlation between *A* and *B*. And suppose, further, that he could give reasons for excluding other hypotheses (most notably here, some other factor *X* causing both *A* and *B*, or the correlation being a coincidence). Then he would no longer have a fallacious *post hoc* argument.

The Fallacies of Composition and Division

The fallacies of composition and division concern reasoning about parts and wholes, or members of a group and the group itself. In the **fallacy of composition,** a conclusion about a whole or group is reached on the basis of premises about parts of that whole, or members of that group. The reasoning goes from the smaller unit to the whole composed of smaller units—from smaller scale to larger scale. (Or, as is often said, from the micro level to the macro level.[15]) In the **fallacy of division,** a conclusion about a part, or member, is reached on the basis of premises about the whole, or group. The reasoning goes from the larger unit to the smaller one. In either case, a fallacy is committed. Both lines of reasoning are faulty insofar as they ignore important distinctions that may exist between parts and wholes or groups and members. Reasoning directly from parts to wholes or from wholes to parts ignores the fact that a whole is often more than the sum of its parts, because it has an entirely different structure and relationships. For an indication of such differences, consider:

(a) The Dutch are extremely tall people. So Holland is a tall country.

Here the premise can be confirmed and is acceptable. But it does not give good reason for the conclusion, which does not even make sense. A country is not the sort of thing that can be tall or short. *Tall* in the premise means "tall compared to other human beings" and the same meaning would not make sense in the conclusion, because a country is not a human being. The conclusion in (a) is based on a category mistake—a misuse, in this context, of the word *tall.* We could not fix matters if we slightly amended the conclusion, avoiding any use of *tall.* Compare:

(b) The Dutch are extremely tall people. So Holland is a large country.

There is no category mistake in (b), even though, in fact, Holland is not large. But in (b) the premise is irrelevant to the conclusion. The height of the individual citizens is irrelevant to the size of their country. Both (a) and (b) commit the fallacy of composition. Consider, now, a slightly different example:

(c) The parts of the chair are brown. So the chair is brown.

In this case, the argument might seem to be better. However there is an element of pure luck in getting to a confirmed conclusion. This case just happens to be one in which the whole does not have relevantly different structures and relationships from the parts. If (c) is based on a general assumption about parts and wholes, it is still objectionable.

Similar comments may be made about inferences from wholes to parts, or from groups to individuals. Consider:

(d) The choir is well balanced. So every choir member is well balanced.

This argument is fallacious because of the way a conclusion about each member of the choir is inferred from a comment about the whole choir. Balance in a choir is a matter of the comparative strength of soprano, alto, bass, and tenor sections. Balance in this sense cannot be a property of individual members, for no individual exemplifies and manifests these parts or the relations between them. Similar comments can be made about (e):

(e) The group reached its own decision and was in that sense autonomous. Therefore, every member of the group reached his or her own decision and was in that sense autonomous.[16]

The group is a group, a composite of a number of individuals. Its individual members are not a group. For the group to reach its own decision requires that it not be manipulated or dominated by some other group. How the group arrives at its decisions tells us nothing about how individual members of the group might arrive at their decisions—in general, or in a particular case. Example (e) illustrates the fallacy of division.

Detecting the fallacy of division can be significant in some important debates about freedom, autonomy, and democracy as (e) above suggests. Another political significant use of the fallacy occurs in the first stages of the following argument:

(f) If groups are held collectively responsible for wrongdoing, then every individual in those groups is responsible for that wrongdoing. For example, if the Serbs are collectively responsible for human rights violations, then every individual Serb is responsible for that ill-treatment. But to hold that every individual Serb is responsible for those violations would be to legitimate prejudice and the stereotyping of Serbs. This would be wrong. Hence we must reject the idea of collective responsibility.

In (f) the implications claimed in the first two statements embrace the fallacy of division. Contrary to what is claimed in these statements, collective responsibility is the *responsibility of a group*, which is not the same thing as, and does not entail, the *responsibility of every individual in that group*.[17] The argument in (f) does not constitute a good reason to reject the notion of collective responsibility.

Objectionable Cause

The **fallacy of objectionable cause** occurs when someone argues for a causal interpretation on the basis of limited evidence and makes no attempt to rule out alternative explanations of the event. Sometimes logicians call this fallacy questionable
cause or false cause. We have not used the label "false cause" because it suggests that
the careless causal reasoning has led to a false conclusion. You might reason carelessly and get a true conclusion—if only by good luck. The problem in objectionable
cause is that the conclusion—even if true—has been reached too hastily.

The fallacy of objectionable cause goes like this:

1. *A* occurred.
2. *B* occurred.
3. We can plausibly connect *A* to *B* in a causal relationship.
Therefore,
4. *A* is the cause of *B*.

If you look at this pattern, you can see the problem. That *A* and *B* have occurred and
can be plausibly connected (in fact, premise 3 risks the plausible scenario error) does
not show that *A* caused *B*. In these premises, there is no basis for ruling out alternative explanations.

A particularly tempting variation on objectionable cause, prominent in political and moral discussions of society and its problems, is as follows:

1. *A* occurred.
2. *B* occurred.
3. Both *A* and *B* are bad things.
4. We can plausibly connect *A* to *B*.
Therefore,
5. *A* is the cause of *B*.

Objectionable cause fallacies of this type are common in election debates. Candidates typically assume that whatever bad things happened when the opponents were
in office were the fault or responsibility of the government. Although this may be
true in some cases, the mere conjunction of a particular group's being in power and
a negative phenomenon of some sort (high unemployment, an increase in crime, or
a dramatic and intractable terrorist episode) does not in itself show that the gov-
erning group caused, or is responsible for, such things. They could have arisen from
many different causes.

When you don't like *A* and you don't like *B* either, it is often tempting to think
that *A* causes *B*. This way, you can link up the things you don't like into a causal
chain, and you will be well on your way to a simple solution that will eliminate these
bad things from the world all at once. A wonderful example of this normative approach to causation may be found in the following argument, which was used by a
panelist on a television show shortly after the nuclear reactor accident at Three Mile
Island in 1979:

> The responsibility for the near catastrophic nuclear accident at Three Mile Island
> rests squarely with the English teachers of America. For years now, they have

been ignoring little flaws of language. They have emphasized self-expression above all else. They have told us that small faults and mistakes do not really matter as long as you communicate your true attitudes and feelings and creatively express your own identity. And the problem at Three Mile Island was, initially, just one of those supposedly little things. One valve was not in the right place. One might think: well, it's just one little thing; it doesn't really matter. But it did matter. That was the problem. It is the teachers of English who have encouraged the attitude that small things don't count, and it is just that attitude which is the underlying cause of the nuclear accident.[18]

The panelist, who obviously had a low opinion of English teachers, did not much like nuclear reactor accidents either. So he jumped to the conclusion that there was a causal connection between these two things. The hastiness of the causal inference here is so obvious that it doesn't need much comment. If there is a common attitude that "little things don't matter," then the existence of this attitude would be a complex social fact, a widespread phenomenon, permeating many aspects of life. It would be amazing indeed if teachers of English had sufficient power to spread such an attitude all by themselves. There are, of course, many more plausible explanations of what happened at Three Mile Island that a careful causal argument would have to rule out.

We all have a craving for explanations for things that happen. Especially tempting are simple, emotionally satisfying explanations of things we don't particularly like. It may seem to "make sense" that they are all linked together, but we cannot assume that just because something makes sense to us, it is true. Such explanations are logically and scientifically of little merit, unless there are good reasons to believe that they are more plausible than significant alternatives. This is an especially important point when we go beyond simple causal explanations to evaluating far-reaching scientific theories. If we can identify an alternative that is more plausible than the theory we are considering, then the existence of that alternative substantially undermines our reason for accepting the initial theory.

Causal Slippery Slope Arguments

So far we have concentrated on arguments in which the conclusion makes a causal claim. Causal claims may also serve as the premises of arguments. One example is the **causal slippery slope fallacy.** In this type of argument, it is alleged in the premises that a proposed action (one that by itself might seem good, or at least acceptable) would be wrong because it would set off a series of side effects, ending ultimately in general calamity. The idea behind the reasoning is that someone who embarks on the action has begun a tumble down a slope of effects, the last of which will be something terrible. Here is a familiar example:

It sounds quite all right, letting people choose to die when they are suffering from painful and incurable diseases and when they are of sound mind. Certainly it would seem a responsible choice if someone in such circumstances chose to kill himself. In fact, the famous author Arthur Koestler recently did just that, and no one blamed him, since he was an old man and was suffering terribly from several diseases. The problem is, though, once you allow voluntary euthanasia the forces are in play, and there will be pressure for assisted voluntary euthanasia. Once this is established, involuntary euthanasia will follow for patients who have incurable diseases but are comatose and cannot make their own decisions. The procedures that permit involuntary euthanasia for those with incurable diseases bring about euthanasia of the retarded and senile, and soon we will be in a state where an individual life has no value at all.

In the premises of this argument, it is alleged that allowing voluntary euthanasia for those patients who can make their own choices will bring about a state in which individual lives have no value. Underlying this claim is the assumption of a causal chain; one change causes a further change, which itself brings more changes. The idea is that the first action is a step down a slippery road to Hell; the first step causes an inevitable slide to the bottom. The problem with such an argument is that the causal claims in the premises are not supported by evidence and are not even very plausible if you think about it. The argument is based on a kind of scare tactic. Actually, the series of dreadful effects is simply invented as an objection to the initial action, which (as the argument admits) is quite desirable when considered on its own. The idea is to intimidate people with the suggested calamity, so that they won't think about the sweeping and implausible nature of the causal claims in the premises.

The way to improve slippery slope arguments is to provide evidence for the causal claims made in the premises, in a subargument—to show why and how one thing would lead to another. Unfortunately, causal slippery slope fallacies can be very effective. One historically prominent example is the domino theory, which was so popular at the time of the Vietnam War. It went something like this:

> If Vietnam becomes communist, then Laos, Cambodia, Burma, India, and all of Southeast Asia will become communist. Then all Asia will be communist, and after that all Europe and the whole world. So even though it might not seem to matter very much whether Vietnam as a single country is or is not communist, we have to stop this thing. It is now or never.

As the Vietnam War came under increased criticism, the domino theory lost credibility. But several decades later, a new version was constructed for Central America. William P. Clark, assistant to President Reagan for national security affairs, put it this way:

> If we lack the resolve and dedication the President asked for in Central America, can we not expect El Salvador to join Nicaragua in targeting other recruits for the Soviet brand of Communism? When, some ask, will Mexico and the United States become the immediate rather than the ultimate targets? President Reagan said: If we cannot defend ourselves (in El Salvador) we cannot expect to prevail elsewhere. Our credibility could collapse, our alliances would crumble, and the safety of our homeland would be put in jeopardy.[19]

More recent versions of this argument refer to the "credibility" of the United States or NATO and make the claim that if no action is taken in some particular case, credibility will be lost so that more and more things will go wrong.

Here is the key premise in a causal slippery slope argument from another period of history:

> Unbridled passion following the wake of birth control will create a useless and effeminate society, or worse, result in the complete extinction of the human race.[20]

This statement was a premise in an argument used decades ago to object to the legalization of birth control. It would not fool anyone today. We have legalized birth control, and neither an effeminate society nor complete extinction has resulted. But contemporary slippery slopes can be more deceptive.

The slippery slope argument was brilliantly satirized by Thomas de Quincy in his essay, *Murder as One of the Fine Arts.* De Quincy wrote:

> If once a man indulges himself in murder,
> Very soon he comes to think little of robbing;
> And from robbing he next comes to drinking and Sabbath breaking.
> And from that to incivility and procrastination.[21]

De Quincy imagined a slide from serious offenses to trivial ones, instead of the other way around. He had obviously heard about, and seen through, more typical causal slippery slope arguments.

EXERCISE SET

Exercise 4

For the following arguments, indicate any causal claims that appear either in the premises or in the conclusion. If causal claims are made in the conclusion, assess the reasoning offered to support them and say if you find examples of *post hoc* or objectionable cause. If causal claims are made in the premises, is the argument an example of causal slippery slope? Why or why not?

Note: Some arguments may contain no causal claims, and some passages may not contain arguments. If either of these is the case, simply note the fact and proceed to the next example.

1. "If the Christian churches wish to refuse ordination of gay people to the clergy, they have a right to their decision, however misguided it may be. But when the churches organize public referendums to repeal the civil rights of homosexual citizens, that's another matter. In Dade County, St. Paul, Wichita, and Eugene, Oregon, the churches openly ran petition drives, distributed the political literature, and raised the funds needed to bring out the public vote that revoked the rights of gays in those places. Unfortunately America is currently besieged by an army of religious zealots who see the Government and the ballot box as instruments for enforcing church dogmas. If the trend continues, we'll have Government-enforced religion and the end of a 200-year-old democratic tradition."
(Letter to the editor, *Time,* June 1978)

2. Since the ABC party took office, the rate of teenage pregnancies in the state has declined by 6 percent. Therefore, the ABC government is responsible for the decline in the rate of teenage pregnancies in the state.

3. "The statement by Archbishop John R. Quinn that Vatican strictures on birth control

are being ignored by many U.S. Catholics reflects the misconception that the doctrines of faith and morals proclaimed by the church are changeable. Yet there has never been an about-face on any of these doctrines. The great secular breakthrough allowed by the promotion and acceptance of contraception has brought us the age of state-countenanced abortion, community-standardized pornography, and a more than embryonic euthanasia movement. This pro-pleasure, antichild mind-set won't intimidate the church of Peter ever to modify the doctrine that sees more to sex than orgasm and more to aging than diminished utilitarianism."
(Letter to the editor, *Time,* November 10, 1980)

4.   If illegal refugees, smuggled into the country, are well treated and given lengthy hearings, then other persons will be encouraged in the trade of smuggling people. If this trade is encouraged, soon we will have not just the occasional ship of smuggled people, but many ships—and truckloads and trainloads as well. Our refugee hearing system and our welfare system could be overwhelmed. So people who enter illegally should simply be made to leave. No free meals, no bureaucracy, no refugee hearings. Keep it short, simple, and sweet, and avoid the floods of people.

*5.   *Background:* The author is asserting that in the period between 1980 and 1986, the quality of the manpower enlisting in U.S. armed forces has improved.

"People can still argue about restoring the draft, but now the arguments are about principles: How should a democracy allot the burden of military service? Is it just and fair to leave the risk of dying to volunteers? The debates are no longer driven by concerns about the quality of people who have volunteered.

"But manpower, though historically the most important factor in military excellence, is not the only one—and certainly is not the principal force behind our increased spending. Pay has gone up—but not stupendously and certainly not by as much as the quality of the force.

From 1980 to 1985 personnel costs rose by less than 20 percent, and as a share of overall defense spending, pay and benefits fell. The improvement in the force, hard to quantify but more like 200 percent than 20, has been due partly to the severe recession of 1982, partly to a sense that the military is "de-civilizing" itself and restoring its standards and self-esteem, and partly to the general resurgence of nationalistic pride."
(James Fallows, "The Spend-up," the *Atlantic,* June 1986, p. 28)

*6.   "On the one hand, although logic and common sense offer excellent solutions when they work, who has not had the frustrating experience of doing his very best in these terms, only to see things going from bad to worse? On the other hand, every once in a while we experience some illogical and surprising but welcome change in a troublesome stalemate. Indeed, the theme of the puzzling, uncommonsensical solution is an archetypical one, reflected in folklore, fairy tales, humor, and many dreams—just as there are both popular and more erudite conceptions of the perversity of other people, the world, or the devil to explain the converse situation. Yet it seems that little serious and systematic inquiry has been focused on this whole matter, which has remained as puzzling and contradictory as ever."
(Paul Watzlawick, John H. Weakland, and Richard Fisch, *Change: Principles of Problem Formulation and Problem Resolution* [New York: Norton, 1974], p. xiii)

7.   *Background:* The following appeared in a letter to the Calgary *Herald,* concerning the showing of Judy Chicago's controversial feminist artwork *The Dinner Party.* The show included a number of plates with symbolic depictions representing female genital organs. The letter was printed on December 10, 1982.

Hint: Concentrate only on the causal reasoning here.

"Re the rave reviews about Judy Chicago's *The Dinner Party.* Certainly the craftsmanship and skills represented deserve praise. I was involved in a campaign of a different nature—

namely the Billy Graham crusade in 1981. I remember the begrudging remarks of our press about it—especially the cost involved and how that money could have been better spent. No such reference to this show's price tag of 393,483 dollars. An irrelevant comparison? They have in common the intention of not just entertaining, but of moving people to a spiritual commitment. May I weigh value by results? Two examples re the Billy Graham crusade, worth mentioning, are that the Calgary crime rate was down both before and after the crusade. In October 1981, an article in the Edmonton *Journal* stated that the Social Services Department had an unusual drop in the number of caseloads last fall, from Red Deer and South, and attributed this to the effects of the crusade. I predict the afterwave of *The Dinner Party* will bring more destruction than healing. Yes, I believe in the equality of the sexes. This show is stirring up attention—but honor to great women? Frankly, it sounds more like Babylon revisited (genitalia were a common sight in the temple worship of Babylon). There has to be a better way."

8. *Background:* This item was part of an advertisement for numerology that appeared in the *Detroit Free Press. Note:* Numerology is a system for predicting what will happen to people on the basis of numbers and letters significantly associated with them.

"We found that numerology is a very useful tool in producing good luck. For example, the letters in the alphabet have assigned numbers. Singer Dionne Warwicke took the advice of her numerologist and added an "e" to the end of her name. She immediately skyrocketed to fame . . . ."

9. *Background:* This argument by Glenn T. Seaborg originally appeared in *Chemical Education News*. It was reprinted in the *Informal Logic Newsletter* Examples Supplement for June 1980:

"Let us say it's a few years hence and all nuclear power plants have been operating safely. But opponents of nuclear power succeed in enforcing a national moratorium on nuclear power. All nuclear power plants are shut down, pending complete re-evaluation in terms of public safety.

"First this moratorium causes a rush by electric utility companies to obtain more fossil fuels—particularly because oil and gas are in tight supply. Coal prices soar, and the government reacts by setting a price ceiling. Coal supplies dwindle, and power cutbacks are put into effect. Finally, restrictions on burning high-sulphur coal are relaxed somewhat, and air pollution rises. Miners, disgruntled over a wage freeze and laxness of employers regarding safety standards, go out on strike. Coal stockpiles diminish, and many power plants are forced to shut down; others, overloaded by power demands, begin to fail. Miners battle with federal troops who have been ordered to take over the mines. A chain of blackouts and brown-outs creeps across the nation. . . .

"Darkened stores are looted at night. At home, people burn candles and wash in cold water. Hospitals begin to use emergency generators, and deaths are reported in intensive care wards because of equipment failure. Ill or injured persons have difficulty getting to a doctor or hospital. Medical supplies begin to lag behind growing demand.

"Children who can get to school wear sweaters and coats in unheated classrooms. At night, there is no television, and people listen to battery powered radios where they hear hope of miners going back to work. But as time goes on, great doubt appears that things will ever be the same again. It's up to you to speculate whether they would be."

*10. "For the past thirty years, six-foot-four John Wayne has stalked through the American imagination as the embodiment of manhood. . . . He has left not only a trail of broken hearts and jaws everywhere, but millions of fractured male egos which could never quite measure up to the two-fisted, ramrod-backed character who conquered the Old West. The truth of the matter is that no man could measure up to that myth in real life—not even John Wayne."

(Tim LaHaye, *Understanding the Male Temperament* [Charlotte, NC: Commission Press, 1977], p. 11)

*11. *Background:* This item appeared in the *Oakland Press* on April 6, 1974, and was reprinted in the *Informal Logic Newsletter* Examples Supplement for 1979:

A Good Way to Cure Colds

University of Michigan medical researchers have discovered that highly educated people with low incomes catch cold more often than others, suggesting that susceptibility to colds might depend on one's frame of mind. Furthermore, more people come down with colds on Monday than any other day.

Well, practically everybody thinks he is not being paid as much as his education calls for, and it's on Monday mornings when this feeling becomes most acute. So obviously, it's not a germ or virus that's causing all our colds but those cold-hearted people in the front office who never seem to realize how smart we are. A cure for colds? One way would be to give everybody a raise and tell them to take Monday off."

12. In 1986, "Farmer John Coombs claims his cow Primrose is curing his baldness—by licking his head. Mr. Coombs, 56, who farms near Salisbury, in southwestern England, says he made the discovery after Primrose licked some cattle food dust off his pate as he was bending down. A few weeks later hair was growing in an area that had been bald for years. The farmer has the whole herd working on the problem now, the *Daily Telegraph* reported yesterday. Mr. Coombs encourages his cows to lick his head every day and believes he will soon have a full head of hair."
(Toronto *Globe and Mail,* March 6, 1987.)

Different Senses of *Inductive*

Before closing this discussion, we should deal with one further complication. You may have heard somewhere that all arguments are either deductive or inductive. In our sense of *inductive,* this statement is not true, as the subjects of the next two chapters will indicate. *A priori* analogies (Chapter 10) and conductive arguments (Chapter 11) are not inductive in our sense, and they are not deductive either. People who say that all arguments are either inductive or deductive use the word *inductive* in a broader meaning than we use it in this book.

The most common broader sense of *inductive* is that in which it simply means "nondeductive." Obviously, if inductive arguments are by definition nondeductive, then, since all arguments must necessarily be either deductive or nondeductive, all arguments will necessarily be either deductive or inductive. (Since deductive and nondeductive express contradictory predicates, these terms will exhaust the possibilities.)

In this book, we have given *inductive* its own definition, which is not formulated by contrast with *deductive.* In our sense, *inductive* and *deductive* are contrary predicates, not contradictory ones. We have made this choice because we find the definition of *inductive* as "nondeductive" too broad to be useful. According to that definition, every argument that is not deductive is an inductive argument. This situation would put conductive arguments, some *ad hominem* arguments, *a priori* analogies, enumerative inductions, cases of guilt by association, explanatory inductions, and many other arguments in the same category. With this definition of *inductive* the category seems too broad to be useful. These various arguments are quite different from each other in a number of ways, as you no doubt realize by now.

Historically, induction has been closely associated with empirical science. Influenced by this association, some modern theorists who have used the broad sense of *inductive* have then gone on to identify inductive arguments with those used in empirical science. The combination of the broad definition of inductive as "nondeductive" and a sensitivity to philosophical tradition has led them to forget the very existence of other arguments commonly used in law, history, ethics, and other fields. Thus the broad category can be quite misleading. We believe that we have excellent reasons not to adopt that system in this book. We have chosen to explain it briefly, however, as you will likely encounter it in other contexts.

In this book, then, *inductive* does not mean "nondeductive." There are deductive arguments, inductive arguments, and other arguments that do not fit in either category. Among these, *a priori* analogies and conductive arguments will be described in Chapters 10 and 11. In our sense, inductive arguments are arguments in which the premises and the conclusion are all empirical propositions; the conclusion is not deductively entailed by the premises; the reasoning used to infer the conclusion from the premises is based on the assumption that the regularities described in the premises will persist; and the inference is either that unexamined cases will resemble examined ones or that a hypothesis is probably true because it has greater explanatory value than competing hypotheses. Given this narrower sense of *inductive*, the inductive-deductive split does not exhaust the possibilities for arguments.

CHAPTER SUMMARY

In this chapter, we described several different types of inductive arguments. These arguments share the property that their evaluation depends greatly on background knowledge, and for this reason, no purely formal method exists for evaluating them.

Inductive arguments have empirical conclusions and empirical premises, and are based, ultimately, on the assumption that unobserved cases will be relevantly similar to observed ones. There are three fundamental types of inductive argument: inductive generalizations, causal inductive arguments, and inductive analogies. Of these, inductive generalizations and causal inductive arguments are described in this chapter. Inductive analogies will be described in Chapter 10. In inductive generalizations, a generalization is made on the basis of observations of a sample, and that pattern observed in the sample is projected onto a broader population. In causal inductive arguments, the premises describe regularities among events and pertinent background knowledge, and the conclusion is that one sort of event causes another.

It is impossible to give completely general rules for the evaluation of inductive generalizations because the factor of background knowledge is so important. The merits of the argument depend more than anything else on the extent to which the sample represents the population. The sample should be large enough and varied enough that it reasonably can be expected to represent the variety that characterizes the target population. An exceedingly small sample leads to the fallacy of hasty generalization; here an attempt at an enumerative inductive generalization fails completely because the sample—which may be based on a single unrepresentative experience—is too small to give a reasonable amount of evidence for the conclusion. When the sample is selective in a way that will predictably distort the evidence in a direction favorable to the arguer's conclusion, it is said to be biased. To obtain representative samples, we have to aim for number and variety in a way that makes sense, given background knowledge relevant to the sample and the population.

Inductive arguments to causal conclusions are especially important and complex. Mill's methods offer strategies for situations where we can reasonably make assumptions about a range of factors likely to include the cause or causes. In a careful causal argument, the conclusion is derived from observed regularities. Causation can never be correctly inferred from correlation alone, because a correlation can have alternative explanations. A reasonable basis must exist for ruling out important alternative explanations if the causal argument is to be justified. A number of interesting and important flaws in argument result when causal arguments are improperly constructed. These include mistaking correlation for cause, engaging in the *post hoc* fallacy or the fallacy of objectionable cause, inferring cause in a question-begging way from a narrative of plausible scenario, and using the causal slippery slope fallacy.

The term *inductive* is sometimes used to mean "nondeductive." If *inductive* is given this meaning, then, by definition, all arguments are either inductive or deductive. In this book, however, the word *inductive* is not defined in this way. It is given its own definition (see Review of Terms Introduced). In our sense of *inductive* and *deductive,* some arguments are neither deductive nor inductive. These include *a priori* analogies and conductive arguments, to be discussed in Chapters 10 and 11.

Review of Terms Introduced

Anecdotal evidence Evidence that is about only a single episode, or only a few episodes, often from within the personal experience of the arguer. Such evidence is too slight to be the basis for a cogent inductive generalization. The (G) condition of argument cogency is not satisfied when evidence is purely anecdotal.

Biased sample A sample that demonstrably and obviously misrepresents the population. Such a sample is unrepresentative because items are not typical of the population, and the ways in which they fail to be typical will affect the reliability of the conclusion. For example, if someone were to question people making purchases at a liquor store in an attempt to find out what percentage of the adult population consumes more than one alcoholic drink a day, he or she would have a biased sample.

Causal inductive argument Inductive argument in which the premises describe regularities or correlations between events of various types, and in which the conclusion is that one event, or sort of event, is the cause of another.

Causal slippery slope fallacy Argument in which it is asserted that a particular action, often acceptable in itself, is unacceptable because it will set off a whole series of other actions, leading in the end to something bad or disastrous. The causal claim that such a series will be the result is not backed up by evidence and is typically implausible on close analysis. Such arguments are not cogent because the sweeping causal premise is not acceptable; the (A) condition of argument cogency is not satisfied.

Correlation   An association of two characteristics, *A* and *B*. If more *A*s than non-*A*s are *B*, there is a positive correlation between being *A* and being *B*. If fewer *A*s than non-*A*s are *B*, there is a negative correlation between being *A* and being *B*. *Note:* It is important not to confuse correlation with causation. Even when *A* and *B* are strongly correlated, this does not show us either that *A* is the cause of *B* or that *B* is the cause of *A*. It is possible that a third thing, *X*, causes both *A* and *B*. Alternately, the correlation might be coincidental.

Fallacy of composition   Inferring a conclusion about a whole or a group from premises about the parts of that whole or the members of that group.

Fallacy of division   Inferring a conclusion about some or all parts of a whole or members of a group from premises about the whole or about the group.

Fallacy of objectionable cause   The fallacy committed when someone argues to a causal conclusion on the basis of evidence that is too slight. It may be committed by inferring causation from correlation alone, or by simply imposing one sort of explanatory interpretation on events and failing to consider others.

Hasty inductive generalization   Inductive generalization in which the evidence in the premises is too slight to support the conclusion, usually because the sample is so small that it is extremely unlikely to be representative. The (G) condition of argument cogency is not satisfied in such a case.

Inductive analogy   Analogy in which the prediction is made that because one case resembles another in some observed respects, it will resemble it in other respects. This is discussed in Chapter 10.

Inductive arguments   Arguments in which the premises and the conclusion are empirical—having to do with observation and experience—and in which the inference to the conclusion is based on an assumption that observed regularities will persist.

Inductive generalization   Inductive argument in which the premises describe a number of cases and a generalization is made, so that in the conclusion there is a claim that some or all further cases will have the same property or properties as the cases cited in the premises.

Inductive reasoning   Reasoning in which we extrapolate from experience to further experience.

Plausible scenario   Form of causal argument that begs the question because the narrative given in the premises assumes the correctness of the causal claim made in the conclusion.

***Post hoc* fallacy**   To infer, from the fact that *A* was followed by *B*, the conclusion that *A* caused *B*. Typically, *A* and *B* are singular events. In effect, the *post hoc* fallacy is an argument that "after this, therefore because of this." Such arguments are not cogent because the (G) condition of argument cogency is not satisfied.

Prediction   Claim that something will happen, or is likely to happen, in the future, based on evidence about what has happened in the past or is happening now.

Pseudoprecision   Claim that appears to be precise due to the use of numbers, but which cannot be precise due to the impossibility of obtaining knowledge with this level of exactness. Often pseudoprecision occurs in contexts where an operational definition is faulty.

Pseudoregularity   An apparent regularity founded on a similarity between cases that is too superficial or of too little scientific significance to be appropriate as the basis for an inductive argument. For example: All these problems occurred on Tuesday, so Tuesday is my bad day.

Random sample   A sample in which every member of the population has an equal chance of being included. Selecting a sample randomly is often the best strategy for approximating representativeness in the sample.

Representativeness   A sample, S, is perfectly representative of a population, P, with respect to a characteristic, x, if the percentage of S that has x is exactly equal to the percentage of P that has x. We are rarely in a position to know that a sample is representative in this strict sense. (If we were, we would not need the sample; this point is often called the paradox of sampling.) We try to make samples representative by choosing them in such a way that the variety in the sample will reflect variety in the population.

Retrodiction   Claim that something happened, or probably happened, in the past, based on evidence about what is happening in the present.

Sample   A subset of cases chosen from an identified population and examined as the basis for an inductive generalization. In an inductive generalization, the cases in the sample are assumed to be representative of a broader group of cases. For example, if we reach a conclusion about U.S. political opinion by a telephone survey of 1,000 people, these 1,000 people are taken as a sample of the broader adult population in the United States.

Stratified sample   A sample selected in such a way that significant characteristics within the population are (approximately) proportionately represented within it.

Target population   All of the cases within the scope of the conclusion of an inductive generalization. The population is the broader group we are reasoning about, on the basis of our evidence concerning the sample. For example, if someone does a television survey of 1,000 adult Canadians to reach a conclusion about Canadian public opinion on a certain matter, the target population is Canadian adults.

Notes

1. Calgary *Herald,* July 8, 1995, "One Horse Race: Klein's Tories Lead in Poll, Despite Opposition Nags."

2. See note 1.

3. These examples were taken from Derek Rowntree, *Statistics without Tears* (London: Pelican Books, 1981).

4. This advertisement appeared in several popular magazines in 1980 and 1981.

5. This item was taken from research summaries in Carol Austin Bridgewater, "When a Man Talks, You Listen," *Psychology Today,* Ziff-Davis Publishing, 1980.

6. Carol Gilligan, *In a Different Voice* (Cambridge, MA: Harvard University Press, 1982). Gilligan's own work was later criticized on various grounds including, notably, the unrepresentativeness of her own samples, which were of white women in a specific geographical region of the United States and did not include African American or native women. Ideally, an empirical study of a female style of moral reasoning (if such, in fact, exists) would involve subjects from various cultural and racial groups.

7. One might, of course, wonder whether looking only at what these people ate might exclude too many other possibilities. This point merits attention and will be considered later.

8. Note that in terms of logic alone, the lettuce or croutons in the Caesar salad could equally well have been identified as a possible cause. It is background knowledge that would lead us to suspect the dressing; for dressing containing sharp cheeses and sauces contain the sorts of ingredients that we would regard as more likely to be associated with stomach illness than lettuce or croutons.

9. Julianne Labreche, "Migraines Linked with Sexual Arousal," *Chatelaine,* October 1980, p. 34. It is important to note that Sicuteri, the researcher, may have made none of the mistakes we find in the report; these may be mistakes that emerge from the way the report was written and edited. However, those mistakes are still worth pointing out because it is through that report that readers are exposed to his research.

10. This passage is taken from a textbook in psychology, one which was widely used in the early 1980s.

11. Gerald S. Lesser, "Stop Picking on Big Bird," *Psychology Today,* March 1979.

12. Toronto *Globe and Mail,* February 23, 1980.

13. Erich von Daniken, *Chariots of the Gods? Unsolved Mysteries of the Past* translated by Michael Heron; paperback reprint of 1969 book (New York: Berkeley Publishing Group, 1984). I owe this example and my interest in the phenomenon of pseudoregularity to Cary McWilliams.

14. Deanna Kuhn, *The Skills of Argument* (New York: Cambridge University Press, 1991), p. 109.

15. The distinction between micro (small) level and macro (large) level is common and thus may facilitate understanding. It is important while employing this decision, however, not to erect a false dichotomy between the micro and the macro levels. There are many levels in between. For instance, we may consider an individual citizen as a member of the state and think of relations between two or three individuals as existing at the micro level of a society. Contrasting macro with micro, we may think of relations between states of the United States or provinces of Canada as existing at the national, or macro, level of society. Obviously there are relationships at intermediate levels, for instance, within and between families, communities, churches, corporations, and professional associations.

16. I owe my interest in this kind of example to Robert X. Ware, who located it in literature about democratic theory and autonomy.

17. This argument was stated at a conference on "Dilemmas of Reconciliation" at the University of Calgary in June 1999 and carried some weight in deliberations.

18. Reported by Joanne Good, Department of Sociology, Trent University, in 1982.

19. Cited by Theodore Draper in "Falling Dominoes," *New York Review of Books,* vol. 15, no. 16, October 27, 1983.

20. This argument was used in the early days of birth control clinics, as reported in a review of a book on Dr. Stopes, an early birth control pioneer. Reviewed by J. Finlayson in the Toronto *Globe and Mail,* January 13, 1979.

21. Thomas de Quincy, *On Murder Considered as One of the Fine Arts* (London: Philip Allan and Co., Quality Court, 1925). De Quincy's essay first appeared in *Blackwood's* magazine in 1827. Thanks to David Hill for this example.

chapter ten
Analogies: Reasoning from Case to Case

I N THIS CHAPTER WE STUDY various ways analogies are used in arguments and in the more general pursuit of knowledge. Also we offer some strategies for grasping the basic structure of an analogy and arriving at a sound critical assessment. We emphasize the important role analogies often play in the reasoning within law and administration and their role in providing grounds for beliefs about phenomena that cannot be studied directly. As well as good arguments from analogy, there are also many arguments from loose and irrelevant analogies that provide only the shakiest base for conclusions. We examine two kinds of cogent analogies, and then go on to discuss some fallacies based on the misuse of analogies.

The Nature and Functions of Analogy

As we saw earlier (Chapters 3 and 6), arguments by **analogy** draw a conclusion about one thing on the basis of a comparison of that thing and another. It is convenient to call the central topic—the one dealt with in the conclusion—the **primary subject,** and the case with which it is compared the **analogue.** In the following unforgettable analogy by C. S. Lewis, the primary subject is the striptease, as it exists in our culture, and the analogue is the unveiling of a mutton chop, as this might exist in an imagined alternative culture:

> You can get a large audience together for a strip-tease act—that is, to watch a girl undress on the stage. Now suppose you came to a country where you could fill a theatre simply by bringing a covered plate onto the stage and then slowly

> lifting the cover so as to let everyone see, just before the lights went out, that it contained a mutton chop or a bit of bacon, would you not think that in that country something had gone wrong with the appetite for food?[1]

Lewis uses our reaction to the analogue to develop a reaction to the primary subject. In the analogous case, we would certainly think that the natural human desire for food had been warped in some way. By drawing an analogy between this case and the case of striptease, which actually exists, he urges us to conclude that our sexual desires in this culture are somehow warped. The answer to the rhetorical question at the end of the passage (would you not think . . . something had gone wrong with the appetite for food?) is clearly supposed to be "yes." The implied conclusion is that in our culture, where the striptease is a form of entertainment, something has gone wrong with the desire for sex.

An argument from analogy begins by using one case (usually agreed on and relatively easy to understand) to illuminate or clarify another (usually less clear). It then seeks to justify a conclusion about the second case on the basis of considerations about the first. The basis for drawing the conclusion is the relevant similarity between the cases, which is regarded as showing a commonality of structure between the two cases compared.

Because this book is about arguments, we concentrate on analogy as a device in argument. However, analogies have many other functions as well. They are of great use in teaching—an analogue may be familiar whereas the primary subject is unfamiliar, so explanations based on analogies are often quite effective. Analogies also are used to illustrate points, or to make a speech or an essay more interesting.

Albert Einstein used an analogy to explain how the enormous energy that is inherent in mass could have gone undetected by physicists until the twentieth century. He said:

> It is as though a man who is fabulously rich should never spend or give away a cent; no one could tell how rich he was.[2]

Here the primary subject is the energy within matter, and the analogue is the unspent money of the rich man. But Einstein was not offering an argument. Rather, he was trying to explain the notion of trapped energy to people who might not be familiar with it—but who would certainly understand the analogue of the fabulously rich man hoarding his money.

In an essay on sampling for opinion polls, Ralph Johnson used the following analogy to explain the concept of a representative sample:

> To take the simplest sort of example, suppose that you were making soup and you wondered whether or not you had put enough thyme in it. You probably first would stir the batch of soup well (the batch is the population) and test a portion that has been well-mixed and hence is a good indicator of the whole batch. In doing this, you would be acknowledging the fundamental principle of sampling, which we will discuss shortly. Next you would select a spoonful of it (the sample), test it (by tasting it) and—based on your perception—project that property back into the population: "There should be more thyme," you might say.

When you stirred the soup, it was to make as sure as you could that your sample was typical of the whole batch. The key feature in construction of a sample is that it be *representative*.[3]

Johnson is not offering an argument in this passage. He is using the familiar activity of tasting soup to explain sampling. Although we concentrate here on analogy as it may be used in argument, much that is said is also applicable to explanatory or illustrative analogies.

Analogy and Consistency

Treating similar cases similarly is a fundamental aspect of rationality. It is by drawing analogies—seeing important similarities and differences—that we determine which are similar cases and which are not. Any application of a general principle or rule—whether in logic, morality, law, or administration—requires that we have a sense of which cases are relevantly similar and merit similar treatment. This is one way that we can see just how fundamental reasoning with analogies is.

In logic, a contradiction, a statement of the type "*P* and not-*P*," is never true.[4] Such a statement both asserts and denies the same thing (for example, "Princess Diana is dead and Princess Diana is not dead"); it is inconsistent and impossible. If we are going to make sense, such inconsistency has to be avoided: one who asserts and denies the very same thing has, in effect, said nothing at all.

However, this is not the only sort of consistency that is essential to the rational life. There is at least one other kind of consistency—that which is involved in treating similar cases similarly. We can be inconsistent by treating similar cases differently—for example, by criticizing in one person behavior we approve in someone else, or by demanding a stiff sentence for one first-time offender while urging probation for another in similar circumstances. If a particular case merits a particular treatment, then consistency demands that relevantly similar cases receive the same treatment.

Often, agreed-on cases are used as the basis for arguments to conclusions about disputed cases. The agreed-on cases serve as the analogues, and on the basis of similarities, one can defend conclusions about the disputed cases. Such arguments **appeal to consistency**: similar cases should be treated similarly.

In fact, this form of argument is common in logic itself. Occasions may arise when we wish to evaluate an argument and we are not certain what to say about it. One technique that may be used is to find a relevantly similar argument on which the verdict is clear and reason from the clear case to the disputed case. The technique of refutation by logical analogy is based on this procedure.

Ethics, Law, and Treating Similar Cases Similarly

The demand for consistency is the basis of many forceful and important moral arguments. These arguments work by bringing an undisputed case to bear on a disputed or problematic case. The cases are considered to be relevantly similar. For example, if an analogue is known to be wrong, and a primary subject is relevantly similar to it, then the primary subject can be known to be wrong too. What matters are relevant similarities.

Jesus used the technique of analogy, implicitly, when he said that a man who lusts after a married woman has already committed adultery with her in his heart. In this comment, Jesus was drawing an analogy between lustful desire and actual adultery in an attempt to get his followers to extend the disapproval they already felt for adultery to lustful thoughts as well.

Dr. Joyce Brothers used a similar technique when she replied to an anxious reader who said, "My problem is that my husband doesn't want to have children because I underwent therapy before we were married and my husband is afraid that my emotional troubles will be passed on to my child." Brothers replied with an analogy:

> When is society going to come out of the dark ages and recognize that mental or emotional problems should be no more stigmatizing to an individual than a case of German measles or pneumonia? We do not shun those who have suffered and been cured of tuberculosis, polio, or other diseases, do we?[5]

Brothers is contending here that emotional problems are relevantly similar to physical diseases and should be treated in the same way. She relies on our acceptance of the belief that people should not be shunned after they have been cured of physical diseases. She draws an undeveloped analogy between emotional and mental problems and these physical diseases, and she urges that we "come out of the dark ages" to make our attitudes consistent. The analogy on which the argument depends may be set out as follows:

ANALOGUE
People with such physical problems as German measles or polio
    suffer
    can recover
    are not shunned by others after they recover

PRIMARY SUBJECT
People with emotional or mental problems
    suffer
    can recover

CONCLUSION
People with emotional or mental problems should not be shunned by others after they recover.

Is this argument a good one? Our assessment will depend on the closeness of the analogy. How similar are physical and emotional diseases with respect to extent of recovery after treatment and possible transferred effect on children? The technique Brothers uses, appealing to consistency of treatment between similar cases, leaves her audience with a choice. The audience can (1) change its attitude toward the primary subject; (2) find a relevant difference between the primary subject and the analogue; (3) change its attitude toward the analogue; or (4) admit that it is inconsistent in its treatment of the analogue and the primary subject. Brothers is counting on people not to opt for (3) or (4) and not to be able to do (2). She presumes that people are committed to rationality with regard to consistency in the treatment of cases. Brothers expects that her readers will choose (1), changing their attitudes about mental illness.

In law, the obligation to treat similar cases similarly is the essence of formal justice. Suppose two people in two separate cases are charged with the same crime. Let us say, for instance, that Jones was arrested for selling liquor to a minor on Monday, and Smith was arrested for selling liquor to a minor on Tuesday. Suppose that Jones is convicted and Smith is not. If there is not some relevant difference between the two cases, this situation constitutes an example of formal injustice. Regardless of the contents of a law, it should be applied consistently. No two accused people are identical; nor will their circumstances be identical. But if they are relevantly similar, they should be treated similarly. If they are not treated similarly, the judge or judges should specify the relevant differences between them. (Perhaps in Smith's case, the minor had convincing identity papers, indicating that he was of age, for instance; that could be a relevant difference justifying the differential treatment for Jones and Smith.)

This consistency in reasoning is the basis of the **precedent** system of law: to preserve formal justice, cases must be resolved as similar cases have been resolved in the past, or a differentiating point must be specified. You can see, then, that picking out central similarities and differences is an extremely important aspect of legal reasoning. Much of legal reasoning is, in effect, reasoning by analogy. The case under discussion in a case constitutes the primary subject, and the issue may be resolved by reference to past cases, which are analogues, or legal precedents.

The same kind of point applies in administrative contexts. Here the context is seldom as structured as requirements for formal justice. Nevertheless, anyone administering a policy seeks to avoid unfairness and the criticism and confusion that will follow if the policy is applied inconsistently. Good administrators will seek to treat similar cases similarly and will sometimes argue against a specific decision on the grounds that it will set a bad precedent. For instance, if the chairperson of a meeting accepts a last-minute addition to its agenda by one committee member on the grounds that it strikes him as important, she may feel compelled to accept many more last-minute additions from others. Presumably everyone who sought a last-minute addition would believe the addition was important. (As we shall see toward the end of this chapter, this kind of appeal to precedent is open to subtle and slippery abuses that lead to fallacious argument.)

Case-by-Case Reasoning and Issues of Classification

Are the economies of Western nations currently in a recession or in a depression? The most straightforward way of resolving this issue of classification is to see how similar and how different our current situation is to that of the 1930s—a classic economic case of a depression. Is a virus an animal? Are Polynesians a distinct race? All these questions have moral, legal, political, or scientific significance, and they call for correct decisions about the application of important concepts—"depression," "animal," "distinct race," and so on. The issues at stake are **conceptual.** Some people regard conceptual issues as unimportant, thinking that they relate only to words and nothing more, and that they cannot be resolved in any reasonable way. However, as we saw in Chapter 4, reasons can be given to back up these classifications. Often such reasons are based on analogies.

If we ask whether a questionable act counts as an act of negligence, for instance, we are raising a conceptual issue, one that often has considerable legal or moral significance. (It might make the difference of several years in jail, or thousands of dollars in fines for an individual or corporation.) One way of resolving such an issue is to compare the act with another that is agreed to be a case of negligence. We then ask how much our problem case is like the standard case, and to what extent it is unlike the standard case. To use this technique is to approach conceptual issues by reasoning from analogy.

Consider a dispute that actually arose regarding some books written about the extermination of Jews during World War II. Some French historians wrote works alleging that six million Jews had not been killed in Nazi death camps and that there had been a conspiracy to fabricate evidence on this matter. Jewish students at the University of Toronto, understandably enraged at the allegation, urged library officials to reclassify the French historians' books, terming them *fiction* instead of *nonfiction*. They believed that the historical claims made in the works were so outrageous that they did not properly qualify as nonfiction. B'nai B'rith officials defended the students' request but did not want to be identified as advocates of censorship. They insisted that reclassifying books was not the same thing as having them unavailable, and therefore reclassification did not amount to censorship.[6]

In this case, both the Jewish students and the B'nai B'rith officials raised questions that were, in effect, about the application of concepts. The Jewish students raised the question of whether books that are about such world events as World War II, but that make outlandish claims about them, are to be regarded as nonfiction (history in this case) or as fiction. What makes a book count as nonfiction? Is it solely the intent of the author to describe the world as it was or is? Or is a certain minimum level of accuracy required? This question could be resolved by looking at clear cases of fiction and nonfiction and reasoning by analogy, or by looking at other borderline cases that have been resolved and using them as precedents, again reasoning by analogy. (The library did not do this, apparently; it simply refused to consider the matter, saying too much public pressure could result.)

B'nai B'rith officials defended what the Jewish students were proposing, but they did not want to allow that it would be censorship. They asserted that reclassification would not be censorship or book banning. Perhaps these officials were right. There is a clear difference between banning or censoring all or part of a book and putting it on the library shelf in one classification rather than another. (Classifying a book as physics rather than chemistry certainly would not amount to censoring it.) In the latter case, the book is still available to readers, and it is this availability that censors wish to prevent.

This example illustrates issues of conceptualization that we might seek to resolve by arguing from agreed-on cases. The pattern of such reasoning, for conceptual issues, is something like this:

1. The analogue has features *a, b,* and *c.*
2. The primary subject has features *a, b,* and *c.*
3. It is by virtue of features *a, b,* and *c* that the analogue is properly classified as a *W.*
So,
4. The primary subject ought to be classified as a *W.*[7]

Sometimes the comparison of cases omits any specification of the similar features and merely sets the cases side by side—the idea being that similarities will be recognized once the two cases are considered together. Thus:

1. The analogue is a clear case of *W.*
2. The primary subject is similar to the analogue.
So,
3. The primary subject is a case of *W.*

Robert Nozick offered a philosophical argument combining conceptual issues with moral ones. He tried to persuade readers that they were far too complacent in accepting the government's policy of redistributing wealth by income taxation. Nozick put his point provocatively by using the following analogy:

> Taxation of earnings from labor is on a par with forced labor. Some persons find this claim obviously true; taking the earnings of *n* hours of labor is like taking *n* hours from the person; it is like forcing the person to work *n* hours for another's purpose. Others find the claim absurd. But even these, if they object to forced labor, would oppose forcing unemployed hippies to work for the benefit of the needy.
>   . . . The man who chooses to work longer to gain an income more than sufficient for his basic needs prefers some extra goods or services to the leisure and activities he could perform during the possible nonworking hours; whereas the man who chooses not to work the extra time prefers the leisure activities to the extra goods or services he could acquire by working more. Given this, if it would be illegitimate for a tax system to seize some of a man's leisure (forced labor) for the purpose of serving the needy, how can it be legitimate for a tax system to seize some of a man's goods for that purpose?[8]

Nozick's analogy can be set out as follows:

ANALOGUE

The government might force a person to work for some number of hours to support the needy.
Point (1): In such a case, a person would labor for some number of hours.
Point (2): The laboring person would not receive the payment for those hours of work; he would receive nothing for himself.

Point (3): The laboring person would be forced by the government to spend his time laboring for others.
Point (4): It obviously would be wrong for the government to put people into forced labor to serve the needy, and the wrongness of this act would be, and is, acknowledged by everybody.

PRIMARY SUBJECT

The government takes the earnings from some number of hours of work to support the needy.
Point (1): A person labors for some number of hours.
Point (2): The laboring person does not receive the payment for those hours of work.
Point (3): ? (How does the analogy hold up here?)

CONCLUSION

Taxing earned income to support the needy is morally wrong.

Nozick's argument may strike you as shocking. After all, we typically accept income tax, which is used (in part) to support such social programs as welfare and medical assistance, and we typically *oppose* forced labor, which we are likely to associate with the concentration camps of totalitarian regimes. Are people being inconsistent in these common attitudes? Nozick is maintaining that they are—that, in fact, labor for which one is not paid because of income tax is just like forced labor and deserves the same bad moral reputation. This is certainly a provocative analogy! To resist it, we must find a relevant dissimilarity between forced labor as in concentration camps and labor that is 100 percent taxed and thus, in effect, unpaid.

Look at the third point for a clue. People do largely *choose* to work at those jobs for which they are taxed, so their actual labor is not forced in the same sense that concentration camp labor is forced. This difference between the primary subject and the analogue is significant; taxed labor is not *forced* labor, because people choose their jobs. The analogy is undermined by this difference: since working at your job during hours when you do not receive pay is something you (typically) choose to do and may enjoy for various reasons, it is not strictly comparable to forced labor. What is forced is not the labor, but the payment of tax. Thus, Nozick's analogy is not fully convincing: we are not inconsistent if we approve of income tax used for redistributive purposes but disapprove of forced labor.

Some arguments make a rather implicit appeal for consistent treatment of cases. Here we often find such phrases as "that's just like saying," "you might as well say," "by the same reasoning," or "according to those standards." Here is an example in which the writer of a letter to *Time* magazine urges that appeals by the chairman of Eastern Airlines for protection from creditors should be rejected.

In seeking protection from Eastern's creditors in bankruptcy court, Lorenzo [chairman of Eastern Airlines] is like the young man who killed his parents and then begged the judge for mercy because he was an orphan. During the last three years, Lorenzo has stripped Eastern of its most valuable assets and then pleaded poverty because the shrunken structure was losing money.[9]

The analogue is the case of a young man who killed his parents and then begged for mercy from the court, saying he is an orphan—seeking pity on the grounds of a state of affairs that he himself caused, since he murdered his parents. The analogue forcefully brings out the general point that one who has caused his own bad situation deserves little pity or mercy from others. The Eastern Airlines case is claimed to be relevantly similar. If it is, clearly Lorenzo would not deserve protection from the court for the bankruptcy caused by his own actions.

Refutation by Logical Analogy

You can sometimes show an argument to be a poor one by comparing it with another argument that is obviously poor. If the two arguments are relevantly similar, then the logical analogy between them will show that the argument in question is poor. It is relevantly similar to another that is obviously poor, so it is poor. In such a procedure the first argument is **refuted by the use of a logical analogy** or, as it is sometimes called, a parallel case.

To see how this works, consider this simple example:

PRIMARY ARGUMENT

You should not take prescription drugs, since these are unnatural substances and as such may be harmful to the body.

The faulty assumption that anything which does not occur in the world "naturally" may be harmful may be exposed by constructing a logical analogy with an argument that is obviously faulty.

ANALOGUE TO PRIMARY ARGUMENT

You should not ride a bicycle, since a bicycle is an unnatural human creation and as such may be harmful to the body.

What is happening here is that there is an argument about two other arguments. The idea is to refute the first argument by showing that it is parallel to a second argument in which a comparable premise leads to a clearly unacceptable conclusion. The structure of the refutation is as follows:

1. The primary argument is like the analogue argument in the basic structure that connects its premises to its conclusion.
2. The analogue argument is incorrect.

So,

3. The primary argument is incorrect.

Provided that we have correctly identified the relevant similarities and are comparing the structure shared by the two arguments, this reasoning about the two arguments is cogent, and shows that the primary argument is incorrect. The technique of refutation by logical analogy can be extremely valuable.

Here is an example in which this technique was used to good effect by a newspaper columnist. The columnist was criticizing a comment by Alberta's energy minister, who had said that since Alberta possessed valuable hydrocarbon resources, it would be silly for the province to develop solar or wind energy. The columnist imagined an ancient character objecting to the development of oil and gas resources in 1914:

> Puffing reflectively on his pipe, he said, "Mark my words. No good will come of this." He said it quite a lot, leaning back in a chair on the front porch of his livery stable.
>
> Of course, anyone who paused to listen stayed to mock, but Max stuck to his guns. "Oil?" he'd say. "What for? We'd look pretty stupid if we came up with anything that reduced the value of our horse resources."
>
> "Alberta is the horse capital of Canada," he'd continue. "Are we supposed to dig up gasoline for the Easterners so they can tell us what we can do with our horses? They'd like that, all right, but why should we oblige them?"[10]

Here the parallel focuses our attention on the basic structure of the minister's argument. A more abstract view of what the minister was saying is: "if something is useful and profitable now, and if some other prospective development could replace that thing, then the prospective development should be abandoned." The columnist's entertaining parallel points out just how silly the original argument is by showing that it is essentially the same argument as one that could have been used to prevent the development of the very hydrocarbon resources the minister was trying to protect.

The technique of refuting an argument by logical analogy is common in everyday conversation and is used quite naturally by people with no formal training in argument skills. Consider, as representative, the following dialogue:

> *Sue:* If God had meant us to have sex with same-sex partners, he never would have created two sexes in the first place. God created two sexes so that men and women could couple and produce children.
>
> *Bob:* Sure. And if God had meant us to wear clothes, we never would have been born naked.

Bob assumes that his argument is both parallel and absurd. No one would accept that God meant us to go nude, or that we should go nude, because we were born naked. The line of reasoning from the circumstance of birth to God's intention in all other circumstances is clearly implausible. Bob is claiming that Sue's argument, inferring God's intentions about intimate partnership from the fact that there are two different sexes, is similarly implausible.

The technique of refutation by logical analogy is intended to bring out the essential reasoning, or structure, of the primary argument and show that, in the analogue argument, the connection required for the argument to work does not hold. The structure is clearly flawed in the analogue argument, and provided that the primary argument has a parallel structure, it is flawed too. To be consistent, we must judge the structure of two arguments in the same way. The trick here, obviously, is to get the parallel between the primary argument and the analogue argument just right. The analogue and the primary subject must be relevantly similar. The real question is when they are relevantly similar and when they are not. To construct a refutation by logical analogy, we need to distinguish between those features of an argument that are merely incidental to its working and those that are central and crucial.

Sometimes an attempt at refutation by logical analogy is not decisive but rather opens further questions for discussion. This aspect of analogical reasoning may be illustrated in an example of some historical importance. During the Cold War (1949–1989) there was a debate about whether nuclear weapons had served to prevent, or deter, war between the United States and the Soviet Union. Those who defended the existence and development of nuclear weapons assumed that they had prevented war; this claim was not accepted by peace researchers and antinuclear activists, who believed that far from preventing war, nuclear weapons were provocative and dangerous. In one of the many debates about the topic, the antinuclear side used the following analogy:

> Saying that nuclear weapons prevented war between the United States and the Soviet Union for forty years, just because we had nuclear weapons and we didn't have war is not a very good argument. For forty years the Canadian Parliament was meeting in Ottawa, and for forty years there were no elephants roaming the streets of Ottawa. You wouldn't say the parliamentary meetings kept the elephants out of Ottawa, would you? Just because you have *A* and you don't have *B,* that doesn't meant that *A* prevented *B*.

In effect, the antinuclear critics were accusing defenders of the nuclear status quo of *post hoc* reasoning. But is the parallel entirely apt? There is a *post hoc* element in both cases. However the primary argument is different from the analogue argument in ways that may be significant for the merits of these arguments. There is, after all, a more plausible line of connection between the absence of war and the existence of nuclear weapons (threat of dreadful retaliation against attack) than there is between the absence of elephants in Ottawa and the existence of meetings of Parliament. Also, there was a genuine possibility of war between the United States and the Soviet Union (something that needed to be prevented), whereas the likelihood of finding elephants roaming the streets of Ottawa is effectively zero whether the Canadian Parliament is meeting there or not. The refutation shows clearly that the argument for nuclear deterrence, in its brief form, is *post hoc*. However, when we think about the difference between the primary subject and the analogue, we can see that the nuclear argument might be adapted and strengthened to make it relevantly different from the analogue argument.

Some Points of Method and Critical Strategy

We have now considered a number of examples of analogies in which a decision about one case is rejected or defended on the basis of consistency considerations. The analogy may be between two real cases or between a real case and a purely hypothetical case. The cases of people being shunned for physical diseases and of unemployed hippies being forced to work for the needy are hypothetical examples; the analogy can work even if these things never happened. Similarly, for the force of the argument about Lorenzo and Eastern Airlines, it does not matter whether, in fact, there ever was a young man who killed his parents and then sought mercy from the court on the grounds that he was an orphan. The analogue may be a real case or an imaginary case: what matters is that the point must be clear, the reasoning about the analogue must be correct, and the analogue must be relevantly similar to the primary case.

The imaginary, or even fanciful, aspect of case-by-case reasoning sometimes confuses and frustrates people, because they cannot understand why purely fictitious examples should be of any importance in rational decision making. But the answer to their puzzlement is not so hard to find. The analogue must above all be a case toward which our attitude is clear: an obviously valid argument, invalid argument, right action, wrong action, legal action, illegal action, correct decision, incorrect decision, or whatever. We will make little progress by comparing one confusing case with another. The analogue must be like the primary subject in those ways that are relevant to the case. Provided these conditions are met, we are pushed by consistency into taking the same stance on the primary subject as we do toward the analogue.

Our attitudes and our moral and logical beliefs are about a whole range of actions, events, and arguments—not just about those that have actually occurred, or existed up to the present moment. For instance, we do not know whether in fact any mother ever killed her newborn baby by boiling it to death in hot lead, but we do know that our attitude toward such an action should be one of extreme repugnance. Any action that can be shown to be relevantly similar to this hypothetical one is also to be condemned.

Because the analogue in this kind of consistency reasoning need not be something that actually happened, the analogy used may be called an ***a priori* analogy.** As we saw in Chapter 5, the words *a priori* in Latin mean "from the first" and are used by philosophers to refer to concepts and beliefs that are independent of sense experience. The analogies examined so far have been *a priori* analogies in the sense that it does not matter whether the analogue describes any real experienced events. What is at issue in these analogies is structure: something we have to reflect on. The analogy will be a good one insofar as the analogue and the primary case share all logically relevant features. Whether this is the case is something we can determine *a priori*, from reflective examination of the cases. The point of classifying these analogies as *a priori* will become more obvious when we look at **inductive analogies,** in which comparisons must be with actual cases. Inductive analogies, which are often used in history and science, form the basis for prediction or retrodiction, rather than decision.

To evaluate an argument from analogy, you can use the ARG conditions as you do for any argument. Suppose that the argument is based on an *a priori* analogy. The conclusion is about one case—the primary subject—and it is reached by comparing that case with another one—the analogue. The premises will describe the analogue and the primary subject. As in any argument, the premises are to be judged for their acceptability. When the analogy is *a priori*, the analogue may be something invented. Thus you cannot question the description of the analogue except on the grounds that it is internally inconsistent and hence contradictory. You can check to see that the primary subject—the case in question—is accurately and fairly described. If the premises assert that similarities exist between the two cases, then you must reflect to determine whether those similarities are genuine.

But the primary issue in these analogies is relevance. In some loose sense, virtually any two things in the universe are alike in some ways. The issue is how relevant the similarities are to the merits of the case. The parallel that is being implicitly or explicitly drawn between the analogue and the primary subject must hold up for the important, essential features of the two cases: those features that are relevant to the issue to be resolved in the conclusion. Think back to the Eastern Airlines case, for instance. Suppose someone were to defend Lorenzo on the ground that like an orphaned young man, he is lonely. This might be a similarity, but such a defense would be flawed, because whether Lorenzo is lonely is irrelevant to the issue of whether he wrongly caused Eastern's financial problems. The analogy between Lorenzo's case and that of the young man who murdered his parents is alleged because both in the primary subject and in the analogue, someone has caused his own problems by wrongdoing and then begs for mercy. If the cases are relevantly similar in these respects, and if there are no relevant differences (such as, for instance, the possibility that Lorenzo was forced into selling Eastern's assets), then the analogy holds and the argument will make its point.

You have to look at what the conclusion asserts about the primary subject, based on the analogy, and reflect on the similarities that hold between the primary subject and the analogue. Ask yourself whether the features of the primary subject that are highlighted by the analogy are relevant to the point asserted in the conclusion. Do those features give reasons to suppose that the conclusion is true of the primary subject? If they seem to, then try to think of relevant differences.

There are always differences between any two things, just as there are always similarities between them. For instance, someone might urge that there is an analogy between traveling and reading, because both provide a person with a chance to leave his ordinary everyday world for another world. No doubt there are many similarities between these activities (both require some education if one is to truly benefit, both cost some amount of money, both give access to other cultures and experiences). Clearly, there are also many differences: traveling typically costs more than reading and provides a fuller, more experiential immersion in a new setting. The question is how relevant, or important, those similarities and differences are to the point at issue in the argument. If someone were trying to argue that because travel is similar to reading and the government subsidizes reading through public libraries, it should subsidize travel too, we would find some similarities (cultural broadening) and differences (cost) *relevant* to assessing the analogy and others (level of physical exertion involved) *irrelevant*.

An analogy encourages you to think of two cases as similar and to reason from one to the other. The similarities between the cases should be real, and there should be a number of relevant similarities if the analogy is to provide the basis for a plausible argument. It is natural to try to refute an argument by analogy by thinking of differences between the primary subject and the analogue, but you cannot refute the argument merely by pointing out that the analogue and the primary subject are different in some respect or other. You have to find differences that are negatively relevant to the conclusion—that is, differences that indicate that the conclusion is false or unacceptable. If you can find decisively relevant differences that upset the analogy in this way, then you can show that the argument fails on the (G) condition. The difference or differences will reveal that the similarities highlighted in the analogy are not sufficient to give good grounds for the conclusion.

Your own reasoning, if this is the line of criticism, will be along the following lines: "The analogue and the primary subject both have features 1, 2, and 3, but the analogue is *x* and the primary subject may well be not-*x*. The reason is that the primary subject has feature 4, which the analogue lacks, and feature 4 may be just the one that indicates that the primary subject is not-*x*, because . . . ."

EXERCISE SET

Exercise 1: Part A

Appraise the following refutations by logical analogy. Find the primary subject and the analogue, and check the refutation by logical analogy using the ARG conditions as they apply to *a priori* analogies.

*1.   Some have concluded that Japanese corporations are more fairly run than American corporations, because in Japanese corporations decisions are typically reached by teams of managers and not just by one top manager, as is typically the case in American corporations. But this is a silly reason for attributing fairness to Japanese corporations. A severely flawed judicial system would not become fair just because teams of judges replaced single judges. Fairness is a matter of the distribution of advantages and disadvantages. It doesn't just depend only on how many people are involved in making decisions.

2.   In the early 1970s, some people claimed that using marijuana caused heroin addiction. They made this claim on the grounds that most people who use heroin first used marijuana. But isn't this a very silly argument? We could just as well argue that using milk causes a person to use cocaine. After all, most people who use cocaine began in life by using milk.

(Adapted from an exchange between Norman Podhoretz and several philosophers in *Commentary* in the late 1960s)

3.   Thinking that an international problem can be solved by bombing is just as ridiculous as thinking that a neighborhood problem can be solved by blowing up someone's house.

*4.   *Background:* The following appeared as a letter to the editor of a Canadian Jesuit magazine. "Grisez (the lay American moral philosopher) follows his master John Ford SJ in holding that the papal teaching about contraception cannot be wrong because "the Church could not have erred so atrociously and for such a long time regarding so serious a matter which imposed very heavy burdens on people." This ignores the fact that on such matters as slavery, torture, and religious liberty the Church was wrong for equally long periods of time—and to its great benefit, has recognized its fallibility."

(*Compass,* March/April 1995)

*5. *Background:* In 1983, there was a movement to achieve nuclear disarmament by the
technique of having a worldwide referendum on
the issue and using the results to put pressure on
politicians. Various arguments were put against
this proposal, including the following one,
which is described here and then contested by a
logical analogy.

"Some have proposed a referendum on the
question of worldwide disarmament. An argument often given against having such a referendum is that almost everyone would vote the
same way: everyone would favor worldwide
disarmament. So this argument is that we
shouldn't have a vote if nearly everybody agrees.
But if general agreement is a reason against
voting on disarmament, there would equally well
be a reason against an election for mayor if the
candidate were likely to win by a very large
majority. Nobody would accept that conclusion!
Similarly, we should not oppose a referendum
just because we expect that almost everyone
would respond to it in the same way."

6. In the fall of 1986, a Canadian cabinet minister, John Crosbie, said that people in Canada's
Atlantic provinces should not complain about
the high level of unemployment in their region.
After all, he said, they were well off compared to
people in Third World countries. Crosbie said
that people in these areas should compare themselves, not with Canadians in central and western Canada, but rather with citizens in poorer
parts of Asia and Africa. Calgary *Herald* columnist Alan Connery satirized Crosbie's comments
by saying it was as if someone defended the
performance of then-Prime Minister Brian
Mulroney by pointing out that he was better
than Hitler and Idi Amin. (Amin was a former
Ugandan ruler responsible for thousands of
tortures and murders.)

Question: Does Connery's satire effectively
constitute a refutation, by logical analogy, of
Crosbie's original argument?

Exercise 1: Part B
Of the following passages, (a) identify those that
contain arguments based on analogy. (b) Then
assess the arguments using the following procedure: identify the analogue and the primary subject; evaluate the argument according to the ARG
conditions. For the (A) condition, check to see
whether the primary subject is accurately described and is similar to the analogue in the ways
the arguer asserts or implies, and determine
whether the analogue is consistently described.
For the (R) condition, determine whether similarities are relevant to the conclusion. For the (G)
condition, use the technique of checking for relevant differences to see whether there are any relevant differences that provide evidence against the
conclusion. *Note:* Not all passages contain arguments. If the passage does not contain any argument, or if it contains an argument that is not
based on analogy, simply say so, and proceed no
further.

1. *Background:* This passage deals with the
issue of whether old people should be cared for
by families or housed in institutions:

"But, we say, old folks get difficult and
senile. Children get difficult and act as if they
were senile, but no one has sanctioned an institution we can send our children to when we no
longer wish to be responsible for them and they
are not yet adults. Turn them out and you will
be charged by the legal system."
(*Informal Logic Newsletter*, June 1979)

2. "The historian J. C. Beckett has argued that
the establishment of Northern Ireland was en-
tered into not 'because anyone wanted it locally,
but because the British Government believed
that it was the only way of reconciling the various interests.' Indeed, given the centuries of
dispute between the Catholics and the Protestants partition did appear inevitable and at least
it was a pragmatic recognition that two variants
of Irish nationalism existed and had to be ac-
commodated."

(Caroline Kennedy-Pipe, *The Origins of the Present Troubles in Northern Ireland* [London: Longman 1997], p. 21)

*3. *Background:* In December 1982, Pierre Trudeau was prime minister of Canada. His government was subjected to extensive criticism, especially because the Canadian economy was quite weak and unemployment was high. Some urged that Trudeau should resign so that his Liberal Party could select a new leader. Others said an election should be called. Trudeau replied:

"People don't change doctors just because they're sick. Particularly if the other doctor down the street is, you know, dropping his pills and breaking his thermometer and he doesn't know what to do."

(Reported in the Toronto *Globe and Mail,* December 21, 1982)

Hint: Assume that Trudeau's conclusion was that the people should not change the prime minister just because the economy was poor.

4. *Background:* The following passage is taken from David Hume's "Dialogues Concerning Natural Religion." In these dialogues, many different analogies are explored as alternative devices for reasoning about gods and the supernatural realm:

"The Brahmins assert that the world arose from an infinite spider, who spun this whole complicated mass from his bowels, and annihilates afterwards the whole or any part of it, by absorbing it again and resolving it into his own essence. Here is a species of cosmogony which appears to us ridiculous because a spider is a little contemptible animal whose operations we are never likely to take for a model of the whole universe. But still, here is a new species of analogy, even in our globe. And were there a planet wholly inhabited by spiders (which is very possible), this inference would then appear as natural and irrefragable as that which in our planet ascribes the origin of all things to design by an orderly system and intelligence. . . . Why an orderly system may not be spun from the belly

as well as from the brain, it will be difficult for him to give a satisfactory reason."

(David Hume, "Dialogues Concerning Natural Religion" in *The Empiricists* [New York: Anchor Press, 1974])

Hint: Assume Hume is comparing reasoning about creation in a world inhabited dominantly by people with reasoning about creation in a world inhabited by spiders.

5. *Background:* The seventeenth-century philosopher Rene Descartes advocated a method of doubt. To build up a system of knowledge, he said, one should begin by doubting all his or her previous beliefs. Some critics objected to this method of doubt, saying that it was unrealistic and extreme. Defending it, Descartes said the following:

"Suppose that a man had a basket of apples, and fearing that some of them were rotten, wanted to take those out lest they might make the rest go bad, how could he do that? Would he not first turn the whole of the apples out of the basket, and look them over one by one, and then having selected those which he saw not to be rotten, place them again in the basket and leave out all the others?"

(Quoted in Anthony Kenny, *Descartes: A Study of His Philosophy* [New York: Random House, 1968], pp. 18–19)

*6. *Background:* The following passage is taken from Howard Gardner, *Multiple Intelligences: The Theory in Practice* (New York: Basic Books, 1993), p. 121.

"In most Western cultures, the task of learning the notational systems is carried out in the relatively decontextualized setting of schools. Many students cannot connect their more commonsense knowledge to cognate concepts presented in a school context. To take one well-known example, when a group of students was presented the problem of how many buses would be required to transport 1,128 soldiers if each bus held thirty-six soldiers, most replied "thirty-one, remainder twelve." These students correctly applied the appropriate arithmetic operation, but without regard for the meaning of their answer."

*7.   *Background:* The following letter appeared in the Calgary *Herald* on March 29, 1999, in response to an article that had criticized teachers.

" 'All lawyers are crooks.' 'Police officers race to line up at the local Tim Horton's (a donut shop).' 'City workers lean on a shovel.' These are all generalizations that rank right up there with Biesbroek's uneducated stereotype of teachers as 'self-absorbed individuals who enjoy telling classes their own opinions and who relish the idea of having the control.' "

8.   *Background:* The following appeared in the *Globe and Mail* for May 27, 1999, as a comment on an article reporting that the Canadian government was going to allow payment for donated sperm:

"If the federal government thinks men should be paid for donating their sperm to reproductive clinics, it should also demand that women be paid for their eggs. If one sex makes money from its genetic material, then the other sex should also be able to. To do otherwise would be to violate the non-discrimination clause in the Charter of Rights and Freedoms as well as the Canadian Human Rights Act. Better still, neither of them should be paid. . . . What appears to be lost in this matter is concern for the children produced by new reproductive and genetic technologies. They have the right to be treated with dignity, not simply as transferred property."

9.   "Suppose that by paying 250 dollars you could go into the largest and most exclusive department store in town and pick out and take home anything you could carry away with you. You would have access to the finest silks, precious jewels, handworked bracelets of gold and platinum, fabulous clothes by the best designers in the world. It would be foolish to the point of imbecility if you paid your money, walked in, and picked out a piece of bubble gum. Well, that's what many college students do, in effect. They pay a nominal amount of money, and by doing so they gain access to some of the greatest treasures of the intellect in the world. Merely by asking, they can discover things that people labored for years to find out. Just by going to class, they can receive the outcome of years of thought and effort of the most outstanding thinkers and scientists the human race has produced. Do they take advantage of this? Often they do not. They merely want to know which courses are the easiest ones, which don't have to be taken, and what are the minimum requirements for graduation. For their money they are offered a fortune, but they choose a piece of mental bubble gum."
(Ronald Munson in *The Way of Words: An Informal Logic* [Boston: Houghton Mifflin, 1976], p. 357)

10.   Responding to violence with more violence is like trying to put out a fire by adding matches. Matches can set off a fire, and when added to a fire, they will only make it burn more intensely. To put out a fire, we need to smother it or pour water on it. That is, we need something different from what's making the fire burn in the first place. And in just the same way, we can't stop violence by replying with more violence. Thus, the way to stop terrorism is not to launch attacks on countries such as Serbia and Sierra Leone, but rather to inject a genuinely new element into the situation. That element is a real desire to work out the underlying political problems that keep terrorism alive.

11.   The human mind has different parts or aspects. Some of these are superior to others. For instance, we have biological drives for food, water, sleep, and sex. We have emotions of fear, anger, hatred, and love. And we have an intellect that can reason. It is the intellect that should dominate in the mind, for this is the superior part of humankind. And similarly, there are different sorts of people in a society. Just as a mind will be disturbed if it is ruled by biological drives, or by emotions unguided by intellect, so society will suffer if it is not controlled by its superior people.
(Adapted from Plato's *Republic*)

*12.   *Background:* The following passage is taken from Amitai Etzioni, *The New Golden Rule* (New York: Basic Books, 1996), p. 129.

"New communities are often limited in scope and reach. Members of one residential community are often also members of other communities—for example, work, ethnic, or religious ones. As a result community members have multiple sources of attachments, and if one threatens to become overwhelming, individuals will tend to draw more on another community for their attachments."

13.   "Smokers should be allowed to smoke only in private where it does not offend anyone else. Would any smoker walk into a restaurant and start eating half-chewed food on someone's plate, or drink a glass of water that previously held someone's teeth? Probably not, yet they expect non-smokers to inhale smoke from the recesses of their lungs. My privilege and right is to choose a clean and healthy life without interference."

(P. T. B., *Cape Town Argus,* quoted in *World Press Review,* January 1988, p. 2)

14.   "We have created a technology to facilitate information transfer, but the end result, ironically, seems to be the opposite. The information overload is jamming our circuitry and paralyzing our ability to communicate meaningfully and to even think about questions that really matter. The tail is really wagging the dog. I still have a few optimistic neurons left, however, and believe that we can address the less desirable aspects of information technology while continuing to enjoy the good parts. The key is to encourage the rigorous teaching of critical thinking in school, beginning as early as Grade 6 or 7, when children begin to think abstractly."

(Letter to the Toronto *Globe and Mail* about information overload, April 2, 1999)

15.   *Background:* This argument deals with the issue of rights over territory acquired by conquest. It was formulated by philosopher John Locke in the eighteenth century.

"That the aggressor, who puts himself into the state of war with another, and unjustly invades another man's right, can, by such an unjust war, never come to have a right over the conquered, will be easily agreed by all men, who will not think that robbers and pirates have a right of empire over whomsoever they have force enough to master, or that men are bound by promises which unlawful force extorts from them. Should a robber break into my house, and, with a dagger at my throat, make me seal a deed to convey my estate to him, would this give him any title? Just such a title by his sword has an unjust conqueror who forces me into submission."

(John Locke, "Of Civil Government" quoted in S. F. Barker, *Elements of Logic.*)

Hint: In the last sentence Locke is saying that an unjust conqueror has a title which is similar to that of a robber who forces someone, at dagger-point, to hand over his estate.

Inductive Analogies

We have now examined a number of *a priori* analogies and arguments based on them. Such arguments support a decision to classify a case in one way or another, or treat an action or argument as good or as poor. But analogies are used as a basis for predictions as well as for decisions. An *a priori* analogy is used to support a decision to treat relevantly similar cases in the same way—logically, morally, legally, or administratively. An inductive analogy provides a basis for prediction: we know that the analogue has certain characteristics, and because the primary subject resembles it in these aspects, we estimate or predict that the primary subject will resemble it in a further related aspect as well.

As we have seen in some of the examples considered, the analogue in an *a priori* analogy is often merely an imagined case. It need not be a real case. In an inductive analogy, however, the analogue must be something that now exists or previously did exist. The factual, empirical properties of the analogue and the primary subject are essential to the way the analogy works.

We often need to make estimations about things that we are not in a position to observe—because they are in the future or in the past, or because there are moral or practical reasons against examining them directly. In such contexts, inductive analogies are important and useful: if we cannot examine A, but we can examine B, and if A is like B in many respects, then, given that B has characteristic x, we estimate or predict that A will have characteristic x. This is reasoning by inductive analogy.

Inductive analogies would not be necessary if we had general laws covering the unknown phenomena. Suppose, for instance, that we need to know whether human beings are adversely affected by toxic emissions from gas flaring, to properly respond to criticisms of practices within the petroleum industry. If we knew that all mammals are adversely affected by the flarings, our problem would be easily solved by a syllogism:

1. All mammals are adversely affected by flarings.
2. All humans are mammals.
Therefore,
3. All humans are adversely affected by flarings.

But we do not know the first premise in this argument to be true. Nor would it be morally or legally permissible to experiment directly on humans to see how they react to exposure to smoke from fires burning off excess materials in the wake of oil and gas extraction. One standard approach in such cases is to reason by analogy: inductive analogy. We might study the effects of the substances on nonhuman animals and then predict what it will be in the case of humans. We will then argue like this:

1. Rats (or some other nonhuman animals) are like humans in respects 1, 2, 3, ...
2. Rats suffer effects x, y, z, when exposed to doses at such-and-such levels of these substances.
3. A dose at so-and-so level in humans is equivalent to a dose at such-and-such levels in rats.
Therefore,
4. Humans will suffer effects x, y, and z when exposed to a dose at so-and-so level of these substances.

In this analogy, the primary subject is human beings and the analogue is rats. The two are being compared with respect to their reactions to exposure to the relevant substances. This inductive analogy differs from *a priori* analogy in a significant respect: the analogue must describe an actual thing and give factual information about it. An inductive analogy is based on information gained from human experience. The conclusion in an inductive analogy cannot be known with complete certainty, but as a basis for prediction, close comparison with a similar case or cases is much better than no information at all.[11]

Inductive analogies are important, and they are a common way of reasoning about human affairs. We use them in simple, practical decision making. For instance, suppose you have twice bought a certain brand of bathing suit, finding that a particular size fits comfortably, that the material wears well, and that the suit is good for active swimming. When shopping again, you may look for the same brand name. You are, in effect, reasoning by inductive analogy: you know the first two suits were a good buy and you infer that the third will be similar to them in its fit, comfort, and so on. Here you are inclined to attribute the good qualities to the manufacturer, so there is a reason for linking the similarities.

Here is an example of a more complex inductive analogy. It is taken from an interview with the American intellectual Noam Chomsky.

> When I'm driving, I sometimes turn on the radio and find that I'm listening to a discussion about sports. People call in and have long and intricate conversations with a high degree of thought and analysis. They know all sorts of complicated details and have far-reaching discussions about whether the coach made the right decisions yesterday and so on. They don't defer to sports experts; they have their own opinions and speak with confidence. These are ordinary people, not professionals, who are applying their intelligence and analytic skills in these areas and accumulating quite a lot of knowledge. On the other hand, when I hear people talk about, say, international affairs or domestic problems, it's at a level of superficiality that is beyond belief. I don't think that international or domestic affairs are much more complicated than sports. And what passes for serious intellectual discourse on these matters does not reflect any deeper level of understanding or knowledge. . . . It does not require extraordinary skill or understanding to take apart the illusions and deception that prevent understanding of contemporary reality. It requires the kind of normal skepticism and willingness to apply one's analytic skills that almost all people have. It just happens that people tend to exercise them in analyzing what, say, the New England Patriots ought to do next Sunday instead of questions that really matter.[12]

Chomsky argues that people are capable of understanding sports and discussing issues of sports in a complex way; therefore, they are probably also capable of understanding political issues and discussing them in a complex way. He attributes the fact that they do not do so to lack of interest, not to lack of ability. (Whether Chomsky is correct in his assumption that political issues are no more complex than sports is debatable. The point here is that Chomsky's argument is an inductive analogy; we are not saying whether it is a cogent argument.) Interestingly, this inductive analogy begins by noting a major difference between discussions of sports and discussions of political policy. The former are carried out with skill; the latter are "superficial beyond belief." The analogy Chomsky appeals to is based on a similarity: the fact that people's capacity for knowledge, analysis, and independent thinking should be the same in both cases.

Within the very sorts of political debates to which Chomsky is referring, inductive analogies are commonly used. Often a past event comes to be a kind of model for a present or future one. When Saddam Hussein of Iraq invaded and then claimed to annex Kuwait in the summer of 1990, many people were reminded of Hitler's annexation of Austria in 1938. Hitler was not stopped right away, and he went on in the next several years to invade Czechoslovakia, Poland, Holland, Belgium, France, and the Soviet Union. Hussein seemed similar to Hitler in running a ruthless government that had engaged in brutality against its own citizens and in being willing to go against moral standards and agreements by the international community. The obvious conclusion of this inductive analogy seemed to be that Hussein should be stopped immediately. This conclusion formed the basis for a United Nations Security Council resolution and the deployment of more than 500,000 U.S. troops in Saudi Arabia and nearby areas.

In 1982, many people opposed U.S. government policy in El Salvador on the grounds of similarities between what was happening there and what happened in Vietnam in the early 1960s. For the Americans considering this analogy, the Vietnam saga was over and—in most people's opinion—American intervention in Vietnam had been a disastrous failure. By pointing out what they regarded as crucial similarities between the Vietnam situation and circumstances in El Salvador, critics predicted failure for the U.S. efforts there also, under the slogan "Not Another Vietnam." The events of Vietnam were known; those of El Salvador were yet to come. Hence the need to use the analogy.

We assess inductive analogies in basically the same way we assess other analogies—that is, by evaluating the significance of relevant similarities and differences between the primary subject and the analogue. With any analogy it is important to reflect on the primary subject and the analogue and try to gain a sense for how the analogy is supposed to work. Often people argue by analogy without ever spelling out the details, and no one takes the time to reflect carefully on the various respects in which the analogue and the primary subject are similar and different. To evaluate any analogy, we should first consider all the relevant similarities and see how they may support the conclusion. We then consider all the relevant differences and consider the extent to which they may undermine the argument. In these respects, evaluating inductive analogies is similar to evaluating *a priori* analogies.

However, some aspects of inductive analogies make their evaluation different. The most obvious of these is that in the inductive analogy, the analogue must describe something real, and the facts cited must be genuine. Imaginary examples are fine for *a priori* analogies, but not for inductive ones. The similarities on which inductive analogies are based are between empirical aspects of the primary subject and the analogue. We cannot determine the extent of the similarity merely by reflecting on structural features, as we can for *a priori* analogies. Our actual experience is our basis for predicting what is likely to happen.

Another significant fact about inductive analogies is that similarities cumulate in an important way. In an *a priori* analogy, what is important is that the similarities relevant to the conclusion hold. If they do, it does not matter whether there are many further similarities or none at all. But in the inductive analogy, the sheer number of similarities does matter. The closer the two cases are, in detail, the more likely it is that the inferred conclusion will be true. This means that the evaluation of inductive analogies depends more on factual background knowledge than does the evaluation of *a priori* analogies. If you do not know the background facts about Hitler and Hussein or about Vietnam and the most current issue regarding military intervention, you will have to do research before you can properly estimate the strength of these analogies.

It is also important that the features cited in the analogies are relevant to the feature predicted in the conclusion; there must be some general basis for thinking that these features and the feature specified in the conclusion are connected to each other. In the simple case of the bathing suits, for instance, the fit, fabric, and design are the responsibility of the manufacturer; hence it is reasonable to expect that a third suit, made by the same manufacturer, will be similar to the first two in these respects. In the case of rats and people, the existence of common underlying physiological traits makes it reasonable to do preliminary experiments on rats when testing drugs intended for people.

To evaluate arguments based on inductive analogy, we first identify the primary subject and the analogue, just as we did for *a priori* analogies. Then, as before, we apply the ARG conditions. At this stage, the difference between *a priori* analogy and inductive analogy becomes significant for our evaluation of arguments. In an inductive analogy, the analogue is a real thing—not a case simply imagined or hypothesized by the arguer. Thus, when we check the premises for acceptability, it is very important to see whether the analogue is accurately described. For example, if someone is using information about two bathing suits to reason to a conclusion about a further suit, it is important that her beliefs about the first suit are correct. (If she thought mistakenly that she had a size 10 and reasoned that since it fit, another 10 would fit, the analogy would likely give a false prediction.)

To determine the relevance of the similarities that exist between the primary subject and the analogue, we have to look closely at the conclusion asserted and reflect on how the features that are similar are related to that conclusion. For instance, suppose a student were to reason by inductive analogy that because Smith is a good instructor in a music course, she will also be a good instructor in an English course. A full evaluation of the relevance of the analogy will require critical thought that goes beyond what is explicitly stated in the premises. To evaluate his argument, he would have to ask himself some questions. In what respects is the primary subject (the instructor's performance in the English course) similar to the analogue (his performance in the music course)? How relevant are those respects to the conclusion—that is, how are they likely to be connected to the property predicted in the conclusion? Class size and subject matter are relevant because there is general reason to suppose that they have some effect on the quality of instruction. The location of the class on one side of the campus or the other is probably irrelevant (why should this affect instruction?). But the talents and qualifications of the instructor will be relevant, and even size and seating layout of the classroom could be relevant.

Some instructors who excel at conducting seminars and are only mediocre at straight lecturing may perform much better in a room with a seminar table or chairs in a circle.

In inductive analogies, our judgments about the relevance of similarities and differences between cases are not made by pure reflection, as they are for *a priori* analogies. Rather, they are made with reference to our background knowledge about how the various properties of things are empirically connected.

If the similarities between the analogue and the primary case are relevant to the property predicted in the conclusion, we still need to see whether they are sufficient to provide good grounds for that conclusion. To determine whether they are sufficient, we reflect on differences that may exist between the primary subject and the analogue. There are bound to be some differences. Here, as with *a priori* analogies, the issue is whether those differences are negatively relevant to the conclusion. The inductive analogy, as explicitly stated in an argument, typically will not mention differences. Like other analogies, it urges us to think of the similarities between the cases compared. We have to think of these differences ourselves to appraise the analogy.

With inductive analogies, finding the differences and determining how relevant they are requires background knowledge. A senior interdisciplinary course is different from a junior philosophy course in that the former will require both a greater breadth of knowledge and a greater ability to respond to complex questions. These differences between the primary subject and the analogue are negatively relevant to the prediction that an instructor who is good in one course will be good in the other. The courses require different knowledge bases and different talents. Thus the differences between the courses tend to undermine the force of the inductive analogy.

When we make such judgments about the cogency of inductive analogies, it is important to note the degree of certainty with which the conclusion is asserted. A student who concluded "Smith is sure to be good as an English instructor because she was terrific as a music instructor" has a different argument from one who asserts "There is some reason to think Smith will be good so far as lecturing in the English course is concerned, because she was terrific as a lecturer in that music course." The second student has a conclusion that is more tentative ("some reason to think" as opposed to "is sure to be") and that is restricted to one aspect of competence: lecturing skill. Since the second argument is already sensitive to the limitations of the inductive analogy, it is less vulnerable to criticism than the first.

EXERCISE SET

Exercise 2

Some of the following passages contain arguments based on inductive analogies. Identify these arguments, and specify the primary subject, the analogue, and relevant similarities and differences between them. Then assess the strength of the inductive analogy as a basis for the conclusion. If the passage does not contain an inductive analogy, comment briefly about what sort of passage it is. Does it contain no argument at all? Or another kind of argument? Or an *a priori* analogy?

1. Studying French without ever speaking the language does not result in a good command of French. Latin is a language too, so studying Latin without ever speaking it will not result in a good command of Latin.

2. In the civil service, people are spending other people's money. Civil servants do not have to earn the money they spend; it is given to them by the government, which raises it from tax dollars. That makes civil servants careless about their expenditures. Universities are like the civil service. Their administrations do not have to earn the money spent. It comes from the government. Therefore, we can expect university administrators to spend money carelessly.

3. A watch could not assemble itself. The complex arrangement of parts into a working watch is possible only because there is a craftsman who designs and constructs the watch. In just the same way, the complicated parts of the world could not arrange themselves into the natural order. So there must be a designer of the world, and that is God.

4. "Zimbabwean ostrich producers may be selling the future of their industry by exporting too many birds. But the money is hard to resist. Europeans and North Americans trying to build their own ostrich industries will pay between 20,000 dollars and 60,000 dollars for a pair. To protect the domestic industry, Zimbabwe had banned the export of live ostriches in 1991. But the ban was lifted this year due to pressure from producers and because Botswana and Namibia have continued to export live birds and eggs. Although they are reaping the profits, some Zimbabwean ostrich farmers fear that the Northern market for meat, hide, and feathers

will dry up now that other countries have built their flocks to meet the demand."
(*World Press Review*, August 1994)

*5. "A majority taken collectively is only an individual whose opinions, and frequently whose interests, are opposed to those of another individual, who is styled a minority. If it be admitted that a man possessing absolute power may misuse that power by wronging his adversaries, why should not a majority be liable to the same reproach? Men do not change their characters by uniting with each other; nor does their patience in the presence of obstacles increase with their strength. For my own part, I cannot believe it; the power to do everything, which I should refuse to one of my equals, I will never grant to any number of them."
(Alexis de Tocqueville, "Democracy in America," quoted in S. F. Barker, *The Elements of Logic*, 3rd ed. [New York: McGraw-Hill, 1980])

6. Slavery was a human institution that existed for thousands of years. Now, slavery is largely eliminated. Morally dedicated citizens in religious and public action groups brought about the end of slavery, even though it was taken for granted as a natural fact of human existence. War, similarly, is a human institution that is taken for granted and that has existed for thousands of years. Morally dedicated citizens in a wide variety of groups, including many that have a religious basis, are working for the elimination of war. And the example of slavery shows that they can succeed.

*7. *Background:* The following is the first part of an advertisement by Foster Parents Plan. The advertisement appeared in *Harper's* magazine in May 1990.

"Here's your chance to achieve a small moral victory. What would you do if you saw a lost, frightened child? You'd probably stop, pick him up, brush away his tears, and help him find his way. Without even thinking about it. And there's a reason. You know what's right. And right now, you can do just that. You can act on instinct . . . by reaching out to one desperately poor child, thousands of miles away. With your personal caring and help. Through Foster Parents Plan, you'll be helping a child who almost never has enough to eat. A decent place to sleep. Medical care. The chance to learn. Or hope. . . . If you saw a helpless child on the street, you wouldn't wait. You'd help that instant. Please don't wait now, either. Achieve a small moral victory!"

*8.   *Background:* This argument was used by Bud Greenspan who sought to show that sports officials cannot be expected to be perfect in their judgment and that it is unrealistic and counterproductive to check their expertise against video replays of the actions they judge.

"Athletes are human. So are officials. If we cannot expect perfection from the performers, how can we expect more from those who officiate? The structure of sports is based on the premise that all one can ask of an athlete is that he or she be dedicated, prepared, talented, and courageous. Can anyone doubt that these qualifications do not hold true for officials?"

(Quoted in Gary Gumpert, *Talking Tombstones and Other Tales of the Media Age* [New York: Oxford University Press, 1987], p. 63)

9.   *Background:* The following passage is taken from Howard Gardner, *Multiple Intelligence: The Theory in Practice* (New York: Basic Books, 1993), p. 31.

"Assessment, then, becomes a central feature of an educational system. We believe that it is essential to depart from standardized testing. We also believe that standard pencil-and-paper short-answer tests sample only a small proportion of intellectual abilities and often reward a certain kind of decontextualized facility. The means of assessment we favor should ultimately search for genuine problem-solving or product-fashioning skills in individuals across a range of materials."

10.   *Background:* The following was a letter on the topic of preserving rain forests.

"The one kind of argument I do not seem to be hearing is one that I believe deserves to be heard when forest policy is being made. That is: Some (a few) of our most ancient and least

disturbed forests in North America are biological communities of living things that have been accumulating and developing almost since the period of our last glacial age, nearly 15,000 years ago. These most ancient communities of living and growing things have been residents of this continent for so much longer than any of us humans that we should consider it our duty to avoid wrecking and pillaging them, simply as the deference owed by very much younger things to those who have lived and sheltered other life and fed nature's multitudes for ages."

(P. H., San Francisco, printed in *World Press Review,* December 1989, p. 2)

Hint: Is this an inductive analogy?

*11.   *Background:* This example is from Arthur Schopenhauer's *The Art of Literature* advocates independent thinking.

"Everyone who really thinks for himself is like a monarch. His position is undelegated and supreme. His judgments, like royal decrees, spring from his own sovereign power and proceed directly from himself. He acknowledges authority as little as a monarch admits a command. He subscribes to nothing but what he has himself authorized. The multitude of common minds, laboring under all sorts of current opinions, authorities, prejudices, is like the people, which silently obeys the law and accepts orders from above."

(Arthur Schopenhauer, *The Art of Literature,* trans. T. Bailey Saunders [Ann Arbor: University of Michigan Press, 1960])

12.   *Background:* The nineteenth-century philosopher Jeremy Bentham wrote primarily about ethics and politics. However, he also wrote a work called *Handbook of Political Fallacies,* in which he set out a number of arguments common in political life and maintained they were fallacious. (Bentham is dealing with the argument—common in his day, apparently—that those who criticize dishonesty in a particular government are seeking to undermine government in general.) This passage is taken from that work:

"In producing a local or temporary debility in the action of the powers of the natural body, in many cases, the honest and skillful physician beholds the only means of curing it; and it would be as reasonable to infer a wish to see the patient perish, from the act of the physician in prescribing a drug, as to infer a wish to see the whole frame of government destroyed or rendered worse, from the act of a statesman who lowers the reputation of an official whom he regards as unfit."

(J. Bentham, *Handbook of Political Fallacies*, rev. and ed. Harold Larrabee [New York: Thomas Y. Crowell, 1971])

*13.   The following item appeared in the Toronto *Globe and Mail* for September 7, 1998:

"In 1960, when a family boat capsized, Roger Woodward of Alabama became the only person to be swept by accident over Niagara Falls and live. He tells Newhouse News: 'I was only seven years old, no one was coming to rescue me, and I knew I was going to die. Your life really does pass before your eyes. I thought about my family, how they were going to miss me. I thought about my dog. I thought about my friends. . . . The water is much calmer before you hit the falls. I guess I suffered vertigo. It was like I was in a cloud . . . . All I remember was that everything went dark. I don't remember hitting, being forced under.' *The Maid of the Mist II* threw the boy a lifeline and he was taken to a Canadian hospital with a minor head injury."

14.   "Suppose that someone tells me that he has had a tooth extracted without an anaesthetic, and I express my sympathy, and suppose that I am then asked, 'How do you know that it hurt him?' I might reasonably reply, 'Well I know that it would hurt me. I have been to the dentist and know how painful it is to have a tooth stopped without an anaesthetic, let alone taken out. And he has the same sort of nervous system as I have. I infer, therefore, that in these conditions he felt considerable pain, just as I should myself.'"

(Alfred J. Ayer, "One's Knowledge of Other Minds," *Theoria*, Vol. 19, 1953; cited by Irving Copi in *Introduction to Logic*, 6th ed. [New York: Macmillan, 1982], p. 394)

15.   *Background:* The following appeared in a column by Naomi Lakritz, in the Calgary *Herald* for September 29, 1998. The columnist favors the proposal to protect taxi drivers by installing a Plexiglass safety shield between the back and front seats of their cabs.

"Do you remember your mother telling you when you first got your driver's licence, that you should never pick up strangers? Well, your mother was right. Cab drivers pick up strangers every day, so it's no wonder they get robbed, beaten up, stabbed and occasionally shot. Sometimes, they're lucky to escape with their lives. Other times, they're not so lucky. But if there's one thing more certain than that Calgary's cabbies will be assaulted, it is that the issue of their safety will likely go nowhere. . . . If any other job came with such occupational hazards, you can bet one incident would be enough. There would be inquests and inquiries, industry regulation and guidelines for safety put in place. Assaults on cabbies are nothing new, yet the dithering over safety goes on. . . . The shields should remain voluntary, but the city really ought to jump in and share costs with the cab companies in a plan to help subsidize them for taxi drivers who want the extra protection."

Further Critical Strategies

An interesting critical strategy that can be applied both to *a priori* analogies and to inductive analogies is that of working out a different analogy that suggests a conclusion contrary to the one in the argument you are examining. This is the technique of **counteranalogy**. When an analogy is drawn, you start to think of the primary subject in a framework suggested by the analogue. In doing so, you begin to transfer concepts and beliefs from the analogue to the primary subject. This analogue will always be one of a number of different possible ones. Adopting an alternative and setting out to conceive the primary subject in terms of that alternative is likely to bring fresh insights and new conclusions.

For instance, we might undermine the comparison between travel and reading, mentioned earlier as a possible basis for urging governments to subsidize travel, by a counteranalogy, comparing travel with play. The counteranalogy will tend to support the conclusion that governments should not subsidize travel, because we do not tend to assume that the government should financially support people for play and leisure. If the conclusions suggested by the counteranalogy are incompatible with those suggested by the original analogue, and the counteranalogy is just as apt as the original, the original analogy is undermined.

This technique of counteranalogies was used to great effect by the philosopher David Hume in his famous "Dialogues Concerning Natural Religion." The "Dialogues" offer a prolonged critical appraisal of one especially famous and important inductive analogy: the argument that because the world is made of organized interconnected parts, like a machine, it must, like a machine, have been designed by an intelligent being. (This argument for God's existence is ordinarily referred to as the Argument from Design.) Hume pointed out that the model of the world as a machine is only one of a great number of possible models, and that other models suggest radically different theological conclusions.[13] He did this in many ways, but one of his most striking strategies was to set forth a number of counteranalogies.

Here is a passage in which Hume employed the technique of counteranalogy:

> Now if we survey the universe, so far as it falls under our knowledge, it bears a great resemblance to an animal or organized body, and seems actuated with a like principle of life and motion. A continual circulation of matter in it produces no disorder; a continual waste in every part is incessantly repaired; the closest sympathy is perceived throughout the entire system; and each part or member, in performing its proper offices, operates both to its own preservation and to that of the whole. The world, therefore, I infer, is an animal, and the Deity is the soul of the world, actuating it, and actuated by it.[14]

In this passage, Hume is saying that you could prove a deity that is understood to be the soul of the world just as well as you could prove a deity who is understood as being an external creator of the world. In effect, neither of these incompatible conclusions is more plausibly supported by analogy than the other. Thus Hume seeks to criticize the machine analogy that supports the Argument from Design. He states his criticism by pointing out that an animal analogy seems just as appropriate as the machine analogy. As stated by Hume, the animal analogy is used to argue for a deity that is located within the world and is a kind of soul of the world. The Argument from Design, which Hume is criticizing, is itself an inductive analogy. Hume constructs an implausible analogue to show that that primary argument is flawed, using the technique of refutation by logical analogy. Hume's argument can be set out as follows:

ANALOGUE

The world is like an animal and must have a soul like an animal. Therefore, there is a deity who is the soul of the world.
   is a possible way of thinking of the world
   highlights some significant features of the world
   leads to a conclusion nobody should take seriously

PRIMARY SUBJECT

The world is like a machine and must have an inventor like a machine. Therefore, there is a deity who is the inventor (creator) of the world.
   is a possible way of thinking of the world
   highlights some significant features of the world

CONCLUSION

The argument that because the world is like a machine it must have an intelligent inventor or creator has a conclusion that nobody should take seriously.

By showing that there are different analogies that seem equally plausible when we try to think of the world as a whole, Hume was pointing out that our experience does not indicate which one of these analogies is the most appropriate one. If we choose to think of the world only as a machine, then, because machines have intelligent designers, we will think that the world must have had an intelligent designer. On the other hand, if we think of the world as an animal we may reach different conclusions. We may conclude that God, or the Deity, is the soul of that animal.[15] Hume's point was that if we find this second conclusion ridiculous—as most religious believers surely would—we should give no more credence to the first conclusion, that the world has a designer. The unpopular argument (that the world comes from sexual generation) is every bit as sensible as the other (that the world was intelligently designed, the way machines are). The two arguments are structurally parallel and, Hume claims, of equal merit. So if one is not cogent, the other isn't either.

An analogy might be thought of as a special sort of screen or filter. (Note the analogy!) Using an analogy, whether in an argument or in an explanation, or merely as a literary device, encourages us to focus on certain aspects of the primary subject—those that are similar to the analogue. An analogy is often said to highlight these aspects. Analogies can be helpful in creative and critical thought when they highlight important features that we might not have attended to before. However, they can also be misleading, in that features not highlighted may also be significant as well. Using different analogies emphasizes different features. Thinking of alternatives can be a liberating and creative experience, especially when language and thought are dominated by one particular analogy.

Thought and language are often dominated by models that we take for granted to such an extent that we do not even realize they are models. We adapt a language from one sort of thing and use it to think and talk about another. In doing so, we may export beliefs and assumptions from one area of knowledge to another, often in an uncritical way. Using a new model may reveal that these assumptions need to be questioned. A new model will sometimes suggest fresh ideas and insights. Thus new analogies can be more than counteranalogies. They may suggest original ways of thinking and talking and new projects and strategies for research.

As a matter of fact, it has been pointed out that our culture and language employ a kind of deep metaphor or analogy that is about argument itself. Argument is assimilated in much of our language to battle or war. Just as people may defend territory in a war, they are said to defend positions in an argument. They may ward off attacks, have opponents, stake out positions, make counterattacks, achieve victories, retreat from positions when attacked, win and lose in debates, and so on. Perhaps we would have a different understanding of argument if we thought of alternative deep metaphors, or models. It is hard to imagine what such metaphors might be because the terminology of attack and defense is deeply ingrained in our language. But there are other models. We might think of persons arguing as negotiators trying to work out a resolution to a common problem, as dancers forming a pleasing pattern, or as quilters making a new design from many individual contributions.[16] If such alternative analogies were explored seriously, new questions about arguments would no doubt arise, and some things like winning an argument or having an opponent when you argue would cease to seem as important as they now do.

Loose and Misleading Analogies

As mentioned earlier, we have developed our treatment of analogy in such a way as to emphasize its serious cognitive uses. On the whole, the arguments from analogy used to illustrate points have been cogent ones. But this should not be taken as an indication that all arguments from analogy are cogent arguments. Many arguments from analogy are quite dreadful, and analogies can be seriously misleading. Now that we have seen how analogies can be important, cogent, and useful, we'll explore some common misuses of analogy.

The Fallacy of Faulty Analogy

Certainly many arguments by analogy are poor; in fact, the special fallacy label **faulty analogy** was invented to describe such cases. Sometimes the analogies on which arguments are based are so loose and far-fetched that it is impossible even to classify them as *a priori* or inductive. It seems as though a gross image of a primary subject is given by the analogue and the unwary audience is supposed to be lulled into a conclusion. Such loose uses of analogy are often discussed as instances of the fallacy of faulty analogy. They involve an appeal to similarities that are highly superficial and give no real support to the conclusion sought.

Here is an example of a grossly flawed argument by analogy. It is taken from a letter to the editor in which the writer urged that the city of Calgary not develop a new subdivision that was proposed to provide housing for 50,000 people:

> Once a pleasant and friendly lady of the foothills, Calgary has become an obese, 200 pound dame and naturally suffers from all the diseases inherent to the distended community: smog breath, body odors, high traffic blood pressure, glandular dollarities, and skin blemishes such as high rises, towers, skyscrapers, and malls. . . . It would be well to consider if this continual expansion of Alberta cities is really needed or just a competitive show-off.[17]

Here the writer uses the analogue of an obese dame to dispute the wisdom of extending the city. He draws out the image in some detail. But it would be hard to take it seriously, either as an *a priori* analogy or as an inductive one. There is no serious demand for consistency between our attitudes toward obesity in people and size in cities! There is no norm of healthy size for cities, nor is there any inductive basis for predicting that the poor health a person is likely to experience as a result of gross obesity will somehow emerge in parallel for a city that undergoes expansion. The notion of "health problems" would be quite dubious in its application to a city. The analogy thus provides no support for the author's stance on the proposed subdivision. It gives him an entertaining and vivid way of stating his point but provides no rational support for it. As far as careful reasoning about the subdivision is concerned, the analogy is simply a distraction.

Loose analogies can be particularly deceptive when the analogue is something toward which people have very strong or settled attitudes. These attitudes carry over too easily to the primary subject, even though there is no significant similarity between it and the analogue. You can see this transfer happening in the following argument, which was put forward in the seventeenth century by essayist Francis Bacon:

> Nobody can be healthy without exercise, neither natural body nor politic; and certainly to a kingdom or estate, a just and honourable war is true exercise. A civil war, indeed, is like the heat of a fever, but a fever of war is like the heat of exercise, and serveth to keep the body in health; for in slothful peace, both courage will effeminate and manners corrupt.[18]

How is the analogue similar to the primary subject? What, precisely, do they have in common? Do these common features have anything to do with the conclusion reached about the primary subject? Do they give sufficient grounds to support that conclusion? Many analogies between the body and the state are so loose that they cannot support specific conclusions.

It is obvious and well known that the healthy human body requires exercise. Bacon exploits this common knowledge to try to show that the political organism also needs exercise, and he then contends that war constitutes this exercise. However, there is at best a loose similarity between the primary subject and the analogue in this case; again, there is no clear standard of health for the primary subject, the state. Furthermore, even if we were to grant that a state or kingdom does need exercise, it is surely not clear that war would be the best form such exercise could take. Internal campaigns to eliminate poverty or pollution might be just as energetic and unslothful as war. These critical remarks are really quite obvious, but the danger is that because of the familiarity of the fact that human bodies do need exercise, and the difficulty of thinking about the state or kingdom as a whole without some analogy, one might believe that Bacon has established his point. Asking how the similarity alleged would function to establish the conclusion can expose the superficiality of the resemblance.

In addition to this kind of suggestive and loose use of analogy there are several more specific fallacies of reasoning that involve the misuse of analogy.

The Fallacy of Two Wrongs Make a Right

We have seen that there is a legitimate way of using analogies to push for consistency between relevantly similar cases. But a common type of argument, easily confused with legitimate consistency arguments, amounts to a fallacy of reasoning. This is the **fallacy of two wrongs make a right.** It is committed when a person tries to defend one thing that is allegedly wrong by pointing out that another thing that is wrong has been done or has been accepted. In doing so, he is in effect reasoning that since we have allowed some wrong, we should (to be consistent) permit more. The following example shows this kind of misuse of analogy. The context is a discussion of a rock concert. A reviewer had criticized the performers for using offensive language and for encouraging fantasies of sex and drug use in the audience. A young rock fan, writing to defend the concert, said:

> There's not a thing wrong with what Roth did in front of 15,000 people. After all, don't millions of people see worse stuff in front of the television every day?[19]

The writer draws an analogy between Roth's performance at the rock show and things that are shown on television. She is trying to reply to the suggestion that the performance is immoral by saying that it is not wrong because it is not worse than something else that is tolerated.

This argument illustrates the fallacy that two wrongs make a right. There is an appeal to consistency here. However, this sort of argument differs from cogent consistency arguments in a subtle but crucial way. The writer says that on television there is "worse stuff," thereby granting that some material on television is bad. If Roth's performance is similar in the respect of being tasteless, as she says it is, the correct conclusion to draw would be that Roth's performance is also bad. You should suspect that something has gone wrong when you note that this conclusion is just the opposite of the conclusion drawn for the analogue; the arguer thinks much material on television is pretty bad.

Two-wrongs arguments are common in areas where abuses are spread across many institutions, countries, persons, and contexts. If someone attacks one instance of the abuse, claiming that it is wrong and that reform is necessary, he is often criticized by those who use two-wrongs arguments. For instance, when Greenpeace campaigned against the killing of baby seals for pelts, many people pointed out that the killing of baby seals is by no means the only instance when humans treat animals cruelly. Animals raised and slaughtered for food are often very cruelly treated, and this cruelty is tolerated. Critics in effect demanded consistency from Greenpeace, asking, "If you tolerate slaughter for food, why criticize killing animals for their pelts?" This demand for consistency is fair enough. But it is a mistake to infer from the social toleration of killing animals for food (which, in the eyes of this critic is wrong) that killing animals for pelts (which, in involving the deliberate killing of animals by humans is similar) should not be criticized. If one practice is wrong and another is relevantly similar to it, then a correct appeal to consistency will imply that the other is wrong too. Two wrongs do not make one right. Two wrongs make two wrongs. There is no ethical or logical justification for multiplying wrongs in the name of consistency.

Consider two proposed actions: (a) and (b). If both are wrong, and similarly wrong, then the best thing would be to prevent both from occurring. Ideally, then, activist groups such as Greenpeace would work against the slaughter of animals for meat and against the seal hunt—granting that both involve unnecessary and wrongful cruelty to animals. But due to scarce resources and other factors, this may not be possible. If anything is to be done, some choice must be made. One of several wrongs will therefore have to be selected as the target of action. When this selection happens, critics may allege that the choice of targets is inappropriate. For instance, they may want to accuse the group of unduly emphasizing a problem that is not as important as some others, and this kind of criticism is, in principle, fair enough. But it is not appropriate to argue that because there is more than one wrong, nothing should be done about that wrong. Reform has to start somewhere; rarely can it start everywhere at once. Following through on two-wrongs thinking would commit us to perpetuating immoral practices in the name of consistency. It is fallacious to infer that one wrong should be condoned because there are other similar ones. The existence of some wrongs is no reason to condone or tolerate others.

The Fallacy of Slippery Assimilation

Perhaps you have heard of the so-called proof that no one is bald. It goes like this: consider a person with 50,000 hairs on his head. If you take away one of these hairs, that will not make him into a bald person. Now suppose you keep pulling out hairs, one at a time. Suppose you get the poor fellow down to the point where he has only 200 hairs left. He won't look very hairy at this point. But is he bald? How can he be? All you do is pull out one hair at a time, and no one hair will make the difference between being hairy and being bald. You are sliding along evenly from a state of hairiness. With no obvious stop along the slide, how do you stop calling the man hairy? If the first hair doesn't make the difference, neither does the second. Nor the third. Nor the fourth. Each hair is just like the one before it. It would surely be arbitrary to say that the 40,004th hair could make the difference when the first or the tenth could not. This argument seems to provide a proof that no one can be bald— very consoling to older men, perhaps, but paradoxical for philosophers and logicians.

In fact, logicians have been puzzled about this kind of argument for several thousand years. It is sometimes referred to as the paradox of the heap because an early form of the argument was that you could never get a heap of grain from an accumulation of individual grains. No one grain would make the difference between having just a few separate grains and having a heap. Clearly, something has gone wrong with the argument. We indicate this fact by referring to an argument of this type as a **fallacy of slippery assimilation.**

Let's take a more abstract look at this puzzling line of reasoning:

1. Case (a) differs from case (b) only by amount *x*.
2. Case (b) differs from case (c) only by amount *x*.
3. Case (c) differs from case (d) only by amount *x*.
4. There is a whole series of cases (a) to (*n* . . .).
5. Within the series (a) to (*n* . . .) each member differs from those preceding and following it only by amount *x*.
6. Amount *x* is a small, even trivial, amount.
7. Case (a) is a clear case of *W*.
Therefore,
8. All the other cases in the series, from (b) to (*n* . . .) are also clear cases of *W*.

As for the baldness example, the series would be long indeed. Each member would have one less hair than the one before; the conclusion would be that no one is bald. (The absurdity of the argument can also be pointed out by the fact that you could use it in reverse to prove that everybody is bald. Start with a completely bald person and add one hair at a time. No one hair makes the difference between being bald and being nonbald. Hence, no matter how many more hairs a person has than the bald man, he will turn out still to be bald!)

Such arguments urge us to *assimilate* all the members in the conceptual series to the first member. (To assimilate them means to gloss over, or blur over, the differences between them.) The reason for the assimilation is that the difference between a member and its successor is slight or trivial; if the first case is *W* and the second one differs from it only slightly, the second one is *W*—and so on for all the further cases. What is wrong with the argument is its implicit reliance on the assumption that differences that are individually trivial are not trivial when many of them are taken together. The argument ignores the fact that differences that are separately insignificant can (and often do) *cumulate* to be significant. Pulling out one hair at a time is not significant, but the *cumulative* effect of pulling out 40,000 hairs surely will be. Think of the point in another context: gaining an ounce would not affect your appearance, but if you gain an ounce a day for 1,000 days, the cumulative effect (more than 60 pounds) will certainly be noticeable. Even if you were slim at the beginning of this process, by the end of it you would be round and plump. There is a difference between being hairy and being bald, and a difference between being slim and being plump, even though it is impossible to say that any one hair or ounce makes the difference.[20]

You probably have heard logically similar arguments in debates about abortion. The strategy is to insist that fetal development is gradual and that each stage of development differs only slightly from those preceding and succeeding it. It is alleged that because of this gradual development we cannot "draw a line." (In fact, a clue to the presence of a slippery assimilation argument is the question "But where can you draw the line?") It is arbitrary to select any one stage or moment in the nine months of development and say that at that point, the fetus becomes a human being. Many antiabortionists infer from these facts that the fetus is a human person from the moment of conception; since we cannot draw a line, all stages represent a person. (Could we equally well infer that all stages represent a nonperson, since the change into a person occurs at no one point?) These two inferences would be logically parallel. Both are mistaken, and both involve the fallacy of slippery assimilation.

The tacit argument underlying the question "Where can you draw the line?" is usually that you can't plausibly specify *one precise point* where a line should be drawn, and that for this reason the distinction in question should not be made at all. But something has clearly gone wrong here. The mistake in the fallacy of slippery assimilation is one of ignoring the fact that differences that are separately trivial can cumulate to be significant. The argument from slippery assimilation indicates that it will be debatable where distinctions are made. It indicates that there will be borderline cases, things which are neither clearly *W* nor clearly non-*W*. The existence of these borderline cases is an important phenomenon. (For one thing, borderline cases help us to avoid false dichotomies, as discussed in Chapter 7. There are people who are neither clearly hairy nor clearly bald, neither clearly slim nor clearly plump, neither clearly beautiful nor clearly ugly, and so on.) But the existence of small differences and borderline cases does not show that all the items in a conceptual series must be classified in the same way because of considerations of consistency.

The Fallacy of Slippery Precedent

A related abuse of consistency reasoning comes when a specific case is considered in relation to a whole series of further cases, some of which are morally very different from the original one. It is sometimes allowed that a particular action would, when considered by itself, be a good one to perform. This good action would, nevertheless, set a dangerous precedent, since consistency would make us slide on allowing further actions that do not share the moral value of the original one. On such grounds it is often urged that even though the action in question is admitted to be good, it should not be taken because it is too closely related to further actions that are not so good. We shall call this the **fallacy of slippery precedent.** Like the slippery assimilation argument, slippery precedent has some resemblance to the legitimate uses of an *a priori* analogy. It relies on a series of cases, using the existence of a related series to justify a conclusion about a member in the series. We slide easily from one case to others; the way is slippery. It also bears a relation to the causal slippery slope, because often an assumption underlying slippery precedent is that the apparently similarity of cases will mean that when we allow some, we will be led (caused) to allow others that are apparently similar.

Here is an example of this slippery use of precedent:

> As a student whose parents are undergoing divorce, and who has suffered from mononucleosis this term, you clearly would deserve an extension on your deadline. However, even though it would be fine for me to allow you this extension, if I did that, I would be bound to give an extension to every student who asked for one. I would wind up giving extensions to students who were just disorganized or who had been out drinking at parties, and soon my deadline would be completely meaningless.

We can easily imagine the familiar scene in which a professor uses this argument to reply to a student's plea for an extension. The professor acknowledges that, considered by itself, the student's request is legitimate and would merit the extension. But he then insists that this legitimate extension would set a bad precedent, because it would provide a basis for further illegitimate extensions, which, for consistency, would have to be allowed. The professor ignores the possibility of considering the case on its own merits.

See if you can detect the same kind of reasoning in this next example, which moves up one level in the university hierarchy. (This one was used by a dean commenting on an action taken by a professor in his faculty.)

> A faculty member has launched an appeal concerning his salary. He says that he did not, in the past, receive all the special merit increments to which he was entitled and he wants to receive back pay. In fact, this professor is disliked by the chairman of his department, and that chairman has admitted that in the past not all deserved increments were given to the man. If you consider his appeal by itself, just on its own merits, you have to admit that he deserves to win it. But the problem is, if he can appeal his salary and claim back pay as a result of a successful appeal, all the other professors with a wage complaint can do that too. To grant his appeal will set the precedent that faculty members can squeal and protest whenever they don't get just what they want from the salary committee. If that precedent is set, we'll soon be granting every appeal, and the very point of having such a committee will be defeated. The system would become completely unworkable. Therefore, even though this single appeal is well founded, it should not be granted because of the precedent it sets.

In these arguments, a case that is admitted to be legitimate is assimilated to further cases that are similar in some respects but obviously not legitimate. The initial case is then set in the context of these others, and the arguer insists that it would set a precedent for them. Since these further cases are not to be allowed, it is inferred that the initial case should not be allowed either on the grounds that it would set a bad precedent.

When we reflect on such arguments, we realize that something must be wrong with them. The problem is that the premises are implicitly inconsistent. Therefore, they cannot all be acceptable; such arguments cannot satisfy the (A) condition. If case (a) is legitimate and cases (b), (c), and (d) are not legitimate, then these cases cannot all be relevantly similar to each other. There must be a relevant difference between them: something about the first that makes it legitimate when the others are not. Given this relevant difference, the first case cannot be a precedent for the others.

To see the significance of the relevant difference, look back at the example of the student and her deadline. If the student has serious family problems and has been ill during the term, then those factors distinguish her case from another one in which a student is pressed for time just because he was disorganized. If there are other students relevantly similar to her, they deserve extensions, and granting such extensions will not make the deadline collapse. To allow an extension in a hardship case is not a precedent for allowing it in every case, provided we are clear about what the hardship is, and why the extension is being allowed for hardship.

Precedent reasoning is legitimate in general and profoundly important in legal contexts. However, it is misapplied in slippery precedent arguments. The reason is simple: cases that are straightforwardly deserving must be relevantly different from other cases that are straightforwardly undeserving. The former cannot set a genuine precedent for the latter. When an arguer admits that a case under consideration is legitimate, but urges that this legitimate case would set a bad or unmanageable precedent, something has gone wrong. Relevant differences have been ignored or compromise solutions have gone unconsidered.

EXERCISE SET

Exercise 3

Of the following passages, first identify those that contain arguments by analogy. For each argument by analogy, identify the primary subject and the analogue, mention key relevant similarities and differences between the primary subject and the analogue, and comment on the merits of the argument. If any passage contains a fallacy such as two wrongs, slippery assimilation, or slippery precedent, point this out and explain how the fallacy is committed in that particular case.

1. "Consider this scenario of a crime. A man decides to rob a store and uses a handgun to carry out his intent. He pulls the trigger and wounds, perhaps kills, someone. A man, a gun, and a bullet are involved in the crime—two inanimate objects and a human being. All the laws in the world wouldn't prevent that man from obtaining a weapon to carry out his intent. Laws do not stop heroin addicts from obtaining heroin; they do not stop motorists from speeding. It is illogical and foolish to think that re-strictive handgun laws will prevent handgun crimes. We must focus our efforts on the people who commit crimes, instead of on the inanimate objects they abuse while breaking the law."

(Cited in the *Informal Logic Newsletter,* July 1983, p. 43)

2. The altos and tenors in a choir are like the filling in a sandwich. When you first see a sandwich you notice the bread. And, of course, the taste of a sandwich depends very much on the taste of the bread. But what would a sandwich be without a filling of delicious roast beef, cheese, or peanut butter? Just nothing at all. And in the same way, the altos and tenors make a choir's music meaningful. Maybe you don't notice these middle parts as much as you notice the sopranos and basses, but without them, the performance would be empty. So the altos and tenors should take care to sing well.

(Calgary choir director, Jim Monro, on the importance of alto and tenor parts in a choir)

*3. "It is of course quite true that the majority of women are kind to children and prefer their own to other people's. But exactly the same thing is true of the majority of men, who nevertheless do not consider that their proper sphere is the nursery. The case may be illustrated more grotesquely by the fact that the majority of women who have dogs are kind to them and prefer their own dogs to other people's. Yet it is not proposed that women should restrict their activities to the rearing of puppies."

(G. B. Shaw, "The Womanly Woman," in *Masculine/ Feminine*, ed. Betty Roszak and Theodore Roszak [New York: Harper & Row, 1969])

Question: Here Shaw is alleging that other people use a faulty argument. Do you agree with him?

4. Obviously, very small organisms, such as algae, do not think. From algae, we progress by small degrees to small sea creatures, insects, birds, reptiles, mammals, and human beings. The behavior of all these creatures exhibits changes only by degrees. Therefore, if we deny mind to algae, we must deny it also to human beings. And if we grant mind to human beings, we must grant it also to algae.

5. "Handgun control doesn't necessarily mean taking the guns away from everybody. It can mean simply to license these weapons, making it unlawful to own one without proper registration. After all, what's the big deal? You need a license to get married. You need a license for your dog. You need one for your vehicle and your business. You need permits for nearly everything. Nobody seems to suffer too much. Drivers must meet certain standards in order to obtain a permit to drive. As a result, thousands of lives are saved every year. So why not similarly license handguns? It'll cost a little, be a little inconvenient, and maybe it'll save a few lives. It really is the least we can do."

(Letter to the editor, *Los Angeles Times*, January 23, 1981, cited in the *Informal Logic Newsletter*, Examples Supplement, November 1981)

6. "It's sort of like the Theory of Relativity. With relativity, it's like this: If you go fast enough, time slows down. With Enriched Fla-

vor, it's like this: The taste stays just as rich as you like even though the tar goes down. What could be simpler? Enriched Flavor, low tar. A solution with Merit."

(Advertisement for Merit cigarettes, printed in *Harper's* magazine, March 1990)

7. *Background:* A contentious issue in Toronto city politics in 1989 was whether to build a domed stadium. Some critics of the stadium had urged that opera was more worthwhile than football and baseball; in response to these comments, newspaper columnist Michael Shapcott had said that no one ever died from lack of opera—that is, opera is not really a necessity of life. The following letter on the issue appeared in a Toronto paper:

"Michael Shapcott is right. No one has ever died from lack of opera. Nor, might I add, have the morgues ever been overpopulated with guests suffering from terminal lack of a domed stadium. Opera is meant to be enjoyed by everyone. . . . Unfortunately, opera gets littered with snobberies, and some wonderful music gets lost in the shuffle. If children were exposed to as much opera as they are to baseball, hockey, and football, opera would rapidly lose its image of being esoteric and intimidating."

(A. C., letter to the Toronto *Star*, reprinted in *World Press Review*, December 1988, p. 8)

*8. *Background:* The following letter appeared in the Calgary *Herald* for October 7, 1998, in response to a suggestion by Nelson Riis that the voting age in Canada be lowered from 18 years to 16 years.

"Riis says there's no reason why 16- and 17-year-olds shouldn't be allowed to vote because in his experience that age group contains many bright, articulate people who have much to contribute to society. There's no question his assessment of the talents of 16- and 17-year-olds is accurate: most we have met are intelligent and well-spoken, are already making a great contribution to society and will do so even more effectively when they grow up. For mature they must. What Riis and other self-styled progressives overlook are the consequences of their actions. If we were to accept that today's generation is two years more mature than those previous and thus worthy of the vote, we must then accept that 16-year-olds should be allowed to go drinking in bars, that they should be jailed for life when they commit murder and that the age for driver's licence should be lowered from 16 to 14. And then, why not lower the already irresponsible legal age for consensual sex from 14 to 12? You see where this leads. That's why Riis is wrong."

*9.   *Background:* Here is a piece on the subject of the moral status of animals. It was written by Lewis Carroll, the author of *Alice in Wonderland.* Carroll was also a logician of considerable accomplishments. This passage is taken from his essay, "Some Popular Fallacies about Vivisection":

"In discussing the rights of animals, I think I may pass by, as needing to remark, the so-called right of a race of animals to be perpetuated and the still more shadowy right of a non-existent animal to come into existence. The only question worth consideration is whether the killing of an animal is a real infringement of a right. Once grant this, and a *reductio ad absurdum* is imminent, unless we are illogical enough to assign rights to animals in proportion to their size. Never may we destroy, for our convenience, some of a litter of puppies, or open a score of oysters when nineteen would have sufficed, or light a candle in a summer evening for mere pleasure, less some hapless moth should rush to an untimely end! Nay, we must not even take a walk, with the certainty of crushing many an insect in our path, unless for really important business! Surely all this is childish. In the absolute hopelessness of drawing a line anywhere, I conclude (and I believe that many, on considering the point, will agree with me) that man has an absolute right to inflict death on animals, without assigning any reason provided that it be a painless death. But any infliction of pain needs its special justification."

(Lewis Carroll, "Some Popular Fallacies about Vivisection," *The Complete Works of Lewis Carroll* [New York: Random House, 1957])

10.   *Background:* Author Edward DeBono is discussing whether thinking can be taught:

"If thinking is indeed a skill, how is it that we do not acquire this skill in the normal course of events? We develop skill in walking by practice. . . . We develop skill in talking by communication. . . . Surely we must develop skill in thinking by coping with the world around us? The answer is that we do. But we must distinguish between a 'full' skill and a two-finger skill. Many people who teach themselves to type early in life learn to type with two fingers. This is because they do not set out to learn typing as such but to use typing in their work. With two fingers they can more quickly acquire a more tolerable level of competence than if they tried to develop skill with all ten fingers. . . . They learn a two-finger skill. Yet a girl who trains to be a typist can, within a few weeks, develop a much higher degree of touch-typing skill, or what we call a 'full' skill. The two-finger journalist has acquired skill in the course of dealing with a limited situation and his skill is only just sufficient to cope with that situation. . . . Similarly the academic idiom taught at schools and refined in universities is a sort of two-finger skill. It is excellent at coping with closed situations where all the information is supplied, but it is very inefficient in dealing with open-ended situations where only part of the information is given, yet a decision still has to be made."

(Edward DeBono, *Teaching Thinking* [Harmondsworth, England: Penguin Books, 1984], p. 47)

*11.   *Background:* Author Donald Griffin is discussing whether animals are conscious and what sorts of thoughts they might have if they are:

"The content of much human consciousness does not conform to objective reality. Fear of ghosts and monsters is very basic and widespread in our species. Demons, spirits, miracles, and voices of departed ancestors are real and important to many people, as are religious beliefs. . . . Yet when we speculate about animal thoughts, we usually assume that they would necessarily involve practical down-to-earth matters, such as how to get food or escape predators. . . . But there is really no reason to assume that animal thoughts are rigoristically realistic. Apes and porpoises often seem playful, mischievous, and fickle, and anything but businesslike, practical, and objective. Insofar as animals do think and feel, they may fear imaginary predators, imagine unrealistically delicious foods, or think about objects and events that do not actually occur in the real world around them."

(Donald Griffin, *Animal Thinking* [Cambridge, MA: Harvard University Press, 1984], pp. 202–203)

12.   If a 10-year-old can get away with writing on a school fence, then an 11-year-old can get away with breaking windows, a 12-year-old can pull off an unpunished mugging, and a 13-year-old can get away with murder. Casual vandalism must be punished.

13.   *Background:* In 1974, Canadian Agriculture Minister Eugene Whelan was criticized because 27 million eggs had been allowed to spoil. He replied to criticism as follows:

"I wouldn't call that a surplus. It was only two days consumption for the whole province of Ontario. They think that's a lot, but how many billions, and I mean billions, of potatoes were dumped in Prince Edward Island years ago. Nothing was said about that."

(Cited in Ralph H. Johnson and J. Anthony Blair, *Logical Self-Defense,* 2nd ed. [Toronto: McGraw-Hill-Ryerson, 1983], p. 105)

14.   *Background:* Here is an excerpt from a letter on the abortion issue, taken from the Calgary *Herald*, January 25, 1983. It was written to argue against the position of a previous writer, Ross, who had urged that a fertilized egg becomes a person at the moment of conception.

". . . That single cell is not a baby; it is simply a cell, which, if conditions permit, may become a baby. In other words, it is a "potential baby" and it is the destruction of this potential baby that Ross calls infanticide. But as he himself puts it, there can be no "cut off" point in the development of a baby, so why not go one step further and consider the unfertilized ovum? The ovum is half a human cell which, if conditions permit, may become a baby—it too is a potential baby. Following Ross's own logic, the destruction of an ovum would entail infanticide. Does he then denounce the birth control pill (which interferes with the release of the ovum) as infanticide?"

15.   *Background:* During discussions of Cold War politics of the 1980s, the following analogy was used to try to show that problems between the Soviet Union and the United States are not best addressed by experts on weaponry.

"If you had a husband and wife who'd been quarrelling, and they were collecting crockery to throw at each other—more and more plates, bowls, heavy pottery, mugs—one subject would be crockery control. Let's limit the weight of the mugs; let's substitute plastic dishes for the heavy plates, and that would be crockery control. And on that I would welcome the advice of ceramic engineers as to how to design plates adequately without making them dangerous. But anyone realizes what the true problem is: what we need is family counselling. We need to deal with the differences that are bound to come up between husband and wife, or between neighbours, or between us and the Soviets—how to deal with those differences in such a way that nobody will reach for the crockery. And, on that subject, don't ask for a ceramic engineer or a pottery manufacturer. You don't ask for a military man to give us expert advice on how to deal with our differences. That's a subject for every human being who has kids with whom they quarrel, parents, neighbors, boss and secretary; we know more about how to deal with differences than a nuclear physicist who does nothing but study nuclear particles. The more he narrows his mind down to the hardware, the less he understands the problem."

(Roger Fisher, quoted in *Nuclear Peace* [Toronto: CBC Transcripts, 1982])

▓▓▓▓▓▓▓ CHAPTER SUMMARY

There are both legitimate and illegitimate uses of analogy. *A priori* and inductive analogies are fundamental in the construction of human knowledge. *A priori* analogies depend on an appeal to consistency, a demand that relevantly similar cases should be treated similarly. They are important in logic, ethics, law, and administration and may be used to resolve important conceptual disputes. A refutation by logical analogy can constitute a conclusive refutation of an argument. This technique is common in logic itself and was used to good effect by the philosopher David Hume in his famous work, "Dialogues Concerning Natural Religion."

Inductive analogies are indispensable in enabling us to bring known cases to bear on the unknown, giving us a basis for estimates that cannot be based on universal or general statements because we do not have sufficient evidence to render those statements acceptable. Whereas an *a priori* analogy demands a decision made in consistency with that in an analogous case, an inductive analogy is used as the basis for a prediction. With inductive analogies, the merits of the argument cannot be determined by reflection alone but must be assessed with consideration for the actual features of the cases compared, using empirical background knowledge. Inductive analogies are used in ordinary life, in scientific reasoning, and in policy reasoning when historical cases are brought to bear on present problems.

Analogies can also be misused. Some arguments are based on analogies so loose and remote that it is hard even to classify them as either *a priori* or inductive. These analogies are deemed to be fallacious. In fact, a special fallacy category, "faulty analogy," is defined to include them. Other faulty uses of analogy, such as the two-wrongs fallacy and the slippery uses of assimilation and precedent, involve more subtle abuses of the inherently legitimate case-by-case technique.

Review of Terms Introduced

Analogue   In an argument by analogy, the thing to which the primary subject is compared and on the basis of which the arguer reasons to the conclusion about the primary subject. Some arguments by analogy use several analogues.

Analogy   A parallel or comparison between two cases. Analogies may be used as the basis for arguments when people reason from one case to a conclusion about another deemed to be similar to the first. In addition, analogies are used in explanations, or as illustrations, or in descriptions.

Appeals to consistency   Arguments relying on analogy and urging that similar cases be treated similarly. If *A* is relevantly similar to *B,* and if *B* has been treated as *x* then, as a matter of consistency, *A* should also be treated as *x*. Appeals to consistency are especially common in logic, law, ethics, and administration.

***A priori* analogy**   An argument by analogy in which there is an appeal to consistency and in which the analogue may be entirely hypothetical or fictitious without undermining the logical force of the argument.

Conceptual issue   An issue in which the question at stake is how a concept should be applied or how it should be articulated.

Counteranalogy   An analogy different from the one on which an argument is based, and leading plausibly to a conclusion different from, or contrary to, that of the original argument. If the counteranalogy is as well founded as the original one, and if it leads to a different conclusion, an argument based on a counteranalogy will constitute a powerful criticism of the original argument.

Fallacy of slippery assimilation   Argument based on the logical error of assuming that because cases can be arranged in a series, where the difference between successive members of the series is small, the cases should all be assimilated. This is a mistaken appeal to consistency. It ignores the fact that small differences can accumulate to be significant.

Fallacy of slippery precedent   Argument based on claiming that an action, though good, should not be permitted because it will set a precedent for further similar actions that are bad. Such arguments are flawed in that they use implicitly inconsistent premises. A good action cannot be relevantly similar to a bad action; there must be some relevant difference between them.

Fallacy of two wrongs make a right   Mistake of inferring that because two wrong things are similar and one is tolerated, the other should be tolerated as well. This sort of argument misuses the appeal to consistency.

Faulty analogy   Name for a fallacious argument in which the analogy is so loose and remote that there is virtually no support for the conclusion.

Inductive analogy   An argument by analogy in which the conclusion is predicted on the basis of experience. The analogue must be a real case, and the factual features of the analogue and the primary subject are essential for determining the strength of the argument.

Precedent   A relevantly similar case that has already been resolved. Reasoning by precedent is particularly common and important in law.

Primary subject   In an argument by analogy, the topic that the conclusion is about.

Refutation by logical analogy   The refutation of one argument by the construction of another that is parallel to it in reasoning and that is clearly flawed.

Notes

1. C. S. Lewis, *Mere Christianity* (New York: Macmillan, 1952), p. 75.
2. Albert Einstein, as quoted by Jonathan Schell in *The Fate of the Earth* (New York: Knopf, 1982), p. 10.
3. Ralph Johnson, "Poll-ution: Coping with Surveys and Polls," in Trudy Govier, editor, *Selected Issues in Logic and Communication* (Belmont, CA: Wadsworth, 1988), p. 164.
4. A truth table construction can be used to show that any statement of the form "$P-P$" is always false.

5. This advice was reprinted in the *Informal Logic Newsletter* in the Examples Supplement for 1979.

6. These events were described in the Toronto *Globe and Mail* for February 8, 1982.

7. *For instructors.* It may be misleading, from the point of view of theory, to assume that the pertinent features of the analogy can be picked out as easily as this model would suggest. Cf. "Euclid's Disease and Desperate Violinists," in Trudy Govier, *The Philosophy of Argument* (Newport News, VA: Vale Press, 1999.)

8. Robert Nozick, *Anarchy State and Utopia* (New York: Basic Books, 1974), pp. 169–170.

9. Letter to *Time* magazine, April 10, 1989.

10. Alan Connery, Calgary *Herald,* July 6, 1969. Reprinted with permission of the Calgary *Herald.*

11. Often, in inductive analogies, several analogue cases are cited; in fact, this strengthens the argument when the various analogue cases differ from each other (there is a greater variety of evidence for the conclusion). To avoid complications, inductive analogies considered in this chapter have only one analogue. Risa Kawchuk points out that structurally, arguments from multiple analogies are interestingly similar to conductive arguments.

12. From "Monday Morning Policy Wonks," *Harper's* magazine, March 1993. Excerpted from an interview with Noam Chomsky in David Barbanian, *Chronicler of Dissent* (Monroe, Maine: Common Courage Press, 1992).

13. The use of inductive and *a priori* analogies by Hume in the "Dialogues" is clearly and interestingly discussed by Stephen F. Barker in "Reasoning by Analogy in Hume's Dialogues," in *Informal Logic* Vol. XI no. 3 (Fall 1989), pp. 173–184.

14. David Hume, "Dialogues Concerning Natural Religion" in *The Empiricists* (New York: Anchor Press, 1974), p. 467.

15. The conclusion is interestingly parallel to the pantheistic doctrine that God is in all things.

16. This point is discussed in an interesting way by Maryann Ayim in "Violence and Domination in Academic Discourse," in Trudy Govier (ed.), *Selected Issues in Logic and Communication* (Belmont, CA: Wadsworth, 1988), pp. 184–195.

17. Letter to the Calgary *Herald,* March 12, 1976.

18. Francis Bacon, *The True Greatness of Kingdoms,* quoted by Susan Stebbing in *Thinking to Some Purpose* (London: Pelican Books, 1983), p. 123.

19. Letter to the Calgary *Herald,* May 7, 1984.

20. The fallacies of slippery assimilation and slippery precedent are sometimes referred to as the slippery slope fallacy. What is called in Chapter 9 "causal slippery slope" is often similarly described. I have preserved the word *slippery* in my descriptions. However, slippery assimilation, slippery precedent, and causal slippery slope are distinguished in this book, because they differ in important ways. The first involves issues about the application of concepts, and vagueness; the second involves uses of analogy; the third involves causal sequences. Some mixed "slippery slopes" mingle these aspects. An articulation of my views on slippery slope fallacies can be found in "What's Wrong with Slippery Slope Arguments?" in Trudy Govier, *The Philosophy of Argument* (Newport News, VA: Vale Press, 1999).

chapter eleven

Conductive Arguments and Counterconsiderations

THE NOTION OF CONDUCTIVE ARGUMENTS was defined and developed by the American philosopher Carl Wellman several decades ago.[1] We have mentioned conductive arguments several times already in this book, most notably in Chapters 2 and 6.

To understand more clearly what a conductive argument is, think back to the convergent support pattern that we defined in Chapter 2. In **conductive arguments,** the support for the conclusion is always convergent.[2] This means that the premises count separately in favor of the conclusion; they are put forward as separately relevant to it and need not be linked to offer support. If one or more premises were to be removed from the argument, the relevance to the conclusion of the remaining premises would be unaffected. As you may remember from Chapter 2, this is not the case in linked arguments. In such deductively valid arguments, inductive arguments, and analogies that have several premises, the support provided by premises is nearly always linked.

In a conductive argument, the premises are put forward as convergently supporting the conclusion. They do not entail the conclusion or support it by inductive generalization or analogy. It is useful to make reference to the ARG conditions when we reflect on the assessment of conductive arguments. As for (A), we assess the premises of conductive arguments just as we would those of any other argument. As for (R), we assess the relevance of the premises by considering each premise separately. As for (G), we consider the premises together, in the light of other evidence that might count against the conclusion.

Here is a simple example of a conductive argument:

(1) She never takes her eyes off him in a crowd, and (2) she is continually restless when he is out of town. (3) At any opportunity, she will introduce his name in a conversation. (4) And no other man has ever occupied her attention for so long. You can tell (5) she is in love with him.

The issue here is whether someone is in love. The arguer has offered several pieces of evidence to support his conclusion. Even if one premise were false or unacceptable, the others would still count in support of his conclusion. Each piece of information is both collectively relevant and separately relevant to establishing the conclusion. This argument proceeds by specifying a number of relevant factors. To evaluate it, we have to see whether each premise is acceptable and relevant, and then judge the strength of the reasons they collectively provide for the conclusion. The argument just described can be represented pictorially as shown in Figure 11.1.

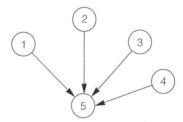

FIGURE 11.1

Some philosophers have referred to conductive arguments as *good reasons arguments*. The name makes sense in a way: the relevant factors are stated as providing good reasons for the conclusion, though they do not support it in virtue of deductive entailment, inductive regularities, or analogy. There are problems with the "good reasons" label, however: it suggests that all conductive arguments are based on *good* reasons. They are not. With other sorts of arguments, we have seen that some are cogent, whereas others are not. The same is true for conductive arguments.

Some conductive arguments provide relevant and good reasons to support a conclusion, but others are flawed. For instance, a conductive argument may specify that certain factors are relevant when actually they are irrelevant—as when straw man, *ad hominem*, and guilt-by-association fallacies are used. In such cases, the (R) condition is not satisfied. Other conductive arguments may provide premises that are genuinely relevant but do not add up to give enough support for the conclusion. In such cases, the (G) condition is not satisfied.

Other names sometimes given to conductive arguments are *cumulation of consideration* arguments or *balance of consideration* arguments. Various factors cumulate to support the conclusion, and typically these have to be assessed in the light of other factors that counter against it. As our description continues, you will understand why these names might be appropriate. Here, we will use the name *conductive*. We have emphasized that in conductive arguments the premises are put forward as being separately relevant to the conclusion. This aspect of conductive arguments has led some commentators to wonder whether such arguments should be broken down into a number of separate ones, each with one premise. Applying this idea to the example about being in love, one would understand it as four separate arguments, each with one premise and one conclusion. The arguer is clearly saying that (1) is a reason for (5); (2) is a reason for (5); (3) is a reason for (5); and (4) is a reason for (5). It has been suggested that in such a case, a person is putting forth four arguments instead of one.

There are three reasons that we have not adopted the approach of breaking down conductive arguments into smaller ones. (Note that this itself is a conductive argument!) The first reason is that in practice, diverse considerations in such arguments are characteristically put forward together. The implication is that their collective bearing on the conclusion should be taken into account when we are deciding whether to accept the conclusion. The second reason is that a number of credible authors on normative reasoning and critical thinking (including Michael Scriven, James Freeman, Kurt Baier, and Stephen Thomas) have acknowledged the existence of these arguments, understanding them to be a distinct type. The third reason we take to be the most significant: were we to break such a conductive argument into separate arguments, we would only later come back to the point where, in effect, we had to consider the various premises together. That happens when we try to decide, on the basis of the various factors put forward, whether the conclusion is acceptable. Think, for instance, of the example just cited. Is this woman in love with this man, with whom she seems to be preoccupied? Whether we say there is one argument or four arguments, it remains true that four reasons have been put forward to support the conclusion; when we come to make a decision about the conclusion, we have to consider these four reasons together and ask ourselves how compelling they are.

Conductive arguments are common in reasoning about practical affairs, where a number of separate factors seem to have a bearing on our decisions about what to do. They are also common in contexts where there are disputes about the interpretation of human behavior or literary texts. Arguments about values and interpretation of actions are prominent in social theory, in politics, and in history. Such arguments frequently draw together several independently relevant factors because there are several distinct pieces of evidence that count for or against one interpretation or the other.

Here is an example of a conductive argument. The author is arguing that the myth of Santa Claus is not harmful to children and when parents lie to children about Santa, their lies can be regarded as white lies.

Usually the Santa lie, befitting Christmas, is a white one.
   (1) For starters, the lie is only temporary. You tell kids about Santa now, but you'll straighten them out later. The deception isn't forever. (2) And the deception is a mild one. You don't take a falsehood and call it truth; you take a

fiction and call it truth—a smaller distortion. This means the loss of the illusion is gentler. When kids are older they don't lose Santa entirely, they just think of him in a different way. (3) Finally, the deception is good for kids. Believing in Santa adds magic and excitement to Christmas; the anticipation is keener, the delight sharper. Parental love is fine and even profound, but a gift from the North Pole is far more exotic.[3]

The structure here is clear. The conclusion is stated in the first sentence. Three distinct reasons are given for it. The first is introduced with "For starters," the second with "And," and the third with "Finally." Each premise considered by itself provides some reason to accept the conclusion: that is what makes these premises *separately relevant*. Taken together—as they should be, because they are put forward to support one single conclusion—they provide better support, though not proving for certain that the conclusion is true. See Figure 11.2.

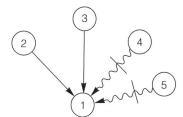

FIGURE 11.2

Counterconsiderations

Thinking back to the discussion of relevance in Chapter 6, you will recall the distinction between positive and negative relevance. In the understanding and evaluation of conductive arguments, relevance is a central critical concept. In a cogent conductive argument, the premises must be positively relevant to the conclusion. How strongly they support that conclusion can be determined only by considering them in the light of points that are negatively relevant to that conclusion. We call negatively relevant points **counterconsiderations**, or objections. Counterconsiderations count against the conclusion being put forward.

In many conductive arguments, some counterconsiderations are acknowledged by the arguer, who accepts that they have a bearing on his or her conclusion and, in fact, count against it. Words such as *though, although, even though, despite the fact that,* and *notwithstanding the fact that* are often used to introduce counterconsiderations. Suppose someone were to say:

I think (1) Bill is annoyed, because (2) he seems to tense up whenever he sees me and (3) he never invites me for coffee the way he used to. Even though (4) he still says hello and (5) we work fairly effectively together, (1) he just seems annoyed.

This person has given reasons for thinking Bill is annoyed but has acknowledged two counterconsiderations: (4) and (5).[4]

When we represent conductive arguments pictorially, we can include counterconsiderations by using wavy lines and a bar, to indicate that they count against the conclusion rather than for it. Counterconsiderations should not be regarded as premises of an argument, because they do not support the conclusion and are not put forward by the arguer as supporting the conclusion. Figure 11.3 pictorially represents the conductive argument just stated, which has two premises and two counterconsiderations. Statement (1) is the conclusion; (2) and (3) are the premises; and (4) and (5) represent counterconsiderations, or objections to the conclusion.

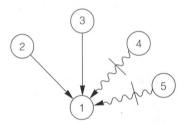

FIGURE 11.3

A person who acknowledges counterconsiderations and nevertheless still wishes to put forward the argument that his conclusion is supported by positively relevant premises is committed to the judgment that the supporting (positively relevant) premises outweigh the counterconsiderations. To speak of "outweighing" is, of course, to use figurative language. We cannot literally measure, or quantify, the strength or merits of the various premises against counterconsiderations. An arguer who offers reasons and explicitly acknowledges counterconsiderations is implicitly claiming that although there are reasons for his conclusion and reasons against it, the reasons for it are stronger and more convincing than the reasons against it. In other words, he has judged, and is implying, that the pros outweigh the cons. The "weighing" or "balancing" of various considerations is admittedly hard to understand or explain in nonmetaphorical terms, but it is in fact something we do all the time.

It's important to recognize that acknowledging counterconsiderations does not necessarily weaken your case. Often it strengthens it, because in understanding the counterconsiderations and reflecting on how well your premises support your conclusion despite these factors, you can gain a more accurate understanding of the issue. Also, you may improve your credibility, showing your audience that you are broad-minded and flexible enough to understand some of the objections to your view, and that you have taken these into account in making up your mind and formulating your argument. Negatively relevant points, which count against the conclusion, are of crucial importance when we come to evaluate conductive arguments. The arguer has put forward premises he takes to be positively relevant to the conclusion. He is committed to the view that his premises give us good reason to accept the conclusion—whatever the counterconsiderations might be. As his audience or critics, we have to evaluate the argument he gives.

With conductive arguments, we evaluate the acceptability and relevance of the premises, as we would for any other argument. But when we come to the (G) condition and seek to evaluate the cumulative strength of the reasons provided, we have to consider whether negatively relevant points outweigh the positively relevant ones.[5] We may begin by evaluating any counterconsiderations acknowledged by the arguer himself. To arrive at a judgment about the merits of the argument, we have to ask ourselves whether we agree with his view that his premises provide better grounds for the conclusion than his counterconsiderations provide for its denial. But there is a further evaluative task that requires creativity and imagination. We have to think of what other counterconsiderations there might be. We should seek out, and reflect on, negatively relevant factors not acknowledged by the arguer, and try to estimate how seriously these would undermine his conclusion.

It is difficult to give completely general guidelines for appraising conductive arguments. We evaluate (A), the acceptability of premises, as we would in any other argument. We evaluate the (R) condition using our normal understanding of relevance, but considering each premise separately. The main difference arises when we consider the (G) condition; what we have to determine is the cumulative strength of the reasons stated in the premises when assessed in the light of counterconsiderations. In a conductive argument, there are nearly always counterconsiderations that are negatively relevant to the conclusion—whether they are acknowledged by the arguer or not.

We'll illustrate these themes by considering an example:

(1) Voluntary euthanasia, in which a terminally ill patient consciously chooses to die, should be made legal. (2) Responsible adult people should be able to choose whether to live or die. Also (3), voluntary euthanasia would save many patients from unbearable pain. (4) It would cut social costs. (5) It would save relatives the agony of watching people they love die an intolerable and undignified death. Even though (6) there is some danger of abuse, and despite the fact that (7) we do not know for certain that a cure for the patient's disease will not be found, (1) voluntary euthanasia should be a legal option for the terminally ill patient.

This argument may be pictorially represented as shown in Figure 11.4.

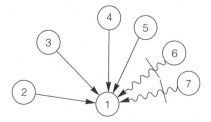

FIGURE 11.4

In this argument, four factors are cited as support for the normative conclusion that voluntary euthanasia should be legalized. The last statement acknowledges two counterconsiderations. Their role as counterconsiderations is made clear by the words *even though* and *despite the fact that*. To accept the conclusion on the basis of the supporting premises, we must judge that the reasons provided in the supporting premises outweigh in significance both the stated counterconsiderations and any other pertinent counterconsiderations. Clearly, a person who would put forward the above argument supporting voluntary euthanasia is one who would believe that the alleviation of pain and the recognition of the right to life are more important, on balance, than the risk that voluntary euthanasia might lead to abuses and the chance that a cure might be found so that the patient would not have had to die. To evaluate this argument, we have to reflect on that judgment. Obviously, there is no formula or rule that we can apply to determine whether reasons for the conclusion outweigh reasons against it.

What more can be said at this point? Several preliminaries can be recalled. First, it is important not to fall into the trap of a false dichotomy here. There are no precise rules for the evaluation of conductive arguments—but that does not mean that the whole matter is hopelessly subjective or merely a matter of emotion. It is not true that every evaluating process is either rule-based or purely subjective, and there is nothing else. There is such a thing as judgment—and people have better or worse judgment about the merits of arguments, just as they do about other matters.

Second, for any judgment or claim we feel uncertain about, we can always try to construct a subargument to support it. For example, if you believe that saving suffering is a *poor* reason for legalizing voluntary euthanasia, ask yourself why, and see what justification you can come up with. While acknowledging that we are dealing here with *judgment* rather than *proof*, we will suggest a strategy for evaluating the reasons put forward in conductive arguments.[6] These reasons are put forward by the arguer as being separately relevant to the conclusion. Reasons have an element of **generality,** and this provides the possibility of some degree of attachment when we come to evaluate them. In the argument about euthanasia, there are four premises: (2), (3), (4), and (5). These premises are put forward to state reasons why voluntary euthanasia should be made legal:

2. Insofar as voluntary euthanasia is chosen, it should be legalized.
3. Insofar as voluntary euthanasia would save many patients from great pain, it should be legalized.
4. Insofar as voluntary euthanasia would cut social costs, it should be legalized.
5. Insofar as voluntary euthanasia would avoid suffering on the part of relatives of the dying, it should be legalized.

The fact that reasons have an element of generality can help us to evaluate their strength in conductive arguments. The argument is about the desirability of making voluntary euthanasia legal. Reasons are given for making this practice legal, and if these reasons hold in the case of voluntary euthanasia, they should hold for other cases too. In effect, the argument assumes:

2a. Other things being equal, insofar as a practice consists of voluntary or chosen actions, it should be legalized.

3a. Other things being equal, insofar as a practice would save people from great pain, it should be legalized.

4a. Other things being equal, insofar as a practice would cut social costs, it should be legalized.

5a. Other things being equal, insofar as a practice would avoid suffering, it should be legalized.

These broad assumptions underlie the original argument. By spelling them out, we can see what sorts of general principles the original argument depends on. Getting away from the specific topic of voluntary euthanasia provides a broader perspective on the issue, and this broader perspective is helpful when we ask, "How strong, or compelling, are these reasons?"

Think carefully about these assumptions. Clearly not everything that will save money should be legalized; nor should everything that will prevent pain be legalized. You will certainly be able to come up with exceptions and counterexamples, and the phrase "other things being equal" is inserted in the assumptions to acknowledge that fact. In Latin, the expression for "other things being equal" is *ceteris paribus* (pronounced "ket-er-iss pair-i-bus"). A *ceteris paribus* **clause** is often inserted in statements of reasons, or in statements of principle. Such a clause expresses recognition of the fact that different things are appropriate in relevantly different circumstances. (For example: other things being equal, we should keep our promises. But if keeping a promise would cause someone to die, other things are not equal; we should not keep this promise.) Often when *ceteris paribus* clauses are not explicit, they are, in effect, assumed.

In the light of these considerations, let us reflect on (4a). For example, there are social practices that deny medical treatment to mentally handicapped children, abolishing schools for the blind, eliminating pension benefits for all citizens over eighty—that would save money but that we would not want to support. Other things are not equal in such cases; the human lives of the people who are aided are regarded as having a dignity and a value, and the aid is seen as morally appropriate or required. To better understand what is presumed in (4a), we should reflect on these counterexamples and ask ourselves just why they are counterexamples.

We can easily generate objections to (4a), and this is also the case for (2a), (3a), and (5a). (Try it; it is a useful mental exercise.) Now it is also important to see the significance of our objections at this point. They do not exactly show that these assumptions are false or unacceptable, because of the *ceteris paribus* clause. The presence of this clause makes it clear that the reasons are not taken to be sufficient or conclusive reasons for legalization. The original argument did not assume that everything that saves money should be legal! In each case, the assumption is only that such-and-such is "a reason" for legalization—a supporting consideration, one factor that counts in favor of legalizing the practice. Insofar as something will save money, that is some reason for doing it; if legalizing voluntary euthanasia will cut social costs, that is some reason for legalizing voluntary euthanasia. Other things being equal, saving money gives a reason for doing something—but what are these "other things" that would have to be equal? In this case, they are many indeed: the practice would have to be socially acceptable, not cruel, not in contravention of recognized human rights, without significant negative social consequences, and so on. There is a false dichotomy that we may lapse into: thinking that the "bottom line" (saving money) either counts for *everything* in decision making or counts for *nothing*. The truth, for most issues, is that saving money counts not for everything, and not for nothing, but for something. Understanding the *ceteris paribus* clause helps us to appreciate this fact.

A striking and important feature of *ceteris paribus* clauses is that such conditions are not typically completely spelled out. In fact, to do this is usually not possible. For (4a), we can see that the class of exceptions will be wide. For this reason, we can say that premise (4) offers only a weak reason for the conclusion. We can go through such a process for (2a), (3a), and (5a). (Do this as a mental exercise; in the interest of saving space, we do not give all the details here.)

Testing the assumptions against objections and counterexamples is one way of trying to evaluate how strong a reason the related premise can offer in support of the conclusion. Using this process, we estimate that (3a) and (5a) have a narrower range of "other things" than do (2a) and (4a). Thus, we estimate that (3) and (5) offer stronger reasons to support the conclusion than do (2) and (4). This process, although slightly cumbersome, provides useful insights into the basis of our reasons, and gives some method—albeit an informal one—for evaluating the strength of the reasons.

Clearly this case is one in which it is crucial to recall that there are counterconsiderations other than those acknowledged by the arguer. For instance, there is concern that if doctors have a role in assisting disabled patients to end their lives, their primary role as healers and savers of lives will be compromised. Furthermore, patients undergoing severe pain may not be capable of making rational decisions about their lives, so that voluntary euthanasia would not really be voluntary after all. Other objections to the conclusion may be raised. Evaluating this argument will involve making a number of sensitive judgments.

In most cases where we are making practical or ethical decisions, conductive arguments are applicable and important. In fact the failure to appreciate this mode of argument can lead to a basic sort of mistake, a kind of **tunnel vision.** This mistake occurs when we consider only one factor and exaggerate its significance. An example can be found in a discussion at a western Canadian university, about censorship of materials available on the Internet. Extraordinarily explicit and brutal visual materials about bondage, bestiality, and sexual violence were available on the Internet to students, who were given accounts in connection with their university work. The president of the Faculty Association, who was also a professor of computer science, was concerned about the availability of this material, for a variety of reasons. Among these were the following: students accessing the Internet to look at pornography were using electronic resources that were then not available for real academic work;

student viewing of pornography using university resources could be used by a hostile critic to cause serious political trouble for the university; the university could be construed as approving the offensive material by facilitating its availability on university equipment; the material might cause copycat offenses of a criminal nature, seriously injuring or even killing victims.

When he raised these concerns, the president found that many people refused to consider them. Instead, they sought to resolve the issue by saying that they were against censorship, and to limit the availability of these Internet materials would amount to censorship. This "tunnel vision" approach does indeed "solve" the practical problem quite neatly. It can be summed up in the following argument:

1. To limit availability of pornographic materials on the Internet would be censorship.
2. Censorship is wrong.
Therefore,
3. The university should not limit the availability of pornographic materials on the Internet.

This argument is deductively valid and makes the whole problem of whether to censor Internet material seem very simple. If we understand the issue as one of censorship and censorship alone, and if we accept that censorship is always bad, no matter what, the issue is clear. How would you respond to this argument? "BUT surely it isn't quite that simple," is what you should be saying. What the issue calls for is conductive argument, not deductive argument. Conductive argument would be appropriate in this context because there are a number of factors relevant to the decision. One, but only one, of these is censorship.

What is wrong with the deductive argument cited above is that premise (2) should have a *ceteris paribus* clause, but if it does, the conclusion will not deductively follow from the premises. The possibilities noted by the Faculty Association president are relevant to the issue and should be considered. Tunnel vision distorts the situation and will almost certainly lead to unwise decisions.

"What is the answer?" you may ask. Should voluntary euthanasia be legalized? Should materials on the Internet be censored? We are not going to say: for you, that will depend on your own decision as to whether to accept the conclusion. Clearly, there is no simple recipe for arriving at a definite answer, especially in the case of issues as profound as these. Our decisions must emerge from our judgment about strength of the reasons put forward, assessed in the light of counterconsiderations. We can set out a logical structure for raising questions about conductive arguments, and the structure is a useful guide for thought.

In essence, the method for appraising conductive arguments is as follows:

1. Determine whether the premises offered to support the conclusion are acceptable.
2. Determine whether the premises offered to support the conclusion are positively relevant to it, and assess the strength of the reasons.

3. Determine whether any counterconsiderations acknowledged by the arguer are negatively relevant to the conclusion.

4. Think what additional counterconsiderations, not acknowledged by the arguer, are negatively relevant to the conclusion.

5. Reflect on whether the premises, taken together, outweigh the counterconsiderations, taken together, and make a judgment. Try to articulate good reasons for that judgment.

6. If you judge that the premises do outweigh the counterconsiderations, you have judged that the (R) and (G) conditions are satisfied. Provided that (A) is also satisfied, you deem the argument cogent. Otherwise, you deem it not to be cogent.

Following this procedure does not quite take you to the stage of determining whether the conclusion is true or whether you have good reasons to accept it. It takes you only to the stage of determining whether the stated premises provide good grounds for accepting the conclusion. If you think the argument as stated is cogent, then you do think there are good reasons to accept the conclusion; presumably you will accept it on the basis of the argument. (You could think of more reasons; this often happens in discussion.) But if you think the argument is not cogent, you may wish to proceed further to see whether the conclusion could be supported by other evidence or reasons not stated in the original argument.

To proceed, you have to reflect on whether there are further considerations, not stated in the argument, that would count in favor of the conclusion and would outweigh any counterconsiderations. Doing so takes you beyond appraising the stated argument. It moves you to a new stage where you are amending or reconstructing that argument by adding more premises of your own. It is a crucially important stage, of course, when your real interest is in whether you should accept the conclusion and not merely in whether the conclusion is well supported by the particular argument you are evaluating.

Weighing pros and cons is nearly always a feature of practical decision making. It is sometimes simple, sometimes difficult, and it is nearly always open to debate. The fact that evaluating conductive arguments depends on our making judgments of relevance and significance does not mean that evaluation is an impossible task, that it is purely subjective, or that agreement can never be achieved. It does mean that those evaluations are open to discussion and revision. Conductive arguments are likely to occur anywhere in which we have distinct factors that count in favor of a conclusion and other distinct factors that count against it. You are likely to find yourself using conductive arguments when you are aware of several distinct reasons that count in favor of a decision or conclusion, especially one concerning what is to be done. Should you make a major purchase, or enroll in a new course? There will be reasons in favor and reasons against. The notion of counterconsideration is important to remember in such contexts, especially when you are strongly inclined toward some particular course of action. It can remind you to think in terms of cons or negatives, as well as pros or positives, and to be aware of the need for judgments about the significance of the various factors. If you are quite convinced that the positives outweigh the negatives, it is worth stopping to ask yourself why you think this and to consider whether there are any additional factors you might have neglected to consider.

EXERCISE SET

Exercise 1

Diagram, and then evaluate the following conductive arguments. Be sure to indicate any counterconsiderations with a wavy line and a bar. (a) State any counterconsiderations on which your evaluation depends, and note whether these are your own contributions or whether they are explicitly acknowledged by the author of the argument. (b) State whether the premises are positively relevant to the conclusion and whether, considered together, in light of counterconsiderations, they provide adequate grounds for the conclusion. (c) If you believe that you lack the background knowledge necessary to evaluate the argument, state what sort of knowledge you would need.

1. Susan must be angry with John because she persistently refuses to talk to him and she goes out of her way to avoid him. Even though she used to be his best friend, and even though she still spends a lot of time with his mother, I think she is really annoyed with him right now.

*2. There is no point in giving money to charity. Some charitable organizations waste it. Besides, when people are really needy, governments should support them and not rely on charity to do it. In addition, the advertisements put out by some of these charities are so emotional that they are positively manipulative.

3. You should return books to the library on time. When borrowing them, you in effect contract to do so. Also, other people may need them, and you can avoid expensive fines by being prompt.

4. Interdisciplinary courses, in which several different academic subjects are supposedly taught together, are not worth taking. They are hard for professors to teach. They are hard for students to understand. They demand so much extra research, for essays, that students do not have a hope of getting a good mark. Besides, many interdisciplinary courses try to combine so many different things that they wind up being a mishmash of unrelated theories and ideas.

5. *Background:* The following argument appeared in a letter to *China Daily,* reprinted in *World Press Review* (December 1989):

"We should smile sincerely at visitors from abroad. However, Chinese drivers, hotel clerks, and sellers should not distinguish between compatriots and foreigners. At present, some Chinese taxi drivers turn their backs if the clients approaching their cars are Chinese. Hotel guards quite rudely prevent Chinese people from entering. Some clerks in friendship stores turn up their noses at Chinese customers. I think, as a Chinese, that those who do such things are disgracing themselves. We may not be as wealthy as foreigners. But there are many kinds of wealth, and money is by no means the only representation of it. A person who looks down upon his compatriots will be cast aside by society and despised by the fair-minded foreigners as well."

Hint: Concentrate on the part after "we may not be as wealthy" and regard earlier sections as introduction.

*6. There is no free will. Why not? First because there are no uncaused events. And furthermore, people sometimes act out of control and can't fully choose what they do. Look at alcoholics, for instance.

*7.   The American Revolution was not a typical revolution. For one thing, the people in revolt were mainly middle class or upper class—not peasants. For another, the object of attack was something far away—a government in England—and not the close structure of the society in which the war occurred. In addition, the internal workings of the society did not change very much after the revolution. Despite the fact that it is called a revolution, and despite its great importance for the history of the world, the American Revolution should not be thought of as a model for other revolutions.

8.   *Background:* The author is discussing the problem of rape and the question of whether rape is due to natural psychological impulses:

"Rape is held to be natural behavior, and not to rape must be learned. But in truth, rape is not universal to the human species. Moreover, studies of rape in our culture reveal that, far from being impulsive behavior, most rape is planned. Professor Amir's study reveals that in cases of group rape (the 'gangbang' of masculine slang), 90 percent of the rapes were planned; in pair rapes, 83 percent were planned; and in single rapes, 58 percent were planned. These figures should significantly discredit the image of the rapist as a man who is suddenly overcome by sexual needs society does not allow him to fulfill."

(Susan Griffin, "Rape: The All-American Crime," in M. Vetterling-Braggin, F. Elliston, and J. English, eds., *Feminism and Philosophy* [Totowa, NJ: Littlefield Adams, 1977], p. 315)

Hint: There is a subargument here.

9.   There are many reasons to doubt whether teachers should be subjected to tests of competence after they have been teaching for some years. After all, teachers were tested at colleges and universities before they became teachers. Furthermore, other professions are not tested in midstream. Some teachers have been given legal

and moral guarantees of continued positions, and the tests jeopardize them. In addition, tests for teachers are unreliable. Another problem is that if teachers fail, poor salary conditions may mean that the new teachers hired to replace them are just as ill-qualified as the fired ones.

(Adapted from "When Testing Teachers May Be a Hoax," by Albert Shanker, *New York Times*, July 21, 1984. Shanker wrote about a teacher test given in Arkansas. Of 28,000 teachers given a three-part test in reading, writing, and math, 10 percent failed.)

10.   Consensus is the best approach to making decisions in small groups. For one thing, no view or person is overpowered by the majority. For another, the discussion and reflection required to reach a consensus help to establish understanding of the subject under discussion. Another positive factor is that the process of respectfully listening to others and considering their views cultivates good relationships between the people in the group. Even though working by consensus may be slow, it is worthwhile.

11.   *Background:* In this column from the *Ottawa Citizen,* reprinted in the Calgary *Herald* for January 4, 1999, David Warren writes about a woman born in 1899, who retains her curiosity about the years after 2000, but lives for the present.

"We don't have a choice about steering ahead, into the void that will soon contain us; it is just that we cannot see. No one, no genius however great, can foresee the consequences of his own tiny life. And the future will continue not to exist, no matter how long we sail towards it; only our view of the past will have changed. We live, on the same terms as that old lady, for the sake of completing the story of the past, riding along with the crash of it, our own wills against the ocean of time. My own resolution for this last New Year in the 1990's is to try to stop living in the future."

*12.   The Bible is among the most trustworthy of ancient documents. We can see that this statement is true for a number of reasons. First, the New Testament was written only 20 to 70

years after the events it records. Second, the oldest manuscript of the New Testament is a copy of originals that were made about 250 years after these originals were written. It is closer to the time of the original than other ancient manuscripts, such as those of Aristotle's *Metaphysics*, for instance. Third, there are more than 13,000 surviving copies of various portions of the New Testament, which date from ancient and medieval times. This fact means that it is highly probable that the original documents are well represented.
(Based on a leaflet distributed by the Inter-Varsity Christian Fellowship)

13. *Background:* The following argument is taken from a philosophical article about punishment, by Russ Schafer-Landau. Schafer-Landau is arguing that judges cannot tailor their sentences precisely to fit the individual cases of the prisoners whom they sentence.

"Tailoring sentences to the particular facts of each case is highly impractical. Judges lack the time to get sufficiently acquainted with an offender's history to make such individuated sentences. Even with adequate time on their hands, most judges will lack the creativity and ingenuity required of those who would hand down such punishments. Further, assuming both adequate information and a robust creativity, many offenses seem incapable of being correlated to such unconventional punishments. What, for instance, are we to do to a counterfeiter, a tax cheat, or a criminal trespasser? It seems doubtful whether there are any nonincarcerative punishments specially suited to effect a moral education for such offenders."
("Can Punishment Morally Educate?" in Michael J. Gore and Stirling Harwood, editors, *Crime and Punishment: Philosophic Explorations* [Boston: Jones and Partlett, 1995], pp. 375–390)

14. "Regardless of their intentions, if one or two members of a democratic group become relatively powerful, more than the equality of final decision-making authority is at stake. Imbalances in influence and expertise can limit less powerful members' ability to obtain and understand information relevant to group decisions. In addition, the more powerful individuals are more likely to take away others' opportunities to talk by dominating both the establishment and discussion of the agenda."
(John Gastill, *Democracy in Small Groups: Participation, Decision Making and Communication* [Gabriola Island, BC: New Society Publishers, 1993], p. 106)

More about Counterconsiderations

It is easy to explain the significance of counterconsiderations in conductive arguments, because of the particular structure those arguments have. But it is not only for conductive arguments that objections and counterconsiderations are important. They arise for every type of argument, and assessing their strength is always crucial when we seek an overall evaluation of the argument.

In deductively valid arguments, the premises entail the conclusion and thus, if true or acceptable, render the conclusion true or acceptable. This is a logical fact that is not affected by addition of new claims to the premises. In this respect, deductively valid arguments are unlike inductive and conductive ones. But that is not to say that there are no objections or counterconsiderations. It merely means that these are pertinent in a different way. In a deductively valid argument, only the premises need to be considered for acceptability. The (R) and (G) conditions are satisfied, given that it is deductively valid; therefore, we must look at the (A) condition to make sure that the premises are acceptable. Anything that is negatively relevant to the premises becomes an objection, or counterconsideration, to the argument itself.

Consider, for instance, the following:

> No one who enjoys free unstructured time should become a parent. Anyone who likes to go out for coffee and movies on short notice enjoys free unstructured time. Therefore, no one who likes to go out for coffee and movies on short notice should become a parent.

This argument is a valid syllogism, as you will be able to prove, using either Venn diagrams or the Rules of the Syllogism. Granting the premises, the conclusion must hold as well. But this validity does not mean that there is no way of objecting to the argument. There are counterconsiderations; we are led to appreciate them by reflecting on the (A) condition, the acceptability of the premises. The premises are:

1. No one who enjoys free unstructured time should become a parent.

And

2. Anyone who likes to go out for coffee and movies on short notice enjoys free unstructured time.

Looking carefully at these premises, we note that the first is, in effect, a judgment of prudence or morality, whereas the second is a generalization about people, presumed to have some inductive basis in experience and observation. A critic might allege that this argument is based on tunnel vision because it represents one reason (liking to do things spontaneously) against becoming a parent as an overwhelming reason not to become a parent. It presumes that "other things are equal"; factors that might count in favor of becoming a parent (wanting the joy of doing things with one's own child, wanting to help one's own child develop into adulthood) are ignored.

All of this is not to say that we are simply rejecting the argument. It is merely to say that the argument is open to objections. Like every other argument, it can usefully be reconsidered in the light of objections brought to bear on it. Interestingly, when we come to appraise objections to premise (1) we will be doing much the same sort of thing that we do when appraising conductive arguments. We will be weighing the significance of pros and cons. Do the benefits and joys of parenthood outweigh the loss of spontaneity and other costs? Some say they do. Many would say they do, and that premise (1) is not acceptable unless it is understood as containing a *ceteris paribus* clause. Counterconsiderations, in the form of objections to the premises, are relevant to the evaluation of this argument, despite the fact that it is a valid syllogism.

As for inductive arguments, obviously objections can be made to their premises. Counterconsiderations can bear on the (A) condition for inductive arguments, just as they can for deductive ones. But in these arguments, unlike deductive ones, counterconsiderations may bear on the (R) and (G) conditions. Most characteristically, they affect (G). A crucial difference between deductively valid arguments and inductive arguments is that for the latter, additional information dramatically affects the strength of the argument. Consider, for instance, the following example:

1. John is a Pole.
2. Ninety percent of Poles are Catholic.
Therefore, probably,
Conclusion: John is Catholic.

As far as (R) and (G) are concerned, this argument is inductively strong; without further information, we could infer that the chances of John being Catholic are about 90 percent. But then suppose we add new information to the argument.

1. John is a Pole.
2. Ninety percent of Poles are Catholic.
3. John is an intellectual.
4. Fifty percent of Polish intellectuals are Catholic.
Therefore, probably,
Conclusion: John is Catholic.

The argument has now been weakened considerably. Statements (3) and (4) are, in effect, undermining the original argument; they function as objections to it and show a need for revisions. Something has to change; in the light of this new information, we know that John is a Polish intellectual. Given his inclusion in this narrower subgroup, the chances of his being Catholic are only about 50 percent.

Some theories of inductive argument incorporate a **total evidence requirement,** stipulating that the support from the premises for the conclusion is to be assessed with regard to the total evidence relevant to the conclusion. In practice, satisfying this condition is nearly always impossible. But the requirement is useful in reminding us that the premises of inductive arguments virtually never state all the information that bears on the conclusion. The strength of the inference from the premises to the conclusion can be undermined by new information, as in the example above. When that happens, the new information plays the role of a counterconsideration to the original argument.

Much the same can be said about inductive analogies. The new information will be some point of difference between the primary subject and the analogue, a difference that is negatively relevant to the conclusion. Suppose, for instance, that we were testing artificial sugars on rats, with a view to determining their suitability for human use, and we came to discover an enzyme essential for digestion in rats that had no counterpart in human beings. If we were to discover such a fact, it would weaken the analogy; it amounts to a counterconsideration. In light of this fact, the analogy would have to be reevaluated and our estimation of its inductive strength might change.

In *a priori* analogies, counterconsiderations may also bear on the (R) and (G) conditions. There will be differences between the primary subject and the analogue; the relevance of these differences to the conclusion has to be determined. Any difference that is negatively relevant to the conclusion is, in effect, a counterconsideration, and its significance has to be judged or "weighed." Suppose, for instance, someone were to argue that students should not opt for the easiest courses at university because doing so is "just like" being offered a precious treasure and choosing bubble gum. One might object that even the harder courses at university are flawed in various ways and not like "treasure"; or that getting poor marks in a hard course can jeopardize a student's whole career, whereas one's future would be secure if one chose a treasure. These differences, which are negatively relevant to the conclusion, would be counterconsiderations.

Counterconsiderations, then, may bear on all the different types of arguments described in this book. Thinking of these negatively relevant points, stating them clearly, and rethinking the premises and inferences in arguments accordingly are fundamental parts of argument evaluation. One thing that makes counterconsiderations especially important is the fact that we tend to have various biases that frequently affect our thought and reasoning. One is the so-called **confirmation bias**. When we believe something (call it X), we tend to notice and remember evidence and arguments that support X, and we tend not to notice and remember evidence and arguments that would refute X. We may even avoid reading sources or listening to people who are against X. We tend, then, to be selective in a biased way; we find out more and more that supports X and less and less that disconfirms X. The tendency is likely to make us feel more certain than we should about what we believe. It also means that we are unlikely to have a good appreciation of how strong the evidence and arguments for X really are.

The confirmation bias appears to be deeply natural.[7] As human beings, we are all affected by it to some degree. We are naturally attached to our own attitudes and opinions, and we have only so much attention and mental energy available. Few conservatives use their leisure time seeking out the arguments and analyses of liberals when it comes to social policy; for that matter, few liberals are keen to find and appreciate conservative accounts of such matters. Life is short. Why go out of our way to pay attention to things that we (supposedly) "know" we are going to disagree with? Although the confirmation bias is natural, it contributes to self-indulgence, illusion, and prejudice. When we attend only to data that seem to support what we already believe, and protect ourselves from objections and counterarguments, we deprive ourselves of the opportunity to have well-reasoned, fair, and accurate beliefs. In the struggle to be open-minded and reflect on problems and issues in a fair and balanced way, we should try to avoid the confirmation bias. Consciously seeking out counterconsiderations for our own positions and arguments is one excellent way to counter this natural bias.

To reach reasonable beliefs and opinions, we have to attend to and engage in arguments. A central and essential part of all judgment and balanced argument is the consideration and evaluations of reasons and counterconsiderations. We have to weigh the significance of alternative reasons, evidence, and claims, and do our best to make careful judgments about which arguments are most cogent and which claims are most convincing.

In her interviews on causal reasoning, researcher Deanna Kuhn found that of her 160 subjects, between 30 and 40 percent were unable to state a position or theory alternative to the one they held. Half could not state a counterconsideration that would tend to disconfirm their own view. Let's reflect on the meaning of these results. Suppose you are being interviewed because someone wishes to explore your skills in argument. The interviewer says, in effect, "Yes, I know you believe *X;* what are some other ideas about this problem? What would someone who disagrees with you about *X* say is the case?" Your challenge at this point is not to state *X* again; it is not to present an argument defending *X;* it is not to explain why you think *X;* it is not to tell a story showing why *X* is plausible; it is not to try to rebut some argument you might imagine against *X.* Your challenge is simply to imagine and articulate a position *different from* and *incompatible with* your own. People interviewed by Kuhn and her colleagues were asked, in effect, to think of the issue or problem as someone else might think of it—someone different from them, who would understand this aspect of the world differently from the way they understand it. To do this requires some degree of imagination and empathy, some ability to see things from a point of view that is not one's own. The interview question asks the subject to make a distinction between what happens and what he or she thinks about what happens.

What Kuhn's research suggested at this point was rather depressing. There was some variety, depending on the topic considered (school failure, recidivism, or unemployment), but overall, between 30 and 40 percent of people interviewed were *unable to state a theory alternative to their own.* Some could say only a few words of something different without lapsing back into their own view. Others were unwilling even to try. To give an idea of the problem at its most serious, here are some of the inadequate responses:

(a) They might say that . . . hmmm . . . whatever ideas there are . . . I mean, I tried to cover a lot of angles, so I'm trying to think what other ideas there are . . . .
(b) I don't know. I seem to have covered everything.
(c) I think they'll say the same thing I would say. It's the atmosphere (criminals return to).
(d) I have no idea. But I'm sure that they would have every argument in the book, every possible argument, and still would not persuade me.[8]

Such responses are disappointing and even a little sad, because they indicate dogmatism and a lack of imagination, and strongly suggest a lack of sympathy and empathy for other people's views.

It is always worth remembering that our own opinions and beliefs are not the only ones. On most complex topics, people hold a wide variety of views, and many of these can be supported by some good reasons and arguments. This is not to say that every opinion and belief is as good as every other, or that every argument is as good as every other. But it does mean that it is important to use our imagination, struggle against the confirmation bias, and appreciate the distinction between what we think, the way the world is, and what others may think. By actively seeking out counterconsiderations to our own arguments, and by remaining open to alternative pictures of reality and new arguments, we can improve our thought and understanding. If we cannot do this, we may have many beliefs and opinions, but we will not have good reasons for them. In fact, we will then fail even to understand our own beliefs. Counterconsiderations are negatively relevant to our arguments and our beliefs, but positively relevant to the balance and accuracy of our thinking.

CHAPTER SUMMARY

In this chapter, we have described and discussed conductive arguments and counterconsiderations. In conductive arguments, several factors are drawn together to support the conclusion. They are put forward as relevant reasons, reasons making the conclusion plausible or sensible. When X is a reason for Y, this means that, other things being equal, if X then Y. The Latin expression for "other things being equal" is *ceteris paribus*.

Conductive arguments are common in many contexts: they are especially prevalent in reasoning about practical decisions, policy issues, and problems of interpretation. Sometimes conductive arguments include reference to counterconsiderations, factors that are negatively relevant to the conclusion. To evaluate a conductive argument, we have to determine whether the premises are acceptable, whether they are positively relevant to the conclusion (this is determined separately for each premise), and how strongly they support that conclusion when counterconsiderations are taken into account. At this last stage (G), the strength of supporting reasons must be estimated and evaluated in the light of counterconsiderations.

The notions of counterconsiderations, counterarguments, and *ceteris paribus* clauses apply not only to conductive arguments but also to all the other sorts of arguments discussed in this book. It is especially important to construct and reflect on counterconsiderations to our own arguments and beliefs. By doing so, we can help ourselves to overcome the confirmation bias—our natural tendency to attend selectively to things that support our own positions, while ignoring evidence against them.

Review of Terms Introduced

Ceteris paribus   Latin expression that means "other things being equal."

Ceteris paribus **clause**   Clause specifying that a principle or connection holds "other things being equal." Most "reasons" statements have an implicit *ceteris paribus* clause. To say that X is a reason for doing A is to say that other things being equal, if X then we should do A. The *ceteris paribus* clause recognizes that there can be a range of exceptions: those cases in which other things are not equal. Example: Other things being equal, if a practice alleviates serious pain, it should be legally permissible.

Conductive argument   Argument in which the pattern of support is convergent (not linked; compare Chapter 2) and premises are put forward as being separately relevant to the conclusion. Counterconsiderations may be acknowledged by the arguer. Conductive arguments are sometimes called good reasons arguments, cumulation of consideration arguments, or balance of consideration arguments.

Confirmation bias   Tendency to notice, credit, and recall information and arguments that support one's beliefs and opinions while ignoring, forgetting, or discrediting information and arguments that disconfirm those beliefs and opinions.

Counterconsideration   Claim that is negatively relevant to the conclusion of an argument. Counterconsiderations may be explicitly acknowledged by an arguer, as is reasonably common in conductive arguments. In this case, the arguer is committed to the claim that his stated premises outweigh the counterconsiderations. Often arguers fail to acknowledge or mention counterconsiderations, and critics have to discover them for themselves to fully evaluate an argument.

Generality of reasons   Refers to the fact that a reason is never a reason solely in one case. If X is a reason for doing A in one circumstance, then X is, other things being equal, a reason for doing A in other circumstances. This point may be stated in another way: if X is a reason for doing A in one circumstance, then X is a reason for doing A in any other relevantly similar circumstance. Relevantly similar circumstances are the circumstances in which other things are equal. The questions that arise are: What are the other things that have to be equal? What are the relevant similarities between circumstances with respect to doing A?

Total evidence requirement   Requirement that an inductive argument be appraised with reference to the total evidence that counts for or against its conclusion. This principle is theoretically important, but not strictly applicable in practice.

Tunnel vision   Single-minded view of an issue that takes one relevant factor and exaggerates its importance to make it the only relevant factor. With tunnel vision, we oversimplify. One manifestation of tunnel vision is to attempt to resolve complex issues with deductive arguments when conductive ones, including counterconsiderations, would be more appropriate.

Notes

1. For further reflections on conductive arguments, consult Carl Wellman, *Challenge and Response: Justification in Ethics* (Carbondale, IL: Southern Illinois University Press, 1971) and Trudy Govier, "Reasoning with Pros and Cons: Conductive Arguments Revisited," in *The Philosophy of Argument* (Newport News, VA: Vale Press, 1999).

2. *For instructors.* The converse is not true. Not all arguments exemplifying the convergent support pattern are conductive. One might have

an argument with several distinct premises, each of which separately deductively entails the conclusion. In such a case, the argument would be deductively valid and hence would not be a conductive argument, as defined here. However, it would exemplify convergent support.

3. Thomas Hurka, "Is It Wrong to Lie about Santa Claus?" as reprinted in the fourth edition of this text (Wadsworth, 1997), pp. 447–449.

4. We may distinguish between a stronger and a weaker sense of acknowledging counterconsid-

erations. In the stronger sense, which is meant here, the arguer allows that these really are objections to his or her position. In the weaker sense, the arguer allows only that other people think these are objections to his or her position.

5   No implication that we can mathematically measure or judge the relevance and comparative strength of various reasons or counterconsiderations is intended.

6.   The general direction of these developments was suggested by David Hitchcock. I have benefited from discussions of conductive arguments with him and with Marius Vermaak.

7.   For a discussion of the confirmation bias, see R. Nisbett and L. Ross, *Human Inference: Strategies and Shortcomings of Social Judgment* (Englewood Cliffs, NJ: Prentice-Hall, 1980).

8.   Deanna Kuhn, *The Skills of Argument* (New York: Cambridge University Press, 1991), pp. 109–111. Letters (a) and so on have been inserted.

chapter twelve
Reflective Analysis
of Longer Works

O
UR ATTENTION IN THIS BOOK thus far has been concentrated on passages and arguments that are relatively short. To have examples of a manageable size and level of difficulty, and in the interest of efficiency, we have selected illustrations of a few sentences or, at most, several paragraphs, in length. We hope that the many illustrations and exercises have made the distinctions and logical points come alive for you, in addition to giving a variety of material for you to analyze and evaluate. But to effectively use the knowledge and skills developed thus far in this book, you need to work on applying them to lengthier materials. The purpose of this chapter is to take some steps in this direction. We develop a number of points about the understanding and evaluation of essay-length works and then treat one essay-length example using the method described. Several interesting essays are appended to the chapter to give you good material to work from.

Introduction

There are some ways in which appraising a lengthier essay is easier than working on a short passage. Most significantly, there is the matter of context. It probably has not escaped your attention that when one or two paragraphs are excerpted from a book, editorial, or letter, it is often not clear what point is at issue or why the author is attending to the subject at all. We have tried to address this problem by selecting carefully and by giving appropriate background information. The advantage with a longer selection is that claims and arguments you need to evaluate are located within a richer and more informative context. You do not have to guess at why the author or speaker is dealing with the topic or where he or she is going once a key argument has been given, because you have a lengthier, more substantial work to deal with. In addition, you are likely to have developed background knowledge that bears on the issue discussed because you are probably reading the longer piece as part of an ongoing interest in the topic.

There are, of course, features that make the analysis of longer pieces difficult as compared with that of shorter ones. You cannot work through a lengthy piece sentence by sentence or even paragraph by paragraph. You cannot consider and carefully evaluate every argument in a longer piece. Typically, there are too many distinct arguments; to locate every one, work out a standardized version, and appraise it using the ARG conditions would be too cumbersome a task. If you were to do this, an essay describing your results probably would be painfully boring for your readers. To reflectively and rationally evaluate an essay-length work, you have to be **selective** in what you address. You have to understand the essay well enough to identify the author's most important claims and arguments and then concentrate your attention on them. Selectivity requires sensitive, accurate understanding and good judgment.

In this chapter, we describe techniques for understanding and appraising essays, on the assumption that the immediate application of these skills will be an analytic evaluative essay of your own. There is no single recipe for getting a good result: we are offering guidelines that we hope will be helpful.

Reading for Understanding

To work out a reflective and well-reasoned response to an essay-length work, the first step is to read the work carefully and make sure that you understand it. For most substantive essays, genuine understanding requires more than one reading.

We often think of reading as a passive activity. In fact, there are various ways of reading actively. When you first read for understanding, relax and try to enter into the thinking of the author. Try to go along with his or her point of view, to engage in it as though it were your own. We call this sort of reading empathetic. (Empathy is the identification with the feelings, beliefs, and point of view of another person; we empathize with someone when we understand, feel, and respond to something from his or her point of view.) Reading something empathetically does not imply that you ultimately are going to agree with it—after understanding, you may agree or disagree. What it means is going along, at least temporarily, with the thoughts and ideas of the writer, entering into his or her frame of reference and working through the flow of ideas and feelings. Doing this is an important device for understanding the work.

When you have read an essay using this empathetic approach, you should then try to state its main point *in your own words*. What is the author trying to say? What is his or her main idea? You should be able to state this **thesis** in your own words without looking back at the written work. A test of whether you have understood the essay is that you can state its main point without looking back at the original. If you find that you cannot do this, you need to read the essay again—perhaps several more times—until its point becomes clear to you.

Let's assume that you have identified the thesis of the essay and can state it in your own words.

Essentially, *X* says that *C*.

But in a good essay, there is not only a thesis, there are reasons given in its support. The author does not just pull a central claim out of nowhere; he or she develops and defends the point. If you understand the essay, on the basis of careful **empathetic reading**, you will be able to state the major reasons for this central claim. You should be able to put in your own words a statement of the following form:

Essentially, *X* says that *C,* because *R*.

In this formula, *X* represents the author, *C* represents the thesis, and *R* represents the reasons for it. The word *essentially* is present to indicate that you are trying to capture the main points of the author; you are not including every strand of supporting argument or every detail. You are attributing an argument to the author: *C* (conclusion) because *R* (premises). This argument is one you have stated in your own words; it represents your attempt to grasp the central point of the essay, so it will necessarily omit many details and qualifications. We'll refer to this construction as the **core thesis argument.**

When you have arrived at a version of the core thesis argument, reread the essay to check your statement against the original. As you read, keep asking yourself whether the author is really saying what you have understood him or her to be saying. This is a stage in which you have to be careful not to commit the straw man fallacy. Especially if you are inclined to disagree with the author and have found empathy in reading difficult to achieve, you should crosscheck your statement of the core thesis argument against the original to ensure that you have not misrepresented him or her. Look for evidence that the author has indeed said what you have attributed to him or her.

There is a balancing act here—one requiring judgment and care on your part. You must use your own words and you must be selective; therefore, your statement cannot represent every detail of support, every nuance, and every qualification in the original. On the other hand, you should not omit essential aspects of the core argument. You will be committing the straw man fallacy if you overstate the thesis or if you omit a central reason. If appropriate, revise your statement of the core thesis argument on the basis of rereading. You will use the core thesis argument for the next stages of analysis and appraisal, so it is important to get it right.

In this process, there are several sorts of essays that pose special problems. You may find that you have great difficulty attributing a thesis statement to the author. Such difficulties may arise for various reasons. The essay may be inexplicit in its statement of a point of view; the author may make a point through satire or ridicule, for instance. Or, the essay may be confusingly written or even contradictory, so that you cannot identify a single clear thesis. Before going on, we take a brief detour to say something about these special cases.

The Inexplicit Essay

This type of essay has no obvious, directly stated central claim or supporting argument. Such an essay often will be written from a distinctive point of view but does not directly, explicitly state a central thesis claim or supporting argument. It may seem to be making a point but will not state that point directly. We'll refer to such essays as **inexplicit essays**. They make a point but make it indirectly by using irony, ridicule, or satire. An essayist may implicitly criticize a policy or practice by drawing it out to extremes and making fun of it. You can, perhaps, get a better grasp of what is meant here by reading the following few paragraphs from one such essay.

These excerpts are taken from an essay called "Isn't Biotechnology Wonderful?" by Bob Bragg.[1] Bragg's essay begins as follows:

> Q: What do you get when you cross a tiger with a parrot?
> A: I don't know, but when it talks I listen.

After this provocative introduction, Bragg goes on to say that there is news from Italy to the effect that biogenetic scientists—using refined techniques of artificial fertilization—have crossed a chimpanzee with a human being. The experiments were interrupted at the embryo stage for ethical reasons, but were said in a report to be capable of creating a new breed of slaves, or a subhuman species to do boring chores for human beings. Bragg writes a lively set of witty comments on the situation, but he never says directly that the biogeneticists were ethically or scientifically wrong in pursuing this line of research. (Skepticism about their approach is indicated in the title of his own essay, which appears to be sarcastic.)

We cannot reprint the whole essay here, but the following passages will give you an idea:

> "It seems like a real life case of Dr. Frankenstein. Another sorcerer's apprentice ignorantly toying with high technology yielding unforeseen consequences and a host of new, insoluble problems.
> "But I wasn't shocked. As a matter of fact, I was encouraged. Biotechnology offers solutions to problems which have plagued mankind for millennia. Now the monkey's play looks like the helping hand. Science offers us the means to avoid the pain and turmoil so common in this vale of tears. . . .
> "Take famine, for example. We no longer need to have millions of humans die off in Ethiopia and Mozambique. We simply cross humans with camels and produce a stubborn creature that can go for weeks without a drink. Will that be one hump or two?"

The rest of the essay continues in the same vein. The final sentence is "Isn't science wonderful?"

After the author has mentioned camels crossed with Africans, politicians produced by crossing chameleons with parrots (they could change rapidly and aptly echo the voice of the people), and teenagers with army ants, the reader will suspect that the hopes of these scientists are being satirized as ridiculously unrealistic. As a reader, you will have to attribute both a central claim and (if appropriate) a supporting argument to such an entertaining author. As it stands, the essay explicitly states neither. Yet Bragg is clearly quite skeptical and cynical about the value of such scientific experiments as these. He seems to be implying some such thesis as:

> Experiments to blend different species genetically to produce some result useful to our own species are of dubious success and value.

If this is his thesis, then we have to read the essay to see whether any reasons for it are given directly or indirectly in the satirical and witty remarks the author makes. In fact, the author does not seem to give reasons: instead of arguing against the genetic experimentation, he ridicules it.

Another indirect approach is found in the essay that, in effect, makes a point by *redescription*. A commonly accepted practice is redescribed in terms and in a context designed to make readers see the phenomenon differently, setting it in a new light. Such redescription can make a familiar accepted practice seem unattractive, controversial, wrong, or just plain silly. Some such essays are brilliant and entertaining, though they contain no statement of a thesis and no direct argument on its behalf.

The strategy of essay evaluation described in this chapter has been designed primarily for direct argumentative essays. From our point of view, inexplicit essays are special cases; this book is primarily about arguments, and these inexplicit essays are nonargumentative in form. But when you try to evaluate longer works you may find some of this type, so we will try to give a few helpful tips about them.

First, we recommend careful reading to see whether you can fairly attribute a central claim to the author, even though he or she does not state it in so many words. (It does seem possible to do this with Bragg's essay.) Reading carefully and imaginatively, you often can attribute a thesis to the author of a satirical or redescriptive essay, and sometimes you can attribute reasons for that thesis as well. If you can attribute a thesis, but no argument, then part of your appraisal of the essay will depend on your assessment of whether that thesis needs to be supported by an argument. If the claim does not seem acceptable without further reason and evidence, and you cannot plausibly attribute any argument to the author on the basis of his or her work, then the essay will be flawed because of its failure to give any rational support for its thesis. (In fact, this might be a criticism of Bragg's essay, charming and entertaining though it is.) Other aspects of the methods described in this chapter can be fairly readily adapted to fit the inexplicit essay.

The Confused or Contradictory Essay

A second kind of problem essay is one that is **confusingly** written or **contradictory** in its content to such an extent that its thesis is unclear. If you are unable to state the thesis of an essay and you suspect that your problems are actually the fault of the author, read the essay again with a critical eye. Leave the empathetic view behind and look carefully through the work with the specific goal of trying to identify a central thesis. If you cannot find a central claim, or if you find several that are inconsistent with each other, the essay fails to make a point—or at least fails to make it clearly—and your evaluation will be a negative one, pointing out confusion or contradictoriness in the original.

Reading for Appraisal

At this stage, you set aside empathy and read the essay from the point of view of a critic. You may find it useful to pretend that you are a teacher who has the task of marking the essay, or a reviewer for a newspaper who is going to write a piece evaluating the essay for prospective readers. You have a statement of the main claim and the core thesis argument, and you keep these in mind. On the assumption that this is the claim the author is putting forward, and these are the sorts of reasons he or she is giving for it, you want to look at the essay *critically* to get a sense of how well the argument is expressed. You want, tentatively, to reach an evaluation of the essay.

An essay is not evaluated solely on the basis of its logic and argument. Logic and argument are important aspects, but features such as organization, style, tone, interest, balance, and judgment also need to be considered. A good essay is one that makes a significant and important point in a plausible and interesting way, that engages the reader—or perhaps even captivates him or her. If an essay is awkwardly written or disorganized, or if it is boring, monotonous, or repetitious, these are flaws.

Other flaws closer to logic as such are the use of emotionally charged language in place of argument, explanation, or analysis; *ad hominem* or straw man misrepresentations of those with whom the author disagrees; or a pervasive failure even to consider plausible alternative interpretations and theories and objections to the author's own position. Such topics have been discussed in this book, and we hope and expect that our discussions will be helpful to you in appreciating these features of longer works.

We suggest the following **features list** as a guide for appraisal:

1. *Interest, importance, and plausibility of thesis.*
2. *Quality of core supporting argument.* Use ARG conditions.
3. *Apparent quality of further arguments.*
4. *Accuracy.* Plausibility of claims, acceptability of statements, documentation of claims (where appropriate).
5. *Clarity and organization.* Are points developed in an orderly way? Are background information, description, and explanatory material included where needed?

6. *Coherence and consistency.* Does the essay hold together? Explicit or implicit contradictions are a serious flaw.
7. *Balance.* Does the author consider objections to his or her position? Is the treatment of opposing views fair and accurate? Are counterarguments carefully developed, if appropriate?

Features 1 to 7 are, in a broad sense, logical: they are concerned with the quality and reasonableness of statements, arguments, and reasons. In addition, essays can be evaluated for more literary aspects. These have not been emphasized in this text because our main topic is logic and argument, not literary style as such. However, as a careful and attentive reader of an essay, you are bound to be somewhat aware of its literary features—aspects dealing with word choice, imagery, grammatical structure, and general style. These are important dimensions of any essay. In recognition of this fact, we can add to our features list:

8. *Word choice.* Is the language well chosen? Is the tone appropriate to the topic and context? (In most contexts it would be inappropriate to discuss a Shakespearean play in the latest teenage slang, or a serious problem such as capital punishment in humorous terms.) Is excessively emotional language avoided? Is the level of language appropriate for the intended readership? Is excessive repetition of key terms avoided?
9. *Grammatical structures.* Are sentences clearly constructed so as to be fairly easily understood? Is there sufficient variety (for instance, between short sentences and longer ones) to avoid monotony and achieve interest? Are paragraphs about the right length? Do they flow naturally from each other?
10. *Impact.* Is there anything that demands and receives the reader's attention? (Impact can be achieved by stylistic strength, by vividness of imagery, by interest of the "voice" or person of the author, by originality of argument and topic, or in various other ways.)

As you read the essay critically, continue asking yourself the following question: Given that *X* is trying to show that *C* because *R,* do the style, organization, and language of *X's* essay contribute positively to the achievement of this goal? The features list given here is not intended to exhaust the possibilities; you may wish to add elements or features if that seems appropriate for the particular essay you are analyzing. The features list, or an appropriate adaptation of it, is a useful guide for **critical reading**. You can use it to gain an overall impression of the quality of the essay. Make notes as you check the essay with regard to the features list; these can be used at a later stage of your work.

The features list directs your attention to different aspects of the essay. Obviously, an analysis using such a list can give various results. It is rather unlikely that all the aspects you note will point in the same direction, so you will have to examine your notes and reflect on them to reach an overall judgment. If an essay seems cogent in its argumentation and accurate in its claims, but is disorganized and worded in an awkward and uninteresting way, what is your overall judgment going to be? You have to evaluate the importance of these factors and reflect on their respective significance with regard both to the topic and to the purpose for which the essay was written.

On the basis of your understanding of the core thesis argument and a careful critical reading of the essay, *tentatively* put the essay in one of the following three categories: good, mixed, or poor. This tentative evaluation gives you the basis to make an outline of your own essay, offering a reflective analysis and evaluation of the author's work.

Developing an Outline for Your Essay

You now work from the tentative evaluation of the essay toward an outline for an essay of your own. Evaluations you have made using the features list are tentative because you may wish to alter them on the basis of closer study. For example, you might have judged an essay to be of poor quality; you might later find, when you try to identify specific flawed claims and arguments, that the style and content were better than you had thought. You can then revise your assessment to "mixed"—or even "good"—if the faults you thought you had identified turn out, on closer analysis, not to be there or not to be serious.

There are many ways in which essays can be set out. As you gain experience in writing reflective or critical essays, you may develop confidence and a sense of your own preferred organization and style. Here, we offer several alternate models, or pattern outlines, just to get you started. We think these models are quite useful; however, they should not be regarded as rigid patterns—just as suggestions intended to be helpful. We call these models **heuristic** because they are intended to give preliminary guidance, and we recognize that they can be amended and developed in various ways, as appropriate.

Our three heuristic models are based on the three evaluation categories of good, mixed, and poor. We suggest a different model for each category.

Appreciative Essay

When you have judged an essay to be good, you have found it to be well written and well organized, and to make a plausible central claim, based on what struck you, on reading, as convincing arguments and balanced considerations. In many cases, you will be disposed to agree with the central claim. If you did not agree with it prior to studying the essay, you are likely to agree on reflection; the organized presentation and arguments in the essay are likely to have convinced you. In such circumstances, you might wonder what you have to say. If the essay is good—or even terrific—then what can you write about it?

This apparent problem, which occurs to many people when they are asked to respond to a very good essay or other piece of work, is actually not as difficult as it seems. In fact, we think it is not really a problem at all. The problem seems to arise because people make a false assumption—the assumption that the only way to say something interesting and original about another person's work is to *negatively* criticize it. Though we often tend to assume that commenting means criticizing and criticizing means negative criticism, we can comment positively. We can point out interesting, original, or important aspects of another person's work and say why we think those aspects are significant. We can also go on from the author's claim to add further suggestions about related points. A reflective essay can be appreciative—and that is the appropriate form if the work you are studying strikes you, on careful reflection, as good.

Like any essay, an **appreciative essay** reveals something about its author. It shows a generosity of spirit, a willingness to recognize and appreciate another's accomplishments, and an openness to the ideas and arguments of other people. An appreciative essay is not likely to display your penetrating critical intelligence or logical sharpness, but it does convey understanding, a sense of judgment, fairness, and accuracy, and—if carefully constructed—at least a modest amount of originality. Such an essay may not seem to you to be brilliant, but it is a worthy form, one that has been used to good effect by famous critics and social theorists. If you honestly find an essay to be good, and you tend to agree with the central thesis and the core argument on its behalf, then the appropriate response in your own essay is one of appreciation.

Here is a suggested plan for an appreciative essay:

OUTLINE PATTERN FOR THE APPRECIATIVE ESSAY

i.   Introduction
     Say whose essay you are evaluating, and state its title, where you found it, the context in which it was written, and the topic or problem it addresses. State the central claim and the core argument, doing so in such a way that your reader will be able to achieve a good and accurate understanding of these points even if he or she has not read the essay on which you are commenting. Briefly state that in your opinion the essay is excellent and does a good job of establishing its point. If appropriate, add a personal touch by describing why you found the essay of interest and how it helped you change your mind or come to a new understanding of an issue.

ii. Explanation for your judgment
     Cite notable argumentative features that you think contribute to making the essay a good one. That is, mention any arguments that are essential to establishing the author's position or are striking in their originality, vividness, or form. Add any comment you may have on the strength of the arguments the author has given. Say why you think the central claim is interesting and important and, if appropriate, add clarification or emphasis. Cite any notable stylistic and organization features that, in your opinion, contribute to making the essay a good one.

iii. Any minor doubts or qualifications

Even in an essay you have judged to be good, you may have minor doubts about the claims or presentation made. Qualify your overall judgment if appropriate. Cite details, specifically, to provide reasons for your minor doubts or qualifications.

iv. Additional reflections and suggestions
Try to provide additional evidence that would bear on the thesis, or interesting illustrations of the point made by the author.

v. Further implications of the work
Given that you have positively evaluated the author's contribution, after careful analysis, conclude by making some suggestions about its practical or theoretical implications. How could the central claim be applied? Taken further? Related to other important or interesting issues?

On the basis of this outline, you should be able to write a reasonably good appreciative essay. The appreciative model is appropriate when your basic judgment about the essay you are analyzing is, simply, that it is a good one.

How might the ARG conditions of argument cogency be used in all this? As mentioned earlier, it is not possible to evaluate every argument in an essay; the task is just too long and cumbersome. But you can use the ARG conditions in evaluating the core argument; if this argument is not cogent, the essay will not be deemed to be good, but rather to be of mixed or poor quality. In addition, you may use the ARG conditions when locating occasional details that are flawed—in the event that any of those details involved arguments used along the way. A further application for ARG is in the evaluation of your own work. When you have written a draft of your essay, try to read your own work from the point of view of a critic: look at your own arguments and ask yourself whether they are cogent according to the ARG criteria.

Mixed Reaction Essay

A **mixed reaction essay** is appropriate when you have judged the quality of the essay you are evaluating to be mixed; you have checked through the features list and have found both significant strengths and significant weaknesses. (In our experience, this is likely to be a common reaction; few essays are just plain good or just plain poor.) In the nature of the case, the "mixed" category can include considerable variety. Look at your features list and the notes you have made, and reflect on the thesis claim and the core argument. Ask yourself whether your overall sense of the quality of the essay tends more toward the positive or toward the negative. If you have a clear tendency in either direction, it is helpful to recognize it, as it can be relevant to the organization of your points and the emphasis you give them.

Here is a suggested model for the mixed reaction essay:

OUTLINE PATTERN FOR THE MIXED REACTION ESSAY

i. Introduction
State whose essay you are evaluating, give its title, and explain the context in which it appeared and the problem or issue the author discusses. Briefly

state the thesis claim and core argument of the essay. Briefly state your judgment about the essay. This will be of the "It is good on the whole, but has such-and-such flaws" or of the "It is in many ways flawed, but has such-and-such virtues" variety. Or, if you cannot see a preponderance either way, you may say your reaction is mixed because of a mixture of good features and flaws. (You do not need to justify these comments in your introduction; you will justify them later.)

ii. Detailing the essay's flaws

You probably cannot mention every single relevant detail here. Try to choose aspects that are significant and serious as far as the argument, style, and clarity of the essay are concerned. Back up your points with specific details, using brief quotations if this is feasible. If you are saying there are flaws in the argument, defend your criticisms by showing (in effect) how the argument fails on the ARG conditions. (Do not use these terms, of course; you cannot assume that all your readers will have read this textbook.)

iii. Detailing the essay's good features

These can be stylistic, organizational, or argumentative features, or they can deal with the interest of its thesis claim and argument. You may deem an argument as lacking cogency but as interesting because of its original structure or challenging line of thought. You may deem an essay to be weak in argument and logical organization but to be vivid and attractive in style. Or you may think an argument cogent, but deem its style boring and its central claim obvious and not worth making. Say which aspects of the essay you appreciate and why you appreciate them. Back up your comments with specific details. (The notes you made using the features list should be helpful at this stage.)

iv. Summary statement, bringing (ii) and (iii) together

If appropriate, make a qualified judgment of the merits of the work, all things considered. Do you accept the thesis put forward by the author, despite the various flaws you have found? If so, why?

v. Further implications or suggestions

If you have criticized the arguments offered, have you any suggestions as to how they might be improved so that the central claim would be adequately supported? Would you recommend restricting or amending the central claim? Can you suggest (briefly) other arguments in its support? Do you have a counterclaim, or counterarguments, you wish to put forward? If your criticisms have not been directed primarily against the thesis of the essay, and if you have basically accepted it, then are there interesting applications or further ramifications of this thesis that might be mentioned?

The mixed reaction essay displays the balanced, careful, reasoned judgment of the author. A danger is that such an essay may turn out to be too wishy-washy and look as if it is saying nothing. You can avoid giving such an impression by being as specific as possible in your comments as to what is good and what is poor and by striving for some sort of overall response that accurately reflects both the original piece and your own comments about it.

Negatively Critical Essay

Sometimes an essay will strike you as just plain poor. When you are asked to write an appraisal of it, your evaluation in such a case will be mainly negative; it will consist of critical arguments from you, showing how and why the original essay is flawed. There are several risks, or dangers, in writing this sort of essay. One is that you might inadvertently commit the straw man fallacy; you have a negative view toward the central claim, or the argument, or the style of the original, and you lapse into such a mood of rejection that you distort the position or miss essential qualifying details. It is important to check your features list and core central argument against the original essay to make sure that your allegations are fair. A second danger when your essay is primarily critical is that you might lapse into *ad hominem* attacks on the author, or into belligerent, exaggerated, emotionally loaded language. Make sure that you do not slide into attacking the author, as opposed to his or her work, and that your language remains polite and temperate.

Here is a suggested outline for a **negatively critical essay**, the sort you will write if you judge the overall quality of the essay to be poor:

OUTLINE PATTERN FOR THE NEGATIVELY CRITICAL ESSAY

i.   Introduction
     Give the title, author, and context of the essay. State, in neutral terms, the problem or issue addressed and the central claim and core thesis argument. State that in your judgment the essay is of poor quality and does not succeed in accomplishing its purpose.

ii. Justification for your negative appraisal
     Here you can cite in more detail features that, in your opinion, show that the essay is flawed. Failures in argument should be mentioned: if it is your judgment that the author did not succeed in giving good reasons for the central thesis, then you should offer your critique of this argument. Why and how does it fail to be cogent? (Work out your critique using the ARG conditions, but do not state it in these terms; just point out problems of acceptability, relevance, or sufficiency of grounds by explaining, in nontechnical language, how they arise.) Other evidence that the essay merits negative evaluation should be given: check your features list and cite aspects of style, language, organization, tone, or additional argumentative flaws. For any objection that you raise, you should think through and describe why it is an objection. (Keep checking back against the original to make sure your evaluation is not too harsh.)

iii. Mention of any redeeming or positive features of the essay
     Usually, even when an essay is quite poor, it has some redeeming features. It may be well written, though illogical in its argument. Or it may be enter-

taining, or have a novel illustration, despite flaws in other areas. If you can find any such features, identify them and express your appreciation.

iv. Suggestions as to how the essay might be improved
Are there ways in which the author could have strengthened his or her core argument? Are there other arguments, not mentioned by the author, that might support the thesis claim? Briefly mention any constructive suggestions you might have about the work. (Be careful to point out that these are your own amendments, and say why you think they would improve the argument or arguments offered by the author.)

v. Summary conclusion

We will illustrate our technique of essay appraisal with reference to a sample essay, set out in the following section. We do not offer a full example of an appraisal, but we do set out a representative outline. Several interesting recent essays are appended to this chapter as works for you to use to practice the techniques suggested here.

A Sample Essay

The following essay on morality and animals was written by Rose Kemp of Peterborough, Ontario, and adapted for this volume.

MORALITY, ANIMALS, AND THE RIGHT TO LIFE

Traditionally it has been thought that moral relations are relations between people. We have our morally significant relationships with each other—with our friends, lovers, husbands, wives, and colleagues—that is to say with other fairly well-developed members of the human species. However, morality is not restricted only to others who are mature and relatively independent human beings. Morality extends to children, to helpless adults, and to seriously mentally handicapped adults. But what the exact boundaries of morality are is not entirely clear. Are human embryos and fetuses entities with whom we have moral relations? What about God, the Devil, and angels, if they exist? What about animals—individual animals and animal species? Or future people, who do not exist yet? Nation-states? Or plants? Is it morally wrong to cut down a 1000-year-old tree and use the wood to make toilet paper? If this is wrong, is it because we wrong the tree itself?

Just what the boundaries of morality are is itself a moral question. This is obvious in the context of the abortion debate, where controversy rages, both in the popular press and amongst philosophers, as to whether a woman has a moral obligation to the fetus developing in her body and whether we condone murder if we condone abortion. Abortion is not the only controversy that involves an issue of moral boundaries. In current policy and politics, the status of future people, animals, animal species, and plants are also important—and in dispute. In this essay I shall not comment on the moral status of the embryo or fetus or of future people, God or angels, nation-states or plants. My present topic is that of animals.

Our whole culture is based on the assumption that animals other than human beings lack the moral status that human beings have. We human beings treat other animals quite differently from the way we treat each other. We cultivate animals for food and clothing, raise them to be killed, keep them in confining and uncomfortable conditions on factory farms, use them experimentally for teaching and research, exhibit them in zoos, and keep them as pets. All these things would be unacceptable if we did them to people. Experimentation is a possible exception—but a controversial one. Ethical restrictions on experiments on people are quite strict and nearly always require that subjects of experiments give informed consent. Can animals consent to experiments done on them? Of course not—and furthermore, some of these experiments impose terrible pain and suffering on their innocent victims.

We do not kill people in order to eat them, nor exhibit them in zoos, nor deprive them of material affection in order to satisfy our scientific curiosity as to what the effects of that deprivation might just happen to be. This difference is because of our own basic assumption about the moral status of animals. We do not think of animals as beings with an intrinsic worth, beings whom we should not hurt or wrong. There is something absurd in the idea that a squirrel or cat is a moral being. When one reads—as I did several years ago—that a dog was tried for murder, the story seems bizarre and incredible. Yet this underlying assumption about animals has been exposed over the past several decades, because some eloquent voices have spoken out against it. Many people are extremely upset and concerned when they see animals suffering or being cruelly treated. This kind of reaction is not new; it has been going on in Western societies for at least a century. In fact, humane societies for the protection of animals existed before the institutionalization of groups for the protection of human children.

The famous humanitarian Albert Schweitzer, who gave up a rewarding intellectual life in Europe to work with lepers in tropical Africa, believed that *life itself*, not just human life, was worthy of respect. He was unwilling to kill even the tropical insects whose presence hindered his medical work on behalf of leprous human beings. Peter Singer, an Australian philosopher and activist, wrote in his book *Animal Liberation* a fervent and dramatic appeal for attention to the prolonged and cruel suffering of animals in scientists' laboratories and on factory farms. Singer argued that our common assumption about animals is just plain wrong and convinced many of his readers that vegetarianism is a morally obligatory lifestyle. His vivid portrayals of the horrible conditions in which some animals lead their lives are unforgettable. Singer argued that animals can suffer, that they do suffer, that they merit moral consideration, and that we should act to end their suffering.

There are good reasons for these conclusions. Consider the basic human right: the right to life. There is no reasonable basis for giving this right to humans and denying it to animals. To say that all human beings have a right to life, a right that is a natural human right, is to say that it is wrong to take the life of a human being without some particularly compelling reason to do so, and that the wrongness of doing this does not depend on any particular legal system or social code. Certainly, to understand more fully what a natural right to life is, we would need to clarify what *particularly compelling reasons* might justify the taking of human life. And we need to explore why this right is natural or universal. But however problematic such aspects of a natural human right to life might be, many people do believe in it. It is enshrined in the United Nations Declaration of Human Rights, to which the United States and Canada are both signatories. The right to life is important and basic. All other rights seem, in fact, to presuppose it. If one is not alive, one cannot exercise other rights such as the freedom of speech and worship, or the right to vote, or get an education and a job.

The right to life is commonly believed to belong to all human beings. Such a right is acknowledged in national and international law, and it is basic and minimal. Many of us do assume that all human beings have a right to life. But our way of life requires that nonhuman animals lack this right. If we thought they had a right to life, we would not kill them for food and clothing, or in the course of experiments. Is this position about the moral status of human beings and animals a consistent one?

If human beings have a natural right to life, then all human beings have this right. And "all" really means all: the severely retarded, newborn infants, the very senile, the morally wicked, the grossly deformed—every last one of them. It may sometimes be justified to take human life, even given this natural right to life—if we had to kill another human being in self-defense, or to save him or her from an agonizingly prolonged and painful death, this might be morally permissible. But we cannot reconcile killing humans as a source of food or of pleasure, or in the course of experiments, or because it is convenient or efficient, with our basic belief that human beings have a natural right to life. We do these things to animals, so obviously we think that animals do not have a natural right to life. Why not? What's the difference?

One common rationalization is that the difference is in the humans' capacity to reason. Another is that humans, unlike nonhuman animals, have the capacity to make moral decisions, to reflect on their actions, to take the needs of others into account. In short human beings, unlike animals, are *moral agents*. But neither of these ideas stands up to analysis. The reason is simple: not all humans are rational and not all humans have moral capacity. (Infants and the severely retarded do not have these qualities; nor do those who are comatose, or extremely senile.) Yet all humans are believed to have the natural right to life. If this natural right to life is to apply to all of us, it must be founded on a feature that we all have, and since we do not all have either rationality or moral capacity, it cannot be exclusively founded on these features.

How can we possibly justify giving a right to life to a tiny human infant, or a seriously mentally retarded human being, and refusing it to a normal adult dog or chimpanzee? There is no general difference that would justify making such an enormously important moral distinction. The adult chimpanzee behaves in a more complex way than the human infant, he gives more evidence of desires and intentions, and his capacities for action and relationship are more fully developed. What feature could we possibly find that a human infant would have, and a chimpanzee lack, that could justify giving the human infant a right to life that the chimpanzee does not have? None: that is the answer.

There is no relevant difference that applies to all human beings and to no nonhuman animals and that would make us consistent in saying all human beings have a natural right to life, whereas no animals do. To be consistent, we should either admit that some human beings do not have a natural right to life or concede that some nonhuman animals do have this right.

If all human beings have a natural right to life, then nonhuman animals have that right too. Now, many people are not going to like this position. They are going to find it radical and strange, and they are going to see that taking it seriously would require extreme changes in lifestyle. So they are going to resist it. What can be said on the other side? A common response is, "Come on, human beings are human, and rats and chimpanzees are only animals. They can't have rights." But this statement expresses nothing more than chauvinistic mysticism. What's so special about being human, about being within one biological species rather than another?

Singer said that giving one species a privileged moral status was just the same thing as giving one race or sex a privileged status. He coined a term for the practice: *speciesism*. Downgrading animals, as less worthy of consideration than people, is speciesism, and speciesism is objectionable, just like racism or sexism. Just being human is no more morally relevant than just being white or just being male.

If animals have a natural right to life, they are within the moral sphere, and it becomes a moral question whether we are justified in killing them in order to eat them. Unless it could be shown that animals provide a necessary element in human diet, the answer to this question should be a firm no. Even if meat were strictly necessary for the continuance of human life—it isn't, in fact—we would have a conflict of rights situation. To think that human interests always supersede those of animals is not only selfish, it is biased and arbitrary.

Save us, you will say, kind reader. Save us from this relentless and impractical logic. For the absence of a distinction between all humans on the one hand and all nonhuman animals on the other, we are going to change our eating habits, our farming habits, our whole way of life? Must we follow Singer into impractical and self-sacrificing idealism?

One who takes a different view is, by coincidence, another Australian, John Passmore. In a book called *Man's Responsibility to Nature*, Passmore said that moral obligations and responsibilities arise only within communities. If I am to have an obligation to you, you and I have to be connected, or related in some way; we must be members of the same community. There must be at least a chance of reciprocity. And, according to Passmore, "Men, plants, animals, and soil do not form a community; bacteria and men do not recognise mutual obligations nor do they have common interests." If we treated plants and animals and landscapes as part of our community, Passmore says, we could not "civilise the world." This seems, incidentally, to be quite a revealing phrase. Strip mining, deforestation, the hole in the ozone layer, pollution, factory farming—these count as civilizing the world? Then, God save us from civilization! Passmore argues that if we were to accept animals and plants as members of our moral community, we couldn't even go on living.

The implicit assumption underlying Passmore's idea that moral relationships must be within communities is that moral relationships must be reciprocal; they must be able to work both ways. According to this view, I have no duty to respect the right to life of a tiger, because a tiger is never going to have a duty to respect my right to life—and he's not going to respect it either. Tigers have no duties. Animals are not in moral communities with respect to one another, and they are certainly not in moral communities with respect to human beings. That's why we don't think a wolf is failing morally if it kills the lamb for food; the wolf is not a moral being and cannot have a duty to recognize any natural right to life that we think the lamb might have. And that's why it really would be ridiculous to try a dog for murder.

Those who want to go on enjoying steaks, leather coats, pets, and zoos would no doubt like to think that Passmore is right; his claim that morality requires reciprocity seems to give a compelling reason not to allow animals to count as moral beings. But the matter is not quite so simple. There is a striking and fatal counterexample to Passmore's assumption that moral relations require reciprocity. It is the case of children. Most parents love their children and want to care for them; we commonly believe that parents have duties toward their children and children have a right to nutrition, education, love, and basic care. Yet children cannot accept duties with respect to us. Nor can they rise to make moral claims; they are for many years not capable of proclaiming their moral status. And yet we do believe in obligations to children and we do think that they have rights. Children who are not full-fledged moral agents are nevertheless within our moral community.

It might seem that we have an argument, from Passmore, for keeping animals out of the moral sphere. But if we follow that argument, we are going to keep some human beings out of the moral sphere too. And this we are not going to countenance. So presuming that we do not wish to alter our beliefs about our obligations to infant humans, we are going to have to alter our beliefs about animals. This is just where the whole discussion started: how can we be consistent in keeping all humans within the bounds of morality while keeping all animals outside it?

Animals are not just like people; they are certainly importantly different from mature human beings, who can make moral choices and assume responsibilities, and deliberate on their actions. People's concepts are much more elaborate and sophisticated than those of animals, and their emotional range and the range of their interest is vastly greater. Only human beings can speculate about free will and the meaning of life; wolves and tigers and cows and pigs do not do this. Presumably this was the sort of thing the famous political philosopher John Stuart Mill had in mind when he made his famous remark that it would be better to be Socrates dissatisfied than a pig satisfied. Socrates wondered about the meaning of it all: pigs do not.

But that does not prove that pigs and other animals are right outside the moral order, that they are lower beings deserving no moral consideration. The problem about morality and animals is not that there are no differences between typical animals and typical people. It is, rather, that there are no differences that are relevant to our current practices with regard to animals—relevant in the sense of counting towards the justification of those practices—and that are also universally characteristic of human beings as contrasted with other animals. Why do these facts constitute a problem? Because we cannot accept them and continue with our current practices towards animals. Because they are uncomfortable for us to think about. Because they make us uneasy. They show our need to reform our cruel practices, to revise our way of life with its inhumanity to nonhumans.

There is no way to avoid this problem. If all human beings have moral status, then animals have moral status. All human beings do have moral status. Human beings have, among other things, the right to life. So, accordingly, do nonhuman animals. The challenge we face is to change our thought and action to take these animal rights seriously. It will not be easy, but it has to be done.

Working through an Example

We shall now use the techniques described earlier in this chapter to analyze and evaluate Kemp's essay on morality and animals.

Finding and Stating the Main Thesis and Core Supporting Argument

Once we have read the essay empathetically several times, we try to state its main thesis. The main thesis of Kemp's essay is:

Animals have a moral right to life.

On the basis of this thesis, Kemp also states related ideas, such as the need for reform of social practices like scientific experimentation on animals and factory farming. But her main claim is for the moral status of animals. Kemp's main argument is essentially as follows:

1. It is a basic assumption in social and moral life that all human beings have moral status and have a right to life.
2. There is no difference between all human beings on the one hand and all nonhuman animals, on the other hand, that would support giving all humans a right to life and giving no animals a right to life.

So,

3. We cannot consistently maintain that all humans have a right to life and no animals have a right to life.

Therefore,

4. We should achieve consistency by acknowledging that animals have a right to life.

This statement of Kemp's thesis and core supporting argument seems accurate even after reading her essay again. Of course, such a core statement necessarily ignores aspects of the essay, the author's references to Singer, Schweitzer, and Passmore, and her counterargument against Passmore; her reference to specific social practices (zoos, use of leather, experimentation, eating meat) needing reform; and her reference to related problems of moral status (children, future people, angels, nation-states, plants) mentioned in the introduction. Nevertheless, this core argument statement reflects the main point Kemp is trying to establish and the main line of argument for it.

Detailed Critical Scrutiny Using the Features List

We now move past the state of empathetic reading to more critical reading where we take notes and document aspects of the essay that strike us as especially good or especially bad or in some other way worthy of note. In doing this, we can use the features list as a guide. For convenience, here it is again, in short form:

FEATURES LIST

1. Interest, importance, and plausibility of thesis
2. Quality of core supporting argument
3. Apparent quality of further arguments
4. Accuracy of claims and documentation
5. Clarity and organization
6. Coherence and consistency
7. Balance
8. Word choice
9. Grammatical structures
10. Impact

We read through Kemp's essay, noting details that are positively or negatively relevant to these features. This, of course, often involves individual preference. Different readers find different aspects interesting or important and will note different details. The matter depends on judgments about various details: which details we pick out can obviously vary. But to give you an idea of how to go about it, here is a checklist for Kemp's essay. (When making up such a list, you may wish also to include page numbers and specific phrases if your eventual essay is going to include documentation.)

1. *Interest, importance, and plausibility of thesis.* Interesting; somewhat plausible, given her argument. Should differentiate between some animals and others. (Insects, crabs, and slugs surely aren't like pigs, tigers, cows, and cats.)
2. *Quality of core supporting argument.* Conclusion needs restriction to some animals, not all. Argument too indirect?
3. *Apparent quality of further arguments.* Consider: Are Singer and Schweitzer erroneously appealed to as authorities? Singer—"speciesism" only a label? Straw man in the "humans are human" view? Passmore refutation adequate? (Check out.)
4. *Accuracy.* No obvious inaccuracy. No documentation about what exactly Singer, Schweitzer, and Passmore said and where (no references). Brutality toward animals on factory farms and in science labs? No specific abuse is described or documented.
5. *Clarity and organization.* Basically all right. A little long and repetitive, but clearly written.
6. *Coherence and consistency.* Good.
7. *Balance.* Important in light of the sweeping and radical claim Kemp defends. She does consider counterarguments to her position, but only two counterarguments are treated: "humans are special just because they are humans" and Passmore's argument about community. Other counterarguments? Especially, practical considerations: what would be the consequences if we started to treat animals as moral beings?

8. *Word choice.* Not inspired but mostly unobjectionable. Slightly uneven; there are occasional rhetorical bits. The prose is quite emphatic and clear. The style is unpretentious.

9. *Grammatical structures.* Good.

10. *Impact.* Fairly strong, for readers to whom a defense of animal rights is new. Slightly derivative—relies a lot on Singer. Style adequate, not memorable. Needs more specific details, and documentation of what Kemp sees as immoral abuse of animals.

On the basis of this list, we can now reach an overall appraisal of Kemp's essay. It is relatively easy, given the points above, to see that the essay would go in the "mixed" category; it is neither strikingly good nor strikingly poor.

Preparing an Outline

Since we have judged Kemp's essay to be mixed in quality, we shall follow the model outline for the mixed reaction essay. (*Note:* this is an outline and only an outline; you would use it to write an essay in which all points were fully explained in clear, complete sentences, and in which you paid careful attention to your own literary style. Do not mistake our outline for a complete essay!)

We shall prepare an outline in five sections that, as indicated earlier in the chapter, will be:

i.   Introduction
ii. Detailing of flaws
iii. Detailing of the essay's good features
iv. Summary statement, giving overall judgment based on (ii) and (iii)
v.   Further implications

As we emphasized before, there are many possible strategies for responding to an essay such as Kemp's. Our approach here is only one of various possibilities: it is recommended here not as a formula to use in all contexts, but rather as a reasonable way to get started if you are inexperienced.

Here is a sample outline, filled in with reference to specific details about Kemp's essay, as noted on the features list.

SAMPLE OUTLINE FOR RESPONSE TO "MORALITY, ANIMALS, AND THE RIGHT TO LIFE"

i.   Introduction
     Essay will respond to "Morality, Animals, and the Right to Life," by Rose Kemp. Kemp's essay was adapted for Govier's textbook, *A Practical Study of Argument* (Fifth Edition, 2001). Kemp: animals have a moral right to life. Her argument: we assume that human beings have this moral right, and that there is no relevant difference between all nonhuman animals and all human beings to which we can appeal to make us consistent if we deny the right to nonhuman animals. Reaction to this essay: mixed. It is provocative,

clearly written, and somewhat interesting; yet there are some basic flaws in argumentation, both regarding clarification of the central thesis and argument for it, and regarding consideration of positions opposed to her own.

ii. Flaws

(a) Central claim needs clarifying: all nonhuman animals or just some? Crucial problem: if it is all animals, the claim is implausible and intolerably impractical, whereas if it is some animals, we aren't told which ones and how to distinguish them.

(b) Defense of claim that all human beings have a moral right to life? We are only told that we all assume this. The argument is an appeal for consistency. We could become consistent by revising our beliefs about human beings' right to life. Why not? Kemp doesn't say.

(c) Counterarguments. Only Passmore seems to be dealt with seriously. Are there no other serious counterarguments? Kemp should deal with allegation that it would be totally impractical for humans to respect a right to life on the part of all animals. Also, she should deal with the claim that even though both animals and humans have a right to life, the right to life of humans outweighs that of animals. Not enough counterconsiderations are taken seriously.

(d) Flaws in argument: Straw man re "humans are human": does anybody really say this? Kemp follows Singer, who argues against this view only by stipulating a negative name for it: "speciesism"; an inappropriate kind of appeal to Singer's authority seems to be working here. Also the reply to Passmore could be strengthened by using an example other than children. Children do grow up to be in reciprocal relation with the adults who have cared for them, so Passmore could fit the case of children into his theory by saying that they are potentially reciprocal members of a moral community. The case of the seriously mentally handicapped might be a more convincing example to argue against Passmore. They are typically seen as having moral status even though they do not reciprocate and never will.

(e) Minor flaw: no documentation regarding Schweitzer, Singer, Passmore. No direct quotations. No details regarding animal suffering in labs or factory farms. Detail and documentation would make essay more vivid and convincing.

iii. Good features

(a) Interesting, readable essay about an important subject.

(b) Challenging argument, gives lots to think about. If we are going to restrict conclusion to some animals, we have to think about which ones; also, we do, as she says, believe in a human right to life. We have to think about that too.

(c) Gives knowledge of what some important other people have said about an important problem.

(d) Well organized, consistent, coherent, clearly written, grammatical. Style is unpretentious and interesting. Straightforward, fair language, on the whole.

iv. Summary statement
Reaction is mixed: although the essay is enjoyable and teaches and challenges the reader, its arguments and, to a lesser extent, its presentation could have been strengthened in significant ways as described above: clearer more qualified conclusion, subargument for premise about human right to life, broader consideration of counterconsiderations, more accurate refutation of Passmore, and more documented, specific information about how animals are mistreated.

v. Further implications
Reader will remember and appreciate this essay: challenging. What is the human moral right to life and where does it come from? If only some humans or some animals have a moral right to life, which ones are they and why? How would we have to revise our lifestyle to acknowledge these rights properly, and how practical would such revisions be? Don't know the answers to these questions, but Kemp's essay shows they are interesting and important.

We shall not go through the next stage of essay writing, where you fill in your outline with fuller, more complete sentences and arguments and with illustrations and other features designed to add interest and further evidence for the claims noted in point form in your outline. This stage is something each writer will complete in his or her own way. Using a detailed outline makes it easier to write an essay that is logically ordered and touches on all the points you want to include from working with your features list.

Checking Your Work

When you have finished writing your essay, you have to check your own work—not only for spelling, grammar, style, and accuracy, but also for readability, interest, accuracy of claims, and quality of argument. In fact, you can use the features list given here as a checklist for editing your own essay—in addition to reflecting on your own arguments using the ARG conditions.

It is often hard to read your own work in this way; as its author, you tend to be too close to it to be able to read it from a detached, critical point of view. Just trying to read your own work from the point of view of a critic is worthwhile and illuminating, however; you probably will find some errors that you can eliminate in the final version of your work. You may do better as your own critic and editor if you allow a few days between writing a draft essay and editing it.

■■■■■■■■ CHAPTER SUMMARY

For the most part, this book has emphasized the analysis and evaluation of fairly short arguments—those of a few sentences or, at most, a few paragraphs in length.

For the concepts and skills you have learned here to be useful in further work you will do—both inside and outside universities and colleges—you need to adapt these techniques to longer works. We have tried, in this chapter, to assist you in beginning this process by describing a technique for appraising an essay-length work.

To use argument analysis and evaluation for a whole essay, you must be selective. You cannot carefully work through every single argument in the essay using the ARG conditions because that would take too long and, if used as the basis for your own work, probably would bore your readers unbearably. Read the essay several times, first empathetically, to gain a good understanding and determine what its central claim, or thesis, and core supporting argument are. You can then employ a list of salient features—we call it the features list—to look for details on the basis of which you will evaluate the essay. Checking through the features list, you note the good and bad aspects of logical argument and organization, and also some of the literary features of the work. Then you consider the list and make a tentative judgment as to whether you would classify the essay as good, mixed, or poor.

Prepare an outline in which you organize and (if necessary) further select which of the noted features you wish to discuss in your own responsive essay. On the basis of your outline, write your response. When your own essay is done, you can use your understanding of the ARG conditions and the features list to check your own work. Before writing a final version of your essay, you should be your own editor—not just for spelling and grammar but for these other aspects as well.

The methods described in this chapter are guidelines that we think are useful for beginners. Experienced writers will have their own personal approaches and strategies. The guidelines here are not meant to be rigid rules: we offer, for those who might need it, a way to begin.

Review of Terms Introduced

Appreciative essay   Essay in response to another that you think is basically good.

Confused or contradictory essay   Essay that has no thesis because it is too unclear or contradictory to make any definite point.

Core thesis argument   The main argument offered by an author for his or her central claim or thesis. The core thesis argument is stated in the form "Essentially, X says C because R" where X is the author, C is the central claim, and R are the reasons, or premises, put forward to support the central claim. The word *essentially* reflects the fact that you must be selective in stating the core thesis argument.

Critical reading   Reading, after the first empathetic readings, in which the reader notes good and poor aspects of a work. A features list may be used to assist in this process.

Empathetic reading   Reading in which the reader tries to enter into the author's point of view as though it were the reader's own. As described here, empathetic reading is used as a device for understanding what the author is trying to say.

Features list   Checklist of aspects to look for when reading critically. Features (1) to (7) are, in a broad sense, logical; features (8) to (10) are, in a broad sense, stylistic or literary. A reader may wish to add further aspects to this list. Features specified in the chapter are:

1. Interest, importance, and plausibility of thesis
2. Quality of core supporting argument
3. Apparent quality of further arguments
4. Accuracy
5. Clarity and organization
6. Coherence and consistency
7. Balance
8. Word choice
9. Grammatical structures
10. Impact

Heuristic device or strategy   Device or technique adopted to give preliminary guidance. A heuristic device is not based on fixed and absolute rules. It can be adapted or even abandoned when it ceases to serve its purpose.

Inexplicit essay   Essay that makes its point indirectly, sometimes by satire or ridicule, or by redescription. The inexplicit essay has no explicitly, or directly, stated thesis or core supporting argument. Often, however, it is possible to attribute a thesis or supporting argument to the author.

Mixed reaction essay   Essay in response to another to which you have a mixed response.

Negatively critical essay   Essay in response to another that you think is basically poor.

Selective   Refers to the fact that only some claims and arguments can be treated when you write an essay responding to another essay or longer work.

Thesis   The main point or main conclusion of a longer work.

Note

1. Bob Bragg, "Isn't Biotechnology Wonderful?"
   Calgary *Herald*, May 17, 1987.

appendix A
A Summary of Fallacies

Many texts on practical logic have a separate chapter on fallacies. Because we wished to explain the various fallacies against the background of the appropriate related standards of good reasoning, we have not treated fallacies in any single chapter. As a result, there is no one place where various fallacies are collected together. For your convenience, here is a list of the various fallacies treated in this text, together with a brief definition of each one and a reference to the chapter in which it is explained in more detail. This set of brief explanations is provided only as a convenient summary and tool for remembering the fallacies; it is not a substitute for the more complete treatment given each fallacy in the appropriate section of the text.

Ad Hominem

(Chapter 6) An *ad hominem* argument is one in which a premise or premises about a person's character or background are used to cast doubt on his argument or theory, and in which those premises are irrelevant to the merits of the position taken. Premises of such a type are irrelevant, except in the special case where those theories and arguments happen to be about the person himself. But specific points about a person's background may bear on the reliability of his or her testimony or the legitimacy of his or her authority. In that case, they may be relevant to our decision whether to accept claims on his or her testimony or authority, even though they are not directly relevant to the question of whether those claims are true or false. To reason from premises about the background, personality, or character of people to substantive conclusions about their arguments or theories is to commit the *ad hominem* fallacy, unless the premises are relevant to the conclusion in one of the ways just described. Abusive *ad hominem* arguments attack the character or background of an arguer; circumstantial *ad hominem* arguments attack the arguer's circumstances or actions.

Affirming the Consequent

(Chapter 8) An argument having the form "$P \supset Q$; Q; therefore, P" is an instance of the fallacy of affirming the consequent. For example, "If you have tuberculosis, you are unhealthy. You are unhealthy. Therefore, you have tuberculosis." The mistake comes in affirming the consequent of a conditional and believing that from the conditional and the consequent one may infer the antecedent of the conditional. This is not a valid form of argument, as you can see from testing it on a truth table. It probably seems valid because of its superficial similarity to "$P \supset Q$; P; therefore, Q" (*modus ponens*), which is valid.

Appeal to Fear

(Chapter 6) A fallacy that occurs when there is an attempt to threaten or to inspire fear in order to induce belief in a conclusion and when little or no evidence is supplied to render that conclusion rationally acceptable.

Appeal to Pity

(Chapter 6) A fallacy that occurs when there is an attempt to inspire or evoke feelings of pity or sympathy in order to induce belief in a conclusion and when little or no evidence is supplied to render that conclusion rationally acceptable.

Appeal to Popularity

(Chapter 6) A fallacy that occurs when premises describing the popularity of a product or belief are used to justify a conclusion that states, or requires, that the product or belief has real merit. Such arguments are fallacious because popularity is irrelevant to real merit. This fallacy is sometimes called the *bandwagon appeal* or the *fallacy of jumping on a bandwagon.* It is also a fallacy to infer lack of merit from unpopularity.

Appeal to Tradition

(Chapter 6) A fallacy that occurs when premises describe the fact that a product, belief, or practice was common in the past and those premises are used in an attempt to argue that that product, belief, or practice is appropriate in the present. Prevalence in the past is irrelevant to merit, which is why appeals to tradition are fallacious. It is also a fallacy to infer lack of suitability for the present from lack of popularity in the past.

Authority

(Chapters 5 and 6) An appeal to authority is fallacious when any one of the following conditions is satisfied:

1. The claim, P, which the arguer is trying to justify, does not fall within a subject area that constitutes a recognized body of knowledge.

2   The person cited as an authority is not an expert within the particular subject area in which the claim, *P*, falls—even though he or she may be an expert about some other area of knowledge.

3.   Even though the claim, *P*, falls within an area of knowledge and even though the person cited as an authority is an expert in that particular area, it so happens that the experts in that area disagree as to whether *P* is true.

4.   The person cited as an authority has a vested interest in the issue of whether *P* is true—either because he or she is paid by another interested party or because he or she has some other personal stake in the matter.

Begging the Question

(Chapter 5) Begging the question is a fallacy that occurs when the premise or premises either state the conclusion (usually in slightly different words) or logically presuppose that the conclusion is true. The conclusion cannot get any real support from the premise or premises because it needs to be accepted in order for those premises to be accepted. In a cogent argument, the premises have a greater initial acceptability than the conclusion—they should be more acceptable, to the intended audience, than the conclusion. When an argument begs the question, the logical relationship between the question-begging premise and the conclusion is so close that this greater acceptability is simply not possible. Example: The best jobs are those that pay the highest salaries, because the only good thing about a job is the money you can make from it.

Causal Slippery Slope

(Chapter 9) In this type of argument, it is alleged in the premises that a proposed action—which, considered in itself, might seem good—would set off a series of further actions culminating in calamity. For this reason, it is concluded that the proposed action is wrong or should not be done. The idea behind the reasoning is that someone who undertakes the proposed action will unwittingly set off a series of effects that will be disastrous. The proposed action is, therefore, the first step down a slippery slope to Hell. The problem with such arguments occurs when the causal claim in the premises is not properly substantiated. Actually, the argument amounts to a kind of scare tactic: the series of dreadful effects is invented by the arguer, who has no real foundation for his causal premise asserting that the proposed action will lead to these effects.

Composition

(Chapter 9) In this type of argument the premises are about the parts of a whole or the members of a group and the conclusion is drawn, directly from those premises, about the whole, or about the group. This type of argument is fallacious because it is insensitive to the differences between wholes and their parts. It ignores the fact that wholes, or groups, very often have properties and structures different from those of their parts.

Confusing Correlation and Cause

(Chapter 9) A correlational statement tells you that two things are associated. For instance, being a drinker is positively correlated with having high blood pressure if a higher proportion of drinkers than nondrinkers have high blood pressure. A causal statement tells you that one thing produces, or helps to produce, another. Since a positive correlation may exist for various reasons, you cannot simply infer a causal relationship from such a correlation. If there is a correlation between being A and being B, then there are four possible explanations for the correlation: either A causes B or B causes A, or something else causes both A and B, or the correlation is a matter of chance. Since three of these four possibilities do not involve A being the cause of B, it is a fallacy to infer that A causes B from the fact that A is positively correlated with B.

Denying the Antecedent

(Chapter 8) An argument having the form "$P \supset Q$; $-P$; therefore $-Q$" is an instance of the formal fallacy of denying the antecedent. For example, "If machines can think, machines can correct some of their own mistakes. Machines cannot think; therefore, machines cannot correct some of their own mistakes." Someone who reasons this way thinks that by asserting a conditional and denying its antecedent, you can properly infer that the consequent is false also. This inference is a mistake, as a truth table analysis will reveal. The inference probably seems plausible because it superficially resembles "$P \supset Q$; $-Q$; therefore $-P$ (*modus tollens*), which is a deductively valid inference.

Division

(Chapter 9) An argument in which the premises are about a whole, or a group, and a conclusion is derived directly from those premises, about the parts of the whole or the members of the group. This kind of argument is fallacious because it ignores the logical distinction between wholes and parts, or groups and members. Often wholes, or groups, have structures, relationships, and properties different from those of the constituent elements that compose them.

Equivocation

(Chapter 4) A fallacy of equivocation is committed when a key word in an argument is used in two or more senses and the premises appear to support the conclusion only because the senses are not distinguished. The argument is likely to seem cogent if the ambiguity is not noticed.

False Dichotomy

(Chapters 7 and 8) A false dichotomy is not, by itself, a fallacy; it is simply a false belief. Believing in false dichotomies may easily lead to faults in argument, however, because a false dichotomy can be a key premise in deductively valid arguments that seem extremely convincing because of their logical validity. A false dichotomy is a statement of the type "It is either X or Y" where the two alternatives X and Y do not exhaust the possibilities. For instance, to say that a man must be either ugly or handsome is to construct a false dichotomy; people can be of average or moderate attractiveness. One common source of false dichotomies is mistaking contrary predicates (for example, good and evil) for contradictory predicates (for example, good and nongood). A dichotomy will always hold if it is based on the purely logical opposition of a predicate and its logical complement. That is, a person will always be either X or non-X for any predicate X. But a predicate Y that is in some general sense the opposite of X is often not its logical complement. For example, *unhappy* is the opposite, but not the logical complement, of *happy*. *Ugly* is the opposite, but not the logical complement, of *beautiful*; and so on. *Communist* is not the logical complement of *capitalist*. One may criticize capitalism without being a communist. To think that a person must either be a capitalist or a communist is to endorse a false dichotomy. False dichotomies may be due to our tendency to oversimplify: we tend to polarize issues, seeing the world in *black and white, and omitting to consider crucially relevant shades of gray.*

Faulty Analogy

(Chapter 10) A faulty analogy is an argument by analogy in which the similarities between the primary subject and the analogue (two things compared) are too superficial to support the conclusion. The two things have only a very loose and general similarity, and there are enough relevant differences between them that the comparison can lend no credibility to the conclusion. Analogies like this do no more than suggest an image in which we can think of a topic, and are often seriously misleading, especially when the analogue is something toward which we have very strong attitudes or feelings.

Guilt by Association

(Chapter 6) The fallacy of guilt by association is committed when a person or her views are criticized on the basis of a supposed link between that person and a group or movement that is believed by the arguer and the audience to be disreputable. The poor reputation of any group is irrelevant to the substantive correctness either of its own views or of the views of any member of the group. It is certainly irrelevant to the substantive correctness of the views of those people or groups who are only very loosely associated with it.

Hasty Inductive Generalization

(Chapter 9) A hasty inductive generalization occurs when a person generalizes from a single anecdote or experience, or from a sample that is too small or too unrepresentative to support his conclusion. Too narrow a range of human experience is taken as a basis for reaching a conclusion about all experiences of a given type. The fallacy occurs when we either forget the need to obtain a representative sample or too quickly assume that a small or biased sample is representative. For example, "Boys are more aggressive than girls, because my two sons were far more disposed to play with guns and watch violent television shows than my two daughters."

Ignorance

(Chapter 6) Fallacious appeals to ignorance are arguments in which the premises describe our ignorance regarding a proposition, P, and the conclusion makes a substantive claim about the truth or falsity of P. Often, not-P is inferred from our ignorance of P, or P is inferred from our ignorance of not-P. For instance, people may infer from the fact that we do not know there are no ghosts that there are ghosts; or they may move from the fact that an event has no known natural cause to the conclusion that it has a supernatural cause. Such inferences are fallacious because our ignorance is irrelevant to the issue of the substantive truth, or even the substantive probability, of claims.

Objectionable Cause

(Chapter 9) The fallacy of objectionable cause occurs when a reasoner imposes a causal interpretation on a set of events and makes no attempt to rule out alternative explanations of those events. Sometimes this fallacy is called *false cause*. We changed the name because you do not always get the cause wrong by this procedure. You may be right, but it will be by accident. In effect, reasoning to a cause too hastily, as in objectionable cause, goes like this: "A occurred; B occurred; A and B can plausibly be connected; therefore, A caused B." The pattern of argument is fallacious because there may be other explanations of the joint occurrence of A and B, and no basis is given in this kind of argument to rule out alternatives.

Post Hoc

(Chapter 9) This is the fallacy of reasoning that simply because one thing precedes another, it must have caused it. Or, to put it differently, you reason that because A

preceded *B*, then *A* must have caused *B*. The argument is a fallacy because it takes far more than mere succession in time to justify a causal conclusion. The conclusion states that *A* produced, or brought about, *B*, and the premise gives information only about sequence in time. To know that one thing causes another, you have to know that the sequence in time is typical and that the causal relation that you allege is the best explanation of the fact that the two elements occurred together. To know that the causal relation is the best explanation, you have to have a basis for ruling out other explanations.

Pseudoprecision

(Chapter 9) Expression of information in numerical terms suggesting a level of precision that would be impossible to achieve. Sometimes pseudoprecision is a result of a combination of questionable operational definitions. Such definitions permit measurement in contexts in which the terms operationally defined (for example, *hyperactive, creative*) have contestable qualitative meanings that would make the application of quantitative measurement unrealistic and inappropriate. Example: "After the new text was introduced, members of Smith's class were 22.5 percent more creative than they had been previously."

Slippery Assimilation

(Chapter 10) The fallacy of slippery assimilation occurs when someone reasons that because there is a series of cases differing only slightly from each other, all cases in the series are the same. For example, "Because there is a gradual progression, ounce by ounce, from weighing 100 pounds to weighing 300 pounds, there is no one spot where you can draw the line between being thin and being fat. Therefore, everyone is really fat." (Or, alternatively, everyone is really thin.) The fallacy here occurs because the argument proceeds as though differences that are separately insignificant could not cumulate to be significant. Obviously, as the weight example indicates, they can. The argument may show that there will be borderline cases, but it does not show that there is no distinction to be drawn. Cases are falsely assimilated in this argument.

Slippery Precedent

(Chapter 10) In slippery precedent arguments, a case that is acknowledged to be good, or deserving, when considered alone is rejected on the grounds that it would set a precedent for permitting further cases that are not good or deserving. The premises compare the case in question to further cases, maintain that the cases in question would set a precedent for allowing those further cases, and claim that the further cases are bad. The conclusion rejects the case in question; what was initially deserving has become undeserving on the grounds that it would set a bad precedent.

Slippery precedent arguments have inconsistent premises, because a case that is good cannot set a precedent for others that are bad. There must necessarily be a relevant difference between the cases that are compared, and this relevant difference is neglected in the premises of the argument, which slide from the initial case to the other ones as though there were no relevant difference between them.

Straw Man

(Chapter 6) The straw man fallacy is committed when a person misrepresents the argument or theory of another person and then, on the basis of his misrepresentation, purports to refute the real argument or theory. The refutation is irrelevant to the merits of the real theory because the view in question has been misdescribed. The way to avoid straw man is to interpret the writings and sayings of other people carefully and accurately and to make sure that you take a strong and representative version of any general theory you criticize.

Two Wrongs Make a Right

(Chapter 10) In this fallacious argument, we see a misplaced appeal to consistency. A person is urged to accept, or condone, one thing that is wrong because another similar thing, also wrong, has occurred, or has been accepted and condoned. For example: "Animals are ill-treated when they are raised for food, so it is all right for animals to be ill-treated when they are kept in zoos." This is a misuse of analogy. If the treatment of animals when they are raised for food is faulty and the treatment of animals in zoos is relevantly similar to it, then the right conclusion to reach is that reform is needed in both cases. It is not that the second wrong should be accepted because the first one has been accepted. The two-wrongs argument seems to rely on the supposition that the world is a better place with sets of similar wrongs in it than it would be with some of these wrongs corrected and the others left in place. But there is no point in multiplying wrongs just to preserve consistency.

Undistributed Middle

(Chapter 7) The fallacy of the undistributed middle is committed in a categorical syllogism in which the middle term is not distributed in at least one of the premises. The middle term is the term that appears in both premises of a syllogism, and it is distributed when it appears in such a way that it applies to all things within the category that the term designates. The subject term is distributed in A (universal affirmative) and E (universal negative) statements, and the predicate term is distributed in E (universal negative) and O (particular negative) statements. An example of the fallacy of the undistributed middle is "All teachers are prompt; all lawyers are prompt; therefore, all lawyers are teachers." Here the middle term, *prompt*, is not distributed in either premise. The syllogism is invalid.

Vagueness

(Chapter 4) Vagueness arises when a word, as used, has a meaning that is insufficiently clear to convey the necessary information in that context of use. If a statement is expressed in vague language, and there is no clue in the context as to what it is supposed to mean, then we cannot tell whether the statement is true or false, because we will not have an adequate understanding of it. Vagueness as such is a fault when it goes to this point, but it is not as such a fallacy. Vagueness contributes to mistakes in reasoning when key terms are not precise enough in the context for us to judge whether the premises and conclusions are acceptable. As used in the argument, the terms are not sufficiently precise to enable us to understand the boundaries of their application. Arguments can trade on vagueness by using terms that cannot be pinned down sufficiently; meanings may become so indeterminate that we go along with the argument simply because we don't know exactly what is being said. At this point, vagueness contributes to mistaken judgments about the merits of reasoning.

appendix B
Selected Essays for Analysis

How Patriarchy Becomes Santa Claus:
Why a Myth Is as Good as Its Smile

Janet D. Sisson

Like many small children in England, I was taken by my parents to 'visit Santa.' He sat in a store, dressed up in a red coat and trousers, with a large fake-fur-trimmed hat and a long beard. Over several years, I came to dislike the idea of sitting on some strange male knee, bad breath whispered into my face. I knew that the "Santas" were different each year, and all imposters, but I put up with the unpleasant farce for the sake of the small gifts that accompanied a "visit to Santa." It was a first introduction to the shameful fact that I would put up with attentions I disliked for the sake of presents. Soon, I decided that the benefits were not worth the costs. Santa came to embody the manipulative aspects of Christmas, and I have wondered about them ever since.

My reading group was looking for a topic for their Christmas meeting; I found myself muttering "let's deconstruct Santa Claus." My friend Laurie suggested I look for a couple of pages for us to discuss, but instead I was soon busy writing. Deconstruction is not my usual way of thinking, and the original suggestion was something of a joke: the result, though still ironic in intent, was less humorous, I discovered.

Originally Saint Nicholas sought out poor children in need of assistance. At a time when gifts showed status, and offering gifts bestowed honour on the receiver, not the giver, Nicholas' acts were real acts of charity, or caring for those less fortunate in life's lottery. Later, he reached colder climes and became a judge of worthiness to receive, making his gifts deserved, not freely given. Nowadays, the grim old "Sinter Klaus" of Northern Europe has become a pudgy grinning idiot, with a house in the earth's most distant suburbs. His world has no place for women—nor men, except as shrunken elves and gnomes. "Visiting Santa" provides a fitting introduction to one great reality of life: you have to cozy up to fat old men in order to get what you want (sometimes known as the Boris Yeltsin syndrome).

The market loves Santa. He works from home in a small business, but his goods are supplied without a need to attend to cash flow. Children learn that presents arrive miraculously, from nowhere. The dark shadows of bankruptcy are never seen in the bright winter night where the reindeer fly. There are gift wraps, but no shops, workers—elves and gnomes—but no paychecks, and the reindeer shit never falls to earth. Santa must be fed, with the cake and beer his red nose and swollen belly attest only too clearly. He receives no payment for his long night's journey of deliveries, no credit for his talent for being in many places at once. Like the forces of the market he works unseen to bring gifts to all.

How many fat old men, dressed in fake beards and tight costumes, have leered and crouched beneath the mistletoe, to fall upon a chosen one with ill-concealed glee? A mask of joviality hides the lust, as patriarchy masks its longing for domination by a pretence that it protects all. Those who do not receive gifts are the disowned of the earth, a luckless crew, not deserving the bounty of the overweight saint. We can enjoy Christmas, knowing that everything is in its (disempowered) place. Santa, smiling and joyous, distracts us from the naked power beneath the red coat and from our subservience to the trading balances of international companies, whose attentions we must collectively suffer to stay solvent.

Once it was different. Gifts were the product of mother earth, or of the goddess Ceres, who cared for crops and harvests. Ceres' daughter, Persephone, died every year in order that the crops might come back. As the Greek and Roman story went, Pluto, the king of all the dead, stole Persephone away to be his bride. Did Ceres pat Persephone on the head and say how pleased she should be to become the mighty Queen of Hades? Far from it: Ceres went straight off to complain to the assembled gods and brought her daughter back up to the sunshine. Unfortunately, Persephone had eaten six pomegranate seeds while in Hades and this act forced her ever after to stay below for six months every year. To ancient Mediterranean peoples, then, gifts came at a price. The harvest is succeeded by scarcity, one must store goods for the future, and prepare the ground for the next year. Ceres, unlike Santa, must work and sorrow for her gifts. What if Santa was forced to spend six months of every year in Hell?

Janet Sisson was a lecturer in Philosophy at the University of Glasgow, and has also taught at the Universities of Kansas, Alberta, and Calgary. She now lives and works in Calgary, Canada. "How Patriarchy Becomes Santa Claus: Why a Myth Is as Good as Its Smile" reprinted by permission of the author.

Abortion and Violence

Henry Morgentaler

At a time when access to safe, medical abortion is being threatened by murderous attacks on doctors providing this service, it would be worthwhile to recapitulate the enormous benefits brought about by legal abortion. I think one of the most important consequences is the declining violent crime rate. This decline has lasted for six years in Canada and the United States.

Is there a relationship between the statistically proven decline in crime rates and access to abortion? For the last six years, in both the United States and Canada, the crime rate has steadily decreased—in particular for crimes of violence, such as assault, rape, and murder. Some demographers explain this by the fact that there are fewer young men around, and it is mostly young men who commit crimes. No doubt this is true, but what is even more important is that, among these young men likely to commit offenses, there are fewer who carry an inner rage and vengeance in their hearts from having been abused or cruelly treated as children.

Why is that? Because many women who a generation ago were obliged to carry any pregnancy to term now have the opportunity to choose medical abortion when they are not ready to assume the burden and obligation of motherhood. It is well documented that unwanted children are more likely to be abandoned, neglected, and abused. Such children inevitably develop an inner rage that in later years may result in violent behavior against people and society. Crimes of violence are very often perpetrated by persons who unconsciously want revenge for the wrongs they suffered as children. This need to satisfy an inner urge for vengeance results in violence against children, women, members of minority groups, or anyone who becomes a target of hate by the perpetrator.

Children who are given love and affection, good nurturing, and a nice, supportive home atmosphere usually grow up to become caring, emotionally responsible members of the community. They care about others because they have been well cared for. Children who have been deprived of love and good care, who have been neglected or abused, suffer tremendous harm that may cause mental illness, difficulty in living, and an inner rage that eventually erupts in violence when they become adolescents and adults.

Most serial killers were neglected and abused children, deprived of love. Both Hitler and Stalin were cruelly beaten by their fathers and carried so much hate in their hearts that, when they attained power, without remorse they caused millions of people to die. It is accepted wisdom that prevention is better than a cure. To prevent the birth of unwanted children through family planning, birth control, and abortion is preventive medicine, preventive psychiatry, and prevention of violent crime.

I predicted a decline in crime and mental illness thirty years ago when I started my campaign to make abortion in Canada legal and safe. It took a long time for this prediction to come true. I expect that things will get better as more and more children are born into families that want and desire them and receive them with joy and anticipation.

It is important that we continue as a society to safeguard the rights and access of women to safe, medical abortion. Not many people realize the enormous benefits to women's health resulting from such good access:

- Disappearance of deaths due to illegal abortions.
- Reduced complication rate attending upon medical abortion, which has become one of the safest surgical procedures.
- Decreased mortality of women giving birth.
- Decreased mortality of babies during childbirth.

Add to this the decrease in crime rates and, most probably, although not statistically proven yet, a significant decrease in mental and emotional illness.

When Canada is rated first in the world by a United Nations agency as to quality of life, part of the rating is due to the increased safety of women due to good access to quality abortion care.

Dr. Henry Morgentaler is a prominent Canadian abortion provider and the 1975 Humanist of the Year. This column is adapted from an editorial that appeared in numerous Canadian newspapers on November 5, 1998. Reprinted by permission of the author.

Believing in the Goddess?

Trudy Govier

Remember the joke about the man who saw God and was asked to describe the vision? "You won't like it," he said, "She's black." To some, this is more than a joke: the original religion was goddess worship, emerging from traditions in Africa.

Belief in a Great Goddess is quite fashionable these days. The notion of an Earth Mother is extremely attractive: it removes divinity from associations with male power, domination and war, and puts worship closer to life and the earth. For many women, the Mother Goddess has extraordinary appeal, soothing and healing the wounds of millennia of woman-hating.

Books and lectures on goddess religion tend to avoid intellectualized theology. Mysticism, motive, and wishful thinking are more conspicuous than clear straightforward arguments for the existence of a goddess. For me, this is a serious gap. Historical points about goddess worship in the past are fascinating but they do not prove, or even suggest, the metaphysical reality of a Goddess to be worshipped today.

Goddesses are to be found in nearly all major cultural traditions—Egyptian, Greek, Hindu, Chinese, Babylonian, Buddhist, and Native American. A Great Goddess of Life was worshipped in many parts of Europe between 50,000 and 5,000 B.C. One can take goddess tours and view pertinent sites in Britain, France, Spain, the Czech Republic, Greece, Turkey, Malta and elsewhere. The history and archaeology of goddess religions has only recently become a popular topic, and it is an absorbing one. The worship of a divine female is one of many things historians tended not to emphasize. Like other aspects, of women's history, it is a fascinating thing to rediscover.

The Goddess or Earth Mother was a Goddess of life, birth, menstrual blood, and sexuality. In Old Europe, goddess figurines were heavy with middle age and had massive breasts, hips, and thighs. The Goddess was often shown with a snake, a symbol of male sexuality not, in this context, regarded as evil. When the patriarchal Jewish religion replaced goddess worship in the Middle East, the symbol of the woman with the snake was adapted to have a different meaning. The snake in the Garden of Eden lured Eve to evil, persuading her to taste forbidden fruit. Because Eve succumbed to this temptation, she and Adam lost their innocence, thereby bequeathing to all their human descendents a heritage of sin. The story of Adam and Eve in the Garden has served anti-female propaganda purposes ever since. With the ascendancy of patriarchal religions, worship of the earthly mother of life was replaced by worship of the transcendent father, principle of authority and power.

That the divine female is virtually absent from Christianity is no accident. Christianity, like the Judaism from which it emerged, is a patriarchal religion. The Christian God is God the Father. There is a limited, and derivative, female principle in the figure of Mary—tender Mary, loving, forgiving, approachable, the recipient of passionate prayers and supplications. Mary's very considerable appeal to rural Catholics seems to amount to a recognition that, for many, male images and symbols omit something important.

Especially intriguing in this connection is the Black Madonna, venerated by rural Catholics in many parts of the world. The Black Madonna is a figure close to the earth, a kind of earth mother within Christianity. The Black Madonna tradition may be a relic of pagan religion and even the original earthly Black Goddess of Africa. Suggestively, shrines to the Black Madonna are often underground. Writing of an isolated area in southern Italy during the thirties, Carlo Levi reported that humble peasant dwellings featured only two pictures. One was a picture of Roosevelt (a benefactor of expatriate Italians in America and, vicariously, of those they had left behind); the other a Black Madonna. She was their link to God. Poland is another place where the Black Madonna is immensely popular. Each summer some 35,000 Poles walk for nearly two weeks on a grueling pilgrimage from Warsaw to Czestochowa to see the shrine of the Black Madonna of Jasna Gora.

There are fabulous historical questions to be asked about goddess religions in ancient times and their vestiges in modern culture. But what does all this tell us about the reality of a Goddess? It is not always easy to tell whether goddess enthusiasts actually believe that a Great Cosmic Mother exists or whether they only believe that many other people, long ago and far away, and all over the earth, used to believe in Her. To me this question matters.

Given that human beings long ago believed in a Goddess, does that give us reason to believe in one today? Apparently many people think so. Several substantial books describing goddess religions of the past move on to describe goddess worship by feminists today without every raising the reality issue. Based on goddess religions thousands of years ago, there are renascent goddess cults and worshippers today. Books showing their art and ceremonies are easy to find; many educated people, especially those sympathetic to New Age trends, will find goddess worshippers among their friends and acquaintances. But is there a Goddess? Should we believe in Goddess?

In their book *The Great Cosmic Mother*, Monica Sjoo and Barbara Mor advise modern women to "return to the Mother who gives us life." As they see it, western culture is based on the death of nature and the exploitation of women, and can retrieve itself only by returning to its maternal beginnings. Describing patriarchal gods and their earthly priests as war-like, women-hating, punitive, domineering, and life-destroying, Sjoo and Mor urge women to build their own church and develop the "goddess within."

Like these authors and other feminists, I'm deeply moved and inspired by visions of long-ago cultures in which women were models for a religion of life-giving. Like them, I mourn the current ecological tragedy; like them, I'm infuriated by misogynistic currents in contemporary Christianity and other religions. But when I start to think about all this, these feelings and attitudes seem to provide only *motives*, not *reasons*, to believe in a Goddess. What interests me is reasons.

The area of spirituality and worship is not one where cogent arguments abound these days. It may seem curiously old-fashioned to ask, bluntly, whether the Goddess *exists* and *why*. Saint Thomas Aquinas, with his five Proofs for God's Existence, was a product of a simpler age. In the light of skepticism about Reason in some feminist circles, perhaps it is not surprising that arguments for the Existence of Goddess are hard to find.

My search for arguments in support of Goddess worship, has revealed four:

One: "People practiced goddess worship in many parts of the world over tens of thousands of years."

There was obviously a strong tendency for early human beings to worship earth as the giver of life, and to link the earth and nature with a woman who gives birth. This is the ancient notion of the Mother Earth. Matriarchal religion came first and was natural for human beings. Patriarchal religions were later and less natural in the way they defined the divine as separate from the experienced world. Because Goddess worship is the primary and natural religion for humanity, it is to this religion that human beings should return.

Purportedly, goddess religions are natural and (or so it is implied) what is natural is correct. The problem with this argument is obvious: what's natural may not be correct. Rape or child-beating are natural in this historical sense, but that fact does not show either to be right. Arguing from the naturalness of something to its rightness is such a well-known fallacy that it has been given a name all its own: the Naturalistic Fallacy.

Two: "We have a genetic memory of goddess worship. Somehow, deep in our collective unconscious, we know that worshipping an earth goddess is true and right. So the Goddess exists."

But our genes are tiny biological units, not minds in their own right. They are neither conscious nor unconscious, and they do not remember. And even if we were to assume that there is such a thing as a collective human memory, that would not show that ideas about a Great Cosmic Mother are contained within it. Current interest in the Goddess does not come from our genes: after all, we had these same genes for decades when there was no interest in the Goddess. Rather, it comes from research in archaeology and art, books, and conversations. Interest in the Goddess is spurred not by genes, but by social trends and public discussion.

Three: "Because Goddess religions are respectful of nature and women, they uphold values indispensable in the current world crisis. We should change our religious orientation and worship a life-loving, nature-bound goddess because only by doing so can we change our thinking and productively deal with the global crisis."

Nor is this argument convincing. For one thing, spiritual reorientation toward a Goddess is not the only way of altering human priorities and practices. And even if Goddess worship did turn out to be politically and ecologically useful, that would not show it to be true.

Four: "Established patriarchal religions have been grossly misogynistic. To develop spiritually, women must leave these repressive and insulting traditions. Goddess religion is the obvious alternative."

This argument, like the previous one, makes a claim for the usefulness of Goddess religion and not for its truth. Besides, Goddess worship is not the only alternative to established religions. Women could seek reform in established churches, start a new religion based on a gender-neutral divine, or become agnostics or atheists.

So I have not found any good arguments yet for believing in Goddess. However, there is more to be said. The obvious first. Arguments for the patriarchal God of Judaism, Christianity, and Islam may fare no better than these arguments for Goddess. None offers compelling watertight proof of a divine creator, much less a Fatherly One presiding in Power and Glory over Heaven and Earth. From a rational perspective, Goddess religions would seem to have no shakier basis than traditional patriarchal religions. Insisting that there be cogent arguments for the Existence of Goddess and that these be able to move the mind of a logically demanding agnostic may be asking too much. Perhaps belief in God or a Goddess must come in another way.

What is it to believe? I tend first look at belief from a logical perspective. On this model, we should have reasons or evidence, or a cogent argument, for a belief. The argument has a conclusion. If we deem the argument cogent, we have reasons to accept that conclusion. We may believe it, for these reasons. Of course we may acquire beliefs in other ways—through custom, tradition, being told, training, or experience. But insofar as these beliefs are reasonable, they must stand the test of criticism. This rationalist model presumes that belief is, more than anything else, a matter of accepting propositions, which should be based on reasons. To believe is to accept that something is the case. I believe, for instance, *that* there is a severe famine in North Korea, or *that* there is a short growing season on the North American prairies. Or *that* God exists. Or *that* Goddess exists. Belief is a matter of entertaining and accepting propositions, which we should accept only if we have good reasons to support the idea that they are true.

Is that all there is to belief? Reasons and propositions? It would seem not. Beliefs affect our attitudes, emotions, commitments, and actions. In some areas—of which religion is clearly one—they affect our whole attitude of life and the world. Some beliefs are myths we use to make sense of the world. And these are no mere propositions. Perhaps we can construct and choose our own myths, even while recognizing that they are myths and cannot be held out as true or provable in the absence of cogent supporting arguments.

This notion of myth construction is, I suspect, how many spiritual women approach the Goddess. The notion of a broad-hipped Goddess of Life, source of nature, sexuality, birth, and death satisfies the passionate spiritual longings felt by many contemporary women. These women want to make sense of the world and themselves as worthy creatures within it. They have come to resist the notion of an all-powerful male God on high who demands perpetual recognition of His tremendous power and glory, and created Eve only to serve Adam. They want a tradition without such images of patriarchal power and the humility of women. If they cannot find it in contemporary established religions, they will use resources of the distant human past to develop it for themselves.

So far as I can tell, Goddess religions have no cogent theological edifice founded on rational arguments. They offer a mythology of life and nature which expresses values many women treasure in their own earthly lives and do not include the worship of male power. No more Lord of All Creation, Vengeful God, or Angry Father. No more Nature at the service of Man or Eve handmaiden to Adam. No Woman source of temptation and evil. Instead a Goddess of earth and life, nature, birth, and life.

For many, this will be a more attractive mythology.

An earlier version of this essay appeared in the Globe and Mail *in 1993.*

Clash over Climate Change: Singer Article Clouds the Picture

Andrew Weaver

As a climate scientist, I was taken aback by "New Heat on Global Warming" (Aug. 7) by S. Fred Singer, who advocates postponing action on climate change until the scientific picture is much clearer. While I won't presume to dictate policy, the scientific consensus is far more clear than Dr. Singer suggests.

First, I don't understand Dr. Singer's suspicion of government-funded scientists, nor his criticism of the climate change information on Environment Canada's Web site. Conspiracies require a motive, and I can't fathom what advantage would accrue from a government plot of climate change misinformation. Though I escape Dr. Singer's criticism because I am not a government scientist, I know that most basic research is by necessity government-funded—and is peer reviewed before funding.

I do not subscribe to Dr. Singer's claim that "governments are unlikely to fund researchers who are not already concerned about global warming." On the other hand, I know industry-funded research is usually aimed at a corporate mission.

An overwhelming body of evidence points to significant warming over the past century, including tree ring analyses by Michael Mann and colleagues that reconstruct northern temperatures during the past 1,000 years. They show a dramatic increase in Northern Hemisphere temperatures at the turn of this century. In the 1,000-year record, 1998 represented the warmest year, the 1990s the warmest decade and the 20th century the warmest century.

While Dr. Singer correctly notes that natural oscillations play a significant role in determining climate, data analyzed by paleoclimatologist Jonathan Overpeck of the National Atmospheric and Ocean Administration have failed to identify any natural mechanism for the unprecedented warming that led to 1998 being the warmest year in at least the past 1,200.

Dr. Singer argues that, so far, natural climate variability appears to dominate over any human effect. Simon Tett and colleagues of the prestigious Hadley Centre for Climate Prediction and Research disagree. In their paper published recently in the journal *Nature*, the authors exclude purely natural causes for warming from 1946 to 1996, and attribute it largely to human factors.

Reaffirming these results, Mike Lockwood of the Rutherford Appleton Laboratory in England told *New Scientist* magazine, "Whatever has happened in the past, the greenhouse effect is now the dominant cause of warming." Referring to his research published recently in *Nature*, Dr. Lockwood said that since 1970, when the pace of climate change began to accelerate, solar changes have caused less than one-third of the observed warming.

These and numerous other recent reports support and strengthen the 1995 United Nations Intergovernmental Panel on Climate Change statement that the balance of evidence suggests a discernible climate change due to human activities. As James Hansen of NASA's Goddard Institute for Space Studies says, "the rapid warming of the past 25 years undercuts the argument of the 'greenhouse skeptics' who have maintained that most global warming occurred early this century when greenhouse gases were increasing more slowly—in fact, the fastest warming is occurring just when it is expected."

I would like to clarify Dr. Singer's assertion that a warming trend recorded by ground instruments is not borne out by data from satellites. Dr. Singer is right that a discrepancy in ground/satellite trends did cause confusion—until researchers corrected errors in satellite orbital calculations. Once corrected, the satellite and ground data both showed warming trends. Nonetheless, these satellite data are still at an experimental stage. And while Dr. Singer is correct that urban environments are relatively warm, he failed to mention that rural temperature instruments, especially those in sparsely populated, high northern latitudes, also reveal a warming trend.

I am puzzled by Dr. Singer's statement that "ongoing sea-level rise slows during warmer periods." If this were true, then it follows that sea-level rise would increase during cool periods. It is now well known that 21,000 years ago, when much of Canada lay frozen under a vast ice sheet and global temperatures were about 5C lower, sea levels were about 120 metres lower. The scientific research on current trends shows that the total sum of glacier and ice sheet melting is causing the sea to rise. Best estimates of sea-level rise by 2100 are 50 centimetres.

As for Dr. Singer's reference to the 17,000-plus scientists who signed the petition last year against the 1997 Kyoto Protocol, I would add that the U.S. National Academy of Sciences, on one of whose boards I serve, took the unprecedented step of disassociating itself from this petition. The academy concluded that "greenhouse warming poses a potential threat sufficient to merit prompt responses."

Dr. Singer says the effects of climate change would be, on the whole, positive. I counter that scientists lack the ability to predict definitively how global warming will affect regional climates and extreme weather events, or what major climate surprises might be in store. So it surprises me that any economic analysis, which must make assumptions on all of these, is possible at all.

The embattled global insurance industry, however, is less reticent than we scientists to make the global warming/extreme weather connection. Until 1988, a loss of more than $1-billion (US) on a single natural disaster was unheard of. Yet between 1988 and 1996, 15 such events occurred. Deducing that climate change is responsible for the 50-fold increase in economic losses to natural disasters during the past 30 years, the global insurance industry has pressed for greenhouse gas reductions.

Unfortunately, as we move toward ratification of the Kyoto Protocol, more and more skeptics will put public pressure on government because of its implications for industries dependent on fossil fuels. I suspect the anti-global warming campaign will employ the tactics of a legal defence team that knows it has lost its case. Numerous questions of doubt, whether they are well-founded or not, will be aimed at the public jury, with the desperate hope that one will produce a not-guilty verdict on society's influence on climate.

I fear corporate lobbying has already created an era of misinformation, and am extremely concerned about the disproportionate coverage the mainstream media gives to what is, in reality, negligible scientific controversy. Scientists are debating climate change in peer-reviewed, international journals. Yet this debate is not about *if* human-caused climate change is happening—but rather how quickly, to what magnitude, with what regional implications and with what threats to humanity.

Andrew Weaver is a professor at the School of Earth and Ocean Sciences at the University of Victoria, Canada. This article first appeared in the Financial Post *for September 2, 1999. Reprinted by permission of the author.*

Global Warming Proof Still Suspect

S. Fred Singer

As a lead author of the 1995 UN-IPCC climate report, Andrew Weaver understandably downplays its scientific uncertainties. Many of his IPCC colleagues are not so sanguine. The prestigious journal *Science* (May 16, 1997) interviewed IPCC participants and got rather skeptical reactions to the IPCC's conclusions. It's therefore disingenuous of Dr. Weaver to accuse scientific skeptics of pursuing an industry agenda while considering government bureaucracies to be free of hidden motives. For the record, my organization, the Science and Environmental Policy Project, is supported entirely by private donations and non-profit foundations.

This is not the place to enter into a detailed scientific debate. My arguments are spelled out in my recent book, *Hot Talk, Cold Science: Global Warming's Unfinished Debate* and on our Web site.

However, many of Dr. Weaver's arguments are easily disposed of. If 1998 was the warmest year and 1999 is cooler, does that mean that the globe is cooling? One year does not make a trend. We all agree that there was substantial warming between 1900 and 1940. This warming marked the end of the Little Ice Age (LIA), which began around 1000 AD. But let's be honest. We had no global temperature measurements until weather satellites started regular observations in 1979. The reconstructions published by Michael Mann are based on proxy data such as the width of tree rings, and fail to even document the LIA; other researchers get quite different results. For example, Dorthe Dahl-Jensen and her colleagues, who used data from thermometers in bore holes of Greenland ice cores, clearly showed the LIA and the warming before 1940 (*Science*, Oct. 9, 1998). The authors remark explicitly that temperatures fell between 1940 and 1995.

Dr. Weaver is not quite up-to-date on the analysis of satellite data. Even after corrections, they still show no sustained warming trend in the past 20 years. Quite independently, balloon-borne radiosondes give similar results. Climate modellers are trying to fit their computer results to the data by introducing questionable corrections (or forcings) from various aerosols, stratospheric ozone, and so on. I consider these efforts to be little more than curve-fitting exercises. As global warming guru James Hansen of NASA, who wrote last year in the *Proceedings of the U.S. National Academy of Sciences:* "The forcings that drive long-term climate change are not known with an accuracy sufficient to define future climate change."

I can clarify the sea-level issue that is puzzling Dr. Weaver. He is correct in stating that sea levels were 120 metres lower some 20,000 years ago and have been rising steadily since then, the peak of the last ice age. Sea levels will continue to rise as more of the remaining polar ice melts, especially in the Antarctic ice sheets. If our present warm interglacial period continues for a few more millennia, sea levels may rise another 10 metres, and we can do nothing about it.

But, as I pointed out in my article, when we analyze sea-level data on a time scale of decades rather than millennia, we find that this long-term rise decreases markedly during a warming period (for example, between 1900 and 1940). The warming causes more evaporation from oceans, hence more global rainfall, and therefore more (short-term) ice accumulation on the Antarctic continent. Apparently, this transfer of water from the ocean to continental ice outweighs the effects of the melting mountain glaciers that raise sea levels. So it is all a matter of time scale. Any man-made (or natural) warming over the next century will slow down the inexorable rise of sea levels.

As an aside, I find it strange that Dr. Weaver, who is so skeptical about the profit-seeking fossil-fuel industry, is so open to the arguments of the profit-seeking insurance industry. Could the reason be that they support his global warming fears? We should recognize their climate change arguments as self-serving, as they try to squeeze higher rates out of government regulators. In fact, hurricanes have been diminishing in frequency and intensity over the past 50 years, according to the UN-IPCC report. Population growth and increased investment, not global warming, have caused higher insurance losses.

To sum up, the crucial question is whether climate models can reproduce observations. So far at least, they have not only failed to do so, but their predictions differ from each other by several hundred percent.

Until climate models are reasonably well validated, we cannot accept their predictions, nor base far-reaching and costly policies on them. Under the circumstances, we should follow economically sound, "no-regrets" policies, such as cost-effective investments in energy conservation.

S. Fred Singer, PhD, is an atmospheric physicist, professor emeritus of environmental sciences at the University of Virginia, and president of the Fairfax-based Science & Environmental Policy Project, a nonprofit policy institute. Reprinted by permission of the author.

Answers to Selected Exercises

CHAPTER 1

Exercise 1: Part A

2. This passage does not contain an argument. It is a description of a physical environment, with the attribution of awareness of the environment to a subject.

4. This passage contains an argument. The conclusion is that any diet poses some problems. This conclusion is stated both at the beginning and (in slightly different words) at the end of the passage. The word *therefore* indicates the conclusion, where the specific problem is inferred from the alternatives considered.

6. This passage does not contain an argument. It offers an account of how physicians arrive at an estimation of one's risk of osteoporosis.

10. This passage does not contain an argument. The first sentence tells how we can understand the relationship of a reactor to a steam generator and makes a comparison. The second sentence elaborates slightly on the comparison.

13. This passage offers an argument that people today are different in significant ways from people thousands of years ago. The evidence is in differences in technology, powers, global consciousness, and intellectual and material wealth.

15. The passage does not contain an argument. It illustrates the possibility of getting a pattern without deliberately trying to. If the passage were set in a larger context in which this possibility were in doubt, it might be interpreted as an attempt to prove that not every resemblance is the result of an intentional depiction.

18. This passage does not contain an argument. It describes an experience in the man's life, giving background information about him, and says that in light of this background, what he is doing now is surprising. There is no attempt to give reasons or evidence for any point that is being debated or questioned.

Exercise 2: Part A

4. This passage does not contain an argument. It explains how two different people's measurements can fit together into invariant patterns, which are the laws of physics and are the same for all observers.

5. There is an argument. The expression "given this evidence" functions here as a logical indicator. The conclusion is "it is likely that men's brains are organized differently from women's brains."

10. The passage contains no argument. The word *because* is part of an explanation as to why she did not develop this independence.

12. This passage does contain an argument. The conclusion is that mountain climbers have accepted a risk of death. The indicator word *so* is a clue. The reasons are neatly set out: first some general conditions of accepting risk are announced; then it is stated that these conditions apply to mountain climbers; then the conclusion is drawn.

14. There is no argument. This is a descriptive passage, depicting the desperate character of peasant life.

15. There is an argument. The conclusion is that there should be freedom of expression of opinion. The reasons are that not to have this would be an evil that would rob us of opportunities either to discover error or to appreciate the truth more fully. (*Note:* This argument is an especially famous one that you are sure to encounter again if you go on to study political theory.)

18. There is no argument here. The passage is a descriptive one, from a science fantasy.

19. There is no argument here. The passage tries to explain how these famous comic strip characters handle life and says they are all right because they set up safety valves for themselves. The word *because* is not a logical indicator; it is part of an explanation.

CHAPTER 2

Exercise 1: Part A

1. Standardization:
   1. If a car has reliable brakes, it has brakes that work in wet weather.
   2. The brakes on my car do not work well in wet weather.
   Therefore,
   3. My car does not have reliable brakes.

3. Standardization:
   1. When unemployment among youth goes up, hooliganism and gang violence go up too.
   So,
   2. Unemployment is probably a major cause of hooliganism and gang violence.
   There is also an argument, from (2) to the conclusion that
   3. Gang violence among youth is not caused by drugs.
   Thus, there is a subargument from (1) to (2) and a main argument from (2) to (3).

5. Standardization:
   1. Every logic book I have ever read was written by a woman.
   Therefore,
   2. All logicians are women.
   This argument will be rather weak unless the arguer has read a great many logic books, but it is clearly an argument.

9. Standardization:
   1. The main feathers of the archaeopteryx show the asymmetric aerodynamic form typical of modern birds.
   So,
   2. The feathers of the archaeopteryx were used for flying.

10. Standardization:
    1. People do science.
    Therefore,
    2. Science is a socially embedded activity.
    The indicator word is *since,* which introduces the premise.

13. The passage does not contain an argument. It describes the San Andreas fault in California.

15. Standardization:
    1. Genes in a lab plant called arabidosis are turned on when the plant's leaves are touched.
    Therefore,
    2. Plants may respond, at a genetic level, to stimuli.

Exercise 1: Part B

Note: These answers are partial because of the nature of the exercise. We have simply tried to indicate where we think a subargument is needed, and why.

2. In response to Peter's last question, Juan could use a subargument to support his claim that polls do not provide information needed to make a decision about which candidate can best deal with important issues. Juan might say, for instance, that polls give information about how popular a candidate is with voters, but they do not give information about substantive issues such as tax policy, environmental cleanup, or foreign policy.

3. No subargument is needed. Nancy seems prepared to believe Catherine's story, and the dialogue does not really contain arguments.

5. No argument is given, so no subargument is needed.

Exercise 2: Part A

1. Somewhat tentative, as indicated by the phrase "if the stories my daughter has to tell are anything to go by."

4. Quite definite commitment to the claim that they will *probably* help.

6. Very definite commitment, as indicated by "no doubt" and "is murder." To make it absolutely clear that he does not want to qualify the judgment, the speaker includes "pure and simple."

10. Very tentative; "could be" indicates that this factor in allergies is being put forward as a possibility.

Exercise 2: Part B

3. There is an argument:
   1. Logicians say *true* and *false* apply only to statements.
   2. (Implicit) Logicians are right.
   3. Pictures are not statements.
   Therefore,
   4. Pictures cannot be true or false.

4. The argument is:
   1. Scientific knowledge is a very cooperative enterprise.
   2. Scientific propositions often must be accepted on the basis of evidence that only others have.
   So,
   3. Cooperation in science is possible only on the basis of reliance of others testimony.
   Thus,
   4. A scientific community often has no alternative to trust, including trust in the character of its members.

5. The argument is:
   1. People who wear high platform shoes are not comfortable in them.
   So,
   2. Flat, colorful, comfortable Keds have never gone out of style.

7. The passage does not contain an argument. It sets forth a kind of thought exercise for the reader. The authors want the readers to do something (that is, repeat the word *chair* in their minds), and they offer a descriptive prediction about what will happen when this is done.

8. The argument is:
   1. CBS Cable lost $30 million when its chairman tried to produce high-quality cultural programming.
   2. The Entertainment Channel with BBC and Broadway material went out of business.

3. Tele-France USA had to give up its attempt to present French cultural programs on television.
Thus,
4. It is not likely that mass media will be able to produce more meaningful artistic products.
The conclusion is taken as indicated by the first two sentences, especially the phrase "economics still guides and strangles" and by our sense of the point of evidence cited about business failures.

Exercise 3

2. Argument:
   1. Individuals are not reliable in their judgment.
   2. Groups are made up of individuals.
   So, probably,
   3. Groups are not reliable in their judgment.
   The premises are linked to support the conclusion.

4. Argument:
   1. The black hole concept is virtually impossible for nonexperts to comprehend.
   2. The notion of antimatter is paradoxical.
   3. In the context of elementary particles, it is impossible to understand what causation means.
   Thus,
   4. Modern physics is a mysterious subject.
   The premises are convergent in their support.

7. Argument:
   1. There would be no practical consequence were the right hand to attempt to give the left hand money as a gift.
   So,
   2. The right hand cannot give the left hand money as a gift. (Hard)
   The conclusion is implied by the questions in the first sentence and in the final sentence.

10. Argument, with subarguments:
   1. There could be no meaning if words could mean just anything.
   So,
   2. Language requires rules.
   3. A single person could make anything he wanted right.
   So,
   4. A single person cannot follow a rule.

Thus,

5. Rules require more than one person.
Therefore,

6. A private language is impossible.

There is a subargument from (1) to (2), another from (3) to (4), and a third from (4) to (5). In the main argument, (2) and (5) link to support (6), the main conclusion.

Exercise 4

2. 1. Butterflies need warm air and sunlight to breed.
    2. (Implicit) The conservatory at the zoo has warm air and sunlight.
    Therefore,
    3. The conservatory at the zoo is the perfect place for butterflies to breed.

5. 1. If God had meant people to fly through the air, they would have been born with wings.
    2. (Implicit) People were not born with wings.
    So,
    3. People were not meant to fly through the air.

8. The argument is:
    1. Only businesses compete, in the economic sense.
    2. A country is not a business.
    Therefore,
    3. To speak of the competitiveness of countries is a mistake.

10. 1. Understanding other people's ideas requires listening and trying to experience another person's world as he or she experiences it.
    2. Resolving conflicts requires understanding other people's ideas.
    3. (Implicit) We are not good at listening to others and trying to experience the world as they experience it.
    Thus,
    4. It is unlikely that we will be able to work out, and fully resolve, conflicts.

Exercise 5

1. Like many ads, this one is very brief, but it seeks to establish a point and is best seen as an argument with unexpressed parts.
    Standardization:
    1. Bananas contain everything NutraSweet contains.

2. Bananas are not dangerous to eat. (inserted)
Therefore,
3. NutraSweet is not dangerous to eat. (inserted)

The missing premise is common knowledge. Also, we attribute it to the ad because it supplies the obvious rationale for comparing NutraSweet and bananas in the first place. The missing conclusion is attributed because we know ads are used to make people seek to consume the products, and we know that there has been some controversy about the safety of artificial sweeteners and other additives.

4. Standardization:
    1. The teenage crime rate is going up.
    2. Teenage theft is rising.
    3. Teenage crime is connected to drug use. (inserted)
    So,
    4. Teenage drug use is not declining.

    Premise (2) is taken as a statement on the assumption that the last question is a rhetorical question assuming a negative answer. This also provides the interpretive basis for (3) and (4).

7. 1. Some nonsmokers suffer headaches, runny noses, and itchy eyes as a result of exposure to secondhand smoke.
    So,
    2. Secondhand smoke can cause minor health problems in nonsmokers.
    3. Secondhand smoke can cause lung cancer in nonsmokers regularly exposed to smoke.
    4. We have good reason to ban activities that cause health problems for vulnerable nonparticipants. (inserted)
    Therefore,
    5. We have good reason to ban smoking in public places.

    (1) supports (2) in a subargument. (4) is a missing premise. (2), (3), and (4) link to support (5).

9. 1. Joyce Brothers thinks Weight Loss Clinic has what a weight loss clinic needs for success.
    2. Joyce Brothers was impressed with Weight Loss Clinic.
    So,
    3. You too should be impressed by Weight Loss Clinic.

    Since the passage is an advertisement, we might add a further missing conclusion that if you need to lose weight, you should go to Weight Loss Clinic.

10. 1. If man were born to be happy, he would not be born to die.

2. Man's body is doomed to die.

So,

3. Man's task on earth is not physical. (inserted)

4. Man's task on earth must be physical or spiritual. (inserted)

Therefore,

5. Man's task on earth must be spiritual.

<u>6.</u> If man were born to be happy, his task on earth would not be spiritual. (inserted)

Therefore,

<u>7.</u> Man is not born to be happy. (inserted)

Note: The fact that we have had to insert two extra premises and two implicit conclusions to render these comments into a clear logical argument is evidence that the original argument was not clearly expressed.

12. This passage does not contain an argument. The character speaking compares Socrates to a kind of stinging fish.

15. The passage does not contain an argument. Rushdie is describing human needs and questions to which he thinks religious beliefs have been a response.

CHAPTER 3

Exercise 1

4. In the context, assume acceptability. The argument fails on (R); the information in (1) and (2) may show that the teacher is inexperienced as a teacher, but it has no bearing at all on the issue of how much she knows about philosophy. In (3) the information is entirely irrelevant to the issue of the instructor's competence in her subject. Because the argument fails on (R), it necessarily fails on (G) as well.

6. The premises are acceptable (A) and they are somewhat relevant (R), because all have to do with unexpected technological breakthroughs. But they do not give adequate grounds (G) because only three cases are described. Cases in which breakthroughs were sought but not obtained are not described, and AIDS may be different from the other problems in ways that make it less amenable to a breakthrough.

9. Assume acceptability (A)—it is an invented example. Premises are relevant (R). However, (G) is not satisfied because the people questioned in the poll may not believe, or may not have been aware when responding to the question asked in the poll, that doctors perform essential services.

10. The argument fails on all three conditions. (A) is not satisfied because we have no good reason to believe that all thinking is divided into only two types. No evidence is given for this, and it is not something known by common experience or known on the basis of reasoning from concepts. (*A priori*—see Chapter 5.) The argument fails on (R) because the premises are about methods of thinking, whereas the conclusion is about the subject matter of thinking. And for the same reason, it fails on (G).

11. 1. In schools in Cuba, girls far outstrip boys in their achievements.

2. Cuba is a socialist state in which equality of the sexes is a matter of law.

3. In Cuba, men are legally required to do their share of the housework.

Therefore,

4. Under socialism and true equality of opportunity, women will show up as superior to men.

We cannot say whether the premises are acceptable unless we have more than just common knowledge regarding Cuba. However, we can accept them provisionally. Clearly, they are relevant to the conclusion. They do not, however, give adequate grounds: the argument fails on (G) because the premises are about only one socialist state, whereas the conclusion is about socialist states generally.

15. The argument passes on (A) and (R) but fails on (G) because other sorts of businesses (for example, multinationals) may not feel pressures in the same way. Other factors such as resource depletion, pollution, and unemployment are not considered. Yet the argument reaches the conclusion that competition is valuable overall.

Exercise 2: Part A

1. Bob does not respond to Caroline's argument. He merely expresses his own dislike of mathe-

matics and explains why he doesn't like it. In the last sentence, Bob hints at (but does not really express) an argument as to why mathematics should not be required.

4. In this case, Juan does meet the challenge of argument. He contests Prahdeep's premise that a good novel should be easy to read, and contests the idea, assumed in another premise, that Prahdeep's experience in finding modern novels difficult to follow is representative.

6. Sheila does meet the challenge of argument. She gives reasons to think finding a counsellor could be counterproductive, and she contests the link between this couple having children and the idea that it would be unfortunate if they split up, by saying that children are better off with divorced parents than with parents who are quarreling and unhappy.

CHAPTER 4

Exercise 1

3. (d) The term would not be suitable for ostensive definition. It is too abstract, too subtle, and not something you can point to. Even if you were in the presence of a person who was wise, and acknowledged to be so, you could hardly define *wisdom* by pointing to him or her, because the person on whose behalf you were defining the word would not know which aspect you were pointing to.

4. (a) This definition is too broad because exchanges can be made using virtually anything as a medium—cattle or foodstuffs, for instance. Such things would not be regarded as money according to ordinary usage, since they would not be integrated into the functioning of an economy.

4. (d) This definition is too narrow. It requires that we concentrate very hard in order to be studying. But people can study provided they concentrate somewhat; in ordinary usage, this is still called studying. The definition also seems narrow in making memory the goal of studying. Sometimes we study for other purposes—for example, to get a better understanding.

5. (c) The new fruit could be called anything you like, but it would be natural to make up a name

that reflects its origin and nature. You might call it a *prapple* or a *papple* or an *appear,* for instance. Then you can stipulate a definition by saying, for instance, "A prapple is a fruit that is a cross between an apple and a pear." Your definition might also refer to properties the fruit has: "a juicy green fruit that is a cross . . . "

6. (c) This statement is not a persuasive definition. It is probably not a definition at all, but just a statement about coffee. If taken as a reportive definition, it could be criticized as too narrow because coffee is consumed in places other than Europe and North America, and by people other than writers and intellectuals.

6. (e) This statement is a persuasive definition that, in effect, seeks to evoke negative attitudes toward the police through emotionally negative terms such as *criminal* and *license to kill.* It ignores the social importance of having police, ignores the checks on police power, and may be inaccurate in its implication that police function only to implement their own personal judgments, and not to enforce the law.

6. (h) This statement is a disguised persuasive definition of art. It claims that real or authentic art must be an artificial representation of reality; photography is natural (thus not artificial and not selecting among the aspects of reality to be presented), so it is not art. (*Note:* It is not at all clear how the word *artificial* is being used here.) A clue to the presence of persuasive definition is the word *authentic.*

6. (k) This is a persuasive definition. A radical is described in negative terms, to discourage anyone from wanting to be a radical.

Exercise 2: Part A

3. The passage does not contain flaws in language.

4. This passage does not contain any argument to show flaws in Carl Sagan's show. The writer obviously believes that the show was cheap and poor, and he conveys this opinion with loaded language—*posture, gimmicks, schmaltz, cheapens, razzle-dazzle,* and *bubble gum mentality.* The emotional language hides the lack of argument.

5. There is a negatively persuasive definition of *nationalism,* as is suggested by the expression

"nothing but." Because *nationalism* is defined in terms of discrimination, intolerance, and prejudice, the author can easily conclude that it has no proper place in the contemporary world. Because it is based solely on a persuasive definition, the argument is not cogent.

6. Here we find two different uses of *natural* and *unnatural*. In the first sentence, *natural* is used to mean "occurs in the natural world"; in this sense, something natural is neither good nor bad as such. In the second sentence, a common belief about homosexuality being unnatural is alluded to. In that sense, *unnatural* means wrong. The argument that homosexual acts are natural and therefore good is based on equivocation between the first sense and the second one, and is thus not a cogent argument.

7. The passage is not exactly based on any flawed definition or flawed use of language. However, in the final part of the argument, the writer exploits an ambiguity in the word *forgive*. We may speak of forgiving a debt, in the sense of cancelling it, which is what is at issue in the question of debt relief for poor nations. Or we may speak of forgiving acts and policies that were wrong, in the sense of relinquishing our resentment and sense of grievance regarding those policies. In the final argument, the author uses these two senses of *forgive* to state his point. However, his argument that people in the West might need forgiveness from those in poor countries is not based simply on an equivocation. Rather, his reasons are that the West loaned money to despots who used it to enrich themselves and keep their power.

12. The ad exemplifies structural ambiguity. It is unclear whether it is the dress or the grandmother that is in beautiful condition.

14. The phrase "independent thinking" is ambiguous. As commonly understood, independent thinking means not believing everything one reads or is told but being willing to question some things and to search out evidence and arguments to arrive at one's own beliefs—at least when the issue is important and there is reason to question what one is told. As used in the premises, though, "independent thinking" is said to involve questioning everything one is told, so that one would have to start from scratch. This is, in effect, a stipulation that is

unreasonable and that avoids the real topic of the argument.

Exercise 2: Part B

3. Negative emotionally charged language is present in "illiterate peewee critics."

6. No euphemism or emotionally charged language is present.

7. There are two euphemisms: "let go" and "freed his future"; both are euphemisms for his being fired. Both euphemistic expressions suggest release and freedom, whereas in reality losing one's job is usually a painful experience.

CHAPTER 5

Exercise 1: Part A

4. This statement is not *a priori* true. Legal responsibility is established by the state. Whether one has contributed the ovum or sperm to create the child is a biological issue. There is no fixed logical connection between a biological fact and a legal fact. For instance, a twelve-year-old could be a biological parent but, because of her young age, not be a legal parent in some jurisdictions. Those who have adopted children are the legal parents of children of whom they are not the biological parents, which also illustrates that these two concepts are distinct.

7. This statement is *a priori* true. If a person fails to be grateful, he is not grateful.

10. We understand this statement to say, figuratively, that no man (or person) is isolated and stands alone. Expressed in non-figurative language, the statement is no true *a priori*; it is empirical.

11. The statement is *a priori* true. It expresses the logical connection between cause and effect. If an action has a cause, it is the effect of that cause and it therefore must be the effect of something that precedes it, because a cause precedes its effect.

14. This statement is not *a priori*. It makes the claim that a space station is needed and gives some reason for that. Value judgments are at stake here.

15. This sentence does not state a claim that is *a priori*. Nor does it express an empirical claim. Rather, it expresses a wish.

Exercise 1: Part B

1. The premise is a matter of common knowledge and would be acceptable.
2. A contestable case. It can be argued that the claim is knowable *a priori*. If we consider a person now and a person in a previous life to be the same person, and we consider that these bodily existences are different ones, then for the same person to be present twice, his or her soul or personality would have to survive (in some sense) between the two bodily lives. At least enough of the person would have to survive for him or her to be capable of being reincarnated. One might dispute this argument by saying that a soul could pop into life after a period of non-existence.
4. The claim is not acceptable *a priori* nor on the basis of common knowledge or authority; in the context there is no subargument. If it were defended by someone on the basis of testimony, it would not thereby become acceptable, because it goes far beyond testimony in its sweeping metaphysical implications. The only way the claim could be acceptable would be provisionally; but it is so sweeping and controversial that even provisional acceptance would not be reasonable.
6. This claim is acceptable as common knowledge.

Exercise 2: Part A

1. These statements are not inconsistent.
4. There is no inconsistency in these statements. The expectation of improvement, and success of some African Americans, is contrasted with the greater effect of unemployment on African Americans.
7. There is an implicit inconsistency between the second statement and the third one. If God created all the goodness in the world, He would have had to create His own goodness, which would mean existing before He existed. (One could escape this contradiction if one assumed that God is not part of this world.) On the assumption that creation requires a creative

act, the third sentence is inconsistent with the fourth one.
9. These statements are not implicitly inconsistent. They do, however, impose an impossible demand on knowledge.
10. There is no inconsistency. The passage merely describes the pros and cons of visiting earth from the point of view of an imagined civilization.
12. There is no inconsistency. The passage describes a terrible civil war in which both sides committed atrocities but those of the rebel troops were especially long-lasting and awful.
13. The first three statements are consistent with each other; in fact, they make much the same point using different words in each case. But the last sentence, from "capital punishment is morally permissible" is inconsistent with the rest of the passage, because capital punishment does involve deliberately taking a life. Also, "wars in self-defense are sometimes necessary" is inconsistent with the first three statements if we understand "necessary" to imply "morally permissible."

Exercise 2: Part B

1. Yes, you can refute this statement by counterexample. People may get cancer from exposure to chemicals over which they have no control. Also, some diseases are genetic or congenital.
2. Yes, you can refute this statement by counterexample. Many who pursue logic are women— as for example, is the author of this book.
5. Yes, you can refute this statement by counterexample. Some long-distance colleges and universities offer courses on television. In addition, new public affairs shows and documentaries provide valuable information. Furthermore, even in the case of shows for pure entertainment, not all entertainment is a waste of time.
9. This statement can be refuted by counterexample. Pakistan is a Muslim country, and Benazir Bhutto was its leader for a number of years. Also, Turkey, which is officially secular, but which is a country in which the majority of people are Muslim, had a woman leader for several years.

Exercise 2: Part C

3. The premises are "withholding information is just the same as lying" and "lying is wrong." If these are taken to be universal statements, covering all cases of withholding information and lying, they are both easily refutable and hence unacceptable.

8. The statement that nothing that is private and intimate should be discussed publicly is not acceptable. Some things that are private and intimate are nevertheless of such great social importance that it is not reasonable to accept a ban on discussing them publicly, and some aspects of sexual relationships fall into this category. It is true that sex is a private matter if by private we mean that it is done apart from public view; it is another thing to say that it is private in the sense of not being open to public discussion. Any temptation to accept the first and third premises probably comes from the exploitation of the ambiguity in *private;* the argument may be said, in this regard, to be based on the fallacy of equivocation.

11. Two premises are unacceptable: "No one knows why some persons of all strata of society become addicts" and "This slipping away from personal responsibility is unjust." The former is unacceptable because it presupposes that experts are incorrect, which is one of the points the author is trying to prove. The latter is unacceptable because it presupposes that people are individually responsible for their actions, which is one of the things the experts deny. Neither of these claims can be taken as acceptable within the context of this argument. (*Note:* They might be true, nevertheless.)

12. The conclusion of this argument is that there is no need for moral concern about the killing of turkeys. The subconclusion is that turkeys are very stupid. Of three premises put forward for this subconclusion, two are based on the author's personal experience, on episodes in which turkeys he observed showed no intelligence. We might accept these anecdotes as testimony, though the author's loaded language counts to some extent against his being an unbiased observer of turkey behavior. The third premise is based on combining those anecdotes with a comparison with flowers, which "know how" to hope and close. In that premise "know how" is used vaguely. All premises of the argument are open to some question. A further objection to the argument is that the sub-conclusion that turkeys are very stupid does not give sufficient reason to believe that there is no need for moral concern about them.

14. The premises are clearly acceptable on the basis of common knowledge. (The argument may be criticized on the (G) condition; other sports are not considered.)

CHAPTER 6

Exercise 1: Part A

1. Statement (a) is relevant to statement (b) because it gives some reason to suppose that (b) is true. The natural interpretation of the behavior described is that elephants are hiding others because the others are not living. If this interpretation is correct, then elephants have the concept "not living," which is, essentially, the concept "dead."

5. Statement (a) is irrelevant to (b). The impossibility of pronouncing words for various ingredients has no bearing at all on the issue of whether these ingredients are dangerous.

6. Statement (a) is not relevant to statement (b) even though they both deal with the Holocaust. Statement (a) is about a dispute among French historians, and (b) considers what would have happened without protective activities by some courageous people. These themes are distinct, and the disagreement among historians provides no evidence concerning what would have happened if some courageous people had acted differently.

9. Statement (a) is clearly relevant to statement (b), because (a) claims that remains of these bones were found; the remains would be evidence that rhinoceri lived there. Note that the remains would not be sufficient or adequate grounds. (a) is relevant and only relevant, because there is some possibility, for instance, that the charred bones could have been planted.

Exercise 1: Part B

1. The argument is:
   1. A number of different religious denominations are represented within the public school system.
   Therefore,
   2. The public school system must be secular.
   As stated, (1) is not relevant to (2), since having different religions is not a reason for having no religion at all. We could make (1) relevant by reading in a missing premise to the effect that only a secular system will be tolerable by all the different denominations. This extra premise, however, would be easily refutable because some denominations feel very strongly about having some religion in education—so much so that they might prefer a religion other than their own to none at all.

5. *Note:* The conclusion is provided in the background information. The premises are relevant to the conclusion, because they give an example that is one of a specious and insignificant connection, and yet shows only four degrees of separation.

9. The premises are irrelevant because fish are an entirely different species from humans, not close in an evolutionary sense and inhabiting an entirely different kind of environment.

10. The conclusion is that a complete proof of Christian beliefs would destroy the Christian religion. The fanciful story about thunderbolts is relevant; it serves to establish that belief based on evidence that is too compelling would not be free belief.

14. The reviewer quoted is arguing in effect that (1) people are no longer seeking to realize a national identity because (2) the culture the University was meant to preserve is global and transnational, so therefore (3) there is no point (or role) for the University. There is a subargument from (2) to (1). (2) is relevant to (1); the main argument is from (1) to (3). (1) is relevant to (3) only if we assume that a major role for the University was the realization of a national identity. That assumption is very questionable. Thus, (1) should not be regarded as relevant to (3).

Exercise 2

1. This passage does not contain an argument.

3. There is no irrelevance in Jones's argument. Smith does not really address that argument. Instead, he himself offers several different arguments to contradict Jones's conclusion. There are numerous flaws of relevance. What animals do to each other is irrelevant to what people should do to animals, because animals do not have a sense of morality and cannot reason about what they ought and ought not to do. What people do naturally (being omnivores) is irrelevant to what they ought to do. There is also an argument from ignorance at the one point where Smith does tie his comments to Jones's argument. The fact that we don't know what sort of consciousness animals may have is not a reason for concluding that they have none or for concluding that they feel no pain.

6. The author is arguing that (1) space is not our final frontier. A number of sentences here are not, however, parts of the argument. The reason that space is not the final frontier is that (2) the oceans, which are here on earth, constitute a vast frontier. That premise is supported by the claim (3) that diversity of life in the oceans may hold the promise of new pharmaceutical interventions in disease treatment. Thus (3) is put forward to support (2), which is put forward to support (1). There are no problems of relevance here. Other sentences are most plausibly regarded as offering additional comment, rather than premises or conclusion.

8. There is an implied conclusion in the rhetorical question that ends the passage. The conclusion is that there is a problem in an attractive woman telling other women not to worry about looking attractive. The premises are (1) Wolf has argued that women harm themselves when they try to live up to high standards of beauty, and (2) Wolf is beautiful and slender. If we assume that one cannot be beautiful and slender without (in some sense) worrying about making oneself beautiful and slender, then these premises suggest that Wolf does not practice what she preaches. There is a kind of contradiction here, which is in some sense a

problem; thus the premises are relevant to the conclusion. We might expect that the argument is a circumstantial *ad hominem*. But given the wording of the conclusion, that is not the case. If the argument were to be a circumstantial *ad hominem*, the conclusion would have to be "Wolf's beliefs about women and beauty are mistaken."

13. Here the premise is relevant to the conclusion. If the only people who know art and art education are art professors or art instructors, that fact is a very good reason for concluding that art colleges should be administered by them.

15. The argument is that (1) Hillary Clinton is a strong effective advocate and for this reason, so (2) she would be a better representative than someone whose main qualifications are that they are due to address or accident of birth a real New Yorker. Premise (1) is relevant to the conclusion (2) because being strong and effective as an advocate are important qualities needed to be a good representative.

CHAPTER 7

Exercise 1

2. Some students are persons who came to the office asking to be excused from the final examination. (*I*)
5. All persons who can afford to stay at London's prestigious hotels are rich persons. (*A*)
6. Some evangelists are not poets. (*O*)
10. Some textbooks are not boring books. (*O*)
12. All mathematicians are persons who love abstraction. (*A*) This sentence is somewhat ambiguous as to scope; it might assert "Some mathematicians are persons who love abstraction." (*I*)
15. All women with jobs outside the home and no assistance with household work are persons burdened with at least two jobs. (*A*)
16. All persons who are friends of yours are persons who are friends of mine. (*A*)
19. All things that are roses called by any name other than *rose* are things that are as sweet as roses. (*A*)
20. No tasks that are ours are tasks that involve wondering why. (*E*) All tasks that are ours are tasks that involve doing or dying. (*A*) (Hard.)

Exercise 2: Part A

1. All pilgrims who came to Massachusetts are persons who left England of their own free will. (*A*)
3. Some things that are technical innovations are not things that are needed. (*O*)
5. Some professors are not persons who are impractical. (*O*)
7. All things that are art are things that are done in the pursuit of beauty and truth. (*A*)
8. All beliefs that are nationalistic are beliefs that are fervent and concern doubtful matters. (*A*)
10. No people that are proles are human beings. (*E*)

Exercise 2: Part B

1. All *T* are *E*. (*T* represents those people who understand the new technology; *E* represents experts.) Converse: All *E* are *T*; not equivalent. Contrapositive: All non-*E* are non-*T*; equivalent to original. The original is an *A* statement; so too are the converse and the contrapositive.
4. All *W* are *D*. (*W* represents whales; *D* represents creatures in danger of extinction.) Converse: All *D* are *W*; not equivalent to original. Contrapositive: All non-*W* are non-*D*. Original is an *A* statement; so too are the converse and the contrapositive.
6. Some *C* are *F*. (*C* represents court proceedings; *F* represents things so complex as to be inefficient.) Converse: Some *F* are *C*; equivalent to original. Contrapositive: Some non-*F* are non-*C*; not equivalent to original. The original is an *I* statement; so too are the converse and the contrapositive.
7. Some *S* are not *C*. (*S* represents students; *C* represents competitive persons.) Converse: Some *C* are not *S*; not equivalent to original. Contrapositive: Some non-*C* are not non-*S*; equivalent to original. The original is an *O* statement; so too are the converse and the contrapositive.
8. No *R* are *D*. (*R* represents Russian authors; *D* represents those insensitive to nature.) Converse: No *D* are *R*. Contrapositive: No non-*D* are non-*R*. The converse is equivalent to the original, and the contrapositive is not. All are *E* statements.

Exercise 2: Part C

1. All *V* are *U*. (*V* represents advice given to young parents by so-called experts; *U* represents things that are unreliable.)
    This is an *A* statement.
    The contradictory is an *O* statement.
    Contradictory: Some *V* are not *U*.
3. Some *C* are *T*. (*C* represents crops; *T* represents things best grown on land that has been left fallow for one season.)
    This is an *I* statement.
    The contradictory is an *E* statement.
    Contradictory: No *C* are *T*.
5. All *P* are *T*. (*P* represents persons who are productive and innovative scientists; *T* represents persons who enjoy freedom of thought and are not afraid to risk pursuing new ideas.)
    This is an *A* statement.
    The contradictory is an *O* statement.
    Contradictory: Some *P* are not *T*.

Exercise 3

2. The argument in categorical form:
    1. Some mothers are persons who find small children extremely irritating.
    2. Some persons who find small children extremely irritating are persons who just cannot control themselves and suppress their rage.
    Therefore,
    3. Some mothers are persons who just cannot control themselves and suppress their rage.
    Venn diagram of premises: *M* represents mothers; *C* represents persons who find small children extremely irritating; *J* represents persons who cannot control themselves and suppress their rage.

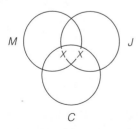

The argument is invalid. It would be possible for the premises to be true and the conclusion false because the *x*'s are on the line and there is

no guarantee they will fall into the areas required for the truth of the conclusion.

7. The argument in categorical form:
    1. All well-educated persons are persons who can read.
    2. All persons who can read are persons who have heard of Hitler.
    Therefore,
    3. Some well-educated persons are persons who have heard of Hitler.
    Venn diagram of premises: *W* represents well-educated persons; *R* represents persons who can read; *H* represents persons who have heard of Hitler.

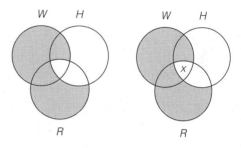

The argument is valid only if we adopt the existential interpretation and assume that there are well-educated persons and there are persons who can read. With this interpretation, we can add *x* and the argument is valid.

9. All *V* are *T*; all *T* are *R*; therefore, all *V* are *R*. (*V* represents acts of sunbathing; *T* represents things that carry a risk of skin cancer; *R* represents things that are dangerous.)

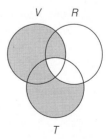

The argument is valid. Given the shading for the premises, we can see that all *V* are *R*. There is no area of the *V* circle left unshaded outside the *R* circle.

12. The argument in categorical form:
    1. Some doctors are unhappy persons. (Some *D* are *U*.)
    2. No unhappy persons are persons who find it easy to express sympathy for others. (No *U* are *E*.)
    So,
    3. Some doctors are not persons who find it easy to express sympathy for others. (Some *D* are not *E*.) Venn diagram of premises: *D* represents doctors; *U* represents unhappy persons; *E* represents persons who find it easy to express sympathy for others.

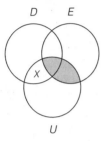

D   E

X

U

The argument is valid. The diagram of the premises shows an *x* in the area representing those who are doctors and who do not find it easy to express sympathy for others; the conclusion states there are persons in this area.

16. All positions involving power and influence in government are positions that should be allotted on the basis of elections (all *P* are *E*); all positions of being the spouse of the mayor are positions involving power and influence in government (all *O* are *P*); so, all positions of being the spouse of the mayor are positions that should be allotted on the basis of elections (all *O* are *E*).

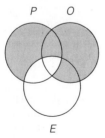

P   O

E

The argument is valid. To dispute the argument, one would most naturally dispute the second premise.

17. Some *R* are *D*; no *D* are *C*; therefore, some *R* are not *C*. (*R* represents religious people; *D* represents people who believe morality depends on religion; *C* represents people who have a true view of morality.)

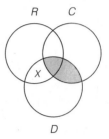

R   C

X

D

Valid.

Exercise 4

1. Some problems experienced by human beings are problems that result from climate (some *P* are *R*); no problems that result from climate are problems that result from abuses of human rights (no *R* are *A*); so, some problems experienced by human beings are not a result of abuses of human rights (some *P* are not *A*).

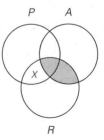

P   A

X

R

Valid.

2. All men who are other than *I* are men who die (all *M* are *D*); no men who are identical to *I* are men who are other than *I* (no *I* are *M*); therefore, no *I* are *D* ("I shall not die").

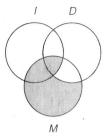

M

Invalid.

6. The argument in categorical form:
   1. Some double letters are letters compounded of two vowels. (Some *D* are *C*.)
   2. No double letters are vowels. (No *D* are *V*.)
   Therefore,
   3. Some letters compounded of two vowels are not vowels. (Some *C* are not *V*.)
   Venn diagram of premises: *D* represents double letters; *C* represents letters compounded of two vowels; *V* represents vowels.

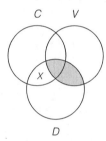

D

The argument is valid because this diagram shows an *x* in the area that is *C* and is not *V*, as is required for the conclusion to be true.

7. Stated premise: All *L* are *T* (where *L* represents leaders of our country and *T* represents persons who have not told the citizens where they want to lead us.)
   Stated conclusion: All *L* are *C* (where *C* represents persons who are totally confused).
   The argument can be turned into a valid syllogism by adding "all *T* are *C*" as a missing premise. The argument is then: all *L* are *T*; all *T* are *C*. Therefore, all *L* are *C*.
   This syllogism is valid. We check this one with reference to the rules. The middle term is *T*; it is distributed in the second premise. The term

L is distributed in the conclusion; it is also distributed in the first premise—thus satisfying the second rule. At least one premise is affirmative; the conclusion is not negative, so we do not need a negative premise. In addition, the syllogism does not have two universal premises and a particular conclusion; its conclusion is universal.

12. Premises: No persons who are lazy are persons who will pass the degree in physics (no *L* are *D*). Some persons who are students in the physics program are persons who are lazy (some *S* are *L*). Conclusion: Some *S* are not *D*.

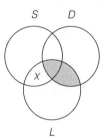

L

Valid.

13. With additions, this passage may be cast as two syllogisms. The context—namely that the author is writing about Canada—is used to supply added premises. *N* represents nations permitting the showing of violence night after night and not permitting the showing of love-making scenes. *C* represents nations that are Canada. *P* represents nations that are guilty of practicing obscenity and hypocrisy. *W* represents things without redeeming social value.
   The first syllogism is: All *N* are *P*;
   All *C* are *N* (inserted);
   Therefore,
   All *C* are *P*.
   (This is valid.)
   The second syllogism is: All *C* are *P*;
   All *P* are *W* (inserted);
   Therefore,
   All *C* are *W*.
   In this case, insertions are made first because of the immediate inference made from the hypocrisy and obscenity to being without redeeming social value, and second because of

the strongly implied criticism of Canada, in the context. (The second syllogism is also valid.) Whether these are cogent arguments will depend entirely on our appraisal of the premises.

CHAPTER 8

Exercise 1: Part A

4. J represents "Joshua will organize the demonstration"; N represents "Noleen will take a petition to all the members of the group"; M represents "Media will probably attend"; G represents "Noleen will likely get many signatures." $J \lor N$; $(J \supset M) \cdot (N \supset G)$

8. E represents "Extensive public relations efforts are being made on behalf of the nuclear industry"; C represents "Efforts being made on behalf of the nuclear industry are convincing the public"; T represents "The nuclear industry is in trouble." The argument is: $E \cdot -C$; $(E \lor -C) \supset T$; so, T.

Exercise 1: Part B

2. M represents "You master calculus"; D represents "You have some difficulty with the mathematical aspects of first year university physics." The argument can then be represented as:
$M \supset -D$; M; therefore $-D$.

The argument is valid. There is no row where the conclusion is false and the premises are true.

8. S represents "You are a suitable student of philosophy of science"; K represents "You know philosophy"; C represents "You know

science." The argument can then be represented as: $S \supset (K \lor C)$; $-K \cdot -C$; therefore $-S$.

S	K	C	$K \lor C$	$S \supset (K \lor C)$	$-K$	$-C$	$-S$	$-K \cdot -C$
T	T	T	T	T	F	F	F	F
T	T	F	T	T	F	T	F	F
T	F	T	T	T	T	F	F	F
T	F	F	F	F	T	T	F	T
F	T	T	T	T	F	F	T	F
F	T	F	T	T	F	T	T	F
F	F	T	T	T	T	F	T	F
F	F	F	F	T	T	T	T	T

The argument is valid. There is no row where the conclusion is false and the premises are true.

9. Let M = Medical authorities change their minds too often; P = People are willing to follow medical advice about a healthy diet and lifestyle; R = People have respect for doctors. The argument is:
$M \supset P$; $-P$; $-R$; therefore, M. The truth table is:

M	P	R	$-P$	$-R$	$M \supset -P$
T	T	T	F	F	F
T	T	F	F	T	F
T	F	T	T	F	T
T	F	F	T	T	F
F	T	T	F	F	T
F	T	F	F	T	T
F	F	T	T	F	T
Ⓕ	F	F	Ⓣ	Ⓣ	Ⓣ

The argument is not valid. In the bottom row of the truth table, the conclusion is false and all the premises are true.

10. Let N represent "The negotiations will be successful," C represent "The problem will continue to be unresolved with the situation at a standoff," and E represent "The situation will escalate into violence." The argument is then represented as:
$(N \lor C) \lor E$; N; therefore, $-C$.

N	C	E	N∨C	(N∨C)∨E	−C
T	T	T	T	T	F
Ⓣ	T	F	T	Ⓣ	Ⓕ
T	F	T	T	T	T
T	F	F	T	T	T
F	T	T	T	T	F
F	T	F	T	T	F
F	F	T	F	T	T
F	F	F	F	F	T

↑ Premise   ↑ Premise   ↑ Conclusion

The argument is invalid, as is apparent from the first and second rows of the truth table, where the premises are true and the conclusion is false.

Exercise 1: Part C

1. Let U = "the United States subsidizes grain sales to Russia"; C = "Canadian farmers will receive less than they presently receive for the grain they sell to Russia"; B = "Some Canadian farmers will go bankrupt"; and A = "Taxpayers will be called on to help Canadian farmers." The argument is:

   $U \supset C$
   $C \supset B$
   $B \supset A$
   U
   Therefore,
   A

   If we set A false, there is no way to make all the premises true, because if A is false, B must be false in order for the third premise to be true; then C must be false in order for the second premise to be true; then U must be false in order for the first premise to be true. However, U is the fourth premise and must be true for the fourth premise to be true. There is no consistent assignment of truth values that will make the conclusion false and the premises true. So the argument is valid.

3. Let I = "Science teaching will improve"; L = "We are going to have a society that is effec-

tively scientifically illiterate"; S = "Teachers' salaries are increased"; A = "There is a chance of attracting good science students into teaching"; G = "Governments are cutting funds for education." Assume that $-A$ can represent "We do not attract good science students into teaching." The argument, formalized, is:

   $I \vee L$
   $(-S \supset -A) \cdot (-A \supset -I)$
   $G \cdot (G \supset -S)$
   Therefore,
   L

   Valid. To make the conclusion false, make L false. If L is false, I must be true to make the first premise, $I \vee L$, true. If I is true, $-I$ is false. Thus $-A$ must be false (and A true) to make the second conjunct of the second premise true. If $-A$ is false, then $-S$ must be false (and S true) to make the first conjunct of the second premise true. If $-S$ is false, then G must be false, to make the second conjunct of the third premise true. But if G is false, then the first conjunct of the third premise is not true. Hence, we cannot make all the premises true when the conclusion is false.

5. Let K represent "The murderer used a kitchen knife"; U represent "The murderer carried an unusually large pocket knife"; L represent "The murderer was wearing loose clothes"; N represent "The murderer was noticed"; T represent "The murderer was very thin"; and W represent "The murderer was wearing clothes found at the scene of the crime." The argument is then formally represented as $K \vee U$; $U \supset (L \vee N)$; $-N$; $L \supset (T \vee -W) -L \cdot -K$; therefore, $-W$.

   To test by the shorter truth table technique, set the conclusion false; that is, set W true. Then, set both L and K false to make the premise $(-L \cdot -K)$ true; set N false to make the premise $-N$ true. If K is false, U must be true to make the first premise true. If U is true, then either L or N must be true, to make the second premise true. But both L and N have been set as false. Hence, it is not possible to consistently assign truth values so that the premises come out true and the conclusion false. The argument is valid.

Exercise 2: Part A

5. $\{(P \cdot C) \vee (C \cdot B) \vee (B \cdot P)\} \supset -(F \cdot G); \{(C \cdot P) \vee (C \cdot B) \vee (P \cdot B)\} \supset \{(F \vee G) \cdot -(F \cdot G)\}$ where P represents "You take physics"; C represents "You take chemistry"; B represents "You take biology"; F represents "You take French"; and G represents "You take German."

8. $(-R \cdot D) \supset (C \vee E); (C \supset A) \cdot (E \supset S); -G \supset (A \vee S);$ so, $-R \supset -D.$ Here R represents "Land claims are resolved"; D represents "Native leaders continue to distrust the government"; C represents "There will be continued nonviolent blockades"; E represents "There will be an escalation of the problem into terrorist action"; G represents "The government can inspire more confidence from native leaders"; A represents "Antagonism between whites and natives will increase"; S represents "The whole country will be adversely affected in a most serious way."

Exercise 2: Part B

3. Let S = "The book was a success." Let L = "The book was a failure." The argument is then "$-S$; therefore L." It is not valid. Note that two different statement letters are needed because "the book was a failure" is not the logical contradictory of "the book was a success."

8. Let D = "International politics is a difficult academic subject"; let M = "International politics is such a mishmash that no one can understand it at all"; let R = "Respected academics study international politics." The argument is then represented as: $D \vee M; R \supset -M; R;$ therefore, $-M \cdot D.$
    The argument is valid. For the conclusion to be false, either M must be true or D must be false. If M is true, the first premise is true. Then, for the second premise to be true, R must be false. Given these assignments, the third premise will be false. If D is false, then M must be true to make the first premise true. Then R must be false in order for the second premise to be true, and, as before, this case will result in the third premise being false. It is not possible to make the premises true and the conclusion false; therefore, the argument is valid.

15. Let S = "Socrates influenced Plato"; I = "Plato influenced Aristotle"; and A = "Socrates influ-

enced Aristotle." The argument is then formally represented as: $(S \cdot I) \supset A; (S \cdot I);$ therefore, $A.$ It is valid. For the conclusion to be false, either S or I will have to be false for the first premise to be true. But given this, you cannot make the second premise true.

17. Let W = "Saudi Arabia loses power in the Gulf"; let B = "The balance of power in the Gulf will be upset"; let I = "There will be increasing political ambition on the part of fundamentalist Islamic groups"; let U = "Saudi Arabia is unable to fund fundamentalist Islamic groups"; let A = "Fundamentalist groups will be unable to carry out their ambitions." The argument is then formally represented as: $W \supset B; B \supset I; (W \cdot U) \supset A; W \cdot U;$ therefore, $I \cdot A.$ For the conclusion to be false, either I must be false or A must be false. For the fourth premise to be true, W must be true and U must be true. Given W, U true, then for the third premise to be true A must be true. Given W true, then for the first premise to be true, B must be true, and given B true, then for the second premise to be true, I must be true. But for the conclusion to be false, either A or I must be false. So it is not possible for the premises all to be true when the conclusion is false. The argument is valid.

19. There are two arguments here. Let D = "Fred goes on a diet for more than two months"; S = "Fred's metabolism will slow down"; L = "Fred will need less food than he does now"; G = "Fred will gain weight on what he eats now"; U = "Fred's dieting is futile." The first argument is formally represented as $D \supset S; S \supset L; L \supset G;$ therefore, $D \supset G.$ It is valid. The second argument is $(D \supset G) \supset U; D;$ therefore U (taken from the first argument); therefore, $U.$ For the first argument, to make conclusion false, set D true and G false. If D is true S must be true, for the first premise; if S is true, L must be true, for the second premise; if L is true, G must be true, for the third premise. Yet G has been set as false. So the premises can't all be true when the conclusion is false and thus the first argument is valid. To check the second argument set U false to make the conclusion false. To make premises true, set D true, for second premise. Given U is false, first premise is true, given D true and G true. So the premises

can be true when the conclusion is false. The second argument is not valid.

Exercise 3

1. *E* represents "Elephants have been known to bury their dead"; *C* represents "Elephants have a concept of their own species"; *U* represents "Elephants understand what death means"; *S* represents "Elephants have a substantial capacity for abstraction." The argument is formally represented as: E; $E \supset (C \cdot U)$; $U \supset S$; therefore, S.
   The argument is valid.

3. Let S = "It rains all day." Let N = "The flowers, trees, and grass will benefit from the moisture." Let R = "The sun shines." Let I = "We enjoy being out." Let G = "Something good will have come." The argument is then symbolized as $S \supset N$; $(-S \cdot R) \supset I$; $(N \lor I) \supset G$; therefore $(S \lor (-S \cdot R)) \supset G$.
   If we set G as false, S as false, and R as true, the conclusion will be false. If S is false the first premise, $S \supset N$, is true. If S is false, R is true, and I is true, the second premise, $(-S \cdot R) \supset I$, is also true. And if I is true, and G is true, the third premise, $(N \lor I) \supset G$, is true whether N is true. Thus the conclusion could be false while all the premises were true. The argument is invalid.

5. Let E = "He exercises regularly." Let I = "His heart condition will improve." Let H = "He is likely to have a heart attack." Let R = "He is likely to be at serious risk of having a heart attack." The argument is then: $-E \supset -I$; $-I \supset (H \lor R)$; $(-H \cdot -R) \supset E$. The argument is valid. To make the conclusion false we would have to set E as false and H and R as false. If we did this, the first premise would be true if I were false. The second premise would be true if either H or R were true. But both H and R have been set as false. Therefore, the premises could not be true when the conclusion is false, so the argument is valid.

7. *W* represents "Workers agree not to strike within the next decade"; *D* represents "Prospects for the recovery of the plant are dim"; *M* represents "Management agrees to forgo special parking and washroom privileges." In this context, "management does its part" is taken to mean that management agrees to forgo special parking and washroom privileges and is thus represented by *M*. *Note:* "There can be a recovery of the plant" is taken to be the contradictory of "Prospects for the recovery of the plant are dim" and is represented as $-D$. The argument is: $-W \supset D$; $-M \supset -W$; therefore, $-D \supset M$.
   The argument is valid.

12. Let S = "Science can be about the objective world." Let O = "An objective world exists." Let I = "There are objects independent of human perceptions and beliefs." Let E = "Objects exist outside minds." Let T = "Tables are inside minds." The argument is (1) $(S \supset O) \cdot (O \supset I)$; (2) $E \supset I$; (3) $-T \supset O$; (4) $-T$; (5) $-T \supset O$; (6) O; therefore S. To check, set S false to make conclusion false. Set O true to make sixth premise true. Set T false to make fourth premise true. Then fifth premise will be true, and third premise will be true if O is true. Given O true, I must be true for the second conjunct of the first premise to be true. If I is true, the second premise is true. Hence it is possible to make all the premises true when the conclusion is false, and the argument is not valid.

13. Let I represent "Television programs improve in quality and appeal"; L represent "Large networks will lose their markets to video"; B represent "Programming budgeting increases"; and A represent "Advertisers are willing to pay more." The argument is then represented as: $(I \lor L)$; $(I \supset B) \cdot (-A \supset -B)$; $-A$; $-B$; $-I$; therefore, L. The argument is valid. We cannot make the premises all true and the conclusion false. For the conclusion to be false, L would have to be false. For the sixth premise, $-I$, to be true, I would have to be false. But if both I and L are false, the first premise, $I \lor L$, is false.

15. Let R = "The artist is talented." Let A = "People are likely to admire the work of the artist." Let P = "The artist gets paid for her work." Let B = "Someone wants to buy this work." The argument is then: $R \supset A$; $-R \supset -A$; P; $P \supset B$; $B \supset A$; therefore, R. The argument is valid. To see why, making the conclusion false requires setting R as false. The first premise, $R \supset A$, is then true whether A is true or false. The second premise, $-R \supset -A$, is true only if A is false; the

third premise, *P*, is true only if *P* is true; the fourth premise, $P \supset B$, is then true only if *B* is true; the fifth premise, $B \supset A$, is true only if *A* is true. But in order to make the second premise true, *A* has been set as false. So the assignment of truth values is inconsistent. Thus the conclusion cannot be false when all the premises are true, and the argument is valid.

18. The passage does not express an argument.

Exercise 4: Part A

2. 1. $-A \cdot -B$
    2. $-B \supset C$ (*C* is to be proven)
    3. $-B$ from (1) by simplification
    4. *C* from (3) and (2) by *modus ponens*

5. 1. $(A \vee B) \supset D$
    2. $-D$
    3. $-B \supset (A \supset X)$
    4. $(A \cdot B) \vee X$ (*X* is to be proven)
    5. $-(A \vee B)$ from (1) and (2) by *modus tollens*
    6. $-A \cdot -B$ from (5) by De Morgan
    7. $-A$ from (6) by simplification
    8. $-A \vee -B$ from (7) by addition
    9. $-(A \cdot B)$ from (8) by De Morgan
    10. *X* from (4) and (9) by disjunctive syllogism

7. 1. $(D \cdot E) \supset (F \vee G)$
    2. $-D \supset F$
    3. $-(D \vee E)$ (to be proven: $F \vee G$)
    4. $-D \cdot -E$ from (3) by De Morgan
    5. $-D$ from (4) by simplification
    6. *F* from (2) and (5) by *modus ponens*
    7. $F \vee G$ from (6) by addition

9. 1. $A \supset B$
    2. $C \supset D$
    3. $(B \vee D) \supset E$
    4. $-E$ to be proven: $-A \vee C$
    5. $-(B \vee D)$ from (3) and (4) by *modus tollens*
    6. $-B \cdot -D$ from (5) by De Morgan
    7. $-B$ from (6) by simplification
    8. $-A$ from (7) and (1) by *modus tollens*
    9. $-A \vee C$ from (8) by addition

Exercise 4: Part B

4. Let *O* = "Words refer only to private sensations in the minds of speakers"; let *I* = "Understanding is impossible." Then the first premise is $O \supset I$—and the second premise is $-I$. We can easily derive the stated conclusion from premises (1) and (2). In fact, it takes one line:

3. $-O$, from (1) and (2) by *modus tollens*
    The only trick in this example is in formalizing; we have to see that the second premise negates the consequent of the first.

6. Let *I* = "The world's weather is increasingly erratic." Let *G* = "The global warming effect is real." Let *M* = "The global warming effect is measurable." Let *E* = "Scientific instrumentation is quite elaborate." The argument is: $I \supset G$; $-I \supset -G$; $(G \supset M) \cdot (-E \supset -M)$; *E*; *M*; therefore *I*.
    1. $I \supset G$
    2. $-I \supset -G$
    3. $(G \supset M) \cdot (-E \supset -M)$
    4. *E*
    5. *M* (to be proven: *I*)

    This argument is not valid and so cannot be proven valid. To see that it is not valid, set the conclusion, *I*, as false. The first premise is then true. The second premise is true provided *G* is false. The third premise is true provided *E* is true and *M* is either true or false. The fourth premise is true, provided *E* is true. The fifth premise requires *M* to be true, which is consistent with requirements for the third premise.

8. Let *K* represent "I know this pencil exists," and let *H* represent "Hume's principles are true."
    1. *K*
    2. $H \supset -K$ (to be proven, $-H$)
    3. $--K$ from (1) by double negation
    4. $-H$ from (3) and (2) by *modus tollens*

12. *G* = "The group decided to undertake the action." *H* = "The group hired Jones to carry out the action." *D* = "The group funded and directed Jones in carrying out this action." *R* = "The group bears responsibility for the action." The argument is *G*; *H*; *D*; $((G \cdot H) \cdot D) \supset R$; therefore *R*.
    1. *G*
    2. *H*
    3. *D*
    4. $((G \cdot H) \cdot D) \supset R$ to be proven *R*
    5. $G \cdot H$. 1,2, Conjunction
    6. $(G \cdot H) \cdot D$ 5, 3 Conjunction
    7. *R* 4, 6 *Modus Ponens*

14. Let *B* represent "She can become a good mathematician"; *S* represent "She studies hard"; *L* represent "Her family life is happy"; *H* represent "Her general health is good"; *E* represent

"She gets exercise"; and D represent "She gets decent food."

1. $B \supset S$
2. $S \supset (L \cdot H)$
3. $H \supset (E \cdot D)$
4. $-E \cdot -D$ (to be proven, $-B$)
5. $B \supset (L \cdot H)$ from (1) and (2) by hypothetical syllogism
6. B assume
7. $L \cdot H$ from (5) and (6) by *modus ponens*
8. H from (7) by simplification
9. $B \supset H$ from (6) to (8) by conditional proof
10. $B \supset (E \cdot D)$ from (9) and (3) by hypothetical syllogism
11. $-E$ from (4) by simplification
12. $-E \vee -D$ from (11) by addition
13. $-(E \cdot D)$ from (12) by De Morgan
14. $-B$ from (10) and (13) by *modus tollens*

CHAPTER 9

Exercise 1: Part A

1. The sample would be unrepresentative because it would overrepresent cities and under-represent rural areas. It could be improved if one were to advertise in rural papers. In addition, job search bulletin boards will be read only by those unemployed people who are still seeking work. Some may have given up; they would not read such boards. Such people might be reached through newspapers, support groups for the unemployed, or counseling groups.

3. The areas he studies are used by humans—especially the campsites. This could affect the presence of elk. At campsites there might be more than the usual number of elk, if they were looking for garbage. Along trails, there might be less than the usual number, if they were frightened of humans. Perhaps these problems would cancel each other out to some extent. Still, the naturalist might improve the representativeness of his sample by attempting to enter some park areas not normally accessed by humans.

5. There are crucial differences in the situations of Professor X and Professor Y, which will likely affect the sorts of students who are filling out these evaluations. X's students had to take the course and are in a large class. Y's students chose to take the course and are in a small class. When we look at the evaluations we should take these differences into account. X's sample is likely to overrepresent less keen students working under less-than-ideal conditions, whereas Y's sample is likely to overrepresent enthusiastic students working under good conditions. The evaluations should not be compared because, given the sampling, it is entirely possible that X's is lower than it should be, whereas Y's is higher. If we are determined to make the comparison, we might try seeking out students in X's class who chose the course and consider only their evaluations. (However, this would not address the problem of different conditions.)

Exercise 1: Part B

2. The size and location (rural, urban, suburban) of the schools; the economic level and age of the students; the principals' definition of, and attitude toward, discipline problems; the practical value of knowledge of foreign languages for students in the area in question. The population would be highly variable.

4. Whether in shallow or deep water, the species of otter, the temperature of the water, currents, the age and size of the otters, their food, the situation of their natural predators. Quite variable.

Exercise 1: Part C

4. The sample is 300 people. The population is (adult) Americans. There is an argument. The sample is reasonably large, but it is likely to be somewhat unrepresentative. For one thing, only one region of the country (south central) is represented. In addition, subjects were sought in libraries, schools, and office buildings. This strategy is likely to overrepresent educational and professional workers and under-represent rural people and those in blue-collar occupations. The argument is not strong.

5. The sample is the time in which Linda was observed during eight visits to the office. The population is Linda's working time over 8 months (8 times approximately 20 mornings per month, or approximately 160 mornings).

The sample is not likely biased, but it is very small. Thus, the argument is inductively weak.

10. The sample is 12,500 nurses. The population is nurses in the United States in 1981. The conclusion is quite tentative, and the sample is very large. No evidence is given as to the representativeness of the sample, but given its size, it is unlikely to be seriously unrepresentative. The argument is inductively strong.

Exercise 2

1. Applying Mill's Method of Agreement would lead to the causal hypothesis that mosquito bites caused the allergic reaction.

2. This new information would lead you to modify the hypothesis. Mosquito bites could not have been the sole cause. An alternate hypothesis would be that a combination of factors, mosquito bites and some sort of scent or perfume, caused the reaction. You could explore this hypothesis using Mill's Method of Difference. What is the difference between the cases where she was bitten by mosquitoes and did not have a reaction, and the cases where she was bitten by mosquitoes and did have a reaction?

4. Using the Method of Agreement, we would conclude that ice makes them feel good, because according to the way events have been described, ice is the common element. What has gone wrong is that gin, rum, scotch, and vodka are all types of alcohol, but they have been given different descriptions here, since they are all different types. The concepts used to state the problem are too specific. We could reformulate the question, calling them all alcohol. Applying the Method of Agreement then would reveal two causal factors: ice and alcohol. These could be investigated further using Mill's methods. We could test to see whether people still felt good when they had ice without alcohol and when they had alcohol without ice.

   Variations on this example are often cited in discussions of Mill's methods. The example is a bit of a joke, because the effects of alcohol on mood are known. It shows (a) that Mill's methods need to be applied in the light of background knowledge and (b) that Mill's

methods can be applied to new data if an implausible hypothesis is generated.

Exercise 3: Part A

1. The sentence beginning with "Nearly" makes a correlational claim. In the first sentence, the word *linked* is ambiguous; it is unclear whether it is a causal claim or a correlational claim. This statement hints at a causal claim. The correlational information would not be sufficient to support a causal claim.

3. Various correlates of church attendance are stated.

6. The passage is essentially a denial that there is a positive correlation between having a death penalty and having a lower annual murder rate. It says, also, that this is evidence that the death penalty does not lower the murder rate. The denial of a correlational claim is good evidence for the denial of a causal claim. The argument is a good one. Although positive correlation is not sufficient for causation, it is necessary for it, so if positive correlation is not present, there is no causal relationship.

13. This passage is descriptive of inductive reasoning, but it does not contain any causal claim, correlational claim, or inductive generalization.

Exercise 3: Part B

1. No problem with unacceptable premises.

3. The observational statements are somewhat unreliable. A child is complaining to his mother who, because of her concern and involvement with him, may take his complaints too seriously. This is not to say that the child's complaints or the mother's concerns should simply be dismissed. But because the observations may be somewhat unreliable, they should be supplemented with reactions from other participants and parents. This would make the argument stronger.

6. The premises describe how a poor person would feel miserable and resentful and be led to commit arson. The conclusion is that the cause of people committing arson is that the poor resent the rich. The premises describe a plausible scenario, based on the assumption that the causal conclusion is true. They are question-begging and therefore not acceptable.

10. Plausible scenario mistake. The friends are described in a way that presupposes the conclusion that materialism and consumerism are what causes the people to leave the churches. This makes the premises unacceptable with regard to justifying the conclusion, because in the context of the argument they are question-begging.

Exercise 4

5. Causal claims are made about the improvement in manpower in the American armed forces. First, the author makes a negative causal claim. The improvements don't result from increased spending. The reasons are that quality has gone up more than spending, which has gone up by less than 20 percent. (The premise is not acceptable because it involves implicit pseudoprecision: we cannot precisely quantify an increase in quality.) If the premise were acceptable, it would be relevant but it would show only that increased spending is not the sole cause of the improvement. A positive causal claim is made in the last sentence, where the author hypothesizes three factors—recession, decivilianization, and nationalistic pride—as causally contributing to the improvement in the forces. No evidence is given for this conclusion. The whole argument assumes that the quality of manpower in the armed forces has improved very much, and this assumption is something for which evidence could have been given if, indeed, it is true at all.

6. This passage does not contain an argument. The authors describe a phenomenon that they say has been given little attention and is puzzling. They do not argue for any explanation of it; nor are there inductive arguments of any other kind.

10. A causal claim is implicit in "He has left a trail . . ." The passage says that the presence of John Wayne in the American imagination has resulted in broken hearts and jaws (presumably figuratively, in movies) and (more seriously) in millions of injured male egos. The only evidence given is that no real man could measure up to John Wayne's image. This evidence is relevant only if we assume that real men were trying to measure up to that image—something we do not know. The causal claim is not adequately supported.

11. The passage is jocular in tone and probably not meant seriously. Two correlational claims are made: that highly educated people with low incomes catch colds more frequently than others do, and that more people catch colds on Monday than on other days. The article makes a (probably nonserious) suggestion, on the basis of the correlational data, that colds are caused by dissatisfaction with one's job. The reasoning would not be adequate, but this passage probably does not contain serious reasoning from correlated data to a causal conclusion.

CHAPTER 10

Exercise 1: Part A

1. The primary subject is the argument that Japanese corporations are more fairly run than American ones because decisions are typically reached by teams rather than by high-ranking individuals. The analogue is the argument that a hypothetical judicial system would not become fairer just because judicial decisions were made by a team of judges and not one high-ranking judge. (Laws administered might be flawed, or decisions might be flawed, even if made by a group instead of an individual.) The premises of the primary argument are acceptable, and it is genuinely similar to the analogue argument in that the key feature of having groups, rather than individuals, make decisions is retained. The analogue shows that more than group procedure is needed for fairness. This is a successful refutation by logical analogy of the original argument.

4. The primary subject is the argument that the Catholic church cannot be wrong about contraception because this is a serious matter imposing heavy burdens on people and the church has promulgated these teachings for a long time. The analogues are slavery, torture, and religious freedom. Slavery and torture are serious, imposed heavy burdens on people, and they were defended by the church for a long time—but then they were recognized as wrong.

There is a refutation by logical analogy of the argument that the church cannot be wrong about contraception; this refutation passes on the ARG conditions.

5.   The primary subject is the argument that a disarmament referendum should not be held because nearly everyone would support disarmament. The analogue is the argument that a mayoralty election should not be held because nearly everyone would vote for the same candidate. No one would accept the analogue argument, which is indeed parallel to the primary argument (in both cases the inference would be from a large majority to the absence of a need for a vote). The refutation by logical analogy is a good one.

Exercise 1: Part B

3.   The primary subject is Trudeau's continuing as prime minister and liberal leader when Canada had a troubled economy and the opposition was said (by Trudeau) to be fumbling. The analogue is a doctor's continuing as a patient's doctor when that patient is sick and the doctor down the street is fumbling. Trudeau's point was that you would not change doctors, so you should not change prime ministers. Trudeau's argument is poor. In terms of acceptability of premises, we should not accept on his testimony or authority that the opposition is fumbling (conflict of interest). Also, his assumption, built into the analogue case, that a patient does not change his doctor when sick, may be questioned. A desperate patient might change doctors, even if the doctor down the street, to whom he was changing, had given signs of fumbling. More fundamentally, however, the analogy can be challenged for its relevance. The two relationships (politician, country/patient, doctor) are too different for a convincing analogy. A doctor is a qualified, trained professional in a one-on-one relationship with a patient. A politician is an elected person, rarely chosen mainly for competence. Furthermore, there are no clear standards for the health and management of an economy as there are for a sick person.

6.   The passage does not contain an argument by analogy. The example of the bus transportation

claim is used to support the claim that students cannot connect their commonsense knowledge to cognate concepts presented in a school context.

7.   This passage uses several logical analogies. The statements about lawyers, police officers, and city workers are cited as false stereotypes. The point is that the claim that teachers are self-absorbed individuals who enjoy telling classes their own opinions and who relish the idea of having control is, analogous, a false stereotype.

12. This passage does not contain an argument.

Exercise 2

5.   This passage contains an inductive analogy. The comparison is between an individual who may abuse power (the analogue) and a majority of a group of individuals (the primary subject) who, it is inferred, might abuse power. The point is that because (for the analogue) it would not be reasonable to give absolute power to an individual, neither would it be reasonable to give absolute power to a majority (the primary subject). This argument seems to be a strong one because the differences that do exist between groups and individuals do not undermine the basic similarity on which the argument depends: their capacity to abuse power.

7.   This argument is not really an inductive analogy; it is an *a priori* analogy. The primary subject is giving your money to Foster Parents Plan, which the argument urges you to do. The analogue is helping, on the basis of emotion and instinct, a lost child who is in tears. You are urged to support Foster Parents Plan out of consistency with what would be your instinctive emotional response to a hurt child. The most relevant differences between the cases is that you do not immediately, in person, encounter the child to whom Foster Parents Plan would direct your money. If you give to the Plan, you have to depend on their organization to direct you to the right child and to administer the money you give. Though these tasks may be well done by Foster Parents Plan, the fact that you depend on an institutional network in the primary case and not in the analogue case constitutes a difference that undermines the analogy. The instinctive emotional response to

a lost child says nothing about the reliability of the institution, which is crucial in the rationality of giving money to Foster Parents Plan. Compare this example with the discussion of Appeals to Pity in Chapter 6.

8. The analogue is athletes, and the primary subject is officials in athletic competitions. The two are urged to be similar, as human beings who are not perfect; the conclusion is, in fact, quite modest, urging only that officials should not be expected to be perfect. The analogy does give adequate support for this conclusion.

11. This passage does contain an analogy, but it is not clear that the analogy is part of an argument. The analogue is a monarch who makes judgments and decrees all by himself. The primary subject is the person who thinks for himself, who makes judgments without attending to popular opinions and prejudices. Clearly, the tone of the passage and choice of analogue show that Schopenhauer is in favor of thinking for yourself. However, it does not appear that the analogy is put forward as a reason for this view; it seems more like a vivid way of stating the view.

13. This passage does not contain an argument. It is a vivid story, told by a survivor.

Exercise 3

3. There are two analogues here as well as a primary subject. The primary subject is the argument that since the majority of women are kind to children and prefer their own children to other people's, women's proper sphere of activity is "the nursery" (taking care of their own children). The first analogue is as above, except that it substitutes men for women. When this substitution is made, the argument is one no one would accept. The second analogue is as above, except that it substitutes dogs for children. Again, nobody would take the analogue seriously. From the two analogue arguments and the fact that they are parallel in structure to the primary argument, it is inferred that the primary argument is a poor argument.

8. The argument begins with "If we were to accept"; sentences previous to this one are

background and acknowledge that there is something correct in Riis's ideas. The argument is a clear example of the slippery precedent fallacy. Letting 16- and 17-year-olds vote would be a precedent for letting 16-year-olds drink in bars, be subject to adult penalties for murder, . . . and then for a lower age for driver's licenses and consensual sex. There are relevant differences between these cases, so that the first need not set a precedent for the others.

9. This passage illustrates the fallacy of slippery assimilation. Because the destruction of a litter of puppies is similar to the opening of a score of oysters, which in turn is similar to killing a moth, Carroll contends that we cannot draw a line between these three actions. Either all of these actions are morally permissible, or all are morally wrong. This conclusion is based on slippery assimilation. Carroll infers that all killings of animals by humans are morally permissible, provided the deaths are painless.

11. The conclusion is that animals may think about fictitious objects and events. Part of the support for this conclusion comes from a premise that is about animal behavior (the apparent playfulness of apes and porpoises) and does not depend on an analogy. However, part comes from an analogy with humans. In this part of the argument, animals are the primary subject and humans are the analogue. This appears to be an inductive analogy; however, it is flawed because of the immense differences between animals and humans with regard to such relevant features as culture, complexity of language, and sophistication of brain. Thus, part of the argument only appeals to an inductive analogy; the direct nonanalogous part of the argument is more cogent.

CHAPTER 11

Exercise 1

2. There are three supporting premises for the first statement, which is the conclusion. The argument is:
(1) Some charitable organizations waste money.
(2) When people are really needy governments should support them. (3) Some charities use

emotionally manipulative advertisements. So, (4) There is no point in giving money to charity.

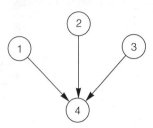

The first and third premises, qualified with "some," are acceptable as known on the basis of common experience. The second is more controversial, but even if acceptable, it is not relevant in any context in which charities do support the needy and do need financial help in doing so. The third premise is not relevant to whether you should give to charity; it is about the quality of ads. There are many counterconsiderations not mentioned in the argument: how needy people are, the fact that their needs may go unmet if you do not give to charity, the fact that other uses you might have for your money are often trivial compared to people's needs, and the sense of social contribution and self-worth that you may derive from giving to charity. The single relevant supporting conclusion is not enough to outweigh these. Thus argument falls down on (A), on (R), and on (G); it is a weak argument.

6. The argument is (1) There are no uncaused events; and (2) Some people are alcoholics, so (3) Some people act out of control and cannot fully choose what they do. Thus, (4) There is no free will. The argument from (2) to (3) is a subargument.

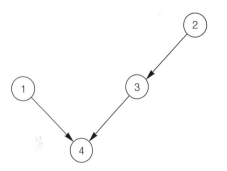

If we assume that having free will would require uncaused events, (1) is positively relevant to the conclusion. But (1) is not acceptable just as it stands; it needs support. (2) is supported in a subargument by (3), which is a matter of common knowledge and can render (2) acceptable. Both premises are positively relevant to the conclusion, but (1), being unacceptable, gives it no support. We are left, then, with only the second premise. It does not have the strength to outweigh counterconsiderations, and there are several, not mentioned by the arguer, that bear significantly on the issue. For instance, there is the fact that human beings experience a sense of being able to deliberate and choose what they do; also, human actions are notoriously hard to predict. The argument is not cogent. It is weak.

7. The argument is (1) The people in revolt in the American Revolution were mainly middle class or upper class and were not peasants; (2) What was attacked in the American Revolution was not the structure of society, but a government far away in England; (3) The internal workings of American society did not change very much after the American Revolution; so (4) The American Revolution was not a typical revolution; then (5) The American Revolution should not be thought of as a model for other revolutions. There are two counterconsiderations: (6) The American Revolution is called a revolution, and (7) The American Revolution is greatly important for the history of the world.

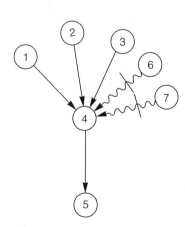

The first three supporting premises are acceptable and could be verified as such by checking standard sources on American history; these are relevant to the conclusion (4) on the assumption that typical revolutions involve the poor, aim at the structure of the society in question, and result in internal changes. This assumption is acceptable. Hence the premises satisfy (A) and (R) so far as supporting (4) is concerned. The counterconsideration in (6) is obviously true and is relevant, but it is far too slight to outweigh the supporting considerations. Whether there are more counterconsiderations that outweigh the premises seems unlikely, but we could consult accounts of revolution by historians and political scientists to find out. The counterconsideration in (7) is not relevant, because the importance of the events for world history has nothing to do with this issue of whether this revolution was typical or not. The counterconsiderations do not outweigh (1), (2), and (3), so the argument from them to (4) may be deemed cogent. (4) is thereby rendered acceptable; clearly (4) is relevant to (5). So the only question that remains is whether the argument from (4) to (5) satisfies (G). It does: a revolution that is not typical can hardly be thought to be a model for others.

12. The conclusion that the New Testament is reliable in the sense that it reliably represents ancient texts. Note that reliability in this sense is NOT the same as reliability in the sense of making true theological or moral claims. The argument is: (1) The New Testament was written 20 to 70 years after the events it records. (2) The oldest manuscript of the New Testament is a copy of originals that were made about 250 years after these originals were written. (3) The oldest manuscript of the New Testament is closer to the time of the original than is common for other ancient manuscripts. (4) There are more than 13,000 surviving copies of various portions of the New Testament dating from ancient and medieval times, so (5) It is highly probable that the original documents are well represented in the New Testament. The structure of the argument is:

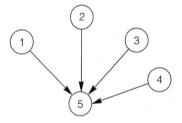

Provisionally, we will accept all premises; should we wish to check these, scholarly sources would be necessary. Premise (4) is not relevant; there could be many copies of something inaccurate or unreliable. Premise (3) is not relevant either unless we assume that other ancient manuscripts are reliable in the sense in question. Premises (1) and (2) offer only slight support, because it would be easy for various errors to slip in under these circumstances. Even granting the premises for the sake of argument, and even without considering possible counterconsiderations, we can see that the argument is weak.

Index